This is an introduction to the aesthetics and sociology of music of the German philosopher and music theorist T. W. Adorno. The aim of the study is to offer a conceptual context within which to situate Adorno's writings on music. Starting with a thematic survey of the early writings from the 1920s, the music of Bartók, Hindemith, Stravinsky and the Second Viennese School is discussed in relation to the philosophical influences which Adorno had absorbed at this time. Adorno's idiosyncratic reception of Marx and Freud is examined in the context of his aesthetic theory. The central part of the book discusses Adorno's approach to analysis, his approach to a sociology of music (through a study of the relation between autonomous musical works and their social function as commodity) and his philosophy of history. The study closes with a critical assessment of Adorno's concept of musical material in the context of his best-known book *Philosophy of New Music*.

Adorno's aesthetics of music

Adorno's aesthetics of music

Max Paddison
University of Durham

CAMBRIDGE
UNIVERSITY PRESS

Published by the Press Syndicate of the University of Cambridge
The Pitt Building, Trumpington Street, Cambridge CB2 1RP
40 West 20th Street, New York, NY 10011–4211, USA
10 Stamford Road, Oakleigh, Melbourne 3166, Australia

First published 1993
Reprinted 1995
First paperback edition 1997

Printed in Great Britain at the University Press, Cambridge

A catalogue record for this book is available from the British Library

Library of Congress cataloguing in publication data
Paddison, Max.
Adorno's aesthetics of music / Max Paddison.
    p.   cm.
Includes bibliographical references and index.
ISBN 0 521 43321 5 (hardback)
1. Adorno, Theodor W., 1903–1969.   2. Music – Philosophy and
aesthetics.   I. Title.
ML423.A33P2   1993
78.1'7'092 – dc20   92–46202 CIP MN

ISBN 0 521 43321 5 hardback
ISBN 0 521 62608 0 paperback

To Linda and Joseph
and
For my mother
and in memory of my father

Contents

Acknowledgements   *page* xi

Introduction   1
1   Adorno in context   3
2   Reading Adorno   13
3   Considerations on method   16

1   Constellations: towards a critical method   21
1   The writings on music: a thematic outline   22
2   History, nature, second nature: the debates with
    Lukács and Benjamin   29
3   The problem of form: Bartók, Hindemith, Stravinsky
    and the Second Viennese School   37
4   Towards a critical method: levels of interpretation   52

2   The development of a theory of musical material   65
1   Theories of artistic material: precursors and contemporaries   66
2   The Adorno–Krenek debate   81
3   On the social situation of music   97

3   The problem of mediation   108
1   Hegel: mediation and the dialectic   109
2   Adorno's Marxian model: the social mediation of music   121
3   Freud: art and sublimation   128
4   Max Weber adapted; rationality and mimesis   135

4   A material theory of form   149
1   The immanent dialectic of musical material   149
2   Immanent analysis: Berg, Sonata op. 1   158
3   Adorno's interpretation of Berg: critique and commentary   168
4   Proposals for a material theory of musical form   174

5 Social content and social function   184
  1 The social dialectic of musical material   185
  2 Musical production   187
  3 Musical reproduction (I): performance   192
  4 Musical reproduction (II): distribution   198
  5 Musical consumption   207

6 The historical dialectic of musical material   218
  1 Adorno's philosophy of music history   219
  2 Bach and the *style galant*   225
  3 Beethoven and Berlioz   233
  4 Wagner and Brahms   242
  5 Debussy and Mahler   256

7 The disintegration of musical material   263
  1 Issues in the philosophy of New Music   265
  2 The decline of the modern   271
  3 Concluding remarks   276

  Appendix   279

Notes   285
Bibliography   330
Index of names   365
Subject index   368

Acknowledgements

This book was long in the making, and many people have inspired and helped the process at different stages. I am particularly indebted to Jim Samson, whose advice and guidance have proved invaluable throughout. I am also indebted to Peter Siebenhühner, who unwittingly launched me on this project, and to Thomas Müller for many intensive discussions on Adorno's sociology of music in Frankfurt. I am not a professional philosopher, and owe a considerable debt of gratitude to Raymond Geuss, whose generous and detailed critical comments on the philosophical aspects of this study were gratefully received and acted on. Others who have commented on this work at various stages, and whose advice has been appreciated are John Deathridge and Jonathan Dunsby. All mistakes are, or course, my own.

Particular thanks must also go to Morris Kahn of Kahn & Averill for his kind encouragement of this project over many years, and to Penny Souster at Cambridge University Press for her unfailing support in seeing the book through to completion. I am also most grateful to Ann Lewis at Cambridge for her careful copy-editing.

I wish to thank the Deutscher Akademischer Austauschdienst for the Stipendium which enabled me to pursue research at the University of Frankfurt in 1979–80. I am also grateful to David Horn and Berndt Ostendorf for facilitating periods of study at the University of Frankfurt. The lectures and seminars of Jürgen Ritsert on Adorno's sociology of music provided much inspiration in the early stages of this research in Frankfurt, as did those of Brigitte Scheer on Adorno's aesthetic theory. I should also like to acknowledge the kind help of Ludwig Finscher on certain points of translation, and of Hans Ulrich Engelmann for suggestions concerning Adorno's concept of material. I am also grateful to Frau Reul at the library of the Musikhochschule for making tape recordings of lectures given by Adorno at the Hochschule in the 1960s available to me.

It is in the nature of a book of this kind, focusing as it does on the work of a single thinker, that freedom to quote extensively from the collected writings has been essential. I should therefore like to express my appreciation of the kind permissions granted by Suhrkamp Verlag of Frankfurt and the Adorno Foundation to cite and translate from Adorno's work. I am also grateful to the editor of *Music Analysis* for permission to cite from my translation of Adorno's talk 'Zum Probleme der musikalischen Analyse' (*Music Analysis* 1/2 1982). Whenever existing published translations have been used, these are, of course, fully acknowledged in the normal manner.

I should like to thank the staff and students of Dartington College of Arts for their tolerance and interest, and in particular Jack Dobbs, Janet Ritterman and Peter Hulton for arranging periods of sabbatical leave. Paul Doe's encouragement in the early stages of my research at Exeter University was also much appreciated.

Finally, I am deeply indebted to the support and patience of Linda Marks. Not only have her critical comments as a sociologist proved an invaluable corrective to the worst excesses of Frankfurt philosophical and sociological prose, but the arrival of our son, Joseph, served to put this lengthy project into perspective. I dedicate this book to them both, and to my parents.

The publication of a paperback edition of this book has provided the opportunity to correct some minor errors. While much has happened in Adorno scholarship during those four years – notably the publication of Adorno's *Beethoven: Philosophie der Musik* fragments edited by Rolf Tiedemann (Frankfurt/Main: Suhrkamp Verlag, 1993), and *Aesthetic Theory*, newly translated, edited, and with a translator's introduction by Robert Hullot-Kentor (London: The Athlone Press, 1997) – I have resisted the temptation to go in for any bibliographical updating at this stage.

Introduction

> ...philosophy persistently and with the claim of truth, must proceed interpretively without ever possessing a sure key to interpretation. ... The text which philosophy has to read is incomplete, contradictory and fragmentary...[1]   Adorno, 'The actuality of philosophy' (1932)

In a well-known scene in Thomas Mann's novel *Doktor Faustus*, the Devil, in one of his transformations before the troubled composer Adrian Leverkühn, appears as the philosopher Adorno. With delicate understatement and a hint of caricature, Mann sketches the contradictory character of this most influential and controversial of twentieth-century writers on music. He highlights the extremes: intellectual sharpness combined with vulnerability, a cultivated tone which threatens to flip over into stridency, and fleeting visions of art's 'promise of happiness' juxtaposed with a cultural pessimism which sees the 'new music' on course for oblivion. 'What is art today?', asks Adorno as Devil, and declares: 'the decent impotence of those who scorn to cloak the general sickness under colour of a dignified mummery'.[2]

In his most famous book on music, *Philosophie der neuen Musik* (on which Thomas Mann had drawn heavily in the writing of *Doktor Faustus*),[3] Adorno uses the metaphor of the stranded sailor's 'bottle-post': radical works are like messages in bottles thrown into the sea, such is the extremity of their alienation.[4] They tell the truth about our predicament in the world, but do so indirectly, in cipher form. It is the task of a critical philosophical aesthetics to decode and interpret these fragmentary 'messages', which nevertheless resist interpretation and retain something of a riddle-character. Adorno is the Devil in *Doktor Faustus* because his philosophy condemns the composer to impotence and alienation, apparently without hope of redemption, while nevertheless compelling him willy-nilly to relate to the outside world from within the autonomous sphere of the musical work. Musical material becomes the stage on which the interaction with society is acted out, blindly, as it were, and in purely musical terms. Music is thus 'condemned to meaning', whatever the intentions of its creators.[5]

1

Adorno is indeed a troubling figure. His philosophy allows for no resolution of the tensions it identifies between autonomous music and the social relations of its production and reception. Any analysis of his work presents a daunting challenge.[6] Adorno himself, in his essay 'Ohne Leitbild', argued that it was impossible for him to contemplate writing a normative aesthetics today. He insisted that he could 'only discuss models [*Leitbilder*] and norms, and then only fragmentarily, as *problematics*'.[7] Taking this position as a constant point of reference, the method employed here is to identify concepts through problematizing them, locating them in the context of Adorno's work and the world of ideas on which he drew. But the need to contextualize concepts is not the same as to define them – the definitive account which leaves no room for contradiction. To contextualize is to interpret through revealing problems and connections; it makes no claim to finality, and it aims to focus polarities and contradictions.

The fundamental problem addressed by Adorno's aesthetics is how to philosophize about art in the absence of aesthetic norms. Aesthetics, as a branch of philosophy, traditionally deals with questions of value and judgement in our experience of art and nature, and is concerned with the evaluation of qualities and attributes like 'beauty', 'proportion' and 'truth' in art. It is occupied with the ontological question of what art 'is' (and what art works are 'in themselves'), as well as with epistemological questions concerning the character of aesthetic experience and the experience of natural beauty: that is, it seeks to understand what is 'subjective' and what is 'objective' in art, as a relationship between Subject and Object.* It asks whether art can be regarded as a mode of knowledge, and whether its relation to the world is mimetic, expressive, or purely formal and symbolic. And it also touches on moral questions raised by art works, indicating the close connection between aesthetic and ethical judgements. Adorno's aesthetic theory, which draws critically on Hegelian dialectics, the sociologies of Marx and Weber, and aspects of Freudian psychoanalytical theory, engages with these long-standing concerns, but, rather than putting forward a system of its own, operates through a critique of existing systems.

Adorno's dialectical aesthetics is critical of 'traditional' aesthetic theories in three main respects. First, traditional philosophies of art have neglected the specificity of art works, preferring to deal with art at a level of generality and universality. Adorno counters this through an emphasis on particular works by means of what he calls 'immanent analysis' (although he is certainly also occupied with the problem of universals). Second,

---

* Initial capitals are used throughout to indicate the Subject–Object relation of German Idealist philosophy. Initial lower case is used for 'object' when reference is to the German terms *Gegenstand* or *Sache*.

traditional aesthetics has tended to ignore the socially conditioned character both of art and its institutions – and, indeed, of aesthetics itself as a discipline. Adorno insists on the necessity for a sociological critique of art through seeing it also in the context of its use and function in industrialized societies; however, unlike more orthodox Marxist theorists, he also insists that art's apparent autonomy in the West cannot simply be dismissed as mere ideology but that it also has a critical function. And third, traditional aesthetics has tended to avoid addressing the historicality of art and its definitions, seeking instead to found itself on absolute values beyond history. Adorno, on the contrary, sees the activity of art as part of a historical process of change which involves art at the same time in a process of constant redefinition of itself, both as reflection of, and in opposition to, the world outside. To this extent Adorno's philosophy of art is also an aesthetics of modernism, in that it seeks to understand the fragmentation and alienation which characterizes Western art in the twentieth century. That Adorno should take music as the primary reference point for his modernist aesthetics is not surprising, given his early musical training, his own experience as a composer and his close involvement with the key figures of musical modernism. Autonomous music ('autonomous' in the sense of a tradition of purely instrumental music having freed itself since the eighteenth century from any direct social function in religious ritual, work, dance, etc., and developing its own 'inner logic') seems to represent the most hermetic and abstract of the arts, the furthest removed from any 'representation' of the outside world and from any political involvement. It was in the tensions within the musical work and in the interaction between composer and musical material that Adorno claimed to discern the contradictions of a fragmented and unreconciled society.

While this book addresses the key concepts and underlying methodology of Adorno's 'sociological aesthetics', the focus is on the musical writings (and in particular on his notion of 'musical material'). The aim is to provide a context of ideas within which to situate the writings on music.

1   Adorno in context

In spite of the centrality of music to his work overall, Adorno is probably still better known as philosopher, sociologist and psychologist. Although biographical detail is not a primary concern of this study, some consideration of the historical and social circumstances in which Adorno's thought developed may help at this stage to cast light on the way in which the diverse strands of his work interrelate.

Biographical sketch: the early years

Born Theodor Ludwig Adorno Wiesengrund[8] on 11 September 1903 in Frankfurt am Main in the confident pre-war years of Wilhelmine Germany, Adorno grew up in a cultured and prosperous bourgeois family steeped in the traditions of Austro-German music and literature. His father, an assimilated Jew, was a successful businessman in the wine trade. His mother (born Maria Calvelli-Adorno) was of mixed Corsican-German Catholic parentage and was a professional singer. An only child, Adorno was brought up mainly by his mother and her unmarried sister, a pianist. His father appears to have been a rather distant figure, although Adorno's childhood was by all accounts a contented one. He learned to play the piano and read music from a very early age, becoming familiar with the Classical and Romantic chamber and orchestral repertoire through playing piano-duet arrangements with his aunt. In 1933 he wrote of this experience: 'Playing piano duets laid before me in the cradle the geniuses of the bourgeois nineteenth century as a present in the twentieth century just beginning'.[9] While still at school he developed an intense interest in philosophy, and every week on Saturday afternoons studied Kant with the philosopher Siegfried Kracauer,[10] a friend of the family. These two childhood enthusiasms, music and philosophy, provided the foundation for his future development.

In 1921 Adorno became a student at the University of Frankfurt, a recently founded and relatively radical institution, where he studied philosophy, sociology, psychology and musicology. At the same time he also continued his studies in composition and piano with Hindemith's former teacher, Bernhard Sekles. From this period date the very early published articles (although his first publication had appeared while he was still at school).[11] The majority of these articles, which continued to appear throughout the 1920s and early 1930s under the name Theodor Wiesengrund, are concerned with the problems of contemporary music. He also produced a large number of concert, opera and book reviews which were published during these years in a variety of journals and newspapers. At this time he also came under the influence of Ernst Bloch,[12] a philosopher whose unique blend of Hegelian-Marxism, a prose-style influenced by Expressionism, and frequent reference to music, made a lasting impression (although their friendship later became strained in the years following the Second World War).

Two further decisive friendships date from these early university years: with Max Horkheimer[13] and Walter Benjamin.[14] Adorno met Horkheimer (with whom he was later to collaborate on a number of projects) in the seminars of Hans Cornelius, Professor of Philosophy at Frankfurt. It was through Horkheimer that Adorno became interested in the philosophy of Edmund Husserl.[15] The immediate outcome of this was his doctoral dissertation, 'Die Transzendenz des Dinglichen und Noematischen in Husserls Phänomenologie',[16] submitted and accepted in 1924. Walter Benjamin and Adorno first met in 1923. It was the beginning of an exchange of ideas which culminated in the intensive correspondence between the two men in the 1930s concerning Benjamin's work on the relationship between Baudelaire's poetry and the Paris of the Second Empire,[17] his essay on art and its technical reproducibility,[18] and Adorno's work on the commodification and fetishization of music and the regression of listening.[19]

Studies with Berg

In 1924, after a performance in Frankfurt of the three orchestral fragments from *Wozzeck*, Adorno was introduced to Alban Berg. Adorno asked if Berg would accept him as a composition pupil, and the matter was agreed on the spot. Studies commenced in Vienna the following year, and continued over a period of three years, while the close acquaintance with the composer lasted until Berg's death in 1935. In later years Adorno wrote:

If I try to recall the impulse that drew me spontaneously to him I am sure it was exceedingly naive, but it was related to something very essential about Berg: the *Wozzeck* pieces, above all the introduction to the March and then the March itself, struck me as a combination of Schoenberg and Mahler, and at that time that was my ideal of genuine new music.[20]

Adorno had ability as a composer, and appeared to be highly regarded by Berg. His compositional output was small, however, and by the mid-1930s Adorno had virtually ceased composing as his theoretical and philosophical interests finally dominated. Nevertheless, the works are of interest in themselves. The *Sechs Bagatellen*, for voice and piano, op. 6 (1923)[21] demonstrate a close motivic–thematic working within a freely atonal idiom, while his *Sechs kurze Orchesterstücke* op. 4 (1929),[22] are particularly effective in their economy of gesture and confident use of the orchestra. These latter pieces show the strong influence of Berg, and, in spite of his hostility to neoclassicism, show distinct traces of traditional forms and genres. There are sketches for a projected opera on Mark Twain's *Huckleberry Finn*, entitled *Der Schatz des Indianer-Joe* (1932–3),[23] of which two songs are complete. The idiom of most of his pieces is firmly based in the heyday of Second Viennese School free atonality pre-1914, the period he regarded as the radical high-point of twentieth-century music from which composers had subsequently retreated into diverse attempts to systematize their compositional procedures.

Susan Buck-Morss has suggested that 'Adorno was perhaps too reflective, too self-conscious, and lacked the spontaneity necessary for uninhibited composing'.[24] Whatever the reasons for his ceasing to compose, it is certain that his early experience as a composer had a profound influence on his music-theoretical work. It influenced not only his writings on music, but also the manner in which he actually composed and structured the texts themselves, with their literary versions of dense motivic working and even the use of the equivalents of inversion and retrograde. René Leibowitz has argued that: 'The fact that his compositions have remained almost completely unknown says nothing regarding their significance; if we had not had this unknown music, then neither would we possess his well-known writings on music'.[25]

While in Vienna studying composition with Berg, Adorno also contributed regularly to the music periodicals *Anbruch* and *Pult und Taktstock*. During this time he studied piano with Eduard Steuermann, the pianist who had given so many first performances of works by radical contemporary composers, and also came into contact with the composer Ernst Krenek. It was from his debates with Krenek in the late 1920s and early 1930s, largely centred around the music of Schoenberg, that he developed his distinctive concept of musical material. During this period Adorno also began work on his *Habilitationsschrift* (the necessary thesis for applicants wishing to be considered for teaching posts in German universities). This took the form of a critique of Kantian Idealism, and showed the increasing influence of Marx and Freud on Adorno's thought. 'Der Begriff des Unbewußten in der transzendentalen Seelenlehre' (The Concept of the Unconscious in the Transcendental Theory of Mind)[26] was submitted in 1927, but was not accepted.

Over the next four years Adorno spent much of his time in Berlin. As well as Benjamin, Bloch and Kracauer, the circle of his acquaintances there included Otto Klemperer, Moholy-Nagy, Bertolt Brecht, Hanns Eisler, Kurt Weill and Lotte Lenya. It was also at this time that he came under the influence of Georg Lukács,[27] the Hungarian neo-Marxist literary and culture critic. As Lukács developed a more anti-modernist stance after the Second World War in his critical writings on modern European literature, however, and moved towards a more orthodox Marxist position, Adorno became openly critical of his work.[28]

Having completed and submitted a second *Habilitationsschrift* in 1931, a critique of Kierkegaard's existentialist argument for 'subjective inwardness' ('Kierkegaard: Konstruktion des Ästhetischen'),[29] Adorno was successful in his application, and almost immediately joined the Philosophy Faculty of Frankfurt University. The same year Horkheimer became director of the Institut für Sozialforschung, and from now on Adorno's own development became increasingly linked with that of the Institut.

The Institute for Social Research

The Institut für Sozialforschung had originally been formed in Frankfurt in 1923 by Felix Weil, and it was run on relatively orthodox Marxist lines by its first director, Carl Grünberg.[30] When Max Horkheimer took over the directorship in 1931 there began the period of the Institut's greatest distinction and productivity. Horkheimer was highly successful in attracting a brilliant group of scholars from many different disciplines. Notable among the members of the Institut at this time were Herbert Marcuse,[31], Erich Fromm,[32] Leo Löwenthal,[33] Friedrich Pollock[34] and Adorno himself. Walter Benjamin was never actually a member, but was closely associated with the Institut until his death in 1940. Much of the work of the members of the Institut and those connected with it (and who became known as the Frankfurt School of Critical Theory) was published in the *Zeitschrift für Sozialforschung*, which first appeared in 1932. Paul Connerton identifies the aims of the Institut and of the Zeitschrift at this period in a summary worth citing at some length:

Despite its scope, the Zeitschrift retained a degree of cohesion by steering between two extreme positions which at that time typified the relationship between philosophy and the social sciences. One pole, represented by German Lebens-philosophie and Phenomenology, was contemptuous of empiricism and pragmatism; the other was represented by the empirical orientation of American social research. Ignoring – or overriding – the seeming disjunction between philosophical speculation and empiricism, the Institute aimed at a fertilizing interpenetration of theoretical and empirical work. It sought to foster by its organizational structure the programme of a 'Critical Theory' which found its paradigm in Marx's *Critique of Political Economy* and its concept of totality in the Hegelian-Marxism of the young Lukács. Common to all three aspects of this programme was the belief that no partial aspect of social life and no isolated phenomenon may be comprehended unless it is related to the historical whole, to the social structure conceived as a global entity.[35]

The Institut, which was initially independent of the university, operated as a kind of community of scholars, taking an interdisciplinary approach to current social issues of importance. The most fundamental of their shared concerns was the rise of Fascism in Europe and of authoritarianism in general (including its manifestation in the Soviet Union under Stalin). They sought to understand the effects upon the individual of propaganda and mass culture (two areas they sometimes tended to conflate), and also how powerful tendencies within the social totality manifested within individual areas of social life. To this extent their approach could be labelled 'ideology critique'. The central problem was that of *mediation*, how the whole is contained, in indirect, mediated form, within the part. From these shared concerns resulted Adorno's partly empirical studies of popular culture, of the mass media, and of the effects of technical reproduction on the quality of experience. These studies made particular use of the concepts 'standardization', 'pseudo-individualization' and 'fetishization' in an attempt to identify the ideological content both of listening habits and of the formal features of popular music. It is an area of his work that has attracted much criticism.

Exile in America

When Hitler came to power in 1933 with the fall of the Weimar Republic, Adorno, like all academics of Jewish extraction, lost his post at the university. Initially he found it very difficult to conceive of leaving Germany and going into exile, in part because his work was so strongly dependent on the German language and German culture. In 1935 he did leave, however, to settle initially in Oxford. He began to prepare for an Oxford D.Phil., but did not complete it. In 1938 he left England, where he had never felt the intellectual climate suitable for his work, and emigrated to the United States. The same year he also married Gretel Karplus, whom he had first met in his Berlin circle of acquaintances in the 1920s.

The Institut für Sozialforschung had moved to the United States earlier, and Adorno had been in regular contact with Horkheimer since they had both left Germany.[36] Horkheimer was able to provide some support for him in America, and Adorno now became a full member of the Institut. He also became director of the Princeton Radio Research Project, working with Paul Lazarsfeld.[37] The partnership was not successful due to friction between Lazarsfeld's empirical approach and Adorno's speculative theoretical bias.[38] Nevertheless, contact with American empirical sociology and psychology did have some influence on his own theoretical approach. This was later to show some benefit in his contributions for *The Authoritarian Personality* (1950),[39] the Institut's major psychological study of intolerance and prejudice. Its effect on his musical writings, however, was limited, and he became increasingly critical of positivist approaches to sociology.[40]

At this time he took to using his mother's maiden name, Adorno (although he had already in the 1920s begun to use the hyphenated form Wiesengrund-Adorno). In the 1930s he had also briefly written under the pseudonym 'Hektor Rottweiler' (1937–8).

In 1941 he moved to Los Angeles, and lived in the same neighbourhood as both Schoenberg and Thomas Mann. He had little personal contact with Schoenberg.[41] With Mann, however, there was frequent contact, and, as we have seen, Adorno acted as musical adviser for the musical sections of *Doktor Faustus*.[42] Adorno's most important work on music to emerge from this period was *Philosophie der neuen Musik*, although the partly empirical projects on popular music and film music (with Hanns Eisler) are also significant.[43]

The American years were not, on the whole, a highly productive period for Adorno. There is no doubt that he missed Germany and German culture acutely. At the same time, however, it gave him an important new perspective on all that he had previously taken for granted about European culture. In a later essay about this stage in his life, 'Wissenschaftliche Erfahrungen in Amerika', he wrote:

In America I was freed from culture-bound naivety, and acquired the ability to see culture from the outside. To give an illustration of what I mean: for me, in spite of all social criticism and consciousness of the predominance of the economy, the absolute relevance of spirit [*Geist*] had always been self-evident. That such self-evidence no longer had any validity at all was something I was apprised of in America, where there was no tacit respect for anything to do with spirit [*Geist*], unlike in Central and Western Europe across the so-called educated classes; the absence of this respect induced the spirit towards critical self-determination.[44]

Return to Germany: methodological disputes

When, in 1949, he was invited to return to Frankfurt he accepted gladly, as did Horkheimer. Adorno became Professor of Philosophy at the University of Frankfurt and co-director with Horkheimer of the re-established Institut für Sozialforschung. Now began a new period of influence of the Frankfurt School on German academic life. Adorno's teaching (and that of Horkheimer) had a profound effect on a whole new generation of students throughout the 1950s and 1960s. The Frankfurt School in exile in the United States had succeeded in keeping alive aspects of German cultural life which Hitler had set out to destroy in Germany itself, and Critical Theory had preserved a thread of continuity which it considered important to re-establish in post-war Germany. The Institut now became affiliated to Frankfurt University.

During the 1950s and 1960s Adorno also taught composition and gave lectures on music criticism and serialism at the Darmstadt Summer School. His output during these years was remarkable, and he produced a constant flow of articles, essays, papers and books, while continuing his lecture series on philosophy and sociology at the university and giving occasional talks on music at the Hochschule für Musik und darstellende Kunst in Frankfurt. His university lecture course in the winter semester of 1961–2, for example, was on the sociology of music (published in 1962 as *Einleitung in die Musiksoziologie*),[45] while a later series (in the winter semester of 1967–8) was on aesthetics.[46]

This was the period of the so-called 'positivist dispute' (*Positivismusstreit*) in German sociology, a series of public debates between the Critical Theorists (represented by, among others, Adorno and Habermas) and the scientific rationalist position (represented in particular by the philosopher of science, Karl Popper). Adorno's reservations regarding the limitations of empirical scientific research methods as applied to sociology and psychology (especially in relation to the reception of music) had intensified since his return to Germany from the United States, even though he and Horkheimer had initially been instrumental in encouraging the use of empirical methodology in post-war German academic research. He criticized scientific positivism for its assumption that the world can be studied in purely objective terms, unaffected by the conditioned nature of the Subject and its forms of consciousness. Adorno played a central role in the dispute, which was launched in Tübingen in 1961 and culminated in the publication of the proceedings in 1969.[47] In what descended into a long drawn out and inconclusive altercation, characterized by polemics, the differences themselves were often difficult to disentangle. The opposing positions have been broadly summarized by Martin Jay, who writes: 'whereas the Popperians contended that scientists in an "open society" would engage in the rational pursuit of scientific truth (or more precisely, the falsification of scientific error), Adorno continued to insist that "the idea of scientific truth cannot be split off from that of a true society"'.[48]

It was also in the post-war years that Adorno renewed his attack on phenomenology and existentialism, a critique begun in the 1930s with his work on Kierkegaard. In his book *Jargon der Eigentlichkeit: Zur deutschen Ideologie* (1964) he criticized, in particular, Heidegger for an obscurantist and 'magical' use of language which attempted to conjure up the immediate presence of the object in the written word (as the identity of concept and object of cognition) while ignoring the historically and socially mediated character of the relationship between Subject and Object. He argued that the identity of Subject and Object was inconceivable under current historical and social conditions, and that the appearance of their reconciliation in philosophy and in art would lead to both serving political ends (just as, indeed, Heidegger's philosophical vocabulary had been so easily assimilated to Nazi ideology). In the two major works that occupied him in his last decade, *Negative Dialektik* (1966) and the unfinished *Ästhetische Theorie* (1970), Adorno took his critique of identity theory and of ontology a stage further. In formulating his philosophy and his aesthetic theory at length in these two works, he set out to confront the problem of how to philosophize in the absence of ontological 'givens', and how to write an aesthetics after the destruction of aesthetic norms. Aesthetics today, according to Adorno, has the problem of understanding 'a situation where art revolts against its essential concepts while at the same time being inconceivable without them'.[49] The result, as Georg Picht has expressed it, is 'atonal philosophy'.[50] An endless dialectical 'working out' pervades Adorno's writings, allowing no resting place in ontological certainties.

In 1967–8 Adorno and Horkheimer came under attack from the New Left student movement for refusing to commit themselves to political action during the student revolution of the late 1960s. While Marcuse (who had remained in the United States) viewed similar developments on American campuses as something to be encouraged, Adorno and Horkheimer were disturbed by the direction things were taking in Frankfurt. They had never considered Critical Theory to be a model for political action and were dismayed at the possibility of their ideas providing an excuse for the use of violence to bring about political change. Adorno's statement at that time, that 'I had set up a theoretical model, but I could not suspect people would want to put it into action with Molotov cocktails',[51] has often been quoted. He saw the aim of Critical Theory as bringing about an initial change in consciousness, rather than attempting directly to change society itself. The Institut was occupied and Adorno's lectures disrupted. In April 1969 he was denounced and humiliated by revolutionary students distributing a leaflet entitled 'Adorno als Institution ist tot' (Adorno as an institution is dead).[52] He died later that year, on 6 August 1969, of a heart attack while on holiday in Switzerland.

Adorno's work suffered a brief decline of interest in Germany in the decade immediately following his death (although a number of significant commentaries on his philosophy and aesthetics were nevertheless produced during the 1970s).[53] In the United States there was an upsurge of interest in the Frankfurt School, fuelled in part by the appearance of English translations of a number of Adorno's books, including *Philosophie der neuen Musik* (in a much criticized version as *Philosophy of Modern Music*)[54] and by the publication of Martin Jay's highly acclaimed *The Dialectical Imagination: A History of the Frankfurt School and the Institute of Social Research 1923–1950*,[55] both in 1973. Two further works which helped to sustain this interest were Susan Buck-Morss's *The Origin of Negative Dialectics*[56] (a detailed enquiry into the early development of Adorno's thought, including discussion of the early writings on music) and, in Britain, Gillian Rose's *The Melancholy Science*,[57] both of which appeared in the late 1970s. Rose Rosengard Subotnik's series of essays on Adorno and music also began to appear at this time.[58]

Critical Theory, modernism and postmodernism

While the Frankfurt School project has been taken in new directions by the 'second generation' of Critical Theorists, Albrecht Wellmer, Alfred Schmidt and, in particular, Jürgen Habermas, the modernist position represented by Adorno, especially by his writings on aesthetics, has itself now become historically situated, and in the process has been labelled 'classical modernism'. It is nevertheless clear that his work remains central to current debates on modernism and postmodernism – particularly to the continuing exchange between Jürgen Habermas and Jean-François Lyotard.[59] Yet Critical Theory remains largely hostile to 'postmodernist' theories. This is due, at least in part, to the relativism implied in the postmodernist position – especially postmodernism as style removed from any sense of historical necessity. It is also partly due to Critical Theory's retention of the concept of the Subject, problematic and fractured as it has become, over the postmodernists' celebration of its disappearance.[60]

The project of the Critical Theory of the Frankfurt School, and of Adorno's own version of it, negative dialectics, was concerned above all with the survival of the autonomous individual, the self-reflecting Subject, in the face of false forms of consciousness, as ideology. The aim of Critical Theory was emancipation from false consciousness, the abolition of alienation, and the recovery of wholeness.[61] In so far as 'the true field of philosophy' is 'the teaching of the good life',[62] as Adorno puts it in *Minima Moralia*, Critical Theory can claim its origins in Plato and classical Greek philosophy. But in what Adorno calls 'the administered world' such wholeness, as the unity of Subject and Object, is presented as already achieved, and is regarded by him as a travesty of true wholeness and absence of alienation. This is the false consciousness which the ideology critique of the Frankfurt School set out to reveal, by casting light on the contradictions underlying a deceptive surface appearance of totality. At the same time, Critical Theory differs from positivist, scientific theories, in that it also reflects critically upon its own terms, upon the assumptions brought to bear by the Subject to the Object of enquiry, rather than primarily seeking empirical verification and control of the Object. Indeed, Raymond Geuss has defined Critical Theory as 'a reflective theory which gives agents a kind of knowledge inherently productive of enlightenment and emancipation'.[63] There is also, therefore, a utopian vision implicit in Critical Theory, which is to be found in both Marx and Hegel, and which can also be traced back to Plato. While the possible shape of such a vision was to some extent made explicit in the thinking of certain of Adorno's Frankfurt School colleagues (and former colleagues) like Fromm, Marcuse and Horkheimer[64] in their later work, Adorno himself refused all such recourse to consolation. Even the aesthetic sphere, to which, as to religion, humanity had traditionally turned for respite from the horrors of reality, and which Freud had labelled as 'escape from the reality principle' through sublimation or repression, was no longer able to fulfil that role. In *Minima Moralia* Adorno writes: 'there is no longer beauty or consolation except in the gaze falling on horror, withstanding it, and in unalleviated consciousness of negativity holding fast to the possibility of what is better'.[65]

2   Reading Adorno

The reception of Adorno's writings on music has long been characterized by controversy and polarization of views. While the well-known split between British and American empiricism and pragmatism on the one hand and continental Idealist and rationalist theories on the other is certainly fundamental to this polarization, the controversy also goes beyond this gulf between cultures and their modes of theorizing. Criticisms of Adorno tend to come from both sides of the cultural divide. Those who dismiss his work often do so on grounds of what they regard as its stylistic obscurantism and methodological inconsistency. This is frequently combined with criticism of what is perceived as the political slant of his writing. While the liberal, 'common-sense' view particularly prevalent in Britain and the United States, which considers music largely in isolation from any socio-political context, tends to be suspicious of Adorno's Marxian analysis of culture, orthodox Marxists have always dismissed his idiosyncratic and selective reading of Marx (essentially a Hegelian reading, with an admixture of Nietzsche and Max Weber). They complain that Adorno's sociological aesthetics remains entirely dependent on the musical values of the bourgeois period.[66] On the other hand, those who embrace Adorno's work unreservedly tend to celebrate its stylistic features above any consideration of method. They admire Adorno's poetic use of language, his delight in paradox and metaphor, and the way in which his writing about music mimetically traces the cracks and fissures of the modernist work of art. This is sometimes combined with a stress on the Freudian influences on his work and a down-playing of the importance of Marx. Indeed, there is a noticeable tendency to fetishize the prose style itself.[67]

Difficulties

Adorno's writing is undeniably difficult. It is characterized by ellipsis and hyperbole, and his dialectical method is founded on antinomy. His texts are constructed in such a way as to resist appropriation and exploitation by uncritical and unreflective modes of thought. Systematization is, for him, a political issue. 'Power and knowledge are synonymous', he writes in *Dialektik der Aufklärung*, citing Francis Bacon.[68] He argues that to systematize is to impose a unity upon the dissimilar, a false totality which betrays difference in the interests of equivalence and exchangeability. At the same time, however, Adorno's writings demand a systematic – that is, active, detailed and critical – reading, and anything less is to betray them equally effectively through fetishizing their complexity as poetic obscurity.[69]

The motivating force of his aesthetics and sociology of music is the desire to illuminate the complex web of meaning which relates autonomous musical works to the socio-political totality, and which he argues is inherent (that is, 'immanent') in the material of music itself. However, in the crossfire between those who denigrate Adorno's work as incoherent, and those who elevate it to the status of poetic literature, the possibility of a thoroughgoing reading of Adorno, where his writings on music are understood as part of a larger context of ideas, becomes endlessly deferred. As a result, Adorno's work has become a happy hunting ground for those in search of quotable aphorisms. When taken out of context, these fragments serve to obscure the larger movement of his thought. As Samuel Beckett said of the work of the painter Tal Coat: 'Total object, complete with missing parts, instead of partial object. Question of degree.'[70] Likewise with Adorno's writings: their fragmentation needs to be understood against a sense of a missing totality, their negativity against an absent utopian affirmation.

When seen as a 'whole', albeit a fractured one, Adorno's work has, in the main, a consistency in its use of concepts which should be seen as the necessary counterpole to the fragmentation which characterizes its mode of expression. It is the tension between these two aspects which gives to Adorno's texts their peculiar compulsion. However, the attempt to reveal the integrative features underlying a body of writing which otherwise emphasizes fragmentation, both stylistically and structurally, should not be misconstrued as a search for a 'system', wherein concepts have fixed positions and function as 'invariants' or ontological absolutes. On the contrary, in Adorno's 'constellations' (his own term for the principle through which each of his texts finds its unique form in relation to its 'object') the concepts are fluid, taking their meanings from their relationship to other concepts, and interacting constantly. Adorno's constellations are characterized by gravitational pulls towards certain recurring problems, like force-fields within which each concept takes on meaning both in relation to a central 'problem' and in relation to its changing philosophical usage over time. Concepts are thus to be understood as inherently contradictory, defined as much by what they exclude as by what they encompass, constantly needing renegotiation in relation to the object they attempt to grasp, but which they ultimately fail to 'identify'. This is Adorno's dialectic of identity and non-identity.[71]

Concepts and the non-conceptual

The contradiction at the heart of Adorno's whole enterprise, and one which is directly linked to the stylistic virtuosity of his writing, is that, for a philosopher, the only access to the non-conceptual is via the concept. This, to use a favourite phrase of Adorno's, is what constitutes the *tour de force* of his texts – that they attempt to use the power of the concept to undermine the concept and thereby enable the non-conceptual to speak. For Adorno, the epitome of the 'non-conceptual' and 'non-identical' is art, and in particular the 'autonomous' music of the bourgeois period,[72] regarded as a mode of 'cognition without concepts' (*begriffslose Erkenntnis*). Thus the interpretation of music and of musical works hits up against the problem of conceptualizing the non-conceptual, of 'identifying the non-identical', in its most extreme form. In *Negative Dialektik* Adorno writes:

Cognition does not contain its objects [*Gegenstände*] within itself. It should not set out to prepare the phantasm of the whole. Thus it cannot be the task of a philosophical interpretation of art works to fabricate their identity with the concept and to absorb them into the concept. However, it is only by means of interpretation that the truth of the work unfolds.[73]

For Adorno, truth lies in the particular which evades the universalizing tendency of conceptual thought. But the 'truth content' of musical works is historical, and concerns the way in which works, through the particularity of their form, attempt to deal with the antinomies of the handed-down musical material, which are seen as social in origin. It is in this way Adorno regards music as a kind of 'unconscious writing of history', in need of philosophical interpretation to reveal its 'truth content'. Hence, in his writings on music, he seeks to decipher the traces of the universal (as social totality) within the apparently self-contained world of the particular musical work. He seeks to do this not through abstraction, but through a form of 'micrological analysis' which grounds the concept within the materiality of musical works and within the tiniest, and apparently most insignificant, details of musical life. He sees the concept as the result of dialectical thinking: it is neither the abstract universal nor the concrete particular, but instead a product of the interaction of the two, which serves fleetingly to reveal the complex relations between part and whole. His claim is to discover the universal within the particular, i.e. *immanently*, without doing violence to the particular by imposing the concept from the outside. That there are problems with this claim cannot be denied – problems of a 'practical' as well as theoretical nature which will be considered during the course of this study. Indeed, one such problem area is Adorno's own musical analyses. In essence, however, his method may be described as a 'logic of disintegration' (*Logik des Zerfalls*).[74] Adorno saw the 'crisis of modernism' as a breakdown of established meanings – a recognition of the inadequacy of received concepts and systems of thought to contain the contradictions of perceived reality. This process of disintegration, as slippage between concept and referent, was one he also discerned within the apparently self-contained material of music. There it manifested as what he called, following Lukács, a 'rupture between self and forms':[75] the expressive needs of the composer as expressive Subject were no longer served by the handed-down genres and formal types representing the objectivity of the social totality. It is in this sense that Adorno claims to derive the 'concept' from the experience of the object itself, and to trace the 'universal' tendency of the whole within the material of the particular musical work.

3   Considerations on method

There are a number of important considerations, some already touched on, which have shaped the approach taken in this study. First, the interdisciplinary character of the work needed to be confronted, as Adorno's writings on music cannot be taken in total isolation from his work in the areas of philosophy, sociology, psychology, literary and art criticism – nor in isolation from other systems of thought on which he has drawn. In particular, the concepts used call for a grounding in the tradition of German Idealist philosophy, as well as the tradition of the Frankfurt School in German sociology. This raised the question of how best to integrate the expository material needed to place the musical writings in their interdisciplinary context. Second, there was the sheer size of Adorno's output, the bulk of which, as well as commentaries on it, still remains untranslated. Third, there was the question of translating Adorno. His work has suffered badly in translation, and existing translations are often unsatisfactory and even misleading, thus adding to misconceptions about Adorno's work still rife in the English-speaking world. And fourth, there was the problem of the complexity of Adorno's writing – how best to deal with the question of the irreducibility of the ideas to a form other than that of their original presentation.

Interdisciplinary character: the collected writings

The interdisciplinary character of Adorno's work is all-pervading, even in those texts which, on one level, seem straightforwardly 'musical'. Indeed, it could be argued that the writings on music have suffered more misunderstanding on this account than his more obviously philosophical and sociological writings. The problem with the musical texts is that, to what could already be seen as decidedly arcane and highly specialized areas of philosophy, sociology and psychology, they add a further level of exclusiveness – that of the specialized technical terminology and 'body of knowledge' of music. This has meant that scholars from other disciplines – with some notable exceptions[76] – have been understandably reluctant to give Adorno's texts on music detailed consideration because of a lack of musical expertise. On the other hand, a traditional musical training hardly equips a musician or musicologist to take on critical theory.[77] The need to understand Adorno's musical writings in a larger context of ideas is therefore evident. While links between the musical and the 'non-musical' texts, and between Adorno's thought as a whole and the larger world of ideas on which he drew, are made throughout this study, the main expository material occurs in the first three chapters.

Adorno wrote a lot, and the collected writings, including the philosophical, sociological, psychological and literary critical texts as well as the writings on music, have now been issued in twenty volumes as T. W. Adorno, *Gesammelte Schriften*, edited by Rolf Tiedemann (Frankfurt am Main: Suhrkamp Verlag, 1970–86). Over half of these volumes are made up of texts on music. The *Gesammelte Schriften* still do not contain Adorno's total output, however, and there remains a substantial amount of work, now the responsibility of the Theodor W. Adorno Archiv in Frankfurt, yet to be published.[78] Material being edited includes three unfinished books: *Beethoven: Philosophie der Musik* (pub. 1993); *Theorie der musikalischen Reproduktion*; and (in English, and dating from Adorno's years in the United States) *Current of Music: Elements of a Radio Theory*. I did not have access to these in writing the present book. Parts of *Current of Music: Elements of a Radio Theory* were published (in English) during the early 1940s in various American journals and in German after the Second World War and I have referred to these, although they do not play a central role in this study. The English-language essays from this project have been omitted from the *Gesammelte Schriften*, as has, for example, the exchange of letters between Adorno and Krenek published separately as *Briefwechsel* (1974). I have made selective reference to the whole range of Adorno's published writings on music, as well as referring to many of his overtly philosophical, sociological, psychological, literary and art critical texts.

Adorno as literature and the problem of translation

Existing translations of a number of important works by Adorno turned out in some instances to need adapting when compared with the original texts. This raises the whole issue of the 'impossibility' of translating Adorno into English, eloquently discussed by Samuel Weber in his prefatory essay to his own translation of *Prismen*, entitled 'Translating the untranslatable'.[79] Other available translations of Adorno's writings, both of the larger-scale works as well as of individual shorter articles published in various periodicals and collections of Frankfurt School texts, have also been drawn on where appropriate and are gratefully acknowledged. For the rest, I have provided my own translations.

It is the vexed question of Adorno's literary style that is inevitably raised yet again by any discussion of the problem of translation. Adorno's style is cryptic and paratactical, and his aphoristic and eccentric use of the German language owes much to Nietzsche.[80] The tendency to proceed by means of tersely constructed, mutually contradictory assertions designed in part to disrupt normal reading habits and to 'shock' the reader into an active relationship with the text, is a feature of all Adorno's writings. The following passage from the Preface to Nietzsche's *Zur Genealogie der Moral* offers advice which could apply just as well to the interpretation of Adorno's texts:

the aphoristic form may present a stumbling block, the difficulty being that this form is no longer taken 'hard' enough. An aphorism that has been honestly struck cannot be deciphered simply by reading it off; this is only the beginning of the work of interpretation proper, which requires a whole science of hermeneutics.[81]

Perhaps the most impressive, and indeed successful example of Adorno's use of aphorism is to be found in *Minima Moralia* (1951), his most 'literary' and poetic book. Although not a 'text on music', it is certainly a most 'musical text', with its wordplays, grammatical inversions and ellipses, its exaggerations and analogies taken to extremes. Furthermore, its translation into English, by E. F. N. Jephcott (1974), has proved to be one of the most successful renderings of all Adorno's books – an occasion where a translator has risen magnificently to an impossible task.

The difficulty in reading Adorno comes from the fact that the texts do not pretend to be neutral, transparent vehicles for an 'objective' content. Instead, his writing takes upon itself a self-reflective role, whereby it constantly seems to negate and consume itself in search of its 'object'. It has to be admitted, however, that this feature of Adorno's style, as well as having its attractions, can also prove intensely frustrating. While it is essential to be aware of the self-reflexive and contradictory character of his literary style in order to understand his texts at all, there are certainly occasions when one wishes that he would simply say what he means in more direct terms. That he was also capable of remarkable directness and clarity without loss of dialectical tension is clearly in evidence in his letters (e.g. to

Krenek[82] and to Benjamin[83]), in the radio talks and available transcripts of his lectures,[84] and also in the talk 'Zum Probleme der musikalischen Analyse' [1969].[85] As Krenek commented concerning Adorno's style in his foreword to the *Briefwechsel*:

His eloquence was phenomenal: he spoke in a style that could be immediately written down and printed. At the same time it must also be said that much of what he delivered to the printer advanced far beyond the style of his spoken language into that region of hermetic cipher which bordered on mannerism and which makes the reading of his work as attractive as it is difficult.[86]

Fragmentation and antisystematization

This brings us back again to the related question of the structure of Adorno's texts, their larger-scale organization. Adorno deliberately set out to avoid the 'totalizing' form of the academic treatise in his work. He favoured instead the fragmentary forms of the essay[87] and the aphorism where, as he put it in his inaugural lecture to the Faculty of Philosophy at Frankfurt University in 1931, 'it may be possible to penetrate the detail, to explode in miniature the mass of merely existing reality'.[88] Even his large-scale books (apart, that is, from the early academic dissertations) usually turn out to be constructed from self-contained essays and fragments. This is straightforward enough in the case of obvious collections of previously published essays and articles, like *Moments musicaux* (1964) and *Impromptus* (1968). It becomes, however, a structural principle in philosophical works of a kind which one would normally expect to contain an argued-through thesis in the traditional manner. Typical examples of this are to be seen in the structure of books like *Dialektik der Aufklärung* (1947), *Negative Dialektik* (1966) and the unfinished *Ästhetische Theorie* (1970).[89] This does not mean that Adorno was at heart a miniaturist, unable or unwilling to think on a larger scale. It is rather that he considered the claim that the 'whole' represents the 'truth' in a fragmented world is necessarily false.[90] The claim to truth made by totalizing systems, whether as philosophical systems, art works or political systems, he saw as ideological not only in relation to the *content* of, for example, a philosophical text, but also in terms of the traditional *forms* employed to express and materialize this content. Thus the argued-through academic treatise was rejected in favour of the idea of the 'constellation' of fragments, each equidistant from an unstated centre, marking the place of the object of enquiry, whose presence is conjured up and at the same time negated by a text which constantly denies identity with the object. And what goes for the structure of the individual texts also goes for what one must call, paradoxically, the 'fragmented whole' of Adorno's output. As

Fredric Jameson has put it, 'it is unavailable as a separate thesis of a general nature'.[91]

The dilemma this presents has a touch of the absurd about it. As we have established, Adorno's work is anti-systematic and resists systematization. An analysis of his work must, of its very nature, be systematic. Put in this way, the problem would seem to be insoluble. Nevertheless, it is in a sense a false dilemma. Because Adorno's work resists totalization, this does not mean that it is unsystematic in its own terms, or indeed that it is irrational and exists outside any conceptual frame of reference. To treat Adorno's texts unsystematically, and to read them in a conceptual vacuum in the belief that this is what they demand from the reader, would be seriously to misunderstand them. It would, moreover, lead precisely to the kind of uncritical and unreflective 'identification with the object' which the texts themselves criticize. The present study proceeds in the conviction that Adorno needs – to adapt a phrase of Walter Benjamin – to be read against the grain.[92] That is to say, the texts need to be read dialectically and their underlying structure be made apparent through placing them within a larger theoretical context. As Max Horkheimer puts it in his essay 'Zum Problem der Wahrheit':

Separated from a particular theory of society as a whole, every theory of cognition remains formalistic and abstract. . . . The dialectical proposition that every concept possesses real validity only as a part of a theoretical whole and arrives at its real significance only when, by its interconnection with other concepts, a theoretical unity has been reached and its role in this is known, is valid here too.[93]

Given the impossibility of presenting Adorno's ideas as a staged linear sequence – at least, without distorting the dialectical character of the ideas themselves – the strategy adopted here has been to keep the 'totality' of Adorno's thought circulating within each chapter. On one level this has inevitably resulted in some repetition. On another level, however, it needs to be seen more in terms of 'variations on a theme'. As the study progresses towards its conclusions it is hoped that fresh light is shed on the whole at each varied restatement of its fragmented parts.

1   Constellations: towards a critical method

> Second nature is, in truth, first nature. The historical dialectic is not
> simply a renewed interest in reinterpreted historical materials, rather the
> historical materials transform themselves into the mythical and natural-
> historical.[1]   Adorno, 'The idea of natural-history' (1932)

A casual survey of Adorno's writings on music could well give the
impression that his theoretical concerns emerged fully formed in the 1920s
and did not change substantially thereafter. There is some truth in
Friedemann Grenz's observation that 'Adorno's thought had remained
always constant, without periods of change, that there had been no
development in it'.[2] Indeed, the unity of thought throughout his work is
striking, and there are evident connections between even the most
occasional of the early pieces and the large-scale philosophical writings of
his last years.[3] Nevertheless, there is also a sense in which Adorno's work
does show development over time. It moves from the early non-Marxian
writings to an idiosyncratic reception of Marx and Hegel influenced by the
neo-Marxism of Lukács and by the attempt of the Frankfurt School to
bring about a fusion of Marx and Freud. In addition, Adorno's emigration
years in the United States were marked by an abrupt encounter with
empirical sociology and psychology, while the period of his return to
Frankfurt in the post-war years was characterized by a certain consolidation in his philosophical and critical method in works like *Negative
Dialektik* and *Ästhetische Theorie*. All these developments have implications for his aesthetics of music.

The aim of this chapter is to identify the key concerns of Adorno's early
writings on music, and to chart the search for a 'method' (the principle of
the 'constellation') seen in the context of his work as a whole. The central
concepts initially employed by him in the texts from the 1920s and 1930s –
nature, history, second nature, and what he calls 'the rupture between self
and forms' – are located in his reception of the early Lukács and Benjamin.
Issues raised by the music of Bartók, Hindemith, Stravinsky, Schoenberg,
Berg and Webern in his writings of this period need to be considered in the

21

light of these concepts. From an examination of the early writings it becomes apparent that Adorno was already grappling with the problem of how society as a totality can be understood to be 'mediated' in aesthetic artefacts, and it is clear that the beginnings of his notion of 'musical material' as historically mediated 'second nature' also date from this time. These central concepts (nature, history, mediation, material) need also to be viewed from the perspective of his later work (especially *Ästhetische Theorie*) in relation to the idea that works of art have a 'truth content'. In order to clarify these connections I put forward a schematic model for what can be seen as three interacting levels in Adorno's critical aesthetics of music – 'immanent' analysis, sociological critique and philosophical-historical interpretation – taken in conjunction with three of the most value-laden and problematic terms of his aesthetic theory: consistency, ideology and authenticity.

1   The writings on music: a thematic outline

A chronological survey of the writings on music is no straightforward matter. Adorno frequently rewrote earlier texts for inclusion in later collections, and often recycled material which he had written years before (and perhaps never published) through juxtaposing it with later material. Indeed, a number of his books are made up either of collections of essays published originally over a period of many years (like *Prismen* (1955), *Dissonanzen* (1956), *Klangfiguren* (1959), *Quasi una Fantasia* (1963), *Moments musicaux* (1964) and *Impromptus* (1968)), or of sections which were written earlier but then substantially revised and published in a new context towards the end of his life (e.g. *Berg: Der Meister des kleinsten Übergangs* (1937–68); *Versuch über Wagner* (1939–52)). As has already been emphasized, Adorno's work in many ways defies categorization over time because its underlying themes do not develop chronologically, but are all present to varying degrees at every point in his writings, even though new influences may have been taken on and different emphases made. With these reservations in mind, the following outline of Adorno's musical writings makes no claim to be anything more than a cursory and selective overview. Its main purpose is that of orientation and the identification of broad themes, before going on to consider in more detail the philosophical issues which occupy the rest of the chapter.

Composers and compositions

Adorno's musical writings of the 1920s and early 1930s are primarily concerned with the problems of the 'new music' from the perspective of someone involved in the practical and 'immanent' musical issues of the time. While the extent of his practical musical involvement should not be over-emphasized, Adorno was nevertheless in direct contact with composers, including Schoenberg, Berg, Webern, Hindemith, Eisler, Weill and Krenek, and the musical writings from this period are predominantly concerned with compositional questions and problems of performance. While often taking the form of brief reviews or technical analyses, they are usually at the same time tightly interwoven with critical commentary and philosophical interpretation. This is of a kind which not only connects the musical texts with Adorno's more overtly philosophical writings of the period, but which also reveals the musical problems discussed to have provided, in a certain sense, the material sources of his philosophical approach. Musical phenomena were not simply subsumed under abstract philosophical categories, but, as Susan Buck-Morss has expressed it, 'were interpreted as themselves concrete and physical representations of the categories'.[4] The details on which Adorno focused in his 'micrological analyses' of musical phenomena were seen by him as historical 'images' (*Bilder*) of the concepts.[5]

In the period from the early 1920s up to his emigration to the United States in the late 1930s, Adorno published over a hundred articles and essays on music (a figure which does not include the many shorter reviews he also published regularly during this time). The earliest of these articles, dating from 1921–2, include two on Bernhard Sekles,[6] and one each on Bartók[7] and Hindemith.[8] He subsequently published three more articles on Bartók up to 1929[9] and two more on Hindemith up to 1932,[10] as well as frequently reviewing performances and scores of their music during the 1920s and 1930s.[11] The main issues raised in these articles (together with the slightly later ones on Berg, Schoenberg and Webern) concern what he calls 'the rupture between self and forms' – that is, the split between the expressive needs of composers and the reified character of the handed-down traditional forms and genres. (This will be discussed later in the present chapter through concrete 'case studies' in Adorno's philosophical interpretation of tendencies in contemporary music of the time.) Adorno's engagement with the music of Bartók and Hindemith noticeably subsides during this period, however, and early on gives way to a spate of articles on Schoenberg, Berg and Webern. Nevertheless, he remained a lifelong admirer of Bartók's music and was in personal contact with the composer in the United States during the 1940s.[12] Of Hindemith he became more critical, and his 'compilation' essay in *Impromptus* (1968), 'Ad vocem Hindemith: Eine Dokumentation',[13] includes his previously published articles on the composer, together with a critical review of *Unterweisung im Tonsatz* written in 1939 but previously unpublished, flanked by new introductory and concluding material (entitled 'Präludium' and 'Post-ludium' as references to Hindemith's piano work, *Ludus tonalis*). Adorno also published articles in the pre-war period on the composers of the 'Great Tradition' of bourgeois art music (as well as on composers who sought directly to continue that tradition in the twentieth century). He ranges widely, and the list includes Bach,[14] Beethoven,[15] Schubert,[16] Wagner,[17] Offenbach,[18] Mascagni,[19] Ravel,[20] Mahler,[21] Richard Strauss[22] and Sibelius.[23] He was also particularly interested in the music of his direct contemporaries, and published a number of articles on Hanns Eisler,[24] Kurt Weill[25] and Ernst Krenek.[26] The bulk of the writing, however, was increasingly on the music of the Second Viennese School.

The first essays on Schoenberg[27] and Berg[28] appeared in 1925, and the first on Webern[29] in 1926. During the next twelve years or so he published twelve articles on Schoenberg, fourteen on Berg and four on Webern.[30] These ranged from introductory and analytical pieces to philosophical–interpretational studies like 'Der dialektische Komponist',[31] and they clearly indicate the centrality of these composers (especially Schoenberg and Berg – Webern seems to occupy a more peripheral role) to Adorno's music theory as it developed during this period. Again, the focus is on 'the rupture between self and forms', and also on the increasingly rigorous control of musical material (seen in the light of the opposed concepts 'history' and 'nature'). Oddly, however, the composer who features as the counterpole to Schoenberg in the full-length study which was later to develop out of these concerns – *Philosophie der neuen Musik* – does not merit an essay at this stage: Igor Stravinsky. His presence is, nevertheless, to be felt, in that he is referred to frequently (especially in 'Zur gesellschaftlichen Lage der Musik'[32] of 1932), and the important position he comes to occupy in *Philosophie der neuen Musik* is already implied. Likewise, Debussy receives no essay devoted to his music; he is, however, often drawn into the discussion of other composers, and a certain picture of him within Adorno's thought does emerge, particularly in relation to Wagner and Stravinsky.[33]

Apart from articles on the music of particular composers, there are also essays on aspects of musical life which, increasingly during this period, tend more towards sociological questions (although they can hardly be said at this stage to constitute a sociology of music). One of the earliest of these writings is the essay 'Zum Problem der Reproduktion' of 1925.[34] This puts forward ideas towards a 'theory of reproduction' – i.e. of musical performance and interpretation – which Adorno initially developed in conjunction with the violinist Rudolph Kolisch, leader of the Kolisch Quartet.[35] He continued to add to the project over a period of many years, intending to write a full-length study of musical performance. The fragments remained incomplete at his death, however.[36] Aspects of 'Zum Problem der Reproduktion' will be considered in more detail in Chapter 5.

A somewhat whimsical piece from this period, discussing mechanical reproduction, is 'Nadelkurven' of 1928,[37] an interpretation of the gramophone. An essay from 1930, 'Bewußtsein des Konzerthörers',[38] focuses on the sphere of reception/consumption and considers the experience of the concert-goer, while a further essay from the same year, 'Arbeitsprobleme des Komponisten: Gespräch über Musik und soziale Situation,' written with Ernst Krenek (and to be examined in some detail in Chapter 2), focuses on the sphere of musical production, specifically the problematic character of composition in relation to the social situation.[39] The late 1920s and the early 1930s were the period of Adorno's intensive debate with Ernst Krenek. Apart from the exchange of letters (published posthumously), a number of articles resulted, including 'Arbeitsprobleme des Komponisten' referred to above. Most important among these are 'Reaktion und Fortschritt' of 1930[40] (a companion to Krenek's essay 'Fortschritt und Reaktion')[41] and the extended essay 'Zur gesellschaftlichen Lage der Musik' of 1932.

Towards a sociology of music

It is with 'Zur gesellschaftlichen Lage der Musik' that Adorno's 'music theory' could be said to come of age, because here he attempts to bring together his thinking on music and its relation to society in a large-scale piece of writing for the first time. Although still an 'essay', there is a definite intention to produce a systematic synthesis of his thinking up to this point – in spite of the often-misunderstood claim of his theory to be 'anti-systematic'. At the same time, it is also a 'fragment' – 'the draft of a finished musical sociology', as he later put it when referring to the article in *Einleitung in die Musiksoziologie* in 1962.[42] The essay also demonstrates Adorno's further attempts to apply a Marxian analysis to music and the conditions of its production, reproduction, distribution and consumption. This text occupies a central position in Adorno's writings on music and, even though he did not permit it to be republished during his lifetime because of what he later came to see as its rather crude application of Marxian theory, its influence is to be felt on all his subsequent work. *Einleitung in die Musiksoziologie* and shorter pieces like 'Ideen zur Musiksoziologie' (1958)[43] and 'Thesen zur Kunstsoziologie' (1967)[44] have to be seen as extended footnotes to 'Zur gesellschaftlichen Lage der Musik'. The essay is examined in some detail at the end of Chapter 2.

Adorno's sociologically orientated writings on music arise from a consideration of the problem of the composer's relation to musical material and of the performer's dual relation to the musical work (as score) and to the audience, in the social context of the commodification of music and the effects of what he came to call the 'culture industry'. These effects included what he called, using a mixture of Marxian and Freudian terminology, the fetishization of music and the 'regression of listening', resulting in a change in the function of music – the triumph of exchange value over use value.[45] They were explored at some length in Adorno's most substantial essay on music up to this point after 'Zur gesellschaftlichen Lage der Musik': 'Über den Fetischcharakter in der Musik und die Regression des Hörens' of 1938.[46] These themes were further developed in the late 1930s and in the 1940s, partly through Adorno's direct encounter with empirical ap-proaches to sociology and psychology in his period of exile in the United States. From the empirically based Princeton Radio Research Project resulted the extended study which remained incomplete and unpublished in his lifetime – *Current of Music: Elements of a Radio Theory*. Parts of this study were published separately, however, in English as 'The Radio Symphony' (1941),[47] 'On popular music' (with the assistance of George Simpson; 1941),[48] and 'A social critique of radio music' (1945).[49] A second project in which he was involved was the Film Music Project of the New School for Social Research, together with Hanns Eisler. From their collaboration resulted a book written in 1944, but only published in 1947 in English and under Eisler's name alone – *Composing for the Films*, a work subsequently published in its original German version under both Adorno's and Eisler's names as *Komposition für den Film* in 1969.[50]

Popular music

Related to the increasingly 'sociological' writings are those on aspects of folk music, 'popular music' and jazz. There are, of course, very different categories of music involved here – categories which Adorno sometimes distinguished between, but often did not. Interesting for its relation to Adorno's assessment of Bartók, as well as for his use of concepts like 'the rupture between self and forms', is his early review of published collections of folk music entitled 'Volksliedersammlungen', dating from 1925.[51] However, for Adorno folk music had itself in the industrialized West been subjected to the process of increasing rationalization which characterizes the modern world, and he argues in 'Zur gesellschaftlichen Lage der Musik' that there is now no 'folk' left anyway.[52] 'Folk music' as a category increasingly tends in the later writings to blur into a general concept of 'popular music' which is itself very hazy, and Adorno sometimes seems to make little distinction between popular songs (*Schlager*), jazz, and 'light music' (*leichte Musik*).[53] 'Folk music' is discussed in the early writings, however, where 'folk' is identified with 'nature', with 'community' (*Gemeinschaft*), and with the 'collectivity', an identification which, so Adorno argues, now belongs to a heroic, mythical past. In the 1929 essay 'Schlageranalysen'[54] Adorno analyses the lyrics and music of three popular songs of the period (including the famous *Valencia* of 1925) using these categories in conjunction with the concept of 'kitsch'. Of the first song, for example ('Ich weiß auf der Wieden ein kleines Hotel' of 1915), he writes: 'In kitsch the refrain still always preserves the memory of the collective power of music, while the narrative verses undertake the expression of the individual, who in truth remains separate from this collectivity: in this way the hit song form tries to create totality'.[55] In an article written probably in 1932 but only published posthumously, Adorno expands on the concept of musical 'kitsch': 'Its task, above all, is: to awake, through the retention of old and superannuated formal types, the impression of an attested collective binding force'.[56] This it achieves through its use of musical 'small change' – formulae which have become so familiar through over-use that they have become stereotypes, including, for example, the pseudo-folksong. By 1932, in 'Zur gesellschaftlichen Lage der Musik', Adorno has extended this analysis by the use of Marxian concepts, and later by the use of psychoanalytical concepts. His much-criticized notion of the 'jazz subject' – lonely and isolated but becoming psychologically submerged in the bogus collectivity of a music which barely disguises its dependence on the military march, in spite of the apparent freedom of its improvised solos – is a contentious image which features in all Adorno's essays on jazz: 'Abschied vom Jazz' (1933),[57] 'Über Jazz' (1937),[58] 'On popular music' (1941) and 'Zeitlose Mode: Zum Jazz' (1953).[59] It is also an image which is used in his critique of Stravinsky's music, particularly in *Philosophie der neuen Musik*.

Philosophy of 'new music' as philosophy of history

Also a product of his 'American Period' are the primarily 'philosophical' texts on music – again, a further reworking of motifs developed in the earlier writings,[60] but now influenced by his own 'rupture' from European (and particularly Austro-German) culture as a result of the Second World War,[61] and his contact with and reaction to the 'consumer society' and 'popular culture' of the United States. These texts are not always directly 'about' the new music of the period, but they are always informed by a position which views music of the past from the perspective of the contemporary avant-garde. Thus the 'philosophy of new music' is also a philosophy of history. These texts, of which *Philosophie der neuen Musik* (1941–8, published 1949) is the most central, include 'Bach gegen seine

Liebhaber verteidigt' (1951),[62] *Versuch über Wagner* (published 1952, although parts of it had been written in 1937),[63] 'Arnold Schönberg, 1874–1951' (1953),[64] 'Das Altern der neuen Musik' (1954–5),[65] 'Musik und Technik' (1958),[66] 'Verfremdetes Hauptwerk: Zur Missa Solemnis' (1959),[67] *Mahler: Eine musikalische Physiognomik* (1960),[68] 'Musik und neue Musik' (1960),[69] 'Vers une musique informelle' (1961),[70] 'Richard Strauss: Zum hundertsten Geburtstag: 11. Juni 1964' (1964)[71] and *Berg: Der Meister des kleinsten Übergangs* (1968, although most of the technical–analytical sections had originally appeared in 1937). The approach used in many of these texts, and in particular in *Philosophie der neuen Musik*, owes much to the book Adorno wrote in collaboration with Max Horkheimer in the United States and published in 1947: *Dialektik der Aufklärung*.[72]

The 'dialectic of the Enlightenment' is seen by Adorno and Horkheimer as the dialectic of history and nature in the particular form of rationality and myth, through which reason has ended up by betraying its own promise of progress towards freedom and is now characterized by repression. They argue that rationality, in liberating itself historically from myth through the progressive domination of nature, has lost its power of critical self-reflection and has become itself part of unreflective 'nature'. Domination of nature has become self-domination, and rationality has ended up serving irrational and repressive ends. Thus the historical progress of the Enlightenment has itself become a regression to myth. This thesis was applied by Adorno and Horkheimer to an analysis of what they saw as significant aspects of Western culture, and the book contains a particularly seminal essay (to be discussed in Chapter 5) on what the authors call the 'culture industry'. The critique of the music of Schoenberg and Stravinsky in *Philosophie der neuen Musik* is a direct outcome of the thesis put forward by Adorno and Horkheimer in their joint project. As Adorno puts it in the preface to *Philosophie der neuen Musik*, 'the book should be read as an extended excursus to *Dialektik der Aufklärung*'.[73]

The fragment as critique of totality

One of the first books to appear after Adorno's return to Frankfurt from the United States was *Minima Moralia* (1951). The book is aphoristic, cryptic and fragmented in form, and is a product of Adorno's experience of enforced emigration and exile in America. The starting point for each section is always a concrete, individual, and usually private experience. This is taken as the material for dialectical reflection which both reveals the 'mediatedness' of the experience, and touches its 'immediacy' through an interpretation which breaks off without linking up with some overarching philosophical totality. The book in a sense provides the model for much of

Adorno's later writing on music and aesthetics, although, as pointed out earlier, it is not itself a text on music. Its central philosophical concern is 'truth', as revealed in individual, concrete experience, but a truth which is always historically mediated and seen as part of a fractured and fragmented totality. In the opening pages of the book he writes:

He who wishes to know the truth about life in its immediacy must scrutinize its estranged form, the objective powers that determine individual existence even in its most hidden recesses. To speak immediately of the immediate is to behave much as those novelists who drape their marionettes in imitated bygone passions like cheap jewellery, and make people who are no more than component parts of the machinery act as if they still had the capacity to act as Subjects, and as if something depended on their actions.[74]

During the 1950s and 1960s these themes were continued in both the philosophical and the musical writings. Adorno's critiques of ontology and of the belief in philosophical 'first principles' (as 'unmediated immediacy') were taken further in extended studies like *Zur Metakritik der Erkenntnistheorie* (1956, although much of the book dates from the 1930s when Adorno was at Oxford),[75] a study of the 'antinomies' of Husserl's phenomenology, and *Jargon der Eigentlichkeit: Zur deutschen Ideologie* (1964),[76] an attack on the concept of 'authenticity' (*Eigentlichkeit*) used by German existentialists like Heidegger. The concerns of these books are also to be discovered in musical texts like 'Über das gegenwärtige Verhältnis von Philosophie und Musik' (1953)[77] and 'Fragment über Musik und Sprache' (1956),[78] as well as in the studies of individual composers Adorno published at this time (see above). They reach back to unpublished texts from the early 1930s like 'Die Aktualität der Philosophie' [1931] and 'Die Idee der Naturgeschichte' [1932], motifs from which will be examined in the following section in relation to the underlying philosophical concerns of Adorno's music theory. These concerns are focused in Adorno's two large projects of the 1960s – *Negative Dialektik* (1966) and *Ästhetische Theorie* (1970). Consideration of concepts like 'non-identity', 'semblance of nature' and 'truth content' as they occur in these important texts will be reserved for the final section of this chapter, where they will be discussed in relation to Adorno's interpretative method. First, it is necessary to return to the issues raised in the early writings on music, the concepts used and their place within the larger context of Adorno's philosophy.

2   History, nature, second nature: the debates with Lukács and Benjamin

In Adorno's writings on 'new music' in the 1920s and 1930s two issues emerge as central. First, there is the problematical relation between *history* and *nature*; and second, there is the equally problematical relation of the composer to handed-down forms, identified by Adorno as 'the rupture between self and forms'. These two issues, as we shall see, are closely connected, and indeed can be understood as two aspects of the same problem.

The idea of natural history

In July 1932 Adorno gave a philosophical paper at the Frankfurt chapter of the Kantgesellschaft entitled 'Die Idee der Naturgeschichte'.[79] Starting from a critique of Heidegger's ontology, and arguing that the concept of Being (*Sein*) in the then dominant Heideggerian philosophy could be quite simply subsumed under the concept of 'nature', he put forward a dialectical theory of the mediation of nature and history which owed much to Lukács and Benjamin.

For Adorno, the concept of 'nature' indicates that which is static, timeless, unchanging and apparently beyond history. It is not nature as implied in the 'natural sciences', or in the term 'natural history' as normally understood. It can, in fact, be further subsumed under the concept 'myth':

> The concept of nature that is to be dissolved is one that, if I translated it into standard philosophical terminology, would come closest to the concept of myth. This concept is also vague and its exact sense can not be given in preliminary definitions but only in the course of analysis. By it is meant what has always been, what as fatefully arranged predetermined being underlies history and appears in history; it is substance in history. What is delimited by these expressions is what I mean here by 'nature'.[80]

The concept of 'nature' is seen by Adorno as itself a historical construct – a construct which, in his later writings, he came to see in a rather different way as 'socially necessary illusion', or 'semblance' (*Schein*). At this stage, however, the appeal to 'nature' – usually under the guise of the ontological notion of 'pure being' (*Sein*) in Heidegger, or 'immediacy' in Husserl, and manifested in composers like Stravinsky as the folkloric, archaic or hieratic and in Hindemith as 'natural material' and 'community' – is regarded by Adorno as the attempt to evade history, and has ideological implications in terms of a reactionary impulse to preserve the status quo and to conceal the real relations of power within modern society (implications which were to be taken up in later writings like *Philosophie der neuen Musik*). The concept of 'history', on the other hand, refers to that which is dynamic and which changes over time, and can be understood as the interaction of 'consciousness' and 'nature', as 'culture' (in the sociological and anthropological senses of the term). Adorno identifies 'history' in relation to 'nature' in the following terms, placing particular emphasis on the concept of 'the new':

history means that mode of conduct established by tradition that is characterized primarily by the occurrence of the qualitatively new; it is a movement that does not play itself out in mere identity, mere reproduction of what has always been, but rather one in which the new occurs; it is a movement that gains its true character through what appears in it as new.[81]

Adorno's interest in these two concepts is in their *mediation*, in the sense in which this term is being used in this study and which is to be examined in particular detail in Chapter 3. That is to say, Adorno is interested in the interaction of the concepts as opposites, whereby nature comes to be seen as historical, and history comes to be taken as nature. He writes, typically:

wherever I operate with the concepts of nature and history, no ultimate definitions are meant, rather I am pursuing the intention of pushing these concepts to a point where they are mediated in their apparent difference.[82]

The second of the two issues which dominate Adorno's music writings of this period is that of the rupture between what he calls the 'I' or 'self' (as individual subjectivity) and 'forms' (as handed-down forms representing a collective objectivity) (*der Bruch zwischen Ich und Formen*). This refers to the disintegration of traditional genres, formal types and schemata and their loss of meaning as shared norms, and their inability to meet the expressive demands placed upon them in the 'modernist' period. The 'rupture between self and forms' is the manifestation of alienation in music and an aspect of the fragmentation of modern life. At the same time, however, the disintegration of forms serves to reveal their historicity, and the breakdown of a 'referential system' like tonality serves to reveal its apparently 'natural' foundations as, in fact, historical – that is, as a 'second nature' tied to particular cultural determinants. The concept of 'second nature' is one Adorno derived from Lukács (although it is to be found in Hegel and, interestingly, the idea also appears in Schoenberg's *Harmonielehre*).[83]

Lukács and second nature

As we have seen, like many other intellectuals of his generation Adorno was profoundly influenced by Georg Lukács's *Geschichte und Klassenbewußtsein* of 1923.[84] Indeed, the Lukácsian concepts of reification[85] and commodity fetishism[86] were the filters through which he initially received Marx.[87] It is nevertheless in the pre-Marxian Lukács that we find the most important source of influence on Adorno's concepts of 'nature' and 'history', together with his notion of the fragmentary character of art. In *Theorie des Romans* (*Theory of the Novel*), which initially appeared in 1916 (it was later published in book form in 1920),[88] Lukács puts forward a critique of the novel which sees the emergence and decline of the genre as a manifestation of the historically changing relationship of the self to the world. The central concept is that of 'totality':[89] the breakdown of a homogeneous world-view (he starts, for example, from a discussion of the epic in relation to communities in the ancient world), has compelled art to create totality independently within its own forms. Lukács writes:

Art, the visionary reality of the world made to our measure, has thus become independent: it is no longer a copy, for all the models have gone; it is a created totality, for the natural unity of the metaphysical spheres has been destroyed forever.[90]

Art works, which have now become autonomous, can no longer mirror a given, accepted external totality within their form, because such a totality no longer exists in a fragmented world. Lukács sees only two possibilities for responding to the situation:

they must either narrow down and volatise whatever has to be given form to the point where they can encompass it, or else they must show polemically the impossibility of achieving their necessary object and the inner nullity of their own means. And in this case they carry the fragmentary nature of the world's structure into the world of forms.[91]

As a result of this break between self and the world, and between the 'autonomy' of art and the 'heteronomy' of empirical reality, art forms become part of a historical dialectic, resulting in a complex and mediated relation between genres and the socio-historical conditions in which they originated and from which they took their meaning. The link between the self and the external world of forms, taken for granted, for example, in the age of the heroic epic with the rootedness of its shared meanings in the community, is now lost, or has become at very least highly complex. As Lukács puts it: 'Artistic genres now cut across one another, with a complexity that cannot be disentangled, and become traces of authentic or false searching for an aim that is no longer clearly and unequivocally given'.[92] In becoming self-contained totalities, the forms of art become 'meaningless' in themselves: their meaning, which has now become symbolic (in that the forms no longer have a direct social function), has to be deciphered historically in relation to the larger totality of which it is part – a totality which is itself fragmented:

as the objective world breaks down, so the [S]ubject, too, becomes a fragment; only the 'I' continues to exist, but its existence is then lost in the insubstantiality of its self-created world of ruins. Such subjectivity wants to give form to everything, and precisely for this reason succeeds only in mirroring a segment of the world.[93]

Lukács can be interpreted here in the following terms: the forms of art become marked by their difference from life (as empirical reality), while at the same time mirroring the fragmentation of life and resolving this 'dissonance' within the alienated unity and totality of their own forms.[94] However, as the forms of art 'lose their obvious roots in supra-personal ideal necessities' they become merely existent and 'form the world of convention'.[95] As such they become recognizable but incomprehensible, and form what he calls a 'second nature' of meaningless necessities which have forgotten their origin. This 'world of convention', in not being recognized as the exteriorization of previous interiority, as the objectification of previous subjectivity, is called by Lukács 'a charnel-house of long-dead interiorities'.[96] Nature as 'first nature', as the set of laws known to the natural sciences, is also, however, seen by Lukács as 'alienated nature':

Estrangement from nature (the first nature), the modern sentimental attitude to nature, is only a projection of man's experience of his self-made environment as a prison instead of as a parental home.[97]

And by the time he has embraced Marxism in the early 1920s, he has modified his concept of 'second nature' so that it becomes 'nature' in Geschichte und Klassenbewußtsein:

Nature is a societal category. That is to say, whatever is held to be natural at any given stage of social development, however this nature is related to man and whatever form his involvement with it takes, i.e. nature's form, its content, its range and its objectivity are all socially conditioned.[98]

Thus, Lukács's concept of 'second nature' (and indeed of 'nature' in the later work) can be understood as reified history and society. Adorno takes over the concept directly, but has reservations concerning Lukács's suggestion in Theorie des Romans that perhaps there exists the possibility of 'a metaphysical act of reawakening the spiritual element that created or maintained [second nature] in its earlier or ideal existence'.[99] In 'Die Idee der Naturgeschichte' Adorno argues that:

The problem of this awakening, which Lukács grants to be a metaphysical possibility, is the problem that determines what is here understood by natural-history. Lukács envisioned the metamorphosis of the historical qua past into nature; petrified history is nature, or the petrified life of nature is a mere product of historical development. The reference to the charnel-house includes the elements of the cipher: everything must mean something, just what, however, must first be extracted. Lukács can only think of this charnel-house in terms of a theological resurrection, in an eschatological context.[100]

Adorno considered that Lukács had recognized how what is historical becomes petrified into what seems to be 'natural', but that he was unable to show how this 'second nature' is to be decoded, apart from resorting to the metaphysical notion of 'totality'. It was Walter Benjamin, so he argued, who offered an approach to the deciphering of 'natural-history' which stayed close to the object of cognition in all its concrete particularity.

Benjamin and the history of nature

Although Adorno had first met Benjamin in 1923 in Frankfurt,[101] it was not until 1928, the period of their adoption of Marxism, that Benjamin's influence on him became particularly apparent.[102] The years that followed, up to Benjamin's death in 1940, were marked by an intense exchange of ideas between the two men, initiated by their 'unforgettable conversations'[103] in September and October of 1929 in the village of Königstein in the Taunus, and culminating in the famous exchange of letters in the late 1930s centred particularly upon Benjamin's work on Baudelaire and his essay 'Das Kunstwerk im Zeitalter seiner technischen Reproduzierbarkeit', and Adorno's 'Über den Fetischcharakter in der Musik und die Regression des Hörens'.[104] At this stage, however, in his 'Die Idee der Naturgeschichte', it is Benjamin's *Ursprung des deutschen Trauerspiels* of 1928[105] on which Adorno is drawing.

Adorno takes the concept of *Naturgeschichte* directly from Benjamin's *Trauerspiel* study. Gillian Rose explains the concept as follows:

In the book *Origin of German Tragic Drama* Benjamin argues that Greek tragedy and Baroque *Trauerspiel* are each determined by their time in the sense that they present the predominant myth of the time.... The myth comprises the history of the significance which the society of the time has given to nature, and, as a myth, presents that significance as eternal. Benjamin calls this *Naturgeschichte* (the history of nature).[106]

In Benjamin's concept of *Naturgeschichte* Adorno sees the idea of the *transience* of nature as the key to nature's historicality, arguing that:

If Lukács demonstrates the retransformation of the historical, as that which has been, into nature, then here is the other side of the phenomenon: nature itself is seen as transitory nature, as history.[107]

To indicate how Benjamin's approach goes beyond Lukács's concept of 'second nature', Adorno introduces two more Benjaminian concepts from the *Trauerspiel* book: *allegory* and *cipher*. Benjamin's insight, Adorno argues, is that the meaning of nature = *transience*, and that the allegorical is not merely an abstract and arbitrary symbol, but is rather the *expression* of something concrete and historical. The purpose of critical philosophical interpretation, as Adorno sees it, is to understand the world of convention, i.e. 'second nature', as a cipher for the historical relation to nature, a cipher which needs to be deciphered. Adorno writes:

What is expressed in the allegorical sphere is nothing but an historical relationship. The theme of the allegorical is, simply, history. At issue is an historical relationship between what appears – nature – and its meaning, i.e. transience.[108]

Second nature, as 'objective' conventions, is made up, as we have seen, of previous subjectivity which has forgotten its origins in subjectivity. This previous subjectivity, or interiority, has rigidified into a cipher, a secret language, but one which, as in works of art for example, expresses the relation between 'nature' – that is, appearance or semblance (*Schein*) as 'second nature' – and its historical meaning, which is that nature equals transience. The deciphering of this relation between 'nature' and its historical meaning is what Adorno is indicating when he calls his hermeneutical method a 'musical physiognomics', as, for example, in his book *Mahler: Eine musikalische Physiognomik* (1960). His approach attempts to interpret, to 'decipher', the surface appearance of music, its 'illusion' or 'semblance', as the petrified expression of a historical response to the experience of 'nature' as transience. According to Rose: 'Adorno generalises Benjamin's theory of seventeenth-century *Trauerspiel*, so that all history is the history of the fall of nature. Each generation sees this history on the face of nature.'[109]

Beginnings of a method: constellations

In Adorno's critique of Heidegger's ontology, and in his reception of Lukács's and Benjamin's concepts of nature, history, second nature and allegory, is to be seen the emergence of his distinctive critical method. These influences are focused in 'Die Idee der Naturgeschichte', which also contains a critique, at times more implicit than explicit, of aspects of Lukács and Benjamin's positions. Briefly put, what Adorno takes from Lukács and Benjamin is the conception of a dialectical relation between 'nature' and 'history', whereby the two poles are mediated through their opposites. But in his own application of this dialectical principle Adorno is really putting forward a 'negative dialectic' in which the opposites negate each other while simultaneously refusing reconcilement. That is to say, the concept of 'nature' is negated and dissolved by revealing nature to be myth, a 'second nature' of historically created conventions now unaware of their origin. Thus 'nature' is shown to be in fact history, created by human labour, and its ontological status as an invariant is destroyed. On the other hand, the concept of 'history' is also negated and dissolved by revealing notions such as 'historical progress' and 'historical continuity' likewise to be myth. History is seen by Adorno to be discontinuous, fragmented, and made up of concrete, material phenomena which do not lead smoothly and seamlessly towards some preordained end. His view of history is not teleological, in spite of impressions to the contrary. At the same time, history is also shown to become naturalized, in that it becomes taken as 'natural', while it also contains the traces of nature within it as the remains of that which has passed away. In a sense, therefore, 'history', as transience, can also be seen as nature, and not as part of some higher metaphysical unity or totality, in the Hegelian sense, within which all antagonisms will be reconciled. This was Adorno's criticism of Lukács's view of history – that it posited just such a totalizing concept of history. On the other hand, his subsequent criticism of Benjamin's view of 'natural history' was that it risked becoming static and was in danger of losing dialectical tension through its emphasis on the 'naturalness' of the historical phenomena under examination, as what Benjamin called 'original-history' (*Urgeschichte*).[110]

Adorno argues that in order to bring out the dual character of the concepts he is using – that is, their mediatedness – he cannot resort to the traditional structure of discursive logical argument. This is because, he implies, traditional forms of theory work against the contradictory character of the concepts themselves and serve to betray the uniqueness of the 'concrete object' of cognition by subsuming it completely under abstract categories. In place of traditional logic Adorno puts forward an alternative logical structure: that of the 'constellation'. He describes this as follows, in relation to the concepts he has derived from Lukács and Benjamin:

It is not a matter of clarifying concepts out of one another, but of the constellation of ideas, namely those of transience, signification, the idea of nature and the idea of history. One does not refer back to these ideas as 'invariants'; the issue is not to define them, rather they gather around a concrete historical facticity that, in the context of these elements, will reveal itself in its uniqueness. How do these elements cohere? According to Benjamin, nature, as creation, carries the mark of transience. Nature itself is transitory. Thus it includes the element of history. Whenever an historical element appears it refers back to the natural element that passes away within it. Likewise the reverse: whenever 'second nature' appears, when the world of convention approaches, it can be deciphered in that its meaning is shown to be precisely its transience.[111]

Although Adorno first clearly formulates the distinctive features of his philosophical–interpretative approach in the early 1930s, in essays like 'Die Idee der Naturgeschichte' and 'Die Aktualität der Philosophie', the essays on music from the early 1920s onwards are already manifestations of the constructional principle of the 'constellation'. The central concepts, as we have seen, are those of the relation between history and nature, and the rupture between the self and forms – concepts which later come to be subsumed under Adorno's critique of the Hegelian Subject–Object relationship. It is to Adorno's application of the 'alternative logical structure', of the constellation – what was in due course to become his 'negative dialectics' – and of the contradictory pairs of concepts examined above to the 'concrete historical facticity' of particular musical works and aspects of musical life, that we now turn.

3   The problem of form: Bartók, Hindemith, Stravinsky and the Second Viennese School

The dialectical tension between 'history' and 'nature' which is such a feature of Adorno's early writings, together with the alienation of the self from the world of established forms, can also be seen as the persistent themes of his subsequent work. His suspicion of all appeals to 'nature' and the 'natural', and of any recourse to notions of 'pure being' beyond history, grew out of a conviction that the attempt to reconstruct such absolutes and invariants had ideological implications. The search for 'natural laws' represented for him a retreat into myth, a refusal to confront the disintegration of accepted meanings which characterized the modern world. He saw it as an attempt to mask alienation and fragmentation under the veil of a reassuring but false totality – a tendency which he viewed in the context of the subjugation of the individual and the rise of totalitarian regimes which characterized the European political landscape of the 1920s and 1930s.[112]

Just as in his own philosophical position he had rejected ontological 'first principles' and systematization, and had founded his thought on the oscillating principle of the 'constellation', so in his small output as a composer he had rejected tonality and had likewise refused the systematiz-ation of the twelve-tone technique, preferring to remain in the uncharted territory of free atonality. While recognizing the undesirability of remain-ing in this state of unreconciled tension without hope of resolution (in spite of Lukács's quip about the Critical Theorists taking up residence in *Grand Hotel Abgrund*, a luxury hotel on the edge of the Abyss from where they were able to contemplate the void 'between excellent meals or artistic entertainments'),[113] Adorno at the same time refused what he saw as any premature reconciliation of 'the rupture between self and forms'. One of these 'premature reconciliations' he considered to be the unreflective use of folk music to symbolize a state of nature or the resolution of the tension between self and others in terms of a notion of the ideal 'natural community' (*Naturgemeinschaft*). (Folk music was being used politically at this period to foster a sense of national identity by both fascist and communist regimes alike.) He considered that another false reconciliation was that represented by the attempt to claim legitimacy for systems of composition, whether new or old, on the grounds that they were founded in the laws of acoustics (as the 'laws of nature'). Yet another was developments like *Gebrauchsmusik* and *Gemeinschaftsmusik*, as attempts to create a lost social function for music beyond that of the commodity, based either on a suspect craft ethic or on some notion of political community. And finally, there was the possibility of a retreat into subjectivity so complete that the rupture between the 'self' and forms became total. It was this last possibility which, he considered, paradoxically showed the way towards a more 'authentic' attempt to confront the fragmentation of established musical forms within the musical material itself. It will be useful at this point to ground these ideas in Adorno's writings of this period through a brief examination of his interpretation of the music of a number of his contemporaries.

Bartók

In Bartók's music, in spite of its 'folkloristic inclinations', Adorno saw a mode of organization which had 'a power of alienation which places it in the company of the avant-garde and not that of nationalistic reaction'.[114] He considered that Bartók – like Janáček – was able to make use of folk music as a valid source of musical material because South-East Europe at that period remained largely untouched by the process of industrialization which had transformed Western Europe and North America. Because East European folk music had largely fallen outside the dominant process of rationalization it could be used critically by Bartók and Janáček for radical and progressive ends. This was Adorno's gloss on Bartók as it appears in a footnote in *Philosophie der neuen Musik*, however – a book in which the composer hardly features at all. It is to the early writings we must look for a detailed picture.

In 1921, in one of his earliest essays, Adorno writes of Bartók concerning *Bluebeard's Castle*: 'His eternal theme is the eruption into the human world of the eternally natural, a theme in which, doubtless unconsciously, the spiritual situation of his people has been concentrated'.[115] Adorno saw Bartók's music as an attempt to span the gulf between, on the one hand, the ahistorical, epic 'natural community' (*Naturgemeinschaft*)[116] of the pre-industrial world, where the 'individual' is represented by the hero, who speaks unproblematically for the community as a whole, and, on the other hand, the highly industrialized societies of the modern world, within which the individual, whose sense of the 'social whole' is now always partial and fragmented, exists in a state of alienation. Technically, this rupture manifests itself within Bartók's music in terms of the relation to its materials. Specifically, this means the relation between the handed-down genres, formal types and tonal schemata of the Western high art-music tradition, and the material from his East European folk-music researches. In his 1921 article and in an article of 1925 on Bartók's *Dance Suite*, Adorno suggests that the result of this confrontation in the case of the first two string quartets and the two sonatas for violin and piano is a critique of sonata form 'pursued to the rhapsodic dissolution [*Auflösung*] of all pre-given form'.[117] On the other hand, in the case of what he calls an 'occasional' work like the *Dance Suite* (written to celebrate the fiftieth anniversary of the unification of Buda and Pest) Bartók could have been expected to retreat from the confrontation with handed-down forms, given the opportunity to make exclusive use of 'folk' material, and instead to allow himself to sink into the attractions of the folk material without concerning himself with the problem of the loss of meaning of traditional forms. The composer nevertheless retains his integrity, Adorno maintains, and approaches the problem of 'form' from two different directions:

He knows – not through reflection, certainly, but rather as creative artist [*als Gestalter*] – that the forms, which have been torn away from [their relation to] the self [*vom Ich*] and have become rigidified in themselves, have lost their power over the self; that, in their own terms, no reality inheres in them any more; and he refuses to avail himself of them as if they were real. But he also knows that the forms are still there residually, even though they no longer exist; that they still continue to make their demands on the self, even though the self cannot meet their demands – just as they can no longer satisfy the demands of the self. The zone of reconciliation remains open to him, but it grants him no peaceful abode; he must strive constantly to burst out of it from both sides. If he passes into the sphere of pure subjectivity, then his national commitment is strengthened; if he enters the sphere of dead forms, then his 'self' is preserved alive.[118]

Adorno argues that a sense of 'alienation' in the *Dance Suite* is achieved by means of an ironic distancing from the material, through *play*, in a manner not unlike the use of irony in certain of Stravinsky's pre-neoclassical works:

Instead of pathetically fighting for the reality of the forms, or of romantically deluding himself of their reality, he *plays* with them, lets them emerge from the occasion, now become the symbol of chance which alone still controls the relation to such forms. He does not attempt to burden them subjectively and to break through them, but reveals himself precisely in the prudent irony with which he conceals himself.[119]

At the same time, however, Adorno considers that Bartók succeeds in remaining true to his folk-derived material, in spite of the alienating effect of the playful irony with which he treats his material. He concludes:

And again the ethnic foundations [of his music] support him; his alienation from the forms is not complete, and there remains a part of him within them and a part of them within him. His 'play' does not become an empty game.[120]

The reference to 'empty game' (*Spielerei*) has Stravinsky in mind. Already by the mid-1920s Adorno had identified the polarities of his 'philosophy of the new music' as Stravinsky and Schoenberg, with Bartók somewhere in the middle – a mediating figure, perhaps, but not to be seen simply as a compromise between the extremes. Faced with the same basic problem of how to deal with the fragmentation of the musical material handed down from Romanticism, a fragmentation which manifested itself as a rupture between the 'self' and the handed-down forms, the three composers had responded very differently. Schoenberg, according to Adorno, had attempted to deal with the problem 'from within', by compelling the material to yield up its own solution (in the form of total thematicism and the twelve-tone technique), while Stravinsky had tried to deal with it 'from without', by imposing outmoded forms upon the chaos of the material, as a kind of ironic game with masks. Bartók's attempted solution was to retreat into himself, into the material of his folk-music collecting, where he 'researched what in reality there remained left over', as form.[121]

Adorno maintains, straightforwardly enough, that folk-music elements are never used in Bartók's music simply as superficial stylistic ornamentation, but instead are embraced by the subjective process of composition, in terms of the interpenetration of 'self' and objectivity. He goes on to suggest that the relation between the self and forms within this material is remarkably homogeneous, in that Bartók consistently avails himself of only three distinctive formal types, defined by the folk material itself: that is to say, declamatory rhapsody, song-like monody and impassioned dance (as *czardas*).[122] Adorno then argues that these three formal types function in Bartók's music as a critique of three Western instrumental formal types: the sonata first-movement, the adagio, and the combination of scherzo and rondo:

Bartók's [compositional] means exhaust themselves in the radical execution of this critique, in the pure representation of the [formal] types; he has really only written three pieces, and his development is nothing other than the path from the hidden seed to the lucid coming into view of these pieces.[123]

Adorno applies this interpretative framework to a number of Bartók's works up to the late 1920s, culminating in a discussion of the Third String Quartet in a brief essay published in 1929. Of the quartet he writes: 'Hungarian (formal) types and German sonata are melted down in the fire of impatient compositional effort; from these elements is produced a truly contemporary form'.[124]

Bartók's use of folk music as an extension of his musical material manages to avoid the danger of succumbing to a romantic nostalgia for a 'state of nature' beyond history, according to Adorno. The folk material and the 'natural community' it signifies are brought into confrontation with the 'dead forms' of the fragmented musical material of Western art music. Adorno argues that the resulting fusion, brought about through the force of Bartók's compositional process, does not conceal alienation under the mask of a false reconciliation of the epic and the modern. Rather, in using the folk material as a critique of the 'dead forms' of Western art music, it throws alienation into relief, while at the same time also forging a new and integrated musical language which does not in the process hide the fractured character of its elements.

Hindemith

Adorno's account of Hindemith's significance in the music of the first half of the twentieth century is complex and, unlike his interpretation of Bartók, lacks consistency in certain respects. In his early 1922 article[125] on Hindemith Adorno demonstrates an esteem for the composer's music which he later found embarrassingly effusive and uncritical.[126] This is, however, moderated in the 1926 essay 'Kammermusik von Paul Hindemith',[127] where Adorno expresses reservations about the composer's turn to neoclassicism and his emphasis on the 'mechanical objectivity' of technique at the expense of subjective expression. He writes concerning Hindemith's attempt to mix formal types like sonata and fugue and to draw on the gestures of Bachian counterpoint:

The works from Hindemith's 'classicist' epoch make their entry with the claim to play among the forms, and in fact merely play with forms. For this reason he only has the choice of given forms, as form is not given to him, just as little as it is to anyone else.[128]

Hindemith's 'new objectivity' (*neue Sachlichkeit*) and his 'music to sing and play' (*Sing- und Spielmusik*, originally called, significantly, *Haus- und Gemeinschaftsmusik* by the composer)[129] of the late 1920s and early 1930s were heavily criticized in Adorno's 1932 essay 'Kritik des Musikanten'.[130] By now, as a result of his belief that the Second Viennese School offered the most convincing response to the current crisis of musical language, Adorno had clearly formulated his opposition to 'classicism' and what he saw as its offshoots, *neue Sachlichkeit* and *Gebrauchsmusik*, with their stress on 'craft' and the need for the composer to turn his hand to anything that came his way, irrespective of content or ideological implications. Adorno criticized *Musikantentum*, which was understood by Hindemith as music-making directed particularly at amateurs, on several grounds. In the first place, he pointed out that the idea of the *Musikant* – a term difficult to translate, but which contains the idea of the spontaneous 'music-maker', with definite skills applied at a level of immediately functional music-making (but not at the elevated level of the *Musiker*, the professionally trained musician) – has associations with the Romantic period which contradict the ideals of *neue Sachlichkeit*. (Furthermore, although Adorno does not emphasize this, it should also be pointed out that the archetypal *Musikanten* are gypsy musicians and town bands, who are hardly amateurs in the sense in which Hindemith uses the idea.)[131] There is in the terms *Musikant* and *musizieren*, Adorno suggests, an attempt to deny the complexity of contemporary social relations and to retreat into notions of ahistorical community and 'natural musicianship' where people make music with improvisatory freedom and communicate in primitive immediacy. Thus, in the second place, he questioned the idea of *Gebrauchsmusik*, as 'music for immediate use', put forward by Hindemith and others. Using his recently acquired Marxism, and making passing reference to Krenek's highly successful 'jazz opera' *Jonny spielt auf* and to the enormously popular and commercially successful dance band of the American band-leader Paul Whiteman (the so-called 'King of Jazz'),[132] he argues that:

Jonny in reality does not 'strike up'; Whiteman gives concerts and people dance to his tune. Music only has use-value [*Gebrauchswert*] where it may serve to teach other people to play music, through instruction; the music which finally emerges from this has again no use-value, and even puts pedagogical values into question. But overall, music has become exchangeable as a commodity against abstract units [of exchange] which are utterly foreign to its use [*Gebrauch*]: i.e. money.[133]

Seen in this way, the real 'use' to which music is put in complex modern societies is not the 'immediate' one of providing music for amateurs to sing and play, but is the 'mediated' one of the commodity, of use for its exchange-value (Adorno's employment of Marxian terminology will be discussed in later chapters). Thirdly, Adorno maintains that, in its rejection of subjective expression, and in its attempt to break down the division of labour between composer and public, the music of Hindemith and composers like him absolutized the idea of the 'community' and the collectivity. In taking the idea of the 'collectivity' or the 'community' as a given, 'one deifies the existing powers as such, and persuades the collectivity, which is in itself empty of meaning, that its very collectivity is its meaning'.[134] And fourthly, Adorno argues that there is a problem in the relation of form to content in such music: it is designed to '"fill" the flow of empty, anxiety-producing time'.[135] This manifests itself in the music through the use of traditional structuring devices, like the sequence, which come into conflict with the disintegrating harmonic and melodic tendencies of the musical material at the present stage of its historical development.

Adorno argues that 'the *Musikanten* want to construct enclaves within rationalized society which side-step the power of the *ratio* for a hollow artlessness [*Natürlichkeit*]; alternatively, they want to pass off the blind rationalization process itself as "tempo of the time", as natural-mythical, and to glorify it'.[136] He suggests that, perhaps for this reason, they let themselves be seen as a substitute for 'folklorism' in the highly rationalized industrial countries of the West. He concludes the 1932 essay as follows:

The formal canon, which is broken, and which the *Musikanten* cannot summon up of themselves, has been replaced by an empty schema not grounded in the material.[137]

Adorno's diagnosis of the reactionary implications of Hindemith's music of the late 1920s and early 1930s, in terms of what he saw as a self-deluding attempt to deal with musical material as if it were an ahistorical 'given', and to claim that music had an 'immediacy' of social function within an idealized *Gemeinschaft*, was borne out, he considered, by the composer's codification of his musical practice in his book *Unterweisung im Tonsatz*, which appeared in 1937. Adorno's review of the book, written in 1939 for the *Zeitschrift für Sozialforschung* but only published in 1968 in *Impromptus*,[138] strongly criticized Hindemith's attempt to justify his particular system of 'extended tonality' in terms of the 'natural laws' of the harmonic series. Adorno accused Hindemith of trying to produce a theory of harmony 'which normalizes the material available today under general rules',[139] and which does not recognize the historical character of all such theories.

It [Hindemith's book] becomes reactionary the moment it puts forward the organizing schemata as norms. Its prohibitions are fetters on the musical forces of production: by means of meagre auxiliary constructions a limited and conventionally orientated compositional experience is elevated to the status of an ontological principle.[140]

In absolutizing as a static 'natural law' what is in reality a moment in a dynamic historical process, Hindemith's music demonstrated tendencies which, Adorno insisted, had many parallels with the dominant political tendencies of its period. In brief, these tendencies may be characterized as the attempt by authoritarian regimes in the Europe of the 1920s and 1930s to legitimize themselves historically through appealing to some mythical sense of 'shared community' (*Gemeinschaft*) and through claiming a foundation in the purity of 'natural laws'. The implications of Hindemith's position were politically reactionary and naïve, Adorno maintained, however 'neutral' and 'objective' his works might appear to be within the limited sphere of musical practice, and however apparently unpolitical their composer's motivations. The case of Hindemith has considerable importance in the early development of Adorno's concept of 'musical material', because the composer's music and his theory of harmony (as put forward in *Unterweisung im Tonsatz*) fulfil the role of antithesis to the position represented by the music of the Second Viennese School and the theory of harmony put forward by Schoenberg in his *Harmonielehre*. The dichotomy will be returned to in the course of Chapter 2.

Stravinsky and the 'stabilized music'

For Adorno, Hindemith and Bartók clearly represent two larger general tendencies within the 'new music' as discussed in his early writings. However, in spite of the obvious fact that Adorno is favourably disposed towards Bartók and (after initial ambivalence) hostile towards Hindemith, the two tendencies they represent are not to be understood as opposites. Rather, they need to be seen as two aspects of one broad category of 'new music' during the first half of the twentieth century which, in a previously unpublished essay of 1928, Adorno had called *die stabilisierte Musik*: 'stabilized music'. He explained this with the aid of a somewhat dramatic metaphor:

the high tide of musical history, which had overflowed the dams of society, is now ebbing back from those dams, after having deposited its most exposed works out there, where they now remain isolated; but the river has rediscovered its old course. Music has become *stabilized*, and become subjected to the demands of a just as freshly stabilized society ....[141]

The exposed and isolated works deposited by the torrent outside 'the dams of society' in Adorno's metaphor are clearly those of the Second Viennese School, particularly in the freely atonal pieces up to 1914: indeed, Adorno emphasizes very strongly that Schoenberg, Berg and Webern – even in their twelve-tone works – do *not* belong to his category of 'stabilized music'. The two general tendencies which make up the category Adorno labels classicism and folklorism:

Sociologically, 'classicism' is to be understood as the form stabilization takes in the most advanced, rationally enlightened states, while the less advanced, essentially agrarian countries – also, oddly enough, the Soviet Union – together with those states which belong to the fascist reaction, are included under 'folklorism'.[142]

Adorno admits that this is a rather crude classification, and it was probably because he found it unsatisfactory that it does not play a very big part in this form in his later work. Nevertheless, it is implied in the essay 'Kritik des Musikanten' examined above in relation to Hindemith, occurs again in 'Zur gesellschaftlichen Lage der Musik' of 1932 (to be discussed at the end of Chapter 2), and is retained in principle in *Philosophie der neuen Musik*,[143] where the case of Bartók, together with that of Janáček, is touched on briefly in these terms. With a few notable exceptions (e.g. Bartók and

Janáček, and the Stravinsky of *Renard* and *L'histoire du soldat*), composers included in the category of 'stabilized music' were considered by Adorno to be reactionary in that, so he argued, (a) the music did not question formal norms within its structure, and this resulted in technical inconsistencies and inadequacies in relation to the demands of the musical material at the current stage of its historical development; and (b) for this same reason such music uncritically affirmed, and became easily assimilated to, the dominant ideologies of current social and political reality.

Adorno delineated the characteristic features of 'classicism' (i.e. neoclassicism) as follows:

(i) it turned to old forms, due to the impossibility of finding new ones that could be easily grasped by existing society;
(ii) it rejected psychological expression and stressed the character of music as *play*;
(iii) it criticized private individualism in favour of a sense of the collectivity;
(iv) it avoided confronting the seriousness of current developments, the 'crisis' of modernism, through recourse to unrelenting cheerfulness (*Heiterkeit*); and
(v) it responded to the need for luxury goods of a new bourgeoisie no longer served by 'inwardness' (*Innerlichkeit*).[144]

Apart from these general features, Adorno considered that music that came within this category could not be seen as being part of a coherent group or type. He saw Stravinsky as its most characteristic representative, and *Oedipus Rex* as its most typical work up to that point – a work in which he maintained that the tendency towards 'musical masks', taken to an extreme with the literal use of theatrical masks and of a specially written Latin text, also resulted in a loss of irony, 'in place of which emerges the rigid shaping of forms which lack credibility'.[145] However, in contrast to the virulent attack on what are seen to be the reactionary and regressive aspects of Stravinsky's music in the second part of *Philosophie der neuen Musik*, Adorno's assessment of the composer at this early stage, as the following extract clearly shows, was moderate and almost sympathetic in tone:

If finally it is Stravinsky who, in spite of all, comes nearer to the truth than any other of the 'classicist' composers, it is because he constantly preserves the character [of the music] as *play* [*Spielcharakter*], and even his self-disclosures never come across as being so grand and obligatory that they could not stand being laughed at in a cabaret...[146]

On the other hand, even though Adorno does not suggest it in this instance, Stravinsky can also be seen as a representative, in certain of his earlier works, of the 'folklorist' tendency within the category of 'stabilized music', even if not as convincingly as Bartók or Janáček. Adorno described 'folklorism' as stabilizing itself 'insofar as it reaches back to the natural sources of music-making which seem to it to be eternally fresh; here individualism wants to find its corrective in a nationalism which is of the same stock as itself'.[147] Furthermore, Adorno questionably included the use of *jazz* within 'folklorism', citing the example of Kurt Weill's use of popular elements in *Mahagonny*, and presumably having in mind Stravinsky's use of popular material in *Ragtime* and *L'histoire du soldat*. (Although he acknowledged that jazz is no longer 'folk music', it is difficult not to see this as another example of the confusion and vagueness at the heart of his concept of 'popular music', raised earlier in this chapter and to be discussed further in Chapter 5.) In 'Zur gesellschaftlichen Lage der Musik', however, Adorno recognized that Stravinsky's music at different times had manifested elements of both 'folklorism' and 'classicism', both of which he included within the second of the four categories put forward in his typology of forms of 'serious music' which express alienation in relation to the 'law of the market'. This was the category of 'objectivism', which contains the two directions of 'stabilized music' being discussed here. He wrote: 'the most effective author of objectivism who in a highly revealing manner manifests each of these major directions – one after the other, but never simultaneously – is Igor Stravinsky'.[148]

Adorno's category of 'stabilized music' – as represented by composers like Stravinsky, Bartók, Janáček, Hindemith and Weill – is a difficult concept to employ in the form in which it appears in the 1928 essay 'Die stabilisierte Musik' because it really contains two distinct ideas which tend constantly to cancel each other out. First, 'stabilized music' is seen as a retreat from the advanced position achieved by radical music in the period immediately leading up to the First World War. It represents the consolidation of a more moderate position which seeks some kind of accommodation with existing society through appealing, in musical terms, to notions of 'collectivity', 'community', 'naturalness', 'immediacy', 'use-fulness', 'playfulness' or 'authenticity' (in the Heideggerian sense of *Eigentlichkeit*) – either by drawing on forms from the past or by drawing on forms derived from folk (or even popular) music. In this sense such music is 'ideological', according to the meaning Adorno gives to the term in 'Zur gesellschaftlichen Lage der Musik':

The ideological essence of musical life is its ability to satisfy the needs of the bourgeoisie adequately, but to do so by means of a form of satisfaction which accepts and stabilizes the existing consciousness, rather than revealing through its own form social contradictions, translating them into form and cognition regarding the structure of society.[149]

Secondly, however, the category included works which were regarded by Adorno as 'authentic' and 'true', in that they expressed alienation and opposed assimilation to the market forces of society through their critical relation to established musical forms. As we have already seen, Adorno considered that Bartók's music achieved this in many instances – e.g. in the string quartets, the sonatas for violin and piano, and the *Dance Suite*. Also, according to Adorno, Stravinsky expressed alienation through irony and fragmentation in relation to his material in a work like *L'histoire du soldat*, Weill similarly in *Mahagonny*, and even to some extent Hindemith in the early one-act operas (*Mörder, Hoffnung der Frauen; Das Nusch-Nuschi*; and *Sancta Susanna*). The contradiction between these two aspects of the concept of 'stabilized music' cannot simply be explained away by Adorno's methodological use of contradiction discussed earlier in the present chapter. It has more to do with the crudity of the categorization itself. The slightly more elaborate typology put forward in 'Zur gesellschaftlichen Lage der Musik', to be discussed in Chapter 2, seems to be an attempt by Adorno to refine and extend the tendencies identified in his earlier scheme.

Schoenberg: 'the dialectical composer'

That the example of Schoenberg's musical development, from the world of *fin-de-siècle* Romanticism up to the emergence of the twelve-tone technique in the 1920s, represented for Adorno the most radical and 'authentic' response at that time to the problem thrown up by the 'rupture between self and forms', is evident in his earliest article on the composer, 'Schönberg: Serenade, op. 24', published in 1925. Like the two Bartók essays from the same year discussed above, the Schoenberg article considers the problem of form in music since 'the crisis of romantic expressive music' from the perspective of *irony*. He suggests that the possibility of irony has been thrown into question since the handed-down forms lost their binding power, their shared meanings. He points out that, even in the case of Mahler, irony in music depends greatly for its effect on the shared conceptual associations that come partly from commentaries on music, from literary programmes. In a discussion of one of Schoenberg's most recent works up to that point, the *Serenade* op. 24, Adorno seeks to identify the nature of irony in Schoenberg's music:

In the face of the experience that no form exists any longer, unless it is to arise from the abyss of subjective inwardness [*Innerlichkeit*], he also has the experience of the most extreme opposite: that no inwardness can live here and achieve duration in terms of aesthetic representation, unless it is to find objective points of containment outside itself. The dialectic of these contrary fundamental experiences – fundamental experiences not as psychological acts but of a self-unfolding essence achieved in terms of the purest material immanence – becomes the source of Schoenberg's irony.[150]

The implication here is that Schoenberg's return to earlier forms in the *Serenade* (as indeed in op. 23 no. 5 and in parts of *Pierrot lunaire*) is a necessary development from the freely atonal Expressionist works (a view which Adorno had modified considerably by the time he came to write *Philosophie der neuen Musik*), but at the same time it presents the problem of how to relate to the handed-down forms. Adorno points out that normally irony in music can be understood as the exploitation of a resistance between an intended meaning and the associations of the form in which the music is cast (*ästhetischer Widerstreit von Gemeintem und Form*) – a strategy which, one might add, is dependent, if it is to be understood, upon a shared context of meaning (for example, as shared associations between composer and listeners). In the Schoenberg *Serenade*, Adorno argues, the opposition is not between the understood intention and the forms used. Instead, the ironic relation between 'self', as subjective expression, and forms is 'worked out' entirely within the structure of the music itself. As he puts it:

The form is transparent and lets the Subject shine through constantly at all points; the Subject, no longer manifest as surface appearance, restricts itself and pulls back, as the form, easily and lucidly, allows it to do.[151]

According to Adorno, it is the control of the material, through the thematic development of the piece, its guiding idea or 'concept', which constitutes the 'Subject' within the structure of the work. That is to say – and this is very much an interpretation of Adorno's meaning, as it is by no means itself transparent – the irony of the piece is constructed through the opposition within the work between the handed-down form or genre (e.g. the March) and the process of thematic development which constitutes its concealed subjective 'content'.

By 1934, in a brief but significant essay entitled 'Der dialektische Komponist', Adorno has given the concept of 'material' central place in his thinking on music:

What ... in truth characterizes Schoenberg, what needs to be understood as the origin of his stylistic history and of his technique, ... is historically and in principle a highly exemplary change in the manner in which the composer relates to his material.[152]

Adorno makes less use of the concept of irony from the late 1920s onwards. Instead he emphasizes increasingly the dialectical opposition of technique and expression, of rationality and mimesis within the work, understood as an increasingly rigorous control of musical material, as 'domination of nature'. This is evident, for example, in his 1927 analysis of Schoenberg's Fünf Orchesterstücke, op. 16, where he argues that the 'themes', as *Grundgestalten*, provide the organizing principle of the pieces in a manner already very similar to the twelve-tone technique.[153] The suggestion is that the extreme economy of means manifest in the construction of the op. 16 pieces, as an aspect of the increasing control of material, arises as an expressive necessity out of the composer's practical relation to his material, and 'not out of abstract calculation'.[154] At this stage, however, the concept of musical material, as the dialectic of 'history' and 'nature', has not yet been invested by Adorno with that almost metaphysical sense of historical 'self-locomotion' it later comes to assume in *Philosophie der neuen Musik*. The development of the concept of material will be pursued in detail in later chapters of this study.

The concept of a 'rupture between self and forms', as the alienation of avant-garde composers from handed-down formal schemes, itself becomes absorbed into Adorno's notion of the split between music's 'autonomy character' and its 'commodity character', and ultimately into the Hegelian Subject–Object relationship – pairs of concepts which belong within his concept of mediation as the 'mediation of opposites through their extremes'. For the moment, however, it remains to follow up Adorno's notion of the 'rupture between self and forms' and its relation to the increasing rationalization of musical material through a consideration of his view of the musical relationship between Schoenberg and his pupils, Berg and Webern.

Berg and Webern – Schoenberg's heirs

In an article published in English in 1930, entitled 'Berg and Webern – Schönberg's heirs', Adorno argued that Schoenberg had 'utilized the elements of the composer's material – melody and harmony, counterpoint and formal structure, orchestration and instrumental timbre'[155] more completely and consistently than any of his contemporaries. As each 'logical step' of what he was later to call 'the idea of a rational and thorough organization of the total musical material [*die Idee einer rationalen Durchorganisation des gesamten musikalischen Materials*]'[156] is made, so this narrows further the available possibilities. Schoenberg often does not stop to follow up stylistic possibilities which appear as a result of his technical innovations, preferring to pursue the new compositional problems thrown up by the material. Adorno writes:

Not many of his works correspond to each logical step of his development, sometimes only one. When the possibility of a whole new music arises, he contents himself with presenting an outline as a sample, worked out once, in order that he may attack the new technical problems which grow out of it. Plans for complete works well on their way to conclusion vanish when the idea of the piece in question has been realized.[157]

The relation betwen Schoenberg and his pupils is thus seen as important, for it is the pupils, through both their adherence to and independence from Schoenberg's work and his teaching, who 'concretely fulfill what he offers as a possibility, realizes but once, and which can survive only when their own substance fills in the outlines of his pattern'.[158] Adorno suggests that the separate developments of the music of Berg and Webern, 'representing the extreme poles of Schönberg's domain',[159] can be traced in their origins from particular single works of Schoenberg. With Berg it is the First Chamber Symphony op. 9 that is seen as seminal – an uncontroversial view shared by, among others, Perle,[160] Redlich[161] and Leibowitz[162] (who is echoing Adorno's analyses in Willi Reich's book on Berg of 1937). Adorno considers Berg to be a less 'dialectical' composer than Schoenberg due to his focus on the 'smallest transition', whereby contrast and 'difference' are always dissolved back into the amorphous and the undifferentiated (an observation which resembles Adorno's criticism of what he regarded as the undialectical and static aspects of Walter Benjamin's writing).[163] In this connection he contrasts Berg with Schoenberg, where the music 'on the basis of incessantly changing and contrasting figures, develops a principle of construction which is dominant even throughout the continual motive transformations and transitions of the *Chamber Symphony*'.[164] With Webern, Adorno finds the relation to Schoenberg less easy to pin down. He identifies what he calls 'the "released" style of Opus 11 to Opus 20',[165] but then goes on to point out that 'the form of the "short" pieces, as it appears in Schönberg's piano work, Opus 19, and in the *Herzgewächsen* [sic], was elaborated in its purest development first by Webern and only later by Schönberg himself'.[166] However, Adorno concludes, 'the technical problem of this style is already formulated in the last piano piece of Opus 11; on the other hand it is also found in the early works of Webern, as in the double canon, *Entflieht auf leichten Kähnen*'.[167]

Adorno sees Berg and Webern as presenting commentaries on Schoenberg. Thus, 'Berg unites him with Mahler on the one hand and on the other with the great music drama and legitimizes him from this point',[168] while Webern 'pursues to its furthest extreme the subjectivism which Schönberg first released in ironic play in *Pierrot*'.[169] The image of the relationship conjured up by Adorno is in some ways that of the great Renaissance painter's studio, where apprentices fill in the detail of the master's sketched outline. To see it in this way would, however, be misleading. The pupils in this case, although strictly adhering to the master's teaching, are creatively independent, their work having more the character of *excurses* on the problems raised by the master. Adorno suggests that

Neither excursion is bound to the work of the master; in actual creation the original nature of the interpreter comes to light, just as in the great commentaries of philosophical literature, those of Plato and Aristotle, for example, the personality of each author breaks through the text.[170]

Berg's initial 'commentary' on Schoenberg's Chamber Symphony op. 9 will be examined in detail in Chapter 4 through a consideration of Adorno's analysis of the Piano Sonata op. 1 – a case study for Adorno's approach to music analysis. Little space need be devoted to Berg at this stage, therefore, in view of the lengthy discussion which comes later.

In the case of Webern, Adorno argues that he 'is the only one to propound musical expressionism in its strictest sense, carrying it to such a point that it reverts of its own weight to a new objectivity'.[171] In his earliest article on the composer, 'Anton Webern: Zur Aufführung der Fünf Orchesterstücke, op. 10, in Zürich' of 1926, Adorno discusses the difficulties of Webern's music, employing yet again the concept of a 'rupture between self and forms':

The difficulty and exclusiveness of the works of Anton Webern has to do with the fact that in them the tension between given form and personal freedom is completely dissolved, because they allot the form-giving right alone to the individual. Whereas it is normally precisely through the tension which governs the relation between the community [*Gemeinschaft*] and the individual [*dem Einzelnen*] that the intelligibility of music [*die Verständlichkeit von Musik*] finds its completion, that which the community finds intelligible serves to ratify the individual and opens the community to the explosive will of the individual. In Webern's case, the will of the individual has definitively exploded the constitutive range of forms corresponding to the community.[172]

Adorno considers that the extreme individualism and concentration of Webern's works constitutes a fulfilment of a tendency inherent in Romanticism and extended by Expressionism. In taking Expressionism to the point where extreme subjectivity turns inside out, so to speak, and through doing so by means of the strict logic demanded by the material, Webern 'objectifies subjectivity' – that is, he achieves what Adorno calls 'the pure representation of the subjective'.[173] Adorno maintains that this objectification of subjectivity 'is realized faithfully, precisely, and without concession to the inert self-definition of the material'.[174] And he continues: 'In such limitation it seems to be outside history; truly the absolute lyric and, following this idea, only intelligible in terms of itself'.[175]

Thus Webern's music may be seen as the extreme extension of the position put forward originally, Adorno suggests, in the third piano piece of Schoenberg's op. 11 – that is, the eradication of pre-given form. Webern, therefore, in one sense represents also the most extreme case of the 'rupture between self and forms', as the alienation of subjectivity from handed-down formal schemata and genres. At the same time, however, he also represents for Adorno the most extreme example of the domination of musical material, whereby 'the immanent consistency of the [musical] structure [*die immanente Stimmigkeit des Gebildes*] is controlled by the degree of subjective intention'.[176]

4   Towards a critical method: levels of interpretation

From the above thematic analysis of Adorno's work, which has focused on the early writings on music and situated them in relation to influences from Lukács and Benjamin, a number of key concepts have emerged. It now remains to see these in the larger context of Adorno's later work, within which the centrality of particular concepts (for example, 'mediation', 'musical material' and 'form') can be made evident. The aim here is to put forward a schematic model through which to understand the oppositional interpretative levels on which Adorno's music theory operates. This entails supplementing the concepts taken from the early writings by introducing further concepts from texts like *Negative Dialektik* and *Ästhetische Theorie*, and taking a further look at the concepts of 'history' and 'nature' in relation to the concept of 'truth content'. The conceptual context and 'schematic model' offered here will then serve as a scaffolding for the rest of this study.

Conceptual context

The concepts so far examined have fallen into two interrelated groups, forming the oppositional pairs: history–nature; and self–world of forms. It has been argued that the relation between the terms of each of these 'binary oppositions' is interactive and (in the Hegelian sense of the term as used by Lukács) contradictory in character: that is to say, dialectical. Through considering their use in the work of Lukács and Benjamin, and through examining briefly their early application by Adorno to the analysis, critique and interpretation both of the music of the avant-garde and of the 'popular' music of the 1920s and 1930s, we have seen furthermore that these two pairs of concepts are themselves related to each other, that they call for further groups of concepts for their extension and for an understanding of the character of their interaction, and that they need to be understood in the context of concrete examples.

In our study of the contradictory relation of history and nature in Adorno's philosophy, several features have emerged as being of particular significance. In the first place, 'nature' is seen to be a historical category; nature is the world of established convention, now having 'forgotten' its historical origins. The link with the other pair of 'binary oppositions', self–world of forms, lies in the character of the process of interaction itself: 'nature' is the result of the historical interaction of the 'self' and the given 'world of forms', and is called by Lukács 'second nature'. In Lukács's Hegelian terms, 'second nature' is the product of the historical interaction of 'Subject' and 'Object', and '[h]istory is viewed as one all-embracing process, in which an historical [S]ubject realizes itself'.[177] This is what Adorno, following Hegel and Lukács, calls 'the objectification of the Subject', and it is a process he attempts to map both within individual compositions and as the 'historical dialectic' of musical material. In the second place, however, 'history', as the interaction of Subject and Object, self and forms, consciousness and 'nature', can be seen to partake of a number of the characteristics normally attributed to 'nature'. These characteristics, as one might expect, are contradictory: they can be subsumed under the concepts *invariance* and *transience*. On the one hand, 'history', as the 'world of forms', the product of the interaction of self and world, Subject and Object, becomes reified (*verdinglicht*) as the world of conventions, and becomes taken as a static absolute, as an unquestioned (and indeed unquestionable) given – i.e. as an invariant. That is to say, it becomes taken as 'natural', timeless and unchanging. On the other hand, 'history', as a process which takes place in time, to which the passing of time is intrinsic, is, like 'nature', characterized by the 'passing away' of things in time, their decay (*Verfall*) and disintegration (*Zerfall*) – i.e. by transience. This process of interaction through opposition, in both the above cases, is called by Adorno 'mediation'.

The characteristics which have emerged above – 'transience' and, in particular, 'invariance' – are seen by Adorno as having ideological implications. The term 'ideology', as has become apparent in the course of this chapter, occupies an important position in Adorno's theory. It needs to be understood here in its specialized sociological sense: i.e. vested socio-cultural interests masquerading as objective or disinterested attitudes, or claiming to be in accord with 'natural laws' or 'common sense'.[178] The distinguishing feature of ideology in this sense is that it is to be understood not as a consciously held system of beliefs, but instead as *a lived system of values of which we are largely unconscious*, which forms our sense of identity, and in relation to which we are normally unable to take a critical and self-reflective position. Ideology understood in this way thus serves to legitimize as natural, universal and unchanging something which is, in a very particularized sense, cultural and historical in origin, and thus subject to change. Adorno uses the term in association with the Hegelian concept 'illusion' or 'semblance' (*Schein*) and the Marxian concept 'false consciousness' (*falsches Bewußtsein*). It has also to be understood in relation to the Marxian (economic) base and (ideological) superstructure: the ideological superstructure of society (e.g. law, politics, religion, art) is an outcome of the forces and relations of production which constitute the economic base, while at the same time the superstructure serves to mystify the real social relations of production which underlie it. For Adorno, although he was certainly no vulgar Marxist reductionist, art, and indeed 'cultural life' as a whole, cannot escape ideology because of 'universal mediation'. That is to say, all aspects of 'culture' (taken in the sociological/anthropological sense of 'whole way of life',[179] and not only as the 'high arts') partake of the dominant ideologies of society through their participation in, and internalization of, social relations. This idea will be examined in more detail in Chapter 3.

Viewed in this context, the idea of 'invariance', as the natural and unchanging, is seen to be associated with the idea of 'community' (*Gemeinschaft*), as the traditionally ordained and naturally regulated relations between human beings within a form of social collectivity where communication and understanding are direct and immediate, based on eternal principles outside history. The relation between the individual and the community is seen as an integrated one, and the collectivity is expressed by the individual either as heroic figure through the epic, or as humble craftsman or *Musikant* through awareness of immediate, functional needs.

This notion of 'community' is ideological, according to Adorno, because to project a conception of the idealized community of the pre-industrial world on to modern industrialized society serves to conceal and mystify the true character of human relations in the modern world. Modern society (*Gesellschaft*) is characterized by transience, by change, fragmentation and alienation; communication and understanding are indirect – i.e. mediated – in all respects. Furthermore, industrial capitalism demands a high degree of rationalization and control (manifest as bureaucracy, administration and conformity), while at the same time emphasizing 'individualization' and 'freedom' as key values. Underlying Adorno's argument is the assumption that capitalism transforms all reality into material for functional use, and all values become commodified in a society dominated by mass production, mass marketing and mass consumption – including, of course, notions like 'the individual', 'freedom' and 'community'.

For Adorno, modern society is expressed culturally through the extremes of two mutually exclusive 'forms': the *commodity* form (which offers a false appearance of integration and wholeness based on exchange, and which magically conceals the labour which went into its production), and the autonomous art of the *avant-garde* (which takes fragmentation and disintegration into its own 'immanent law of form', and which does not seek to conceal the fact that it is something made). 'Commodity' art accepts its function within the dominant relations of production of society uncritically, and evokes, so Adorno argues, an uncritical and standardized response from its public. Avant-garde art resists its commodity-character through taking a critical position towards the handed-down artistic material within its own structure, and demands a critical, interpretative and self-reflective mode of reception.

In the application of these concepts to the specific case of autonomous art music in the West Adorno takes, as we have seen, the perspective of the avant-garde. The relation between history and nature, and the 'rupture between self and forms', as well as being interpreted in sociological terms by means of the concept of ideology, are also understood in purely 'immanent' terms, by means of the concept of *immanent consistency*. Although this concept did not feature greatly in Adorno's writings of the early 1920s, it had emerged by the late 1920s as important, because with it Adorno implies that the ideological aspects of art are grounded in the technical structure of art works. At the same time, however, he also implies that it is through the technical consistency of the work, the identity of the structure of the work with its guiding idea (or 'concept'), that a critical relation to the handed-down material is achieved. Art works – and, in particular, musical works as the most self-referential mode of art – derive their material from the 'outside world' of functional empirical reality and, through the consistency of their form, at the same time separate themselves from empirical reality (Adorno employs here the metaphor of the Leibnizian *monad*).[180] It is therefore in the material of music, in the historical process of the increasing technical control of 'musical nature', that the mediation of music and society, as the contradictory dialectic of the self (as Subject) and the world of forms (as Object), takes place. This process of mediation is also a process of demythologization of handed-down forms, and in the avant-garde art work serves to reveal ideology through its critical relation to its material. What characterizes the 'authentic' work for Adorno is that it does not accept the handed-down material as a given, but questions it 'immanently' within its structure.

Thus the notion of 'authenticity' also needs to be considered here, although it is a concept which encompasses issues of extreme complexity in Adorno's thought and no single account of it can claim adequacy. In spite of Adorno's criticism of Heidegger's concept of *Eigenlichkeit*, his own use of the term 'authenticity' (*Authentizität*) does appear to contain the existentialist sense of 'truth to self', as consistency of action in the face of the meaninglessness and horror of the world. This could be translated into musical terms as follows: since the breakdown of the validity and binding force of traditional forms and conventions, the 'authentic' musical work has had no choice but to forge its own internal consistency. Nevertheless, it is a consistency which, while it cannot help but draw on the material of handed-down conventions, does so with full cognizance of their loss of meaning (hence the often ironic stance of much modernist music). But this is not to say that Adorno shares the existentialists' ontology, whereby, in spite of all, the business of 'being-in-the-world' and the *Angst* of existence can ultimately, so he argues, be reconciled and accepted as part of a natural order of things outside history. For him no reconcilement is possible in a world that has produced Auschwitz. The apparent 'meaninglessness' of much radical art in the twentieth century is not an acceptance of the meaninglessness of existence and a heroic attempt on the part of the isolated individual to forge meaning nonetheless. Rather it is a mute protest against the false consciousness which prevents a better world. Adorno insists that

an unbroken relation to the aesthetic sphere is no longer possible. The concept of a culture after Auschwitz is illusory and nonsensical, and for this reason any creation [*Gebilde*] that arises at all has to pay the bitter price. However, because the world has survived its own demise, it yet has need of art as its unconscious recording of history. The authentic artists of the present are those in whose works there shudders the aftershock of the most extreme terror.[181]

'Authentic' art for Adorno always has an echo of the outside world within its material, but sublimated and reconciled by the individual work's law of form. As he put it in a discussion with the critic Lucien Goldmann: 'I would say that the rank or quality of works of art is measured – if one can employ this flat term – according to the degree in which antagonisms are formed within the work, and in which their unity is attained through antagonisms rather than remaining external to them'.[182] But today, so he argues, the tensions between outer and inner no longer allow for reconciliation within the work of art, and its form shatters. In fact the existence of art itself becomes problematic, at least as expressive art. This is because to be true today it has not only to be internally consistent, but must also express suffering of an order which goes beyond what it is possible for its form to contain. It is in this sense Adorno contends that the authentic works now are the failures. 'Authenticity' understood in this way needs to be taken together with the concept of a 'truth content' in art works.

Art, the semblance of nature, and truth content

The concept of 'truth content' (*Wahrheitsgehalt*) does not feature very prominently in the early writings, but, because of its importance to

Adorno's aesthetics overall, it demands to be introduced at this point in order for us to be in a position to put forward a 'model' of his interpretative method. This entails drawing on *Negative Dialektik* and *Ästhetische Theorie*, and specifically on the treatment in those books of the concepts of 'spiritualization' (*Vergeistigung*), 'non-identity' (*Nicht-Identität*) and 'semblance' (*Schein*).

One aspect of an art work's 'truth' is its consistency, the result of the domination of its material by technique. Paradoxically, however, it is this technical domination of material, its 'spiritualization' as Adorno puts it in *Ästhetische Theorie*, which lends to art works something of the status of 'natural' objects. In the apparent inevitability and necessity of their structure and in the seamlessness of their construction, autonomous art works (at least in the 'bourgeois period' of the eighteenth and nineteenth centuries) acquired a 'naturalness' and spontaneity which belied the fact that they were something made, put together. That is to say, art acquired the 'semblance', 'appearance' or 'illusion' (*Schein*) of nature (this applies particularly to the music of the Austro-German tradition, with its strong emphasis on 'organicism'). To put the paradox another way: while autonomous art works are formed through the most extreme technical domination and manipulation of material, this domination has as its end, its 'purpose', the creation of something which is without direct 'purpose' or 'function'. This idea relates directly to Kant's notion (in *Kritik der Urteilskraft*) of art and art works as 'purposefulness (or *purposiveness*) without a purpose' (*Zweckmäßigkeit ohne Zweck*).[183]

For Adorno, as we have seen, 'nature' is the Lukácsian–Marxian 'second nature'; significantly, however, his concept of nature also takes on distinctly Freudian associations, as a projection of the repressed contents of the unconscious. It is understood as non-identity, that which is left out, discarded, repressed or occluded by the dominant mode of rationality, and which escapes becoming 'functionalized' by it. 'Nature' becomes the repository of our longings, the screen upon which historically we project our deepest needs as well as our anxieties and insecurities. It is that region to which are consigned those things rejected or repressed by society in its dominant form. Psychoanalytically speaking, the bringing to consciousness of that which has been repressed, its recovery and formulation, results in a sense of freedom, of emancipation from the power of the repressed contents of the unconscious. For Adorno, the 'truth' of art appears to lie in this 'bringing to speech' of nature – a nature, however, which is itself the projection of that which has been repressed and rejected by society. Art is therefore not pure expression, but is also a mode of cognition through which we can understand things about the world. The 'truth' of art in this sense, its domination of material to produce a consistent form, is to recover that which has been rejected or repressed, and to reveal it through featuring it as the central problem around which the work of art is formed – even, paradoxically, at the expense of the work's formal consistency. Fundamental aesthetic criteria are implied when Adorno writes that

Spiritualization in art is not some linear progress. Its criterion of success is the ability of art to incorporate into its formal language those phenomena that bourgeois society outlaws, revealing in them a natural other, the suppression of which is truly evil.[184]

On the one hand, autonomous art is different from and stands apart from empirical reality because it is not obviously functional; at the same time it is different from 'nature' in that it is 'artificial' and highly contrived. On the other hand, art resembles the 'functionality' of empirical reality in that it partakes of its 'purposefulness' and rationality, particularly as technique and technology; at the same time it also resembles nature, in that it achieves, traditionally at least, the appearance of natural beauty. The paradox is twofold: (i) the purpose to which art's purposefulness, its rationality, is put is the creation of something which is apparently without purpose or function; and (ii) the artifice of art is dedicated to the production of something which seems natural and spontaneous. According to Adorno, art achieves this 'spontaneity' only through the most rigorous control and domination of its material – that is, of 'nature' as 'second nature'. But the 'end' to which this domination of nature is directed, its 'purpose', is, he argues, the rescue of what the idea of nature signifies to us; beauty, spontaneity, freedom, transience and, in particular, *immediacy* – as well as the recovery of that which has been outlawed and repressed. Adorno argues that such a seemingly perverse 'purpose', which, in the face of the dominant means-ends rationality[185] is no purpose at all, serves as a critique of the false immediacy of empirical reality (as society, history) through negation:

It sides with repressed nature. ... Art is the redemption of nature and immediacy through a process of negation. Hence art is total mediatedness; it assimilates itself to the non-repressed by exerting unlimited sway over its material.[186]

Thus, the interaction of 'nature' and 'history', as examined earlier in this chapter, is taken full circle. On the one hand, 'nature' is revealed by art and critical philosophy to be historical in origin, as mediated 'second nature', a projection of historical needs not met by society. On the other hand, 'history', as the movement of *Geist* (see Chapter 3), of increasing 'consciousness of self', is revealed as becoming the 'semblance' of nature in two ways: (i) at any particular stage human consciousness (as 'society') may tend to think of itself as absolute, as a 'given', and become reified; and (ii) human history may be seen as the attempt to redeem 'nature', as the identity of Subject and Object, in an ideal, utopian society (the myth of the biblical Fall). Art works, as a special case of this 'progress of self-consciousness' which is history, aspire through extreme artifice to become 'nature-like'. This is an 'illusion' (*Schein*), in the sense that they are not nature, but it is also the 'truth' of art works, in that art works represent our attempt both to capture the transience of nature and to express the gap between 'history' and the myth of 'nature'. Thus it is the 'semblance' or 'illusion' of art works which constitutes not only their 'ideological moment', but also their 'truth content' – a truth which is historical, and which is not to be arrived at apart from the complex of mediations through which it is expressed.

A dialectical model

From the above observation concerning the conceptual context underlying Adorno's writings on music, and making use of terminology from Adorno's later philosophical and sociological as well as musical texts – in particular, *Philosophie der neuen Musik, Zur Metakritik der Erkenntnistheorie, Einleitung in die Musiksoziologie, Negative Dialektik*, and *Ästhetische Theorie* – it is possible to construct a 'dialectical model' of his theoretical approach, to uncover the different levels on which his interpretative method operates in relation to the 'truth content' of musical works. The model is concerned with three levels of interpretation: (1) immanent (including technical) analysis, (2) sociological critique and (3) philosophical-historical interpretation.[187] And as the 'truth content' of musical works is always historically mediated, these levels of interpretation are concerned to decipher different aspects of the mediation of music. These aspects, or 'moments',[188] have been focused here under the concepts *consistency, ideology* and *authenticity.*

It should be stressed that the 'levels' put forward in this model operate to some extent in all Adorno's texts on music, whatever their period, particular emphasis or point of focus. In separating them out, therefore, the model is quite calculatedly 'going against the grain' of Adorno's thinking. The purpose, however, is not prescriptive, in that it definitely does not seek to offer an abstract formula in its own right to be applied as a working method apart from the understanding of Adorno's thought. Neither is it intended to be descriptive, in that one does not discover the model directly stated in this form in Adorno's writings. Its purpose is rather heuristic and interpretative, in that it seeks to uncover the unifying 'method' hidden beneath the fragmented surface of Adorno's writings on music (and, more broadly speaking, his texts on aesthetics). While this cannot be called a 'fundamental principle' underlying his work in the philosophical sense of a *Grundsatz*, simply because Adorno's negative dialectics operates against any such principle, it does nevertheless point to the consistency of his approach, and this is something that can legitimately be called a 'method'.

(1)   Immanent analysis   At this level, the 'truth' of the musical work means its inner *consistency (Stimmigkeit)*. By this is meant the consistency with which the 'idea' (i.e. the 'concept') of the work, in purely musical terms, is realized through the technical structure of the work. This notion of the truth of the work corresponds to the traditional philosophical definition of truth as 'the identity of the concept with the object of cognition'. This is what is known as *identity theory*: i.e. A = A. Because the musical work, as epitomized by the rise to dominance of 'absolute' instrumental music in the bourgeois period, has an *autonomy character* (freed from its functional and auratic origins, for example, in magic, ritual, religion, work or dance), it has no directly identifiable external referent. Thus the truth of the work understood in this context is its identity with its own form, the unity and logical consistency of idea and technical structure. The truth (or 'untruth') of the work is revealed at this level through immanent technical analysis.

Critical note   In using the term 'immanent' analysis, Adorno means more than simply uncovering the 'facts' of the work's structure as an end in itself. 'Immanent' analysis goes beyond technical analysis through interpretation and therefore can be understood as involving the whole of Adorno's hermeneutic enterprise. In *Philosophie der neuen Musik* Adorno writes: 'Technical analysis is assumed at all times and often demonstrated. It needs, however, to be supplemented by interpretation of the smallest details if it is to go beyond mere humanistic stock-taking and to express the relationship of the object [*Sache*] to truth.'[189] Nevertheless, in spite of his insistence on the importance of technical analysis, Adorno's own analyses are frequently sketchy and do not always convincingly bridge the gap between technical detail and philosophical interpretation.[190] This problem will be returned to in later chapters, and in particular in Chapter 4.

(2)   Sociological critique   At this level, the 'truth' of the musical work is, paradoxically, its 'untruth', as *ideology (Ideologie)*. Its ideological 'moment' can be understood as the way in which the self-contained particularity of the work appears to put itself forward as a universal principle. In one sense, therefore, *all* art is ideological, in that it posits a 'closed world', consistent in itself, which lays claim to an ideal relationship

of part to whole which does not exist in the world of everyday, empirical reality – an ideal relationship which is, however, appropriated by dominant ideologies for their own purposes. Furthermore, the closed world of autonomous music appears to deny its heteronomous origins in previous social function. It is in this sense that autonomous music may be understood as 'ideological', and therefore 'untrue': it is 'false consciousness', in that, in Marxian terms, it serves to conceal the true nature of social relations within existing society. At the same time, however, the contradictions of social reality may also be understood as being present in musical works and in musical material, and it is in this sense that music may be understood as 'true', in that it contains society 'unconsciously' within itself, as what Adorno calls 'objective Spirit' (*objektiver Geist*). It is the concern of Adorno's sociology of music, as ideology critique, to explore the contradictory relation of autonomous music to social reality in terms of (i) how society inheres in musical works and in musical material (i.e. music's *social content*), and (ii) how music is assimilated by (or indeed, opposes) the relations of production of existing society (i.e. music's *social function as commodity*). Thus, in demystifying music through revealing its connections with that which apparently lies outside itself – i.e. society – a further aspect of its 'truth' is uncovered.

   Critical note   Although claiming to deal with musical works and musical life as 'social facts', Adorno's sociology of music is essentially speculative rather than empirical in its orientation (in spite of its forays into empirical methodology in the United States during the late 1930s and early 1940s). His approach is more that of a critical social philosophy, throwing up problems on a theoretical level which it leaves to empirical sociology to verify experimentally. In his 'Vorrede' to *Einleitung in die Musiksoziologie*, Adorno writes concerning the relation to empirical sociology: 'The author is conceited enough to believe that he is supplying the musical branch of that discipline with enough fruitful questions to keep it meaningfully occupied for some time and to advance the link between theory and fact-finding – a link that is constantly called for and constantly put off again'.[191] Nevertheless, the lack of empirical data to back up many of his assertions inevitably means that Adorno's sociology of music is particularly value-laden.[192] It is therefore important that his judgements should be seen within the context of a larger conceptual context – a context which can serve to identify the assumptions and values which underlie his theory. Such a context has already been suggested in the present chapter and is further developed in subsequent chapters of this study, while Adorno's sociology of music is examined in some detail in Chapter 5.

(3)   Philosophical-historical interpretation   At this level, the 'truth' of
the musical work is related to the work's *authenticity (Authentizität)*. This
does not mean 'truth to material' in any traditional sense, a 'consistency of
form' in relation to handed-down models or to the physical laws of
acoustics. Nor does it mean 'truth to social function' as a simple
identification with dominant ideologies. Instead, what is meant is – if one
may put it so obliquely – truth to the *split* between these two extremes, in
view of the 'rupture between self and forms', between individual and social
totality, and between Subject and Object, which Adorno sees as the
dominant characteristic of the 'modernist' period. The truth, quality and
authenticity of the work are gauged according to the extent to which the
work succeeds in incorporating this conflict within its 'immanent law of
form', and to the extent to which its form and structure arise out of this
conflict, as a 'force field', rather than remaining external to it through
resorting to handed-down formulae or through attempting to be accessible.
At this level, the 'truth' of the work is revealed through philosophical
interpretation. This both makes use of immanent analysis and sociological
critique as well as going beyond them to suggest how the 'authentic'
autonomous musical work is not only isolated from society (even though
deriving its material from society), but also points to something beyond
existing society through its emphasis on non-identity. Thus, philosophical
interpretation seeks to reveal the emancipatory potential of the authentic
work of art through reflection upon the manner in which the work deals
'internally' with the conflicting demands of autonomy and social function.
It is this emancipatory potential within art works that is seen as
'progressive'. Its manifestation within the art work is, however, to be
understood as a technical relation of Subject and Object, composer and
material. Emancipation, as progress towards freedom of the Subject
through its objectification as the structure of the work, is to be understood,
paradoxically, as a process of increasing technical control of material, a
process which is simultaneously one of rationalization and demythologization of handed-down material. This process is historical in character, and
thus the philosophical interpretation of music also constitutes a philosophy
of music history.

Critical note   Overall, Adorno's 'philosophy of music' has to be
understood as embracing all the levels outlined here, as analysis, critique
and interpretation. Indeed, more specifically, we are referring to his
aesthetics, understanding the term as meaning that branch of philosophy
occupied with questions of value and judgement in relation to both art and
nature. Aesthetics, as we have seen, has traditionally been concerned with

the question of universals in art, and with the attempt to systematize these in terms of abstract categories. Adorno argues that universals are one pole of a fundamental dialectic in both art and in aesthetics. At the same time, however, aesthetics has to establish its connection with the particularity of art works, and to learn to grasp what he calls the 'micrological figures' (*die mikrologischen Figuren*),[193] the tiniest details of the structure of art works.[194] Furthermore, art works are not created or experienced in a vacuum: their context and their relation to that which lies outside their 'monadic' isolation is part of their complex of meaning. Adorno maintains that art works, already mediated in terms of their material and their form, call for a further level of mediation – that of concepts, as the 'second reflection' (*zweite Reflektion*) provided by a philosophical aesthetics. He argues that

artistic experience in general is by no means as immediate as suggested by the official art religion. Experience of an art work always involves experience of the latter's ambience, its place and function in the environment. This tends to be denied by the zealous defenders of *naïveté* who would rather venerate art than understand it.... Implied in the idea of an aesthetics is the notion of liberating art by means of theory from the kind of rigidification that befalls it through the inescapable division of labour.[195]

The problem here is the familiar one of the 'hermeneutic circle': on the one hand, art works need to be understood in order for us to enter into their problematic in the first place; on the other hand, any appropriate form of understanding needs to be derived from, and grounded in, the works themselves. In other words, is Adorno's aesthetic theory (incorporating his immanent analysis, sociological critique and philosophical interpretation) derived from the works themselves, or is it imposed upon them as a pre-established system of values from the outside?[196] In *Vorlesungen zur Ästhetik (1967–68)* he argues that, while the hermeneutic circle cannot be escaped, it can at least be accounted for 'through a theory in which the traditional philosophical distinction between "first thing" and "derivation" is shown dialectically to be invalid'.[197] Adorno's dialectical theory, outlined here in very schematic form as a 'model', denies the validity of philosophical 'first things', putting in their place the Hegelian concept of universal mediation. Thus, his philosophical interpretation of music history does not argue, as he claims the traditional view of history does, that one thing is derived from or follows on from another in a continuous sequence of direct causes and effects founded on some notion of ontological absolutes. Instead, he interprets history in reverse in terms of its 'discontinuities', and sees the 'historical dialectic of musical material' from the perspective of the avant-garde and in the context of commodity fetishism. Thus, for example, Bach is seen in the light of Schoenberg, Wagner with reference to the Hollywood movie, extreme motivic–thematic integration in the context of the disintegration of musical material.

Aspects of Adorno's 'philosophy of history', as his 'theory of the avant-garde', have been discussed in the present chapter. They will be returned to in more detail in Chapters 6 and 7.

In conclusion

As well as being interpretative and heuristic in intention, the above 'model' also has a *critical* purpose. The tension between surface appearance and underlying structure in Adorno's work, suggested by the model, may itself be seen in two ways. On the one hand, it could be argued, it can be seen as a blind spot, and therefore as ideological: his espousal of the 'fragment' as critique of all totalizing systems could be understood as a form of mystification, in that underlying it is an allegiance to totality and to all-embracing 'organic' unity every bit as thorough-going as that of the grand tradition of German Idealist philosophy from which Adorno himself can be seen to emerge. On the other hand, the same feature can also be seen as pointing to the consistency of his work. That is to say, there is no fundamental principle underlying Adorno's work as such, no allegiance to any notion of 'first things'. The fragment is its form, but underpinning this is an interpretative method, that of the 'constellation', which relates unity and fragmentation, integration and disintegration, continuity and discontinuity through their opposition. This could be seen as constituting the *authenticity* of Adorno's work: that is, its truth to its underlying and all-pervading compositional 'idea' – the dialectical method itself.

This double possibility for the understanding of Adorno's aesthetics of music runs throughout the remaining chapters of this study.

2   The development of a theory of musical material

> The assumption of an historical tendency in musical material contradicts the traditional conception of the material of music. This material is traditionally defined ... as the sum of all sounds at the disposal of the composer. The actual compositional material, however, is as different from this sum as is language from its total supply of sounds. ... All its specific characteristics are indications of the historical process. ... Music recognizes no natural law...[1]   Adorno, *Philosophy of New Music* (1949)

In Adorno's very early writings the idea of 'musical material' itself remains as yet rather unfocused. It is only later that the concept receives its most comprehensive formulation – that is, in *Philosophie der neuen Musik*. Indeed, the whole argument of that book is predicated on the idea that it is not what 'musical sounds' are in themselves – their natural, physical qualities – that is significant, but rather what they have *become* in any particular instance. Adorno maintains that it is in the relationships of sounds one to another, which are historical in character, that social relations are sedimented, albeit in purely musical terms. Nevertheless, although *Philosophie der neuen Musik* offers a version of the concept in its apparently most complete form, it is argued here that a clearer understanding of what is meant by 'musical material' is to be gained from a careful examination of how the idea of the mediation of music and society unfolds in Adorno's work from the late 1920s up to the period of his exile from Germany in the mid-1930s.

Adorno's theory of material developed out of his intensive debates with the composer Ernst Krenek, culminating in the important essay 'Zur gesellschaftlichen Lage der Musik' of 1932, his first attempt to provide a systematic account of his ideas on music and its social situation. However, both this essay and the Adorno–Krenek debates need to be placed within the terms of an already existing debate concerning the nature of 'artistic material', and of the relationship of 'technique' to 'expression'. Adorno frequently leaves his sources unacknowledged, especially when they are assumed to be common property and part of the intellectual ambience of the early twentieth century. Some familiarity with this ambience, the larger debate over 'artistic material', is nevertheless important for an understanding of Adorno's own particular theory. This is not to suggest, however, that Adorno was necessarily influenced directly by all the positions discussed below, even though obviously familiar with them – the politically committed position of Hanns Eisler is a case in point, as is the traditionalist stance of Paul Hindemith. The intention in the first part of this chapter is rather to provide a sense of the range of debate on 'material' at the *fin de siècle* and the first four decades of the twentieth century, within which Adorno's contribution can then be situated.

1   Theories of artistic material: precursors and contemporaries

It can certainly be argued that Adorno's concept of musical material as the 'objectification of the Subject' and as the 'spiritualization of matter' can be traced back to Eduard Hanslick. In his *Vom Musikalisch-Schönen* Hanslick writes that

Composing is the working of the spirit in material capable of being spiritualized [*ein Arbeiten des Geistes in geistfähigem Material*]. . . . As the creation of a thinking and feeling spirit it follows from this that a musical composition has to a high degree the capacity itself to be intelligent [*geistvoll*] and expressive [*gefühlvoll*].[2]

In its common usage among creative artists, however, the general concept of 'artistic material' has remained rather ill defined (as opposed, for example, to more pressing concerns with 'technique', 'structure', 'form' and 'content' – i.e. concepts to do with the process of 'shaping' the material). The concept of 'material' seems to have been taken as a given, and either has remained largely unquestioned or has included a notion of the 'material' as 'raw material', the basic natural 'stuff' at the artist's disposal before actually beginning work in any particular medium.[3] A version of artistic material which, in musical terms, perhaps comes nearest to the rather straightforward 'sculptural' conception of material is the idea that the basic stuff of music is simply its 'sounding material'. It is often claimed that the task of the artist in the shaping process is to remain 'true' to the demands of the material. These demands are usually considered, however, to stem entirely from the natural properties of the material, from the natural physiological limitations of our organs of perception, and from a somewhat static view of the psychology of perception. It is a composer like Hindemith who serves to focus the 'traditional' side of the debate most clearly in its extreme form, in that he represents the polar opposite of Adorno's 'radical' concept of musical material.

Hindemith's craft of musical composition

As we have seen in Chapter 1, Adorno had been interested in Hindemith's work from very early on, and had increasingly criticized the composer's music during the 1920s and early 1930s for its ahistorical claims and its treatment of musical material as if it were a natural 'given'. The publication of *Unterweisung im Tonsatz*, as Hindemith's attempt to formulate theoretically his practical compositional principles, as a 'theory of harmony', only served to confirm the accuracy of Adorno's early insights, based as they were on a critical consideration of the music itself. Adorno was not, of course, 'influenced' by Hindemith's book – it appeared in 1937, by which time he had already formulated the essential features of his own theory. However, a brief consideration of Hindemith's position as presented in *Unterweisung im Tonsatz* will serve admirably to throw into relief the other positions to be examined below.

Hindemith unequivocally states his intentions in the opening pages, indicating the pedagogical purpose of the work:

The teacher will find in this book basic principles of composition [*Grundzüge des Tonsatzes*], derived from the natural characteristics of tones, and consequently valid for all periods. To the harmony and counterpoint he has already learned – which have been purely studies in the history of style ... – he must now add a new technique, which, proceeding from the firm foundation of the laws of nature, will enable him to make expeditions into domains of composition which have not hitherto been open to orderly penetration.[4]

The emphasis on 'natural laws' (here as *Naturgebundenheit*, and a little later as *Naturgesetz*), and on the validity of the 'natural characteristics of tones' for all periods, taken together with his concept of 'material' as *Werkstoff* (unfortunately translated in the 1942 English version as 'the medium') or as *Tonrohstoff* ('tonal raw material'), reveals the extent to which Hindemith believes that the artist has direct, unmediated access to the 'raw material' of art, seen as part of nature as yet uninfluenced by history, culture or society. Corresponding to this belief is a belief in a universality of psychological responses to music – that is, to the intervals of music, certain of which 'make similar impressions upon all men ... even the man at the lowest level of civilization ...'.[5] Certain intervals – octave, fifth and major third – Hindemith sees as invariants, they are immutable and have the elemental power of nature behind them:

the major triad ... is to the trained and the naïve listener alike, one of the most impressive phenomena of Nature, simple and elemental as rain, snow, and wind. Music, as long as it exists, will always take its departure from the major triad and return to it. The musician cannot escape it any more than the painter his primary colours, or the architect his three dimensions. In composition, the triad or its direct extensions can never be avoided for more than a short time without completely confusing the listener . . . In the world of tones, the triad corresponds to the force of gravity. It serves as our constant guiding point, our unit of measure, and our goal, in even those sections of compositions which avoid it.[6]

Hindemith, in his 'interval series', attributes *a fixed* value to each interval, according to the degree of 'tension' he considers it to contain, rationally derived, he claims, from the overtone series. In his search for absolutes, for ontological certainties, he replaces tonality with a system which dispenses with the relativity of tonal relations and establishes a theory of harmony as rigid, in its own way, as the mediaeval view of the universe. He writes:

We may state the result of our investigations into the qualities of simultaneous tone combinations as follows: In contrast to the conventional theory of harmony, in which all tones are ranked according to their relation to an *a priori* tonal scheme, and thus have only relative values, our system attributes a fixed value to each. Between those of highest and those of lowest value we recognize a great number of gradations, each of which has a constant value.[7]

Hindemith's position, founded on a vision of music as the embodiment of static, immutable and universal truths rooted in the eternal laws of nature, can be summarized most concisely in his own words:

We have seen that tonal relations are founded in Nature, in the characteristics of sounding materials and of the ear, as in the pure relations of abstract numerical groups. We cannot escape the relationship of tones. . . . Tonality is a natural force, like gravity.[8]

Adorno's response to *Unterweisung im Tonsatz* was predictable in view of his previous criticisms of Hindemith's music. In his 1939 review of the book he wrote:

The 'faithful master musician' [*der 'gläubige Musikus'*] is transformed into a raging rationalist as soon as it has anything to do with chords, or even mere intervals, in which historical experiences have been precipitated, and which carry the trace of historical suffering. They must at all costs be proved to be the product of pure laws, even when they have long since become socially so rigidified as 'second nature' that they are in no need of any support from 'first nature'.[9]

That such 'traditional' and relatively unreflective conceptions of artistic material as those of Hindemith should have survived so long into the twentieth century is in itself surprising, in that the view that the material of music is of purely natural origin can be discounted as soon as any sophisticated referential system – like tonality – is examined and its apparently 'natural' characteristics stand revealed as being in fact highly contrived. In a mode of art as dependent on technical means and technology as music, practically everything can be seen to be culturally 'pre-formed' in some way – for example, tuning systems, instrument construction, and the demands and limitations of notational systems. That the argument against the presumed natural foundations of artistic material was already well under way before Adorno began formulating his ideas in the 1920s is evident enough. A number of these positions will be identified briefly in what follows, before focusing on the important debate with Krenek in Section 2.

Paul Valéry and l'art pour l'art

The intensive examination of the structuring principles and inner workings of art works and the process of their making had already by the late nineteenth century led to the recognition of the extreme character of the split between art and life. The *l'art-pour-l'art* position, especially as expressed by the French Symbolists, emphasized both the separation of art from life and the process of progressive control over 'material' (as *matière*, 'matter') which further encouraged the intensive development of the art work as a 'closed world'. This movement was central to the development of a 'modernist aesthetic'. Dating from the late 1840s and early 1850s in the work of Baudelaire, it found its extreme expression in the poetry of Rimbaud, Verlaine and Mallarmé, in the plays of Maeterlinck, and in works like Huysmans's *A Rebours* (translated significantly as *Against Nature*). The position was particularly clearly articulated by Paul Valéry (1871–1945) during the 1890s, and subsequently elaborated by him at great length in his theoretical writings on poetry and art up to the 1940s. What particularly drew Adorno to Valéry's aesthetic project was the latter's attempt to map the perpetual interaction of the sensuous and the rational in the work of art, an interaction which had so characterized the French Symbolist poetry of the *fin de siècle*. The paradox which Valéry identified with such clarity is what Adorno later described as 'the conflict between an objectifying technique and the mimetic essence of art works [which] comes to a head in the endeavour to redeem permanently what is fleeting, epiphenomenal and transitory, and to steel it against the onslaught of the forces of reification'.[10] Adorno continues:

Artistic technique is a labour of Sisyphus; it is akin to the notion of art as a *tour de force*. This is what Valéry's theory – a rational theory of aesthetic irrationality – is all about.[11]

Valéry's oppositional–complementary pairing of *inspiration* and *technique* finds its correspondence in Adorno's dialectical pairing of *expression* and *construction*. As indicated above, for Valéry the poem is a 'closed world' (*un monde fermé*) within which, through the interaction of inspiration and technique, a material (the word, in particular as *sound* in a very musical sense)[12] is shaped and structured to remove it from the domain of 'ordinary life'. As W. N. Ince puts it:

Art and life are separate for ... [Valéry]; he said on various occasions that he disliked 'life' in art, and spoke of eliminating or transcending 'le désordre monotone de la vie extérieure'.[13]

At the same time the exterior world is 'represented' within the closed world of the poem, in that the material, as 'words', also carries meaning as part of ordinary language.

Seen from Adorno's perspective, Valéry's position can also be understood as, paradoxically, incorporating a relationship between art and society, via the concepts of construction and technique, which is oppositional in character. In a passage strangely reminiscent of Adorno's use of Weber's concept of 'rationalization' in relation to art, Valéry wrote in 1935:

Man's control over matter has become continuously stronger and more accurate. Art has benefited from these advantages, and the various techniques created for the needs of practical life have given artists their tools and methods.[14]

Valéry's view of art as a 'closed world', which relates to the real world only through denying it, comes close to what Friedemann Grenz calls 'Adorno's theory of hermetic art'.[15] It can be seen as related (via the version of Symbolism which had taken root in Russia by the early years of the twentieth century) to another particularly influential expression of the concept of material – that put forward by the Russian Formalists in the period 1915–30. How much Adorno was actually influenced by theorists like Tynyanov, Eichenbaum, Shklovsky, Tomasjevsky and Jakobson is difficult to say with any certainty, as he makes practically no direct reference to their writings. That he was certainly aware of their thinking is strongly asserted by Dahlhaus, however,[16] and the similarities between Adorno's concept of 'pre-formed' material and the Formalists' concepts of 'materials' and 'device' or 'technique' (priëm) are very striking. In pointing out that 'the Russian Formalists' concept of material also means something already formed',[17] Peter Bürger, in his essay 'Das Vermittlungsproblem in der Kunstsoziologie Adornos', cites the following passage from an article by Juri Tynyanov:

The originality of a literary work consists in the application of a constructional factor to a material, in the 'formation' (in fact, in the 'de-formation') of this material. ... It is to be understood that 'material' and 'form' are throughout not opposed to one another; that material is itself 'formal', for there is no material apart from construction.[18]

Schoenberg's theory of harmony

It is, however, in Schoenberg's *Harmonielehre* (1911) – a book that Adorno would probably have known in its revised 1922 version[19] – that are to be discovered the most direct influences upon Adorno's concept of musical material. Although the actual term 'material' (*Material*) is employed relatively seldom by Schoenberg in his theoretical writings, it is nevertheless evident that he understands more by it than sound as 'raw material' (*Stoff*) and as 'natural phenomenon'. What Schoenberg brings to bear on the notion of the 'natural' material of music is the concept of historical evolution and of historical necessity.[20] The apparent 'natural laws' are only those 'necessary' at a particular historical moment; they are conventional. What is more, it is not even particularly important whether it can be demonstrated that the material, as for example, tonality, is actually in accordance with 'natural' laws at all. In his discussion of consonance and dissonance in the *Harmonielehre* Schoenberg argues for 'dissonance' as a matter of degree rather than of kind – i.e. as a historical rather than natural category:

The way of history, as we can see it in that which has actually been selected by practice from the practicable dissonances, hardly leads here to a correct judgment of the real relations. That assertion is proved by the incomplete or unusual scales of many other peoples, who have, nevertheless, as much right as we to explain them by appeal to nature. Perhaps their tones are often even more natural than ours (that is, more exact, more correct, better); for the tempered system, which is only an expedient for overcoming the difficulties of the material, has indeed only a limited similarity to nature. That is perhaps an advantage, but hardly a mark of superiority.[21]

What is important for Schoenberg is that music is to be understood as a mode of *cognition* (*Erkenntnis*), and that it is through the medium of form that music acquires meaning. In 1924 Schoenberg had written (in a piece later published in *Style and Idea* as 'Theory of Form'):

A theory of form would have to aim, first and foremost, at showing the significance of all artistic forms – the fact that they try to endow the artistic product (whose shape is conditioned by a material extrinsic to ourselves) with an external and internal constitution permitting us to recognize it as something that corresponds to the qualities of our intellect. Through its relationship, analogy with, similarity to other things we think, feel and sense, we are able to grasp it as similar to us, appropriate to us, and related to us. So one must show how the material, against or in accordance with its own aim, is forced by art – by fulfilling the demands of comprehensibility – to adapt itself to such conditions.[22]

Implied in Schoenberg's position is the idea that the material – whether natural or not – is already 'pre-formed', and contains the historical necessity to go beyond its present stage of development in order to become more appropriate to the expressive needs of the creative Subject. In the *Harmonielehre* he writes: '... we can only base our thought on such conjectures as will satisfy our formal necessity for sense and coherence without their being considered natural laws'.[23] He makes it clear that it is not meaning as enshrined in the laws of nature that interests him, but rather meaning as structured in products of the human spirit (*Geist*), and there is the suggestion that what we take to be natural laws are actually, on the contrary, the result of 'the struggle of the craftsman to shape the material correctly'.[24] The idea is also present that the material itself has a dynamic of its own, that it has immanent demands to which the composer must respond and which are the result not so much of natural forces but rather of cultural and historical forces. Schoenberg argues in the *Harmonielehre* for a process of 'reflection on nature', a process which in effect is a response to the demands of the material, and which reveals the material to be a 'cultural product', rather than 'nature'. Interestingly, Schoenberg uses the term 'second nature' for this historical–cultural product which has come to be taken as natural, in a manner which has some similarities to Lukács's use of the concept in *Theorie des Romans* (see Chapter 1) – a feature which would not have been lost on Adorno. The passage in question is worth citing at length:

> our present-day ear has been educated not only by the conditions nature imposed upon it, but also by those produced by the system, which has become a second nature. At present we can hardly, or just gradually, escape the effect of this artificial, cultural product; and reflection on nature may have value for the theory of knowledge without being thereby necessarily capable of bearing immediate artistic fruits. It is certain that this path, too, will be taken again sooner or later, the path that leads to new secrets of nature. It is certain that these, too, will then be thinned out to make a system; but before anything the old system has got to be got out of the way.[25]

Schoenberg, unlike, for example, Hindemith, presents in embryo a dialectical view of musical material. Whereas Hindemith, in *Unterweisung im Tonsatz*, argues restoratively for physical determinism in terms of the overtone series, and psychological and biological determinism in terms of the fixed values of the intervals and of the manner of their reception, Schoenberg, in the *Harmonielehre* written over a quarter of a century earlier, argues not simply for cultural determinism, but for the dialectical interaction of 'culture' (as 'history', 'consciousness') and 'nature' (as 'second nature'). It is essentially a materialist dialectic, but one which takes place entirely within the hermetic world of the self-sufficient work of art, as an extreme extension of the late nineteenth-century aesthetic of *l'art pour l'art* (Valéry's idea of the art work and the poetic state as *un monde fermé*).

It also constitutes an extension of a long-standing 'formalist' position which can be traced back through the whole Austro-German musical tradition, one theoretical expression of which was the aesthetic stance of Hanslick. It was Schoenberg's thorough-going musical dialectic which appealed so powerfully to the youthful Adorno in the early 1920s, and which doubtless provided the major stimulus for him to develop an elaborated concept of musical material in conjunction with Ernst Krenek between the years 1929 and 1934. Schoenberg brings an almost Hegelian awareness of the dynamic dimension of historical movement to the concept of musical material, together with an emphasis on the cognitive value of music and on the idea of 'progress' – something Adorno later came to formulate as the 'dialectic of construction and expression'.

August Halm's two cultures of music

A further musical influence on Adorno's thinking was the German theorist and music educationist, August Otto Halm. Halm (1869–1929), a contemporary of Schenker, published in 1913 his most influential book: *Von zwei Kulturen der Musik*.[26] In this he put forward a theory of musical form and historical progression which insisted both on the complete autonomy of music and on what he called the 'will of form' (*Formwille*; an idea which comes close to Adorno's notion of the demands of the musical material, and which is clearly greatly influenced by Schopenhauer's notion of music as the most direct manifestation of the Will). When, for example, in *Ästhetische Theorie* Adorno writes that 'there are objective genres and types with a teleology of their own',[27] he acknowledges in a footnote that '[t]his was emphasized in musicology by the unjustly forgotten August Halm'.[28]

Halm's 'two cultures of music' are essentially two formal types: the Baroque fugue, culminating in Bach, and the Classical sonata, culminating in Beethoven. The first he understands as representing unity, the second, conflict. He argues for a necessary historical synthesis of the two, which he sees as being partly realized in the example of Bruckner. He uses the term 'material' (*Material*) in a sense which often seems to prefigure Adorno, particularly when discussing Beethoven (e.g. in relation to the motivic structure of the music). More striking still, however, is Halm's attempt to bring together concepts of motivic development within musical form and of the development of the individual within the state. This foreshadows Adorno's attempt to discuss the fate of the individual, as creative Subject within late capitalist society, in terms of the dialectic of musical material, as progressive rationalization of all aspects of musical form (this will be discussed in detail as the historical dialectic of musical material in Chapter

6). A couple of passages taken from the end of Halm's book will serve to illustrate the correspondences with Adorno. Halm writes:

There is something of the bureaucratic mentality in the Classical sonata. The individual – that is, the theme, the melody – is not so much valued as a 'being for itself' [als ein Wesen für sich], with its own rights and its own life. It is much more a case of it being used, indeed manipulated: its own achievement is circumscribed. It has its place and its function within the whole, and it is often only this function which lends or denies it life. It is at the same time defined and held together by the atmosphere of the total event [des gesamten Geschehens].[29]

And he continues with a further analogy:

Or, if you prefer it, the Classical sonata could just as well be compared with an anthill, which just as much shocks us as leaves us in a state of astonished admiration for its being the embodiment of the division of labour [die verkörperte Arbeitsteilung]. The individual ant, biologically determined, is born to its function within the state.[30]

At the same time Halm interprets the historical 'progress' of musical form in terms of the ideal relationship of the individual to the social totality, the state.[31] There is an increasing awareness by the individual of its function within the social totality, of its ideal role in shaping that totality and of the potential for greater freedom of the part in relation to the whole. That is to say, there is a utopian character to be seen in Halm's concepts of *Formwille* and musical progress towards 'freedom'. Also contained in his thinking is something of the contradictory character of this emancipation, as freedom of part in relation to whole – freedom to shape the whole also containing its opposite, i.e. the part is pre-shaped to fit the 'ideal' whole. Many of these features, particularly the 'utopian' character of musical progress, are to be found in the work of someone who may well have provided the link between Adorno and Halm – the philosopher Ernst Bloch.

Ernst Bloch and the spirit of Utopia

The influence of Ernst Bloch on Adorno's concept of material is complex. Bloch (1885–1977), the so-called 'philosopher of Expressionism', was one of the founding fathers of Western Marxism and a close associate as well as intellectual adversary of Lukács. He published his most celebrated work, *Geist der Utopie*, in 1918.[32] In the extensive 'Philosophy of Music' section of the book Bloch puts forward, in that remarkably torrential prose-style which makes his writing so distinctive, what is in effect a philosophy of music history. Although owing something to Halm in its general sweep and in its emphasis on the historical movement of forms prominently featuring Bach, Beethoven and Bruckner, Bloch's philosophy of music also contains a concept of musical material which is essentially derived from Schoenberg's *Harmonielehre*. That is to say, Bloch's concept of 'material', like Schoenberg's, is founded on the conviction that the material of music is not 'natural' but rather cultural and historical. (Of the *Harmonielehre* he wrote: 'the book was written by a creative composer who only strove for a system of representation and not a system of Nature'.[33])

In fact, the line of influence from Schoenberg and Bloch to Adorno is vividly illustrated by one particular example of the 'decay' of musical material which is common to all three – i.e. the example of the diminished seventh chord. In his *Harmonielehre* (1911) Schoenberg writes:

whenever something difficult had to be done, one enlisted the services of this miracle worker, equal to every task.... But another meaning was also found for it: it was the 'expressive' chord of that time. Whenever one wanted to express pain, excitement, anger, or some other strong feeling – there we find, almost exclusively, the diminished seventh chord. So it is in the music of Bach, Haydn, Mozart, Beethoven, Weber, etc. Even in Wagner's early works it plays the same role. But soon the role was played out. This uncommon, restless, undependable guest, here today, gone tomorrow, settled down, became a citizen, was retired a philistine. The chord had lost the appeal of novelty, hence, it had lost its sharpness, but also its luster. It had nothing more to say to a new era. Thus, it fell from the higher sphere of art music to the lower of music for entertainment. There it remains, as a sentimental expression of sentimental concerns. It became banal and effeminate. *Became* banal! It was not so originally.[34]

Bloch's account of the fate of this chord in *Geist der Utopie* (1918, 1923) is clearly derived directly from Schoenberg, even down to details of wording:

The brilliant and harsh diminished seventh was once new; it gave an impression of novelty and so could represent anything – pain, anger, excitement and all violent emotion – in the music of the classical masters. Now that the radicalism has worn off, it has sunk irretrievably into mere 'light music' as a sentimental expression of sentimental ideas.[35]

Adorno takes up the example in passing in his article 'Reaktion und Fortschritt' (1930) as part of his debate with Krenek as follows:

Regarded in the context of the total level of the material at the time of Beethoven as the strongest tension moment available, it [the diminished seventh] becomes devalued at a later stage of the material to a harmless consonance...[36]

And over a decade later he develops the idea at greater length as part of the section on the 'immanent tendency of musical material' in *Philosophie der neuen Musik* (1941–8, published 1949), revealing even closer similarities to the Schoenberg and Bloch examples given above:

Even the more insensitive ear detects the shabbiness and exhaustion of the diminished seventh chord and certain chromatic modulatory tones in the salon music of the nineteenth century. For the technically trained ear, such vague discomfort is transformed into a prohibitive canon.... The diminished seventh chord, which rings false in salon pieces, is correct and full of every possible expression at the beginning of Beethoven's Sonata op. 111. This chord is not just superimposed and merely the result of the structural disposition of the movement. Rather it is the total *niveau* of Beethoven's technique which gives the chord its specific weight.... But the historical process, through which this weight has been lost, is irreversible. This chord itself, as an obsolete form, represents in its dissolution a state of technique contradictory as a whole to the state of technique actually in practice.[37]

Contained in Bloch's philosophy of 1918 is to be found the idea of music and musical material as 'raw material' permeated by 'Spirit' (*Geist*), in a sense very reminiscent of Hanslick. It is not a question of 'sound' (*Ton*) as discussed by physics, as a natural material, but rather a case of music as the 'metaphysics' of sound. That is to say, in music 'sound' is more than simply 'what it is' – an idea very much present in Adorno's theory of musical material. Bloch puts this position in *Geist der Utopie* as follows:

Little may be achieved, therefore, without our doing creative violence to the note and its related vibrations. To become music it is absolutely dependent on the flesh and blood of the person who takes it and performs it ... any so-called aesthetic physics of the note will be sterile without a new metaphysics of the note, whose servant it is. Hence in the last analysis the life of the note and its own fixedness, its mediumistic, unbroken material idea is – precisely while it is being played – never basically intended.[38]

While it is certainly the case that Bloch's 'philosophy of music' is altogether more overtly 'metaphysical' and transcendent than Adorno's, the utopian dimension of Bloch's thought is nevertheless also very much present in Adorno's theory of material. Bloch expresses his utopian vision of music in the following dramatic terms in *Geist der Utopie*:

The ultimate purpose of music and philosophy is purely the articulating of this basic mystery, this first and last question of all things.... *It is that which does not yet exist, which is lost and dimly sensed, our encounters with the self and the 'we' concealed in the dark and in the latency of every lived instant, our utopia calling to itself through charity, music and metaphysics, but not to be realised on Earth.*[39] (italics in original)

This is what Adorno means when he talks of art's *promesse de bonheur* and its riddle character. It is a 'moment of affirmation' which appears in even the most negative of modern works as the possibility of change, of 'the new', in relation to 'the immutable', the pre-given. As he puts it in *Ästhetische Theorie*:

This relation between the existent and the non-existent is the Utopian figure of art. While art is driven into a position of absolute negativity, it is never absolutely negative precisely because of that negativity. It always has an affirmative residue.[40]

Adorno had first read Bloch's *Geist der Utopie* at the age of eighteen, and, according to David Drew, 'he saw it as a magical and cryptical counterpart to Lukács's *Theory of the Novel*, and doubtless found in it further inducement for embarking on his studies in philosophy, music, sociology, and psychology at the Goethe University in Frankfurt'.[41] Adorno met Bloch through Walter Benjamin in Berlin in 1928, and the two men had a considerable influence upon each other over the next few years, up to 1932 (the period of Adorno's debates with Ernst Krenek). While Bloch's influence at this time, together with that of Lukács, was mainly to confirm Adorno's new-found Marxian approach (leading indirectly to its application in 'Zur gesellschaftlichen Lage der Musik'), Adorno's influence on Bloch is certainly clearly in evidence in *Das Prinzip Hoffnung* of 1938,[42] written shortly after Bloch had emigrated to the United States. Passages like the following show a remarkable accord with Adorno's work of the period 1929–38:

Composers turn music not only into an expression of themselves but also into an expression of the age and society in which it originates. So naturally this expression is not just romantic or quasi-freely subjective. Any number of *human tensions* are added to the tension of the fifth to create a more complicated cadence and thus the history of music. *Social trends themselves* have been reflected and expressed in the sound-material, far beyond the unchanging physical facts and also far beyond a merely romantic espressivo. No other art is conditioned by social factors as much as the purportedly self-acting, even mechanically self-sufficient art of music; historical materialism, with the accent on 'historical', abounds here.[43]

Bloch also offers specific examples – albeit painted with a very broad brush – of how he considers social tendencies are reflected and expressed in the sound-material of music:

The dominance of the melody-carrying upper part and mobility of the other parts correspond to the rise of the entrepreneur, just as the central *cantus firmus* and terraced polyphony corresponded to the hierarchical society. Haydn and Mozart, Handel and Bach, Beethoven and Brahms all had a social mission which was very specific; it extends from the form of performance to the *ductus* of the tonal material and its composition, and to the expression, the statement of the content. Handel's oratorios reflect, in their proud solemnity, the rise of imperialist England and her claim to be the chosen people. There would have been no Brahms without the middle-class concert society and even no musical *neue Sachlichkeit*, no purportedly expressionless music, without the enormous increase in alienation, objectification and reification in late capitalism. It is always the consumer sector and its requirements, the feelings and aims of the ruling class which are expressed in music.[44]

And in characteristic fashion, Bloch also sees something in music of the 'bourgeois period' which transcends ideology through its utopian vision, its offer of hope and solace, even in a context of total negativity:

Yet at the same time, thanks to its capacity for such directly human expression, music surpasses other arts in its ability to absorb the manifold griefs, wishes and rays of hope common to the socially oppressed. And again, no art outstrips a given age and ideology – although this, of course, is an outstripping which never abandons the human sector. It is inherent in the material of hope, even when the music is expressing sorrow at its times, society or world, and even in death.[45]

The relationship between Adorno and Bloch cooled considerably after the Second World War (Bloch, in fact, returned from exile in the United States to live in Communist East Germany, but became disillusioned and later left to live in West Germany). Indeed, it would be safe to say that it was Adorno who had distanced himself from Bloch, rather than the other way round. Nevertheless, the influence of Bloch's *Geist der Utopie* made a lasting mark on Adorno's thought: the 'spirit of Utopia' remained a crucial polarity within his negative dialectics, even though, as with the Jewish *Bilderverbot* (the prohibition on the naming of God) or Beckett's *The Unnameable*, Adorno refuses to give his vision a positive form. The utopian vision, although in a much simpler, more concrete and more practically committed political sense, is also present in the music and thinking of a younger contemporary and friend of Bloch's and later collaborator with Adorno – the composer Hanns Eisler. Eisler's theories from the early 1930s are worth pursuing here briefly, both because of their connection with Bloch and because of certain parallels with Adorno's theory of material.

Hanns Eisler and the social function of music

As we have seen, Adorno knew Eisler through the artistic and intellectual circles in which they both moved in Berlin in the mid-1920s.[46] The question as to whether Eisler exercised any direct influence on Adorno's theory of musical material is difficult to gauge, because the two men both developed a dialectical approach to the problems of music and its social function using a Marxian analysis based on the theory of the commodity at roughly the same time. (Indeed, any influence could well have been in the other direction: in the book they wrote jointly in the United States, and which was published initially in English under Eisler's name alone in 1947 as *Composing for the Films*, it has to be argued that Adorno's contribution was the greater, and that his influence on the manner in which Eisler formulated his ideas was decisive.) But the parallels in their thinking in the early 1930s are worth noting – as long as the divergences in their positions are also borne in mind. In December 1931, for example, some months before the publication of Adorno's essay 'Zur gesellschaftlichen Lage der Musik', Eisler gave a talk in Düsseldorf, where workers' choirs were rehearsing Brecht's *Die Massnahmen* (*The Measures Taken*), entitled 'Die Erbauer einer neuen Musikkultur' ('The builders of a new musical culture').[47] In it he put forward a dialectical theory of music history from the perspective of the 'new music' and the contemporary 'crisis within music' – albeit from a committed Marxist position that was far more reductionist than Adorno's selective use of Marxian ideas and which accords the 'new music' considerably less autonomy than does Adorno's theory. The key concept is that of 'social function'. In his talk Eisler argued that:

history has taught us that every new musical style has not arisen from an aesthetically new point of view and therefore does not represent a material revolution, but the change in the material is conditioned as a matter of course by an historically necessary change in the function of music in society as a whole.[48]

Using the concept of 'social function', Eisler traces the development of Western music from feudal times to the 'bourgeois period' and to what he perceives to be the subsequent degeneration of bourgeois music in the twentieth century. Like Adorno, he argues that 'a certain social situation leads to a certain musical technique which, in turn, when applied in practice makes this particular social situation possible'.[49] Applying this concept to church music in the Middle Ages, for example, he writes:

Music in the church is not directed towards the individual or his individual fate, but has the task of making all participants adopt a certain religious bearing.... This form of music-making corresponded to the class interests of the lords of the manor, the feudal lords, and in practice made feudalism possible and stabilized it again and again. Arising from this social function a certain method of constructing tones arose, which we will simply call musical technique.[50]

The technique in question is a polyphony which uses devices like imitation and canon, without contrast in terms of modulation and timbral 'effects', which, he implies, presents a static and non-individualistic world-view. Against this he opposes historically the new function of music in bourgeois society as 'that of allowing a harmonious development of the individual personality'.[51] He continues:

To describe bourgeois music as graphically as possible, we must say that the term 'commodity' which is indeed the decisive factor in capitalism, has spread into the realm of music. The concert form signifies the introduction of commodity relations into music. Concert ticket-buying, the sale of sheet music, the term music specialist – the producers of music commodities – are all characteristic of this.[52]

The function of music in bourgeois society, he argues, is entertainment and pleasure, and the 'upholding of the individual personality'.[53] Seen in relation to changes in compositional technique, this led to the development of homophonic music. Eisler identifies what he calls the 'bourgeois individual' – a term also employed by Adorno, and equivalent to his 'historical Subject' – and sees as a particular historical development of this the 'early revolutionary individuality', as reflected in the music of the Mannheim School in the mid-eighteenth century. Eisler sees the high point in the development of the bourgeois individual in musical terms in the music of Beethoven:

The greatest heights of bourgeois music were reached in Beethoven's symphonies in which the pleasure was refunctioned to become a kind of philosophical world outlook. While at revolutionary periods revolutionary bourgeois music reflects the great revolutionary individual in his actual struggle against feudalism, by the middle of the nineteenth century it also reflects the disappointed, property-preserving petty bourgeoisie.[54]

Eisler's analysis of the technique and devices used in homophonic music of this period in relation to the concept of 'social function' is interesting in the way in which it corresponds to aspects of Adorno's theory of material, particularly as the 'historical dialectic of material' presented in Chapter 6. Eisler, like Adorno, emphasizes the relation of even the most 'elevated' and serious forms of autonomous music in the bourgeois period to their social function as 'entertainment' (in fact Adorno tends to stress the *origins* of genres and forms like the symphony and sonata in the *divertissements*, serenades and operatic overtures of the *style galant*). Both Eisler and Adorno emphasize the significance of *contrast* in such music. Eisler writes:

It is built on the principle of *contrast* first and foremost. This principle guarantees to a high degree variety and entertainment. The development of harmony and its theoretical derivations make possible ever more new methods of contrast. Finally, contrast is also guaranteed by the technique of instrumentation, which introduces timbre as a musical means of presentation. . . . This style is appropriate, as no other, for appealing to the individual experience and to the individual imagination. The listener is not forced to take a predetermined attitude but an attempt is made to excite him, to entertain him and to create associations for him.[55]

Where Adorno's position diverges considerably from that of Eisler is on the question of direct political commitment. For Eisler, theoretical speculation on the dialectical social function of music was part of a larger project to use music in a politically engaged *praxis*, along the lines of Brecht's 'epic theatre'. For Adorno, such an enterprise ran the risk of degenerating into propaganda and of betraying its own 'law of form' – that is, the demands of its material. He argued that it was through its *form* that art opposed coercion, not through direct intervention. In his essay 'Engagement' of 1962 Adorno wrote: 'It is not the office of art to spotlight alternatives, but to resist by its form alone the course of the world, which permanently puts a pistol to men's heads. In fact, as soon as committed works of art do instigate decisions at their own level, the decisions themselves become interchangeable.'[56]

The affinity between Eisler and Adorno remained strong enough for Eisler to collaborate with Adorno on the Film Music Project of the New School for Social Research in the United States in the 1940s, the fruits of which appeared in *Composing for the Films*. Nevertheless, their differences became pronounced, resulting in a final split between the two men on their return to Germany – East and West – in the immediate post-war years. Eisler settled in East Berlin, having been deported, like Brecht, for his Communist beliefs as a result of the McCarthy trials. Adorno, as we have seen, was invited back to resume his academic career at Frankfurt University.

This cursory examination of precursors and contemporaries of Adorno serves to demonstrate that the development of Adorno's theory of musical material did not occur in isolation. It needs to be seen rather as one particular variant of a common current of thought which was very active during the first three decades of the twentieth century. The question of who might have exercised 'direct influences' on Adorno is ultimately not important. What is important is to see the emergence of the concept of 'material' as part of a continuing debate during this period. Central to this debate is the intensive exchange of ideas between Adorno and the composer Ernst Krenek between the years 1929 and 1932. It is to this dialogue that we now turn.

2   The Adorno–Krenek debate

Adorno first met Ernst Krenek in June 1924 in Frankfurt, where Krenek's opera *Der Sprung über den Schatten* was receiving its first performance. Although they remained in close contact, it was not until the end of 1928 that their frequent correspondence began, probably as a result, Claudia Maurer-Zenck suggests, of Adorno's editorship of the journal *Anbruch*, which started early in 1929; Krenek was contributing an article for the January issue.[57] It was Adorno's essay 'Atonales Intermezzo?',[58] which Krenek had seen before its publication in *Anbruch* in May 1929, that initially stimulated the debate over twelve-tone music and the concept of musical material. Adorno valued Krenek both as composer[59] and as theorist,[60] and, as well as collaborating on *Anbruch* and the journal '23', they contributed significantly to Willi Reich's book on Berg of 1937.[61] Contact was maintained throughout the emigration years in England and the United States, and the two corresponded, albeit no longer regularly, up to the 1960s.

The debate on musical material and the twelve-tone technique took a number of forms. Apart from their meetings, there was the intensive exchange of letters of which the surviving ones were subsequently published (in 1974) as part of the long-standing but sporadic correspondence between the two men up to 1964.[62] At the same time, and often as a direct result of their exchange of ideas, both men published articles on aspects of the problem of musical material, and also gave a number of radio talks (one in the form of a dialogue, subsequently published in the *Frankfurter Zeitung*).[63] The rest of this chapter is an examination and summary of the main issues in the debate, focusing on material from the years 1929–30 and 1932.

The first group of material – a letter from Adorno to Krenek dated 9 April 1929; two articles by Adorno, 'Zur Zwölftontechnik' (1929) and 'Reaktion und Fortschritt' (1930); and the Krenek–Adorno radio discussion in its published form, 'Arbeitsprobleme des Komponisten: Gespräch über Musik und soziale Situation' (10 December 1930) – focuses mainly on the immanent-historical and cognitive dimensions of the musical material (although the radio discussion does begin to take on the social situation of music). The second group – a letter from Krenek dated 11 September 1932 and a letter in response from Adorno dated 30 September 1932, followed by the very substantial Adorno article 'Zur gesellschaftlichen Lage der Musik' (1932) – emphasizes the social dimension of musical material and also the social function of music.

In its early stages the exchange is taken up almost entirely with the clarification of basic concepts (e.g. nature, history, progress, consistency, material), and it takes as its point of departure Schoenberg, atonality and the twelve-tone technique (in accordance with Adorno's view that the material of music is always that at the most advanced stage of its historical development). In its later stages – that is, in 'Zur gesellschaftlichen Lage der Musik' – the debate moves towards a more elaborated theory. In what follows the key concepts in the debate are identified and their development towards a rudimentary theory of the relationship between music and society is mapped out. The occasion has been taken here to present the terms of the discussion in some expository detail, as the Adorno–Krenek *Briefwechsel* and most of the associated articles and talks have not yet appeared in English.[64] The problems raised by Adorno's attempt at this stage to account for the mediation of music and social reality by means of a concept of musical material are taken up in detail in Chapter 3.

Historical necessity and cognitive character

In the course of the letter to Krenek dated 9 April 1929 Adorno writes concerning the problem of atonality:

I am in agreement with you that the overtone theory and other physically based arguments are to be rejected. We are concerned with the phenomena, not with their physical conditions.... I apportion, in the most precise sense, the character of *cognition* [*Erkenntnis*] to any legitimate art. To qualify this I would just like to say that my point of departure is not a free-floating rationality which is able to choose ahistorically between the opportunities offered by the material. Instead, I maintain that the cognitive character of art is defined through its *historical actuality* [*geschichtliche Aktualität*].[65]

Adorno immediately takes up and develops the two aspects of the concept of material already suggested by Schoenberg – *historical necessity* and *cognitive character*. The implications already are that the 'material' (still to be exhaustively explored by Adorno on a conceptual level) is not the sum of all acoustical possibilities and associated compositional techniques to date. The choices, he insists, are limited by the historical stage reached by the material in relation to current expressive needs. In 1929 that stage was the period of the recent development of the twelve-tone technique. It was also, of course, the period of neoclassicism and of various attempts to restore and rationalize a modified tonality.

Actuality

To a question put by Krenek in a previous letter (no longer extant) as to why Adorno considered atonality and the twelve-tone technique to be 'a higher form of thought'[66] than tonality, Adorno answers:

When I maintain that atonality is the only possible manner of composing today, it is not because I consider it ahistorically to be 'better', a handier referential system than tonality. It is rather that I think that tonality has *collapsed*, that every tonal chord has a meaning that we can no longer grasp; that, once we have outgrown the 'natural givens' of the tonal material, we can no more go back into that material than we can return to a form of economic production based on use-value, or (something which I would argue against Karl Kraus) than we are able to speak an objectively given, ontological language, the words for which long ago fell into disuse.[67] (italics in original)

Krenek had previously suggested, concerning the question of criteria for what constituted 'good music', that the 'better' a piece of music, the more advanced it would be, in the sense of using the most developed musical means available.[68] Adorno expanded on this by maintaining that the recognition of the quality of a composition is tied up with the level of what he called its 'inner-historical actuality' (*an dem Stand ihrer innergeschicht-lichen Aktualität*). The collapse of tonality and the subsequent challenge of atonality is directly the result of the demands of the material. Triadic interpolations within an atonal context sound false, he says, and 'this impurity [*Unreinheit*] is not the result of abstract style-critical postulates, but of the compulsion [*Zwang*] to which the material subjects us and which is stamped upon it'.[69]

The issue, Adorno insists, is not to do with the search for a new 'referential system' or 'frame of reference' (*Bezugssystem*) to replace tonality:

> The current argument – which is even used in support of the twelve-tone technique – that without a frame of reference musical form is not possible, is not, in my view, the essential problem that concerns us, because the identity of the octave, the constancy of the individual intervals, high and low registers and so on, constitute in themselves a frame of reference. I cannot see why there should be an a priori need for further frames of reference over and above these.[70]

Rationalization

Although Adorno considered the twelve-tone technique to be an 'inevitable outcome' of the historical pressure from within the material, and to be a manifestation of that tendency towards extreme rationalization of all aspects of social life which Max Weber had identified within Western culture (see Chapter 3), he nevertheless did not seem to regard it as the only form of rationalization possible for atonality. Furthermore, he argues – using imagery surely derived from Bloch's *Geist der Utopie*[71] – that the twelve-tone technique is not to be taken as a substitute for tonality.

> The twelve-tone technique ... is not, even for me, a new shelter in which one can take refuge since the roof fell in on tonality. If it should turn out to be that, then the technique should be dispensed with forthwith – this is no time for building shelters. I regard the twelve-tone technique much more as the rationalization of particular compositional experiences [*Komponiererfahrungen*]: above all of the aversion to the repetition of the same pitch-classes within too short a period ...; and then also of the consequence of variation technique and total thematic economy, as initiated by Brahms. ... In other words, I accept the twelve-tone technique only as the outcome of a consistent [*stimmig*] and inevitable [*zwangsvoll*] musical dialectic, as is the case with Schoenberg's variation technique ... I regard it in no sense as a ready-made, freshly-minted recipe for composition, ahistorical and offering handy advantages over tonality.[72]

Adorno attacks Hauer for the mechanical character of his system and because it is not the result of the demands of the musical material.[73] The twelve-tone technique – or any such similar system – should be the means and not the end of composition. He goes on to argue that there is nothing against rows (he uses the term *Thema* here) with less or even more than twelve pitches, and cites the variation movement from Schoenberg's *Serenade* op. 24 as an example of a piece which is constructed around an eleven-note theme. He states that he would not hesitate to suggest emancipating the technique from the number 12 'if the compositional situation made it necessary'.[74] He makes the point that 'the twelve-tone technique is not an objectively valid compositional canon – something which no longer exists today anyway – and is hardly even a compositional technique at all' (in that more elements than pitch-content enter into the composition of a twelve-tone piece). Adorno sees the technique as a kind of 'purification' of the musical material, whereby it is 'purified of the dross of the merely organic; composition as such, with all its problems, only begins *after* this'.[75]

He argues that the richness of possibilities offered by the technique is also not in itself anything unique, and should not be overstated (in that tonality in its time has also been very rich in 'relational possibilities' (*Beziehungs-reichtum*)). The twelve-tone technique has merely come about as a result of these possibilities, and has provided a formula for their manipulation. He writes: 'That it is possible to get by without it no-one has demonstrated more rigorously than the Schoenberg of *Erwartung* and *Die glückliche Hand* ...'.[76] Adorno considers that the possibilities thrown up by the kind of freely atonal and athematic compositional techniques of *Ewartung* have not really been sufficiently followed up.

Tendency of the material

Adorno identifies an important feature of the twelve-tone technique which formalizes the kind of freedom of possibilities which is so striking about the 'athematicism' of works like *Erwartung*: 'It is precisely the twelve-tone technique ... which offers the splendid dialectical possibility for this, in that it shifts the thematic working behind the compositional scenes, as it were, into the material, with which it can then operate with complete freedom'.[77] This seems to be one of the most significant aspects of the technique for Adorno. That is to say, in rationalizing a tendency which Adorno considers had become an immanent-historical pressure within the material, the basic set, with all its derivatives, now becomes itself the material, functioning both pre-compositionally and at the most fundamental level of the work. A problem which Adorno saw at this point (and this was directly on the heels of Schoenberg's Variations for Orchestra op. 31 of 1928) was the relationship between foreground and background levels in twelve-tone compositions – something he was later to expand in *Philosophie der neuen*

Musik concerning the traditional features of Schoenberg's phraseology at the foreground level in relation to the radical nature of the basic material.

Adorno also addresses himself to the problem of harmony in twelve-tone music (again in response to points raised by Krenek in a previous letter no longer extant). The claim that twelve-tone music is 'aharmonic' or that the harmony is 'functionless' is not valid, he maintains, in that implied in the term 'functionless' is reference to Riemann's *Funktionsbegriff* – a concept which applies only to one form of functional harmony, i.e. tonal harmony. Adorno argues that atonal and twelve-tone harmony is not arbitrary: it has its own form of functionality, and the clue to this lies in the aversion to note-repetitions in atonal music, formalized by the twelve-tone technique:

> The aversion to note-repetitions is itself stamped on one of the most important harmonic principles of the twelve-tone technique: the principle of 'complementary' harmony [*das Prinzip der 'komplementären' Harmonik*]. ... One could perhaps formulate it thus: it requires that each group resolve harmonically through pitches which do not occur within it.[78]

For Adorno this would seem to be one of the principles that would govern the 'correctness' or consistency (*Stimmigkeit*) of twelve-tone harmony. Contained here is also therefore a criterion for value-judgements in relation to such music. As Adorno puts it: 'if twelve-tone music presents itself as harmonically arbitrary, then it is just badly composed'.[79]

Finally, Adorno briefly addresses himself in this letter to the problem of voice-leading and counterpoint. He is critical of the then fashionable view that the 'harmonic arbitrariness' of the 'new music' since the breakdown of tonality is the result of the voice-leading of entirely independent contrapuntal lines. He argues to the contrary that contrapuntal working in atonal music is, in a very precise sense, dependent upon harmonic considerations (that is, the principle of complementary harmony), and 'how, the other way round, harmonic problems are also voice-leading problems'.[80]

On the twelve-tone technique

Adorno wrote up the substance of his debate with Krenek at this stage as the article 'Zur Zwölftontechnik', which he published a few months later in the September–October 1929 issue of the journal *Anbruch*. The striking difference in style is not merely that between a letter (albeit one clearly written with eventual publication in mind) and a published article. Adorno's love of cryptic formulations, which tend to leave the reader in some doubt as to whether their meaning has really been grasped, is very much in evidence in this text, whereas the letters are in the main relatively straightforward (a feature upon which Krenek himself comments in his foreword to the *Briefwechsel*).[81]

'Zur Zwölftontechnik' will not be examined in any detail here because the important general points made in it concerning the concept of musical material have already been summarized as they occur in somewhat less concentrated form in the letter to Krenek of 9 April 1929. One general point from 'Zur Zwölftontechnik' concerning the musical material, although perhaps of relative unimportance, deserves to be made here, however, as it is not emphasized in the letter. This has to do with the common prejudice that the twelve-tone technique is not only a compositional *method*, but that it is also to be understood as being in some way a *mathematical* method. Adorno dismisses this notion, arguing instead for historical necessity:

[The twelve-tone technique] is above all not a positive compositional method, but is rather a historically relevant *pre-forming* [*Vorformung*] of the material which had to be carried through. It is not to be explained mathematically, but historically, and it is not directed at a mathematically formal region of music, but rather aims to make compositional freedom possible.[82]

Nevertheless, Adorno later came to regard the twelve-tone technique as having enchained music in the very act of freeing it.[83] Adorno's attitude to middle-period, serial Schoenberg is decidedly ambivalent, and there is no doubt that he regarded the works of the freely atonal period as holding out the hope of a freedom from which music was soon to retreat. As he puts it in *Ästhetische Theorie*:

An ever-increasing number of things artistic were drawn into an eddy of new taboos, and rather than enjoy their newly won freedom, artists everywhere were quick to look for some presumed foundation for what they were doing. This flight into a new order, however flimsy, is a reflection of the fact that absolute freedom in art – which is a particular – contradicts the abiding unfreedom of the social whole.[84]

Progress and the avant-garde

In focusing on Schoenberg in the letter to Krenek of 9 April 1929 and in the article 'Zur Zwölftontechnik', Adorno makes it clear that in his view the *actual* musical material available to a composer at any particular historical moment is that at the most advanced stage of its development – that is, at the most extreme intersection of expressive needs and technical means. For Adorno, writing in 1929, that point of intersection was seen as embodied in the music of Schoenberg, which becomes the starting point for Adorno's own, conceptual exploration of musical material, viewing music history as he does always from the standpoint of the avant-garde. In the next article to be examined here – 'Reaktion und Fortschritt' of June 1930 – the concept of material is further elaborated, with particular emphasis on the concept of *Stimmigkeit* (consistency, correctness) in relation not only to Schoen-berg but also to other compositional practices of the period. As the title indicates, the article focuses on the idea of 'progress' (*Fortschritt*) in music. This involves further examination of the relationship between history and nature, and also introduces the notion of the historical decay and devaluation (*Entwertung*) of musical material (he later tends to use the terms *Verfall* or *Zerfall des Materials*). In this article (and in those that follow) Adorno is moving towards a more generally applicable notion of musical material, albeit one which, he insists, can only be understood in relation to individual works. There is not at this stage, however, any real attempt to take on the social dimension in any thoroughgoing manner; the idea that the musical material has a *social content* is, nevertheless, already implicit.

The social dimension enters into Adorno's thinking in 'Reaktion und Fortschritt' only to the extent that he suggests that, although one cannot talk of 'progress' in music in terms of composers being 'better' today than they were, say, at the time of Beethoven, one could say, perhaps, that social relations have progressed; it is not, however, very clear what he means by this. What is clear is that for Adorno, progress in music is not at the level of individual works and in the idea that composers are getting better at writing music; it takes place rather at the level of the material. The material may therefore be understood as having a collective content, although at this stage in the discussion the idea is not developed, and the emphasis still tends to be on the expressive Subject as individual in the interaction between composer and musical material. The material is, nevertheless, the precipitate or sediment of previous interactions between composers and the historical 'figurations' they encounter as material, and thus represents the social collectivity:

It is the material which provides the stage for progress in art, not individual works. And this material is not, like the twelve semitones with their physically patterned overtone relationships, unchangeable and identical for all time. On the contrary, history is sedimented in the figurations [*Figuren*] in which the composer encounters the material; the composer never encounters the material separate from such figurations.[85]

It is in these material 'figurations' that progress takes place – and also historical decay within the material (see the example given above of the diminished seventh chord, in relation to Bloch and Schoenberg). For Adorno '[p]rogress means nothing other than always to grasp the material at the most advanced stage of its historical dialectic'.[86] As we have noted, Adorno's emphasis is on the *material* and its historical movement, not on the individual work. This points to an ambivalence at the heart of the concept of musical material: progress takes place in the musical material rather than in the individual work, and yet the only access we have to the progress of the material is through individual works. This problem will be considered in more detail in Chapter 4.

Consistency

This dialectic only takes place, however, as a dialectic between *composer* and material; that is to say, the composer works with particular available material figurations in the shaping of a concrete musical work. Adorno maintains that it is purely in terms of the demands thrown up in the course of this process that the question of progress or reaction is decided – in other words, the work's *consistency*. The reasoning appears to be along the following lines: (i) 'consistency' means the full realization in the structure of the work of its motivating 'idea' or concept; (ii) however, all 'authentic' works of art are the concrete manifestation of an adequate response to the historical demands of the material, the structuring idea of the work being also of necessity an inseparable aspect of this response; (iii) to respond adequately to the historical demands of the material is to be progressive; (iv) thus any work which strives to achieve consistency in its response to the historical demands of the material will thereby show itself to be progressive. Adorno insists that:

it is only in its immanent consistency that a work proves itself as progressive. In each work the material registers concrete demands, and the movement with which each new work manifests these is the sole obligatory shape [*Gestalt*] of history for the author. A work that meets these demands completely is consistent [*stimmig*].[87]

Adorno is putting forward a materialist aesthetic here, which makes the claim that judgements concerning the quality of a work, as consistency and progress (and ultimately as authenticity and 'truth' to the material), can (and indeed must) be grounded in the technical structure of the work. The validity of these judgements must therefore be revealed through 'immanent analysis' (a concept considered briefly in Chapter 1, and which will be examined in greater detail in Chapter 4). As Adorno puts it: 'The fight against aesthetic reaction has to take place centrally in the immanent analysis of works and not in vague judgements about "style"'.[88]

Reaction

'Reaction' in this context has for Adorno the general sense of 'reaction against change'; its particular characteristics could be summarized as (a) a belief in the constancy of musical material based in the unchanging laws of nature; (b) a belief in the constancy of the musical Subject – both as composer and as listener – based in the unchanging nature of expressive needs; and (c) a belief in the unchanging, ahistorical character of the 'truth' of great works of art. Adorno notes two objections which are raised from the reactionary position against the notion of progress as the historical dialectic of musical material. These objections are (i) that in the dialectic of the material the freedom of the composer is forgotten – the composer merely becoming the executor of historical-material laws and demands rather than the 'sovereign maker' he should be; and (ii) that the material dialectic has limitations built into it when it comes to the 'original meaning' (*Ursinn*) of the material itself which, although it may have become distorted and almost lost in the course of history, can nevertheless be grasped and restored by the creative artist. Adorno argues that both these objections can only be met by returning to the object itself – i.e. the work in its historical context. Neither the composer and the myth of his independence from the material, nor the material and the myth of its original meaning can now be restored, Adorno maintains; freedom is not situated somewhere beyond the objectivity of the work, in the psyche of the artist; and an artist who ignores the demands of the material leaves the compositional process of the work up to the blind realization of historical forces. 'The closer the contact with the material', he states, 'the freer the artist'.[89]

Compositional practice and devalued material

At this point Adorno becomes more specific concerning other compositional possibilities for dealing with the material, apart from Schoenberg. He argues that any attempt to establish 'original meaning' in the material can lead to nothing more than a form of literary 'reminiscence technique' – as, for example, if one tries to use the harmonic procedures of Schubert today. Recognizing this, however, Adorno considers that there is one sense in which such a way of using the material can be justified. This is what he calls – by analogy with painting and literature – 'surrealist' music, and he gives in support of this the examples of Weill, Krenek and Stravinsky in certain of their works. Such a form of musical surrealism recognizes that 'original meaning cannot be restored',[90] and therefore juxtaposes its historically devalued fragments in a montage-like manner which enables them to yield up new meanings within a new aesthetic unity (an idea later expanded as part of the typology of composers of 'authentic' music in Part 1 of 'Zur gesellschaftlichen Lage der Musik').

Insofar as surrealist composing makes use of devalued means, it uses these *as* devalued means, and wins its form from the 'scandal' produced when the dead suddenly spring up among the living. . . . But in any case, the 'surrealist' technique is capable of producing constructive unity, consistent precisely in its enlightened and abruptly expounded inconsistency – a montage of the débris of that which once was.[91]

Adorno identifies *pastiche* (*Stilkopie*) as another possibility for restorative practice. But, he argues, even if a pastiche composition should succeed completely in its own terms, 'its means are always in themselves so faded that even the most successful copy is incapable of bringing them back to life'.[92]

Nature and second nature

In his insistence that there can be no direct, unmediated access to nature and to 'original meaning' in art, Adorno, as we have seen in Chapter 1, is working with what is essentially a Lukácsian concept of 'second nature'. That is to say, what is taken to be 'natural' in art is in fact mediated nature, 'second nature', already culturally and socially filtered. In *Geschichte und Klassenbewußtsein* Lukács states that 'nature' is 'a societal category'. He goes on to elaborate on this:

That is to say, whatever is held to be natural at any given stage of social development, however this nature is related to man and whatever form his involvement with it takes, i.e. nature's form, its content, its range and its objectivity are all socially conditioned.[93]

We have seen how Adorno took Lukács's concept of 'second nature' (as it appears in *Theorie des Romans*) as both myth and as 'the world of convention'. As Gillian Rose points out, however, at this point Adorno is 'severely hampered because he has no concept or theory of society or of a mode of production'[94] – something which is apparent in his music theory until the mid-1930s (even 'Zur gesellschaftlichen Lage der Musik' of 1932 has problems formulating the relationship between the aesthetic forces of production and the social forces of production).

Demythologization and emancipation

It is in 'Reaktion und Fortschritt' that Adorno begins decisively to link history and truth in relation to a notion of 'authenticity' (at this stage he uses the term *Echtheit*, but more usually uses the term *Authentizität*). For music to have a 'truth content' it must be interwoven with the historical figuration of the material. This is a process of the freeing of human consciousness from myth, and it constitutes progress. He writes:

Whatever nature may have been at the start, it is only from history that it receives the seal of authenticity [*Echtheit*]. History enters into the constellation of truth: through the dead stare of their speechless eternity the stars will strike down with confusion anyone who tries to partake of truth outside history.[95]

Progress is not to be confused with the individual facts of history, or with individual works of art; it is rather, Adorno maintains, a process of *demythologization*, particularly from the myths of absolute origins and of pure being beyond history:

To rescue musical archetypes from speechless eternity is the true intention of progress in music. Just as the social process is not to be construed as progress in terms of its individual facts or in the sense of thoroughgoing development, but rather as progress in demythologization [*Entmythologisierung*], the same is true of the genesis of music in time.[96]

That the aim of such progress, as demythologization, is emancipation from the myth of nature as 'invariance', the 'spiritualization' of material through shaping it, is clear in the concluding passage of the article:

That which is unchanging in nature can look after itself. It is up to us to change it. But a nature which clings on to itself murkily and oppressively, and fears the light of an illuminating and warming consciousness, is rightly to be distrusted. There will no longer be room for such a view of nature in the art of a real humanism.[97]

The composer's working problems

The radio discussion between Krenek and Adorno entitled 'Arbeitsprobleme des Komponisten: Gespräch über Musik und soziale Situation' was broadcast from Frankfurt on 16 November 1930, and was published the following month in the *Frankfurter Zeitung*. In a letter to Adorno a few weeks before the programme Krenek had suggested that they take up the debate where they had left off in 'Reaktion und Fortschritt' and in Krenek's accompanying article in the same issue of *Anbruch* entitled 'Fortschritt und Reaktion'. Krenek had argued for the relative independence of the musical material and for the improvisatory freedom of the composer. Adorno, on the other hand, had argued for the historical determination of the material and for the obligation of the composer to respond to its historical demands. In the discussion they structure the arguments in the form of a series of alternating theses – a form which for convenience the following summary retains.

Adorno opens the discussion, which, for the first time in their debate (at least, as available in the published letters and articles), introduces the problem of the social situation of music. He emphasizes that the problems faced by the composer are not only to do with purely technical musical issues but that they also involve the relationship to society. Nevertheless, he insists, this social dimension is only graspable in any concrete sense at the level of musical material, even if the sources of that material lie beyond its own immediate sphere.

In response, Krenek sets out to define what is to be understood under the concept of 'material'. He includes 'the totality of all musical expressive means [*Mittel*]: that is, harmony, rhythm and melody as they occur as natural givens, as possibilities for composing at any particular period'.[98] He considers, however, that the objective physical structure of the material is not the determining factor for the composer, but rather its 'subjective manner of appearance'. On the other hand, the material is not itself to be understood as ready-formed, but instead merely represents the *possibility* of form for the composer.[99]

Sedimentation of history

For Adorno, the suggestion that the material is dependent on extra-musical conditions (i.e. Krenek's 'subjective appearance') presupposes another formulation of the concept. If human consciousness is imputed to the material by implying that musical material is more than of merely objective natural origin, then it must also partake of the history of human consciousness. Furthermore, 'consciousness does not have pure natural material, only historical material'.[100] For this reason Adorno considers that it stops being merely 'the possibility of form' (to use Krenek's formulation), and presents itself as something which is already pre-formed (*als bereits Vorgeformtes*). The harmonies available to a composer 300 years ago are no longer the same as those available to a composer today, he maintains – not in the sense that the same chords did not exist 300 years ago, but in the sense that they no longer carry the same meaning today and can no longer be used in the same way. 'The possibilities for composing already contain the sediment of history within them.'[101]

Krenek does not dispute the historical character of meaning in musical material. He maintains, however, that it is possible to put old means to new uses, according to the intention of the composer. Krenek sees the composer as having a necessary degree of independence from the material, although he agrees that the composer is also at the same time dependent on the historical process. This dependency will spontaneously define the choice of the composer's means of expression, and 'should he decide, on the basis of this subjectively free but objectively defined choice, on traditional expressive means, then these will of themselves acquire a new, historically defined meaning precisely through their extra-musical dependency'.[102]

Meaning and historical change

To be able to decide whether musical means of the past are capable of taking on legitimate new meaning, it is not enough, in Adorno's view, simply to consider the formal capacity for change as such. It is the meaning of change itself that is important. Adorno argues that the meaning of the changes in musical material since the emancipation of music from ritual and from nature is inseparable from the process of emancipation of European rationality itself. Adorno sees the meaning of this emancipatory process as *freedom* – not so much in terms of an untrammelled individual 'will to expression', but more in terms of the freeing of human consciousness from the force of mythical bonds. According to Adorno, '[i]t is neither some insight of the composer into the course of history, nor his subjective need for expression which decides on the choice of [available] means. What is decisive is the consistency [*Stimmigkeit*] of the composition [*Gebild*] in itself.'[103]

Krenek acknowledges that the individual 'will to expression' is never free-floating but always verifies itself within the social realities of a particular period. He is, however, of the view that 'these realities are not consciously controlled by individuals, but are spontaneously met'.[104] Krenek maintains that, underlying Adorno's concept of the 'consistency of the composition in itself' as set against subjective expressive needs, there is too restricted a notion of the 'shaping' possibilities in composition (*die Gestaltungsmöglichkeiten*). Krenek would simply include the concept of *Stimmigkeit* (consistency) among the compositional means – that is, as part of the composer's technical capabilities. Krenek also considers that, even though the social structure today is no longer as secure as it was in the first half of the nineteenth century, the composer can even now still rely on certain inbuilt limiting factors – or, indeed, create them for himself. Krenek thus persists in his view of the almost infinite creative freedom of the artist, while at the same time recognizing certain social and historical limiting factors not of the artist's own making and outside his conscious control.

Social reality and artistic freedom

Adorno accepts that the social reality within which the composer stands cannot be abstractly calculated, but can only be spontaneously expressed (he later came to call art works the 'unconscious writing of history'). This does not mean, however, that the will to expression is 'practically limitless', as Krenek puts it. Adorno is not positing *Stimmigkeit* as the goal of artistic production (which may have been the case with *l'art-pour-l'art* theory at the end of the nineteenth century). Instead, he sees in the concept of *Stimmigkeit* the *criterion* by which, practically and concretely, the will to expression of the composer is limited. It is only in the consistency of the work, he insists, that one can read how social reality has asserted its demands in the material. It is in the fulfilment of these demands that

Adorno sees the paradox of the freedom of the composer.[105]

Both Krenek and Adorno agree in general terms that the work of the composer and his compositional decisions stand in a particular relation to social reality. However, what, Krenek asks, would Adorno characterize as the pressing demands of the musical material today, assuming that society manifests itself as demands within the material? Krenek himself considers it probable that these demands are so constituted that, through their realization, a substantial number of other 'shaping' possibilities – especially those previously used – are closed off. Having got Adorno's agreement on this point, Krenek goes on to suggest that such a sacrifice of possibilities could in the end be in vain, because there may be no connection between art and social reality to be won today. Since established social structures have collapsed into a chaos of conflicting claims, there is no other choice, in Krenek's view, but to have recourse to the individual. He further suggests that the connection to society could be seen in terms of the sublation (*Aufhebung*) of social reality through individual artistic creation: the raising of the social and material demands on to a higher level – still manifested, however, in the material.[106]

The principle of construction and the demands of the material

In order to be able to answer Krenek's question concerning the demands of the material today, Adorno feels that a sociological context needs first to be provided. He makes the following observations:

(1) The reason why the compositional realization of the demands of the material may not be able to guarantee any social connection is not because the resulting work is too radical and distanced from real life. It is much more because the relations of power in contemporary society do not allow for such a connection between art (above all, art with a 'truth content') and social reality.

(2) Where art seeks this connection, in terms of general accessibility, there is the suspicion that a deception is being attempted, to persuade people into imagining that the isolation in which they live really adds up to a community (*Gemeinschaft*).

(3) This does not mean that society is chaotic and disorganized, and that everything is now up to the individual (as Krenek had suggested); on the contrary, society is highly organized. It is organized, however, in the sense that it hides the true nature of social relations, and to this end must necessarily frustrate all art which sets out to uncover the social condition.

(4) While Krenek's emphasis on the individual over this ideological collectivity is dialectically correct, and better serves the freedom of

consciousness than does the new belief in nature, there is no guarantee that this individual mode of operation will not end up serving ideologically questionable interests.

(5) The means to safeguard the individual mode of operation, in the sense of genuine freedom, is the postulate of consistency (*Stimmigkeit*).[107]

The demands of the material are, Adorno suggests, that the constructive process of composition controls the 'natural' material as completely as possible, while leaving itself as little as possible under the blind control of the natural 'stuff' of music: this process would, however, emerge from the productive force of the material and not be the result of calculation. All musical means – that is, harmony, melody, counterpoint, rhythm, form and even instrumentation – would be under the control of the constructive principle. 'Blind' principles like tonality would be precluded, and 'nature' would need to stand the test of construction to prove its constructional credentials, instead of being played off ideologically against construction.[108]

A sociology of music

In 'Arbeitsprobleme des Komponisten' Adorno had reached a point where, with the discussion of the ideological dimension of musical material, a coherent sociological theory was noticeably lacking. In the texts so far examined from the period 1929–30 there is a move from a general notion of 'culture' towards a more specific concept of 'society'. Gillian Rose comments on this as a development to be found in the work of Lukács and of Benjamin as well as Adorno. She observes that '[A]fter the adoption of Marxism, culture was predicated on the theory of commodity fetishism and hence on a specific mode of production, or kind of society, but the notion of "culture" retained the more general or universal connotations'.[109] In these early texts and letters of Adorno and Krenek on the concept of material there are increasing references to the relation between music and society and in particular to immanence of society in musical material. There is, however, no real account of how this comes about. In turning to Marx's theory of value and in particular to the concept of commodity fetishism, Adorno found a theoretical approach that enabled him to produce his first extended essay on the sociology of music. This was 'Zur gesellschaftlichen Lage der Musik'.

By 1932 Adorno was writing to Krenek (letter dated 30 September 1932) that the task of sociology 'is not to ask music how it functions, but rather, how it stands in relation to the fundamental antinomies of society; whether it confronts them, masters them or lets them be, or even conceals them'[110] –

all to be understood immanently, in terms of the structure of musical works. The problem of the social function – or apparent lack of function – of music in contemporary society now hinges, for Adorno, on the mode of production in a society based on the exchange of commodities. Adorno writes: 'the commodity character of music is not defined by the fact that it is exchanged, but rather that it is exchanged as an *abstract value*, as Marx had explained the commodity form; that it is not an unmediated but a "reified" exchange relationship that takes place'.[111] Adorno also relates this to the autonomous character of Western high art music, having freed itself historically from its previous bonds with religion and ritual during the period of the rise of capitalism in Europe. Having freed itself from one type of immediate function due to the kind of division of labour which characterizes capitalism, music then acquires another function as a result of the capitalist mode of production: it becomes a commodity. The antinomies between music's autonomous character and its commodity character, and between the consistency with which it deals with its material at the level of musical production and its ideological relation to the social forces and relations of production, provide the starting point for 'Zur gesellschaftlichen Lage der Musik'.

3   On the social situation of music

'Zur gesellschaftlichen Lage der Musik' is divided into two sections: *Production* and *Reproduction/Consumption*. The following account focuses on the arguments presented in the first section, as here, in very concentrated form, is to be found the essence of Adorno's theories on the dilemma of modern music, its alienation from society in view of the contradictions raised by its autonomy-character over the general social function of music as commodity, and its critical function as a form of cognition, paralleling social theory. In the material structures of such music, he maintains, are encoded the antinomies of society itself – this is what he identifies as the 'social content' (or social 'substance' (*Gehalt*)) of musical works.

The immediate value of the article for our present purpose is that it provides a concise sociological framework for a later discussion of the 'dialectic of musical material' (see Chapters 4, 5 and 6) and of Adorno's theory of the avant-garde. It is, however, a framework which, as with all Adorno's theoretical work, needs decanting from its original and densely packed style of formulation into its underlying theses in order to be made available for discussion and analysis. As discussed earlier in the present study, this is a process of reduction which goes against the grain of Adorno's writing, but which at the same time serves to reveal something of its underlying structure. What follows, therefore, is one interpretation of the main stages in his argument: it proceeds by way of contradiction, and for the sake of clarity each step is presented here both as a separate thesis and as a moment within a larger dialectical process of argument.

The autonomy character of music and its social content

Adorno sees the social totality as fractured and contradictory, made up of antagonisms. Music, in its own terms (that is, in its material and structures), 'sketches in the clearest possible lines the contradictions and fractures which cut through present-day society'.[112] Yet autonomous music, since the beginning of the bourgeois period, has been cut off and separated from society by these very same contradictions and 'fractures' (for example, the division of labour) which it re-presents in it own material. Its autonomy has allowed music to develop parallel to society, mirroring its antagonisms, and at the same time to diverge from it, developing an independent dynamic of its own. Although music is autonomous and separate from society, it nevertheless contains society 'sedimented' within its material; this constitutes its *social content* or 'substance' (*Gehalt*).

The social function of music and its commodity character

As a result of its autonomy status, music no longer has a direct function in society, nor does it serve direct (i.e. unmediated) needs. Its role in the social process 'is exclusively that of a commodity; its value is that determined by the market'.[113] Thus, music's immediate *social function* today is that of the commodity, as an abstract unit of exchange on the market.

The alienation of music

The conflict between the autonomy character of music and its commodity character results in a condition of *alienation*; this may also be understood as a conflict between the forces of production and the relations of production, or as the tension between the spheres of production and consumption – an opposition between radical music's social content and its social function. The communication and marketing mechanisms of monopoly capitalism have destroyed music's immediacy through their invasion of the private sphere of the individual – indeed, Adorno maintains that the last bastion of music's immediacy, domestic music-making, has been destroyed. He writes: 'Through the total absorption of both musical production and consumption by the capitalist process, the alienation of music from man has become complete'.[114]

Music's 'coming of age' and its mortality: self-reflection

Historically, music becomes conscious of its alienation, of its isolation from society and of its own reification, and is thus compelled towards *self-reflection*. This is a stage in music's development that Adorno has elsewhere called its 'coming of age', its coming to maturity,[115] as part of the historical dialectic of the material. Furthermore, 'music, lacking proper knowledge of the social process – a condition likewise socially produced and sustained – blamed itself and not society for this situation, thus remaining in the illusion that the isolation of music was itself an isolated matter, i.e. that things could be corrected from the side of music alone with no change in society'.[116] What is called for is not a change in music, but social change, Adorno maintains. However, music can do nothing directly to effect change, either through intervention or through attempts to change itself in order to become accommodating and accessible. The question arises, therefore, as to just what music can do, faced with the awareness of alienation, having been compelled towards self-reflection.

The cognitive character of music

The result of music's historically increasing reflection on its condition of alienation is the emergence of the autonomous musical work as a mode of *cognition*. Adorno writes: 'here and now music is able to do nothing but portray within its own structure the social antinomies which are also responsible for its own isolation'.[117] The antinomies of society are present in the musical material, according to Adorno, and are expressed in music 'in the antinomies of its own formal language'.[118] Music 'fulfils its social function more precisely when it presents social problems through its own material and according to its own formal laws – problems which music contains in the innermost cells of its technique'.[119] Because these problems are already there as antinomies with the musical material, the composer – the radical composer of art music, that is – is confronted with the task of responding to the demands of the material. Adorno underlines the cognitive character of such music when he writes: '[T]he task of music as art thus enters into a parallel relationship to the task of social theory'.[120]

The fetish character of music

In stressing radical music's alienation, together with what could be seen as its formalist problem-solving in isolation from society, Adorno sees the danger of absolutizing its autonomy status through treating music as a purely spiritual phenomenon. He emphasizes that music's immanent and separate development must not be seen as 'the mere reflection of the social process'. To treat it in this way 'would be a sanction of the fetish character of music'.[121] This tendency poses a threat to music's very right to exist, Adorno maintains, and in this sense he regards its fetish character to be music's most fundamental problem.

Music as critical theory: the critical character of radical music

The relation of radical music to society is thus problematical in all its aspects. It both shares the conditions and conflicts of society and its social theory, and, at the same time, it shares the attitudes that society, through its social theory, ought to express towards these conditions and conflicts. What both social theory and radical music have in common, therefore, is that both crudely reflect the aporias of society, and both attempt to articulate and express an attitude *towards* these aporias; they are both therefore self-reflective. When Adorno writes that 'the character of cognition is to be demanded of any music which today wishes to preserve its right to exist',[122] this may be interpreted as meaning that the crude reflection of social tendencies by autonomous music can only lead to such music becoming fetishized and assimilated to the status quo – the situation of jazz and popular music, according to him. A second level of reflection, a critical self-reflection, is necessary at the level of the structure of the music to enable it both to distance itself from social tendencies and to take a critical stance against those tendencies. This position also contains an implicit judgement on society as it is, in that it both reflects society and points beyond it.

Mediation

The cognitive and critical self-reflective character of radical music is achieved, Adorno maintains, through its relation to the musical material. It is the task of such music to give clear and precise form to the problems offered up by the material. In dealing with the material the composer is dealing with historically sedimented conventions, and Adorno stresses again that the musical material 'is itself never purely natural material, but rather a social and historical product'.[123] The solutions that music offers to the problems thrown up by the material have, in musical terms, the status and cognitive character of social theories. And the relationship of these solutions – as 'social postulates' – to praxis is not direct and immediate, in terms of recipes for what is to be done. The relationship is instead an indirect and mediated one. However, as Adorno indicates later in the essay, 'a solution to the problem of mediation in music has by no means been found; it is rather only that the location of the problem has been designated with greater precision'.[124] The concept of 'mediation' (*Vermittlung*) is fundamental to Adorno's music theory, and needs to be taken together with the concept of 'musical material', as it is the material itself that is envisaged as the *locus* of mediation. The pressing concern Adorno expresses in 'Zur gesellschaftlichen Lage der Musik' is that of the connection he had perceived in the 1920s and early 1930s between 'objectivism' in art (e.g. neoclassicism and *neue Sachlichkeit*) and fascism (e.g. the association of neoclassical composers like Casella and, indeed, Stravinsky[125] with extreme right-wing politics). To understand this connection in purely musical terms, he argued, it was necessary to go beyond questions of individual consciousness and to examine instead the *function* of the music, and how this function had been taken into the material itself as a technical–compositional problem. This raises the problem of mediation in acute form. The concept is both elusive and problematic, and it will be examined in detail in Chapter 3.

The unintelligibility of modern music and the limitations of empirical consciousness

Because of the dominance of what he calls 'empirical consciousness' today, and the resulting unintelligibility of music, Adorno maintains that the following kind of faulty reasoning develops: 'such music is incomprehensible, therefore esoteric and private, therefore reactionary and to be rejected'.[126] Adorno considers that this kind of response (and it is a particular response from the orthodox Marxist position) stems from the Romantic vision of primitive musical immediacy that considers the present-day level of empirical consciousness (limited and restricted as he considers it is by a class domination which seeks to preserve such a level of consciousness at any cost) to be the positive yardstick against which a suitable non-alienated music appropriate to free human beings is to be measured. Cognition, and music-as-cognition, he maintains, must not allow itself to be restricted by the limitations of consciousness of the masses and of class domination. In Adorno's view, '[m]usic is under the same obligation as theory to reach out beyond the current consciousness of the masses'.[127]

The dialectic of music and social praxis

Adorno considers that the critical function of radical music lies in its negation of bourgeois musical categories in the face of their historical assimilation and affirmation by the culture industry. Music that has become conscious of its social function must enter into a *dialectical relation to praxis*, he argues. This does not mean making itself 'socially useful' (as, for example, *Gebrauchs-* or *Gemeinschaftsmusik*, in the cases of Hindemith and Eisler discussed earlier in this chapter and in Chapter 1); this would be merely to define itself further as a commodity. Instead, he considers, radical music should develop, in social isolation, 'highly rational and transparent principles of construction' to uncover and negate *within* the material itself 'basic bourgeois categories such as the creative personality and expressing the soul of this personality, the world of private feelings and its transfigured inwardness'.[128] Even such a music as this, though, would still 'remain dependent upon bourgeois production processes and could not, consequently, be viewed as "classless" or the actual music of the future, but rather as music which fulfils its dialectic[al] cognitive function most exactly'.[129] However, Adorno considers that the very fact that such music provokes resistance seems to indicate that it is realizing its social function, even if only as a negative force, and that 'the dialectical function of this music is already perceptible in praxis'.[130]

A typology of music

As a result of his reasoning in 'Zur gesellschaftlichen Lage der Musik', the stages of which are outlined above as opposing theses, Adorno divides musical activity into two opposing categories. Category One contains that 'affirmative' music which accepts its commodity character, is not dialectical, and passively orientates itself to market demands. Category Two contains music which does not accept the demands of the market and which functions dialectically as a negation of bourgeois categories within its own material. Broadly put, Adorno distinguishes between an assimilated music which affirms the status quo and its own commodity character, and a radical music which attempts in various ways to negate the status quo and its own commodity character. The traditional and longstanding distinction between 'popular' and 'serious' music comes to mind here, but Adorno insists that it does not adequately define the situation as he sees it. As he puts it: 'a great share of supposedly "serious" music adjusts itself to the demands of the market in the same manner as the composers of light music'.[131] Adorno in fact regards both 'light' and 'serious' music as the sundered halves of one 'musical globe', viewed 'equally from the perspective of alienation'.[132] They are, however, two halves which can now never be reconstructed into a whole.[133]

Category One: affirmation

The music of Adorno's first category is that which accepts its social function as commodity. It occupies an apparently dominant position in society, in that it is accessible and either orientates itself to market demands or is manipulated by the market. It also serves to conceal alienation by mystifying the true character of the relations of production in society. Adorno distinguishes roughly between three types of music in this category.

(i) The first type includes 'light' or 'popular' music of all kinds (he seems to make no exceptions here – apart from the tiny glimpse of hope he allows in a brief paragraph in the 'Leichte Musik' chapter of *Einleitung in die Musiksoziologie*,[134] written many years later).

(ii) The second type includes 'serious' music of the past which has now acquired the status of museum exhibits and has taken on a commodity character, being marketed and distributed via the same mechanisms of the 'culture industry' as 'light' and 'popular' music, therefore being subjected to the same kinds of consumption patterns.

(iii) And finally, the third type embraces all that 'moderate' modern music which makes compromises in order to be accessible. And there is a paradox here: the unashamed commodity character of 'light' and 'popular' music – which, Adorno maintains, is tolerated by society and at the same time despised and exploited by it in the same way as society uses prostitution – reveals much about the hidden aspects of modern society. It functions to satisfy society's drives (*Triebbefriedungen*), while the official face of society denies the existence of such drives. Adorno writes: '[i]n a certain sense, such music transcends the society it supposedly serves'.[135] On the other hand, that 'serious' music which serves the market does so under cover of 'economically opaque fashion', and its market character as commodity is disguised as something more acceptable. He concludes that '[i]n the distinction between light and serious music, the alienation of man and music is reflected only through distortion – in the same manner, namely, as this alienation is seen by the bourgeoisie'.[136]

Category Two: negation

The music of Adorno's second category is that music which does not submit to the market and which expresses alienation: that is to say, the radical 'serious' music of the avant-garde, as distinct from the bulk of 'moderate' modern music and 'serious' music of the past. He recognizes that this music clearly does not hold a dominant position in society, and he attempts to make a further categorization of it into four distinct types.

(i) The first type 'presents and crystallizes' the problem and its solutions to the contradictions of society immanently, in terms of its own material and structure. Furthermore, it does this 'without consciousness of its social location or out of indifference to it'.[137] This type of autonomous music, like the Leibnizian monad, although a part of the totality is 'blind' to it, containing the totality within itself. And this totality is not presented as a pre-established harmony, but rather as 'a historically produced dissonance'.[138] This type of music is experienced at the level of consumption as a serious shock, and is represented by Schoenberg and the Second Viennese School.

(ii) The second type 'includes music which recognizes the fact of alienation as its own isolation and as "individualism", and further raises this fact to the level of consciousness; it does so, however, only within itself, only in aesthetic and "form-immanent" terms'.[139] It attempts to transcend and sublate this awareness without acknowledging the actual condition of society itself, however. It tends to achieve this by turning to stylistic forms of the past in the belief that such archaic forms have escaped alienation, 'without seeing that such forms cannot be reconstituted within a completely changed society and through completely changed material'.[140] Adorno labels this kind of music 'objectivism', in that it seeks 'to evoke the image of a non-existent "objective" society or ... of a *Gemeinschaft*'.[141] Drawing on the scheme put forward originally in his unpublished essay 'Die stabilisierte Musik' of 1928 (examined in Chapter 1), he maintains that in the capitalist, industrialized societies neoclassicism is the usual form of 'objectivism', while in the underdeveloped agrarian societies it is folk music that provides much of the material. Adorno cites Stravinsky as representative of this type of music, although Bartók is also mentioned.

(iii) The third type Adorno describes as a 'hybrid form'. Like 'objectivist' music, this type recognizes the fact of alienation but at the same time is, unlike the 'objectivist', socially aware. Adorno writes: '[The composer] denies himself the positive solution and contents himself with permitting social flaws [*Brüche*] to manifest themselves by means of a flawed invoice which defines itself as illusory with no attempt at camouflage through attempts at an aesthetic totality'.[142] To achieve this he makes use partly of material from nineteenth-century bourgeois music and partly of the material of present-day consumer music. Such music breaks out of aesthetic immanence, and bursts out of the frame of the autonomous work, so to speak, and in so doing achieves an effect similar to French Surrealism. Adorno suggests that such music stems from the period of Stravinsky's *L'histoire du soldat* and was developed particularly in the works Kurt Weill wrote in conjunction with Bertolt Brecht (e.g. *Dreigroschen Oper* and *Mahagonny*).

(iv) The fourth type, according to Adorno, is a music which attempts 'to break through alienation from within itself, even at the expense of its immanent form'.[143] It is *Gebrauchsmusik* that is being referred to here. This kind of music is, however, dismissed by Adorno on account of its 'obvious dependence upon the market'.[144] Rather more deserving of attention, he maintains, is *Gemeinschaftsmusik*. Adorno considers this to have developed out of neoclassicism, and its representative composers are Hindemith and the Eisler of the proletarian choral works.

The change in the function of expression

From the typology outlined above, it is quite clear that Adorno favours Schoenberg's 'solution' to the problem of music's alienation in contemporary society. According to Adorno, Schoenberg, through his purification of the expressive language of bourgeois music and through pursuing the consequences of that language to the extreme, had raised expression to a new level to create a different music into which 'no social function falls – indeed, which even severs the last communication with the listener'.[145] He achieves this, Adorno maintains, through his extreme clarification and rationalization of the material of bourgeois art music – investing the material with consciousness, as it were. Schoenberg takes control of the expressive material of bourgeois individualism and makes it a vehicle for the 'undisguised and uninhibited expression of the psyche and of the unconscious *per se*'.[146] The works Adorno cites as the most representative examples of this process are all from the period of free atonality in Schoenberg's development – e.g. *Erwartung, Die glückliche Hand, Sechs kleine Klavierstücke* op. 19 – and he sees a direct relationship between the works of this period and psychoanalysis. This process of clarification and rationalization results in the musical work not only becoming separated from society as it is, but also becoming critically opposed to it. It also results in a profound change in musical language, whereby the formalized and mediated language of bourgeois art music becomes the volcanic and immediate expression of suffering. This comes about through Schoenberg's *technical* solutions to musical problems like ornamentation, repetition and symmetrical relationships, which extend from large-scale formal structures to harmony, melody, counterpoint and instrumentation. His use of dissonance as 'the vehicle of the radical principle of Expressionism' undermines tonality itself and is at the same time 'the resolution of objective-material contradictions which continued to exist in the Wagnerian technique of chromatic sequence and in the diatonic technique of variation employed by Brahms as well'.[147] Adorno maintains that, although on the one hand Schoenberg's music is regarded as private and esoteric, it becomes at the same time in fact socially very relevant when the *dialectic of musical material* implied in his music is projected on to and understood in the context of the *social dialectic*. 'This is justified', Adorno writes, 'by the fact that he – in the form of material problems which he inherited, accepted and continued – found present the problems of society that produced this material and in which the contradictions of this society are defined as technical problems'.[148]

Freedom and construction

It is both through the extremes of expression, breaking down the remnants of conventional musical syntax, and through the consistency of its structure, forcing as this does the material to yield up its own radical syntax, that, according to Adorno, Schoenberg's music 'eliminates at least within itself alienation as a matter of subjective formation and objective material'.[149] Adorno sees the following consequences: (i) in overcoming alienation within the hermetic circle of its own immanent structure music moves towards freedom from the arbitrariness of structures imposed from outside; (ii) the radical and immanent character of the solutions to the problem of form forcibly reconstitutes the autonomy of music and sets it in opposition to the commodity fetishism of the 'culture industry'; (iii) the radical character of the music leads, however, to unintelligibility and to its alienation from society; (iv) within the music itself there is the question as to whether it is possible to reconcile its radical solutions to problems of structure with the ideal of the hermetic work of art 'resting within itself' which Schoenberg inherited from classicism, and further, 'whether such a concept of a work of art, as totality and cosmos, can still be upheld at all';[150] and (v) Schoenberg's attempted reconstruction of an autonomous music, through the purification and rationalization of its language, is – like Kraus's search for a pure language – 'a doubtful undertaking', in that it is probably no longer possible; the limits of what is possible 'through music alone' have been reached, in terms of reconcilement with society as it is.[151]

In conclusion

In 'Zur gesellschaftlichen Lage der Musik' Adorno provides a synthesis of his thinking on the situation of music up to 1932, formulating the fruits of his debates with Krenek and of his extensive involvement with the musical life of the time into something approaching a coherent theory of the musical avant-garde and its contradictory relation to social reality. Prior to this essay his ideas had centred around particular aspects of autonomous music, especially of contemporary music, and around the critique of philosophical systems. 'Zur gesellschaftlichen Lage der Musik' brings together the particular and the general, music and society, through its emphasis on a notion of musical material as the *locus* of the mediation of music and society. The crystallization of his ideas in this form was the result of his reception of Marxian theory, particularly as filtered through Lukács and Benjamin. It could well be argued that all his succeeding work on the aesthetics, sociology and immanent analysis of music is predicated on this essay, as a consolidation and refinement of it and as a series of footnotes to it, in spite of his reluctance to allow it to be republished. The problem it throws up, however, is the as yet unresolved question of how the 'mediation' of music and society is to be understood on a theoretical level. A detailed examination of this problem forms the basis of Chapter 3.

3   The problem of mediation

> Because, according to Hegel's dictum, there is nothing between Heaven and Earth which is not mediated, thought only remains true to the idea of immediacy through sustaining itself within the mediate. On the other hand, thought becomes the victim of the mediate as soon as it tries to grasp it immediately, without recognizing it as mediated.[1]
>
> Adorno, 'The essay as form' (1954–8)

The absence of a fully formulated concept of mediation within Adorno's 'Zur gesellschaftlichen Lage der Musik' has been commented on in the previous chapter. As we saw, Adorno had written in 1932 that 'a solution to the problem of mediation in music has by no means been found; it is rather only that the location of the problem has been designated with greater precision'.[2] However, in spite of his recognition of the problematic character of the relation of music to society, and of the 'natural' and 'historical' within musical material, Adorno could be accused of continuing to use the concept of mediation in his subsequent work as though the very application of the term itself served to resolve the underlying problem.[3] In view of this it is important to see the concept as part of a broader historical context of ideas.

Although Adorno claims to focus on the 'unique particular' and insists that mediation cannot be understood in the abstract, but only through the examination of concrete individual instances, there are nevertheless features of the concept and of its context of ideas which can usefully be identified at a level of generality. Taking the tripartite model put forward in Chapter 1, Adorno's concept of mediation can be seen as operating simultaneously on three different levels: (i) musical works are mediated 'in themselves' (as the dialectic of construction and expression); (ii) musical material is culturally and socially mediated (as the relation of musical to social production, reproduction, distribution and consumption); and (iii) musical material is historically mediated, in that its 'progress' can be understood as part of what Adorno and Horkheimer call the 'dialectic of Enlightenment' (the progressive domination of nature and the rationalization of all aspects of social life, as the dialectic of mimesis and rationality).

This model can be seen to underpin the present chapter, and also to shape the successive emphases of the three following chapters. It is because musical material is already historically and socially mediated that it is meaningful and significant.

Although I have schematized aspects of the 'constellation of ideas' to which the concept belongs, it would be misleading to give the impression that what one might be tempted to call Adorno's 'theory of mediation' can really be subsumed within a unified system – or, indeed, be regarded as a theory at all in any usual sense of the term. It remains fragmented in its presentation within Adorno's writings, and only begins to become more comprehensible when the fragments are seen as parts of a dialogue with other systems of ideas. Some parts of this dialogue have already been filled in during the discussion of the concepts of 'nature', 'history' and 'second nature' in Chapter 1 and in the discussion of the concept of 'musical material' in Chapter 2. The intention now is to go back a further stage, and to provide some of the missing parts from Adorno's dialogue with the tradition of German Idealist philosophy, with social philosophy and sociology, and with psychoanalytic theory. This entails the examination of the concept of 'mediation' in the theoretical context of its use in Hegel and Marx, together with other concepts Adorno has taken from Freud and Max Weber in his attempt, as Michael Rosen has put it, 'to solve the twin problems of Idealism: how the *transcendental* interacts with ... the *empirical*, and how that transcendental activity may be rationally recuperated'.[4]

1   Hegel: mediation and the dialectic

The term 'mediation' is the usual English translation of the German word *Vermittlung*. Taken in its broadest and most general sense the term implies interactions, interconnections, interchanges, between otherwise different activities, areas, spheres or processes. It can also have the sense of the reflection of one sphere of activity by another, taken together with the idea of a 'middle term' in which this reflection takes place, or in which shared characteristics of the different spheres converge or coincide as aspects of a larger totality. That these rather general and imprecise senses can also be understood in relation to Adorno's use of the term 'mediation' is not to be disputed. In themselves, however, they do not take us very far, suggesting only that unlike things can in some respects be understood as being related, but without saying much beyond this. Adorno, however, is using the term 'mediation' in the particular Hegelian sense of the interaction of opposites, whereby all apparently 'immediate' givens can be seen on reflection to be the 'mediated' products of the all-embracing process of the dialectic itself.

In its critique of the 'givenness' and 'immediacy' of phenomena, Adorno's speculative approach attempts to release objects from their isolation and to show how their meaning derives from their context, from their relation to the 'whole' – a relation which is not external to phenomena, but immanent. In tracing the markings of the 'whole' within the part, and at the same time using the separateness of the part as a criticism of the 'whole', Adorno inevitably has recourse to metaphor. However, the metaphorical use of language in Adorno's work arises from an underlying conceptual context which is generally consistent. This context derives its essential features from Hegelian dialectical logic. As a critical method Adorno uses this not in any scientific sense of testing hypotheses (for which it is singularly unsuited),[5] but as a way of pursuing contradictions to their extreme, to the point where they shed light on the mediated relationship of part to whole. Difficult as it is to say anything about the concept of mediation in Hegel without tracing the totality of his philosophical system, it is nevertheless essential at this stage at least to provide some account of the relevant Hegelian terminology and of its theoretical context, and to indicate the use Adorno makes of it.

Part and whole

Underlying Adorno's theory of mediation is Hegel's notion of 'the Whole' (*das Ganze*) as a dynamic totality made up of the interaction of diverse particulars. In his concept of material and, related to this, in his theory of form, Adorno seeks to understand the mediation of part and whole, of the particular and the universal, both *within* musical structures, and *between* autonomous musical structures and the heteronomous social totality of which music is part. More precisely, mediation is understood as the historical dialectic of Subject and Object, of the separation of consciousness (as Subject) from itself through its interaction with the world (as Object) and its return to itself at a level of second or 'self' reflection. Indeed, 'mediation' *is* the process of the dialectic, understood as the interaction of opposites through their extremes, whereby the opposites partake of each other, but at the same time retain their identity at a new level of synthesis, or 'sublation' (*Aufhebung*). Thus for Adorno, as for Hegel, mediation does not simply refer to the way in which unlike spheres are connected. It is to be seen rather as the *process* of interaction and interconnection itself, whereby subjectivity and objectivity partake of each other perpetually *within* the hermetically sealed-off and monad-like dialectic of musical material.

In 'Thesen zur Kunstsoziologie' (1967) Adorno writes: 'according to Hegel, mediation is in the object itself [*in der Sache selbst*], not a relation between the object and those to whom it is brought'.[6] Following Hegel,

Adorno insists that, although Objects are necessarily 'Objects to Subjects', mediation is not to be understood simply as the relationship *between* two terms. Neither is mediation to be conceived simply as the Object of experience being 'filtered' through the psychological and cognitive make-up of the experiencing Subject. For Adorno, as for Hegel, 'mediation' is a material process which is manifested concretely 'within the Object' as well as through the experiencing Subject, as the result of previous interactions between Subjects and Objects. In *Negative Dialektik* he formulates this in the following terms:

Mediation of the [O]bject means that it must not be statically, dogmatically hypostatized but can be known only as it entwines with subjectivity; mediation of the [S]ubject means that without the moment of objectivity it would be literally nil.[7]

Thus Adorno insists that the social dimension of autonomous music is not to be sought simply in the 'social function' of musical works – i.e. in their relation to the world via the process of their reproduction, distribution and reception (although this is certainly one aspect of their meaning). It is to be sought rather within the material content or 'substance' (*Gehalt*) of the works themselves, where, he argues, these social relations are sedimented, in musical terms, as 'social content' (*gesellschaftlicher Gehalt*). As Alfred Schmidt emphasizes in discussing Adorno's contradictory concept of 'materialism': 'Art works were for him in the strictest sense "monadological creations"; they mirror the social whole within themselves, but they do not mirror it externally'.[8]

It is the interpretation of this social content which leads, according to Adorno, to insight into the 'meaning' of a work. This is the work's 'truth content' (*Wahrheitsgehalt*) – the interaction of the socially mediated expressive Subject with the objectivity of the historically mediated musical material, as realized in the concrete structure of particular musical works. Because this mediation of Subject and Object within musical works is conceived by Adorno, following Hegel, as a continuing historical process, as a kind of progressive movement of consciousness, it is important to examine some of the assumptions underlying Adorno's Hegelian concept of history. Indeed, the centrality of Hegel to Adorno's 'music theory' is everywhere evident in his work, no more so than in *Philosophie der neuen Musik*, where in the introduction he writes: 'the systematic approach [*die Lehre*] of *Phänomenologie des Geistes* – according to which all immediacy is already mediated in itself – is to be applied to art. In other words, immediacy is a product of domination.'[9] To locate the concept of mediation within Hegel's philosophy will at the same time serve to ground Adorno's concepts of 'truth content' – as examined in the 'interpretative model' put forward in Chapter 1 – and of 'musical material' – as examined in Chapter 2 – firmly in Hegelian logic.[10] This also involves a further consideration of the concepts of 'nature' and 'history'.

Truth, logic and the dialectic

In his *Logik* (*Encyclopaedia*, Part I, 1830) Hegel writes: 'The study of truth, or, as it is here explained to mean, consistency [i.e. the agreement of an object with our conception of it], constitutes the proper problem of logic'.[11] And in *Wissenschaft der Logik* (*Science of Logic*, 1812) we find a similar statement amplified to indicate the inseparability of the act of *thinking* from truth: 'Truth is the agreement of thought with the object, and in order to bring about this agreement – for it does not exist on its own account – thinking is supposed to adapt and accommodate itself to the object'.[12] He identifies three different methods of ascertaining truth: (i) 'experience' (or 'immediate knowledge'), (ii) 'reflection', and (iii) 'philosophical cognition'.[13] These three forms or stages of knowledge correspond to (i) that which is simply given, as immediate material, 'Pure Being' (*Sein*), identical with itself; (ii) the negation of the immediate, the given, through consciousness of itself as non-identical; and (iii) the result of the foregoing process of negation and sublation (*Aufhebung*) as totality, no longer as a simple given but as a dynamic 'synthesis'. This third stage is the outcome of the conflict, or contradiction, between the previous two stages and, as 'knowledge', moves on to a different qualitative level. There is an obvious similarity between stages (i) and (iii), in that (iii) now becomes the basis for a new dialectical interaction. There is, however, a crucial difference, in that (i) is *immediate*, whereas (iii) is *mediated* – or rather, is *mediated immediacy*. In order to clarify further the relation between immediacy and mediation – a relation which, like much else in Hegel's philosophy, is by no means always clear – it is important to recognize that the terms themselves are entirely relative to each other: what is the *mediated* product of one process of identity and negation becomes, relatively speaking, the *immediate* 'given' for a new dialectical process.

The dialectical process is characterized by the fundamental Hegelian notion of *sublation*. The opposition of *identity* and *negativity* (*non-identity*) is raised to a qualitatively new level to become a new totality – that is, the creation of something new through an act of negation and sublation which also retains the original opposition within itself. From this it can be seen that *sublation* and *mediation* are two aspects of the same process.

Adorno's conception of both philosophy and art as modes of knowledge which, through critical self-reflection, open on to an experience of freedom can also be traced to Hegel. That is to say, human consciousness, through its interaction with and negation of the 'given', as nature, advances towards freedom by means of the action of self-reflection and individualization. This process may be described as one of continuing separation from 'nature' (as 'the given') through becoming conscious of difference and through materializing this difference, which then becomes a new given, as 'mediated nature', at a new stage in the dialectic.

The Hegelian dialectic therefore constitutes a process of continuity and change which is *historical* in character. Human consciousness acts on 'nature', and in the process changes both itself and nature. This 'mediated nature' is historical, and is what constitutes 'reality' for us. That is to say, we make reality through the process of our interaction with 'second nature' and through our separation from and reflection upon it. Therefore for Hegel reality is this discourse, in all its diverse and concrete particularity, and it is this dynamic process of *Becoming (Werden)* – as opposed to static *Being (Sein)* – which he means when he uses that most frequently misunderstood of all his concepts, *Spirit (Geist)*.

History and progress

For Hegel, therefore, all history is the history of human consciousness, as the progress of 'Spirit' *(Geist)* towards freedom through the dialectical process of the sublation of antagonisms. It is this process, which contains the idea of the reconciliation of opposites *(Versöhnung)*, that is called 'mediation' by Hegel. We have already noted (in Chapter 2) how the progress of the musical material is seen by Adorno as the interaction of the expressive Subject and the 'objectivity' of handed-down material/compositional procedures (in Hegelian terms as the separation, or 'alienation' *(Entäußerung)*, and 'objectification' of consciousness from itself – i.e. as the art work – through the self-reflection *(Selbstreflexion)* and self-consciousness *(Selbstbewußtsein)* of form). Thus the motor of this historical movement of musical material is the mediation of Subject and Object within individual works and against handed-down tradition. As noted, this inevitably carries with it the idea of progress. However, it needs to be remembered that by 'progress' *(Fortschritt)* Adorno does not mean *qualitative* progress in art works, but rather *technical* progress. He makes this clear in his article 'Fortschritt' (1964):

All progress in the cultural sphere is that of domination of material [*Materialbeherr-schung*], of technique. ... Progress in the domination of material is in no sense directly identical to the progress of art itself.[14]

At the same time, the concept of progress is itself contradictory. On the one hand, 'progress' implies, in the Hegelian sense, progress of 'Spirit' towards freedom. On the other hand, Adorno also uses it to imply technical progress, as techniques for the increasing control and mastery of the material through, in the Weberian sense, the rationalization of all its aspects. The apparent contradiction between these two senses lies in the suggestion put forward by Adorno that progress towards freedom of 'spirit', of consciousness as manifested in art works, is brought about through the historical tendency in the West towards the total rationalization and control of all dimensions of the material of art, seen as part of a larger process of social rationalization and demythologization (a process to be discussed at greater length later in this chapter). As we saw in Chapter 1, Adorno and Horkheimer had argued that this had led to a version of Weber's 'iron cage' of rationality, as 'dialectic of Enlightenment' – a historical dialectic towards freedom which had turned into its opposite during the course of the bourgeois period – total organization and administration. Indeed, in Adorno's Hegelian terms, the 'Object' (whether as 'reality' or as 'material') is objectified subjectivity which has forgotten its origins in subjectivity. This is what he calls 'the movement of Spirit' in art – the reflection by art of social reality, its simultaneous critique of that reality through standing apart from it, and its promise of something beyond current reality.

Spirit

The Hegelian concept 'Spirit' (*Geist*) can therefore be seen to be an important mediating idea as used by Adorno. At the same time, however, it has to be admitted that *Geist* is one of a group of central ideas which smuggles metaphysics back into Adorno's 'materialist aesthetics'. The notion of the 'spiritual' in art is one which has been frequently misunderstood, particularly since the early years of the twentieth century. Kandinsky contributed to this misunderstanding in his *Über das Geistige in der Kunst* (1912), Adorno suggests, and the concept threatened to become inseparable from superstition and the vague need to believe in higher forces.[15] The situation has not been helped by the problem of translating the term *Geist* into English. The choice is limited to the inadequate terms 'mind', 'intellect' or 'spirit', among which 'spirit' is to be preferred in this case, even though it carries with it misleading connotations of religiosity and mysticism which are far from what Adorno (following Hegel) intends by the concept. This needs to be borne in mind in what follows.

The concept is difficult to pin down with any precision, and has to be understood in the dual sense of 'totality' and of 'historical tendency'. For Adorno, *Geist* (as 'progress of spirit') comes to stand for 'historical consciousness' (*Bewußtsein*) and, at the same time, 'rationality' (*Rationalität*) and the historical tendency towards increasing 'rationalization'

(*Rationalisierung*) in Western society. To this 'progress of spirit', as 'historical consciousness' and 'rationalization', Adorno attributes an 'objective' character, something which accounts for his use of that most troublesome of concepts in relation to the dialectic of musical material in *Philosophie der neuen Musik*: 'objective spirit' (*objektiver Geist*). Underlying the concept of 'spirit' is also the dialectical opposition to 'nature', to 'matter' or 'raw material' (*Stoff*). Understood in this way, the 'progress of spirit' as the dialectic of musical material is what Adorno (again following Hegel) calls a 'spiritualization' of material (*Vergeistigung*) – a concept discussed briefly at the end of Chapter 1.

Adorno insists that 'spirit' emerges from the 'configuration' of the work of art, as the tension between its elements. It is neither something which hovers somewhere over the surface of the work, nor is it identical to the work's facticity or materiality. It is rather the mediation of the work's 'sensuous instants' (*sinnliche Augenblicke*) (as *Stoff*) and of form (as *Gestaltung*) – 'mediation understood here in the strict sense of each of these moments requiring its opposite within the work of art'.[16] It is, furthermore, not to be confused with the intentions or consciousness of the individual composer, *Geist*, as 'objective spirit', being rather the point of intersection between the individual and historical/collective Subject.[17] The Hegelian connection here is plain enough. In *Phänomenologie des Geistes*, in the passage discussing spirit in relation to self-consciousness and which leads into the famous 'Master and Slave' section, Hegel writes:

In that a self-consciousness [*Selbstbewußtsein*] is the object [*Gegenstand*], it is just as much 'I' [*Ich*] as it is object. – And with this we already have the concept of Spirit [*Geist*] before us. And what consciousness has further to become aware of is the experience [*Erfahrung*] of what Spirit is, this absolute substance [*Substanz*] which, in the complete freedom and independence of their opposition – that is to say, different for-themselves-existing-consciousnesses – is the unity [*Einheit*] [of these same opposites]; an *I* that is a *We* and a *We* that is an *I*. Consciousness first finds in self-consciousness, as the concept of Spirit, its turning-point [*Wendepunkt*] ... [18]

Adorno clearly has this passage in mind when he writes in 'Ideen zur Musiksoziologie' (1958):

The compositorial Subject is not individual but collective. All music, even that which is the most individualistic stylistically, has an inalienable collective content: each single sound already says 'We'.[19]

And in *Ästhetische Theorie* we find:

The [S]ubject in a work of art is neither the viewer nor the creative artist nor some absolute spirit. It is spirit, to the extent to which it is embedded in, and mediated and preformed by, the object.[20]

But *Geist*, as the intersection of individual and collectivity, is a complex and contradictory concept in relation to actual musical works. For instance, in Mahler Adorno suggests that

there rumbles a collectivity, the movement of the masses ... Mahler's music is the individual's dream of the irresistible collective. But at the same time [his music] is the objective expression 'that identification with [the collective] is impossible ... '[21]

Geist, as 'historical consciousness' and as 'objective spirit', is therefore clearly to be distinguished from *intentionality* at the level of the individual Subject. It concerns rather the idea that dominant socio-historical tendencies become objectified in mediated/sublimated form within cultural artefacts via the interaction between artist (as individual Subject) and material (as collective Object). It would seem that these tendencies do not operate directly at the level of individual consciousness, but can be 'brought to consciousness' as part of the creative process of objectification and critical interpretation as 'second reflection'. This process of 'second reflection' is what, according to Adorno's definition, characterizes both avant-garde art and critical philosophy.

It is without doubt the centrality of Idealist concepts like *Geist*, *Vergeistigung* and *Wahrheitsgehalt* to Adorno's aesthetics which has attracted commentators with a distinctly theological interest in his work (see, for example, Gramer (1976)[22] and Zuidervaart (1981)[23]). The combination of philosophy (as negative dialectics) and music (as the 'autonomous music' of the Western tradition), with their emphasis on non-identity and non-representation, has proved irresistible, offering an apparently blank screen upon which can be projected more positive and metaphysical visions of totality than Adorno claimed to be putting forward. Reasons for this attraction will have become evident enough from the above discussion of the concepts and from the extracts from his work given – that is to say, the metaphysical and theological resonances of the terms are powerful, in spite of all, and any precise meanings are very difficult to pin down. Nevertheless, the concept of *Geist* can be understood in more concrete terms in relation to Adorno's use of the idea of 'mediation' if it is taken in conjunction with the concept of 'rationalization' (*Rationalisierung*), as progress in technique and technology, and the concept of the *avant-garde*.

Progress in technique and the avant-garde

For Adorno, the dialectic of musical material as progress in 'spiritualization' and technique means the avant-garde, which, as he puts it, 'moves in the field of tension between *spleen et idéal*, between spiritualization and obsession with that which is farthest removed from spirit'.[24] As we have seen, Adorno defines the avant-garde and its relation to the musical material as being that music which is at 'the most advanced stage of its historical dialectic'.[25] He considers that, even though the material is always that of the *present*, modernity is itself not chronological. He writes:

Rather, it answers to Rimbaud's postulate that, in relation to its own time, art be the most advanced consciousness where sophisticated technical procedures and equally sophisticated subjective experiences interpenetrate. Rooted in society, these procedures and experiences are critical in orientation. Such truly modern art has to own up to advanced industrial society rather than simply deal with it from an extraneous standpoint.[26]

Thus, at any particular historical period there are, he maintains, only certain kinds of work which meet this criterion – that of the autonomous avant-garde. The requirements are that the composer respond to the historical demands of the material in accordance with the most advanced consciousness of expressive needs and of available techniques of composition and the state of technology. 'The interrelation of music and society', Adorno writes, 'becomes evident in technique. Its unfoldment is the *tertium comparationis* between superstructure and base'.[27] Technology and technique represent the most advanced level reached by the forces of production in a society – the 'progress of spirit' as rationality and rationalization – and as such, in music, it mediates the aesthetic and the material forces of production:

technique always embodies a standard of society as a whole. It socializes even the supposedly lonely composer; he must pay attention to the objective state of the productive forces. As he lifts himself up to the technical standards they merge with his own productive force; in most cases both will so pervade each other during his apprenticeship that they can no longer be disentangled.[28]

The idea of technique and technology as a mediating link between base and superstructure will be taken up in later sections of the present chapter, in relation to Marx and Weber.

The identity of Adorno's 'historical Subject'

For Adorno, therefore, 'progress' of the musical material, as the dialectic of expressive needs and technical procedures, the movement of 'objective spirit', actually means progress in the articulation of the 'historical Subject' as mediated in musical structures. But it is not enough simply to identify this with the avant-garde, as the expression of the most advanced consciousness of expressive needs and technique of its age, because the argument becomes circular. The question of the identity of the 'historical Subject' needs to be taken a stage further.

It is certainly the case that Adorno's concept of musical material is posited on the material of bourgeois art music in the industrially developed countries of the West. He argues that art music in the 'bourgeois period' (that is, from the early eighteenth century to the present) and, in particular, the category of the 'avant-garde' are, by implication, only to be understood in relation to the rise to power of the bourgeoisie, quite irrespective of the class origins of the individual composers themselves. Adorno suggests, in fact, that the class origins of composers have tended as a rule to be 'the petty bourgeois middle class or their own guild'.[29] In *Einleitung in die Musiksoziologie* he writes:

> To be considered first of all is whether, from the viewpoint of the producers' class membership, there has ever been anything other than bourgeois music – a problem, by the way, which affects the sociology of art far beyond music. .... On the other hand, the social status of the proletariat within bourgeois society served largely to impede artistic production by workers and workers' children. The realism taught by want is not as one with the free unfoldment of consciousness.[30]

Thus, in Adorno's view, the historical Subject/Object, as the most advanced consciousness of its period, is represented by the *bourgeois individual*. Michael de la Fontaine has formulated the reasons for Adorno's limitation of his concept of musical material to the material of bourgeois art music on (i) *theoretical/systematic* grounds, and (ii) *historical grounds*.[31] I summarize de la Fontaine's formulation as follows:

(i) The *systematic* grounds maintain that, in the bourgeois era, only the bourgeois individual is the Subject/Object which, in the form of *rationality*, can be seen as representing in its purest form the socially necessary degee of domination and control (also regarded as *self*-domination and control). The proletarian individual, however, is regarded as the socially derived Object, carrying socially superfluous domination within itself.

(ii) The *historical* grounds maintain that, in the early bourgeois period (i.e. the eighteenth and early nineteenth centuries), composers had a productive relationship to folk music. They were thus able constantly to renew their material from the vitality of folk music, sublimating the material of folk music into that of art music. In the period of high capitalism, however (i.e. the late nineteenth and early twentieth centuries), there no longer remained an independent 'folk' 'whose songs and games could be taken up and sublimated by art'.[32] There remained only dependent classes which, because of their dependence, had lost their own means of expression (*Ausdrucksmittel*), and are now controlled 'from above' by the historically 'obsolete and devalued materials of art music'.[33]

For Adorno, therefore, it is the 'bourgeois Subject' that both dominates and expresses the 'objective spirit' of its age, as the embodiment of the rationality principle in the capitalist period. It is also the 'bourgeois Subject' which is embodied in the dialectic of musical material, and which, so he argues, dominates, in obsolete form, even the material of 'popular music'. (The problem of Adorno's critique of popular music and its material has been touched on in Chapter 1, and will be discussed further in Chapter 5.)

De la Fontaine's formulation provides a useful account of Adorno's position. However, it needs to be emphasized that the avant-garde expresses the consciousness of the 'bourgeois individual' as the Subject/Object of history *dialectically* rather than directly – that is, it is a mediated and *contradictory* expression of the dominant tendencies of its period. The avant-garde, it has to be argued, represents the alienation of disaffected and radical art from the social class from which it largely emanates, and for which it was largely created. Furthermore, it is necessary to see de la Fontaine's formulation in the context of Adorno's view of the rise of the bourgeoisie to dominance (a context not provided by de la Fontaine, but one which is needed in order to make sense of Adorno's potentially confusing identification of the 'bourgeois individual' with concepts like the 'historical Subject', 'advanced consciousness', 'critical self-reflection' and the 'avant-garde'). This context will be provided in Chapter 6, by means of an overview of Adorno's dialectic of musical material as philosophy of history.

The historical mediation of Subject and Object, as the rise of the bourgeois individual in the period of industrial capitalism, is what constitutes Adorno's essentially Hegelian philosophy of history, and it is this which provides the theoretical underpinning for his concept of the 'dialectic of musical material'. The 'dialectic of musical material' can be understood as the historical 'objectification' of the bourgeois Subject in musical structures – what Adorno calls the process of 'subject-objectification', an objectification of the Subject which has forgotten its subjective origins. As already emphasized, however, the relation of art to the social totality is, according to Adorno, contradictory – it both reflects the dominant tendencies of social reality and opposes them, while at the same time pointing to something beyond society as it is. While Adorno's dialectical approach to history is clearly Hegelian in origin, the process is not seen as leading to the final reconciliation of opposites within some metaphysical concept of 'the whole'. The whole – in this case the social totality – is fractured, insists Adorno, and access to understanding it is only by way of the fragment, within which the 'fragmented whole' is mediated. To recapitulate, therefore: in more concrete terms, the dialectic is that between history and nature, consciousness and material, while at the most abstract level – that of German Idealist philosophy – it is that between Subject and Object. In music, the locus of this mediation of opposites is the musical material, as the historical dialectic of composer and material, seen from the perspective of the avant-garde. The problem is that of form – essentially, how to create 'integrated' works out of a culturally disintegrating material. The context is that of a society dominated by the exchange of commodities. The 'progress' of the musical material is thus seen as the progress of the 'historical Subject' (i.e. the bourgeois individual) becoming increasingly conscious of its predicament. This is what Adorno means by the contradictory character of the avant-garde, particularly in its relation to the 'culture industry' and to what he tended to avoid calling 'popular culture'.

Mediation through the extremes

As Jürgen Ritsert has pointed out,[34] the emphasis in what Adorno takes from Hegel's logic is not on the *reconciliation* of contradictions, but is rather on the fact that they are *antagonistic*. Indeed, the point of Adorno calling his dialectical method 'negative' is precisely that it admits no 'reconciliation'. For Adorno, Ritsert argues, mediation does not take place in some middle-term (*eine Mitte*) between the extremes, but rather in the extremes themselves. This is to be seen particularly clearly in Adorno's discussion of the split between the avant-garde and popular culture, between the autonomous work and the work as commodity. In a letter to Walter Benjamin in 1936 Adorno wrote:

Both bear the stigmata of capitalism, both contain elements of change (but never, of course, the middle-term between Schönberg and the American film). Both are torn halves of an integral freedom, to which however they do not add up.[35]

The idea is now that of a 'fractured whole', a whole which can only be approached via the fragmented parts rather than through the harmonistic notion of the reconciliation of opposites. Ritsert argues that:

Between the 'incomprehensibility' of the serious products and the 'inescapability' of easy listening there is in the end for Adorno no 'third thing' any more. The mediating middle-term [*die vermittelnde Mitte*], the *tertium comparationis*, is lacking whereby the extremes can be 'reconciled' or the opposites can be 'neutralized'. 'The situation has polarized in the extremes ...'.[36]

In this sense Adorno proceeds through revealing contradiction and identifying the extremes, more often than not by means of hyperbole. As Ritsert puts it: 'The "movement of the contradiction", an expression for the dynamics of the total constellation [*Gesamtkonstellation*], means in this case the *sharpening of antagonisms*.[37] That is to say, the totality of musical life, mapped between the extremes of avant-garde and commodity music, reflects as a whole the tendencies of the social totality. Society is mediated through both these extremes, on the one hand through negation, as non-identity, and on the other hand as affirmation and total identification. In Adorno's terms:

The unity of the two spheres of music is thus that of an unresolved contradiction.... The whole can not be put together by adding the separated halves, but in both there appear, however distantly, the changes of the whole, which only moves in contradiction.[38]

2   Adorno's Marxian model: the social mediation of music

The idea of the 'fractured whole' characterized by antagonisms was a striking feature of the model put forward by Adorno in the essay 'Zur gesellschaftlichen Lage der Musik', presented in summary form at the end of Chapter 2. This model made use of Marx's 'conflict theory' of the antagonistic relationship between the forces and relations of production, itself a materialist version of Hegel's theory of the contradictory character of mediation. It is to the extension of the concept of 'mediation' in Marx, and its reception by Adorno, that we now turn.

Although Marx himself did not produce an aesthetic theory, the fragmentary references to art and literature to be found throughout his work, when taken in conjunction with his socio-economic theories, have provided a rich source of ideas for some of the most penetrating writing on aesthetics and the sociology of art of the twentieth century. While by no means the first to draw on Marx in this respect, Lukács has certainly been seminal. Indeed, apart from the early, pre-Marxian *Theorie des Romans*, the work of Lukács which probably had the most decisive influence on the young Adorno was *Geschichte und Klassenbewußtsein*, a book that is hardly concerned with aesthetics at all. The Hegelian interpretation of Marx which characterizes that work, together with the use it makes of Max Weber's concept of 'rationalization' in its discussion of bureaucracy and technology in relation to reification in capitalist society, provided Adorno with powerful conceptual tools to apply to aesthetics. In looking at the sources of much of Adorno's thinking in Marx, therefore, it needs to be remembered that this is specifically a Hegelian interpretation of Marx filtered through Lukács.

Production, distribution, exchange, consumption

Although Marx often uses the term 'mediation' in the sense of a connection *between* things, the Hegelian sense of mediation as *immanent* – i.e. as inherent in processes themselves – is also very much implied, even though the term itself may often not be used by Marx to indicate this. Both senses are to be understood in the basic model Marx uses to suggest the general ways in which production in society relates to consumption via the spheres of distribution and exchange (a model taken over by Adorno and adapted and extended to discuss the musical relations of production and the social function of music – see Chapter 5). In *Zur Kritik der politischen Okonomie* Marx provides a rough sketch of this familiar model:

Production creates articles corresponding to requirements; distribution allocates them according to social laws; exchange in its turn distributes the goods, which have already been allocated, in conformity with individual needs; finally, in consumption the product leaves this social movement, it becomes the direct object and servant of an individual need, which its use satisfies. Production thus appears as the point of departure, consumption as the goal, distribution and exchange as the middle, which has a dual form since, according to the definition, distribution is actuated by society and exchange is actuated by individuals.[39]

However, Marx immediately qualifies this simple outline by emphasizing the complexity of the real relations between the sphere of production and the other spheres. The model, in a most fundamental sense, is a specific, but 'inverted', form of the abstract Hegelian mediation of Subject and Object. Marx writes that '[i]n production persons acquire an objective aspect, and in consumption objects acquire a subjective aspect; in distribution it is society which by means of dominant general rules mediates between production and consumption; in exchange this mediation occurs as a result of random decisions of individuals'.[40] The apparently separate spheres of production, distribution, exchange and consumption are in reality, he maintains, so closely interlinked that they need to be taken as one entity. Although production is the dominant phase, it not only determines consumption, but is also determined by it. Likewise, distribution, as distribution of products, has to be seen as an aspect of production, while exchange is not only shaped by production but also, as market demands, is able to affect production. Moreover, Marx points out in *Das Kapital* that the production process, in order to be continuous, has to repeat itself and is therefore also a process of *reproduction*: 'When viewed therefore as a connected whole, and in the constant flux of its incessant renewal, every social process of production is at the same time a process of reproduction'.[41]

In his adaptation of Marx's theory of production to the particular case of aesthetic (and, even more specifically, *musical*) production within capitalist society, Adorno is applying it as a convenient means of identifying key spheres within 'musical life'. Like Marx in his discussion of the complexities of social production, Adorno recognizes the limitations of the model in view of the dynamic complexity of real musical relations. In his essay 'Ideen zur Musiksoziologie' he writes:

Even the division into the spheres of production, reproduction and consumption is itself a social product, less to be accepted by sociology than to be deduced [from it]. . . . The individual areas of research are not dealt with as neatly co-ordinated or subordinated fields, but are approached in terms of their dynamic relationship.[42]

Although the model provides the basic skeleton for an essay like 'Zur gesellschaftlichen Lage der Musik', for example, it is not applied particularly systematically and, as with Adorno's use of Hegel, there are lacunae. One of these is his use of the term 'reproduction'. It is clear enough what he intends it to mean – i.e. musical reproduction as (a) interpretation/ performance (of the score) as an aspect of production; and (b) 'technical' reproduction (of the performance) as an aspect of distribution/exchange – but this specialized use of the term in relation to music is not explained in relation to Marx's general use of the concept. For Adorno the spheres identified in the model tend to operate only as useful orientation points. At the same time, however, he is also, like Marx, working against any dogmatic application of these categories through demonstrating how the different spheres interpenetrate and have a reciprocal effect upon each other.

Like Marx, Adorno at the same time insists on the priority of the sphere of production. In *Ästhetische Theorie* he writes: 'Concern with the social explication of art has to address the production of art rather than study its impact (which in many cases diverges completely from art works and their social content, a divergence that can in turn be explained sociologically)'.[43] Adorno considers the spheres of distribution and consumption to be dependent upon the sphere of production and subordinate to it. This is because his focus is on the musical work and its social content (*Gehalt*) and not on the reception of the work. He considers that, because musical reception is itself socially mediated, it cannot as an area of study be a substitute for the analysis of the specificity of the work itself. It is in the musical work and in the dialectic of the musical material that the social significance of music is to be deciphered, in terms of socially sedimented traces within the material, not through focusing exclusively on the conditions of music's reception/consumption. On the other hand, what the study of the distribution and consumption of music does identify is the *function* of music in capitalist society, and this is an aspect of the musical work which has profound implications not only at the level of consumption, but also at the levels of production and reproduction. That is to say, Adorno maintains that the social function of music today is that of the *commodity*: production is the *production of commodities*, and the commodity form is significant because it represents *mediated* labour.

One aspect of the commodity form is certainly the 'natural material' from which it is produced and the material means of production which transformed it into a commodity. To take it on this level of immediacy, however, is, according to Marx, to misunderstand the commodity. As Marx puts it in Chapter 1 of *Das Kapital* (Volume I): 'It is nothing but the definite social relation between men themselves which assumes here, for them, the fantastic [*phantasmagorische*] form of a relation between things'.[44] In being taken as an immediate given and fetishized as a 'thing', the commodity is seen as standing against us as a 'natural phenomenon', and is regarded by Marx as 'alienated labour'.[45] The important aspect of the commodity form was, for Marx, not its 'natural material', but rather its 'mediatedness' as a product of human labour. The defining characteristic of the commodity form is that the labour that went into its production is *concealed*, and that, as a result of this, something that has been made, an artefact, assumes the appearance of nature, as 'natural object'. This is what Marx means when he refers to social relations assuming 'the fantastic form of a relation between things' as a result of commodity fetishism. In using the term *phantasmagorische* Marx also appears to be referring to the nineteenth-century 'phantasmagoria', the creation of 'illusion' for public entertainment using the latest technological means.[46] Adorno's use of the concept of phantasmagoria, derived particularly from Benjamin, will be returned to in the course of Chapter 6.

Forces and relations of production

In identifying *the historical development of human labour* as the key mediating factor between human beings and nature, rather than Hegel's rather mysterious 'Spirit'(*Geist*) (i.e. as 'alienated labour'), Marx considered that he had also identified the material basis for a 'scientific study' of the economic, political and ideological development of human society. The distinction he makes between the forces of production and the relations of production is particularly important:

In the social production of their existence, men inevitably enter into definite relations, which are independent of their will, namely relations of production appropriate to a given stage in the development of their material forces of production. The totality of these relations of production constitutes the economic structure of society, the real foundation, on which arises a legal and political superstructure and to which correspond definite forms of social consciousness.[47]

Marx considers that: 'At a certain stage of development, the material productive forces of society come into conflict with the existing relations of production. . . . From forms of development of the productive forces these relations turn into their fetters.'[48] These 'social antagonisms' come about because developments in the forces of production have outstripped developments in the existing relations of production. The relations of production constitute the economic base of society (although whether the forces of production also belong to the base is disputed);[49] and it is, according to Marx, the economic base which determines social existence and the forms of consciousness which correspond to that existence – that is, what he calls the ideological superstructure. Among the forms consciousness takes in the superstructure of society is art. Thus, changes within art – within, for example, musical structures, and the material of music viewed as historical – would have to be accounted for as a reflection of fundamental transformations going on within the economic base – that is, as conflicts between the means of production of society and its corresponding relations of production. Marx formulates this as follows:

In studying such transformations it is always necessary to distinguish between the material transformation of the economic conditions of production, which can be determined with the precision of natural science, and the legal, political, religious, artistic or philosophic – in short, ideological forms in which men become conscious of this conflict and fight it out. Just as one does not judge an individual by what he thinks about himself, so one cannot judge such a period of transformation by its consciousness, but, on the contrary, this consciousness must be explained from the contradictions of material life, from the conflict existing between the social forces of production and the relations of production.[50]

Adorno's problems with Marx's base-superstructure model were the by now familiar ones of attempting to apply what is in many ways a crude deterministic theory to the case of art – and, in particular, to the extreme case of a 'non-referential' mode of art like autonomous music. Furthermore, Marx's claim to have discovered a 'scientific basis' for the study of human society has positivistic implications quite foreign to Adorno's speculative approach. Interestingly, Marx did seem to recognize that art might be something of a special case, when in *Kritik der politischen Okonomie* he wrote: 'As regards art, it is well known that some of its peaks by no means correspond to the general development of society; nor do they therefore to the material substructure, the skeleton as it were of its organization'.[51]

In focusing on those aspects of Marx's theory which are particularly relevant to the understanding of Adorno's concept of 'mediation' it is also important to be aware of those dimensions of the theory which Adorno's critique either rejects or allows only a minor role in his aesthetics. Most striking is the substitution of a notion of 'critical consciousness' for Marx's notion of the revolutionary role of the proletariat in the class struggle – something which, on the surface at least, is very reminiscent of Hegel's *Geist*. Adorno and Horkheimer argued that the revolutionary potential of the proletariat within highly industrialized capitalist societies has been absorbed and diverted by, among other things, the all-embracing effects of the 'culture industry'. This demonstrated the way in which the high level of development of the forces of production (as technology, scientific knowledge and the organization of labour) had come to legitimize the existing power structure of society through representing the existing relations of production as rational and necessary. As Paul Connerton has put it, instead of the imbalance between the forces of production and the relations of production offering 'grounds for a critique of the power structure ... now they provide a basis for its legitimation'.[52] According to Adorno this oppositional function remains now only in the domain of art (i.e the avant-garde) and theory (i.e. critical philosophical and social theory). The question of Adorno's possible misunderstandings or distortions of Marx has given rise to criticism of Adorno's work as a whole; a detailed consideration of these criticisms would, however, be out of place in a study of this sort.[53] Nevertheless, Adorno's reception of Marx's theory of the forces and relations of production and of the base-superstructure model in terms of its applicability to music is of great importance, and it merits closer examination here.

Adorno and the base-superstructure problem

In 'Zur gesellschaftlichen Lage der Musik' Adorno had made an ambitious, if somewhat unpolished, attempt to apply Marx's model of social/material production to the field of music.[54] Relevant as that essay is in many ways, however, Adorno later came to consider that it was, in one important respect, flawed. In a footnote to *Einleitung in die Musiksoziologie* he discloses why he had never allowed the earlier essay – 'the draft of a finished musical sociology' – to be republished. He states that his error had been the 'flat identification of the concept of musical production with the precedence of the economic sphere of production, without considering how far that which we call [musical] production already presupposes social production and depends on it as much as it is sundered from it'.[55] This realization – that while musical production (as composition and performance) is dependent on the process of social and economic production and is influenced by it, it is not identical to it – led Adorno in his subsequent writings on music to explore in a somewhat less doctrinaire way the complex mediations which relate the musical work and 'musical life' to the social totality. It was also an indication of how much he had relinquished, or at least revised, his early version of Marxism.

As already seen, in Marxian terms the sphere of production embraces the material forces and relations of production, the two existing in an antagonistic relationship. That Adorno also perceives society as 'antagonistic' has already been discussed. What was not clear, either in the debate on musical material between Adorno and Krenek or in 'Zur gesellschaftlichen Lage der Musik', was the location of the antagonisms in relation to music. This gap in Adorno's theory is now to some extent filled. Roughly put, composition and, in part, performance (presumably as techniques and technologies of composition and performance, instruments, notation, and indeed 'musical material') are what he appears to understand as the forces of (musical) production, which, as *aesthetic* forces of production, belong to the ideological superstructure. The form of production epitomized by the 'culture industry', however, he understands as belonging to the economic relations of production, and as such is seen as part of the economic and material *base* of society. Furthermore, the musical forces of production, as aesthetic forces, still derive, at least in part, from an earlier mode of production – that characterized by a master–apprentice, craft ethic, although, of course, continuously modified by technological developments from the capitalist mode of production. Seen in this way, both the forces and the relations of *musical* production come entirely under the sway of the material relations of the capitalist mode of production, in spite of the anachronistic survival within musical composition and performance of pre-capitalist modes of production.

Adorno's Marxian conception of the relation of music to the social totality is thus complex and potentially confusing, given (a) the distinction he maintains between *aesthetic* and *material/economic* production, and (b) the blurring of that distinction through tracing a multiplicity of mediating links between aesthetic and material/economic production. Thus, musical production is part of the ideological superstructure of society and therefore cannot be identified directly with material/economic production. There are, nevertheless, parallels between the ways in which the two operate – for instance, *technology*, as noted above, is seen as a mediating link between superstructure and base. And, just as the material relations of production tend to fetter the material forces of production, so do the musical relations of production (e.g. the 'culture industry') dominate and control the musical forces of production (e.g. composition in relation to musical material, compositional techniques, performance practice, etc.). The antagonisms between the forces and relations of production are seen by Adorno as common to both the musical/aesthetic and the material/economic spheres of production. The key point to grasp in all of this, however, is the following: although musical (i.e. aesthetic) production belongs to the ideological superstructure, the musical relations of production are controlled by the culture industry, which is part of the material/economic base. Adorno formulates the problem of the complex and contradictory relation between musical and social production as follows:

What we call production in music or in art at large, is initially defined as the antithesis of a cultural consumer commodity – which makes it so much less possible to equate it directly with material production. The difference between the two spheres is constitutive: in the aesthetic sphere, whatever art may be it is not in the nature of a thing. In critical social theory, works of art are included in the superstructure and thus distinguished from material production. The antithetical, critical element alone, which is essential to the content of important works of art and opposes them to the [relations] of material production as to the governing practice at large – this alone forbids unthinking talk of production in either case, if confusions are to be avoided.[56]

Thus Adorno rejects crude socio-economic determinism in his interpretation of Marx. In arguing that art not only reflects society but also opposes it, not only converges with society but also diverges from it and develops its own dynamic, Adorno needed to pursue further the interpenetration of the subjective and the objective, and of 'history' and 'nature' in art. In turning to Freud and Max Weber Adorno found concepts which enabled him to discuss, in both 'material' and psychological terms, ways in which the outside world is refracted by the Subject and ways in which 'inner subjectivity' is able to engage with the 'objectivity' of the outside world through the processes of sublimation, repression, mimetic adaptation and rationalization.

3   Freud: art and sublimation

Like other members of the Frankfurt School,[57] Adorno made considerable use of aspects of psychoanalytic theory in conjunction with Marxian theory. In fact it has been argued that he set out in the late 1930s and the 1940s during his period of exile in the United States quite calculatedly to substitute a Freudian approach for his previously more Marxian orientation.[58] The psychoanalytic interpretation of the music of Schoenberg and Stravinsky in terms of progress and reaction – using concepts like sublimation, repression, infantilism, regression, depersonalization and psychosis – is certainly a striking feature of what is perhaps Adorno's most important book to date from this period, *Philosophie der neuen Musik*. At the same time, however, Adorno was very critical of Freud's attempt to interpret art works through a psychoanalysis of the artists' personal lives, and rejected his biographical interpretations of, for example, Leonardo da Vinci, as hopelessly philistine in conception for 'dismissing as neurotics men of art who in fact merely objectified in their work the negativity of life'.[59] He found unacceptable the simplistic prescription that psychoanalysis imposed on art, that it 'should deal affirmatively with the negativity of experience', and the judgement that 'the negative moment is just a mark of the process of repression finding its way into the work of art'.[60] Adorno also argued that psychoanalysis overemphasized the view that art is daydreaming, thus placing too much stress on the fictional aspect of art and on the element of projection involved, while ignoring the art work as 'object'. At the same time, however, he considered that psychoanalytic theory does make a useful contribution to the demythologization of art through penetrating art's hermetically sealed world and relating it to that which is not art – particularly through providing some insight into its connection with the instinctual drives. Adorno argued that '[t]o the extent to which psychoanalysis decodes the social character of a work of art and its author, it is able to furnish concrete, mediating links between the structure of works of art and that of society'.[61] Nevertheless, although psychoanalysis may shed light on the mediation of art and society through its emphasis on instinctual drives, Adorno insisted that art cannot be explained only in such terms: 'In the process of artistic production, unconscious drives are one impetus among many. They become integrated with the work of art through the law of form.'[62] Part of the dynamic tension which characterizes art works is, for Adorno, the tension between the conscious and the unconscious, between, for example, the calculation of construction and the spontaneity of expression. Thus Freud's emphasis on the 'reality principle' is seen by Adorno as an obstacle to the understanding of art, because implied here is the desirability of adaptation to and affirmation of reality as it is, whereas any deviation from the reality principle is regarded as escape. For Adorno this is the most reactionary and restorative aspect of psychoanalysis – the identification of 'imagination' with 'escape', and the non-recognition of art's potential critical character:

The experience of reality is such that it provides all kinds of legitimate grounds for wanting to escape. This exposes the harmonistic ideology behind the psychoanalytic indignation about people's escape mechanisms. . . . It is true, there is an element of escape in imagination, but the two are not synonymous.[63]

It is, however, the theory of *sublimation* that Adorno sees as Freud's most valuable contribution to an understanding of the social dimension of art, and of the way in which social tendencies are mediated by the creative individual at the level of instinctual drives. At the same time Adorno is critical of the theory, and rejects certain key features of it.

Sublimation

Implied in Freud's concept of 'sublimation' is the idea that works of art are not merely direct wish-fulfilment, but that they also transform repressed libido into 'socially productive accomplishments'.[64] However, as with

Marx, what Freud has to say on art is not very systematic, and is largely peripheral to the main body of his work. Furthermore, the concept of 'sublimation' itself, like much of psychoanalytic theory, is ambiguous and very much open to interpretation. What is clear in Freud's own accounts of the concept is that (a) sublimation is characterized as dynamic, developmental and evolutionary; (b) it involves a release of tension and the liberation of energy from purely instinctual activity; (c) instinctual drives become canalized into forms of essentially non-instinctual behaviour; (d) there is a displacement of potentially disruptive energy from activities and objects of primarily sexual interest on to activities and objects which are not primarily sexual and which are socially acceptable and creative; and (e) it is generally positive and non-neurotic in character.[65] In his *Neue Folge der Vorlesungen zur Einführung in die Psychoanalyse* (1933) Freud writes:

The evidence of analytical experience shows that it is an undoubted fact that instinctual impulses from one source attach themselves to those from other sources and share their further vicissitudes and that in general one instinctual satisfaction can be replaced by another. But it must be admitted that we do not understand this very well. The relations of an instinct to its aim and object are also open to alterations; both can be exchanged for other ones, though its relation to its object is nevertheless the more easily loosened. A certain kind of modification of the aim and change of the object, in which our social valuation is taken into account, is described by us as 'sublimation'.[66]

And in his essay on Leonardo da Vinci Freud considers that there are aspects of sublimation which are inaccessible to psychoanalysis because of the essentially biological/organic (as opposed to psychological) foundations of the phenomenon, and that '[s]ince artistic talent and capacity are intimately connected with sublimation we must admit that the nature of the artistic function is also inaccessible to us along psychoanalytical lines'.[67]

In Freudian terms, as we have seen, sublimation constitutes what is described as a 'socially necessary' displacement of instinctual energy on to socially productive – or, at very least, socially acceptable and non-aggressive – forms of behaviour. One is reminded of Adorno's perceptive observation in the opening sentence of 'Über den Fetischcharakter in der Musik und die Regression des Hörens' that 'music represents at once the immediate manifestation of impulse and the locus of its taming'.[68] In this, as Adorno recognized, there is also a distinctly ideological and reactionary element, in that through sublimation (as in regression and repression – the concerns of his 1938 essay on music's fetish-character and the regression of listening) the individual becomes better 'adapted' to the status quo, to the 'rationality' of an irrational society. There is in sublimation, at the same time, however, also the idea of *development*, in a positive sense not contained in the concepts of regression and repression. Sublimation may be seen as the motor, on the individual level, of the creative process itself. In brief, therefore, the process can be understood as containing the following phases: (i) displacement of instinctual drives from the immediate, 'natural' object of desire; (ii) delaying of gratification leading to creation of alternative, non-instinctive patterns of activity, as both escape from and opposition to existing reality; and (iii) ego-development, in terms both of adaptation to reality and of taking an autonomous position in relation to existing reality. Nevertheless, Adorno finds the ambiguity of the concept disturbing, arguing that, in Freud's system,

there is a total lack of any adequate criteria for distinguishing 'positive' from 'negative' ego-functions, above all, sublimation from repression. Instead, the concept of what is socially useful or productive is rather innocently dragged in. But in an irrational society, the ego cannot perform at all adequately the function allotted to it by that society.[69]

Critical Theory and psychoanalysis

Reservations notwithstanding, the concept of 'sublimation' does have its uses for Adorno. By employing it he is able to suggest a relation between the individual subjectivity and the collective objectivity in terms of a theory of psychic life. As we have seen, this is something that was lacking in Marx's socio-economic theory. The Critical Theorists' attempt in the late 1920s and early 1930s to bring about a fusion of Marx and Freud was itself noteworthy, in that, although it is possible to see Freud's approach as being essentially dialectical and dynamic, it also in some key respects seems to run counter to Marx's historical materialism: it can be seen as ahistorical in its emphasis, taking as it does the bourgeois family as a given and absolutizing it. What was urgent at the time, however, was the development of a social psychology which could complement Marx's sociology.[70] Adorno himself had begun to explore psychoanalytic theory quite early on (in 1924),[71] but it was really Erich Fromm who made the first steps towards the integration of Freud into Critical Theory in two articles which appeared in the *Zeitschrift für Sozialforschung* in 1932[72] (the same year as the appearance of Adorno's 'Zur gesellschaftlichen Lage der Musik'). Although Adorno and the rest of the Frankfurt School later came to have fundamental disagreements with Fromm on account of his 'neo-revisionism',[73] at this important period in the development of Critical Theory there is much in Fromm's (early) articles published in the *Zeitschrift* which can be taken as formative. It is for this reason, and for the light it casts on Adorno's use of the concept of 'sublimation' in relation to the Hegelian–Marxian concept of 'mediation', that a brief summary of arguments from one of the early Fromm articles is relevant at this point.

In the article 'Über Methode und Aufgabe einer analytischen Sozial-psychologie' (1932) Fromm writes:

Applying the method of psychoanalytic individual psychology to social phenom-ena, we find that the *phenomena of social psychology are to be understood as processes involving the active and passive adaptation of the instinctual apparatus to the socio-economic situation. In certain fundamental respects, the instinctual apparatus itself is a biological given; but it is highly modifiable. The role of primary formative factors goes to the economic conditions. The family is the essential medium through which the economic situation exerts its formative influence on the individual's psyche. The task of social psychology is to explain the shared, socially relevant, psychic attitudes and ideologies – and their unconscious roots in particular – in terms of the influence of economic conditions on libido strivings.*[74] (italics in original)

Fromm argues that the instinctual drives (the 'libido strivings') constitute 'nature' in the human psyche and are acted upon by socio-economic conditions. He also argues that the instinctual apparatus 'is one of the "natural" conditions that form part of the substructure [*Unterbau*] of the social process',[75] as human resources (together with the material means or forces of production, as tools, technology, etc.). In this way he reasons that the instinctual drives form a crucial link between the 'interiority' of the human individual and the social process, between economic base and ideological superstructure. This is, he maintains, the psychological dimen-sion missing from Marx's economic and sociological model. Through the sublimation of instinctual drives in response to the influence and pressure of socio-economic reality the material base is reflected in the ideological superstructure in the mediated form of intellectual, artistic, legal, religious and political structures. He also argues that this helps account for the way in which ideas (and ideologies) in their turn can affect society. He writes that this is because 'the impact of an idea depends essentially on its unconscious content, which appeals to certain drives; that it is, as it were, the quality and intensity of the libidinal structure of a society which determines the social effect of an ideology'.[76] And what he calls 'the libidinal structure of a society' is not, he argues, a constant, but changes historically as the socio-economic conditions change. He concludes:

Clearly, analytic psychology has its place within the framework of historical materialism. It investigates one of the natural factors that are operative in the relationship between society and nature: the realm of human drives, and the active and passive role they play within the social process. Thus it investigates a factor that plays a decisive mediating role between the economic base and the formation of ideologies. Thus analytic social psychology enables us to understand fully the ideological superstructure in terms of the process that goes on beween society and man's nature.[77]

Fromm's argument in his early articles in the *Zeitschrift für Sozialforschung* that the instinctual drives form a link between base and superstructure, and that the 'libidinal structure of a society' is not a constant, but changes historically as the socio-economic conditions change,[78] would seem, in broad terms, to be in accord with Adorno's own reception of Freud in the late 1920s and early 1930s. The main differences at this stage could be seen to lie in the tone adopted by the two men in their writings. Even in these early texts, Fromm's presentation suggests an essentially positive and affirmative view of 'human nature' and its potential for change under present social conditions which is borne out in his writings in the United States after he left the Institut für Sozialforschung in 1939. Adorno, on the contrary, communicates a sense of dark irony and pessimism in all his work. This comes to a head in a paper he delivered in 1946 in Los Angeles attacking the revisionism of Karen Horney and of Fromm in his later writings – especially their attempt to categorize character types and to construct 'a totalistic theory of character' from Freud's theories.[79] In this paper, entitled 'Social science and sociological tendencies in psychoanalysis',[80] Adorno wrote:

The stress on totality, as against the unique, fragmentary impulse, always implies the harmonistic belief in what might be called the unity of personality, [a unity that] is never realized in our society. It is one of the greatest merits of Freud that he has debunked the myth of this unity.[81]

Regression and de-sublimation

Adorno points out that, as well as going with the idea of ego strength and ego development as a positive value, the process of sublimation in psychoanalytic theory carries with it an aspect of regression: '[p]roductivity is not pure sublimation but entwined with regressive moments, if not with infantile ones'.[82] There is also the possibility of attempting to cope with the tension between the pleasure and reality principles through regression to earlier, infantile channels for the discharge of instinctual/libidinal energy – obsessional and fixated behaviour patterns as a defence mechanism against unacceptable aspects of reality. This kind of regressive behaviour (characterized at the reception stage by what Adorno calls regressive listening and fetishism – see Chapter 5) he also sometimes calls *de-sublimation* (*Entsublimierung*). Adorno uses this concept to discuss the phenomenon of treating art as a source of immediate gratification, of cathartic release, which he considers to be the opposite of sublimation. It particularly informs his critique of 'popular music'. As we have seen, therefore, for Adorno the concept of sublimation contains several separate moments which could be identified as: displacement, delayed gratification, productivity, adaptation, opposition. These contradictory aspects are also contained in his concept of art and the contradictory relation to social reality, which could be summarized as: (i) different from society (displacement), (ii) derived from society (adaptation), (iii) pointing beyond society (opposition). In *Ästhetische Theorie* he puts this in other terms by drawing a connection between sublimation and freedom:

By re-enacting reality's spell, art sublimates it into an image while at the same time freeing itself from it. Sublimation and freedom are therefore two sides of the same coin. The spell art puts upon the *membra disiecta* of reality by virtue of its synthetic tendencies is modelled upon the spell of real life and yet this real life is reduced to the status of a negative utopia.[83]

The concept of sublimation of the instinctual drives seems to provide for Adorno a way of understanding both the socially mediated productive forces for the shaping or 'forming' of the material of art, as well as the expressive and communicative power of the 'formed material' itself. At the same time, however, he was also very suspicious of the 'normative' implications contained in the concept, whereby sublimation was conceived as transforming potentially disruptive desires into 'socially desirable achievements'. To counter this he argued that, in the case of art, the sublimated and displaced drives retain their power to disturb. This is doubtless the origin of his statement in *Minima Moralia*: 'Every work of art is an uncommitted crime.'[84] Art works are both derived from and absorbed by the dominant culture, but at the same time they also oppose assimilation. It becomes apparent, therefore, that the concept of sublimation is remarkably contradictory as Adorno employs it. Indeed, in another striking passage in *Minima Moralia* Adorno attacks the concept and seems to dismiss Freud's use of it altogether. In doing this, however, he makes the concept distinctly his own, and reveals through it the possibility of understanding the activity of art as something far more complex, antagonistic and *critical* than Freud's simplistic notion of it as mere escape from the reality principle:

No work of art, within the organization of society, can escape its involvement in culture, but there is none, if it is more than mere handicraft, which does not make culture a dismissive gesture: that of having become a work of art. Art is as inimical to 'art' as are artists. In renouncing the goal of instinct they remain faithful to it, and unmask the socially desirable activity naïvely glorified by Freud as sublimation – which probably does not exist.[85]

Contradictory and unsatisfactory as it might seem, the concept of sublimation serves to provide a more rational account of a process implied in the somewhat irrationalist concepts employed by Bloch and Halm (e.g. *Formwille*) to explain the dynamic movement of musical forms, and ultimately traceable to Schopenhauer's notion of music as representation of the Will. Adorno's use of Freudian concepts, together with the considerable influence of Hegel and Marx, now needs to be grounded in a more detailed account of his reception of Max Weber.

4   Max Weber adapted; rationality and mimesis

In *Einleitung in die Musiksoziologie* Adorno argues that: 'What carries Spirit [*Geist*] forward in music, the rationality principle which Max Weber rightly recognized as central, is nothing but the unfolding of extra-artistic, social rationality. This is what "appears" in music.'[86] It is Weber's concepts of *rationality* and *rationalization* which provide Adorno with what are probably his most valuable insights into the way in which society 'appears' in music, as he puts it. And, as with the ideas identified earlier in this chapter, these concepts need to be understood as part of the theoretical frame from which they derive – particularly when such concepts are not normally associated with art and art works, where the activity of art is, if anything, viewed rather as an attempt to evade what is generally understood by 'rationality.'

Rationalization and the disenchantment of the world

Although Weber identifies four types of 'rationality' (a typology which will be considered briefly below), in its most common usage the term refers particularly to the relation between means and ends. Martindale and Riedel define the concept (specifically 'means-ends' or 'instrumental' rationality) as follows: 'A social action is rational when the means utilized in the course of action are chosen because of their efficiency or adequacy to the attainment of the ends in view.'[87] They point out that the term is not used in its everyday sense, in that it does not refer to ends or values as such. The focus is on the efficiency and appropriateness of the *means* to achieving particular ends, and therefore the use of the term 'rationality' in this sense has definite *technical* connotations.[88] Thus, actions which may appear irrational from any 'normal' point of view, may be rational in Weber's sense because of the logical nature of the means employed to achieve apparently 'irrational' ends.

Weber argued that the overriding tendency of Western culture was towards the ever-increasing rationalization of all aspects of social life. This was to be seen not only in science, industry, business and government administration, but also in politics, religion and the arts. The process of progressive rationalization was at the same time a process of disenchantment, of demythologization. As Martindale and Riedel put it: 'Old mythologies are exposed, taboos are exploded, magical forms are destroyed, and the colorful and varied forms of old mysteries are clarified in the cold light of scientific day ... a "disenchantment of the world is carried out"'.[89] Weber linked rationalization with religion and the rise of capitalism, and saw the origins of both extreme rationalization and capitalism in the application of the rational and ascetic principles for the strict organization of all aspects of life previously restricted to monastic circles up to the period of the Renaissance in Europe. His thesis, particularly as put forward in *Die protestantische Ethik und der Geist des Kapitalismus* (1904–5), was that the dissolution of the monasteries had led to both the individualization of the principle of rationalization (as Protestantism, thrift and the accumulation of capital) and its secularization (as the increasing organization and control of society and the domination of nature). The most characteristic form of this process of rationalization may be seen in the increase in the efficiency of administration, an all-pervading bureaucratization. It is to this that Adorno is referring when he talks of the 'administered world' (*die verwaltete Welt*).[90] Given the all-embracing character of rationalization, anything that has to some degree escaped the process is regarded by Weber as highly significant. For Adorno this provides a dialectic of rationality and irrationality, as, for instance, history and myth, science and magic, and *ratio* and *mimesis*. Before proceeding to examine the concept of rationalization in relation to Adorno's music theory, however, it is necessary to consider more closely Weber's four types of rationality.

Weber's ideal types of rational social action

In his *Wirtschaft und Gesellschaft* of 1922 Weber identifies four types of social action. These are: (i) that characterized by *means-ends rationality* (*Zweckrationalität*, also translated as goal rationality, or instrumental rationality) – i.e. rationally calculated means to a given end; (ii) that characterized by *value rationality* (*Wertrationalität*) – i.e. a belief in the intrinsic, absolute value of a particular form of behaviour for its own sake, irrespective of ends or consequences; (iii) that which is *affectively determined* – i.e. behaviour determined by spontaneous emotional impulse and states of feeling; and (iv) *tradition* – i.e. behaviour characterized by settled habit patterns, custom, routine.[91]

Weber points out that (iv), *traditional behaviour*, functions as a 'limiting case' within his typology, in that it is not 'rational' in the same sense as (i) and (ii), being simply 'reaction to settled stimuli along lines laid down by settled habits'.[92] Likewise, (iii), *affective behaviour*, is regarded as 'on, or often beyond, the boundary marking out the area of consciously "meaningful" behaviour: it may simply be a spontaneous response to an unusual stimulus'.[93] He suggests, however, that 'affective' behaviour can come close to being rational action in both the 'means-ends' and 'value' senses of (i) and (ii) 'when the affectively determined action results from the *conscious* discharge of emotion'.[94] This special case of 'affective' behaviour he calls *sublimation*.[95]

Comparing (iii), 'affective' action, with (ii), action determined by 'value rationality', Weber maintains that the latter type (ii) is characterized by conscious decision on the ultimate goal of the action and *systematic organization* of action to achieve that goal. In contrast, apart from the special case outlined above (as sublimation), the former (iii) is spontaneous and is not normally conscious. What both types of action have in common, he considers, is that 'the meaning of the action does not lie in the consequences which result from it but is inherent in the specific nature of the action itself'.[96] Among the kinds of examples Weber gives which could be included under these overlapping types (ii) and (iii) are areas of activity that could be considered as falling under the category of the *aesthetic*. Specifically concerning *value rationality* he writes that 'an action which is "rational" in this sense is always performed in obedience to "imperatives" or in fulfilment of "claims" which the agent believes to be imposed on him'.[97] He adds that action of this type, directed towards meeting such claims in the attempt to realize a value, is probably identifiable only in a fairly small, although significant, proportion of actions.

Weber also recognizes that there are aspects that (ii), *value rationality*, and (i), *means-ends rationality*, have in common. What distinguishes actions which are rational in the 'means-ends' sense is that a person, in acting, 'rationally *assesses* means in relation to ends, ends in relation to secondary consequences, and, finally, the various possible ends in relation to each other'.[98] However, aspects of (ii), *value rationality*, are present when there has to be a choice between conflicting ends and consequences; nevertheless, the action may still be rational in respect of its *means*. Furthermore, the conflicting ends could themselves not be regarded as absolute, but instead could be assessed on a scale of their relative values, thus bringing such an action once more firmly under the 'means-ends' type. At the same time, as suggested above, the type of action based on absolute values (ii) uses systematic organization to achieve its absolute value, very much along the lines of 'means-ends' rationality. Nevertheless, the distinguishing feature of (ii) is that the meaning of the action lies in the nature of the action itself, and not in its consequences. Weber points out that, although there are various possible interactions between these two types of rational action, what is particularly significant is that '[f]rom the standpoint of the "means-end" kind of rationality ... the other kind is always *irrational*, and the more so the more it elevates the value by which action is to be guided to the status of an absolute value'.[99] It is this antinomy that Adorno emphasizes in his use of the concept of rationality in relation to art: art works are rationally constructed, but their rationality is irrational from the point of view of the dominant means-ends rationality of social reality.

The rational and social foundations of music

Weber himself, in an appendix to *Wirtschaft und Gesellschaft*, developed the concepts of rationality and rationalization specifically in relation to music in the extended essay, subsequently published separately, entitled *Die rationalen und sozialen Grundlagen der Musik* (written in 1911, but not published until 1921).[100] In this essay Weber applied to the special case of music his thesis that Western culture is characterized by (a) an ever-increasing tendency towards the rationalization of all aspects of society – i.e. of human interrelationships (bureaucratization was only one aspect of this tendency), and (b) the ever-increasing domination of nature which this process implies. He examines these tendencies in music in terms of (i) the relation of melody to harmony, (ii) a comparison of Western and non-Western scale and tuning systems, (iii) polyphony and the development of notational systems, and (iv) the technology of musical instruments and systems of tuning them. Weber's essay applying the concepts of 'rationality' and 'rationalization' to music and musical life has certainly to be viewed as a pioneering effort towards the development of a genuine 'sociology of music', and its significance for the understanding of the mediation of music and society was recognized early on by Adorno and his fellow Critical Theorists at the Institut für Sozialforschung.

The process of progressive rationalization is seen as pivotal by Adorno because it is shared both by the immanent formal/structural processes of music and by the processes of the social totality itself. This does not mean, however, that these processes are to be seen as identical. While both may share the process of the increasing domination of nature (in music, for example, 'human control over phonic materials'),[101] Adorno considers that there is nevertheless a crucial difference between the two types of rationality involved. However, he does not elaborate on this by specifying where 'aesthetic rationality' could fit within Weber's fourfold categorization of different forms of rationality. He clearly sees the dominant form of rationalization in Western society as coming under means-ends rationality (*Zweckrationalität*), but we are left to assume that 'aesthetic rationality', seen in the light of Kant's view of art as 'purposiveness without a purpose' (or 'end-orientatedness without an end' (*Zweckmäßigkeit ohne Zweck*)), corresponds to some extent to Weber's value rationality. But this is already a somewhat crude and ultimately unnecessary attempt to reduce Adorno's use of Weber's concepts to a simple formula, and Weber's own cautionary remarks about his typology need to be borne in mind here: 'the types mentioned are pure abstractions conceived for sociological purposes, to which real action may approximate to a greater or lesser degree or out of which (an even more frequent case) it is compounded'.[102] It is more useful to examine Adorno's notion of 'aesthetic rationality' in the context of his own use of the term and in relation to Weber's dominant category of means-ends rationality.

Adorno points out that music tends to be regarded today as a special 'zone of irrationality' – what the Frankfurt Institut für Sozialforschung in one of their joint publications had described as 'a sort of nature reservation or park in the midst of a highly rationalized society'.[103] Nevertheless, although autonomous music in the West is, in a particular sense, the 'voice of inwardness' (*Innerlichkeit*), an extreme expression of subjectivity, Adorno argues that Weber had demonstrated that its individual and apparently hermetic expressivity presupposes and is determined by rationality in a way which connects it with the dominant means-ends rationality of society itself. That is to say, the material itself is the result of a continuous and progressive process of rationalization. The tendency could be described as a movement towards the rationalization of those elements of music and musical material which were previously, relatively speaking, 'irrational' or, more accurately, 'unrationalized' – elements of the 'sounding material' of music which may have been incorporated or tolerated within compositional or performance practice, but without being controlled or controllable beyond a certain degree. Many examples could be given here in connection with Western art music, but a few must suffice to illustrate the point. It could be argued, for example, that the development of musical instrument technology and of performance technique has been characterized by progressive control over all aspects of the means of sound production, towards the ends of the purest possible sound throughout the whole range of the instrument (the element of control is seen at its extreme in the case of the new technology as applied to music). Also the context within which music is marketed, distributed and consumed represents a high degree of rationalization in the form of the ever-increasing efficiency of the culture industry. A compositional example Adorno gives is that of the techniques of motivic–thematic development and the disintegration of large-scale forms in Austro-German music, progressively rationalized towards total thematicism, the twelve-tone technique and multiple serialism – that is, towards what Adorno called the 'totally integrated work'.[104] The process is historical, and, on one level at least, directed towards greater control and domination of the musical means, greater logicality of form, greater 'comprehensibility', and so forth. To this extent, therefore, one can see parallels with the means-ends rationality of empirical reality, geared as this is towards greater efficiency of production and of (bureaucratic) control. The difference between *aesthetic* rationality and means-ends rationality, however, lies precisely in the relation of ends to means.

Adorno argues that, far from being irrational, 'autonomous' art works are highly rational in terms of the predetermined character of their material (e.g. tuning systems), and in the way in which their material is dominated through the logic of form and compositional techniques. The rationality of art works is, however, irrational, following Weber's argument, from the point of view of means-ends rationality, because the end towards which the highly rationalized means are directed is – if this can be described as an 'end' – a *lack of purpose*, in the sense of Kant's 'purposiveness without a purpose'. In this sense, Adorno argues, the rationality of autonomous art throws into question the (means-ends) rationality of empirical reality. As he puts it: 'Art is rationality criticizing itself without being able to overcome itself'.[105] Thus he argues that while the art work, as a closed system, shares the rationality of the external world like the Leibnizian monad, in that it is also the result of a process of the domination of nature through the application of reason (as, for example, the logic of form), art nevertheless 'does not reproduce the conceptual order of the external world'.[106] Adorno sees the rationality of art – particularly when taken to the extreme – as opposing itself to the instrumental rationality of the real world. Thus the rationality of external reality, as social reality, is both reflected and opposed by the autonomous art work's extreme rationality of form.[107]

'Mimesis' and 'ratio'

In order to discuss the contradictory character of aesthetic rationality and of mediation in relation to art, Adorno uses the traditional aesthetic concept of *mimesis* in conjunction with rationality (as *ratio*). However, Adorno does not use the concept of mimesis in its traditional sense as 'imitation of nature' or as 'representation' or 'reflection'. He uses it rather to indicate a process of 'adaptation to', of 'making oneself similar to the environment' whereby 'the outside serves as a model on to which the inside molds itself'.[108] Michael Cahn argues that 'Adorno's discussion of mimesis takes its starting point from a biological context', and he goes on to suggest that Adorno 'considers *mimicry* to be a prehistorical or zoological version of mimesis'.[109] That is to say, mimesis could be understood as a form of copying, or identifying with, the outside world in order to protect oneself from a threatening environment, as a means of survival. This is the continuation of primitive magic in art, 'an identification with the aggressor' whereby 'becoming one with the enemy immunizes you'.[110] In following the 'logic of the object' through mimicking it, art, according to Adorno, at the same time reflects it, criticizes it, and frees itself from it. In this case, however, what is being mimicked by art works is not a 'thing' which represents a threat, so Adorno argues, but a threatening *process* – the process of rationalization which characterizes the outside world, means-ends rationality itself.

Mimesis can therefore itself be seen, anthropologically speaking, as an earlier form of rationality: primitive man's attempt to gain control over the hostile forces of nature. In fact, taking an anthropological position and starting from Adorno's and Horkheimer's *Dialektik der Aufklärung*, Helga Gripp points to the dual-level character of mimesis/rationalization in Adorno: (i) mimesis as the dawning self-awareness of the Subject, and its movement towards freeing itself, through imitation and magic, from domination by nature; and (ii) rationality as the increasing domination of nature by the Subject through the power of reason as a process of demythologization, of disenchantment.[111] This reveals yet a further aspect of the inherently paradoxical character of art works. On the one hand, their mimetic aspect has itself to be seen as an earlier form of rationality, but of a kind which threatens to fall back into primitive magical suggestion. On the other hand, their rational aspect constantly opposes the 'magic spell' cast by the gestural, mimetic quality of the work by threatening to demystify it. Taking Adorno's statement in *Zur Metakritik der Erkenntnistheorie* that 'rationality is altogether the demythologization of mimetic modes of procedure',[112] Michael Cahn writes:

This secularization is the outcome of the mimetic taboo which purified myth to become enlightenment and simultaneously set them both in an inescapable and ineffaceable opposition.[113]

Aesthetic rationality can also be understood as a return to a form of mimetic adaptation, which has as its aim the 'bringing to speech' of the object through this conflict of opposites. Thus the contradictory character of aesthetic rationality could be formulated as follows: art uses the rationality of the world of empirical reality *mimetically* as a means of freeing itself from the repression of means-ends rationality. Mimetic adaptation constitutes the mediation of Subject and Object within the material structure of the art work. Adorno argues that, in internalizing the rationality of the external world to an extreme degree, the art work sets up resistance to it and at the same time goes beyond it. In *Ästhetische Theorie* he puts this as follows:

Why do works of art have to be rational? Because they need rationality to put up resistance against empirical life. To shape works of art rationally means to elaborate [*Durchformung*] and organize them thoroughly. This sets them off from the environment which is governed by instrumental *ratio* with its tendency to dominate nature. Although the latter is also the matrix of aesthetic rationality, art does gain independence from it. Art works oppose domination by mimetically adapting to it. If they are to produce something that is different in kind from the world of repression, they must assimilate themselves to repressive behaviour. Even those works of art which take a polemical stance against the *status quo* operate according to the principle they oppose. This principle deprives all being of its specific qualities. In sum, aesthetic rationality wants to make amends for the damage done by instrumental rationality outside art.[114]

Adorno also suggests in the essay 'Funktionalismus heute' [1965], that the process through which means-ends rationality finds its way into art works is that of sublimation:

Purposefulness without a purpose constitutes the sublimation of purpose. There is no sphere of the aesthetic in itself; it exists only as the force-field of such sublimation.[115]

Rationalization in art is identified by Adorno with construction, as the activity of 'shaping' or forming (*Gestaltung*) the material, and is associated with a number of related concepts. Self-reflection is implied, as opposed to the 'blindness' of expression; also technique, rationality (as *ratio*) and objectivity. Against this, expression could easily be regarded simply as the 'voice of the Subject', as 'subjective feelings', as opposed to the 'objectivity' of form, rationality and technique. Taking this view of 'expression', the concept of *mimesis* could also be seen as related to it, as the 'miming' of inner, subjective feelings in order to bring them to expression, as well as the 'mimicking' of bodily gestures. In his book on Wagner, Adorno writes:

It is no doubt true that all music has its roots in gesture ... and harbours it within itself. In the West, however, it has been spiritualized [*vergeistigt*] and interiorized [*verinnerlicht*] into expression, while at the same time the principle of construction subjects the overall flow of the music to a process of logical synthesis; great music strives for a balance of the two elements.[116]

But this also raises doubts about the purely 'subjective' character of expression. Adorno suggests that '[a]rt is expressive when a subjectively mediated, objective quality raises its voice to speak ...'.[117] The affective and bodily gestures also have 'objective', socio-cultural and historical significance. He continues:

If expression were merely a duplicate of subjective feelings, it would not amount to anything. ... A better model for understanding expression is to think of it not in terms of subjective feelings, but in terms of ordinary things and situations in which historical processes and functions have been sedimented, endowing them with the potential to speak.[118]

The contradiction presented by the Subject–Object relationship in art works is that rationality (as construction) is geared towards the production of something which is 'irrational' – at least from the perspective of instrumental reason. Adorno sees 'expression' as the result of the conflict between mimesis and rationality within the musical work – it is, as he puts it, a kind of 'interference phenomenon'.[119] This is what gives music its ability to 'speak' to us – what Adorno calls its 'language-character' (*Sprachcharakter*). It is what he identifies as the 'subjective paradox of art':[120]

Art aims at the production of a blind quality (expression) on the basis of reflection (form), the emphasis being on the aesthetic creation of blind expression, not on rationalization; it aims at 'the creation of things of which we do not know what they are'.[121]

This is the expressive quality of art: expression not as pure unmediated subjectivity, but as something which seems, through its formal construction, to have an objective character, and through its articulation as 'form' to transcend the merely personal.

Expression as objectivity: the language-character of music

Adorno argues that art's 'expressivity' is not about expressing specific emotions *per se*. Instead, it is mimesis, the artist's ability to mimic, which constitutes art's 'expressive quality', and 'which sets free in him [the artist] the expressed substance'.[122] This is the 'gestural' aspect of art works, which is one aspect of their 'language-character' – what Adorno calls 'mimetic language'. Musical gestures, for example, are associated with bodily gestures, and these have a further association with previous, extra-musical functionality – for instance, in work, dance, ceremony and ritual. The other aspect of the similarity of art works to language is their rationality, which gives to them the appearance of 'communicative language' through the logicality of their construction, along the lines of conceptual language (but which is, however, largely self-referential, even in modes of art which makes use of words as their material). The gestural, mimetic aspects of the work are mediated through the logicality and rationality of the work's form and structure, however, and are therefore no longer 'immediate'. These two aspects of art's similarity to language – the communicative and the mimetic – are contradictory, Adorno maintains, and he and Horkheimer in *Dialektik der Aufklärung* make a further distinction between them through the use of the terms *sign* (*Zeichen*; i.e. concept) and *image* (*Bild*):

As a system of signs, language is required to resign itself to calculation in order to know nature, and must discard the claim to be like her. As image, it is required to resign itself to mirror imagery in order to be nature entire, and must discard the claim to know her.[123]

Both these moments contribute to the 'expressive power' of art works, Adorno suggests, and the contradiction they embody can be understood in terms of Hegel's identity – non-identity opposition, as the split between concept and object of cognition. Thus, the 'sign', as concept, also has a repressive aspect, as the domination of given material and its rationaliz-ation in the context of a 'language system'. In musical terms, the 'concept', as suggested earlier, can be understood at the level of form, and also at the level of motif or theme and their 'working out'. On the other hand, the 'image', as mute imitation or representation – i.e. mimesis as an earlier, 'non-conceptual' stage in man's attempt to gain control over nature – provides a glimpse of that which lies outside 'concepts'. In this respect it is seen by Adorno as having a 'utopian moment', as non-identity. It points fleetingly to that which has escaped rationalization, as spontaneity and freedom from constraint. The use of the term 'image' suggests a directness and immediacy of expression beyond concepts. At the same time, the mimetic aspect of art is always in danger of falling back into the 'pre-linguistic', as identity with nature. The 'image' is given its power to speak, however, through its articulation and organization within the form and structure of the work, while the 'sign', as part of a system of signs, aspires in art works towards conceptual thought but, in failing, becomes itself an expressive image of communication. As Adorno puts it: 'the true language of art is speechless'.[124] Art works are like the sphinx: they seem to promise meaning through the logic of their form, but it is a meaning which remains concealed. In this way construction and expression converge, paradoxically, in their extremes.

Construction as subjectivity: sense of form

Furthermore, the form-giving aspects of the work are by no means to be regarded as mainly the result of 'conscious' processes of rationalization and control of musical material. Adorno's concept of *Formgefühl* – 'feeling (or sense) of form' – seems to identify important aspects of the compositional process which operate largely at the level of 'intuition' and 'spontaneity'. Adorno formulates the contradiction presented by the concept as follows:

What the theorists view as one big logical contradiction is quite familiar to the practitioners in their day-to-day work: control over the mimetic moment, the spontaneity of which is summoned up, destroyed and redeemed. Wilfulness amid spontaneity – this is the vital element of art. Indeed, its presence is an indication of the subjective ability of the artist, although it should be stressed that this process is objectively determined. Artists are acquainted with that ability; they call it their intuitive understanding of form [*Formgefühl*]. It is a mediating concept that solves the Kantian problem of how it is that art – for Kant an utterly non-conceptual thing – subjectively contains the moment of universality and necessity which is the preserve of discursive knowledge according to Kant's critique of reason.[125]

As is the case with a number of Adorno's concepts, the notion of *Formgefühl* seems to have been taken over directly from Schoenberg. In the fragment entitled 'Theory of Form' (written in 1924, but not published until later) Schoenberg argues that:

A true artist's inborn emotional and intellectual gifts have, by self cultivation and culture, become a faultlessly functioning apparatus that does not need the spur of conscious thought; he is as much at home in the world of the intellect as in the world of emotions, and it is this that distinguishes the true artist from the others.[126]

And in his *Harmonielehre* Schoenberg writes that he believes:

every era has a particular sense of form, a norm which tells the composer of that era how far he must go in working out an idea and how far he may not go.[127]

The concept as both Schoenberg and Adorno use it would seem to bring together several different and contradictory factors. In the light of the Marxian, Freudian and Weberian concepts discussed earlier in this chapter, these factors could be identified as: (i) the sublimation of the instinctual drives, harnessed towards 'positive social ends' (i.e. in this case musical composition) and therefore also shaped by socio-cultural pressures; (ii) the internalization of cultural norms (both the process of rationalization itself, as well as the 'gestures' which, through mimesis, are taken up and sublimated within the work's formal logic); and, following on from these, (iii) because of this absorption of cultural values and the technical training which goes with it, a 'spontaneity' and playfulness results which is able to function both within and against shared cultural assumptions to transcend them and create new forms – new forms which act as criticisms of old ones. *Formgefühl* – vague and all-embracing as it may be as a notion – has therefore to be understood as combining subjective and objective, conscious and unconscious, constructive and expressive features in one concept, particularly through the internalization of cultural norms[128] and the sublimation/repression of instinctual drives. It is therefore, as Adorno says, of particular importance as a mediating concept.

Mediation of opposites

As we have seen, for Adorno 'mediation' in this context is the interaction, through their opposition, of Subject and Object within the structure of art works. He discusses the unstable balance between these two moments in an unusually lucid passage in *Ästhetische Theorie* – a passage which encapsulates much of the area of concern of this chapter, and which is cited here at length:

For the art work as well as for aesthetics, [S]ubject and [O]bject are moments. Their relation is dialectical, which means that the several components of art – material, expression, form or whatever – are each simultaneously subjective and objective. Material is shaped by the hands of those who bring it into the work; expression, while objective in itself, is also a subjective input; similarly, form has to be produced with the necessities of the [O]bject in mind but by a [S]ubject, or else it remains a mechanically imposed mould. Not unlike the construction of a given in epistemology, the material often confronts the artist like an impenetrable wall; but material is also a sedimentation of the [S]ubject. Conversely, in expression which is ostensibly the most subjective component there is objectivity in the sense that the work of art is being transformed, as it incorporates and deals with expression; thus expression turns into a subjective mode of behaviour bearing the imprint of objectivity. The reciprocal relationship of [O]bject and [S]ubject in art works is a precarious balance, not an identity of the two.[129]

Thus the simple dualism suggested by a distinction between expression as subjectivity and construction as objectivity cannot be sustained within a dialectical analysis such as Adorno's. His argument that the opposites mediate each other could be presented in the following terms (drawing freely on a model put forward originally by Jürgen Ritsert):[130] 'form' can be understood as reified or 'congealed' expression, as the 'objectification of the Subject', and must therefore be seen as containing an element of subjectivity; 'expression' can be understood as the result of the tension between mimesis and rationality, as the sublimation of gesture through construction, and must therefore be seen as containing an element of objectivity (in that the rationality of art works is also related to the dominant rationality of empirical, social reality, while the gestures taken up and sublimated by the formal logic of art works are also, in their origins, social gestures).

Taking this a stage further, I suggest that this interaction of the individual and the social, as the Subject–Object relation in Adorno's concept of mediation, can be understood dialectically on three interacting levels:

(1) At the level of empirical reality (i.e. in modern industrialized societies) the relation between the individual and the social totality is alienated and characterized by fragmentation (the relation of artist to society being only a special case of this). The 'total administration' of society is experienced by the individual as Weber's 'iron cage of rationality'. The Subject–Object relationship at this level, i.e. between individual and society, is *antagonistic*.

(2) At the level of the aesthetic, sublimated/repressed social antagonisms and internalized socio-cultural norms (including the process of rationalization itself) are displaced into the arena of the artistic material. The stage on which the conflict now plays itself out is the structure of the work of art, in the tension between mimesis and rationality, expression and construction, as the immanent dialectic of the material. Social antagonisms exist within the art work only in 'cipher' form, as deviations from the handed-down formal norms, as genres, formal types and schemata, to create new or modified forms. The Subject–Object relationship at this level, i.e. between artist and material, becomes *productive*.

(3) Again at the level of empirical reality, individual works of art encounter the dominant modes of production, reproduction, distribution and consumption of society at large. Here the tension is that between, on the one hand, the autonomy of works of art and, on the other, the commodity values of an exchange society in which the works themselves become commodities. Works become assimilated and are themselves transformed into norms for future musical behaviour, becoming part of the historically available material. At the same time, as modes of cognition, art works also implicitly criticize the dominant rationality of empirical reality, but do so through their form, whereby the handed-down material is re-contextualized. The Subject–Object relationship at this level may therefore be seen to have two contradictory aspects: (i) it is *normative* (in the sense of works of art becoming themselves assimilated to the musical material as handed-down norms of musical behaviour); and (ii), it can also be seen as oppositional and *critical* (in the dual sense of the work of art as 'thing' criticizing the means-ends rationality of the outside world through its own 'functionlessness,' and as 'form' deviating from the handed-down formal norms, genres and schemata to create new structures).

In conclusion

I have argued that Adorno's concept of mediation, while essentially derived from Hegel, needs to be understood in conjunction with other ideas taken from Marx, Freud and Max Weber. The concept of 'objective spirit' (*objektiver Geist*) becomes partly identified with Weber's concept of rationalization, in particular as the progress of technique and technology. It is this, as an aspect of the means-ends rationality dominating Western industrialized society, which, in Freudian terms, is sublimated/repressed in autonomous art, and which according to arguments put forward by Critical Theorists in the early 1930s, provides a link between the Marxian economic base and ideological superstructure. The rationality principle, in its sublimated form as aesthetic rationality (Kant's 'purposiveness without a purpose'), then comes to contradict and critically oppose the dominant means-ends rationality of society. Underlying the concept of mediation, in all its versions as discussed here, is the fundamental interaction and opposition of 'nature' and 'history' examined in Chapter 1 in terms of Adorno's debt to Lukács and Benjamin. One particular version of this dialectic is the mediation of expression and construction, as *mimesis* and *ratio* – the sublimation of heteronomous gesture within the formal logic of autonomous music. I have suggested that, in this way, Adorno's concept of mediation converges with his concept of the dialectic of musical material through the concept of *form*.

Nevertheless, the concept of mediation remains highly elusive and, central as it is to his theory of musical material, was never systematically explored by Adorno on a theoretical level.[131] Hence, in this chapter I have attempted to make explicit a context of ideas which, I argue, goes some way towards making sense of a complex and otherwise rather vague concept as generally used. With this context of ideas in mind, we now turn to an examination of Adorno's concept of form.

4   A material theory of form

> In art, the criterion of success is twofold: first, works of art must be able to
> integrate layers of material [*Stoffschichten*] and details into their imma-
> nent law of form; and, second, they must not try to erase the fractures left
> by the process of integration, preserving instead in the aesthetic whole the
> traces of those elements which resisted integration.[1]
>
> Adorno, *Aesthetic Theory* (1970)

'Material refers to all that is being formed', writes Adorno in *Ästhetische
Theorie*.[2] As we have seen, however, Adorno insists that 'material' is not
simply that which is formed and shaped in the compositional process of any
particular musical work, as 'raw material' (*Stoff*); musical material is itself
already historically 'pre-formed'. That is to say, musical material is mediated
not only because it is shaped, more or less consistently, within the form of the
work itself, but precisely because it is already historically and culturally
pre-formed before any individual act of composition even begins.

But here lies the ambiguity: Adorno appears to emphasize the general
concept of material over that of the particular musical work. It is the
'progress of musical material' he seems to see as a manifestation of the
'progress of spirit', rather than the individual musical work.[3] One is left to
assume that the general progress of the material can exist only in and
through its manifestation in particular works, although this is not directly
stated. This relative obscurity in Adorno's concept of musical material can
be clarified through an examination of his concept of form – a concept
which is confusing because it is used by him in two distinct but interrelated
senses: form at the level of the pre-formed musical material, and form at the
level of the individual musical work. The aim here is twofold: to examine
the relationship between these two levels of form, as the mediation of
universal and particular, and to consider the problem of formal integration
in relation to what Adorno sees as the disintegration of musical material.[4]

1   The immanent dialectic of musical material

In opposition to the traditional theory of form (*Formenlehre*), as well as to
the tendency to emphasize pitch as the dominant structuring parameter in

music, Adorno puts forward a concept of form as 'the sum total of all moments of logicality or, more broadly, consistency in art works'.[5] Form is the totality of moments through which a work is organized meaningfully.[6] And in *Ästhetische Theorie* he writes:

Aesthetic form ought to be the objective organization of all that appears in a work of art, with an eye to rendering it consistent and articulate. Form is the non-repressive synthesis of diffuse particulars; it preserves them in their diffuse, divergent and contradictory condition. Form therefore is the unfolding of truth.[7]

As we have seen, Adorno takes over directly Hegel's conception of art as a mode of cognition (*Erkenntnis*), arguing that art is not primarily concerned with pleasure, 'usefulness', or even beauty, but 'with a revelation of truth'.[8] In the conceptual model put forward at the end of Chapter 1, I suggested that the concept of 'truth content' in Adorno's aesthetics needs to be taken on several interacting levels. At the level of the autonomous work truth can be understood, initially at least, as consistency of form, the identity of the 'idea' of the work with its structure. Such an assertion cannot be taken simply at face value, however, as Adorno sees the work of art as a force-field of tensions rendered articulate and meaningful through consistency of form. This complex of ideas needs to be followed through in relation to Adorno's dual-level concept of form.

On one level, 'meaning' is already present in the pre-formed material, in the sense of culturally shared understandings of socially and historically mediated aesthetic norms and conventions. At this level (which could be called the general or universal level), form has to be seen as a fundamental attribute of the material itself. The material is already 'formed' and is not 'natural' – genres, forms and schemata themselves being 'material', as well as tuning systems, compositional techniques and stylistic norms. On another level, these conventional meanings – as musical gestures, figurations, formulae – are dismantled, deconstructed and re-contextualized within the new complex of meaning represented by the 'immanent law of form' of the particular musical work. At this level (which could be called the 'particular' level), form is the articulation, organization and re-contextualization of the historically available 'layers' of material to give them new meaning at the level of the individual composition. It is in the field of tension between these two levels that Adorno appears to locate the 'truth content' of a work: the consistency of its immanent form in relation to the divergent socio-historical tendencies of its pre-formed material. The relationship between these two levels can be examined by means of a number of fundamental binary oppositions.

Material: form and content

Adorno differentiates between 'material' and 'content' (*Inhalt*), in relation to the traditional form–content dichotomy. 'Material' does not simply equal 'content'. While Adorno argues for the unity of form and content, he at the same time insists that they need to be understood as distinct categories, in that the one is mediated by the other. For Adorno 'content' in music is literally 'what is going on' in the piece (*das Geschehende*), what 'happens' to its basic material in the process of its shaping and of its unfolding through time – for example, to its motifs and themes, as developments, transitions, 'workings out', as a process of 'becoming' (*Werden*). That is to say, it is the individual 'structure' of any particular work. 'Material', on the other hand, is what the composer controls and shapes, ranging from sounds (as pitches, timbres, durations, dynamics), through connections of any kind made between them (as melody, harmony, counterpoint, rhythm, texture), up to the most advanced means available for integrating them at the level of form (as we have seen, he considers forms, genres, and also styles to be part of the material, together with compositional procedures, techniques and technology).[9] For Adorno, the material 'is all that the artist is confronted by, all that he must make a decision about, and that includes forms as well, for forms too can become materials'.[10] Nevertheless, the total accumulated stock of musical material is not all available to the composer at any particular period:

The concept of material took on a serious technical connotation in the 1920s. ... What has in fact happened can be described as an enormous expansion of available materials, breaking down the old boundaries between species of art in the wake of the historical emancipation of form in art. People on the outside have tended to overestimate this development. In the actual practice of art there are compensatory factors like the artist's taste and, more important, the state of development of the material. Small, indeed, is the amount of concretely useful material, never mind the plethora that is available *in abstracto*. That small amount must be such as not to collide with the stage of development of spirit [*Geist*].[11]

As we saw in Chapter 2 Adorno contends that the freedom of the composer in relation to the available musical material is not total, as Krenek had argued it was. Adorno insists that the composer's choice of material is always constrained by the stage reached by the development of expressive needs and technical means at any particular historical period (by what he calls, after Hegel, 'the stage of development of spirit').

Like Schoenberg, Adorno argues that form in relation to the individual work is *substantive*, in that it should arise in response to the demands of the historically pre-formed material without doing violence to it or being arbitrarily imposed on it.[12] In this sense it would appear that Adorno is saying that each individual composition should be in effect an indicator of the stage reached by the musical material at any particular historical period. It is a response at the level of form (i.e. its own 'immanent law of form') to the inherent tendencies of the pre-formed material. This response is not simply a reflection of the current state of the material, however. It at the same time also acts as a *critique* of it, in the sense suggested at the end of the previous chapter – that is, it negates and reconceives the pre-formed, handed-down material, as a historically 'necessary' response to the problems posed by the material at its previous stage. In this way it creates a new form which arises out of a critique of the old, and which then contributes itself to the overall dialectical movement of the material. Furthermore, as has been indicated in Chapters 2 and 3, the dialectic of the material is seen simultaneously by Adorno as partaking in the 'progress of spirit', as the dialectic of Enlightenment. That is, form represents the progressive rationalization, integration and control of all aspects of the musical material at the same time as the material itself, as handed-down genres and forms, is tending towards fragmentation and disintegration. For Adorno the 'critical' and 'authentic' work strives for a consistency of form which is achieved without concealing the fragmentary character of its pre-formed, handed-down material.

Thus 'form' cannot in fact be separated from 'content' and from 'material', as a set of abstract and invariant formal categories – even though categories of this kind have undoubtedly had their effect, both as ideal types and as handed-down forms and genres. One of the difficulties, therefore, in discussing form is its very ubiquity: it can seem to apply 'to just about everything that is artlike in art'.[13] This is so, Adorno argues, because art exists only through its form, and our contact with it is only through its form:

Form refutes the view that art works have immediate being. They do not. They owe their existence to form, which is therefore their mediator, the objective condition of their being reflected in themselves. Mediation here refers to the relation of the parts to each other and to the whole, as well as to the elaboration of details.[14]

Adorno defines form as the articulation of a whole into its complexes, its partial totalities, while recognizing also that '[a]rt of the highest calibre pushes beyond totality towards a state of fragmentation'.[15] Thus from the perspective of Adorno's modernist aesthetic there is a historical tendency for 'forms' to become 'second order matter' (*Stoffen zweiten Grades*), and for art to undermine its traditional forms. Thus forms and genres become in their turn part of the available material.

Form and genre

The traditional concept of form, as conveyed by the term *Formenlehre*, contains formal types like song, sonata, rondo, variations, fugue, etc.

which are regarded by Adorno as belonging essentially to the handed-down musical material. And the line between these formal types and the concept of *genre* (*Gattung*) is not always a clear one, at least in the senses in which Adorno uses the terms – whether fugue is to be regarded as a form or a genre is a case in point. The generally accepted distinction between the two – that 'form' in its traditional (architectonic) sense indicates the surface articulation of a piece as a whole into its larger sections and sub-sections, and that 'genre' refers to 'norms of musical behaviour' understood in relation to previous social functions[16] – is recognized by Adorno, although his own dialectical concept of form goes beyond the merely architectonic. His concept of 'form' (which has to be seen as embracing both formal types and genres) is dynamic, in that it focuses on the emergence, development and disintegration of genres and formal types as aspects of the historical dialectic of musical material.

Adorno considers that '[t]he significant aspect of genres and forms can be found in the historical demands of their materials'.[17] He takes the fugue as an example: that it is bound up with tonality and tonal relations, and significantly emerged after the demise of modality to become the most highly rationalized form of polyphony with the rise of tonality. The fugue was both a response to the historical demands of the musical material (as tonality and the requirement that the handed-down contrapuntal practices adapt to meet the possibilities of tonality) and also a legitimation of the new situation.

Adorno argues that genres and formal types, having emerged in response to the historical demands of the material, develop a dynamic of their own. They become 'objective' through consensus. On the one hand, he argues that genres and formal types have long since lost their power as norms, in that the historical tendency towards the extreme individualization and nominalism of art works has served to undermine their validity. On the other hand, he also appears to be saying that the handed-down genres and formal types continue to maintain their influence, if only as a kind of 'negative presence', and it is the subversion of this which gives the work of art its *raison d'être*:

At the present time art is most alive precisely when it subverts the validity of its generic concept. Then again, this subversion is nothing new but a familiar theme in art history: there has always been a tendency to break the taboo on impure or hybrid types.[18]

The search for universals, therefore, has also had to go beyond genres, formal types and stylistic norms to a level which can also account for the disintegration of norms, possibly in terms of some notion of 'invariants'. For Adorno, however, even the notion of invariant factors like *time* in music are suspect. This point will be discussed at greater length later in this chapter.

Thus, to reformulate the dual-level model we have been using so far, Adorno's concept of form can be understood as (i) *normative* – i.e. in the sense of handed-down 'norms of musical behaviour', as genres, formal types and schemata; and (ii) *critical* – i.e. in the sense of deviation from, or subversion of formal norms to create new structures. Adorno sees the relation between these two levels as dynamic and 'progressive', but also, with the breakdown of the binding character of formal norms, as tending towards disintegration. The fundamental problem thrown up by any critical and authentic work of art is how simultaneously to contain and to reveal this disintegration within the consistency of its form.

Universal and particular

Adorno considers nevertheless that genres, formal types and tonal schemata do represent one of the levels of universality which constitute art's 'language-character' (*Sprachcharakter*). It is within and against this that the particularity of the individual work comes into being, as 'content' (*Inhalt*), or specific 'structure' (*Struktur*) – what Adorno calls 'what is going on' (*das Geschehende*) in the piece, as *deviation* from the schema. This level may also be understood as constituting music's 'subjective moment', as 'expression'. (However, as discussed in Chapter 3, 'subjective expression' – as the unique particular of the work – has also to be seen as containing an element of universality and of objectivity, in line with Adorno's assertion that mediation only takes place through and in each of the extremes, without there being some middle term which mediates between them; likewise, the 'objective' formal schemata and genres as handed down must be seen as being a sedimentation of previous subjectivity.) Of genre as a universal Adorno writes:

The individual work that simply subordinates itself to a genre does not do justice to it. It is more fruitful if there is conflict between them. Historically, genre has gone through several phases: from legitimation (of old genres) to creation (of new ones) to destruction (of genres *per se*).[19]

Adorno's model of the interaction between universal and particular levels as constituting music's language-character calls to mind Saussure's *langue–parole* distinction.[20] Like the binary relationships within Saussure's linguistic model, Adorno's oppositional terms can be applied at a number of different levels. At the level of *style*, for example – defined by Adorno as 'conventions in a state of balance, however precarious, with the Subject'[21] – style could be seen as a particular in relation to the general characteristics of tonality as an idiom at a specific historical period (like the Viennese Classicism of the late eighteenth and early nineteenth centuries). On the other hand, the all-pervading style of Viennese Classicism would be a universal within and against which the particularity of a Haydn, Mozart or Beethoven functioned. Likewise, genres could be understood as interacting with style, form with genre, specific structure with conventional forms, and so on.

Although it could be argued that universals in art have no real existence apart from their mediation in particular works of art, they are, Adorno maintains, nevertheless indispensable:

For art, universals such as genres are as indispensable as they are confining. This has something to do with art's similarity to language. Language is both hostile to the particular and concerned with its redemption. Its particularity is mediated by universals; it is a constellation of universals. But language does not do justice to universals, if they are employed rigidly as though they had being in themselves. What it does is use universals by narrowly concentrating on the particular it wants to express. Thus linguistic universals are true to the extent to which they are subject to a countervailing dynamic ...[22]

By 'countervailing dynamic' Adorno means the total negation of universals within the work – that is to say, through the uncompromising dissolution of conventions as part of the compositional process, whereby universals can be understood as an aspect of the material with which, and against which, the composer works.[23]

Schema and deviation

Theory of form, as *Formenlehre*, has come to have the restricted sense of formal *schemata*, a limiting of the concept of form which follows on, Adorno maintains, from equating form as *architectonic schema* with the specificity of the individual work, what is actually 'going on' within the work – its 'content' (*Inhalt*), so to speak. In other words, it simplistically confuses *form* and *content* in two different ways: by suggesting that what is 'going on' in the individual work is identical to its formal stereotype; and, conversely, that content – as 'expressive content' and as 'musical elements' – is something separate from form. Adorno does not deny the significance of the traditional formal types categorized by the *Formenlehre*, both for the music of the 'Great Tradition' and for music since the breakdown of that tradition. He sees the purpose of technical analysis, however, as being the exploration of what he calls the *structure* of the work, as distinct from both formal schemata and from basic musical elements. He defines 'structure' not as 'the mere grouping of musical parts according to traditional formal schemata', but 'rather as having to do with what is going on, musically, *underneath* these formal schemata'.[24] It is in this sense that one can understand a work's 'structure' as being its 'content' (as opposed to its 'form'). But, as Adorno recognizes, there is a risk of over-simplification here – increased by the generally confusing use of the term 'structure' as a replacement for the term 'form' since the 1950s (and Adorno's particular use of the concept 'structure' differs in many respects from Dahlhaus's attempt at a definition of the term in *Darmstädter Beiträge zur Neuen Musik X* of 1966).[25] What Adorno emphasizes is the dialectical character of form, the mediation of the universal and the particular within musical works – i.e. the mediation of form and content, the relationship of schema to what is going on underneath it (*das Geschehende*), and which deviates from it. As he put it in his talk 'Zum Probleme der musikalischen Analyse' [1969]:

For, contrary to widespread belief, even that which is going on underneath is not simply a second and quite different thing, but is in fact mediated by the formal schemata, and is partly, at any given moment, *postulated* by the formal schemata, while on the other hand it consists of deviations which in their turn can only be at all understood through their relationship to the schemata.[26]

The task of technical-immanent analysis is therefore, for Adorno, the investigation of 'this already complex relationship of *deviation* to *schema*, rather than just the one or the other alone'.[27] And while this relationship is at its most obvious in music of the 'Great Tradition', Adorno insists that it can be found to persist in residual form even in music which has broken with that tradition.

The social content of form

In his essay 'Form in der Neuen Musik' Adorno argues that, as instrumental music of the bourgeois period 'knows no content derived immediately from the substance of the outside world', such content (*Gehalt*) has sedimented itself in the handed-down forms.[28] This is to be heard, he claims, as a residual echo in, for example, the rondo as round dance, with its alternation of couplet and refrain. And, following Wagner, he suggests the clatter of dishes can still be detected in autonomous music, given its origins in eighteenth-century *Tafelmusik*.[29] This 'secret content' of genres and formal types, the residue within autonomous music of a previous immediate social function, combined with the normalizing function of the genres, forms and schemata as part of the store of conventions handed down as musical material, constitutes one aspect of the generalized and 'objective', socially mediated dimension of musical works. On the other hand, it is through the logicality of its 'immanent form', the internal consistency of its structure, that art also defines itself as separate and different from the real world, and thus critically opposes empirical reality. In *Ästhetische Theorie* Adorno puts this mediation of opposites as follows:

Assuming that one has to differentiate form from content before grasping their mediation, we can say that art's opposition to the real world is in the realm of form; but this occurs, generally speaking, in a mediated way such that aesthetic form is a sedimentation of content. What seem like pure forms in art, namely those of traditional music ... derive from external content such as dance.[30]

For Adorno, 'musicality'[31] consists in the ability to rediscover the sublimated content of traditional forms and genres and to change their function within the specific shape of the work.[32] This can be seen to operate in a number of ways. It had, he maintains, always been a feature of the works of the 'Great Tradition', but until the second half of the nineteenth century the handed-down forms, although continually transformed, had not disintegrated under the pressure of expressive needs. In the later nineteenth century and early twentieth century, with the disintegration of tonality, genres and formal types had themselves become part of 'content', subjected to displacement and fragmentation within a new context of meaning – for example, the treatment of sonata form, of the symphony, and of genres like ländler, waltz and march in Mahler, Schoenberg and Berg. But it was Wagner, he argues, who prepared the way for this revolutionary change of relationship to handed-down material:

With its hostility to standard forms [*Typen*] and its playful use of them, Wagner's musical form not only does away with the feudal remnants of musical material, it also makes the material incomparably more pliant to the composer's will than ever before.[33]

And at a particular stage – seen at its extreme in the 1950s and early 1960s – formal norms apparently disappear altogether in the attempt to purge the musical material of all conventional/expressive residues. This last development left music with the triumph of construction, Adorno considers, to the extent that the total rationalization of the autonomous work becomes the total rejection of the heteronomous world outside.

The contradictory character of form

As noted in earlier chapters, Adorno argues that, although works of art masquerade as pure spontaneity, as unmediated expression, and as 'nature', this is an illusion, a semblance (*Schein*), in that they are in fact constructed, their expression being an aspect of their structure, and their 'naturalness' being a product of history. They give the appearance of pure immediacy, of pure content, but exist in fact only through their form, which mediates their content, their expression. They give the appearance of utter

uniqueness, but this is the product of the organization and re-contextualization of their pre-formed, socially mediated material, which includes the
conventionalized genres and formal schemata. Authentic autonomous
works function as a critique of the instrumental rationality of the outside
world, although they are mediated by that same rationality through the
logicality of their form. And through 'the law of their form' they construct
a unity, a complex of meaning consistent within itself, yet a unity which,
Adorno maintains, is no longer, contrary to the general view, a synthesis of
diverse particulars in the sense of a harmonistic totality. He considers that
this is the particular problem for the musical work in the modernist period:
to construct a unity which does not conceal the fragmentary and chaotic
state of the handed-down musical material, and yet which does not simply
mirror fragmentation through identification with it, but which is able to
embody, negate and transcend it in the sense of the Hegelian *Aufhebung*.
This, for Adorno, constitutes the critical, self-reflective and cognitive
character of musical form,[34] something he had attempted to formulate in
his early writings on music in the 1920s and 1930s, particularly in relation
to Schoenberg in his essay 'Der dialektische Komponist' (1934). As he was
later to put it in 'Form in der neuen Musik' (1966):

the formal problem for composers today: is disintegration possible through
integration? The position reached by compositional consciousness is such that it is
only through the critical dissolution [*Auflösung*] of the meaning-giving aspects of
the composition, of that context which allows meaning any positive existence, that
the synthesizing, meaning-giving elements of composition hold their own. Integration and disintegration are entwined.[35]

2   Immanent analysis: Berg, Sonata op. 1

Although this question – how to construct integrated musical works in the
face of the disintegration of musical norms – lies at the heart of all Adorno's
writings on music, his analyses of Berg's music are of particular interest
because, it could be argued, they take the composer as a paradigm case for
the process of 'integration through disintegration'. In the main, the Berg
analyses date from the 1930s – a period when Adorno was consolidating his
theory of musical material in relation to the music of the composers of the
Second Viennese School, and when he was still very much under the
influence of Berg as both composer and teacher. (Most of the analyses in
fact date from 1937, when the memory of the composer and his untimely
death was still acute.) Most were published initially as part of Willi Reich's
book on Berg[36] and included in the 1968 Berg[37] book. Some were written in
the intervening years.[38] Overall they are, as Adorno said shortly after the
appearance of the 1968 volume, 'traditional analyses of the kind which

brings the "whole" down to the smallest possible number of what one calls "germinal cells" [*Keimzellen*], and then shows how the music develops out of them'.[39] He also says that 'there is no question but that Berg himself ... would also still have approved of this traditional kind of analysis'.[40] Before discussing the broader implications – as well as the limitations – of Adorno's analyses in relation to the weight of sociological and philosophical interpretation he makes them bear, I will first summarize his analysis of one of Berg's works in some detail: the Piano Sonata op. 1. This draws mainly on the analysis contained in the Berg book,[41] but also makes reference to the 1930 essay discussed in Chapter 1, 'Berg and Webern – Schönberg's heirs'.[42]

Berg: Piano Sonata op. 1

Adorno sees Berg's first published work, dating from 1907–8, as highly significant because he considers that it contains in embryo practically all those processes which distinguish the composer's subsequent work. It is both an 'apprentice piece' – as he puts it, 'one could well imagine that it came out of the solution of a set task on sonata form'[43] – and at the same time a work which convincingly extends its models (in particular Schoenberg's Chamber Symphony of 1906, but also the harmonic world of Wagner's *Tristan*). Although he considers the piece to be very successful in its own terms ('thoroughly articulated up to the last note, it can make the claim to complete success')[44] it also, he maintains, leaves clear traces of the process of its production within its structure:

compulsion and necessity of success are stamped on it; the hand which subdued the reluctant material [*Stoff*] left its traces everywhere in the shape of the work thus won; everywhere the experienced eye becomes aware of the process of production in the product itself.[45]

Adorno argues that in one sense the material of the piece is 'sonata form' itself, especially as handed on by Schoenberg in works like the First String Quartet op. 7, and more particularly the Chamber Symphony op. 9:

To be sure, his indebtedness to Schoenberg in the Sonata lies incomparably deeper than that of the basic musical 'stuff' [*Musikstoff*] they both so strikingly had in common, and indeed transformed in so strikingly similar a manner. It is the idea [*die Idee*] of the sonata itself, characterized as it is by that exclusive through-construction [*Durchkonstruktion*], as motivic–thematic working, which refuses all fortuitousness and economizes with a minimum of given material [*mit einem Minimum von Gegebenem*]...[46]

The 'extended tonality' and intensive motivic working moving towards the total thematicism of Schoenberg's music of this period certainly provided

Berg with his 'material', to the extent that, as Adorno shows, Berg even seems to be borrowing thematic ideas from the First Chamber Symphony. (Apart from the general pervasiveness of the interval of the fourth – perfect and augmented – in both works, specific examples he gives of these references are: a comparison of the opening motif of the Berg (g–c–f♯) with the main theme of the Schoenberg, initially at bar 8, 'cello (a–d–g♯); and a comparison of the semiquaver motif in the second subject at bar 30 of the Berg with what he calls 'the end of the transition theme' (*Schluß des Überleitungsmodells*) of the Schoenberg – presumably the semiquaver figure in the viola and 'cello at the end of bar 38, although it is by no means certain that this is the passage he means.[47]) Adorno points out, however, that although the model on which Berg is drawing is that of the Chamber Symphony, the influence does not run to the large-scale conception of sonata form which characterizes that work. He writes of Berg's op. 1:

> Its didactic unpretentiousness as a sonata movement is unaffected by the principle of the bracketing of several movements into one carried through by Schoenberg's First Quartet and Chamber Symphony. But the Sonata is so indebted to these works in all other respects that the assertion is valid that Berg's stylistic development springs from the compositional problems of the Chamber Symphony...[48]

The Berg Sonata, self-contained as it is, still remains a 'first movement',[49] and Adorno admits that 'its completion through [the addition of] other movements, although certainly not needed, is thoroughly feasible'.[50] The general point, that Berg remained indebted to the formal experimentation of the early Schoenberg in all his subsequent works, is undoubtedly valid.[51]

Adorno identifies the following technical means as being those particularly characteristic of the sonata principle (i.e. by implication that handed on by Brahms and the early Schoenberg): 'the technique of developing variation of the shortest thematic "paradigms" [*Modelle*]; connections made by means of motivic "remnants" [*Reste*]; derivation of all "accompaniment" from the thematic material'.[52] And furthermore, the overriding principle is that 'an expansive profusion of thematic figures should, in the smallest space, be extracted from a minimum of motivic material, but at the same time be brought into a unity of a kind whereby the abundance of shapes does not, in spite of the work's brevity, fall into confusion'.[53] This can be seen as a reformulation of the question posed by Adorno (see above) as the formal problem faced by composers in the modernist period: 'is disintegration possible through integration?'[54]

What Adorno sets out to demonstrate, through an analysis of the exposition of the Sonata, is the way in which Berg's music, even at this early stage, mediates between conventional formal types and new musical means. He argues that Berg does not simply mix the new musical means with the traditional, but 'as the master of the smallest transition he develops them out of the traditional [forms and schemata]; he does not mediate between styles but rather between the new material and the pre-given'.[55] Thus the aim of the analysis is to explore the 'immanent dialectic of the musical material' within the structure of the work, as the mediation of new and old and, effectively – although it is not made particularly explicit in the analysis – the dialectic of expression and construction. This dialectic, as 'mediation of opposites', can be understood on a number of levels.

Above all there is the mediation of, on the one hand, the architectonic scheme of the sonata form, as reified formal archetype (with its clearly articulated sections and sub-sections, differentiated subject-groups, transitions, repeated exposition, etc.) and, on the other hand, the tendency towards rethinking the idea of overall unity 'from the bottom up', so to speak. This is the tendency whereby the motivic power of the thematic material, by means of 'developing variation', threatens the 'top down' unity of the sonata format through blurring or dissolving the distinctions between expository and transitional/developmental areas. Adorno recognizes, of course, that this 'mediation of opposites' had been an important aspect of the evolution of the sonata principle right from the beginning – or certainly since Beethoven – and it is one of those features which he regards as constituting the historical tendency of musical material. His interest in the analysis of the Sonata op. 1 is to identify how Berg re-creates this dynamic aspect of the form by using the most advanced musical means available to him at that time.

A specific aspect of the mediation of formal archetype and new technical means is the way in which the tonal schema underlying the traditional sonata form, and the relations of tonality itself as a system, are modified, extended, and also opposed by new harmonic means. These are, in the case of Berg's Sonata, essentially those of Schoenberg's Chamber Symphony op. 9 – the modification of the hierarchical, non-symmetrical features of traditional tonality by means of non-hierarchical, symmetrical scale and harmonic formations; that is to say, the use of chords built on fourths, the whole-tone scale (and the use of chords built on it, i.e. augmented triads) and an extreme (but still essentially tonal) chromaticism. All of this constitutes what Adorno calls 'the identity of the pre-motivic "material" [*die Identität des vormotivischen* 〉*Materials*〈]',[56] and he points to important differences between Berg's and Schoenberg's handling of the material:

The Chamber Symphony began with fourths: harmonically in the introduction, melodically in the first subject group. They are stated without mediation and with all the confidence of conquest. With Berg, on the other hand, they first appear at b.26 of the Sonata and have a harmonic function. The fourth chord sonority f♯–b–e is introduced in such a way that the critical pitch e, as a suspension to d (that is to say, related to what is admittedly only a somewhat circumscribed tonic chord of the basic tonality of b minor) seems 'foreign' to the harmony.[57]

At the same time, however, the differences between Berg and Schoenberg in the handling of what are essentially the same harmonic materials are also due to the use Berg makes of a noticeably Wagnerian approach to chromaticism – a feature which Adorno emphasizes in his 1930 essay on Berg and Webern, but not in the 1937 analysis. In the 1930 essay he argues that:

the differences are obvious. Not merely in a certain sweetness of the harmony which frequently imposes the whole-tone chord on major ninths and imparts greater significance to the ninth than Schönberg ever did, suggesting Debussy, Skrjabin and even Reger. This harmonic sweetness, which at times frankly exploits the erotic Tristan quality, is not fortuitous. It is conditioned by a harmony essentially chromatic, which does not set forth the independence of neighboring tones so decisively as does Schönberg, but imposes the new chords upon a Wagnerlike continuo on the leading-tone.[58]

Adorno attempts to demonstrate in the course of his analysis how Berg succeeds in generating his fourth-chord sonorities from out of the essentially tonal language with which he is working in the Sonata, allows them points of independence, and then dissolves them back into the 'tonal flux' once more.[59] As he puts it: 'Berg reduces the imposing, piled-up fundamental intervals of the Chamber Symphony to unobtrusive, sliding leading-note relationships'.[60] Adorno also attempts to show how Berg's manipulation of the 'pre-motivic material' is not to be separated from the motivic–thematic processes of the work – how, in fact, the motivic cells of the piece are so designed from the outset to enable this identity of horizontal and vertical to come about, and at the same time to enable endless transitions and connections to be created between apparently disparate ideas. In 1930 he wrote:

With Berg ... the principle of transition, of imperceptible transition, takes precedence from the start, and the residue of harmony based on tonal cadences ... is nothing but an indication of this principle. The units of which his music is built up are ... infinitely small, and, as such are interchanged at will regardless of their differences.[61]

Adorno takes the first four bars of the Sonata (the antecedent phrase of the first subject) and identifies three motifs which he regards as the 'germinal cells' of the whole work and which are related to each other (see Ex. 1).[62] His account of this segmentation is as follows: motif (b) is a free inversion and, he suggests, could also be understood as a retrograde variant of motif (a); motif (c) is derived from the rhythm and the inversion of the minor

Example 1

second step between the final f♯ of motif (a) and the first two g's of motif (b).[63] He then goes on to discuss the consequent phrase of the first subject (bars 4–11) in terms of its derivation from the motivic material of the antecedent. He particularly focuses on the varied repetition of motif (a) (transposed) which appears in bar 6 (r.h., e♭–b♭–a, l.h., b–f♯–f), which he describes as 'somewhere between true repetition and retrograde, something one could call "axis rotation" [*Achsendrehung*]'.[64] This technique of the permutation or 'interversion' of the sequence of intervals in a motif is certainly of great significance in the piece, and Adorno argues that 'one could well see it as a precursor [*eine Vorform*] of the later serial technique; the motif is used in the sense of a "*Grundgestalt*"'.[65] Interversion, together with the recycling of what he calls 'motivic remnants' (*Reste*) and the extension and contraction of the intervals of a motif (so much a feature of the Chamber Symphony), are those techniques, he considers, which enable Berg to 'dissolve' (*auflösen*) one thematic idea almost imperceptibly into another, mediating between what Adorno later came to formulate as 'sameness' and 'difference' by means of 'similarities'.

The analytical points Adorno makes concerning the remainder of the first subject and the beginning of the transition to the second subject can be summarized briefly in the following terms: continuation (*Fortsetzung*) of the consequent is achieved by means of sequences derived from both intervallic and rhythmic aspects of motif (b), counterpointed against motif (c); the whole-tone associations of the two major thirds from motif (b) are exploited and developed melodically into a descending whole-tone scale (bar 8) which later, in varied form, 'has far-reaching consequences' (see Ex. 4 (h)). This forms the first climax of the work, subsiding (motifs (b) and (c)) over pedal points, and serving at the same time, through the use of motif (c), to lead into the transition theme (motif (c), as the minor second interval, being 'the smallest transition *en nuce*').[66]

Concerning the transition itself, Adorno suggests that, given the already developmental character of the exposition so far, Berg faced the problem of needing to 'mediate' between first and second subjects, while at the same time needing to avoid overbalancing 'the briefly established first subject' (presumably bars 1–4 in particular) by yet more transitional/developmental working. He argues that the way in which Berg handles this problem shows his *Formgefühl* – his confidence in being able to work within the traditional sonata scheme with considerable freedom, while still preserving the format: 'the transition and first subject are combined, so that the first subject belatedly takes on a ternary form'[67] (i.e. the 'first subject' returns at bar 17 in the transition, being then subjected to further 'development').

Adorno's analysis of the transition, briefly summarized, is as follows: this section is differentiated from the first subject through its contrasting tempo (a device to which Berg resorts throughout the Sonata). Motivically he considers that it can be understood as beginning with a fresh variant of motif (a) (although he does not demonstrate this analytically), and there is a clear connection with the first subject in the use of the semitone step movement of motif (c). He divides the 'transition theme' into two basic motifs, (c) and (d) (see Ex. 2).[68]

Example 2

He points out that, in further contrast to the first subject, the transition theme is structured after a one-bar pattern, which, rhythmically displaced, is immediately imitated at a distance of two crotchet beats, the added accompaniment in the upper part being a rhythmically augmented inversion of the model or 'paradigm'. At bar 15 the theme settles down to regular sequences using the closing triplet figure of motif (d), and then becomes modified to function as the opening (motif (a)) of the first subject which re-enters at bar 17. The previous six bars prepare for this re-appearance of the first subject, Adorno argues, 'through the use of motif (c)' – presumably through the dotted rhythm which it has in common with motif (a), given that intervallically the two motifs could not be more different. (More detailed analysis on Adorno's part would surely have revealed closer similarities between motif (d) and motif (a) to account for the subtlety of this transformation of one motif into the other – a wonderful example of Berg's 'art of the smallest transition'.)

But to continue with Adorno's account: the return of the first subject material at this point (to complete the third part of the ternary form of this combined first subject/transition section) is at first melodically true to the original version of the antecedent phrase. The consequent is, as he puts it, 'woven into a rich contrapuntal combination with the antecedent, then spun out through imitation'.[69] The climax (*Höhepunkt*) at bar 24 is marked by the re-appearance of the whole-tone scale passage from bar 8, now rhythmically augmented and modified, with the 'transition theme' (motifs (c) and (d)) as counterpoint. The fourth-chord passage emerges out of this, at bar 26 (discussed above), motivically derived from an inversion of the transition theme, and 'the falling augmented fourth of the concluding part of the motif is retained as "remnant" [*Rest*], varied through larger intervals, but then in its *Grundgestalt* becoming the head-motif of the second subject'.[70] This is a further example of what Adorno means by Berg's process of 'permanent dissolution', and of the 'smallest transition'.

Adorno sees the second subject as consisting of three motifs – motif (e) (two versions) and motif (f) (see Ex. 3).[71]

Example 3

He interprets the opening of the second subject group as being related motivically to the opening of the first subject by means of 'axis rotation':

the intervals e–a♯–b amount to – starting with the last note and ascending linearly – those of the head-motif: b–e–a♯ (= g–c–f♯). The second shape of the paradigm (Example 3(f)) is a free variant of the diminution of motif (e). The first sequence (b.32) employs a further axis rotation: d♯–e–a, from e–a–d♯.[72]

A further aspect of the second subject group which he identifies is 'the tendency towards rhythmic rejuvenation' – the sextuplet figure in motif (g) (see Ex. 4) in this sense, he suggests, being traceable to the semiquavers of motif (f). This process pushes the tempo forward and, at bar 39, *rasch*, the closing theme (*Schlußsatz*) of the second subject group is arrived at (see Ex. 4).[73] Briefly summarized, Adorno's account of the final section of the exposition is as follows: this 'closing theme' is made up of the minor second motif from motif (f) (see Ex. 3) and the sextuplet figure which is the culmination of what he calls the 'tendency towards rhythmic rejuvenation' (all of this he labels motif (g)), and then the melodic continuation, motif (h), which he links with the descending whole-tone passage from bar 8, although the intervals are now varied. In a manner similar to its

Example 4

augmentation in bar 24, motif (h) leads towards a passage based on fourth-chord harmony (bar 44), now prepared for by the liquidation of the chord e–ab–db (bar 43, l.h.) into eb–ab–db (bar 44, l.h.) (one assumes that this is what Adorno means here: there is a mistake in his analysis at this point, the bar 40 chord being printed as e♮–ab–db–e instead of eb (es)). Then follows a long diminuendo, three times interrupted by the sextuplet figure, 'then complete dissolution [*Auflösung*] into whole-tone altered chords' (bar 49). The whole-tone harmonies are retained, 'but now only as accompaniment to a dark-toned, expansive *Abgesang* (bar 50, *viel langsamer*)'.[74] The theme of the *Abgesang* is derived directly from motif (g), now rhythmically augmented. Adorno maintains that, of all the themes in the piece, this was the only one not related to the first subject. This connection is now brought about through intervallic variation, in that the second bar (bar 51, r.h.) of the theme, taken as a 'paradigm', is gradually recast into the beginning of the first subject (motif (a)), and thus facilitates the repetition of the exposition.

For the rest of the Sonata Adorno's analysis is much less detailed, focusing on what he sees as particularly significant moments. He suggests that the 'shaping principle' of the development is the opposite of that of the exposition, and that, in spite of the all-pervading character of development and transition in the work as a whole, Berg nevertheless succeeds in creating a distinctive identity and function for the development section proper:

In the layout of the development section Berg's unerring sense of form [*Formgefühl*] is already in evidence. After the combinatorial abundance of the exposition it would be tautological and confusing to attempt to surpass its ingenuity with motivic and contrapuntal work. The shaping principle of the development is precisely the opposite: the themes, having been through the discipline of the exposition, can now breathe and allow themselves to sing out, as anticipated at the end of the exposition. Thus the development achieves its independent function.[75]

He notes the way in which Berg opens the development section by establishing a connection between motif (a) and the descending whole-tone scale passage (initially of bar 8, and what he later labels motif (h)). Then how the *allegro*-character of the piece is gradually re-established through the use of the transition theme (motif (d)), in conjunction with a diminution of motif (b): these, in combination with motif (h), led up to the big climax (bars 89–92) which, he maintains, is essentially homophonic in character, in spite of some imitation. Its effectiveness, he argues, is achieved 'through *simplification* of the compositional texture'.[76] This is followed by a passage built primarily of perfect fourths (bars 95–7) which, he says, acts as a caesura in the piece, very much along the lines of similar passages in Schoenberg's Chamber Symphony op. 9. From this there develops a line which, like the connection of motifs (b) and (h) in bars 8–9, now directly joins up motifs (e) and (g) – the two main components of the second subject group. He points out that the beginning of motif (g) is also the ending of motif (f), both of which are versions of motif (c). The end of the development section and the beginning of the recapitulation are fused by means of 'the smallest transition'.

As we might expect, Adorno's interest in the recapitulation is to consider how the constituent elements of the exposition have been modified 'in the light of that which has happened [to them]'.[77] He points out that the combining of first subject and transition section is now dispensed with:

The first subject has already been sufficiently dealt with; if it stood at the beginning of the Sonata, lapidary and closed, as a motto, then the dynamics of the development have now worked through it, and it is brought into the functional context.[78]

Therefore, he maintains, the 'working out' of the first subject in the recapitulation is restricted, in that it no longer embraces the transition section, while at the same time the first four bars of the theme, the antecedent, as stated at the very beginning of the work (as 'motto'), is made to flow without a break into the consequent phrase, now developed in its own right. The transition section now functions straightforwardly as the link between first and second subjects, and is concentrated into six bars, making use of motif (d) in counterpoint, together with a new and augmented version of motif (c). The second subject reappears in varied form, to avoid 'the rigidity of the recapitulation', as he puts it. The closing section of the second subject is now considerably expanded as a consequence of the big climax in the development section, and taken, by way of the passage in fourths corresponding to bar 44 of the exposition, to a further climax, making use of motif (h) 'which can now no longer just slip by as if nothing had happened'.[79] The *Abgesang* material (motif (g)) returns (bar 168), with two bars as before, two bars with sequence in the bass and then in inversion. Its 'remnants' lead into the final cadence – the first perfect cadence, as Adorno points out, since the antecedent of the first subject in bar 4, and exhibiting 'the inclination to bring the melodic intervals of the head-motif (motif (a)) together in harmonic simultaneity'.

Adorno writes that 'in the sorrow of the ending appears once more, quietly, the promise of serial technique'.[80] And indeed, he sees the whole piece as the prototype for the compositional approach Berg was to develop in the works that follow. Adorno ends his analysis with the observation that:

Under the thin, precarious shell of the pre-given form there lies ready the whole dynamic force [of Berg's music], with all its technical correlatives...[81]

Adorno suggests in his 1930 essay that 'Berg's music may be compared to something that unfolds like a plant. Its scheme is that of the *organism*...'.[82] (italics in original). He considers Berg's music to be less 'dialectical' than that of Schoenberg, 'where the organic substance is fixed dialectically from the outset by the structural motive'.[83] It is this 'organic essence', he maintains, which 'unites him with the nineteenth century and Romanticism'.[84] The link with Wagner, which Adorno unfortunately does not pursue in his analysis, reinforces this. What is particularly intriguing in Adorno's observations on the Sonata is that which is left at the level of suggestion – that is to say, concerning the way in which Berg in his 'apprentice piece' moves back and forth between his models, Schoenberg's Chamber Symphony op. 9 and Wagner's *Tristan*.[85] I have followed up some of the clues left by Adorno concerning the *Tristan* connection in the Appendix.

3   Adorno's interpretation of Berg: critique and commentary

Adorno's analysis of Berg's Sonata op. 1 raises two main issues. The first concerns the nature of Berg's music and the light that Adorno's analysis sheds (or fails to shed) on it; and the second concerns the nature of Adorno's analytical method. I suggest that these two issues cannot be taken entirely separately, at least not beyond the point where only the most broad generalizations can be made. I would certainly argue that Adorno's insights into this music are quite profound in their implications for the understanding of the 'problematic' of modern(ist) music in general and of Berg's music as a paradigmatic case for this: that is to say, the issues he identifies concerning the problem of 'integration through disintegration' in relation to the demands of the musical material, and the particular techniques and compositional procedures Berg developed to deal with this. Also identified is the mediation of universal and particular as that of individual compositional procedure and genre/formal type within the structure of the work – e.g. Berg's re-creation of, and deviation from (in fact, *dissolution* of) the handed-down categories of 'sonata form'. There are difficulties, however, and it has to be admitted that Adorno's technical analyses are sketchy and frequently stop short of providing thorough analytical detail to support his claims at the level of interpretation. While this is not to say that the analyses invalidate the larger claims of his music theory and the insights to which they lead, they do require further elucidation for their secrets to be revealed, and the analytical approach itself demands criticism in relation to Adorno's larger critical aesthetic and sociological theory.

The problem of Adorno's musical analysis

Given the problems raised by Adorno's approach to technical analysis, two criticisms need to be addressed. The first, which concerns his obvious impatience with the process of detailed technical analysis itself, is not, perhaps, so serious. Adorno has a tendency to make sweeping generalizations about the structure of a work, and not to support points made with systematic analysis. His impatience with detailed analytical work should not be seen as hostility to technical analysis in general (he was, in fact, very insistent on the importance of the activity, as the section entitled 'Analyse und Berg'[86] in his book on the composer, and his talk 'Zum Probleme der musikalischen Analyse'[87] clearly indicate). It is more a symptom of his approach overall, in that his writing is characterized by an extreme form of ellipsis, leading his critics – Schoenberg among them – to complain of wilful mystification. That is to say, in the interests of a terse style and densely structured text, Adorno omits what could be regarded as essential expository or explanatory material, and this often results in difficulties in understanding precisely what he means. In his musical analyses leaps are sometimes made, points are not followed through, and there are some vaguenesses and inaccuracies. Frustrating as these features might appear, they are not such a high price to pay if insights into the music itself are forthcoming. Given the value of Adorno's larger emphasis on the contextualization of music, the idiosyncrasies and shortcomings of his technical analyses can be allowed some indulgence.

The second criticism, which concerns the limitations of Adorno's analytical method *per se*, is more serious. One cannot escape the feeling that, even though the analyses themselves tend to be irritatingly fragmentary, the real problem lies in the strange disparity between the sophistication and radicality of his aesthetics and sociology on the one hand, and on the other hand the lack of sophistication and the traditional character of his music-analytical method. These extremes are curiously undialectical, in that they leave a gap which is situated both in the analyses and in his critical commentaries on music. In part, this gap is an inevitable aspect of the hermeneutic activity.[88] But in Adorno's case it is also in part due to the acceptance (at least, in his writings up to the 1950s) of a rather old-fashioned motivic–thematic formal analytical approach, with all its assumptions concerning the existence of separate categories like 'first subject', 'transition section', 'second subject', etc., combined with a highly elaborated aesthetic theory which is founded on a notion of the dissolution and subversion of such apparently invariant formal categories.[89]

The fact is that most of Adorno's technical analyses date from the 1920s and 1930s, and were largely, it would seem, influenced by a version of Schoenberg's analytical teaching, as filtered through Berg. Other analysts and theorists he had read (although not uncritically) were Kurth and Lorenz, and later, Erwin Ratz and Rudolf Stephan. That he was interested by Schenker's work is also clear, although his understanding of it seems to have been somewhat limited.[90] What is obvious is that, unlike his critical theory, the kind of analysis he practised had a rather *ad hoc* and empirical character very much at odds with the general tenor of his work overall. Thus, the disparity between the critical aesthetic and sociological theory on the one hand, and the uncritical analytical texts on the other, can at times appear extreme. That he became increasingly aware of the inadequacy of his technical analyses and of his analytical method during the 1950s and 1960s suggests, however, that the critical dimension of his thought had an impressive capacity for self-renewal. In the last year of his life he said, speaking of analysis in relation to Berg and the problems of the 'new music':

such a structuring of the inner fibre of a music also calls for an analytical practice completely different from the long-established 'motivic–thematic' approach – and I should like expressly to say that it was in the Berg book that I became particularly aware of this necessity. However, I don't in the slightest flatter myself as in any way having succeeded in fulfilling this demand, and what I say here as criticism of analysis in general also applies without reservation as criticism of all the countless analyses that I myself have ever produced.[91]

In defence of Adorno's analyses it needs to be said that, however fragmentary and lacking in precise technical detail, they nevertheless often succeed in spite of all in conveying a compelling sense of the music itself. Particularly in the case of his Berg book, Adorno's intimate understanding of the works he is discussing shines through, and the analytical points he makes usually transcend the inadequacies of his analytical method. Diether de la Motte's suggestion, that in respect of his technical analyses Adorno represents the old-style musical dilettante whose knowledge of a work comes more from what he hears than from a detailed study of the score, rings true.[92] Adorno seems to refer to the score almost as an afterthought, and with the same kind of vagueness with which he uses references and bibliographical details in his work as a whole. But it is not these idiosyncrasies and mannerisms in themselves which limit his technical analyses. The fundamental reservation remains that, apart from 'late thoughts' like the 'Analyse und Berg' section of his Berg book and the talk 'Zum Probleme der musikalischen Analyse', Adorno does not really subject the traditional terms of his inherited analytical approach to the same kind of rigorous, self-reflective critique he brings to his philosophical and sociological methodology.

Adorno's interpretation of Berg

It was in reconsidering for republication in 1968 the analyses of Berg's works he had written thirty years earlier for Willi Reich, that Adorno became particularly aware of characteristics of Berg's music which he felt had eluded traditional forms of motivic analysis – including his own. In 1969 he said:

I saw something that I had, of course, dimly sensed for a long time: namely, that Berg's music is not at all a 'Something' [ein Etwas] which forms itself, so to speak, out of a 'Nothingness' [ein Nichts] of the smallest possible, undifferentiated component elements. It only seems like this at first glance. In reality it accomplishes within itself a process of *permanent dissolution* [permanente Auflösung], rather than achieving a 'synthesis'.... So then, not only does Berg's music start out from the smallest component elements and then immediately further subject these to a kind of 'splitting of the atom', but the whole character of his music is that of a permanent self-retraction or self-cancelling [permanente Selbstzurücknahme]. Its 'Becoming', if I may term it thus – at all events, where it crystallizes-out its idea in its purest form – is *its own negation* [ihre eigene Negation].[93]

Adorno argues that this characteristic of Berg's music, its process of permanent dissolution, is not simply intended by the composer in an allegorical sense, as an external expressive gesture, but is actually the outcome of its most deep-seated and all-pervading structural principle. With Berg's music, the atomization of the material and its integration belong together, not in the sense of recombining its elements into some more positive and powerful totality (as he suggests was the case with Wagner), but rather in the more negative sense of a delicate ambiguity verging on nihilism, imparted, as Adorno puts it, 'by the contrasting message of a powerful musical presence which arises from nothing and trickles back into nothing'.[94] This is what he identifies as Berg's *tone* (the term itself – *Ton* – was a favourite expression of the composer's), and in the opening chapter of his Berg book he writes:

If one immerses oneself in Berg's music one sometimes has the feeling that his voice has a resonance made up of a mixture of tenderness, nihilism and faith in the utmost nullity, seeming to say: 'well, in the end everything is really nothing at all'. Beneath the gaze of analysis this music dissolves away completely, as if it contained no solid elements. It disappears, furthermore, while still in its apparently fixed, objectified state of aggregation [*Aggregatzustand*].⁹⁵

This characteristic, the effect of the permanent and all-pervading process of transition identified in the sub-title of his book on Berg as '*der kleinste Übergang*', Adorno regarded as the realization of a tendency which had been present in autonomous music of the bourgeois period all along. It was Wagner, he points out, who had described music as '*die Kunst des Übergangs*',⁹⁶ and whose music – particularly *Tristan* – had provided Berg with an important model. It was the chromaticism of *Tristan* (in a sense via Mahler and Schoenberg, although Adorno insists that Wagner is the important precursor in this respect) which provided Berg with the technical musical means to achieve this sense of 'dissolution' (see my analysis in the Appendix). This is by means of semitone step movement:

Nullity, or transitoriness [*das Nichtige*] has its equivalent in the musical material in the semitone step ... always ready to melt into the amorphous. Probably alone among the masters of the new music, Berg was a chromaticist through and through; the overwhelming majority of his themes can be reduced to a kernel made up of the semitone step, and for this reason the [functional] character of statement [*Setzung*] given to themes in traditional symphonic music never fits them in Berg's music.⁹⁷

However, Adorno maintains that Berg's music avoids the danger of 'the monotony of extreme chromaticism' (he has Reger in mind here) through its sense of form, through the articulation and structuring of its material. He suggests that the technique Berg had at his disposal was to create distinctive thematic shapes which 'through their own development are drawn back into nothingness'.⁹⁸ This he considers Berg derived from Wagner, as 'continuous transition', but with it combined the extreme motivic economy he had derived from Schoenberg, to produce a synthesis which Adorno regards as quite idiosyncratic, and which he describes in the following terms:

It [Berg's music] retains from each theme a remnant [*ein Rest*], each time less and less, and finally something so small as for there to be only an infinitesimal difference, through which not only the theme declares itself to be nothing, but at the same time the formal relationships between the successive parts become infinitely closely interwoven.⁹⁹

This compositional procedure, the splitting of motifs into ever smaller 'remnants', is also, however, something to be seen at work in Wagner, as a means to continuous transition, as well as in Schoenberg, where it is usually regarded as a means towards ever greater motivic economy.

The importance of Berg's music for Adorno lay precisely in its dissolution of the surface appearance of the characteristic forms and compositional procedures of the Austro-German tradition from Bach to Schoenberg (to be examined in Chapter 6) – a process of disintegration to which Wagner had significantly contributed. Through greatly extending those procedures – by means, for example, of extreme chromaticism and developing variation in large-scale forms – Berg's music seemed to Adorno to reveal, through making it its own fundamental constructive principle, the underlying tendency towards disintegration within motivic–thematic music and its forms. This is what Adorno had called the music's 'death drive' (*Todestrieb*).[100] Berg's music did this, Adorno maintained, through its reversal of the process described by Schoenberg as 'developing variation'. In his Berg book Adorno put it as follows:

To derive a maximum of shapes [*Gestalten*], according to Schoenberg's idea, from a minimum of elements, constitutes only one level of Berg's compositional procedure. The other level goes deeper: that the music dissolves itself as it unfolds. It ends with the minimum, virtually with the single note. In this way the constituent elements come to resemble each other in retrospect and fulfil the economy principle in reverse. With Berg, probably more than with any other composer, the kind of basic element on which analysis focuses is not the primary source of the work but the end result, thoroughly mediated in itself.[101]

The implications of Adorno's study of Berg's music are, however, profoundly paradoxical, and his Berg book needs to be understood in relation to certain comments on the composer which occur in *Philosophie der neuen Musik*. There Adorno suggests that the formal achievements of Berg's music are the result of the fulfilment of tendencies inherent in the works of Schoenberg's Expressionist period. But in the process of developing large-scale forms to extend the fleeting world of the Expressionist miniature or of a work like *Erwartung*, Berg also, so Adorno argues, attenuated the shocks and transfigured the anxieties contained within music of this kind.[102] What are the gestures of direct and 'unmediated suffering' in Schoenberg's music of this period are transformed by Berg, according to Adorno, into musical gestures that can be repeated, and thus tamed – vehicles of expression like the leitmotif (his examples are taken from *Wozzeck*):

The unmediated sketches of the Expressionistic Schoenberg are here [in Berg] mediated to become new images of affects. The security provided by the form turns out to be a medium for shock absorption.[103]

Adorno considers, nevertheless, that 'the impulses of the work [*Wozzeck*], which are alive in its musical atoms, rebel against the work which has developed out of them. They tolerate no outcome.'[104] There is certainly an element of ambiguity here on Adorno's part. His judgement constitutes simultaneously a criticism of the 'traditional' and conciliatory features of Berg's music and a vindication of its tendency towards self-negation. Although Berg's music tempers its response to the strict demands of the musical material with a hint of utopian reconciliation, which Schoenberg's more uncompromising music does not, Adorno is clearly sympathetic to Berg's solution. He seems to be saying that Berg's great achievement, the *tour de force* of his music, was at one and the same time to have undermined traditional formal norms while apparently reinstating them. Berg's 'smallest transitions' serve to reveal the transience and instability of formal norms, genres and schemata through dissolving them back into their smallest constituent elements. The fatalism and delicate nihilism of his technical procedures, Adorno hints, constitute a statement which transcends the hermetic circle of his musical works.

Just as Berg's music in particular, and the 'new music' in general, had undermined and thrown into question the traditional assumptions concerning universals, invariant factors and norms, but without being able to dispense with them entirely, so, according to Adorno, had analysis and aesthetics to do likewise, and develop a new theory of musical form to complement and reflect upon the current instability. As he put it: 'The crisis in composition today ... is also a crisis in analysis'.[105]

4   Proposals for a material theory of musical form

As we have seen, Adorno recognized the inadequacy of his own analyses of Berg's work to deal with the shifting character of the music, its *permanente Auflösung*. He therefore came to see a need for different general categories through which to approach music – categories which, he suggested, should be able to offer pointers for the understanding and identification of all musical processes and not just those aspects privileged by the traditional theory of form. In a sense the conception of such different formal categories had been implicit in his approach all along. It can be detected in his writings on music right from the 1920s. Nevertheless, it still coexists somewhat uneasily with the traditional categories of the *Formenlehre*, as our discussion of the problems raised by his musical analyses has shown. It is not really until the 1960s, however, that his call for a new 'theory of form' becomes more explicit. This occurs particularly strikingly in his book *Mahler: Eine musikalische Physiognomik*, published in 1960, where, in the course of developing specific categories for the understanding of Mahler's music (e.g. *Durchbruch*, *Suspension*, *Erfüllung*), he suggests that:

Out of Mahlerian categories like 'suspension' [*Suspension*] or 'fulfilment' [*Erfüllung*] there arises an idea which could contribute to [the process of] bringing music to speech through theory with implications beyond the confines of [Mahler's] works: the idea of a material theory of musical form – that is, the deduction of formal categories from their meaning [within the context of the work]. This has been neglected by the academic theory of form, which makes do with abstract classificatory divisions like first subject [*Hauptsatz*], transition [*Überleitung*], second subject [*Nebensatz*] and closing theme [*Schlußsatz*] without understanding these segmentations in terms of their function. In Mahler's case the conventional abstract formal categories are overlaid with the material ones. At times these become specifically the bearers of meaning, while at other times the material formal principles also constitute themselves beside or underneath the abstract ones which admittedly continue to provide the scaffolding and to underpin the unity [of the work], but which themselves no longer contribute to the musical complex of meaning [*Sinnzusammenhang*].[106]

Mahler's music, perhaps more than any other, provides Adorno with the ideal subject-matter for his 'material theory of musical form'. This is because Mahler's music, more than any other, brings to the fore the 'second-hand' character of the available musical material. Genres like march, ländler and waltz are used in a way which 'breaks open' their social content and, to use Adorno's term, 'characterizes' it. At the same time it does this within the context of existing formal types like sonata form, rondo, scherzo and Lied in a way which highlights the 'joins' within these forms – that is to say, it emphasizes the fragmentary character which underlies the apparent unity of the traditional formal conventions. Openings, endings, transitions, developments become themselves material, and their functions within the conventional formal types become independently characterized as musical gestures. In the case of Mahler the 'social content' of the music is revealed in Adorno's hermeneutic analysis as, in one sense, clearly derived from the previous 'social function' of its musical material, as genres. In another sense, however, Adorno's 'material theory of musical form' comes out of a need to find categories which go beyond the identification of obviously socially derived musical material, like genres, to identify the basic principles which underlie all other levels of form. This must not be seen, however, as yet another attempt to find a pure realm of musical universals beyond history. He insists that the basic categories at this level of universality only have meaning in relation to the particularity of actual musical works. Nevertheless, it may prove useful to provide an outline of the basic categories of Adorno's 'material theory of musical form' at this point before returning to the discussion of concrete musical examples in later chapters (and to a further brief consideration of Mahler in Chapter 6).

Basic categories

There is no single 'complete' version of the 'material theory of musical form' in Adorno's work. Fragments of it are to be found scattered among his later writings on music. I have here gathered together a number of these fragments. In his talk 'Zum Probleme der musikalischen Analyse' of 1969, for example, he sketches the basic categories for a possible 'material theory of form':

There lies in analysis a moment of the Universal, the General [*das Allgemeine*] – and this goes with the fact that music is certainly also, in essence, a language – and it is, furthermore, precisely in the most specific works that this moment of 'universality' is to be sought. I might attempt to summarize or codify this universality in terms of what I once defined as the 'material theory of form in music': that is, the concrete definition of categories like statement [*Setzung*], continuation [*Fortsetzung*], contrast [*Kontrast*], dissolution [*Auflösung*], succession [*Reihung*], development [*Entwicklung*], recurrence [*Wiederkehr*], modified recurrence [*modifizierter Wieder-kehr*], and however such categories may otherwise be labelled. And so far not even the beginnings of an approach have been made regarding such a 'material theory of form' (as opposed to the architectonic–schematic type of theory). These [i.e. dialectical] categories are more important than knowledge of the traditional forms as such, even though they have naturally developed out of the traditional forms and can always be found in them.[107]

In *Ästhetische Theorie*, on which Adorno was working at the time he gave his talk 'Zum Probleme der musikalischen Analyse', there are several references to the idea, albeit brief. The following example restates some of the above categories while adding to them the terms 'dynamics' (*Dynamik*) and 'statics' (*Statik*):

Even the most asymmetrical and non-harmonious works of art can be described in terms of formal characteristics like similarity and contrast, statics and dynamics, statement [*Setzung*], fields of transition [*Übergangsfeldern*], development [*Entwick-lung*], identity and return [*Rückkunft*]. They are unable to efface the distinction between the first appearance of its [basic] elements and their albeit modified repetition [*modifizierte Wiederholung*].[108]

And the following extract adds significantly to the list of general categories through introducing the problem of *beginning* (*Anfang*) and *ending* (*Schluß*), and also that of distance from the centre (*Mittelpunkt*):

The problem of how to begin and how to close is part of a more comprehensive material aesthetic of forms which is only a desideratum at present. It would deal with categories such as continuation, contrast, transition [*Überleitung*], development and 'knot' [*Knoten*]. It would also look into the problem of whether all elements must be equidistant from the centre or whether they should have different distances, different densities [*Dichte*].[109]

This last category, that of 'distance from the centre', is one that had occupied Adorno since the 1920s and his first contacts with the music of the Second Viennese School. It clearly derived its initial impulse from total thematicism and the development of the twelve-tone technique, but Adorno did not restrict the category only to such music. He saw it rather as applying, in different ways, to all radical music of the period, and uses it in conjunction with the categories 'statics' and 'dynamics'. It refers to the tendency towards symmetry and the suppression of the dynamic progression of the music through time which he considered to be a characteristic feature of the avant-garde: the tendency of the 'totally integrated work' towards 'total standstill'. The following passage from 'Neunzehn Beiträge über neue Musik' [1942][110] is illuminating in this respect:

If it is at all possible to point to something like a [basic] 'idea' underlying the shaping of form in the new music, then one would have to put forward the idea of static form: that is, of a form in which each single event is equidistant from the centre, in which concepts like development [Entwicklung] and progression [Fortgang] – even if for different reasons in the different schools [of composition] – increasingly lose their meaning and in which in a certain sense the music relates indifferently to time. Stravinsky underlines the 'standing still' character of his music through the deliberately undynamic structure of his phrases; in the twelve-tone technique stasis is produced almost against the will of the composer through the density of the material. Remarkably enough, it is precisely through this idea that the new music is most closely related to impressionism – to which in almost every other respect it is opposed. One could regard Schoenberg's most recent work as an attempt to break out of this stasis, while Stravinsky is trying to ordain it as the immutable and obligatory law of the new musical language.[111]

Sameness and difference

Starting from a conception of music as 'language-like', both in terms of its expressive character and of its logicality (and in spite of the attempts of the 'Darmstadt School' to purge it of these features in the 1950s), Adorno put forward the general categories of sameness (Gleichheit) and difference (Ungleichheit) as being the most fundamental to a theory of form. (These categories can be seen, of course, as a version of the identity–non-identity polarity of Hegelian logic.) If invariants are being looked for at a high level of generality, then these categories would certainly fit the requirements; with them also go categories like repetition (Wiederholung) (i.e. with 'sameness'), and contrast (Kontrast) and development (Entwicklung) (i.e. with 'difference'). However, he points out that such invariant categories are of little value in themselves, because they can only be understood within the context of the 'whole': that is, they are always mediated through the totality of the work's structure. What is most significant in musical analysis is actually the recognition of *similarity* (*Ähnlichkeit*). He writes in *Ästhetische Theorie*:

Musical analyses ... have shown that even the most diffuse and dissociated (that is, least repetitious) creations contain similarities, that certain parts are related to others in terms of some specific characteristic, and that, generally, the intended nonidentity is realized only through reference to such identities.[112]

The unity-giving features of musical structures function not simply in terms of 'repetition of the same' interspersed with 'difference' in the architectonic sense, but by means of infinitely subtle degrees of similarity – of difference in sameness and sameness in difference – mediated through each other and through the structure of the whole. Adorno continues:

Devoid of any sameness at all, chaos would reign, and it would itself be an immutable essence. What is more important than any invariance is the difference between manifest repetition imposed from outside and not mediated by specific details and the inevitable determination of difference by a residue or 'remnant' of sameness [*durch einen Rest von Gleichem*].[113]

As we have seen, Adorno insists that the usefulness of such general categories lies in their concrete definition within the structural context of actual works. The categories themselves may be seen as constituting a kind of syntax of possible movement, but they only have any meaning at the level of the particularity of specific pieces of music.

The problem of repetition

Adorno considers that during the Classical and early Romantic periods there existed a lively and vital interaction between the so-called 'big forms' and the individual musical elements which generated the dynamic unfolding of a piece through time. Within this 'dynamic unfolding', however, the problem increasingly became that of the large-scale architectonic repetition represented by the recapitulation. The recapitulation becomes the crucial point – in particular the approach to it via the end of the development section – as it is the static moment within the dynamic form. As Adorno puts it: 'Because the recapitulation is no longer possible it becomes a *tour de force*'.[114] In new music Adorno argues that overt repetition itself becomes unbearable, and yet at the same time 'wherever music articulates itself meaningfully, its inner logicality is tied up with overt or latent repetitions'.[115] This is a problem for new music, partly solved by latent repetition (e.g. the constant presence of the row), and partly, he suggests, by recognizing that the function of reprise can be carried out by other parameters – it does not need to operate only at the level of pitch manipulation:

The ability to sense and utilize quite abstract relationships of symmetry and harmony has grown ever more subtle. In music, for instance, a more or less tangible reprise used to be *de rigueur*, for it helped establish symmetry; nowadays the same result can be achieved through a vague similarity of tone colours [*Klangfarben*] at different points.[116]

Adorno argues that musical form 'is difficult to imagine without similarity or difference', and that 'even the postulate of "repetitionlessness", of absolute difference, demands a moment of "sameness", measured against which difference only becomes difference'.[117] However, this is by no means an argument for the idea of invariants, he maintains – at least in the sense of formal absolutes to be accepted without demur. In fact resistance to invariants is entirely legitimate, he insists, even though it leads to the disintegration of traditional assumptions about 'form' (he cites as examples Beethoven's late piano bagatelles and string quartets, and also Mahler's last works). He argues that the tendency towards the disintegration of musical form is the outcome of the pull towards the detail. What was previously imposed on the material from outside now flies apart: 'Disintegration is immanent to integration, as the unity of the disparate'.[118] Adorno maintains that what he calls 'integral form' emerges out of the specific tendencies of the individual musical elements, and that, after the disintegration of the traditional architectonic formal types, form can only be thought of as 'form from below to above' and not the other way round.[119] This point will be returned to later.

In the same way Adorno argues that 'the articulation of time through repetition, through stasis, and the Utopia of the unrepeatable penetrate each other'.[120] In a sense, the 'ban on repetition' which was observable in much new music, led to stasis due to (a) the generation of constant 'repetition' at a deeper level of structure, and (b) the search for constant difference at the foreground level which, due to the rapid rate of change, produced the impression of constant sameness. Adorno points up this paradox by the formulation that 'because there are no forms any more, everything becomes form'[121] – an outcome of this being both the multiple serialism of the 1950s and its apparent opposite, the use of chance procedures in composition and performance and the attempt to break down the boundaries between the work of art and life.

Beginning and the problem of ending

There remain the categories *beginning* (*Anfang*) and *ending*, or closure (*Schluß*). Adorno suggests that these, in the final analysis, are what provide a musical piece with 'a minimum of form and unity',[122] as the givens of musical time. It would seem that time is the ultimate invariant in music –

the fact that music is a temporal art. But even this undeniable fact, Adorno argues, when taken out of the total context of form-giving moments in music, becomes irrelevant, and 'to take [any invariants] out of the dynamic complexion of history or that of the single work is to misinterpret them'.[123] He points out that 'in actual fact the relation of music to formal musical time is defined not abstractly, but in the context of a concrete musical event'.[124] 'What happens' in the course of a musical work, in the sense of a meaningful sequence of musical events, has itself come to be questioned – i.e. the idea of 'having one event follow logically from another, with the result that the sequence of events would be as irreversible as time itself'.[125] The idea of narrative logic in this sense has, he argues, itself been seen to be fictitious, and is part of the illusory character of art as *Schein*:

Today music is clearly rebelling against the conventional ordering of time, making room for widely diverging approaches in dealing with musical time. The point is that, no matter how doubtful it may be whether art can shake off the invariable of time, it is more useful to regard time as a moment rather than as an a priori assumption of music.[126]

The totality of the musical work is defined temporally through beginning and ending at certain points in time, and is further articulated as a unity through its 'partial totalities', through the partial closure of its individual complexes. Adorno maintains that, since the loss of the binding power provided previously by the traditional formal archetypes, music has been faced by the 'problem of closure' – how to end convincingly – and with it the problem of the integration of the 'partial totalities' within the whole has been thrust to the fore. He sees these as problems which face the musical work and to which there are no convincing solutions today, mainly because they are problems which are not only to do with music. He argues that 'authentic art', as the avant-garde, is compelled by the demands of the material to push beyond totality and integration towards fragmentation and disintegration. Works today are necessarily scarred, and bear the marks of enforced integration or loss of conviction within their form:

The unity of art works cannot be what it must be, i.e. unity of a manifold. By synthesizing the many, unity inflicts damage on what it has synthesized. The works are as deficient in their mediated totality as they are in their immediacy.[127]

Adorno considers that attempts to deal with the problem of unity and of closure through recognizing the demands of the isolated partial moments have likewise not escaped this deficiency. The fragmentary miniature – what he calls Webern's 'notion of intensity without extension'[128] – he sees as an attempt to avoid the dilemma facing large-scale forms altogether. Montage he criticizes because, once it has lost its shock value against the idea of organic unity, it falls back into its indifferent and unbinding elements, as *Stoff*.[129] And he is sceptical of the claim that 'open forms' and works based on chance principles can escape the reification of closed forms. He points out that it was the 'traditional' open forms – that is, those episodic forms like rondo and song forms – which lent themselves most readily to commodification and standardization, while the large developmental 'closed' forms (like the sonata) resisted this to a greater extent.[130] On the other hand, open forms, including the traditional ones like the rondo, act as a critique of the appearance of unity and closure which characterizes 'closed' forms. Through the element of arbitrariness in the structure of open forms (for example, further sections could always be added, or existing sections could be taken away), they throw into question the idea of 'necessity' and inevitability which characterizes the nominalism of closed forms. As Adorno puts it, open forms (and genres) 'free themselves from the lie of being necessary. By the same token, they become more vulnerable to contingency.'[131]

Vers une musique informelle

Broadly speaking, as we have seen earlier, Adorno's concept of form distinguishes between two types: (i) that which goes from 'above to below'; and (ii) that which goes from 'below to above'.[132] The dual-level 'model' put forward at the beginning of this chapter can now be reformulated, with further variations, to reveal connections with Adorno's discussion of 'open' and 'closed' forms, as well as with the 'top down' and 'bottom up' types. The opportunity can also be taken to clarify further what can be understood by Adorno's use of the concepts 'consistency', 'authenticity' and 'immanent critique' in relation to musical form.

The first kind of form can be understood in relation to the handed-down, pre-given genres and formal types, imposed on the material 'from above'. These represent a level of universality (what Adorno calls *schlechte Allgemeinheit*) and are normative, the form being organized from totality to detail. The second can be understood as form which emerges out of the 'inner necessity' of the material, 'from below'. It represents the nominalism (i.e. 'self-identity') of the particular, is critical, and moves from detail towards totality. These two types do not correspond as such to the distinction Adorno makes between 'open' and 'closed' forms; it is rather that the 'openness' or 'closedness' of the forms adds a further critical dimension to the types. What characterizes 'modernist' art for Adorno is that the *inability to close* is 'turned into a freely chosen principle of method and expression'.[133] (This is a principle which Adorno saw at work in Schoenberg – he cites the example of the March from the *Serenade* op. 24 – and, in particular, in the plays of Samuel Beckett.[134]) Thus, Adorno's notions of 'authenticity' and of 'consistency' would seem to favour a nominalistic form 'from below' which freely chooses to go against the tendency of such forms towards integration and closure by denying the reconciliation of opposites and remaining deliberately open and fragmentary. This is seen as acting as an immanent critique of totality, of the universal, and of a wholeness which is seen as false. As an 'immanent critique', however, it operates in purely musical terms, as a critique both of the false totality of traditional forms and of the total determinacy of serialism.

At Darmstadt in 1961 Adorno put forward the concept of what he called *une musique informelle*[135] – that is, 'informal music' in the sense of 'formless music', more accurately form which negates the received formal norms and which emerges from the demands of the material. Growing as it did out of a critique of serial music as well as from a critique of traditional forms, and taking as its starting point Schoenberg's op. 11 no. 3 and his *Erwartung* op. 17, as well as Webern's opp. 7–11, the concept of *une musique informelle*, according to Martin Zenck, can be taken both as a critical judgement on serial and post-serial music and as an 'ideal type' in the Weberian sense of the term. As Zenck puts it: it is 'ideal typical as the direction in which compositional praxis would have to move in order to find its way out of the dead-end of total determinism and fulfil the ideal of *une musique informelle*'.[136] *Musique informelle* in this sense may be understood as the refusal to fall either into what Adorno sees as the positivism and false totality of multiple serialism or back into the 'bad universality' of pre-given, handed-down forms. It is 'informal' in that its form arises out of a denial of pre-determined or pre-existing form, while at the same time developing the equivalents to the old formal categories (which in themselves cannot be restored) according to the needs of the new materials.[137] In this the origins of Adorno's concept of *musique informelle* are clearly to be seen in his 'material theory of musical form'. It is offered by Adorno as the only possibility for an authentic, critical and self-consistent music in an age when any direct representation of wholeness and rounded completion is, so he argues, necessarily ideological. The concept of *musique informelle* was doubtless put forward more as an ideal than as an existing reality. However, as Martin Zenck has argued, its influence on the compositional praxis of the 'New Music' was considerable, particularly on composers like Boulez, Stockhausen and Ligeti.[138]

In conclusion

In examining Adorno's concept of musical material as an immanent dialectic (as the dialectic of universal and particular, genre/formal type and individual structure, construction and expression, and overall as the dialectic of objectivity and subjectivity), we have seen how the concept converges with his concept of form. Form has thus emerged as an important and contradictory concept: it is, in the Hegelian sense, the mediation of opposites in and through their extremes. It is both a universal and a particular. It depends on a process of integration and yet constantly threatens its own identity by dissolving itself to embrace that which lies outside its concept, and thus risks fragmentation and disintegration. It is both a defence against the world of empirical reality, and at the same time its material is already mediated and 'pre-formed' by the real world. However, the internal consistency of the integrated work, as the relation between the work's individual structure and its handed-down, pre-formed material, is also threatened by the tendency towards fragmentation of the handed-down material. It becomes increasingly difficult to produce convincingly integrated structures out of a disintegrating material – a material which is itself shaped by music's function in the world of empirical reality. Thus the idea of the 'truth' of the autonomous work being its 'identity with its own concept' – i.e. its consistency – becomes difficult to sustain in isolation, and needs also to be seen in the context of the way music actually functions in contemporary society. The implications of Adorno's argument are that the internal consistency of the autonomous work of art, while on the one hand constituting its 'truth', is also, due to the separation of the work from the world of empirical reality, its 'untruth' – i.e. *ideology*.

The development of the discussion so far (in Chapters 1–3, and in the present chapter) has been broadly along the following lines: nature/ history→material→mediation→form – these being understood as different aspects of the same fundamental idea. That is to say, musical material is historically mediated 'nature' as form, and thus becomes significative as a mode of cognition. However, Adorno also saw musical form as a homologue of society, and saw freedom of form and its corresponding critique of pre-given form as a metaphor for an ideal, free society, and, simultaneously, as a critique of existing society. But at the same time, through the fetishization of form, music becomes assimilated to society. Thus the next stage in the discussion is to consider the mediation of music and social reality in terms both of the antagonistic relationship to society at the level of autonomous form, and of the assimilated relationship at the level of the commodity. That is to say, the autonomous work and its social content need to be understood in the context of the social forces and relations of production. This provides the focus of Chapter 5, an examination of Adorno's sociology of music as ideology critique.

5   Social content and social function

> Music is not ideology pure and simple; it is ideological only insofar as it is
> false consciousness. Accordingly, a sociology of music would have to set
> in at the fissures and fractures of what is actually going on within the
> music [*des musikalisch Geschehenden*]. ... Sociology of music is social
> critique accomplished through the critique of art.[1]
>
> Adorno, *Introduction to the Sociology of Music* (1962)

In his essay 'Thesen zur Kunstsoziologie' (1967) Adorno writes: 'Sociology
of art, according to the meaning of the words, embraces all aspects of the
relationship between art and society. It is impossible to restrict it to any
simple aspect, such as the social effects of works of art. This effect is itself
only a moment in the totality of that relationship.'[2] Thus there is a sense in
which the concerns of Adorno's sociology of art permeate all levels of what
is here, for convenience, being called his 'aesthetics'. However, as was
suggested in the earlier part of this study, Adorno's 'sociology of music', in
the narrower sense of the term, does also have a very specific focus of its
own: that is, it seeks to reveal the ideological dimension of music. Music's
claim, since the Enlightenment, to be autonomous, is false consciousness
when seen in relation to its social function as commodity. As ideology
critique Adorno's approach is twofold: to examine the *social content* of
musical material, and to consider the *social function* and *context* of music
and musical works. His purpose is to reveal the social relations within
which music functions and which are mediated within musical material, but
which music's autonomy status and character as commodity also serve to
conceal.

As we have seen, Adorno's approach to a sociology of music is essentially
speculative rather than empirical in orientation, and to this extent it could
perhaps be more accurately called a social philosophy of music. Through
critique it seeks to reveal the contradictions inherent in the relation between
music and society, particularly as mediated within musical material and as
problems of musical form. The aim here is to examine Adorno's sociology
of music as ideology critique through focusing in turn on the spheres of
production, reproduction, distribution and consumption.

1   The social dialectic of musical material

It is the antagonistic relationship between the aesthetic forces and relations of production (as the composer's relation to musical material) and the material relations of production (as the culture industry's relation to the musical work) that is here being called the 'social dialectic of musical material'. Implied is a split beween 'autonomous' and 'commodity art' – although, according to Adorno, autonomous art cannot itself escape the effects of commodification and, precisely because of its 'separateness', is always in danger of being assimilated by the culture industry. In fact, the autonomous art work, so he argues, becomes the ultimate commodity. On the other hand, commodity art (as, for example, popular music), even though apparently for immediate use as entertainment, denies, Adorno maintains, the very pleasure it promises. Its 'infinite nearness' is at the same time 'infinite distance', in that the consumer is perpetually separated from the object through the process of fetishization and reification.

At this level – the sociological – mediation has to be understood both in the sense of being immanent to the object (the musical work and its production) and also, with some qualifications, as being a relation between the work and 'musical life' (the conditions of its reproduction, distribution and consumption) – a relation which is, however, reflected in the musical material. Thus Adorno's production–reproduction–distribution–consumption model (adapted, as we have seen, from Marx) offers a way of situating music within a larger context of meaning.

A schematic model

Adorno's sociology of music suggests several levels of mediation. At the level of production it is the mediation of the 'subjectivity' of the composer (in fact already a social product, and constituting an aspect of the musical forces of production in the sense, for example, of technical skills, expressive needs, 'spontaneity') and the 'objectivity' of the musical material (as the handed-down, historically changing set of musical conventions, now 'social property' and having forgotten its previous partly subjective origins). The locus of the mediation at this stage is in one sense the musical work 'in itself', although this immediately presents us with the problem of what a work is – ideal object, technical structure, or score. In another sense, however, the autonomous musical work has to be understood as itself embodying the mediation of opposites through the extremes of expression and construction.

At the level of reproduction as interpretation and performance the emphasis is on the mediation of performer/interpreter (also constituting an aspect of the musical forces of production, as technical skills and handed-down performance practice) and the musical work as score. The locus of the mediation at this stage is again the musical work, but now as 'sounding object', as an actual performance.

At the level of reproduction as distribution the emphasis is on a significantly different form of mediation – that of the 'culture industry' (as 'technical reproduction', recording, radio, television, film, concert agents, marketing, etc.), and the musical work as performance. Again, the locus of the mediation at this stage is the musical work, but now as commodity, with the emphasis on its value in exchange rather than its 'use-value'.

And finally, at the level of consumption/reception, the emphasis is on the mediation of the listener (and here Adorno distinguishes between a number of possible 'listening types', ranging from the 'expert', via the 'culture consumer', to the 'entertainment listener') and the musical work as commodity. At this level the locus of the mediation could be taken as the 'musical experience' itself, whereby music is affectively and conceptually mediated by the socially determined receptive Subject.

While the dangers of such models[3] need to be recognized, in that they easily reduce complex ideas to mere formulae, they do serve a useful if necessarily limited purpose for initial orientation in potentially confusing conceptual terrain. What this model brings into focus is a fundamental antagonism in Adorno's sociology of music – that between, on the one hand, musical production (which includes composition and, to an extent, performance/interpretation) and, on the other hand, the conditions of music's distribution and consumption. At the same time it has to be remembered that the spheres of production, reproduction, distribution and consumption constantly interact – something difficult to superimpose here in graphic form without rendering the whole 'map' unreadable. The following schematic interpretation (see Fig. 1) is therefore put forward with reservations, together with the usual cautionary comment that Adorno hated such diagrammatic representations of his ideas.

As a mapping of the basic terms of Adorno's sociology of music this model does not simply set out to situate music in relation to its social *function* (although it does also do this, in that it identifies music's social function today as that of a commodity). Rather, it sets out to understand music at the same time in its *opposition* to society, in terms of its difference from empirical reality. Thus the mediation of music and society has to be seen as contradictory, the two spheres interpenetrating but at the same time remaining distinct, separate and irreducible. Adorno's sociology of music is elaborated by means of this model in what follows.

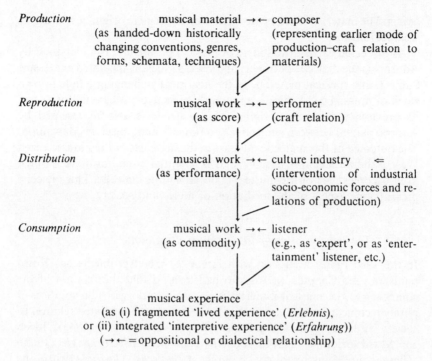

Production musical material →← composer
(as handed-down historically   (representing earlier mode of
changing conventions, genres,   production–craft relation to
forms, schemata, techniques)   materials)

Reproduction musical work →← performer
(as score)   (craft relation)

Distribution musical work →← culture industry   ⇐
(as performance)   (intervention of industrial
socio-economic forces and re-
lations of production)

Consumption musical work →← listener
(as commodity)   (e.g., as 'expert', or as 'entertainment' listener, etc.)

musical experience
(as (i) fragmented 'lived experience' (*Erlebnis*),
or (ii) integrated 'interpretive experience' (*Erfahrung*))
(→← = oppositional or dialectical relationship)

Figure 1

2   Musical production

The relation between musical/aesthetic production and socio-economic
production is, as we have seen, a complex and paradoxical one for Adorno.
On the one hand, the forces and relations of aesthetic production strive to
escape those of socio-economic production, and to oppose them. On the
other hand, artists and art works are *faits sociaux*,[4] and are part of and
derived from society, to the extent that dominant tendencies within social
reality (like the process of means-ends rationalization) are internalized and
subverted by artists and appear in art works in sublimated/repressed form.
However, another way of looking at the relation is, so Adorno argues, to
recognize that the critical and oppositional character of art is a product of
society itself, in that '[t]here are times when aesthetic forces of production
are given completely free rein because the material ones, hemmed in as they
are by existing relations of production, cannot be unleashed'.[5] Through art
are realized things which it is not possible to realize directly in social reality
as it is, and in this utopian sense art comments unfavourably upon society

as it is. The material of art, however, is seen as social in origin, just as are its technical means.

As discussed earlier, the sphere of musical production is understood by Adorno as the dialectic between composer, as socially mediated expressive Subject, and musical material, as the historically changing handed-down stock of musical conventions, apparently objective but having 'forgotten' its previously subjective origins. This dialectic is also represented by Adorno as that between subjective spontaneity and objective convention. The outcome of this dialectic, at least in the high arts of the industrialized West, is the *musical work as score*, and as potential 'sounding object', which itself becomes part of the musical material and its dialectic. This dialectic presents one aspect of the mediation of music and society.

The relation of composer to musical material

In the 1930 radio discussion with Krenek, 'Arbeitsprobleme des Komponisten' (see Chapter 2), Adorno had insisted that the relation of the composer to the musical material is not only to do with the solution of purely technical problems, but that it also involves a mediated relation to society. In later writings (e.g. *Philosophie der neuen Musik* (1949), 'Ideen zur Musiksoziologie' (1958), *Einleitung in die Musiksoziologie* (1962), 'Thesen zur Kunstsoziologie' (1967), *Ästhetische Theorie* (1970)), he explores the relation further. As part of the dialectic of musical material, he argues, the composer, as 'creative Subject', is not a *tabula rasa*, but is, like the musical material, culturally and socially mediated. Adorno also considers the concepts of 'creativity', 'spontaneity' and 'inspiration', as 'free play', themselves to be of dubious value. He emphasizes instead the necessity for the composer to respond and submit to the demands of the material as the crucial factor in great music. In this way the composer's subjectivity, as spontaneity, serves to mediate the contradictions of the material, contradictions which are themselves social and historical in origin. In *Einleitung in die Musiksoziologie* he writes:

What is attempted is the solution of problems. Contradictions that appear as resistance of the material, which is historical in itself, are to be pursued to the point of reconcilement. By virtue of the objectivity of tasks, including the tasks they supposedly set themselves, the artists cease to be private individuals and become either a social subject or its vicar. Hegel already knew that their worth is proportional to their success in this self-relinquishment.[6]

It is the process of rationalization that characterizes both composer and musical material. Thus, through emphasizing the process of rationalization (particularly as technique and technology) as an important factor in the mediation of musical material and society, Adorno considers that the interaction of the composer with the musical material is at the same time an interaction with society – but only, he stresses, to the extent that this interaction (*Auseinandersetzung*) finds expression in the musical work.

In the course of the 'historical dialectic of the musical material' the concept of the composer is transformed. In a sense the composer loses his creative freedom due to 'the rigid demand for compositional accuracy'[7] – what Adorno had elsewhere identified by the concept 'consistency' (*Stimmigkeit*) – which faces him in structural terms in the composition. In *Philosophie der neuen Musik* Adorno formulates the composer's predicament in the following rather dramatic terms:

He is no longer a creator. It is not that the times and society impose external restrictions upon him; it is rather the rigid demand for compositional accuracy made upon him by his structure which limits him. The state of technique appears as a problem in every measure which he dares to conceive: with every measure technique as a whole demands of him that he do it justice and that he give the single correct answer permitted by technique at any given moment. The compositions themselves are nothing but such answers – nothing but the solution of technical picture puzzles – and the composer is the only one who is capable of reading his own compositions and understanding his own music. His efforts find fulfilment in the execution of that which his music objectively demands of him. But such obedience demands of the composer all possible disobedience, independence, and spontaneity. This is the dialectical nature revealed in the unfolding of the musical material.[8]

For Adorno the relation of the composer to society is to be understood as a response to the demands of the musical material. It is irrelevant whether composers are aware of 'social tendencies' or not – Schoenberg's fractious comment: 'Music has no more to do with society than a game of chess'[9] comes to mind here – as both they and the musical material at their disposal, so he argues, are socially and historically mediated anyway.

The musical work

The outcome of the interaction between composer and musical material is the musical work, understood both as *autonomous object* and as *process*. The work is not merely a fixed object, a closed system as text and as artefact; it is also a process, being in a state of constant flux and 'becoming':

Above all, the work of art is processual, in so far as it is a relation between a whole and its parts. In other words, this relation itself is a process of becoming. The work of art is not a totality in the sense of a structure integrating the parts: once objectified, the work keeps on producing itself in response to the tendencies at work in it. By the same token, the parts are not givens but centres of gravity straining towards totality, even though they may also be subject to preformation by the whole. ... Works of art are not fixed once and for all, but are in flux.[10]

Adorno sees the musical work as 'a force-field [*Kraftfeld*] organized around a problem'.[11] Musical analysis is thus regarded as an aspect of the work itself, as a necessary complement to it. Its task is to uncover and understand the 'problem' around which the work is organized. In the light of analysis the work is seen as a dynamic complex of meaning (*dynamischer Sinnzusammenhang*), a context which extends from a core of precise technical detail out through the relationship of parts to whole within the autonomous and hermetically sealed structure of the work understood as 'windowless monad', and beyond this to the multiple mediations through which the technical structure of the work relates to the social totality. Within the conception of the work as a 'complex of meaning' can also be understood the twofold-character of the work, as autonomous artefact and as heteronomous social fact. As discussed in Chapter 3, the art work is understood by Adorno, in Hegelian terms, as an objectification (as *Objektivation* and as *Entäußerung*) of Spirit (*Geist*) and as an expression of individual subjectivity, but also at the same time as a reflection of social tendencies. Art works are in one sense unique and identical only with themselves (hence the nominalism of art works), and yet this identity is brought into focus and sustained by that which is outside their own hermetic and defined structures. In this lies the dynamic quality of the art work:

The processual character of art works is grounded in the fact that they are man-made artefacts; as such they belong by definition to the 'native realm of spirit', but in order to be identical with themselves they need the presence of the heterogeneous, the non-identical, the amorphous. The resistance of the otherness in their midst prompts them to articulate themselves in a language of form, leaving absolutely no blank spots, no areas not touched by form. Dynamic therefore is reciprocity, a restless antithetical process which never comes to a halt in static being.[12]

Nevertheless, there is also a sense in which the autonomous musical work is a 'congealed object' at standstill. As a finished totality within itself, the work acts as a dynamic force-field of tensions precisely because it is finished and self-contained, defined and separated from a larger totality. It is the paradoxical phenomenon of frozen movement; the motion of the work 'must come to a halt and yet remain visible *qua* motion in this standstill'.[13] Because music is an art which unfolds through time, the 'frozen movement' aspect of the work is concealed by the façade of the temporal unfolding of the work in performance. This is particularly apparent in the musical work as *score* – that nodal point within the musical forces and relations of production which, in the high bourgeois period, mediates between the spheres of production and reproduction, composition and interpretation. (The importance of the work as score in relation to the performer, as interpreter, within the forces and relations of musical production will be discussed in the following section on Reproduction.) It is through textual analysis, through technical analysis of the score, that one comes to recognize, as Adorno points out in connection with the motivic–thematic music of the bourgeois period, the similarity of the work to 'the jig-saw puzzle, constructed as it is out of elements over against which dynamic development (which on the face of it predominates to such an extent in this music) reveals itself in many ways to be merely a contrived appearance'.[14] Adorno goes on to expand on this as follows:

It could be said that the character of this 'aesthetic appearance' (which even applies, in spite of all, to an art as far removed from illusion as music . . .) has occurred as the consequence of an increasing 'Becoming' – or development – from out of itself [aus sich Herauswerdendes]. In reality, however, such music could more accurately be said to have been 'put together' [zusammengesetzt] in the quite literal sense of having been 'composed', contrary to the impression more usually associated with it. . . . [A]ll 'Becoming' in music is in fact illusory, insofar as the music, as text, is really fixed and thus is not actually 'becoming' anything as it is already all there.[15]

The tension between movement and stasis, which constitutes one of the paradoxes of the musical work, also constitutes its processual character. This internal dynamic of the work, having severed its 'ties with the empirical world',[16] also constitutes its polemical and critical character over against the empirical world. There is something in the art work, Adorno maintains, which 'in an unconscious way expresses its desire to change the world'.[17] For example, the reconciliation of conflicting forces which characterizes the Classical (and to some extent the Romantic) work both distances it from the world and at the same time acts as a criticism of the real world.

The essential concept is that of *tension* (*Spannung*), in conjunction with the notion of *force-field* (*Kraftfeld*). For Adorno the 'authentic' work of art maintains this tension within its structure, and holds the oppositions within itself unreconciled. As discussed in Chapter 4, it is through the 'immanent logic' of its form that the work both maintains this inner tension, as a world 'in and for itself', and at the same time separates itself from the world outside. The loss of this tension, Adorno argues, compromises the art work and leads to its assimilation by the culture industry (something he considers typical of much post-war art – a preview, perhaps, of postmodernism). But it is in fact the very autonomy and inner consistency of the work of art which renders it vulnerable to commodification. This turns art works of the past into commodities and museum exhibits and also compromises modernist works. As discussed in Chapter 1, one aspect of the truth or untruth of the work lies for Adorno in its technical consistency or inconsistency. But as we have seen, he also emphasizes that, in what he calls 'authentic' music, this consistency cannot be gained through ignoring the tendency towards disintegration which characterizes the stage of historical development reached by the material.

3   Musical reproduction (I): performance

It is in the sphere of musical reproduction, Adorno maintains, that the alienation of music from society actually becomes tangible. Alienation is experienced as a social fact in the relationship between production and consumption, and Adorno sees the sphere of reproduction as mediating between production and consumption. Within the broad sphere of reproduction Adorno makes a further differentiation in distinguishing between reproduction as interpretation/performance and reproduction as distribution/exchange/marketing. It is to reproduction in the first sense that he is referring when he writes of reproduction mediating between production and consumption, as, for example, in 'Zur gesellschaftlichen Lage der Musik':

It serves production, which can become immediately present only through reproduction. Otherwise it would exist only as a dead text or score. Reproduction is further the form of all musical consumption, for society can participate only in reproduced works and never only in the texts. The demand of reproduction – understood as the demand for authenticity – and that of consumption – the demand for comprehensibility [intelligibility, *Verständlichkeit*] – address reproduction to the same degree and intertwine in it.[18]

This section is concerned with reproduction as performance/interpretation. Reproduction in this sense is seen, therefore, as falling partly within the sphere of production. The dialectic here can be understood as that between performer, as interpreter, and the musical work as text, as written score, the outcome being the musical work as performance, as 'sounding object'. The emphasis is on the socio-historical character of this dialectic, as an aspect of the dialectic of musical material.

The relation between performer and score

The work as *text*, Adorno writes, 'is merely a coded script which does not guarantee unequivocal meaning and within which changing thematic contents appear along with the development of the musical dialectic, which in turn encompasses social impulses'.[19] Adorno makes the point that musical performance is not concerned with 'an eternal work *per se* nor with a listener dependent upon constant natural conditions, but rather with historical conditions ... the works themselves have their history and change within it'.[20] The work is both historical and social, and in its reproduction as performance it has to be interpreted accordingly. Not only has the degree of freedom accorded to the interpreter changed – that is, diminished – since the beginning of the bourgeois period; due to the alienation of music from society today, the way in which music of the past can be adequately performed in order to render the work intelligible has also changed, and freedom of interpretation has become drastically limited. As Adorno puts it: 'The change within works themselves is portrayed in reproduction; this happens under the sign of radical alienation as the reduction of reproductive freedom'.[21] In the pre-capitalist period (by which Adorno means the general bass period up to Bach and Handel) '[t]he work did not stand in a state of alienation from society; rather through reproduction it exerted an influence upon production'.[22] Through the domination of pre-capitalist music by the tradition of musical guilds and of individual musical families, '[t]he impulse of tradition guaranteed a continuing stable relation between music and its public within the stability of reproduction'.[23]

Adorno points out that right up to the late eighteenth century production, reproduction and improvisation 'intermingled without fixed boundaries'.[24] He also emphasizes that this interpretative freedom existed not only in Baroque scores, with their open dynamics, tempi and, often, phrasing; it to some extent persisted in the nineteenth century – for example, in Beethoven, where the often sparse markings in his scores need an interpretative understanding based in a knowledge of the ethos of his music.[25] That is to say, even in the case of, for example, Beethoven, an adequate interpretation of certain features of the score as 'sign system' can only come about through a close study of the structure of the work, and within the sign system of Beethoven's scores there still remain elements (especially dynamic markings) which have not been fully rationalized. The regulation of these factors 'is assigned to a tradition which remains irrational for several centuries following the introduction of tempered tuning'.[26] It is, according to Adorno, the rise to power of the bourgeoisie at the end of the eighteenth century that changes all of this (although pockets of irrationality within the material still survive). On the one hand, through increasing rationalization, the musical work achieves its final autonomy, and on the other hand, it at the same time, as 'a rational system of signs, defines itself as commodity in relation to society'.[27] Moreover, free competition on the open market ends the tradition of guilds and the tradition of performer with its close association with the production of musical works. Adorno argues that the intervention of the performer in the

work still persists, but with the increasing rationalization of the work itself
and its autonomy such intervention tends to become arbitrary, and its
effects are no longer necessarily in the interests of the work but pander more
towards the demands of the consumers. As he puts it:

The interpreter has only the choice between two demands of rational character:
either he must limit himself strictly to the realization – at most to the decoding – of
the exact language of musical signs, or he must adjust to the demands which society
as market makes upon him and within which the configuration [Gestalt] of the work
perishes.[28]

The performer/interpreter mediates in several senses: for example, between
the spheres of production and consumption (more particularly between
work-as-score and listener), and also between the autonomous work as
rationalized sign system and the consumer's demand for the performance
of musical works as 'special zones of irrationality' within the total
rationalization of the 'administered world' of advanced capitalism. For
Adorno, the performer, in mediating between these areas, stands as 'the last
musical refuge of irrational reproduction within the capitalist process'.[29]
The relationship of the interpreter to the musical work, which he serves 'by
producing its contents again out of the work itself within the framework of
the prescriptive text and its signs',[30] was still possible even in the nineteenth
century because both interpreter and composer shared the same social
structure, were both in the same way 'bourgeois individuals', and both
accomplished the 'expression of bourgeois individuality in the same way'.[31]
(As examples of composer–performers Adorno suggests Liszt and Rubinstein.) Furthermore, the public to whom they offered their music 'is just as
individualistically conditioned as they are; it recognizes itself in them and
through them it takes possession of the work offered. In the triumphs which
it prepares for the virtuoso – far greater than those with which the
composer is celebrated – it celebrates itself.'[32] Adorno maintains that the
profound change that has affected musical reproduction since the nineteenth century is that which came about in the transition from competitive
to monopoly capitalism.[33] This has affected the balance of the kind of
individualistic society in which the 'interpretive personality' flourished up
to the nineteenth century, and has radically changed the function of the
performer/interpreter. An abyss has opened up between the work and the
interpreter, and between the work and the public – something which applies
not only to contemporary musical production, but which also concerns
music of the past. In 'Zur gesellschaftlichen Lage der Musik' Adorno
writes:

The historical mutation of works within the framework of ambiguous texts is not an
arbitrary process, but rather obeys strictly the insights gained within the realm of

musical production. Subjected to more careful observation, older and, above all, 'classical' German music – if it is to be realized as its construction presents itself to the eye of today – demands the same strict reproduction as does new music, resisting every improvisational freedom of the interpreter.[34]

Adorno argues that the only adequate way to perform the music of the eighteenth and nineteenth centuries today is with the strictest attention to the detail of the score (he talks of 'die Forderung sachlich adäquater Wiedergabe der Werke').[35] And furthermore, he maintains that the need for such a style of performance 'has emancipated itself from the will of the author', and that it is through this kind of detachment that 'the historical character of reproduction is conclusively revealed'.[36] He supports this point with reference to the performance of Beethoven (and also indirectly to certain excesses in the direction of 'historical authenticity' in the performance of early music):

If an early Beethoven piano sonata were to be played today as 'freely', with such arbitrarily improvisational changes – for example, changes of the basic tempi of individual movements – as it was – according to contemporary reports – by Beethoven himself at the piano, the apparently authentic manner of interpretation would strike the listener as contradictory to the meaning of the work in the face of the constructive unity of such movements.[37]

The conclusions Adorno draws from this are important in relation to his concept of the dialectic of musical material. He maintains that it is only in the light of later musical production that the constructive unity of such earlier works has become clearly recognizable; at the time it was probably not the 'organic unity' of Beethoven's music which struck his contemporaries, but rather, as Adorno has put it elsewhere in discussing the analysis of such music, what he calls its 'titanism' (see Chapter 6). Thus Adorno sees a parallel here between the problematical nature of musical production and reproduction, composition and interpretation – between 'the rigid demand for compositional accuracy' made upon the composer faced with the historical demands of the musical material, and the 'strict attention to the detail of the score' demanded of the interpreter of not only twentieth-century music but also the music of earlier historical periods.

Lucia Sziborsky suggests that 'Adorno's theorem concerning the way in which musical works change through history, the roots of which reach back to the year 1925, did not receive its first constitutive impulse from the Marxian theory of the commodity, but from the practical question: how is the past to be interpreted today?'[38] The text to which she is referring is the essay 'Zum Problem der Reproduktion' of 1925[39] (in fact, Adorno had for some time the intention of writing a 'theory of musical reproduction', a project on which at one point, in 1935, he hoped to collaborate with Rudolf

Kolisch).[40] In this early essay Adorno had already sketched the outline of his theory of musical reproduction. In it he insists that it is the *content* (*Inhalt*) of works which finally decides their manner of interpretation, and that the freedom of the interpreter is relative and often overstated. There are demands which come from the structure of the work itself and which limit the freedom of the interpreter and separate him from the realm of improvisation. He writes: 'In what way one is to read the work, what degree of freedom the work allows the interpreter who is to interpret it – to research this seems to be the central task of a theory of reproduction'.[41]

For Adorno, the fundamental problem for a theory of reproduction is what, in his early writings, he had called 'the rupture between self and forms'. This problem was discussed at some length in Chapter 1 in relation to composition, and we must now return to it in the context of performance and interpretation. Adorno's argument is that in earlier historical periods the interpreter had a certain freedom within the transpersonal objectivity of the genres and formal types which constituted, musically speaking, the world outside and beyond his subjectivity, and which was acknowledged and approved by him.

For when the forms allow the self space and are at the same time endorsed, then interpretation has its highest claim on freedom; and also when the composer speaks completely from himself he nevertheless does not speak in isolation, but is perceived and understood; this 'being understood' lives within the work itself as a formal element.[42]

Under the influence of Lukács's *Theorie des Romans* (see Chapter 1)., Adorno argues that the tension in earlier music (for example, in Bach) between the self and its forms – between the composer and the handed-down musical forms – allowed for a degree of flexibility in interpretation, allowed space for *Schein und Spiel* ('illusion and play'). The handed-down forms spoke as 'we', the community, and carried the weight of objectivity; the composing Subject spoke as 'I', the creative individual. Between the two existed both a consensus and a tension which gave room for 'play' (*Spiel*). When, however, the binding force of the musical forms disperses, 'the space between the archetype and the individual work shrinks, or becomes infinite ... no "play" happens any more and the freedom of the interpreter is reduced to the minimum which human dependency cannot do without, even in art'.[43] In many ways, therefore, the theory Adorno puts forward in 'Zum Problem der Reproduktion' can be seen, at the level of reproduction, as complementing as well as presaging his theory of musical material at the level of production. The alienation expressed by the composer at the level of the demands of the musical material, as the 'rupture between self and forms', is experienced at the level of interpretation as lack of improvisatory freedom. Adorno writes: 'the greater the structure of acknowledged objectivity in the musical work, the greater the freedom available to its interpreter. With the fading away of the objectively-given "form world" there also fades away with it the freedom of interpretation.'[44]

The musical work as performance

While it is in the area of performance, as 'sounding object', that the musical work comes particularly under the sway of the 'culture industry', works nevertheless 'need to be played and interpreted in order to unfold their essence'.[45] The notion of consistency (*Stimmigkeit*), as accuracy in meeting the demands of the work as score, may therefore be understood in relation to performance as well as composition. However, while at the level of the work as score multiple and contradictory readings may coexist as infinite potential performances, at the level of the work in performance, as 'sounding object', no particular realization of the piece can fully meet the contradictory demands of the work as score. This impossibility of any completely adequate performance is built into the structure of the work at the level of composition, Adorno maintains, as the relation between substantive content (*Gehalt*) and appearance (*Erscheinung*). This is an aspect of the 'problem' of the work and of its 'riddle character' or enigmatic quality (*Rätselcharakter*). The attempt to cope with the impossibility of the work and to make it possible at the level of performance has, for Adorno, something of the character of a circus act. The central concept he utilizes in conjunction with performance is *tour de force*:

To interpret art correctly for the purpose of reproduction means, first of all, to formulate it as a problem. In every work there are incompatible demands arising from the relation between content and appearance. These incompatible demands pose problems for performance and have to be recognized. In addition, the reproduction of works of art has to uncover the *tour de force* in them; that is, it has to find the point of indifference where the possibility of the impossible lies concealed. Because of the antinomies of works, completely satisfactory performances are actually impossible; of the many conceivable ways of performing one and the same work, each one tends to suppress some contradictory element. The supreme principle of reproduction is therefore that the performance becomes the arena of those conflicts which have been objectified in the work as a *tour de force*.[46]

In his use of the concept '*tour de force*' Adorno is referring not only to obvious virtuosity in musical works and their performance. He insists that the concept is valid even for 'simple' works, as well as for works of the 'great tradition' which may not be virtuosic in any obvious sense at all. As examples of this from the 'great tradition' he refers to the synthesis of the harmonic and the polyphonic in Bach: how the logic of chord-progression, 'as a pure result of part-writing, is freed of its heterogeneous heaviness ... a factor which imbues Bach's works with their peculiarly floating quality';[47] and the 'paradox' of Beethoven's music – 'that something emerges out of nothing', motivically–thematically speaking, he suggests, as a kind of musical verification of Hegelian logic.[48] The aim of an adequate musical performance must therefore be, according to Adorno, the revelation of the 'problem' of the work, as *tour de force*, and the making possible in performance of the impossibility which lies at the heart of the work.

Although the objectification of the work as performance is essential for its processual character to be revealed, Adorno maintains that this at the same time also contributes to the reification of the work. The work 'in itself' is an objectification of the Subject, while the work-as-performance, although a further aspect of this process of objectification, can also serve to 'fix' the work – i.e. to reify it. Although the work as performance is more than the work as printed score, Adorno insists that the work as transcendental 'thing in itself' is more than both. However, the work is not available to us in its immediacy, but only in mediated form, and its materiality – both as performance and as score – is 'the resultant of an inner dynamic'[49] to which we have access only through this materiality, as material structure. Accordingly, Adorno gives priority to the score over its performance, considering the score to come closer to the work 'in itself':

scores are always more than just pointers to performance. In short, they are more nearly coterminous with the artistic phenomenon itself than with performance. There may, incidentally, not be such a great conflict here. To realize music until very recently has meant to realize the interlinear version of the score. The fixation by writing or notation is not extraneous to art, for it enables the work to become independent of its genesis. This alone should argue strongly for the primacy of texts over their reproduction.[50]

4   Musical reproduction (II): distribution

It is with reproduction as distribution and marketing that we move to an account of the musical work as performance which orientates itself more towards consumption than towards the demands of musical production. As suggested above, this process can also be seen as a move from the musical work as an 'in itself', an objectification of the Subject, towards the work as a 'for other', as the reification and standardization of subjectivity in the form of the commodity. This distinction, between *objectification* (as both the *Objektivation* and *Entäußerung* of the expressive Subject in dynamic, processual musical structures) and *reification* (as *Verdinglichung*, the rigidification of dynamic processes into static givens), is crucial to an understanding of Adorno's sociology of music. It goes some way towards explaining Adorno's emphasis on the sphere of production over that of consumption.

In one sense the marketing and distribution of music is already an aspect of the sphere of consumption and cannot really be discussed apart from consumption. In another sense, however, due to the all-important intervention of the culture industry at this point, music falls directly under the control of the mode of production of monopoly capitalism. Thus the musical forces of production and the autonomy of the musical work come under the sway of the culture industry – that is to say, they become part of the process of industrial production itself. The culture industry is seen by Adorno as a kind of filtering mechanism, a process of pre-selection which shapes public taste according to the demands of a capitalist market economy and which has the effect of standardization of taste. This process is an important aspect of the mediation of music and society, and its ramifications are discussed in the following terms in *Einleitung in die Musiksoziologie*:

Until distribution gets to the masses, it is subject to innumerable processes of social selection and guidance by powers such as industries, concert agencies, festival managements, and various other bodies. All this enters into the listeners' preferences; their needs are merely dragged along. Ahead of everything comes the control by the giant concerns in which electrical, recording and broadcasting industries are overtly or covertly merged in the economically most advanced countries. As the concentration and the power of the distributive agencies increase, freedom in the choice of what to hear tends to decrease; in this respect, integrated music no longer differs from any other consumer commodities.[51]

The relation here is therefore understood by Adorno as that primarily between the work as performance and the 'culture industry' as institutionalized marketing. The outcome of this relation is the reified musical work as commodity – the triumph of exchange-value over use-value.

Musical performance and the culture industry

Whereas the musical work as performance was discussed in the previous section from the point of view of its relation to interpretation and its orientation towards musical production and the demands of the work as score, the performance of the work will now be considered from the point of view of distribution and its orientation towards consumption. The work as performance acquires a function within the social relations of production – that of entertainment. This function, Adorno maintains, changes the 'meaning' (*Sinn*) of autonomous music.[52] It fundamentally affects the meaning of 'great music of the past', characterized as it is by its separation from society on account of its very functionlessness:

profit takes the functionless into its service and thereby degrades it to meaningless-ness and irrelevancy. The exploitation of something useless in itself, something sealed and superfluous to the people on whom it is foisted – this is the ground of the fetishism that covers all cultural commodities, and the musical ones in particular. It is tuned to conformism.[53]

He considers that this distorts the meaning of musical works of the past, and, at the same time, leads to the production of music explicitly for the market: 'in music, too, demand has come to be a pretext for the sphere of production'.[54] Fragmented listening habits both change the significance of music of the past and dictate the composition of whole genres of music of the present – that is, that music which accepts its commodity character and is specifically designed for commodity consumption. The culture industry furthermore dictates performance styles, with a concentration on surface effect which is at the expense of structural demands. In the essay 'Über den Fetischcharakter in der Musik und die Regression des Hörens' (1938) Adorno writes (with typical overstatement):

The new fetish is the flawlessly functioning, metallically brilliant apparatus as such, in which all the cog wheels mesh so perfectly that not the slightest hole remains for the meaning of the whole. Perfect, immaculate performance in the latest style presents the work at the price of its definitive reification. It presents it as already complete from the very first note. The performance sounds like its own phonograph record.[55]

And in *Einleitung in die Musiksoziologie* he argues that performers themselves become material for the culture industry, subject to fetishiz-ation:

In the machinery of musical distribution the productive forces of performing artists are transformed into means of production, after the model of movie stars. This effects a qualitative change in them.[56]

Part of this process – that is, the change in compositional and performance styles in the interests of consumption – is the reduction of the particular language of autonomous works to a *generalized* musical language, to the general characteristics of tonal harmony, for example. In Adorno's words:

In the spirit of our time the sole remainder of the autonomous artistic language of music is a communicative language, and that does permit something like a social function. It is the remnant that is left of an art once the artistic element in it has dissolved.[57]

Because social conditions no longer favour autonomous music, those features of the language of autonomous music which were once secondary and associative come to the fore and become dominant. That is, those gestural and mimetic elements, associated with music's previous functionality and which had become sublimated through the 'law of form' of autonomous music, now reappear, given the music's change of function. These in their turn also become part of the musical material available to the composer (see the account of Adorno's discussion of the music of composers like Weill and Eisler under the concept 'surrealist music' in Chapter 2 and the discussion of Mahler's music in Chapters 4 and 6). According to Adorno, this is the disintegration of the material of music into its single 'pre-artistic' elements, to form a second, mass musical language. This is 'communicative' only in the ironic sense of being made up of gestures that have become familiar through repetition and through their association with extra-musical contexts. In contrast, the autonomy of the avant-garde work is maintained through total integration of its elements within the closed world of its form, and through an explicit *refusal* of communication (it needs to be recognized that Adorno's 'heroic' concept of the avant-garde retains a notion of 'development', however fractured, and contrasts in several respects with that derived from Dadaism, which emphasizes the techniques of montage and collage). Adorno writes:

When social conditions have ceased, in the listeners' consciousness, to favour the constitution of the autonomy of music, that extra-artistic side of it necessarily comes to prevail again. The only reason why music's scattered members will fit into something like a second musical mass language is that the esthetic integration of its literally sensual, pre-artistic elements was always precarious – that throughout history, these elements lay waiting for a chance to elude the entelechy of the structure and to disintegrate themselves.[58]

The threat to the 'constitution of the autonomy of music', and the disintegration of musical material to form 'a second musical mass language' is seen by Adorno to be one of the most significant effects of the 'culture industry'. Adorno, together with Horkheimer, first introduced the term 'culture industry' in *Dialektik der Aufklärung*, although his concern with the effects of the mass distribution and mechanical reproduction of art works dates back much earlier and provides the focus for his debate with Walter Benjamin in the mid-1930s. (Adorno's essay 'Über den Fetisch-charakter in der Musik und die Regression des Hörens' of 1938, originating as a critique of the position taken by Benjamin in his 'Das Kunstwerk im Zeitalter seiner technischen Reproduzierbarkeit' of 1936, provides an important intermediate stage in the development of the concept.) In *Dialektik der Aufklärung* (in the chapter 'The culture industry: Enlightenment as mass deception'), Adorno and Horkheimer saw the 'culture industry' (together with what they identified as its equivalent at that time in the 'Eastern bloc' – the centralized political control of arts policy under the doctrine of socialist realism) as the culmination of the process of rationalization of all aspects of culture which had been taking place since the Enlightenment. They argued that this has resulted in the extension of the organizational methods of monopoly and state capitalism even into areas as apparently autonomous and separate from society as the arts. The culture industry levels and renders identical everything that comes under its control:

> for culture now impresses the same stamp on everything. Films, radio and magazines make up a system which is uniform as a whole and in every part. Even the aesthetic activities of political opposites are one in their enthusiastic obedience to the rhythm of the iron system.[59]

The culture industry, Adorno and Horkheimer maintain, brings about 'the false identity of the general and the particular', and serves to conceal the gap between Subject and Object, individual and totality, reality and Utopia. They write: 'Under monopoly all mass culture is identical'.[60] According to Adorno and Horkheimer, the culture industry justifies itself on two counts: (i) in terms of technological reproductive processes; and (ii) in terms of consumer needs and demands. They maintain that these two come together in the kind of explanation put forward by interested parties which involves an appeal both to consumer needs and to the need for efficient management of distribution in order to meet widespread consumer demand:

> It is alleged that because millions participate in it, certain reproduction processes are necessary that inevitably require identical needs in innumerable places to be satisfied with identical goods. The technical contrast between the few production centers and the large number of widely dispersed consumption points is said to demand organization and planning by management. Furthermore, it is claimed that standards were based in the first place on consumers' needs and for that reason were accepted with so little resistance.[61]

Adorno and Horkheimer provide a critique of this kind of justification of the culture industry in the following terms: (i) the process results in a circle of manipulation and dependency which only serves to reinforce the system itself and make it even more powerful; (ii) the system's own justification of itself does not draw attention to the fact that the increasing power of technology over society derives from the power of those who already have economic control in society; (iii) the technological rationale, based on the argument that increased efficiency and control is in response to consumer needs, amounts to 'the rationale of domination itself'.[62] Adorno and Horkheimer argue that, as the centralization and concentration of the control of the production and distribution of culture, and the control of patterns of consumption lie ultimately in the hands of a relatively small number of large industries, the implications are essentially political.

In an article written in 1963, 'Resumé über Kulturindustrie', Adorno reconsidered his ideas on the culture industry, and also revealed that the choice of the term itself (rather than the more innocuous 'mass culture') was the result of a desire to convey a notion of culture manufactured and manipulated from above, and to distinguish it clearly from the idea of 'a culture that arises spontaneously from the masses themselves, the contemporary form of popular art'.[63] Adorno makes it clear in the 1963 article that what is usually regarded as his attack on popular music is really an account of the manipulation of music by the culture industry and not a dismissal of popular music as such. He stresses, in fact, that both 'high' and 'low' art are changed by the culture industry:

To the detriment of both it forces together the spheres of high and low art, separated for thousands of years. The seriousness of high art is destroyed in speculation about its efficacy; the seriousness of the lower perishes with the civilizational constraints imposed on the rebellious resistance inherent within it as long as total control was not yet total. Thus, although the culture industry undeniably speculates on the conscious and unconscious state of the millions towards which it is directed, the masses are not primary, but secondary, they are an object of calculation; an appendage of the machinery.[64]

Characteristic of the culture industry, Adorno maintains, is how it disguises 'sameness' as the 'incessantly new'. What it puts forward as progress is in fact this dressing up of the same basic formula. Adorno explains how the term 'industry' is to be understood in this context. It is not to be taken literally, as it refers rather to 'the standardization of the thing itself – such as that of the Western, familiar to every movie-goer – and to the rationalization of distribution techniques, but not strictly to the production process'.[65] He also points out how film, for example, because of the division of labour involved in its production, resembles industrial–technical processes, but 'individual forms of production are nevertheless maintained'.[66] The term 'culture industry' refers to the rationalization of the work process as much as to what is manufactured. It is industrial in its organization, and it appeals to a sense of order, Adorno maintains, but order without specific content. Its 'message' is conformist, its concepts of order those of the status quo, unquestioned and unanalysed. Adorno writes: 'The power of the culture industry's ideology is such that conformity has replaced consciousness'.[67] The culture industry therefore stands opposed to the concept of the work of art as a mode of cognition, with a 'truth content', and implying a sense of the progress of human consciousness as Enlightenment and emancipation. Adorno argues in 'Resumé über Kulturindustrie' that 'the total effect of the culture industry is one of anti-enlightenment that is the progressive technical domination of nature, becomes mass deception and is turned into a means of fettering consciousness'.[68]

The work as commodity

Adorno considers that the commodity character of art affects all music today, and that, as discussed in Chapters 2 and 3, the stark choice facing any composer conscious of the problem is whether to accept or to oppose music's commodity character. As we have seen, Adorno argues in 'Zur gesellschaftlichen Lage der Musik' that music

> no longer serves direct [unmittelbaren] needs nor benefits from direct application, but rather adjusts to the pressures of exchange of abstract units. Its value wherever such value still exists at all – is determined by use: it subordinates itself to the process of exchange.[69]

Although all music is subject to commodification, Adorno makes the important distinction – already outlined in relation to the typology offered in 'Zur gesellschaftlichen Lage der Musik' discussed in Chapter 2 – between (i) music which is specifically designed at the level of production with its function as commodity in mind, and (ii) music of the past (as well as some 'modern' music) which acquires the function of commodity at the level of its reproduction and distribution, a function which comes into conflict with the immanent demands of the musical work itself.

In the first category Adorno seems to encompass all kinds of popular music – including light music (leichte Musik), 'hit' songs (Schlager) and commercial jazz. The chapter on 'Popular music' in Einleitung in die Musiksoziologie devotes attention to each of these in turn. 'Light music', for example, makes use of the 'devalued' material of high art music, and even up to the mid-nineteenth century it was, in Adorno's view, still possible to produce light music of unpretentious substance – Adorno has Offenbach in mind here, and also Johann Strauss. However, the last period when it was still conceivable for a genuine interaction to take place between the 'lower' and 'higher' spheres of music was, Adorno maintains, in the late eighteenth century with a work like Mozart's The Magic Flute. Already by the later nineteenth century light music in the form of operetta was in decline. One of the reasons for this, he suggests, was the close connection of this music with 'the economic sphere of distribution – more specifically, with the garment business'.[70] But it was the wholesale industrialization of the production and distribution of operetta, in parallel with the industrialization of production in society, which transformed this music, together with the related genres of the revue and the musical, into an essentially mass-produced form geared towards consumer trends. This came about, Adorno argues in 'Zur gesellschaftlichen Lage der Musik', through intense competition which necessitated the kind of team production and advance planning and organization later to be such a feature of the Hollywood film industry, and which 'transformed light music into a market article'.[71] It is this standardization of production which, Adorno considers, is such a feature of the 'hit' song. He attempts to demonstrate this in some musical detail,[72] but somewhat spoils his case by his fervently subjective approach to the material. More convincing are his earlier forays into this area, like the brief essay 'Schlageranalysen' of 1929 (published initially in *Anbruch* 11), discussed in passing in Chapter 1. This analyses and interprets the music and lyrics of three popular song hits from the period 1915–28, including the famous *Valencia*. Here Adorno succeeds in providing real insight into the social significance and effect of such songs in their historical context, and achieves this through a certain detachment and delicate irony of style.

Perhaps most controversial has been the reception of Adorno's critique of jazz.[73] There are misunderstandings, it would seem, on both sides. That is to say, Adorno has courted criticism in articles like 'Über Jazz' (1937) and 'Zeitlose Mode: Zum Jazz' (1953), not to mention 'Über den Fetischcharakter in der Musik und die Regression des Hörens' (1938) and 'On popular music' (1941), where it is fair to say that he at times demonstrates a degree of prejudice and even ignorance of the music which is difficult to defend.[74] There are other moments, however, where he makes perceptive observations which indicate a greater understanding of and sympathy for the possibilities of popular music and jazz than he is given credit for by his numerous critics of this aspect of his work. The following passage, for example, displays a grasp of the complexity of the problem of evaluating jazz as a music with a 'truth content' in the sense in which Adorno uses the concept in conjunction with 'serious' music, and shows Adorno for once applying his own dialectical principles with admirable rigour to a music he clearly dislikes:

The social function of jazz coincides with its history, the history of a heresy that has been received into the mass culture. Certainly, jazz has the potential of a musical breakout from this culture on the part of those who were either refused admittance to it or annoyed by its mendacity. Time and again, however, jazz became a captive of the culture industry and thus of musical and social conformism; famed devices of its phases, such as 'swing', 'bebop', 'cool jazz', are both advertising slogans and marks of that process of absorption. Popular music can no more be exploded from within, on its own premises and with its own habituated means, than its own sphere points beyond it.[75]

Adorno argues elsewhere, however, that, in spite of the insistence by jazz fans that there is a distinction to be made between 'commercial' jazz and the 'pure' article, jazz 'is tied to commercial music by its predominant basic material, the hit songs',[76] and that for this reason jazz is unable to go beyond its own sphere. It could be argued against this position that Adorno appears to be inconsistent on this in relation to his overall theory as put forward in 'Zur gesellschaftlichen Lage der Musik'. If his concept of 'surrealist' music, as described in his third category of 'authentic' music (see Chapter 2, above), is applied to his views on jazz, then it is difficult to see why, if Weill could juxtapose elements of popular music material with historically 'devalued' material and enable them to acquire new meaning by putting them within a new context, jazz or rock musicians should be incapable of doing likewise.[77]

In his second category of music subject to commodification Adorno includes music of the past (and certain contemporary music), now powerless to prevent itself being absorbed and manipulated by the culture industry. The crucial concept for understanding this process of assimilation is *Entkunstung*, a term difficult to translate adequately, but which I shall render here – with reservations – as *de-aestheticization*.[78] The concept refers to the removal of the distinction between autonomous art and other spheres of life or, to put it another way, the removal of the 'art' from art (indeed, if one could get away with it, 'de-artification' might come closer to conveying the sense of *Entkunstung* than 'de-aestheticization', making it clear that 'art' (*Kunst*) is not identical to 'the aesthetic' (*Ästhetik*)). The concept encapsulates, as always with Adorno, two opposing tendencies. On the one hand, a decisive characteristic of modernist art, as the avant-garde, is its negation of its own concept and of the aesthetic categories which hitherto had defined it – a tendency seen at its extreme in the anti-art manifestations of the Dadaists. This is a process which Adorno sees as having started historically with art freeing itself from its auratic and cultic functions and gaining its autonomy from immediate social and religious function. This tendency has distanced art from society. On the other hand, as part of the larger process of social rationalization epitomized by the division of labour, the public finds itself distanced from art, and in particular from the production of art. Adorno argues that, whereas the modernist art work, in reflecting the gulf which separates art from life, succeeds in further distancing itself from the public by presenting an experience of alienation which the public finds unpalatable, the public itself seeks to escape alienation by breaking down the difference between art and life by reducing art to entertainment. Both of these extremes come for Adorno under the concept of *Entkunstung*. Adorno gives the following account of the process in *Ästhetische Theorie*:

Unmistakable symptoms of this tendency are the passionate urge to violate and meddle with the work of art in ways which do not allow it to be what it is; to dress it up; to shorten its distance from the viewer; and so on. The masses want the shameful difference separating art from their lives eliminated, because if art were to have any real effect on them it would be that of instilling a sense of loathing, which is the last thing they want. These are some of the subjective predispositions that make it possible to line up art on the side of consumer goods. Objective vested interests do the rest.[79]

Adorno thus sees a parallel between our relation to art and our relation to consumer commodities. Art's autonomy character (art of the past, that is) now makes art works easily assimilable to the culture industry through the kind of fetishization which turns them into commodities, abstract and interchangeable objects of exchange. This process of *Entkunstung* constitutes an extreme form of reification, Adorno maintains, which has considerable implications within the sphere of consumption/reception in view of the ways in which music is now listened to and experienced.

5   Musical consumption

It is most obviously in its consumption/reception that the musical work becomes the object of musical experience. This is not to say, of course, that musical experience occurs only within what is here being labelled the 'sphere of consumption', as the relation of listener to musical work. It almost goes without saying that it is a precondition of all areas of the relations of musical production: that is to say, of the relation of composer to material; of interpreter to score; and, it must be argued, the relation of culture industry to performance. Thus Adorno's concept of 'musical experience' and his typology of listeners, although examined here mainly in relation to the sphere of consumption, will also need to be understood as applying, with appropriate modifications, to the spheres of production, reproduction and distribution.

Adorno's concerns at this level are to understand modes of listening and types of musical experience in relation to what he considers their adequacy to the demands of the musical work. As already indicated in this chapter, the centrality of the work, and ultimately of the demands of the musical material, characterizes Adorno's dialectical model at each stage of its unfolding – with the important exception of the relation between the culture industry and the musical work as performance, where the relationship is significantly reversed. What Adorno's sociology of music reveals is that the relation between the musical work and the listener is not simple and immediate, in spite of any appearances to the contrary. It is instead a complex and densely mediated relation which, Adorno insists, is now crystallized in the work itself as commodity – the dominant form in which we, as listeners, have access to it. Adorno sees it as his aim, therefore, to identify characteristic modes of listening (as ideal types) which may be considered more or less adequate to the demands of the work and which at the same time may be capable of countering the effects of the culture industry. He also aims to identify the characteristics of a desirable form of musical experience which such a mode of listening presupposes and to which it also may lead. The dialectic here is therefore that between mediated work and mediated listener.

The relation between listener and musical work

In view of the complex of mediations suggested at each stage in the application of Adorno's adapted Marxian model, it will be useful at this stage to review briefly what can now be understood under the concept 'musical work'. As has been shown, Adorno insists that the work is mediated 'within itself', and that mediation is not to be understood simply as being located in the relation between work and, for example, performer or audience. This does, however, need to be correctly interpreted. He understands the work as 'sedimented history and society', and insists furthermore that the pre-compositional 'musical material' available to the composer is itself already historically and socially mediated and has its own demands. This dialectic of expressive needs and technical means, of Subject and Object, which constitutes the 'dialectic of musical material', operates not only between composer and material, but also between work-as-score and interpreter, between work-as-performance and culture industry, and between work-as-commodity and listener. At each of these stages – that is, of production, reproduction, distribution and consumption – the work may be identified at different levels of its mediation. As seen above, however, Adorno places greatest emphasis on the sphere of production because there, in the dialectic of composer and musical material, he sees 'the objective social constitution of music in itself'.[80] The spheres of reproduction, distribution and consumption he considers, as already indicated, to be dependent on the sphere of production, as it is only within the structure of the work, he maintains, that one is able to 'understand' and decipher the work in its relation to society, and not in its effects. The implication here seems to be that the mediations at the level of reproduction, distribution and consumption are not intrinsic to the work in the same way as the mediation of music and society at the level of musical production, in that the former are more in the nature of relations *between* the work and, for example, performer, culture industry or listening public. Also implied here is the suggestion that this form of mediation, as relation between two terms, contains an element of mystification or distortion, particularly in view of the commodification of the musical work via the culture industry. For Adorno, just as it is the task of the composer to respond to the demands of the musical material, and of the performer to respond to the demands of the work-as-score, it is likewise the task of the listener to understand the demands of the work as an 'in itself'. This means demystifying the work as commodity and as performance, and attempting to reach the work in its essential ambiguity and multiple possible readings – the enigmatic quality or 'riddle character' of the art work. This demands, according to Adorno, a particular kind of active listening.

It would, however, be wrong to give the impression that Adorno believes that musical works have any ultimate meaning in an absolute sense, and that it is possible to experience a work apart from its multiple mediations and outside and beyond its historical and social context. Adorno, on the contrary, is insisting that a work needs to be understood as a 'complex of meaning', as mediated. At the same time, however, he maintains that each work makes its own unique *structural* demands upon the listener, and that it is through recognizing and responding to these demands that it is possible to catch a glimpse of the ways in which society is mediated in musical structures. Adorno thus gives priority to the structure of the work at the level of production, maintaining that to do otherwise (i.e. to emphasize distribution or consumption at the expense of the work) is to make the music an arbitrary occasion for the projection of the listener's preconceptions.

Adorno opens the first chapter of his *Einleitung in die Musiksoziologie* with a definition of the area of concern of a sociology of music. He writes that 'one would probably start by defining it as knowledge of the relation between music and the socially organized individuals who listen to it'.[81] He observes that, for such knowledge to exist, extensive empirical research into the nature of this relation would be required. However, for the results of such research to 'rise above the compilation of inarticulate facts',[82] the 'context of problems' involved needs first to be structured at the level of theory. It is to this end that Adorno puts forward his typology of listeners. He insists that such a categorization of 'listening types' is offered in order to be tested empirically, and modified accordingly. As a typology it 'is thus to be understood as merely one of ideal types – a trait it shares with all typologies'.[83] Nevertheless, Adorno is not occupied primarily with the investigation of the 'tastes, preferences, aversions and habits of the audience'[84] in themselves. His concern, as always, is with the demands of the musical work, and with 'the adequacy or inadequacy of the act of listening to what is heard'.[85] Fundamental to his theory is therefore the conviction that 'works are objectively structured things and meaningful in themselves, things that invite analysis and can be perceived and experienced with different degrees of accuracy'.[86]

Adorno's typology of listeners as given in *Einleitung in die Musiksoziologie* contains eight types, ranging from the 'expert' to the 'musically indifferent' listener. There are, however, other versions of such a typology to be found in a number of his writings – for example, in 'Zur gesellschaftlichen Lage der Musik',[87] in 'Über den Fetischcharakter in der Musik und die Regression des Hörens',[88] in 'Anweisungen zum Hören neuer Musik',[89] and at the end of *Philosophie der neuen Musik*.[90] All these versions can be reduced to a fundamental oppositional pair of categories: (i) *adequate* forms of listening, and (ii) *regressive* forms of listening.

(i)   Adequate listening This category includes two main types, labelled in *Einleitung in die Musiksoziologie* the 'expert listener' and the 'good listener'. The *expert listener* is the type Adorno describes as the 'fully adequate listener', fully conscious of what he hears, 'who tends to miss nothing and at the same time, at each moment, accounts to himself for what he has heard'.[91] In other words, this is a type of highly informed and self-reflective listener, able to think along with what is heard and able to understand the individual moments as parts of a 'complex of meaning', a context made up of past, present and future moments which constitute the musical work as it unfolds through time. Such a listener understands what he or she hears as 'necessary', in terms of the concrete technical logic of the work and the demands of its material. It is a mode of conduct that, in the article 'Anweisungen zum Hören neuer Musik', Adorno had labelled 'structural listening'.[92]

The type of listening which would do justice to the ideal of the integrated composition could best be labelled 'structural'. The advice, that listening should be multi-levelled . . . has already identified an essential moment of this listening ideal.[93]

Adorno considers that this type of listener is probably quite rare today, and is likely to be made up of specialists. He suggests that it 'may be more or less limited to the circle of professional musicians', although '[n]ot all of them meet its criteria; indeed, many reproductive artists are apt to resist them'.[94] He is keen, however, to rescue the type from the belief that it is the exclusive privilege of the professional musician to constitute the category of the 'expert listener'. For Adorno, the fact that it is likely to prove difficult to find many listeners who could meet the exacting demands he proposes should not be permitted to discredit the type itself. His reasons for arguing for the validity of this type could be summarized as follows: (a) the increase in the complexity of compositions has itself reduced the number of listeners in this category,[95] and this in itself is a manifestation of the alienation of music from audiences; and (b) as an 'ideal type' it is the only mode of listening fully adequate to the material/structural demands of the music itself, and thus maps one extreme limit of the typological series that follows on from it.

Adorno recognizes that the demands made by the structural complexity of musical works upon the listener are 'not only incompatible with his nature, with his situation, and with the state of nonprofessional musical education, but with individual liberty as well'.[96] This is what, for him, legitimates the type of the 'good listener'. This type is also capable, like the 'expert', of hearing beyond the surface of a piece of music, and of making connections between details and the work as a whole, but 'he is not, or not fully, aware of the technical and structural implications'.[97] His understanding of the 'immanent logic' of a piece of music tends to be spontaneous, and need not involve any conscious knowledge of its grammar and syntax (rather in the way we understand our own language). Adorno identifies this type with what we mean by a 'musical person', and points out that '[h]istorically, such musicality required a certain homogeneity of musical culture'.[98] In his typology as put forward in *Einleitung in die Musik-soziologie*, Adorno suggests that this type, as the musical amateur, is threatened today by the mass media and mechanical reproduction, is unlikely to occur within the petty bourgeoisie, and its 'best chance of survival may be where remnants of an aristocratic society have managed to hold out, as in Vienna'.[99] Adorno's association of the musical amateur specifically with the remnants of the aristocracy, even in Vienna, is rather curious, however, especially in the light of his suggestion in a brief essay dating from 1933, 'Vierhändig, noch einmal',[100] that it was the existence of an informed public actively involved in amateur music-making and drawn primarily from the middle classes (particularly the 'high' bourgeoisie) which provided just that 'homogeneity of musical culture' which was necessary for the development of art music (especially the symphony) in the 'bourgeois period'. This amateur music-making consisted mainly of chamber music and in particular of arrangements of orchestral music for piano duet, and enabled a relationship to exist between composer and informed public which has not survived the modernist period. The loss of the amateur to the practice of radical music is seen by Adorno as further emphasizing the alienation of the composer.

(ii)   Regressive listening This category, according to Adorno, is characterized by the fetishization of music, and is dominated by what he calls the 'entertainment listener'. This type, he suspects, is statistically the most significant, in that the majority of listeners appear to consider the social function of music to be primarily that of entertainment. What is not clear is whether the type is a product of the culture industry, or whether the industry responds to the type. Adorno himself did no empirical research into this, but admits that research is needed.[101] He considers that socially the type represents no particular class, has no particular political affiliations, but will probably be conformist. Its main feature, in all its

manifestations, is 'the need for music as a comfortable distraction'.[102] The type is inseparable from technology, in that it uses music as background music, as a kind of addiction (Brecht and Eisler had both talked of musicians as 'dealers in narcotics').[103] It seems to be an amalgam of several other listening types in Adorno's 'regressive listening' category, or at least to contain elements of them. The 'emotional listener', for example, has some similarities with the 'entertainment listener'. The 'emotional listener' uses music as the occasion for the free flow of associations, and is strongly anti-intellectual, resisting the idea of 'structural listening'. Music is valued as 'a source of irrationality, whereby a man inexorably harnessed to the bustle of rationalistic self-preservation will be enabled to keep having feelings at all'.[104] There are also similarities between the 'entertainment listener' and what Adorno calls the 'culture consumer', but the latter, unlike the straightforward and unrationalized motives of the 'entertainment listener', goes in for the conspicuous consumption of music as 'culture'. Adorno maintains that this type, the 'culture consumer', is the historical and sociological legacy of the amateur as 'good listener', but fetishizes aspects of works like 'theme tunes' or grandiose moments. It is the polar opposite of 'structural listening', in that it is characterized by 'atomistic listening' and is not interested in structure. It also fetishizes performers and aspects of technique. Adorno writes that the milieu of this type of listener is 'the upper and uplifted bourgeoisie, with links to the petty one; their ideology may be reactionary, culture-conservative. Almost always they are enemies of the vulnerable new music.'[105] Other types in Adorno's typology are the 'resentment listener', obsessed with historical authenticity, or with music education, and intent on 'purifying' the performance of music and domesticating it, and the 'popular music' equivalent of this in the 'jazz fan', who seeks to control and domesticate the potentially subversive character of jazz. And finally, there is a catchall type which Adorno calls the 'indifferent listener'. This also includes within it the 'unmusical' and the 'anti-musical' – categories which Adorno also feels need research.

Adorno's sketch for a typology of listeners is speculative and, as we have seen, is not directly grounded in empirical research (although it is clearly based on ideas which emerged from the empirical work he did in the United States for the Princeton Radio Project in the early 1940s). Like all aspects of his work, the typology is heavily value-laden. At the same time, however, it is consistent in all respects with his music theory taken as a whole. That is to say, the conviction underlying it is that musical works are objectively structured and significative, and therefore call for a form of interpretation which is able to follow the inner logic of a work as experience while also being able to reflect upon and account for the experience as understanding. Such a form of experience seeks to understand the 'social content' of a work 'from the inside', and its ideal is a form of 'structural listening'.

Musical experience and understanding

This double problem – that of a fully adequate form of musical experience which involves a total immersion in the dynamic unfolding of the structure of the work, and which, at the same time, is able to go beyond the immediate givens of the experience of the work towards an understanding of its immanent logic – is present both as point of departure and as endpoint of Adorno's aesthetics, sociology and 'immanent analysis' of music. It occurs at this point because it follows on naturally from the questions raised by the typology of listeners outlined above. As already suggested, however, it is quite clear that the question of musical experience and of the understanding of music is not something which is of concern only at the level of musical reception/consumption. It is central, although with different emphases, at each stage of the 'social dialectic' as outlined above – that is, in the spheres of musical production and reproduction (as both interpretation and distribution), as well as in the sphere of reception/consumption. Although Adorno takes the musical work as an 'in itself' as his starting point and constant point of reference, the work itself is, of course, inseparable from the various forms of experience and understanding – and of perception and interpretation – which also constitute its mediation. That is to say, while the form of a work itself constitutes a type of 'second reflection' (*zweite Reflektion*) upon its handed-down material, this also calls for a corresponding form of 'second reflection' in the listener to experience and understand the work's immanent logic.

As is to be expected, the pairs of opposites Adorno has set up in other areas of his music theory, and which have been discussed in previous chapters of the present study, also resonate in his examination of the concepts 'musical experience' and 'understanding.' Along the lines of polarities like 'resigned' art and 'authentic' art, negation or affirmation of the commodity character of art, 'fetish character' and 'cognitive character', it is possible to make similar distinctions within Adorno's concepts of 'musical experience' and 'understanding'.

Like Walter Benjamin, Adorno distinguishes between two types of 'experience' – *Erlebnis* and *Erfahrung*. He is critical of the concept of experience as 'lived experience', as 'the sphere of the given, ... of "*Erlebnis*"',[106] put forward in particular by phenomenologists like Husserl.

For Adorno, experience as *Erlebnis* implies a type of isolated experience bound to sense data and unable to go beyond them. Its epitome he considers to be the kind of atomistic and fragmented listening characteristic, for example, of the 'culture consumer', the 'emotional listener', or the 'entertainment listener', focusing as he suggests these types do upon individual sensuous moments, or fetishizing particular aspects of performance through removing them from their total 'complex of meaning'. Along with this kind of atomized 'lived experience' Adorno places a particular type of 'understanding' characterized by a demand for familiarity, standardization and 'pseudo-individualization' at the level of form. He appears to use the term *Verständnis* to indicate 'intelligibility' or 'comprehensibility', based on acceptance of received conventions and consensus. Thus, to talk of the *Verständlichkeit* of a musical work would be to refer to its intelligibility in relation to traditional or standardized formal types.

Adorno argues that, to meet the immanent demands of the musical work, what is called for is a kind of experience which involves the capacity to immerse oneself within the work, to follow its dynamic unfolding 'blind', as it were, while also being able to grasp it as a whole. This kind of experience he subsumes under the concept *Erfahrung*. This implies for him (as for Walter Benjamin) a mode of experience which can both follow the 'events' of the work from moment to moment as they unfold through time, but which can also transcend this level to relate the individual moments in terms of past, present and future within their total context, 'out of time', so to speak. *Erfahrung* is characterized by what he calls 'mimetic understanding' (*mimetisches Verstehen*), tracing the shape of the work 'from the inside'. This kind of experience implies a mode of understanding – namely *Verstehen* – which is *interpretative*, which is active in relation to the object, and is critical and self-reflective, in that it seeks always to check itself against the assumptions which the Subject brings to the Object of cognition. This combination of *Erfahrung* and *Verstehen* is also, Adorno considers, a necessary aspect of the 'immanent analysis' of music. The analytical act cannot, he suggests, occur simultaneously with *Erfahrung* (although it can be understood as a special case of *Verstehen*). It is, however, an important precondition for the experience of the work, as part of the pre-existing knowledge that is brought to bear on it and which has to be dissolved once more in the experience of the work; it is also a necessary further stage in the understanding of the work, in retrospect, so to speak, having withdrawn once more from the 'blind experience' and 'mimetic understanding' of the dynamic process of the music's unfolding.

Adorno argues that the inner logic of the work, its 'inner structure', is not directly accessible to immediate perception (*Anschauung*). It is only via *Erfahrung*, as interpretative experience, and *Verstehen*, as interpretative understanding, that the materiality of the work, its mediated 'thinglike' (*dinglich*) character, may be transcended: 'every experience of art works has to go beyond their surface aspect [*ihr Anschauliches*]'.[107] Thus the aim of such a form of interpretative (as opposed to 'lived') experience and understanding is to arrive, through a process of 'second reflection', at the point from which the notion of 'lived experience' presumes to start – that is, a direct confrontation with the work 'from the inside'. This notion of 'immanent understanding' needs further clarification. In *Ästhetische Theorie* Adorno writes:

Verstehen of particular art objects is the objective reproduction or re-enactment of a work by experience where experience operates on the inside of the work, just as, in musical terminology, to interpret a piece of music means to play it in accordance with one's understanding of how it was meant to be played.[108]

The notion of 'immanent understanding' is problematic, Adorno maintains, because, operating 'on the *inside* of the work', it must also fall under the spell of the art work. *Truth content*, on the other hand, he sees as standing opposed to the work's magic spell. An 'adequate' understanding of a work of art therefore means, he considers, 'demystifying certain [of its] enigmatic dimensions without trying to shed light on its constitutive enigma'.[109] Adorno insists that he is using the term 'enigma' in a precise sense; not as denoting something ambiguous, but rather in the sense of a riddle or puzzle (something discussed in earlier chapters in relation to the paradoxical aspects of art). *Verstehen* does not cancel this enigmatic quality, or 'riddle character' (*Rätselcharakter*) of art works, he argues. Music, as the non-referential art *par excellence*, presents this riddle character in its most extreme manifestation: 'Music's enigma cannot be solved; it can only be decoded in terms of its shape, and it is here that philosophy of art comes in...'.[110]

In his use of the concepts *Verstehen* and *Erfahrung* Adorno is attempting, as he puts it, to restore the dimension of thought to experience and, in the process, to rescue aesthetic experience from the phenomenologists. His approach to the understanding of art is at the same time a critique of phenomenological approaches, like that of Husserl, in that it insists that the experience of art is always mediated. This does not mean, however, that he believes that art works can be grasped purely in terms of conceptual knowledge – on the contrary, he insists that they demand to be understood structurally, in material, substantive terms. Nevertheless, he argues, this kind of 'thinking experience' of art works 'can be fulfilled only by a twofold approach: specific experience joined to a theory that is able to reflect experience'.[111] This dialectical approach is essential, Adorno maintains, due to the mediated character both of the art work and of aesthetic experience. According to Adorno, the approach demystifies the enigma of the work and, at the same time, locates and identifies it as the problem to which the structure of the work is the concrete answer.

In conclusion

With Adorno's concepts of *Verstehen* and *Erfahrung* we are again brought full circle. 'Mimetic understanding', as the experience of musical structures 'from the inside', returns us once more to the concrete musical work as an 'in itself'. It is a form of experience which gives priority to the Object and to the sphere of musical production, but which, at the same time, through critical interpretation, recognizes the socially and historically mediated character both of the Object and of the experiencing Subject. The model presented in Section 1, and which has provided the structure for the rest of this chapter, represents an attempt to locate key stages in the mediation of Subject and Object through an examination of Adorno's sociology of music. At the same time, however, the interpretation offered here reveals Adorno's sociology to be a trope-like extension of his immanent analysis. Starting always from a focus on the inner consistency of the musical work as Object, his dialectical–interpretative approach attempts to break through the isolation of the work by the force of the work's own contradictions – contradictions which, as technical 'inconsistencies' or unresolved tensions, demand interpretation. Consideration of the reproduction, distribution and consumption of the work thus arises from a focus on the sphere of production and returns to it, the experience of the work now understood in the light of the multiple mediations of which it is constituted. There is, Adorno insists, no access to the work apart from these mediations, which constitute its 'meaning'. Thus the autonomy of the musical work, its isolation, is revealed to be an aspect of the illusory character of art, as ideology, in that its claim to be separate from empirical reality is *false*. Lukács also makes this point in *Geschichte und Klassenbewußtsein*, when he writes:

Mediation would not be possible were it not for the fact that the empirical existence of objects is itself mediated and only appears to be unmediated in so far as the awareness of mediation is lacking so that the objects are torn from the complex of their true determinants and placed in artificial isolation.[112]

On the other hand, as we have seen, Adorno claims that the isolation of autonomous music today is also *true*, in that 'authentic' art stands in critical opposition to empirical reality. It is in the tension between these two 'moments', between *consistency* (as consistency of form) and *ideology*, that Adorno's conception of the 'historical dialectic of musical material', as the mediation of the 'bourgeois Subject' and the objectivity of empirical reality, is to be understood. It is to an interpretation of Adorno's philosophy of history as the historical dialectic of musical material, and in relation to the concept of authenticity, that we now turn.

6   The historical dialectic of musical material

> The historical moment is constitutive of art works. The authentic ones are those which surrender themselves unconditionally to the material content [*Stoffgehalt*] of their time, without the presumption of timelessness. They are the unconscious historiography of their epoch; this, in the end, is what constitutes their mediation as a form of cognition.[1]
>
> Adorno, *Aesthetic Theory* (1970)

'The forms of art record the history of mankind more impartially than do documents',[2] writes Adorno in *Philosophie der neuen Musik*. As we have seen, Adorno argues that the truth and authenticity of art works is not to do with the amount of 'historical relevance' or 'social commitment' consciously invested in them by their creators. It has instead to do with the extent to which the artist responds to the demands of the material 'in itself' – demands which are historical and social in character because the material is already historically pre-formed. Thus, the philosophical interpretation of musical works involves the deciphering of their historical and social content through tracing the mediating links between autonomous works and the heteronomy of empirical reality – links which are embedded, however, in the material and structure of the works themselves.

Although predicated on the music of Schoenberg and the Second Viennese School and viewed from the perspective of the avant-garde, Adorno's concept of musical material does not simply represent the progressive and teleological view of music history characterized by continuity which is suggested by certain commentators (for instance de la Fontaine[3] and others, including Dahlhaus[4]). I argue, on the contrary, that Adorno's philosophy of history takes as its basis the view that the historical development of music in the 'bourgeois period' is characterized also by discontinuity, and that the historical dialectic of musical material is characterized not only by increasing integration of all dimensions of the work, but equally by fragmentation and disintegration at the level of the musical material. To bring this dual-character of Adorno's historical concept of material to the fore I have juxtaposed his philosophical interpretation of Bach with his discussion of the significance of the *style galant*, his interpretation of Beethoven with some scattered but telling comments on Berlioz, and his extended discussion of Wagner with a short but significant essay on Brahms. A brief consideration of his views on Debussy and Mahler leads to a reformulation of the problem Adorno saw facing the 'New Music': how is it possible to construct integrated works out of a disintegrating material? First, however, we need to reconsider the terms of Adorno's philosophy of history in relation to the history of music.

1   Adorno's philosophy of music history

The theoretical basis of Adorno's dialectical philosophy of history has already been discussed in some detail in earlier chapters. Its most complete statement in Adorno's work is to be found in *Dialektik der Aufklärung*, a critique of the idea of history as progress – i.e. of Enlightenment as the progress of reason towards freedom from restraint – carried out in terms of an examination of history in relation to myth, reason in relation to nature, scientific rationality in relation to the irrationality of primitive magic.

As we have seen, the approach taken by Adorno and Horkheimer in *Dialektik der Aufklärung* was that characterized by what I have called the 'mediation of opposites through their extremes'. As well as drawing on Hegel, Marx and Weber – and also, notably, Freud – Adorno and Horkheimer derive much of their approach from Nietzsche, in particular from *Zur Genealogie der Moral* (1887). When Nietzsche writes that 'every step taken on this earth by our ancestors has been paid for with the greatest torments of body and mind',[5] he is referring to the historical progress of civilization as being characterized also by the repression and domination of inner as well as outer nature. A version of this thesis is central to *Dialektik der Aufklärung*, whereby the domination of nature through reason is seen to turn against the bourgeois Subject in the form of domination of self as repression and internalization. This is made clear in the following passage:

The instrument by means of which the bourgeoisie came to power, the liberation of forces, universal freedom, self-determination – in short, the Enlightenment, itself turned aganst the bourgeoisie once, as a system of domination, it had recourse to suppression.[6]

As applied in *Philosophie der neuen Musik* – and indeed in much of the rest of his subsequent writings on music – this thesis can be understood in relation to the schematic model put forward at the end of Chapter 3 (and can also be seen to be related to the 'theses' derived from 'Zur gesellschaftlichen Lage der Musik' at the end of Chapter 2). First, there is the external process of rationalization to which the artist has an ambivalent, if not antagonistic relationship because rationalization constitutes a threat to the 'irrational' (or 'non-rational') aspects of aesthetic activity. Second, the external process of rationalization is internalized/sublimated by the expressive Subject and objectified within the work as the integration of elements previously 'unrationalized' – e.g. as increasing domination of musical material through the logic of form. This process is seen by Adorno as mimetic, in that music 'mimics' the external threat (rationalization) through taking it into itself as its inner 'law of form', at the same time positing 'its own, self-enclosed area, which is withdrawn from the context of profane existence'[7] and which separates and protects it from the outside world, as a form of primitive magic. And third, the outcome of this process has two opposing aspects: (i) the totally rationalized and internally consistent work becomes the total commodity, its 'purposefulness without a purpose' becoming assimilated to the purposes of a totally rationalized society – i.e. as ideology; and (ii) the work resists assimilation to the dominant rationality of society and, through its alienation from society, takes on a critical character – i.e. as what Adorno calls the 'authentic work'. Before examining Adorno's 'historical dialectic of musical material' in these terms, some account is needed of the historical periodization which may be seen to underlie it.

Adorno's historical periodization

The rise of the bourgeoisie and of the 'bourgeois individual' to become the 'Subject/Object' of history, and thus to become the 'expressive Subject' which is 'objectified' in musical material and in autonomous musical structures, is nowhere laid out in explicit terms as a 'scheme' in Adorno's writings. It could, however, be understood as moving through four main stages or periods, with a possible implied fifth – that of the 'pluralism' of the post-1950s.

(i)   The eighteenth century   This is essentially the period of the European Enlightenment up to the 1780s, when the bourgeoisie was gaining economic and scientific–technical–intellectual power but was without political power. During this period musicians were in the employment of the Church, the aristocracy, or the rich merchant classes. In the earlier part of this period they had the status of craftsmen or servants, while later their status began to change in the direction of more entrepreneurial activities. Bach seems to represent most fully the earlier part of this period for Adorno (although Handel functioned at certain points in his career in a distinctly different way – in the free market place, in a commercially advanced England moving towards its Industrial Revolution), when 'art music' still retained some vestiges of a direct social function. Haydn and Mozart represent both its peak and its collapse, and the rapidly increasing tendency, already apparent in the Baroque period, towards the complete autonomy of instrumental music seen in the Classical sonata, and the need for musicians to operate independently in a free market. Adorno's interpretation of the music of this period will be discussed in Section 2 of this chapter.

(ii)   The late eighteenth century to the mid-nineteenth century   This is essentially the period 1789–1848, from the French Revolution and the acquisition of political power by the bourgeoisie, to 'the year of revolutions'. It is also the period of the Industrial Revolution, at first in England, but with gradually increasing influence in the rest of Western Europe. During this period composers and virtuosi acquired independent social status, together with precarious economic power in a free market. Art music at this period can be heard as a celebration of its class, the radical and liberal bourgeoisie in uncertain alliance with 'the people', with aspirations towards 'freedom, equality and universal brotherhood' and with a sense of all-embracing optimism and dynamism. Beethoven most completely represents this spirit for Adorno, with his Ninth Symphony as its most complete expression, while Berlioz represents an anticipation of the 'age of industry'. Adorno's interpretation of the music of these two composers and their relation to their period is discussed in Section 3 of this chapter.

(iii)   The mid-nineteenth century to the early twentieth century   This is essentially the era of rapid industrialization throughout Europe and the USA, the period of high capitalism and imperial expansion. After 1848, Adorno argues, the most advanced consciousness of the period in art, as represented by the avant-garde, was no longer able to identify with the class interests of the bourgeoisie as a whole. After 1848 the bourgeoisie ceased to be a revolutionary class, having achieved economic and political power and having relinquished its previous common interests with the proletariat (or at least with some perhaps romanticized notion of 'the people') for an alliance of interests with the aristocracy. 'Advanced' art, so Adorno argues, is no longer in this period at one with its class and a celebration of it, but becomes torn, tinged with doubt and increasingly suffers a loss of confidence in itself very much at odds with the dominant spirit of optimism and positivism in the science, technology, industry and commerce of the time. The peculiar situation arises whereby an art turns against the culture which produced it, and ultimately even against the concept of art itself. This is, however, not manifested directly with full consciousness of the sources of the predicament, but in mediated/sublimated form within the art work itself and in the artist's relation to the material. It is manifested as a

formal/technical problem, and as the tendency for art to turn in upon itself, leading to a 'crisis within the art'. The dominant aesthetic becomes that of *l'art pour l'art*,[8] and technically the period, particularly in its later stages up to the First World War, is characterized by radical formal experimentation. Thus for Adorno, the concepts of the 'avant-garde', of 'modernism', of 'experimentalism' and of 'the new', can be dated from the change in sensibility he considers to have taken place around 1848, and which is most clearly expressed initially in the poetry of Baudelaire as a sense of alienation and *anomie*, and as the conflict between *spleen et idéal*.[9] Music becomes the ideal mode of art, because it is overtly the most 'self-contained', self-referential and distanced from everyday empirical reality. Adorno considers that both Wagner and Brahms in different ways represent this tendency of autonomous music to turn in upon itself, although the split between the avant-garde (itself a bourgeois category) and the consumers of art, the bourgeoisie, did not occur in music until the *fin-de-siècle*, beginning with Mahler and Debussy, and increasing in intensity with the formal experimentation of Schoenberg and the Second Viennese School, and the innovations of Stravinsky and Bartók. Aspects of Adorno's interpretation of the music of Wagner and Brahms are discussed in Section 4, and of the music of Debussy and Mahler in Section 5. Extended discussion of Adorno's interpretations of the music of Stravinsky, Bartók, Hindemith and the Second Viennese School has occurred in earlier chapters of this study, while a critique of the Schoenberg–Stravinsky polarity as put forward in *Philosophie der neuen Musik* is reserved for Chapter 7.

(iv)   The First World War to the late 1950s This is a period characterized by the collapse of the old economic order based on colonial wealth, the rise of authoritarian regimes in Western Europe and the Soviet Union, monopoly capitalism, and the emergence of a 'mass culture' based on mass production, technological reproducibility, intensive advertising and propaganda, and 'consumerism'. In art music this is a period of further crisis, a further loss of communicative and functional context, combined with and as a partial consequence of the breakdown of the binding features of musical 'idiom'. Adorno considered the situation to present a threat to the survival of art (at least, as anything other than 'museum culture'), through on the one hand art's commodification and on the other hand its alienation. The period is characterized in music by attempts to deal with the crisis of identity through systematization and a search for order, in effect various attempts to restore stability and find a new social function. The period is dominated by the neoclassicisms of Stravinsky and Hindemith, the serialism of the Second Viennese School (which also to an extent has features of neoclassicism), the attempts to assimilate folk music into art

music of Bartók and Janáček, and the Brechtian 'alienation' of popular and nineteenth-century music of Eisler and Weill. Also characteristic of the period were the state-prescribed attempts at accessibility and new simplicity in the socialist realism of Stalinist Russia and the Reichskammer art of Nazi Germany, as well as what Adorno appeared to see as the monopoly capitalist equivalent of these in the free market democracies (especially the USA), the 'culture industry'. Adorno seemed to regard the multiple serialism of the Darmstadt School not only as an attempt to purge musical syntax of any extra-musical accretions and to offer the possibility of a new, totally integrated and autonomous music; he also appeared to see it as the most extreme version yet of the long-standing tendency which he considered to have characterized the whole of this period: that is, to forge a new – and allegedly 'natural' – order out of a disintegrating material. Aspects of part of this 'period' have already been discussed in earlier chapters (in particular Chapters 1 and 2). They will be reconsidered briefly in Chapter 7.

(v)   Post-1950s: the decline of the avant-garde   To this historical scheme could be added a fifth period, clearly implied in Adorno's later work – that characterized by the relativism and pluralism of the post-1950s, by the decline of the avant-garde and of the 'new music', and by the change in the character of musical material. Indeed, such a development had been foreseen by Adorno as far back as 1932, in 'Zur gesellschaftlichen Lage der Musik'. The implications of such a development for Adorno's theory of material will be discussed in Chapter 7.

What is apparent in the above outline is (a) the sense of historical movement as the dialectic of the 'bourgeois Subject' and the objective conditions in which it finds itself, and (b) the rise and decline of the avant-garde as a bourgeois category and its relation to changing social conditions characterized by commodification. We shall shortly turn to a more detailed examination of the articulation of the bourgeois Subject (its 'objectification' through technical rationalization) seen as the historical tendency of musical material.

A pre-history of the 'new music'

As already emphasized, Adorno insists that the material of music is always that of the *present*, at the furthest stage reached by technical means in relation to expressive demands. A perhaps predictable result of this, however, has been the historicizing of the theory itself. Because his theory of musical material was first developed in relation to the music of Schoenberg (in particular in the 1927 analysis of the *Fünf Orchesterstücke* op. 16, in the article 'Zur Zwölftontechnik' of 1929, in the debates with

Krenek of the late 1920s and early 1930s, in 'Zur gesellschaftlichen Lage der Musik' of 1932, and consolidated in *Philosophie der neuen Musik* in the 1940s in relation to the music of Schoenberg and Stravinsky), most of Adorno's commentators have come to see the theory as being limited exclusively to that narrow but important strand of development in Western European art music represented by Austro-German music since the Enlightenment, and culminating in the first half of the twentieth century with the serialism of the Second Viennese School.

In referring to Adorno's writings from the 1920s and early 1930s, for example, Michael de la Fontaine comments that '[t]he focus on Schoenberg is at this period already so strong that "material" in fact really means only that which prepared the way for dodecaphony'.[10] Lambert Zuidervaart considers that 'Adorno's concept of musical material holds less promise for the historiography and sociology of music in general than for one particular philosophy of some modern music [i.e. the Second Viennese School]'.[11] And Carl Dahlhaus suggests that 'one of the basic patterns of his [Adorno's] philosophy of history is to reconstrue aesthetic norms into historical trends to form a basis for a pre-history of the twelve-tone technique'.[12] Adorno certainly seems to provide justification for these interpretations when he writes: 'One can only understand Schoenberg if one understands Bach; one can only understand Bach if one understands Schoenberg'.[13] I would argue, however, that in focusing on Schoenberg in the 1920s, 1930s and 1940s Adorno was taking the composer's music as *the most extreme case available at that time* for what he saw as the dominant tendency in Western industrialized society as a whole: i.e. the tendency towards progressive rationalization. The focus on Schoenberg and the tradition of which he is part, seen as the clearest embodiment of this tendency, does not mean that the concept of musical material only includes that which prepared the way for serialism (I will try to demonstrate this later). It means rather that the Austro-German tradition is seen historically as the most dominant and influential strand within Western art music of the 'bourgeois period', and as that which in its most extreme form epitomizes the process of progressive rationalization. It is the 'turning inward' (*Innerlichkeit*) of autonomous instrumental music, its focus upon its own immanent structuring processes, which enables it, according to Adorno, both to reflect the dominant rationality of its society – i.e. highly rationalized bourgeois society – and at the same time to stand in critical opposition to the dominant rationality. What is significant in Adorno's concept of material, as we have seen in earlier chapters, is that it is founded on an underlying concept of mediation which identifies the rationalization process of empirical reality itself as that which is internalized and sublimated in works of art. In his essay 'Ideen zur Musiksoziologie' (1958) he writes:

The history of music is, without question, that of a process of progressive rationalization. It had stages like the Guidonian reform, the introduction of mensural notation, the invention of the figured bass, of tempered tuning, and finally, since Bach, the irresistible tendency towards integral musical construction which today has been taken to the extreme.[14]

And yet, he goes on to say, 'rationalization – inseparable from the historical process of the *embourgeoisement* of music – denotes only one of its social aspects, just as rationality itself, as Enlightenment, provides only one moment in the history of a society which still remains irrational, in a "state of nature"'.[15] The tendency towards total integration of all parameters of music, which he sees as epitomized in Schoenberg and as reaching its logical fulfilment in the total stasis of the multiple serialism of the early 1950s, embodies, as its 'truth content', only one of these extremes. Its other extreme is the tendency towards reification, fragmentation and disintegration, which is also part of the historical dialectic of musical material. A further manifestation of this is what he sees as the emergence of a new musical 'mass language', as a result of the total commodification of music by the culture industry.

Being essentially a theory of the avant-garde, it is, furthermore, not surprising that Adorno's theory of musical material should itself begin to change, and even appear to disintegrate and lose its validity,[16] at the point when the avant-garde itself becomes seen as historically situated and as a category to be questioned (even though Adorno himself had foreseen this). The broad course of the 'historical dialectic of musical material', as progress of the expressive Subject, is outlined below. I have referred critically to de la Fontaine's account, and also made reference to Dahlhaus, in combination with my interpretation of what I have called Adorno's 'theory of history'. Adorno's 'pre-history'[17] of the twelve-tone technique, as the tendency towards total integration and rationalization, provides one important strand of this dialectic. Equally important, however, is Adorno's account of the commodification of music and the tendency towards reification, fragmentation and disintegration. These two extremes are inextricably entwined in Adorno's theory of the dialectic of musical material, as the following account seeks to demonstrate.

2   Bach and the *style galant*

In some ways Adorno's focus on Bach as the composer whose music provides one of the earliest models for what he calls 'bourgeois subject-objectification' is paradoxical. From the point of view of the composer's own intentions, Bach, with his intense religiosity and pietism, could be seen as standing in opposition to the rational spirit of the Enlightenment. Furthermore, from the point of view of the reception of his music at the time, his style was perceived generally as archaic in relation to the new spirit of the *style galant*. And finally, from the point of view of certain twentieth-century musicological tendencies (particularly those concerned with a notion of authenticity very much at odds with Adorno's), Bach's music is regarded ontologically as having an objective character which transcends subjectivity (e.g. as 'subjective expression' in performance). As Adorno puts it, '[it] is said to be elevated above the [S]ubject and its contingency; in it is expressed not so much the man and his inner life as the order of Being [*Sein*] as such, in its most compelling form'.[18] In his essay 'Bach gegen seine Liebhaber verteidigt', Adorno writes that Bach tends to be seen as 'the revelation – in the middle of the Century of Enlightenment – of the time-honoured bounds of tradition, of the spirit of medieval polyphony, of the theologically vaulted cosmos'.[19]

Archaism and Enlightenment

In reply to the argument that the theological and pietistic impulses of Bach's music stand in direct opposition to the spirit of the Enlightenment, Adorno answers that it has never been the case that a composer's own conception of his music has to 'coincide with its intrinsic nature, with the objective law peculiar to it'.[20] In fact Adorno insists that at the level of its form and of the compositional techniques and musical technology available to it, Bach's music partakes thoroughly of the process of rationalization of its period; *Das Wohltemperierte Klavier* is seen as a classic example of Max Weber's thesis, as put forward in *Die rationalen und sozialen Grundlagen der Musik*, in terms of compositional technique, of developments in the standardization of tuning systems, and of musical instrument technology.

Adorno's response to the point that Bach's 'archaism' in relation to his contemporaries operates against the idea of 'progress' is to argue that herein lies the critical and oppositional character of the music, and also that a more sophisticated theory of musical progress is called for in order to understand Bach's relationship to the larger social tendencies of his time. He suggests that Bach doggedly persisted in following the 'immanent logic' of the musical material in opposition to the 'commodity character' of the *style galant* which was coming to dominate musical life in the mid-eighteenth century. The line of reasoning, as put forward in 'Bach gegen seine Liebhaber verteidigt', is somewhat tortuous:

Among his archaic traits is the attempt to parry the impoverishment and petrification of musical language, the shadow side of its decisive progress. Such traits represent Bach's effort to resist the inexorable growth of the commodity-character of music, a process which was linked to its subjectivization. Yet such features are also identical with Bach's modernity inasmuch as they always serve to defend the right of immanent musical logic against the demands of taste.[21]

The point is clarified in the essay 'Ideen zur Musiksoziologie'. There Adorno argues that 'progress' in music is not a continuum, but is characterized by fractures, by breaks in continuity (*Brüche*). This is because, he explains, while music progresses according to the logic of its own immanent but socially mediated laws (i.e. those of the musical material), it is at the same time also affected – and at times diverted – by what he calls 'social force-fields' (*gesellschaftliche Kraftfelder*).[22] Thus he maintains that the rise of the *style galant*, 'which superseded Bach and the level reached by him in the domination of musical material, is not to be accounted for in terms of musical logic, but in terms of the logic of consumption, in the needs of a bourgeois class of customers'.[23] So Adorno argues that Bach refused to deal with the historical contradictions at the level of the material merely by superficial stylistic means (as, he maintains, did the *galant* composers). Instead, he sought to bring about the reconcilement of the two extreme tendencies within the handed-down material of his time (i.e. the extremes of strict counterpoint and *basso continuo* harmony) purely through the inner logic of form and the demands of the material itself. The need was to create a new formal unity out of the opposing demands of polyphony and tonal harmony. That this set him apart from what had become the dominant musical tendency of the mid-eighteenth century – that is, the demand for a much simpler, less polyphonic and more homophonic style of music, the function of which was entertainment, as *divertissement* – is an example, Adorno argues, of the discontinuity of historical progress in music. 'Progress' does not proceed along the straight line of strict chronological succession, he insists. This argument will be returned to and expanded later in this chapter.

The fugue as 'bourgeois subject-objectification'

Against what he sees as the twentieth-century ontological and historicist (i.e. 'authentic') view of Bach as somehow representing a state of 'transcendent Being' (*Sein*) beyond subjectivity, Adorno argues for a more dynamic conception of the composer. As de la Fontaine puts it, Adorno sees Bach as 'the first protagonist of material self-reflection',[24] and in the Bach fugue he sees 'one of the earliest models of bourgeois subject-objectification'.[25] Adorno identifies the progress of 'subject-objectification' quite directly with the treatment and development of the musical material, as handed-down forms and genres, as harmonic schemata, as compositional techniques (e.g. strict counterpoint) and, in particular, as thematic material. As we have seen, what is significant and meaningful about material, as a form, or as a 'theme' or 'subject', is not simply what it *is*, as Being (*Sein*), but much more the process of development or deviation, as Becoming (*Werden*) (and also, importantly, what does not happen, given the available possibilities – the omissions and 'blind spots' in the piece, as well as its technical inconsistencies).

As already seen (in Chapter 4), Adorno maintains that two distinct tendencies come together in the Bach fugue: the 'archaic' tradition of strict counterpoint as handed down from Palestrina, and the newer harmonic–monodic tradition of the *basso continuo* accompaniment.[26] The problem facing Bach, according to Adorno, was 'how, in terms of *basso continuo* harmony, music could justify the harmonic progressions as meaningful and at the same time organize itself polyphonically, through the simultaneity of independent voices'.[27] Adorno points out that the usual claim, that contrapuntal techniques employed by Bach serve to construct musical objectivity, belies the fact that material is also the result of subjectivization. What is striking about the Bach fugue is its motivic economy. In order for complex polyphony to take place within the harmonic schemata of the *basso continuo*, the theme has to be dismantled and dissected into its smallest component parts, he maintains. The harmonic scheme necessitates the extreme rationalization of the thematic material, to enable the fugue subject (or subjects) to remain identical and identifiable even though being subjected to a process of constant 'tonal' and motivic variation. Adorno argues that the Bach fugue 'is an art of dissection; one could almost say, of dissolving Being, posited as the theme, and hence incompatible with the common belief that this Being maintains itself static and unchanged throughout the fugue'.[28] He suggests that, in comparison to this technique (which he characterizes by Schoenberg's term 'developing variation'), Bach relatively seldom resorts to strict imitation in the 'old style', apart from its use in *stretto* passages[29] and in the canonic writing of the very late works. Adorno considers that 'developing variation', as the basic compositional principle of Viennese Classicism, derives from the motivic economy and dissection which characterizes the Bach fugue theme, which, on its return in the tonic at the end of a fugue, is 'rebuilt over layers of analysis (i.e. dissection) and thematic work ...'.[30]

Adorno thus interprets this technique in Bach as 'the decomposition of the given thematic material through subjective reflection on the motivic work contained therein'[31] – i.e. in Hegelian terms, as a dialectical process of the negation of the 'objectively given', as *Sein*, and its reconstitution through the Subject, as *Werden*. He goes on to suggest that this mediation through the Subject also implies a social mediation:

a social deciphering of Bach would presumably have to establish the link ... [with]
... the change in the work-process that took place during the same epoch through
the emergence of manufacturing, which consisted essentially in breaking down the
old craft operations into [their] smaller component acts. If this resulted in the
rationalization of material production, then Bach was the first to crystallize the idea
of the rationally constituted work, of the aesthetic domination of nature; it was no
accident that he named his major instrumental work after the most important
technical achievement of musical rationalization.[32]

Rationalization and self-reflection

In summary, therefore, Adorno suggests that the 'inner truth' of Bach's
music is that it not only adheres to and embodies the most powerful
tendency of the bourgeois period (i.e. rationalization), taking it to its most
extreme point for the music of its time, but that, through its process of
self-reflection, it provides an image (*Bild*) of the reconcilement of
rationalization with 'the voice of humanity'.[33] The music's 'immanent law
of form' objectifies the Subject and transcends subjectivity, but without
thereby excluding the Subject.[34] Its 'archaism' is at the same time its
modernity – the classical ideal of the '*Versöhnung von Gelehrt und Galant*',[35]
the reconciliation of the learned and the *galant* styles. In 'Bach gegen seine
Liebhaber verteidigt' Adorno writes;

Bach, as the most advanced master of the *basso continuo*, at the same time
renounced his obedience, as antiquated polyphonist, to the tendency of the time
which he himself had shaped, in order to help that tendency reach its own truth, the
emancipation of the Subject towards objectivity in a seamless whole which has its
source in subjectivity itself. ... The distant past is entrusted with the Utopia of the
musical [S]ubject–[O]bject: anachronism becomes a harbinger of things to come.[36]

In brief, Adorno's philosophical/historical interpretation of the mediation
of Subject and Object in Bach's music could be outlined in the following
terms: the Subject in Bach's music, as the 'bourgeois individual', is united
with the objectivity of the universal. This 'objectivity' is not, however, in
spite of the paradoxical claims of the historicizing 'Bach devotees', a
universal in the sense of an absolute, ahistorical, unmediated pure Being.
On the contrary, it is the subjectively mediated objectivity of the early
bourgeois world-view, utopian in character and realized in Bach's music as
a harmonious unity of individual Subject and objective Cosmos, within
which the Subject nevertheless retains its individual freedom. The theological dimension in Bach's music is an aspect of its material (as handed-down
genres) and an obligatory aspect of its time and place (the first half of the
eighteenth century in provincial Lutheran northern Germany): what is
significant, however, is the way in which the composer deals with his

material – the relation to socially mediated compositional techniques and technology. In this lie the progressive and rationalizing tendencies of Bach's music, and his oneness (whatever his religious convictions) with the spirit of the Enlightenment, the 'Age of Reason'. Thus Adorno gives a humanistic interpretation of Bach's music. He also argues that the reconciliation of universal and particular in Bach presents an image of the 'seamless whole' of unity in diversity which was already utopian in relation to the social reality of its time, and which was to be revealed as such in the gradual process of increasing 'material self-reflection' (what he calls, as we have seen, music's 'coming of age' (*Mündigkeit*)) in the later stages of the historical dialectic of musical material.

It must be said that Adorno's sociological and philosophical interpretation of what he sees as the rationalizing tendency within Bach's music does not entirely convince. The problem is the by now familiar one with Adorno's method: the distance between musical structures and social structures is in this case not really bridged at the level of interpretation because, in spite of his insistence that such interpretation must be grounded in the immanent analysis of concrete works, there is little analytical detail. But I have already argued that any possibility of validation in technical–analytical terms is hard to envisage. This is not helped by the brevity of his few texts on Bach, and by the rather undialectical way in which they manage to be both extremely general and extremely particular at the same time, without much contact between the extremes. 'Bach gegen seine Liebhaber verteidigt' (1951) focuses on rescuing the composer from the clutches of the devotees of 'authentic performance', and contains only very general reference to particular works and practically no analytical detail, while 'Johann Sebastian Bach: Präludium und Fuge cis-moll aus dem ersten Teil des Wohltemperierten Klaviers' (1934)[37] provides analytical detail of a descriptive variety, but few clues as to how these details connect with Adorno's larger aesthetic and sociological theory. Such criticisms do not only apply to Adorno's interpretation of Bach, however; they have occurred earlier in relation, for example, to the music of Berg in Chapter 4, and will be returned to later in relation to his music theory as a whole. Adorno's attempt to relate the concept of 'progress' to the idea of 'historical discontinuities', is nevertheless of some sophistication, and has explanatory value when applied to concrete historical contexts.

Style change and change in social function

The 'historical fact'[38] that Bach's complex and scholarly style was superseded by the simple and genteel style of the *galant* composers calls for some kind of interpretation which is able to go beyond the straightforward intra-musical notion of recurrent cycles of reaction against established styles. Adorno argues that through these abrupt style changes (historical discontinuities) there also runs a line of continuity – albeit a continuity which at certain points disappears from view in terms of any direct manifestation in musical works. It is a continuity which can only be inferred from the modified reappearance of a particular line of development of musical logic in musical works at a later period, and from the significant omission or negation of certain features previously considered to have been of central importance. The modified reappearance can now be understood as a synthesis of the earlier manifestation and of that which had reacted against it – synthesis in the Hegelian sense of *Aufhebung*, of simultaneous negation and raising to a new qualitative level. Thus Adorno's Hegelian conception of musical progress (as domination of material) has to be envisaged as being more a spiral than a straight line:

the domination of material increases in a spiral movement which can only be grasped in terms of that which is lost or left by the wayside. When conceived in this way it is above all the antinomies, the necessary contradictions which are the ferment of social cognition.[39]

Seen in this way, the reaction against the High Baroque represented by the *style galant* is to be explained, as outlined above, by a change in the social forces and relations of production and not by invoking the immanent logic of the musical material.[40] That change was brought about, Adorno maintains, by the gradual *embourgeoisement* of music, the move from noble or church patronage to survival in a free market:

For the first time composers were confronted with the anonymous marketplace. Without the protection of a guild or of a prince's favor they had to sense a demand instead of following transparent orders. They had to turn themselves, their very core, into organs of the market; this was what placed the desiderates of the market at the heart of their production.[41]

As well as diverting the material from the line of its apparently logical development, this change in function also itself becomes embedded in the material. In relation to the state of musical material in the mid-eighteenth century Adorno's argument is as follows: the social demand for entertainment (*Unterhaltungsmusik*) became internalized musically in the *style galant*, and manifested not only as greater simplicity, both harmonically and melodically, but also as greater contrast and diversity within and between each movement of a work, as *divertissement*, compared to the relative unity of mood of the Baroque. It was, however, this very variety and diversity, which had its origins in its social function as entertainment or 'conversation music', which in turn 'became the premise of that dynamic relation of unity and diversity which constitutes the law of Viennese classicism'.[42] Thus the dynamic process of 'developing variation', of motivic–thematic working which Adorno perceives in Bach, becomes accelerated through the influence of external determinants like the need for greater variety and contrast to please the new bourgeois audience, and moves towards a new stage in the development of compositional technique in the music of Haydn, Mozart and Beethoven (with, it might be added, a return to a marked use of counterpoint in the later works of these composers). Adorno considers that this constitutes 'an immanent advance in composing, one which compensated, after two generations, for the losses caused by the initial turn in style. It was the source of a way to pose musical problems that has survived to this day.'[43] And at the same time his observation in *Ästhetische Theorie* (paraphrasing Wagner), that 'the greatest part of what passes for musical art today is an echo of the contemptuous clatter of dinner music',[44] serves as a reminder of the functional origins of certain distinctive features of the Classical sonata and the symphony in the *divertissements*, serenades and operatic overtures of the mid-eighteenth century.

What is particularly interesting about this theory of progress in music is that it reveals a contradiction in Adorno's own position, at least as normally perceived. On the one hand, Adorno argues here that the 'commercial influence', the change in the social relations of production, can also prove productive at the level of composition. In fact he goes so far as to insist that:

The customary invectives against commercial mischief in music are superficial. They delude regarding the extent to which phenomena that presuppose commerce, the appeal to an audience already viewed as customers, can turn into compositional qualities unleashing and enhancing a composer's productive force.[45]

On the other hand, Adorno argues elsewhere most forcefully that the influence of commercial factors on music, in the form of the 'culture industry', is altogether malevolent.[46] Further aspects of this contradiction will be considered in the course of this chapter. For the moment, however, Adorno's own formulation of what could be called his 'general law of musical progress' (and it should be remembered that 'progress' refers to progress in technique and as 'demythologization', but not necessarily in 'compositional quality') will serve to take us on to a second stage of his conception of the 'historical tendency of musical material':

social compulsions under which music seems to be placed from without are absorbed by its autonomous logic and the need for compositorial expression, and are transformed into an artistic necessity: into steps of the right consciousness [*in Stufen richtigen Bewußtseins*].[47]

3   Beethoven and Berlioz

As we have already established, Adorno maintains that the relation between musical works and society, and between musical progress and social progress, is not reducible to direct correspondences between the two spheres. It is rather that society as a problem, or 'context of problems' – 'as the entirety of its antagonisms'[48] – appears immanently in the musical material as problems of musical logic, of form.

Musical autonomy and the rise of the bourgeoisie

It is with Beethoven, so Adorno argues, that art music becomes fully autonomous. That is to say, it becomes *aesthetically* autonomous, as what he calls 'an autarchic motivational context',[49] screened off as a separate sphere within society, but a sphere created and maintained as such by the organizing principles underlying bourgeois society itself – e.g. the division of labour. Seen therefore as one sphere within the totality of society, the autonomy of the aesthetic sphere is relative – it is both part of society and separate from it, containing the totality within itself as 'monad'. Adorno writes that:

The kinship with that bourgeois libertarianism which rings all through Beethoven's music is a kinship of the dynamically unfolding totality. It is in fitting together under their own law, as becoming, negating, confirming themselves and the whole without looking outward that his themes [*Sätze*] come to resemble the world whose forces move them; they do not do it by imitating that world.[50]

Although Adorno has an irritating stylistic tendency to anthropomorphize the aesthetic sphere, and habitually talks of 'music' or 'themes' as though they somehow function independently of any human agency, he is in fact also referring to the change in social status of composers themselves in this period following the French Revolution – but a change in status which is part of the change in the position of the bourgeoisie as a rising class. The following passage from *Einleitung in die Musiksoziologie* makes this clear (while at the same time the curious slippage between composer and music is a good illustration of the stylistic feature mentioned above):

Let us reflect further on Beethoven. If he is the musical prototype of the revolutionary bourgeoisie, he is at the same time the prototype of a music that has escaped from its social tutelage and is esthetically fully autonomous, a servant no longer. His work explodes the schema of a complaisant adequacy of music and society.[51]

It is not that Beethoven 'represents' the official spirit of the time – Adorno considers that a composer like Rossini does that more accurately. It is that the process of 'dynamization' which characterized the social revolution of the period in relation to the static nature of existing institutions is to be encountered in Beethoven's autonomous music in very concrete terms, as the way in which he deals with the handed-down musical material and its formal conventions. The state of the musical material faced by Beethoven was 'the state of the problem offered to [him] by the sonata form of Haydn and Mozart, in which diversity balances out into unity, but continues diverging from it, while the form itself remains an abstract cover drawn over diversity'.[52] Adorno suggests that Beethoven's problem was how to take further the state of balance achieved within the dynamic form of the Classical sonata – a state of balance which Adorno, somewhat questionably, seems to equate with a lack of thoroughgoing development and with a sense of stasis resulting from the large-scale repetition and symmetry represented by the recapitulation in Haydn and Mozart.[53] Beethoven's decisive contribution, he maintains, is his extension of the concept of development to the point where it cuts across the conventional sectionalization of the sonata and pervades the form as a whole:

In Beethoven, however, the development, as subjective reflection upon the theme which decides the fate of the theme, becomes central to the entire form. It justifies the form, even where this remains as a pre-given convention, through spontaneously regenerating it.[54]

Musical development as material self-reflection

The significant idea is that of development as *subjective reflection* – something which Adorno recognizes in Bach as motivic–thematic dissection and 'working out', but sees being taken on to a different level in Beethoven via the possibilities exposed by Haydn and Mozart in terms of the dialectical nature of the sonata principle. Adorno sees this process as analogous to philosophical reflection, as a kind of 'conceptless cognition' (*begriffslose Erkenntnis*). Tonality itself is its basic material, the 'objectively given', which, in Kantian terms, 'is thrown into question and has then to be re-created once more by the Subject and its forms'. Adorno argues that 'in Beethoven the forms (particularly the large, dynamic forms like the sonata) could be said to re-emerge from out of the specific process of the composition'.[55] This is made possible, he considers, because of the way in which Beethoven fashions his basic motivic material, the 'particularity' of the thematic material connecting smoothly with the 'universal' as tonality. That is to say, the motivic cells are in themselves quite indifferent, emphasizing the basic stuff of tonality itself – e.g. thirds, scale passages, repeated notes. As he puts it in *Einleitung in die Musiksoziologie*:

The tendency ... is, as far as possible, to dequalify the natural material [*das Naturmaterial*] within which the [thematic] work functions; the seed motifs [*die*

Motivkerne], the Particular, to which each theme [*Satz*] is tied, are themselves identical to the Universal; they are formulae of tonality, reduced to nothingness in terms of things in their own right [*als Eigenes*] and just as much pre-formed by the totality as is the individual in individualistic society.[56]

This is the most fundamental level of 'self-reflection' within Beethoven's music (Adorno is referring particularly to the middle-period works) – the dialectic of universal and particular, as the negation of tonality as immediate 'natural material', and its regeneration from out of itself as mediated 'second nature'. A further level is that of the contrasting first and second subject groups, which tend both to be derived from common 'germ motifs',[57] and thus tend to lose their traditional uniqueness and irreducibility. As de la Fontaine points out, it is to this Adorno is referring when he talks about Beethoven's 'renunciation of the inspired moment' (*Verzicht auf den Einfall*) in *Philosophie der neuen Musik*.[58] *Einfall* is what Adorno sees as 'the irreducibly subjective element' in music, the 'theme' as *Sein*, while the 'working out' (*die Arbeit*) 'represents the process of objectivity and the process of becoming [*Werden*], which, to be sure, contains this subjective moment as a driving force'.[59] Thus Adorno suggests that this irreducible element for Beethoven is in fact the motif, which, due to its identification with tonality itself, has an objective and material character (*Materialcharakter*). In the development section the themes thus lend themselves to fragmentation and further variation until, as de la Fontaine puts it, 'through their opposition [*Gegensätzlichkeit*] they are sublated [*aufgehoben*] into the common material dimension from which they were derived'.[60]

Musical logic as 'philosophical cognition'

And then there is the level of the larger-scale formal structure of the Beethoven sonata. In spite of the character of the basic motivic cells and of the process of development in Beethoven, Adorno acknowledges that the recapitulation is still retained – 'the recurrence, unshaken despite all structural dynamics, of what has been negated and gone beyond [*die Wiederkehr des Aufgehobenen*]' – but at the same time he maintains that it 'is not merely external and conventional'.[61] Adorno considers that the recapitulation is now the result of that which has gone before, and that the themes and motifs have been shaped from the outset with a view to what they are to become; they are 'designed for the instant of the reprise'.[62] (As an example of this he cites 'the overwhelming effect of the recapitulation over the dominant pedal point in the first movement' of the *Appassionata*.[63]) In a sense this is the paradox of Beethoven's music: it seems as though everything develops out of the '"motive-power" [*Triebkraft*] of the individual elements',[64] whereas in fact these elements are also defined in advance by the movement as a dynamic whole (as, he suggests, the sketchbooks indicate, showing a constant re-working of thematic ideas until they prove capable of fitting the requirements of the movement as a whole). Thus the recapitulation acts as an affirmation within the sonata of this process of 'becoming'. As de la Fontaine says: 'When the original themes, which formed the work's point of departure, return in the recapitulation, they do so now in the light of their own previous history [mit ihrer Vorgeschichte]. They are derived from out of themselves and thereby legitimized.'[65] This constitutes the cognitive character of Beethoven's music, Adorno argues; the relationship of part to whole revealed at every instant as a process of musical self-reflection. And he goes as far as to insist that 'in this his music is no mere analogy for, but is in fact directly *identical* to, the structure of Hegelian logic'.[66]

For Adorno, the 'truth' of Beethoven's music concerns the way in which its thematic material, as 'Subject' in both musical and philosophical senses, derives from the 'whole' – i.e. tonality – but at the same time separates itself from it as a conventional system of tonal relations through re-creating the system from out of itself. This it does through a process of development and fragmentation (as 'self-reflection'), reducing given 'being' (*Sein*) to its basic elements and transforming these elements into a process of 'becoming' (*Werden*), before reconciling them once more with the 'whole' in the light of what has happened to them through the process of development (in the recapitulation). In this way the Beethoven sonata form is interpreted by Adorno as an embodiment of the Hegelian dialectic. He has this to say in *Ästhetische Theorie* about the truth content of Beethoven's music in relation to that of Bach:

progress is more than growing technical mastery and spiritualization. It is also the progress of spirit in the Hegelian sense of the term, i.e., an increasing awareness of spirit of its freedom. There is room for endless disagreement on the question of whether Beethoven was superior to Bach in terms of mastery of materials. Each probably mastered dimensions of material, and each probably did so equally well. To ask which of the two ranks more highly is therefore a moot question. It is only when we use the criterion of truth content – the emancipation of the [S]ubject from myth and the reconciliation of both – that Beethoven emerges as the more advanced composer. This criterion outweighs all others in importance.[67]

My account of Adorno's Beethoven critique has so far been taken mainly from the final chapter ('Vermittlung') of *Einleitung in die Musiksoziologie* and from comments scattered throughout *Philosophie der neuen Musik*. De la Fontaine derives his summary almost entirely from these sources. I have also made use of insights from *Ästhetische Theorie* and from the lecture 'Zum Probleme der musikalischen Analyse' [1969]. While all of these indicate the centrality of Beethoven to Adorno's conception of the historical dialectic of musical material, they do not (with the exception of his unfinished project *Beethoven: Philosophie der Musik* published in 1993) provide much detailed analytical reference to individual works. (As we have seen, however, this is a recurring complaint concerning Adorno's writings on music.) There are, nevertheless, a number of short essays on Beethoven which call for some comment here, not because they go into much analytical detail, but rather because they raise significant questions regarding Adorno's method in relation to particular works, and because they provide a fuller and more complex view of the composer than that offered so far in the above account or by de la Fontaine.

Fragmentation and unity in Beethoven's late style

The emphasis up to this point has been on *unity* in Beethoven's music – the usual emphasis, in fact, in a composer whose music has come to be seen as 'integrated' (although, as Adorno points out, this was not the distinguishing characteristic of the music as perceived by his contemporaries in the earlier part of the nineteenth century). Early on, however, Adorno also began to consider those aspects of Beethoven's music (and, indeed, of the whole tradition of art music of the bourgeois period) which work against unity and integration – or, alternatively, which create unity out of disunity, integration out of disintegration. In two brief articles from the 1930s ('Ludwig van Beethoven: Sechs Bagatellen für Klavier, op. 126' [1934][68] and 'Spätstil Beethovens' (1937)[69]). Adorno identifies features of Beethoven's late style which tend towards fragmentation, and from out of which, through the sheer force of construction, the composer creates a sense of unity. These features – the material of the late works – are, according to Adorno, the expressive conventions of the period, taken as the gestures and flourishes (*Floskeln*) of subjectivity which, through construction, are distanced or alienated from their conventional expressive meanings and compelled to speak as themselves.[70] Adorno gives as an example part of the middle section, bars 20–29, of the first Bagatelle op. 126, where the three-note expressive gesture in the right hand at the end of bar 20 is revealed in the next nine bars or so to be just what it is, a cadence figure spun out through repetition and rhythmic diminution to the point where, having been stripped of its conventional expressive attributes, it again assumes expressive power.[71] In these late works, Adorno argues, the process of extension is different from the early and middle period works:

His late work still remains processual; not, however, in the sense of development [*Entwicklung*], but in the sense of an ignition [*Zündung*] between the extremes which out of spontaneity does not tolerate a secure middle [*Mitte*] or harmony.[72]

These 'extremes' are technical features like, for example, polyphony and bare unison/octave passages juxtaposed abruptly without mediation (as in op. 126, no. 4). It is through these fissures in the surface (the 'appearance', (*Schein*)) of the work that subjectivity appears, Adorno argues. He formulates the relation of Subject and Object in the late Beethoven as follows:

This illuminates the absurdity that the late Beethoven can be called both subjective and objective simultaneously. The broken landscape is objective, the sole light by which it glows, subjective. It does not give rise to their synthesis. As the power of dissociation it tears them apart in time, in order perhaps to preserve them for eternity. In the history of art late works are the catastrophes.[73]

Adorno sees this as a feature of the late work of many artists – i.e. the idea of *catastrophe* as *discontinuous, sudden change*. In particular, however, he sees it as a characteristic of the music of Mahler, and indeed of a whole tradition of music itself 'growing old'. This is seen by Adorno as a dimension of Beethoven's music which led to no immediate development at the time, but which remained as a potential in the musical material, taken up by Mahler much later (although certain of its characteristics were to appear in the music of Berlioz, the interpretation of which will be discussed briefly below). It is a further example of Adorno's conception of historical progress as a spiral movement.

The Missa Solemnis: *alienated masterpiece*

Finally, there is the important essay 'Verfremdetes Hauptwerk: Zur Missa Solemnis' of 1959.[74] Here Adorno brings together the two emphases of his Beethoven critique – integration and disintegration. He argues that the *Missa Solemnis* is necessarily a problematical work because it attempts to combine the dynamic and integrative technique of 'developing variation' from basic motifs with the stasis and sectionalization of the archaic genre of the Mass. This results in an unresolved tension in the piece which works against a sense of integrated totality and which accounts for what Adorno considers to be 'flaws' in the composition. He suggests, however, that it is these very 'inconsistencies' when judged by the values of the early and middle period works which, in the *Missa Solemnis*, call for interpretation. He argues that here Beethoven is facing, in purely compositional terms, the problem 'of whether ontology, the objective spiritual order of Being [*die objektive geistige Ordnung des Seins*], is still at all possible'.[75] It is as though Beethoven were trying to evoke the idea of the Absolute, the eternal, the objective cosmos through his use of the liturgy, while at the same time attempting to mediate this objectivity through the subjectivity of motivic–

thematic development. That he does not totally succeed in this is nevertheless, according to Adorno's interpretation, a sign of the work's truth and authenticity. The reasoning behind this apparently perverse conclusion could be argued along the following lines: (i) the Classical ideal in music, to be found in the early and middle period works of Beethoven, is that truth = consistency, the identity and unity of motivating idea and its working out as the dynamic structure of the autonomous work, the objectification of subjectivity; (ii) the archaic genre of the Mass, with its socio-religious function in the liturgy, and its static, non-developmental sequence of sections, represents the *ancien régime*, a world order the stability and objective, absolute truths of which were already perceived as ideological in the post-Enlightenment, post-French Revolution Europe in which Beethoven was working; (iii) the attempt by Beethoven to synthesize these two worlds – the old and the new orders – and to reconceive the static genre of the Mass in terms of the dynamic process of motivic–thematic development, is only partially successful in the *Missa Solemnis*. Gaps remain, and the marks of the unsuccessful struggle to achieve synthesis are evident in the resulting work. These 'flaws' point to a historical truth: that the seamless unity of Subject and Object, of the inner world of the individual subjectivity and the outer world of the objective social order and its forms is no longer possible, and is now fraught with conflict. The autonomous art work – itself a product of the Enlightenment and the end of the old world order – now becomes an arena within which the problematical relation between Subject and Object, the 'self' and the external world of handed-down forms and genres, is fought out. The struggle for technical consistency in the face of the historical impossibility of a synthesis of such conflicting materials, produces a tension within the work which manifests at the level of form as incomplete integration. This nevertheless constitutes the work's authenticity, the mediation of socio-historical context within the 'closed world' of musical form, and tending towards fragmentation. It can be understood as the 'truth content' of Beethoven's late works, and goes beyond mere formal–technical consistency as the sole criterion of truth:

The late Beethoven's demand for truth rejects the illusory appearance of the unity of subjective and objective, a concept practically at one with the classicist idea. A polarization results. Unity transcends into the fragmentary. In the last quartets this takes place by means of the rough, unmediated juxtaposition of callow aphoristic motifs and polyphonic complexes. The gap between both becomes obvious and makes the impossibility of aesthetic harmony into the aesthetic content of the work; makes failure in a highest sense the measure of success. In its way even the *Missa* sacrifices the idea of synthesis.[76]

As Dahlhaus points out, the idea that the *Missa Solemnis* succeeds precisely because of its 'fragmented' character mediates 'a historical–philosophical insight which was not to be won in any other way than through aesthetic failure; this belongs to the central figures of Adorno's argument, to the motifs which run through his entire philosophy'.[77] In Dahlhaus's words, this is an idea, the 'intention of the *work*' (as opposed to the conscious intention of the composer), 'which only unfolds itself in [the work's] after-life or history of effect [*in dessen Nachleben oder Wirkungsge-schichte*]'.[78] The notion of *Wirkungsgeschichte* has also to be seen as an aspect of the historical dialectic of musical material. What is perceived as significant in a composer's work is a reflection of the expressive needs of a period; different facets of the work are seen in retrospect and developed by later composers, thus contributing in concrete terms to the spiral move-ment of musical material. Concerning the historical reception of Beethoven Adorno says that:

initially he achieved his effect through what ... has been called 'titanism', or through his expressivity; and only by means of intensive structural analysis did it then later become clear why his music can, with good reason, be called 'beautiful' and 'true', and also eventually where its limits were to be sought.[79]

Adorno suggests that one immediate response to the 'titanism' of Beethoven's music, as opposed to its sense of unity, was that of Berlioz, 'who outstripped Beethoven's titanic posture to which audiences first responded favourably'.[80] This focus on the dramatic aspects of Beethoven's music, taking dramatic gestures to an extreme, was what, in Adorno's view, made it possible to perceive a deeper structural dimension to the music – as far as dramatic effects were concerned, Beethoven had been outdone at his own game by Berlioz. (Adorno remarks that usually the structural merits of a work 'begin to stand out clearly only after the material has grown old, or when the sensory apparatus has been dulled to the point where it no longer fastens on the most striking feature at the surface'.[81])

Berlioz: a changed conception of technique

The case of Berlioz within Adorno's theory is interesting, as it provides a link between Beethoven, as the 'revolutionary bourgeois', and what could be called 'the age of industry', the rise of industrial capitalism and the commodification of art. Berlioz represents another example of 'historical discontinuity' for Adorno. Just as, he maintains, the *style galant* cannot be understood purely in terms of immanent musical logic and historical continuity following on from the Baroque style, so the phenomenon of Berlioz cannot be understood in purely intra-musical terms as following on from the compositional problems of the Classical style. In 'Ideen zur Musiksoziologie' he writes:

Just as little do the innovations of Hector Berlioz follow from the consequences of Beethoven's compositional problems, but are much more determined by industrial procedures arising outside music, by a radically changed conception of technique compared to that of the Classical art of composition. In him, and in those composers specifically following on from him, Liszt and later Richard Strauss, the achievements of Viennese Classicism are forgotten in a similar manner to the way in which [the *galant* composers] forgot the achievements of Bach.[82]

Quite apart from the questionable blanket inclusion of Liszt among those composers where 'the achievements of Viennese Classicism are forgotten', Adorno unfortunately gives little detail as to how Berlioz's music relates to the industrial procedures of the early nineteenth century. From odd comments in *Einleitung in die Musiksoziologie* one gathers that '[t]he link – notably the kinship of the technological aspect of Berlioz's treatment of the orchestra with industrial procedures – is hard to deny'.[83] Also that '[s]uch essential features as the desultoriness and abruptness of Berlioz's idiom do indeed plainly attest changes in the form of social reaction which he underwent in musical form'.[84] The development of orchestral technique is clearly significant, however, and was Berlioz's vital contribution to the development of musical material and compositional techniques. The link with extra-musical developments is not difficult to identify in the case of musical instrument technology and the development of the orchestra, and constitutes an obvious example of Max Weber's principle of progressive rationalization.

A crisis in musical logic

As well as establishing greater control over the timbral dimension of musical material, however, Berlioz also, Adorno argues, was the first 'modern' composer, in the sense of precipitating 'a crisis of musical logic' through '[t]he attempt of his program music to portray intoxication through opium'.[85] This led to the increasing fragmentation of musical form – a fragmentation brought about by the influence of the exterior literary programme, by the increasing focus on orchestral effects and, paradoxically, through the 'unifying' device of the *idée fixe* (features discussed at much greater length by Adorno in relation to the music of Wagner).[86] These changes, initially externalized aspects compared to the 'immanent musical logic' of form as handed on by Beethoven and Viennese Classicism, then became themselves 'internalized', became part of the dialectic of the material and became part of its complex of problems.[87] In his extended essay on Richard Strauss, dating from the 1960s, Adorno suggests that:

Based on the program, the music of Berlioz and his followers had sought to free itself of the inexorable necessity which, ever since Beethoven, had cast its shadow over the development of rigorous composition. .... In logically consistent music, everything became increasingly determined. ... Berlioz, Liszt, and Strauss kept themselves outside of this very German process. By not accepting the autonomy of form as absolute, by belying it through the introduction of heterogeneous materials which could never be entirely absorbed in music, they sought to retrieve for music some of the freedom it had been forced to relinquish by the law of its reason. In Berlioz this occurred through eruptions and exterritorially...[88]

And these points had been made with even greater clarity in the important essay, 'Musik und Technik' of 1958:

Berlioz was the prime phenomenon of modernity in music; he was the first composer in whom the continuity of tradition and – along with it – the continuity of musical structure broke into fragments. In the most pregnant sense, he created a compositional technique conscious of itself in its disposition over a level of musical material – the level of instrumental realization – which up to that time had been an arbitrary concern. At the same time, he was the first significant composer – if Gluck is disregarded – for whom the technique of composition, the ability to create structures characterized by unity, coherence and consistent development, was insufficient. His was the first music of the more modern age in which the context of musical meaning and musical meaning itself become dubious. ... in his work instrumental organization and compositional disorganization complement each other. It is precisely this [aspect] which explains the modern impression made by his works.[89]

I argue that Adorno's comments on Berlioz – brief and scattered as they are within the total corpus of his writings on music – are of considerable significance for his theory of musical material. The tendency of many of Adorno's commentators (including de la Fontaine and Dahlhaus) has been to ignore or underestimate this aspect of his theory – i.e. that concerning fragmentation and historical discontinuity – in the most undialectical fashion, thus encouraging a very monolithic view of his thinking. Such a view emphasizes the concepts of immanent musical logic, integration, unity and continuity at the expense of their opposites: external influences, disintegration, fragmentation and discontinuity. The result is that the theory is seen as providing little more than a pre-history and legitimation of the serialism of the Second Viennese School. That it does in part serve this purpose is undeniable, especially in relation to *Philosophie der neuen Musik*. However, as I have already suggested, if the emphasis is rather on the concept of *progressive rationalization*, Adorno's theory of musical material can be seen at the same time to embrace music which falls outside the Austro-German tradition, as well as tendencies within that tradition which work against its most central values.

4   Wagner and Brahms

In identifying Berlioz as a key musical figure of the period of early industrialization in Europe, and as a figure whose work simultaneously manifests an intensification of the 'titanic', gestural character of Beethoven's music and a fragmentation of that composer's 'immanent musical logic', Adorno traces what he sees as the spiral movement of musical material in its historical dialectic of progress and regression to its pivotal point in the mid-nineteenth century: Richard Wagner. At the same time, he also traces forward to Brahms, via the lyrical 'inwardness' of Schubert and Schumann, the intensification of Beethoven's process of integration through 'developing variation'. Adorno's interpretation of the music of these two composers emphasizes the contradictory character of both from the perspective of the avant-garde. The difference in the amount of space given to each composer here is, in one sense, simply a reflection of the fact that Adorno wrote a great deal more on Wagner than he did on Brahms. However, this also needs to be seen as an indication of the importance Adorno gives to the understanding of the 'complex of problems' bequeathed by Wagner to the 'New Music' of the twentieth century, and of the 'truth' and 'untruth' of Wagner's music as a cipher for the contradictions of its own historical period, the 'age of industry'.

Progressive rationalization and mimetic regression

With Wagner,[90] Adorno argues, the process of progressive rationalization extends further into the technical structure of the musical work in all its aspects – motivic and harmonic construction, instrumentation and the extension of orchestral forces and development of new instruments and new sonorities, the manipulation of time, and the integration of music, text, dramatic action and stage design into a new totality. And yet, Adorno suggests, the 'progressive' in Wagner's music, as advance in technique, cannot conceal the regressive dimension of its expressive content. Put in oppositional terms, Adorno considers that, on the one hand, the process of rationalization in Wagner's music has as its objective the construction of the appearance of an all-embracing, integrated and organic 'nature'. On the other hand, however, in spite of the 'progressive' and radical character of the technical means developed to achieve this end, Adorno sees what he regards as significant 'blind spots' or inconsistencies in the structure of Wagner's music. His reading of these 'inconsistencies', in terms of their ideological significance, hinges yet again on the manner in which he considers the music's formal logic achieves a new and integrated totality in relation to the pre-formed, handed-down musical material as reified genres, formal types and tonal schemata. One of the dominant concepts he employs in his interpretation of Wagner's music is that of gesture (*Gestus, Geste*) – a concept discussed earlier in the present study (see Chapter 3) in relation to the oppositional pairs *mimesis–ratio* and *expression–construc-*

tion. First, however, we need to see Adorno's critique of Wagner in more general terms through the pairs of concepts *history–nature* and *Sein–Werden*, in relation to the important concept of *phantasmagoria* (*Phantasmagorie*) as concealment of labour through increasing technical domination of material.

The rejection of history for the myth of nature

The rejection of history in favour of mythical nature can be understood in Wagner's case in several ways. First, there is what Adorno calls 'the tendency towards an allegorical return to unarticulated natural material'.[91] This can be seen clearly, of course, in the symbolism of the *Ring*:

> If we were to summarize the 'idea' of the *Ring* in simple words we would say that man emancipates himself from the blind identity with nature only to succumb to her in the long run. The allegory of the *Ring* asserts the dominion over nature and subjugation by nature are one and the same.[92]

However, the rejection of history in favour of nature also underlies, Adorno maintains, what he describes as the 'elemental' character of much of Wagner's motivic material. He argues that the motifs are always threatening to fall back into the undifferentiated basic material of tonality itself: examples he offers are *Urmotive* of the triadic kind which opens *Rheingold*, or of the chromatic kind which opens *Tristan*. The contradiction he sees here is that the leitmotif has to be distinctive and arresting in order to be recognized on subsequent and varied appearances over long stretches of time; at the same time, however, the tendency of Wagner's technique of 'the art of transition' is 'to dissolve everything definite and specific into an undifferentiated mass, whether into the "*Ur*-triad" or into chromaticism'.[93] Adorno argues that 'Wagner's hostility to standard forms ends in absurdity, in the nameless, the unspecific and the abstract',[94] and that the legacy is to be heard, via Reger, in the banalities of Strauss and Pfitzner,[95] and also in the techniques of film music.[96] In this he sees Wagner's music as prefiguring the historical 'disintegration' of musical material.

Phantasmagoria and the concealment of labour

Secondly, there is what Adorno sees as Wagner's attempt to present art as 'nature', as seamless, timeless and ahistorical, and to conceal the process of production, the labour that went into the creation of the product. He argues: 'the concealment of production through the surface appearance of the product is what constitutes the law of form of Richard Wagner's music'.[97] A manifestation of this is the idea of the *Gesamtkunstwerk* itself, where the 'blending' of essentially different modes of art into a new synthesis also has as its intention the concealing of the joins, and of the artifice of the process of artistic production itself. The contradiction here is that the concealment of artifice through the illusion of 'nature' results in the art work as separate, distinct and alienated from nature. As Adorno puts it:

in seeking an aesthetic interchangeability, and by striving for an artifice so perfect that it conceals all the sutures in the final artefact and even blurs the difference between it and nature itself, it presupposes the same radical alienation from anything natural that its attempt to establish itself as a unified 'second nature' sets out to obscure.[98]

This 'perfection of illusion' (*Vollendung des Scheins*) which magically conceals artifice Adorno calls (using Walter Benjamin's concept) *phantasmagoria*[99] (see Chapter 3). On the one hand, Wagner's 'perfection of illusion' as phantasmagoria derives from the fantastic aspects of Romanticism, the attempt to transcend everyday reality through the creation of a magical alternative reality. On the other hand, however, Adorno suggests that it also signals the birth of realism, in that '[t]he Wagnerian phantasmagorias are among the earliest "wonders of technology" to gain admittance to great art'.[100] Wagner's 'illusionism' is achieved through technical and *technological* domination of the musical material – in particular the orchestra. (An example cited by Adorno is the phantasmagorical character of the *Venusberg* music from *Tannhäuser*, where, he suggests, the effect of 'loudness from afar' is created through the use of the high woodwind – especially piccolo – and through omitting the bass instruments.[101]) The illusory and fantastic character of Wagner's music, its 'imitation of nature' and its concealment of its own process of production, is what Adorno sees as also constituting its commodity character – indeed, Adorno's description of the phantasmagoria clearly derives in part also from Marx's famous description of the commodity in *Das Kapital* Volume I: 'It is nothing but the definite social relation between men themselves which assumes here, for them, the fantastic [i.e., *phantasmagorische*] form of a relation between things'.[102]

Society, nature, fate

Thirdly, and more generally, there is Wagner's rejection of the historical and political present for an ahistorical and mythical past in the face of the frustration of his own political activities up to 1848. Adorno sees in this the contradictory character of Wagner's radical position, at once both progressive and regressive. He argues that Wagner equates society with 'nature', and thus sees both in terms of the idea of 'fate' (*Schicksal*). His radicalism, suggests Adorno, is at the same time both a rebellion against authority (as convention), and a reaffirmation of authority:

The parable of the man who dominates nature only to relapse into a state of natural bondage gains an historical dimension in the action of the *Ring*: with the victory of the bourgeoisie, the idea that society is like a natural process, something 'fated', is reaffirmed, despite the conquest of particular aspects of nature. The catastrophe arises at the moment when this much-vaunted 'natural process' is revealed to be the mere product and stigma of an all-knowing authority. It is in this context that the musical gesture of retraction that lies at the heart of Wagner's music becomes fully comprehensible in social terms.[103]

Adorno sees Wagner – both the man and his music (a dual focus which has given rise to much criticism of his approach in this instance)[104] – as the paradigmatic figure for the post-1848 period. In him converge the contradictions of the age of industrial capitalism following the period of revolutionary upheaval and early industrialization during which the bourgeoisie had established itself politically. Striking among these contradictions is the evident subject-matter of Wagner's operas and music dramas in relation to their period. In *Versuch über Wagner* Adorno writes: 'There can be no doubt that the elimination of the political from Wagner's own work was, in part at least, the result of the disillusionment of the bourgeoisie after 1848, a disappointment outspokenly reflected in his correspondence'.[105] Furthermore, argues Adorno, the recourse to myth is at the same time a rejection of history: the search for the 'universally human', as essence, 'requires the dismantling of what he supposes to be the relative and contingent in favour of the idea of an unvarying human nature'.[106]

Being and Becoming

The emphasis in Wagner's work on static Being (*Sein*) over dynamic Becoming (*Werden*) is seen by Adorno not only as a feature of the 'subject-matter' of the music dramas, but also as a feature of the motivic material and of the larger formal design of the music itself.[107] The ontological emphasis on *Sein* over *Werden*, and on 'nature' over 'history' is understood by Adorno in musical terms as an emphasis on a deliberately 'allegorical' – and therefore, he maintains, static – use of motivic material over a 'developmental' and dynamic (i.e. Beethovenian) one. Adorno argues, for example, that the device of the leitmotif is, of its very nature, resistant to development, in spite of the overall impression given by Wagner's music, which is that of perpetual development:

Beneath the thin shell of continuous movement [*Verlauf*] Wagner has fragmented the composition into allegorical leitmotifs strung together like discrete objects.

These defy the claims of a totalizing musical form no less than the aesthetic claims of 'symbolism' – in short, the claims of the handed-down tradition of German Idealism. Even though Wagner's music is thoroughly perfected as style, this style is not a system in the sense of being a thoroughly consistent and self-contained totality, a purely immanent context of part and whole.[108]

In his talk 'Zum Probleme der musikalischen Analyse' Adorno specifically contrasts Wagner's compositional procedures with those of Beethoven:

I have just spoken of the 'indifference' of the material in Beethoven. With Wagner, the basic motifs [Urmotive] which are supposed to represent the primeval world [das Urweltliche] of Wotan and the Valhalla domain in the Ring are kept within a certain ... undifferentiated, or 'unspecific Universality'. But in Wagner's case they are not, by a long way, as legitimate as they are with Beethoven because Wagner's individual motifs have the significance and weight of symbols, and contain basically the whole idea of the germinal cell of the romantic Lied. For this reason they have pretensions to a 'Beingness' [Sein] 'in and for themselves' much more than is ever the case with Beethoven.[109]

And he continues:

this weakness, inherent in the themes and contradicting their own claim to just 'being there' [da zu sein], points, moreover, to their real weakness as regards substance, in view of what happens to them and what they become – something that one would not think of in connection with Beethoven, because with him the priority of 'Becoming' over that which simply is is already established right from the start.[110]

Unsublimated gestures

Adorno identifies the origins of what he sees as the 'static' and 'regressive' aspect of Wagner's music as lying in its 'gestural character'. As discussed in Chapter 3, Adorno understands the language-like aspect of autonomous music as being in part the outcome of the interaction of two opposing 'moments': the mimetic and the rational. The 'mimetic moment' he sees as the survival of gestural, pre-linguistic elements within the increasingly rationalized structures of autonomous music. These elements, the remnants of autonomous music's heteronomous origins in previous social function, are now sublimated and absorbed within the music's all-embracing formal logic – that is to say, they are mediated through the work's 'law of form' (Formgesetz). In Wagner's case, however, Adorno argues that the assimilation of these gestural elements into the overall formal logic of the music has been incompletely carried through. This results, he maintains, in technical inconsistencies in Wagner's work, as faults in compositional technique. These 'inconsistencies' he sees as indicators of the 'ideological moment' in Wagner's music.

But what does Adorno mean when he talks of the 'unsublimated gestures' of Wagner's music? And indeed, what does he mean in more concrete terms by the concept of 'gesture' overall? He refers, for example, to 'the gesture of beating time that dominates his [Wagner's] work',[111] and argues that:

Wagner's use of the beat to control time is abstract; it is no more than the idea of time as something articulated by the beat and then projected onto the larger periods. . . . the measure to which he subjects time does not derive from the musical content, but from the reified order of time itself.[112]

Thus Adorno, using the image of the conductor (and in particular of Wagner as the celebrated conductor) as 'heroic' representative of the public within the orchestra, suggests that the large-scale 'gesture' of Wagner's music is in one sense that of the conductor's controlling and regular beat – a beat which is itself inscribed in the structure of the music and which controls it 'from above'.[113] This is manifest in the music, he maintains, through its division into large stretches of time dominated by regular beats, and punctuated by the reified gestures of incidental music – e.g. 'flourishes, signals and fanfares' – which 'survive in the midst of the *durchkomponiert* style in which they are deposited like sediment'.[114] Among the examples he cites are the introduction to Act III scene 3 of *Lohengrin*, and Siegfried's Journey to the Rhine in *Götterdämmerung*.[115] Adorno argues that material 'residues' of this kind, the fanfare-like public gestures of incidental music which have remained unsublimated by the work's formal logic, indicate the regressive aspect of Wagner's music, in that they resist the process of rationalization and remain on a mimetic, pre-linguistic level of signification. He writes:

An element of unsublimated [material] is scattered within the highly organized style. Wagner's musical consciousness succumbs to a peculiar kind of regression [*Rückbildung*]: it is as if the aversion to mimicry, which became increasingly strong with the historical process of Western rationalization and which contributed in no small way to the crystallization of an autonomous, language-like musical logic, did not have complete power over him. His compositional approach falls back into the pre-linguistic, without, however, being able to rid itself completely of language-like elements.[116]

Technical inconsistency

We need also to examine further what Adorno understands by 'technical inconsistency' in Wagner's music. To grasp Adorno's argument here we need first to recall the discussion in Chapter 3 concerning the dialectic of *construction* and *expression* in relation to the concept of gesture, and that in Chapter 4 concerning the two levels on which it was argued his concept of 'form' needs to be taken – the universal and the particular. Adorno's use of the concepts 'gesture' and 'expression' will certainly lead to confusion if not understood in relation to his concept of form.

Expression, according to Adorno, is a kind of 'interference phenomenon', the resultant of the tension between mimesis and rationality within the structure of the work. It is the sublimation of the mimetic, gestural elements of the musical material through the rationality of construction (see Chapter 3). As we have seen, he maintains that, although all music probably has its roots in gesture, 'in the West ... it has been spiritualized [*vergeistigt*] and interiorized [*verinnerlicht*] into expression, while at the same time the principle of construction subjects the overall flow of the music to a process of logical synthesis'.[117] He suggests furthermore that great music strives to achieve a balance of these two elements – that is to say, of the mimetic and the rational – through the logic of form. The idea implied here, that 'expression' is created through the subjection of handed-down musical gestures to the logic of construction through *development*, may also seem to suggest that the gestures are not *in themselves* 'expressive'. Expression would therefore seem to be the product of development. This has led Dahlhaus to the view that Adorno's critique of Wagner is at very least ambiguous in its use of the concepts 'gesture' and 'expression':

> expression, as Adorno understands it, is inseparable from development [*Entwicklung*]. And the opposition which he astonishingly sets up between expression and gesture says nothing more or less than that musical expression derives not so much from a theme or motif in its first, immediate shape, but owes much more to [the process of] developing variation into which the theme is drawn. Against the popular notion that expressivity is a quality of melodic inspiration [*Einfall*], Adorno, admittedly without saying so unambiguously, seems to be convinced that it arises from [the process of] musical construction which serves in the first place to uncover whatever may be concealed in an 'inspired' initial idea [*Einfall*].[118]

Dahlhaus's confusion – the result, in this instance, of his undialectical approach to Adorno's work – arises from the straight opposition he sees between the two concepts 'gesture' and 'expression'. They are, indeed, opposed by Adorno, but *dialectically*: that is to say, they must be understood as interacting through their extremes. As we have seen, in Adorno's Hegelian use of concepts each concept contains its opposite, and can be understood in two apparently opposed senses, depending on whether, relatively speaking, it is taken as (i) immediate, given 'being' (*Sein*), or (ii) mediated 'becoming' (*Werden*), as the outcome of a process of development, of sublimation and, in the Hegelian sense, of sublation. What Dahlhaus emphasizes in his reading of Adorno in this instance is the idea of expression as outcome of development, as *Werden*, to which he opposes the idea of gesture as immediate given. This gives only half of the picture, and therefore distorts both concepts as Adorno employs them. Any material which provides the starting point for a process of development may be seen conveniently as an immediate 'given' which then becomes something new through its mediation as form. At the same time, however, its immediacy and 'givenness' have to be seen as relative, in that the given material is itself already historically preformed, as mediated 'second nature', while on the other hand the outcome of the process of development of the 'given' material contributes itself to the historical dialectic of material, and becomes itself a new 'given' in joining the stock of handed-down conventions. Thus, seen in relation to Adorno's 'theory of form' as put forward in Chapter 4, 'gesture' and 'expression' may be understood in the following two senses: (i) at the 'universal' or general level of form, gestures as, for example, the handed-down conventions of incidental music, are 'expressive' only in that they carry the conventional expressive meanings associated with their previous functionality; and (ii) at the level of the form of particular musical works, expression is the outcome of the development and recontextualization of handed-down material, as the expression of new 'meanings' – meanings which themselves constitute new expressive gestures.

The ideology of immediacy

Adorno's critique of Wagner rests precisely on the argument that what Wagner himself takes as a natural, immediate 'given' and to which, as *Urmotive*, he attributes absolute symbolic meaning, is in fact reified 'second nature'. Furthermore, Adorno insists, the process of development in Wagner's music – for example, through the use of leitmotif and sequence – does not serve to uncover the mediated character of its original material, but rather serves to conceal it under the cloak of absolute and timeless values. Adorno argues that the appearance of development is achieved in Wagner's music through the use of *sequence* – a device which, so he maintains, conceals the fact that nothing essential has changed by means of increasing expressive intensity through repetition of the same material at a different pitch. As has been seen, however, Adorno takes Beethoven as his model in his discussion of 'development', and in this he could be accused of absolutizing the historically situated symphonic ideal of what Schoenberg had called 'developing variation' and of applying it inappropriately to Wagner. Dahlhaus formulates his uneasiness concerning this aspect of Adorno's critique of Wagner in the following terms:

The suspicion nevertheless automatically forces itself upon one that the tradition and idea of developmental form to which Adorno orientates his critique of the form of Wagner's music may in fact be foreign to opera, and that therefore Adorno's critique may rest on a confusion of generic norms: a suspicion which, while to some extent certainly allowing itself to be allayed by the objection that the music drama as conceived by Wagner may be a different genre to opera, cannot be completely suppressed.[119]

As Dahlhaus points out, Adorno's critique of Wagner takes the composer strictly at his word, in that the music drama is understood as the historical consummation of the symphony.[120] These underlying assumptions need therefore to be kept in mind in his interpretation of Wagner's music, and it also needs to be remembered that his conception of the 'historical dialectic of musical material' is centred around the notion of 'progress of spirit', as both progress in rationalization and progress of the expressive Subject (see above and Chapter 3). Within the structure of musical works the Subject is identified with the theme/motif, and what becomes of it in the process of thematic development – a process which Adorno understands as the 'objectification of the Subject'. *Einfall*, it will be recalled, as the theme or motif, is seen as 'the irreducibly subjective element' in music, the initial 'inspired idea',[121] and its development is what constitutes its objectification through the logic of form – a 'logic' in part contained as potential in the initial idea as *Einfall*, and which in part may also be seen as having shaped the initial idea from the outset to enable it to fulfil its role within the overall formal logic of the work.[122] Contained in Adorno's notion of the 'progress of spirit' are, therefore, two different aspects: (i) increasing rationalization and control of the musical material as historical progress in technique (and technology); and (ii) increasing objectification of the expressive Subject as the structure of the work, manifesting as increasing awareness of the demands of the material through the 'self-reflection' of form. It would seem – although Adorno does not formulate it in these terms – that, although these two aspects of the 'progress of spirit' in music belong together, they can also diverge and come to contradict one another. It is in this sense that Wagner could be understood as being simultaneously progressive and regressive. In terms of rationalization, as increasing control of the material, Wagner's music is perceived by Adorno to be progressive – indeed, revolutionary. In terms of the self-reflection of the Subject, however, it is judged to be regressive. That is to say, the apparently dynamic and integrated form of Wagner's music, in terms, for example, of the working out of its fundamental motivic material, the leitmotif, is considered by Adorno to conceal static and unintegrated elements. It is these features that he seeks to identify, and which, so he argues, constitute the technical inconsistencies in the structure of Wagner's music, in view of the claims made *by the works themselves* to be integrated and developmental.

The technification of inwardness

The central argument in Adorno's critique of Wagner is that the ideological moment in the music lies in the falseness of the unity of the subjective and the objective, between the 'self' as *Einfall* and 'form' as construction, development or working out. That is to say, Wagner's music seeks to convince us of a smooth continuity between 'inwardness' (*Innerlichkeit*) – the inner world of the individual, of the Subject – and the external world (*Äußerlichkeit*), as Object, empirical reality. (Indeed, it is interesting to compare his critique of Wagner in this respect with his critique of Beethoven, especially regarding the *Missa Solemnis*.) Adorno maintains that Wagner's large-scale musical gesture is that of incorporating the public into the music, of 'dominating' the audience through making use of handed-down conventions derived from incidental music and opera, and which are employed to contrive a link between the extra-musical and the interior world of the music itself. Adorno considers that what characterizes Wagner's musical (and indeed personal) pose in relation to the public is the attempt to embody the heroic individual as directly representing the values of the collectivity, of the ideal community. While on the one hand Wagner's music represents the most extreme example of the attempt to 'objectify subjectivity', to externalize the inner world of the individual and to express this 'inwardness' on a grandiose scale, on the other hand the very technical control of the material which enables him to achieve this public expression of inner subjectivity also contributes to its commodification and reification. Adorno argues that the phantasmagorical world of Wagner's music is a kind of 'technification of inwardness' which the public can enter to marvel at and be overwhelmed by, very much in the spirit of the great world exhibitions of the second half of the nineteenth century. Indeed, in a passage in his 'Paris, capital of the nineteenth century' which had undoubtedly impressed Adorno, Walter Benjamin had written:

The world exhibitions glorify the exchange value of commodities. They create a framework in which commodities' intrinsic value is eclipsed. They open up a phantasmagoria that people enter to be amused. The entertainment industry facilitates this by elevating people to the level of commodities.[123]

The commodification of expression: music's 'coming of age'

In *Minima Moralia* Adorno expands on the idea that the intensification of expression through the 'technification of inwardness' as spectacle on the scale of Wagner's *Gesamtkunstwerk* leads to the commodification of art in line with the production process of capitalist society. He argues that

the more artists have journeyed into the interior, the more they have learned to forego the infantile fun of imitating external reality. But at the same time, by dint of reflecting on the psyche, they have found out more and more how to control themselves. The progress in technique that brought them ever greater freedom and independence of anything heterogeneous, has resulted in a kind of reification, technification of the inward as such. The more masterfully the artist expresses himself, the less he has to 'be' what he expresses, and the more what he expresses, indeed the content of subjectivity itself, becomes a mere function of the production process.[124]

It is in this sense that Wagner's music is understood as both a reflection of and a retreat from the dominant tendencies of its period. Adorno's critique of Wagner should therefore not be misconstrued as a polemical attack on the composer and a dismissal of his music – although it has to be conceded that there are times when the casual reader could be excused for taking *Versuch über Wagner* in this way. Although Wagner 'withdraws from history' and from the political realities of his time, Adorno argues that the contradictions of the rejected empirical reality reappear in mediated form within the apparently self-contained, mythical world of the music drama and, what is more, within the structure of the music itself. Thus, what may be seen, in Marxian terms, as the 'false consciousness' of Wagner's music, its ideological moment, may also be understood through Adorno's dialectical critique as an aspect of the music's 'truth content'. The omissions, contradictions and inconsistencies of Wagner's music – its 'absences' – are seen to be as significant as its genuinely radical implications, in that they are the scars left within the musical structures of the dominant historical and social tendencies of the real world of his day. Adorno continues:

Nietzsche had an inkling of this when he taxed Wagner, that tamer of expression, with hypocrisy, without perceiving that this was not a matter of psychology, but of a historical tendency. The transformation of expressive content from an undirected impulse into material for manipulation makes it palpable, exhibitable, saleable.[125]

It is with Wagner, therefore, that the commodity character of music first becomes clearly apparent, so Adorno argues, as an aspect of music's 'coming of age' in a society dominated by the exchange of commodities. At the same time, however, its commodity character can be seen as one outcome of music's alienation from society and its retreat into autonomy, into the total rationalization and 'technification' of the work of art. According to Adorno, Wagner's legacy includes the extremes of the avant-garde art work and mass culture, Schoenberg and the Hollywood movie. After Wagner, its commodity character becomes part of autonomous music's context of problems, to be confronted in the compositional process as a tendency within the handed-down musical material.

Brahms the progressive

If Wagner's music manifests historical discontinuities, it is Brahms, at first sight at least, who represents a line of historical continuity for Adorno, linking Beethoven and Schoenberg through the increasingly all-encompassing function of motivic–thematic development. At the same time, however, his interpretation of Brahms leads itself to paradoxical conclusions, and merits at least a brief consideration here, in spite of the small amount of space given to the composer in Adorno's writings.

Considering the historical importance of Brahms, it may seem strange that Adorno devoted only one short text wholly to the discussion of his music (apart, that is, from a short article on Eduard Steuermann's *Brahms-Ausgabe* (1932)).[126] In fact the essay, 'Brahms aktuell',[127] was written in 1934 (although only published posthumously) specifically to counter what was at that time a generally held view of the composer as the academic traditionalist, and in this Adorno anticipates Schoenberg's similarly motivated essay of 1947, 'Brahms the progressive'.[128] Adorno's essay, like Schoenberg's, emphasizes the hidden legacy of Brahms to the New Music, and the essence of its argument reappears in the course of later and more important texts like *Philosophie der neuen Musik*[129] and *Einleitung in die Musiksoziologie*.[130]

The retreat into inwardness

Adorno argues that Brahms's starting material is derived from the intensely subjective lyricism of Schumann and, to some extent, that of Schubert – a subjectivity which, as an expression of the self-enclosed, private world of the bourgeois individual, threatens the objectivity of handed-down formal types.[131] Brahms's problem, according to Adorno, was: how to reconstitute the sense of totality and objectivity represented by the Beethovenian sonata form, but from the position of the isolated subjectivity expressed, for example, in the Schumannesque and Schubertian Lied. Adorno suggests that Brahms's solution was to turn inwards, and that his music is characterized by a total immersion (*Versenkung*) within, and intensive reflection (*Besinnung*) upon his material – i.e. the subjectivity of the Schumann lyric song:

His music examines its material – precisely that of the high Romanticism of Schumann – profoundly in its self-giveness until it becomes objectified: objectification of the Subject. What is achieved in Wagner through a dynamic tempest is achieved in Brahms through stubborn insistence.[132]

This reflection upon the material, as 'objectification of subjectivity' is achieved by means of an extension of Beethoven's process of development to every aspect of form. In *Philosophie der neuen Musik* Adorno relates Schoenberg to Brahms in the following terms:

[Brahms] consequently becomes the advocate of universal economy, rejecting all fortuitous elements [*Momente*] in the music, and yet developing the most extreme multiplicity . . . from materials the identity of which is preserved. There is no longer anything which is unthematic; nothing which cannot be understood as derived from the identity [of the basic thematic material], no matter how latent. Schoenberg develops the tendencies of Beethoven and Brahms; in so doing he can lay claim to the heritage of classic bourgeois music – in a sense very similar to that in which dialectical materialism is related to Hegel.[133]

What is preserved in Brahms, according to Adorno, is a balance of subjective expression in relation to the 'objectivity' of tonality, 'forcing the lyric intermezzo and academic formal technique [*Satz*] into meaningful union'.[134] In this Brahms succeeds impressively in reconstituting a sense of totality which is technically consistent – unlike the appearance of totality constructed by Wagner, maintains Adorno. However, in *Einleitung in die Musiksoziologie* Adorno subjects Brahms likewise to ideology critique to reveal the price of his achievement of totality:

That Brahms – like the entire evolution since Schumann, even since Schubert – bears the mark of bourgeois society's individualistic phase is indisputable enough to have become a platitude. In Beethoven the category of totality still preserves a picture of the right society; in Brahms it fades increasingly into a self-sufficiently esthetic principle for the organization of private feelings. This is the academic side of Brahms. His music beats a mournful retreat to the individual, but as the individual is falsely absolutized over society Brahms's work too is surely part of a false consciousness – of one from which no modern art can escape without sacrificing itself.[135]

This is the ideological aspect of Brahms's music – that its achievement of a well-balanced and technically consistent totality has to be at the cost of the retreat of the individual from a society which is not 'whole'. But at the same time Adorno argues, as in the case of Wagner, that the synthesis of private and public world was not historically possible at this period, unlike at the period of Mozart and even the early and middle period Beethoven, because the idea of social 'wholeness' was by now an illusion. Thus the removal of the individual into the interior of the work of art was the only recourse available, in different ways, to both Brahms and Wagner.

The establishment of laws and the loss of necessity

But the authenticity of Brahms's music lies, for Adorno, in its legacy – a legacy which can also be seen as paradoxical. Part of this legacy is Brahms's contribution to music's 'coming of age'. Adorno considers that, by his extension of the control of musical material into the 'innermost cells' of the work through the process of developing variation, Brahms further stripped music of its 'naïvety' and increased its cognitive character (*Erkenntnischarakter*).[136] Thus Brahms can be seen as partaking in the process of music's 'demythologization'. It is this which constitutes Brahms's lasting influence on the New Music, in the sense of 'the establishment of laws', as Adorno puts it, and not through any overt stylistic influences.[137] This is Brahms 'the progressive'. At the same time, however, as Rose Rosengard Subotnik has suggested in her reading of Adorno, in moving towards the 'total development' of the musical work 'Brahms actually emphasized the arbitrariness of the connections between this material and its largely traditional forms of organization, which was [sic] not commensurately individualized. And individual configurations characterized by arbitrariness cannot be considered necessary.'[138] Thus, it can be argued, Brahms, like Wagner, also contributes towards the disintegration of musical material through throwing into question the 'necessary' character of its relations.

5   Debussy and Mahler

Before going on to consider the implications for the New Music of the 'historical tendency of musical material' towards what Adorno identifies as the total integration of the musical work and the disintegration of the musical material, we should first briefly register certain of his observations on two composers of the *fin de siècle* – Debussy and Mahler – whose music could be seen as offering very contrasting responses to the problems thrown up in particular by Wagner. It is through Debussy that Stravinsky can be seen to relate to Wagner, Adorno argues, while Schoenberg's relation to Wagner is in part filtered through Mahler. As is the case throughout Adorno's philosophical interpretations, the discussion hinges on what he sees as the underlying relationship of Subject to Object. Thus, in *Philosophie der neuen Musik* Schoenberg's music is interpreted as an intensification of the survival of the expressive Subject to be found in the alienated subjectivity of Mahler's late works,[139] while Stravinsky's music is interpreted as an extension of the capitulation of the Subject to the 'culinary' objectivity of 'elementary tonal combinations' to be found in the mature works of Debussy.[140]

Debussy: capitulation to the Object

Adorno's comments on Debussy are not to be discovered in any developed form, as he wrote no single essay or article devoted to the composer's music. Instead, Debussy appears as part of the discussion of other composers – in particular Wagner and Stravinsky. Adorno, predictably enough, emphasizes the 'sensuous'[141] and 'undynamic'[142] aspects of Debussy's music – and, indeed, of French music in general. He sees

Debussy as the link between what he considers Wagner's lack of true dynamic development through emphasis on the essentially 'static' and symbolic leitmotif and on instrumental colour, and Stravinsky's obsessive repetitions. Common to all three composers he sees a desire to represent the archaic, mythical and ahistorical in music, and to signify 'nature' and 'fate'[143] (in Debussy's case he would appear particularly to have *Pelléas et Mélisande* in mind).

Adorno maintains that Debussy's music is essentially undialectical in its relation to its material. The material is seen as a highly refined extension of what he calls the 'culinary' aspects of the bourgeois art music tradition, and of nineteenth-century salon music. Although radically modernist in its implications (that is, in its structural principles – for example, 'the atomization of thematic substance' in *Jeux*, the technique of juxtaposition, and the questioning of notions of temporal succession),[144] the immaculate surface of the music leaves no 'fractures' which might indicate the traces of its struggle to integrate the contradictions of the socially mediated musical material into its immanent law of form. He suggests that, although, as an extreme manifestation of *l'art pour l'art*, Debussy's music sets itself apart from society, in his case this is a sign of a polemical rather than an alienated relation. Indeed, Adorno had argued in 'Zur gesellschaftlichen Lage der Musik' that autonomous music in *fin-de-siècle* France was not as alienated from bourgeois society as music in Germany, because industrialization was not so advanced at that stage in France:

French music, not yet isolated and not dialectical within itself by virtue of its polemic[al] position toward society, could sublimate the means of this society within itself without making a substantial attack upon society. Debussy, an autonomous artist like the Impressionist painters, whose technology he transposes into music, can take with him into his highly fastidious artistic method elements of bourgeois culinary music and even of salon music in terms of sound and melody. Of course, just as in Strauss, the diatonic emerges in Debussy too – barren and archaic. This happens in his theory as well – in the dogma of natural overtones and the resulting Rousseauean diction, the consequence of the total sublimation of the primal musical material of the bourgeoisie.[145]

Adorno's claim, that the undialectical character of Debussy's music – and indeed of French music as a whole at this period – can be explained ultimately by the fact that France might not have been as industrially advanced as Germany and therefore that 'alienation' was not experienced so acutely, needs to be treated with some caution. It was, after all, the France of the late nineteenth century that had provided the material for Durkheim's sociological studies into the condition of *anomie*, and Paris, the 'capital of the nineteenth century' and city of the great world exhibitions, which had also produced the Baudelairean conflict of *spleen et idéal*. Nevertheless, Adorno's main point is made clearly enough: fastidious in the organization of its material, guided by the principle of 'taste', Debussy's music is easily assimilated by society because structurally it avoids the contradictory character of its musical material and does not take it into its 'law of form'. In this, like Stravinsky's music which in certain respects it prefigures, Debussy's music has an objective character, argues Adorno, in that it reflects social contradictions in its material, but does not critically reflect upon these contradictions dialectically within the structure of the work.

Mahler: the survival of the expressive Subject

In the music of Gustav Mahler,[146] on the other hand, Adorno sees a dialectical relationship to a fundamentally tonal and expressively exhausted material. In *Mahler: Eine musikalische Physiognomik* he writes:

Mahler's atmosphere is the illusion of the intelligible, of the already known [*der Schein des Verständlichen*], in which the 'other' [*das Andere*] clothes itself. Shockingly he anticipates that which is to come with the means of the past. . . . The tone is new. He charges tonality with an expressiveness which, of itself, it is no longer capable of delivering.[147]

Although 'nature' is a constant theme in his work (to be heard, for example, in the 'nature sounds' of his orchestration), Adorno argues that Mahler reveals his musical material always as mediated 'second nature' – the 'denaturalization of second nature',[148] as he puts it. Mahler displaces the familiar and makes it unfamiliar, thus rendering it capable of expression once more. Mahler exhibits the opposite of Debussy's fastidious 'taste'. For his material he takes the left-overs, the second hand and the vulgarized – in a word, kitsch:

After the destruction of musical culture, degraded to ideology, a second 'whole' builds itself up out of the fragments and scraps of memory. Subjective organizing power enables culture to reappear within this second 'whole', against which art protests but which it does not destroy. Each Mahler symphony asks how a living totality can emerge out of the ruins and debris of the musical world of things [*aus den Trümmern der musikalischen Dingwelt*]. Mahler's music is great not in spite of the kitsch to which it is inclined, but in that its construction enables kitsch to speak, loosens its tongue and sets free the longing which commerce merely exploits and which kitsch serves. The process of development of Mahler's symphonic movements traces out deliverance on the strength of dehumanization.[149]

Although, for reasons of space, I have chosen here not to refer to discussion of particular works by Mahler, in many ways Adorno's 'physiognomical' analyses of Mahler's music represent some of his most satisfying philosophical interpretations, in that they come closest to deriving their categories from the musical works themselves. As suggested in Chapter 4, this is doubtless because Mahler's music, more than any other of its period (except possibly that of Charles Ives), makes use of 'second order matter' in a way which lends itself more easily to such interpretation. (It is noticeable that Adorno has more problems in 'concretizing' his interpretation of Schoenberg's serial works in *Philosophie der neuen Musik*, and has correspondingly been criticized on account of the excessive abstraction of the concept of musical material in that book.[150]) In Mahler, for example, the problem of closure is brought to the fore in very concrete terms because part of his material is the formula of the tonal cadence itself, together with the ritualized character of the reprise within the sonata schema. Extrapolating from his discussion of Mahler's Sixth Symphony, Adorno writes:

In the reprise, music, as a form of ritualized bourgeois freedom like the society of which it is part and which is contained within it, remains in bondage to the mythical unfreedom. It manipulates the 'natural context' [*Naturzusammenhang*] circling within it as if the returning material [*das Wiederkehrende*], on the strength of its mere return [*Wiederkehr*], were more than it merely is, as if it were metaphysical meaning itself, the 'Idea'. Conversely, however, music without reprise retains something which is not merely unsatisfactory, and disproportionate, abrupt in a culinary sense, as if something were missing, as if it were not going to have an ending. In fact, all new music is tortured by the question of how it will be able to end, and not merely stop, now that the cadential closing formulae can no longer accomplish this...[151]

In his acceptance of the fragmentary character of the musical material and his displacement of it in relation to the handed-down formal schemata, and in his refusal of closure in favour of forms kept deliberately open, Mahler confronts the modernist dilemma, albeit through the debris of an essentially traditional tonal material. This is what constitutes for Adorno the authenticity of Mahler's music. The expressive Subject survives in Mahler through compelling the expressively exhausted gestures of late nineteenth-century tonal material, now commodified and degenerated to kitsch, to speak for a second time. The vehicle for the expression of the Subject in Mahler is the traditional but exhausted one of Romantic melody, the enforced and independent use of which in his music has radical harmonic implications which were taken further in the early works of Schoenberg. 'Schoenberg was actually the first to emancipate *melos*', Adorno argues; 'in the process, however, he liberated the harmonic dimension itself'.[152] But, as we have seen, melody, as theme or motivic–thematic development, is what, for Adorno, constitutes the expressive Subject, as objectified in musical structures. Thus, the emancipation of *melos* is simultaneously the emancipation of the Subject – but only within the confines of the musical work. The contradictory implications of this, in terms of Adorno's interpretation of Schoenberg's serialism in *Philosophie der neuen Musik*, will be considered in the concluding chapter.

The problem of the New Music

According to Adorno's interpretation, the problem thrown up by Wagner and Brahms as music's 'coming of age' (*Mündigkeit*) is the problem bequeathed to the 'New Music' via composers like Debussy and Mahler. The 'problem' can be posed in the following terms as a question: how is it possible to compose autonomous, integrated and consistent musical works in the face of, on the one hand, the disintegration of musical material and, on the other hand, the degeneration of music to ideology as a result of its commodification? Adorno was clearly sympathetic towards Mahler's compositional strategies for dealing with a disintegrating material (just as he was towards Kurt Weill's brittle juxtapositions and displacements of late nineteenth-century sentimentality and popular vulgarity). And perhaps, in a different sense, one could also include here Adorno's affection for Berg's romantic nostalgia for a lost totality – the attempt at 'integration through disintegration' through subjecting the remnants of a late nineteenth-century material to a process of dissolution (*Auflösung*) by means of the most 'infinitesimal transitions'. While Adorno cites Berg as saying 'it is plain common sense for an artist to make sure the nails don't stick out and the glue doesn't stink',[153] he also writes in *Ästhetische Theorie* that '[i]n sharp contrast to traditional art, modern art does not hide the fact that it is something made and produced; on the contrary, it underscores this fact'.[154] It is particularly this latter feature of modernist art works which is so strikingly evident in a composer like Mahler, and which constitutes for Adorno one aspect of modernist music's 'critical character', its rejection of closure and 'completeness'. From the perspective of Adorno's Hegelian interpretation, the truth of Mahler's music, its authenticity, lies precisely in the 'ruptures', the fractures (*Brüche*) in the totality of its form. As in Hegelian logic, truth is not simply the identity of the concept with the object of cognition (as 'consistency'); it is also their non-identity, that which is 'other' (*das Andere*) and which has not yet been assimilated. In other words, it points to the New, to that which is not yet:

As was the case for Hegel in his critique of identity theory, truth for Mahler is the 'other' [*das Andere*], that which is not immanent but which arises out of immanence: in a similar manner the Kantian doctrine of the synthesis is reflected in Hegel. Something exists only as the outcome of a process of becoming [*als Gewordenes*], instead of merely becoming [*bloß zu werden*]. The economical principle of traditional music, its mode of determination, exhausts itself in exchanging the one for the other, from which nothing is left over. The one goes into the other without remainder, rather than the one illuminating the other. The New, which traditional music is unable fully to dominate, is shunned. In this respect even great music was tautological up to Mahler. This was its consistency: that of the uncontradictory system. With Mahler we are given notice that the rupture [*der Bruch*] acquires the status of a formal law.[155]

In conclusion

In the above examination of Adorno's philosophical interpretation of music of the 'bourgeois period' I have tried to show how the idea of historical necessity and continuity, of progressive integration of material, is only one aspect of his philosophy of history as the 'dialectic of Enlightenment'. The other 'pole' of the dialectic – and the aspect of his theory, I have suggested, that is frequently ignored or underestimated – is the emphasis on historical discontinuity and the tendency towards the disintegration of musical material, towards fragmentation. Adorno's concept of 'the tendency of the material' needs to be understood as containing both these moments – integration and disintegration – to the extent that, due to the antagonistic and unreconciled existence of both within the musical work, they are seen to constitute a new 'law of form'. That is to say, the form contains ruptures and fractures, and thus denies itself finality and completion. This is not, however, if we are to understand Adorno correctly here, only the 'law of form' of authentic works of the modernist period. It is also to be found, he maintains, in the late works of Beethoven, in the programmatic symphonies of Berlioz, and in what he sees as the 'inconsistencies' of Wagner's music dramas. This is because, he argues, art works are the 'unconscious writing of history', and without needing to know anything of society directly, they nevertheless mediate society within their form because both the artist and the material are already socially mediated. In *Ästhetische Theorie* he sees these inconsistencies in terms of discontinuities:

Society's discontinuities, its untruths and ideologies, emerge in the work as structural discontinuities, as deficiencies. This is so because the orientation of works of art, their 'stance towards objectivity', remains a stance towards reality.[156]

I have suggested at several points in this study that it may assist our understanding of Adorno's concepts of 'musical material', 'mediation' and 'form' if we take them at the level of homology or of metaphor in their relation to society.[157] It needs to be stressed, however, that for Adorno art works are not simply 'representations of' society, or 'similar to' society in their structure. Although he insists that the relation of art works to society is thoroughly contradictory in all respects, in that they are separate from society (through their autonomous form), derived from society (through their pre-formed, heteronomous material), and point beyond society (through the critique practised by the freedom of their autonomous form on the manifest 'unfreedom' of existing forms of society), he nevertheless at the same time insists that society is also 'inscribed' within art works. This is because, he argues, art works, through the self-reflection of their form as the 'objectification of the Subject', are a mode of cognition. This is the 'second reflection' practised by the immanent form of the work itself (as a parallel to the 'second reflection' of critical philosophical theory) which serves to denaturalize and recontextualize the pre-formed, socially mediated material available to it. As a form of cognition, autonomous art works also provide us with knowledge of empirical reality, even in the process of attempting to distance themselves from that reality.

As we have seen, the idea which dominates Adorno's concept of the historical dialectic of musical material is that of the historical 'movement' of the expressive Subject as objectified in musical structures. This is what is to be understood by the concept 'mediation': that is, Subject-objectification, the externalization of the expressive Subject in concrete musical structures. Furthermore, the presence of the Subject at all points within the structure of the work, as the self-reflection of form, is what constitutes the emancipation of the Subject as a process of 'demythologization' of the material. At the same time, however, this process of demythologization and rationalization, as the total domination of musical material by the Subject, is seen by Adorno to lead to the total alienation of the Subject within the structure of the work. While this is the 'truth' of the work, in that it corresponds, Adorno maintains, to existing social reality, it also results in the Subject's enchainment within the structure of the totally organized work.

In the final chapter of this study, which also serves as its concluding remarks, I shall take this contradiction one stage further, in relation to Schoenberg and Stravinsky. I shall do this through a reconsideration of certain issues in *Philosophie der neuen Musik*, before drawing the study to a close with a return to the problem of form through a discussion of Adorno's notion of the disintegration of material (*Zerfall des Materials*) in relation to the decline of the avant-garde.

The aesthetic categories have lost their a priori validity. Now the same can be said of artistic materials themselves. The disintegration of materials is the triumph of their being-for-other.[1]   Adorno, *Aesthetic Theory* (1970)

Adorno's interpretation of Mahler's music would seem to legitimize as 'authentic' a very different relationship to material and a very different conception of form from that suggested by his interpretation of Schoenberg. This difference, which has the character of a contradiction, calls for examination, as it has implications both for the concept of musical material since the 'demise of modernism', and for the theoretical consistency of Adorno's dialectical aesthetics. As a conclusion to this study I shall focus the discussion particularly on issues arising from *Philosophie der neuen Musik*, drawing also on the views of a number of Adorno's critics.

In very general terms, I suggest that the contradictory character of Adorno's work needs to be seen in two ways. On the one hand, as has been emphasized throughout this study, contradiction is a calculated feature of Adorno's methodology. He understands the object of enquiry itself to embody the contradictions of the social forces and relations of production, and his interpretative method aims to reveal and decipher this 'contradictoriness' as the 'mediation of opposites through their extremes'. The concepts he employs can themselves only be understood when seen within the larger conceptual context which, I have argued, underlies all his writings, and which is itself characterized by the idea of the 'constellation' of opposites within which each concept takes its meaning. That is to say, Adorno does not posit 'absolute meanings', in any ontological sense; there are no philosophical 'first causes', and 'natural givens' – for example, invariants like the overtone series or the dimension of time in music – are not accorded any privileged status. The musical work as Object is itself seen dialectically as the outcome of a historical and material process, the objectification of the socially and historically constituted Subject. This is what Adorno calls the 'progress of Spirit', as *objektiver Geist* – the historical mediation of Subject and Object in material terms. As Michael

Rosen has put it, referring to *Negative Dialektik*, Adorno's ambition 'is no less than to bring together the *Idealist* concept of transcendentalist subjectivity with the great *sociological* theme of the division of labour'.[2] As we have seen, this project, when understood in relation to his aesthetics of music, argues that the mediation of music and society takes place at the level of musical form. The 'immanent form' of the individual work is a reflection upon, and recontextualization of, musical material, itself already historically 'pre-formed'. In this way, Adorno maintains, each work, as a mode of cognition, is a critique both of previous works and of social reality itself.

On the other hand, contradiction is also 'inscribed' in Adorno's work in another sense: in spite of the consistency with which, in the main, he uses concepts, there are, nevertheless, certain blind spots in his approach, and these manifest as gaps in his theory which stubbornly resist closure. This could be seen as the ideological aspect of Adorno's aesthetics of music: the approach itself, which elevates fragmentation to the status of a structural principle, a 'law of form', also serves to conceal inconsistencies in the general logic of its own argument. As I suggested at the end of Chapter 1, the suspicion persists that, in spite of Adorno's espousal of the fragment as critique of all totalizing systems, underlying his own work there is, nevertheless, an allegiance to totality and organic unity which derives from German Idealist philosophy and from the emphasis on motivic–thematic integration in the tradition of Austro-German instrumental music. It could be argued that problems at the generalized level of the philosophical concept – e.g. that of the Hegelian *Geist* – manifest as 'practical' problems at the particularized levels of immanent analysis and sociological critique. That is to say, in spite of his best efforts, Adorno often fails to bridge the gap between technical analysis and the sociological critique and philosophical interpretation of particular musical works. It is difficult to resist Martin Jay's suggestion here, that the flawed character of Adorno's own work can also take on a larger historical meaning: 'As a social physiognomy', Jay writes, 'it could scarcely avoid replicating in some respects the society it both described and hoped to change'.[3]

It is the aim of this closing chapter to identify some of the hiatuses in Adorno's aesthetics of music and to suggest reasons for their resistance to the dialectical logic of his theory. Issues in *Philosophie der neuen Musik* are discussed in relation to the Schoenberg–Stravinsky polarization, and in relation to problems arising from Adorno's concept of *objektiver Geist*. This leads to a reconsideration of Adorno's concepts of material and of form in relation to his theory of the avant-garde, in the context of the 'decline of modernism'.

1   Issues in the philosophy of New Music

In the Introduction to this study I argued that the polemical stance taken by Adorno in *Philosophie der neuen Musik* would almost certainly be misinterpreted unless understood within a conceptual context derived in large part from his earlier writings.[4] Having provided such a context in previous chapters, it will now be useful to examine certain issues in *Philosophie der neuen Musik* in relation to Adorno's larger theoretical position.

The impact of *Philosophie der neuen Musik* in the years immediately following its publication in 1949 appears to have been considerable. There were reports of young composers learning German specially in order to be able to read the book in the original language.[5] Its two main themes – the historical tendency of musical material as progress, culminating in serialism and the total control of all parameters of music; and the attack on neoclassicism as regression – found a ready audience among the generation of composers and musicians that was emerging in the immediate post-war years and which was centred on Darmstadt. *Philosophie der neuen Musik* seemed to provide the theoretical and philosophical legitimation for the experiments with multiple serialism which followed the appearance of Messiaen's *Mode de valeurs et d'intensités* (also in 1949) in the work of Boulez and Stockhausen in the early 1950s – even though, of course, the development of Adorno's theory of musical material had antedated these events by over twenty years.

While it is possible to argue that much of the book's influence (as well as the controversy it aroused) was due to misunderstanding, it must also be acknowledged that the manner in which Adorno presented his theory – that is, by means of a polarization of tendencies represented in their most extreme forms for their period by the music of Schoenberg and Stravinsky, and expressed in a style which is distinctly polemical – contributed significantly to this misunderstanding. It has been argued so far that Adorno's theory of material lays its emphasis as much on the 'disintegration' of musical material and on the discontinuities of its historical tendency, as on the continuities of its historical dialectic as progress towards the total integration and rationalization of the musical work. While both these emphases are still present in *Philosophie der neuen Musik*, their extreme polarization in this case causes them to become frozen. The moment of stasis, as the denial of the dimension of time which Adorno had recognized in the New Music, is actually written into *Philosophie der neuen Musik* itself. The dialectic of material is brought to a standstill, like Hegel's vision of the 'end of history'. Unlike Hegel, however, there is no ultimate reconciliation of antitheses within the Whole, as Absolute Spirit, but only an absolutizing of the antitheses themselves in their mutual and total alienation. The extremes, as total integration and total disintegration, become final, and no way forward is offered. Adorno's absolutizing of the repressive aspects of the 'dialectic of Enlightenment' as rationalization and total integration – which Jürgen Habermas has criticized by pointing out that rationalization also has a liberating aspect[6] – leads to what he sees as the stalemate of serialism (and ultimately, of multiple serialism). His absolutizing of distintegration implies the total commodification of musical language as kitsch.

The Schoenberg–Stravinsky polarization

In the Introduction to *Philosophie der neuen Musik* Adorno insists that 'it is only through the extremes that the essence of this music finds itself revealed; they alone allow the cognition of its truth content'.[7] Having written the Schoenberg section originally in 1940–41 as a self-contained extended essay, he later decided to add an essay on Stravinsky and to frame the whole with an introductory section. There can be little doubt that it was this particular process of construction which gave the book its polemical character, unusual even for Adorno, and which lent it something of the air of a manifesto – features which very likely also account for its influence as a rallying cry for the New Music in the immediate post-war years. Although the book functions according to Adorno's usual dialectical method, the extremes are even more sharply drawn than usual, are dealt with separately and at length in the two main sections of the book, and, although each essay can be understood as proceeding dialectically within itself, there is little genuine 'dialectical interaction' with the Stravinsky essay to be found within the Schoenberg essay (understandably perhaps, in view of its genesis). Given the centrality of the Schoenberg essay, however, this leads to the feeling that an alien set of criteria is being somewhat dogmatically applied to Stravinsky's music. This is unfortunate, because Adorno applies his method with powerful logic to the music of Schoenberg, and with illuminating results.

Adorno argues in the Schoenberg essay that with serialism the historical tendency towards the ever-increasing domination of musical material approaches its extreme. There is no longer room for 'illusion and play' (*Schein und Spiel*), in that construction reaches all aspects of the material, all conventional and decorative elements are negated, and the extreme compression which characterizes the resulting work affects the nature of expression itself. The composer, as 'expressive Subject', having become emancipated along with the material in the period of free atonality and Expressionism, can now only respond to the demands of the material in the strictest possible manner. Adorno sees this as the outcome of a historical process of increasing rationalization, whereby subjective expression objectifies itself through construction, to the point where the extreme 'inwardness' (*Innerlichkeit*) of the lonely Subject of Expressionism becomes totally 'externalized' (*entäußert*) and objectified:

The Subject of the New Music, for which the music presents itself as a case study, is the emancipated, lonely, concrete Subject of the late bourgeois phase. This concrete subjectivity, and the material which it so radically and thoroughly shapes, supplies Schoenberg with the canon of aesthetic objectification.[8]

Adorno follows through the thesis of *Dialektik der Aufklärung* relentlessly in *Philosophie der neuen Musik*. The total domination of material is at the same time the self-domination of the expressive Subject. The total objectification of the Subject results in the Subject's loss of freedom. The truth of Schoenberg's serial music, the total consistency of its structure in its search for an all-encompassing unity, also results in the alienation of the Subject within the objectivity of the structure. Adorno writes:

Twelve-tone technique is truly the fate of music. It enchains it by liberating it. The [S]ubject dominates music through the rationality of the system, only in order to succumb to the rational system itself.[9]

And the material itself, now pre-formed by the technique, is returned to the realm of nature, as *Stoff*, the historical necessity of the material now reduced to total control and, curiously, to a certain arbitrariness and lack of necessity. As Adorno puts it: 'From the procedures which broke the blind domination of tonal material [*die blinde Herrschaft des Stoffs der Töne*] there evolves a second blind nature by means of this regulatory system'.[10] Thus Adorno argues that the 'correctness' and consistency of Schoenberg's solution leads to a music which comes close to *neue Sachlichkeit* and to the positivism of Stravinsky. And yet, he insists, the 'failure' of Schoenberg's music nevertheless constitutes its 'truth content', its authenticity. Schoenberg's music makes concrete the alienation of the Subject through its determination to preserve the Subject by extending its control to every corner of the material. At the same time, however, it is a dead end: total stasis. As with Beckett's *Endgame*, the expression of suffering becomes frozen and timeless.

Adorno's interpretation of Stravinsky's music in *Philosophie der neuen Musik* is also contradictory, but in a different way. As with the case of Schoenberg, a few examples must suffice to demonstrate this. Although his assessment of the composer had never been particularly generous, Stravinsky had been treated in 'Zur gesellschaftlichen Lage der Musik' as representing at least two of Adorno's four categories of music which are

dialectical in their relation to society and which resist commodification –
the categories of 'objectivism' and 'surrealism'.[11] In 1932 Adorno had
cautiously praised Stravinsky's music – especially *L'histoire du soldat* –
even allowing it a certain 'logical consistence' in its critical, ironic and
dialectical relation to society:

In his best and most exposed works – such as *L'histoire du soldat* – he provokes
contradiction. In contrast to all other objectivist authors, Stravinsky's superiority
within his métier threatens the consistent ideological positivity of his style, as this is
demanded of him by society; consequently, in his case as well, artistic logical
consistence [*Folgerichtigkeit*] becomes socially dialectical.[12]

In *Philosophie der neuen Musik*, however, Adorno assesses the work
differently:

L'histoire is Stravinsky's pivotal work, but at the same time it scorns the concept of
a *chef d'œuvre* as *Sacre* still had hopes of being. *L'histoire* sheds light upon
Stravinsky's total production. There is hardly a schizophrenic mechanism . . . which
does not find therein a highly valid equivalent. The negative objectivity of the work
of art recalls in itself the phenomenon of regression. In the psychiatric theory of
schizophrenia, this is known as 'depersonalization' according to Fenichel, it is a
defensive reaction against the omnipotence of narcissism. The alienation of music
from the [S]ubject and, at the same time, its relationship to physical sensations find a
pathological analogy in the illusory sensations of those who are conscious of their
own body as an alien object.[13]

Stravinsky's music is presented here as undialectical, in that Adorno argues
that it expresses the total alienation of the Subject but *without the Subject's
awareness of its alienation*. The split is so complete, the Subject so
'depersonalized', that it can now only be adequately described in
psychoanalytical terms. The suffering of the expressive Subject is repressed;
instead of being worked through 'from within', as he maintains is the case
with Schoenberg (particularly in the freely atonal works), the Subject
regresses to the repetitive behaviour of the infantile state, and to notions of
the archaic and the primitive 'beyond history'. The music is seen as a sterile
game of permutations with the worn-out fragments of handed-down
material.

At the same time, however, Stravinsky's music is also presented in
Philosophie der neuen Musik as an urbane and sophisticated conjuring trick
which, without concealing the fragmented character of its construction,
nevertheless has the intention 'emphatically to reconstruct the authenticity
of music – to impose upon it the character of outside confirmation, to
fortify it with the power of being-so-and-not-being-able-to-be-other-
wise'.[14] This is what Adorno regards as authenticity gained at the expense
of the Subject: the Subject is sacrificed to the regressive, pre-individual
objectivity of the collective (a sacrifice clearly contained in the 'programme'

of *Sacre du Printemps*). Adorno's assessment of Stravinsky in *Philosophie der neuen Musik*, particularly through the emphasis on what is seen as the affirmative and reactionary aspects of folklorism and, in particular, of neoclassicism, effectively excludes his music from the arena of the radical avant-garde and from a place within modernist art. Alfred Huber, in his article 'Adornos Polemik gegen Strawinsky', expresses a familiar (if unusually restrained) protest at Adorno's treatment of Stravinsky's music in *Philosophie der neuen Musik*:

Stravinsky's music is also an expression of progressive individual construction [*Gestaltung*], and to complain of its 'absence of suffering' betrays a patchily informed understanding. That Adorno failed to recognize this is not so much due to a lack of intensity, but rather to a lack in his philosophical system which, through its dogmatically inflexible bearing, failed to notice the presence in Stravinsky's work of original, progressive thinking. Aspects of his materially orientated critique may well be thoroughly applicable to the object [*in der Sache*], but the effect is diminished through the application of a pattern of experience from outside which is alien to Stravinsky.[15]

In the late essay 'Strawinsky: Ein dialektisches Bild'[16] of 1962, however, Adorno again revises his interpretation of Stravinsky. While still critical in his attitude, he now sees Stravinsky again as a 'dialectical composer', and re-establishes him in the third of his four categories of radical music in 'Zur gesellschaftlichen Lage der Musik', that of 'surrealist music'. As Peter Bürger puts it in his essay 'Das Altern der Moderne':

in his late essay on Stravinsky ... he proposes a completely different interpretation of neo-classicism: Stravinsky's music is not the reconstruction of a binding musical language but an artist's sovereign play with pre-given forms of the past. ... By explicitly locating Stravinsky's as well as Picasso's neo-classicism in the vicinity of surrealism, Adorno now assigns the latter a place *within* modern art. That the two interpretations are incompatible is obvious, and so is the superiority of the latter interpretation. Whereas the polemical interpretation proceeds in a globalizing fashion, understanding neo-classicism as a unitary movement, the second interpretation seeks differentiation. It leaves open at least the possibility of seeing more in neo-classical works than a sheer relapse into a reactionary thinking of order.[17]

While Adorno's interpretation of Stravinsky in *Philosophie der neuen Musik* relates him to what are seen as the 'regressive' aspects of the music of Debussy and, through this, to the music of Wagner, this second interpretation (to be found in 'Zur gesellschaftlichen Lage der Musik' as well as in 'Strawinsky: Ein dialektisches Bild') could be seen to link him in certain respects with Mahler (a link, however, not made directly by Adorno). While Adorno remains suspicious of the urbane and detached objectivity of Stravinsky's style, he seems now to discern a 'moment of truth' in the way in which the composer manipulates the debris of a culturally exhausted and disintegrating material. Although Adorno does not acknowledge this himself, the approaches to a disintegrating material taken in different ways by Mahler and by Stravinsky could be seen as offering a possibility for going beyond the stalemate of serialism. This possibility – modest as it is – will be returned to in Section 2 in relation to Adorno's concept of *une musique informelle* and his admiration for the work of Samuel Beckett.

Finally, quite apart from inconsistencies in his treatment of Stravinsky, the approach taken by Adorno in *Philosophie der neuen Musik* is abstract and lacks real grounding in concrete musical examples. (Furthermore, Adorno's theory does not account satisfactorily for the tonal works which Schoenberg continued to write from time to time throughout the period of his twelve-tone works.) This abstraction and lack of emphasis on the 'concrete particular' of individual works certainly goes against Adorno's own claims for his approach in the book, made in the introductory essay. There he writes: 'Truth or untruth – whether Schoenberg's or Stravinsky's – cannot be determined by a mere discussion of categories, such as atonality, twelve-tone technique, or neo-classicism; but only in the concrete crystallization of such categories in the structure of the music itself'.[18] Adorno came to recognize this as an unsatisfactory feature of *Philosophie der neuen Musik*, and commented critically on it in 1953 in his essay 'Über das gegenwärtige Verhältnis von Philosophie und Musik', where he wrote that 'the book did not obey its own principle as strictly as it was duty-bound to do'.[19]

Misunderstandings

In 1950, in the March issue of the journal *Melos*, Adorno published a brief article entitled 'Mißverständnisse'[20] in order to counter what he saw as the misunderstandings which had characterized the reception of *Philosophie der neuen Musik*. The immediate occasion for the article was a critical review of *Philosophie der neuen Musik* which had appeared the previous year in *Melos* by Walther Harth.[21] Harth, Adorno claimed, had misunderstood the intention of the book in two important respects: he had interpreted Adorno as setting Schoenberg's freely atonal, Expressionist works against the serial works; and he had criticized Adorno's use of psychoanalytic categories to discuss the music of Stravinsky as dangerously insubstantial, and had interpreted their use as an attack on Stravinsky personally. Underlying both these misunderstandings, maintains Adorno, is a third and more fundamental one: that is, a misunderstanding of the concept of 'objective Spirit' (*der Begriff des objektiven Geistes*):

As a consequence of the philosophy for which I am responsible, I have applied a concept of 'objective Spirit' to music, although without making it explicit: an 'objective Spirit' which prevails over the heads of the individual artists and also beyond the merits of the individual works. This concept is as foreign to public awareness today as it is taken for granted in my own experience. Had I given thought to the communication of the ideas and not merely to that which seemed to me to be the appropriate expression of the object [*Sache*], then I would have had to articulate this concept.[22]

Adorno's admission, that he had not made sufficiently explicit the central concept of *objektiver Geist* which underpins his theory of musical material, is typically accompanied by the implication that such concerns with 'communication', with spelling out the concepts themselves, ought not really to be necessary, given an informed readership. It is this refusal to compromise which has led to misunderstanding of his work as a whole, not just of *Philosophie der neuen Musik*. A less charitable view, however, might see it as Adorno's refusal to make clear his terms of reference, and might well regard such an attitude to the reader as unacceptably élitist. Either way, the misunderstandings, if such they are, are inevitably compounded when Adorno's work is translated into a language as unsympathetic to dialectical thought as English, and received by English-speaking cultures where concepts like 'objective Spirit' and 'historical dialectic' lack any meaningful context.

Furthermore, Adorno's unwillingness to clarify the concept of *objektiver Geist* encourages almost wilful misunderstanding. Dahlhaus, for example, complains of 'the transformation of musical works, in which subjective spirit [*subjectiver Geist*] realizes itself, into an anonymous material, which later composers encounter as objective spirit [*objektiver Geist*]'.[23] I have suggested earlier (in Chapter 3) that it is most profitable to view the concept of *objektiver Geist* in relation to Adorno's use of Max Weber's concept of rationalization. *Geist* is the objectification of the Subject through increasing technical control of musical material. It is not that the material is anonymous – Adorno makes it quite clear, for example, in his discussion of Brahms that the material in this instance is specifically that of Beethoven, Schubert and, in particular, Schumann. It is also, however, a question of responding to technical demands, which are part of the material as Adorno sees it – technical demands which, as compositional technique and technology, also share in the advanced stages of technical development and of progressive rationalization which characterize empirical reality itself. As we have seen, for Adorno, *objektiver Geist*, in part at least as progressive rationalization – that is, increasing technical control – of material, is identified with the avant-garde.

2   The decline of the modern

In his book *Theorie der Avantgarde* Peter Bürger argues that Adorno's theory of the avant-garde has now to be seen as historically situated. He takes Adorno's emphasis on the autonomy of art as evidence that Adorno (like Lukács) was unable to question the institution of art itself – its social function, in other words. For this very reason, he maintains, Adorno could not help but affirm and argue within the institution that is art.[24] While in certain respects Bürger's argument is persuasive, it does nevertheless seem to understate the extent to which Adorno had actually considered music's social function (see my account of Adorno's sociology of music in Chapter 5), as well as the degree to which he had predicted the end of the avant-garde. Indeed, in *Ästhetische Theorie* Adorno also suggests that the survival of 'great music' itself as an art form may well be threatened, because the historical conditions which gave rise to it in the first place have changed (conditions which, one might assume, would include both 'art as bourgeois institution' and the social institutions which sustained bourgeois art historically). He writes:

A latecomer among the arts, great music may well turn out to be an art form that was possible only during a limited period of human history. The revolt of art which programmatically defined itself in terms of a new stance towards the objective, historical world has become a revolt against art. Whether art will survive these developments is anybody's guess.[25]

The historical character of the avant-garde

Adorno had foreseen the decline of the avant-garde quite early on. There are indications of his recognition of the precariousness of the modernist venture as early as 1932 in 'Zur gesellschaftlichen Lage der Musik', and in 1954 he took the bold step of giving a lecture at the Stuttgart New Music Week entitled 'Das Altern der neuen Musik'.[26] This was the outcome of his conviction that the musical avant-garde of the early 1950s – particularly the multiple serialists of the Darmstadt School – were, in their attempt to purge musical material of its historically acquired meanings, seeking to return to a mythical state of 'musical nature'. At the same time, through the standardizing effects of the culture industry, Adorno saw a change in the traditional 'language' of music, as the 'decomposition' of the material of 'autonomous' music. For example, tonality in traditional autonomous works he saw as having been reduced in the twentieth century to a generalized musical language (see Chapter 5). This he describes as a 'mass musical language' made up of those aspects of the musical material which were previously secondary and associative but which have now become dominant. They consist, he suggests, not only of standardized progressions in tonal harmony, but whole genres and styles of music, which, in their disintegration from the 'logic of form', and through their function in, for example, advertising and film, have become available now as cultural relics which, even though culturally mediated, appear to communicate on a level of resistance-free immediacy. Historically this is seen as a result of music's change of function, together with the corresponding loss of dialectical tension between the autonomy of the musical work and the heteronomy of its pre-formed material. As Adorno puts it:

As a rule, ... authentic works cannot wipe out the memory that they originated in some heteronomous social purpose of the kind that underlies Beethoven's drum rolls. The residual *divertissement* that so irked Richard Wagner in Mozart is by no means confined to Mozart and his epoch. Even those works that broke consciously with the notion of *divertissement* are subject to the suspicion of secretly continuing the tradition of heteronomy. The position of artists in society – to the extent to which they have any mass appeal – tends to revert to heteronomy after the age of autonomy has come to an end. Before the French Revolution artists were retainers: today they are entertainers.[27]

Adorno leaves us, once again, with an unreconciled contradiction. The musical avant-garde, at least in the sense in which it existed in the 1950s and early 1960s, has grown old. 'Classical' modernism has become a historical category, and the tension between radical art and social norms has been reduced through a return to accessibility. At the same time, a mass musical language, fragmented and operating largely at an iconic level of meaning, has emerged. This new communicative language contains not only the mainly tonal gestures of so-called 'popular' or 'light' music, and of the well-known museum repertoire of the Classical and Romantic traditions. It can be argued that it has now gone considerably beyond Adorno's original description of it in his 1932 essay, and has assimilated and historicized many of the typical gestures of what was once the radical avant-garde, the extremes of expression and technical experimentation now reduced to an unambiguous and restricted range of meanings through functioning, for example, as 'sound tracks' for powerful visual imagery on film and television.

In their book *Composing for the Films* Eisler and Adorno had argued in relation to film music that 'composing has become so logical that it need no longer be the consequence of its material and can, figuratively speaking, dominate every type of material to which it is applied'.[28] This separation between compositional techniques and musical material, seen by Eisler and Adorno in part as a consequence of the particular demands of music for the cinema and in part as a result of the general process of fragmentation which has come to characterize music in the twentieth century since its commodification, has now to be seen as affecting all music, including that of the avant-garde. It was a tendency which Adorno had recognized in both Wagner and Brahms, and which was rationalized in the development of the twelve-tone technique – a technique which, he argued, had developed from the immanent demands of the material itself.

Changing concepts of material and form

Although Adorno's concept of the historical tendency of musical material was derived from one particularly inward-looking and uncompromising strand of the European avant-garde – that is to say, that of the Austro-German tradition – I would suggest that, in predicting the demise of that tradition and the rise to dominance of a second, mass musical language made up, as he put it in 1932, of the 'ruins and external remains'[29] of the previous musical culture, Adorno's 'conflict theory' of musical progress and regression still has a relevance for the pluralism which characterizes music in the late twentieth century. Its relevance is that it points both to the total negation of musical material in any traditional sense and, simultaneously, to the total expansion of musical material 'to embrace everything',[30] as Heinz-Klaus Metzger has put it. It could well be that a critical and self-reflective music today has had to give up the dream of a coherent and integrated, internally consistent musical language. In its place, it can be argued, there is, as material, only the used and the second hand, the found objects and 'ready mades' from the cultural scrap heap.[31] But, as we have seen, Adorno seemed also to have sensed even this possibility when, in 1938, he wrote of Gustav Mahler that 'his themes are expropriated ones ... the used parts win a second life as variants'.[32]

Heinz-Klaus Metzger, that protagonist of the avant-garde of the 1950s who had responded indignantly in 1954 to Adorno's suggestion that 'new music was growing old' with an article in *Die Reihe* suggesting that it was perhaps Adorno who was getting old,[33] has subsequently used Adorno's concept of musical material to discuss the music of John Cage. The immediate occasion for this was the performance of Cage's *Europeras 1 & 2* at the Frankfurter Oper in the 1987/8 season, and Metzger wryly concludes his essay with the suggestion that 'it may well be that there is no longer any material, if indeed there ever was any. Presumably only the belief that material existed existed – and the belief's quotable.'[34]

The implications of this view are that the material of music has become totally relativized and lacking in 'historical necessity' to the point where it ceases to have any meaning in the sense in which Adorno had used the term 'material'. But in the process of articulating this position – one certainly implied in Adorno's work – Metzger appears to have reverted to a concept of material as mere 'matter', as *Stoff* – that is, 'naturalized' and removed from history. While using Adorno's concept of musical material from *Philosophie der neuen Musik* to interpret Cage's approach in the *Europeras*, he has at the same time also adopted Cage's own notion of musical material[35] – one diametrically opposed to that of Adorno. As Dahlhaus has put it, 'Adorno's concept of material is a historical category, whereas

Cage's idea of matter is a natural one'.[36] In taking as his material for *Europeras 1 & 2* chance-derived fragments from the scores, libretti, set and costume designs of the 'great operas' of the standard historical repertoire, Cage has removed historically loaded material gestures from history and, perversely enough, naturalized them. He has followed the disintegration of historically mediated materials to the extreme, to the point where the historically expressive gestures are separated from the compositional techniques which traditionally organized them and gave them their historical meaning. They are both decontextualized and, at the same time, recontextualized, 'the relics of a tradition', as Metzger puts it, now become 'the products of the most recent history – indeed, following the decline of the idea of the coherently integrated artwork, they are truly the most advanced of all: computer-assisted chance operations'.[37] There is a sense in which Cage has revealed the process of disintegration through formalizing and distancing it in his *Europeras* within the detached structures generated by his chance operations. At the same time, however, the structure, as in all Cage's work, is designed to bypass the Subject. As in Adorno's interpretation of Stravinsky in *Philosophie der neuen Musik*, it could be said of Cage that '[a]uthenticity is gained surreptitiously through the denial of the subjective pole'.[38]

Cage's relation to material is holistic and non-dialectical, and through his music he seeks to annul the separation of art from life. Adorno's notion of authenticity, on the contrary, is dialectical and humanistic in orientation, emphasizing the autonomy of the work of art and the emancipation of the Subject from 'mere existence' (*bloßes Dasein*). The relationship of Subject and Object takes place within the work itself. It is, in Adorno's view, necessarily an antagonistic relationship today, characterized by the conflicting demands for unity of form (as Subject) in the face of the need to remain true to a disintegrating material (as Object). That is to say, the 'form' of the integrated work, to be 'authentic' (that is, true to the demands of its material), must now incorporate its apparent opposite – disintegration, fragmentation, chaos, along the lines of his ideal of *une musique informelle*.

Although Adorno had derived the concept of *musique informelle* from the freely atonal works of Arnold Schoenberg's Expressionist period, it is nevertheless in the work of Samuel Beckett, that most musical of writers and the person to whom *Ästhetische Theorie* was to have been dedicated, that he claimed to discover its most convincing realization outside music. In 'Versuch, das Endspiel zu verstehen', Adorno suggests that Beckett's work has affinities with the music of both Stravinsky and Schoenberg, combining Stravinsky's 'frightening stasis of disintegrating continuity' with Schoenberg's advanced techniques of construction and expression.[39]

He talks of Beckett transforming thought into a kind of 'second-order matter', arguing that he uses thoughts as the fragmented materials of the interior monologue 'to which spirit [*Geist*] itself has been reduced by the reified remains of culture [*dinghafter Rückstand von Bildung*]'.[40]

In the final analysis, Adorno's aesthetics, like Beckett's 'interior monologue', addresses the problem of form not only at a level of philosophical abstraction but also in the most material and concrete terms. The texts themselves embody the problem of form, and it is the resulting tension between form and material which doubtless accounts for the disturbing effect of the work of both writers. It is a tension which refuses resolution. Furthermore, it is through the 'force-field' of its form, so Adorno argues in *Ästhetische Theorie*, that art both mediates society and liberates itself from it, in the sense of showing a different set of potential relations to those which dominate existing society:

All genuinely new art seeks the liberation of form. This trend is a cipher for the liberation of society, for form – the aesthetic complex of particulars – represents the relation that the work of art has to society. It is for this reason that liberated form is objectionable to the status quo.[41]

In 'reflecting' the fragmented character of its socially mediated material, such a notion of form is at the same time also *self*-reflective. That is to say, the fractured form is not identical to its fragmented material, because through the self-consciousness of construction it separates itself from the chaos of the material while at the same time 'expressing' it. In a discussion with his unofficial biographer, Deirdre Bair, Beckett is reported as having talked of the problem of 'form' in his work, referring to the tension between what he called 'mess' and form. In talking of his novel *How It Is*, Beckett here comes probably closer than anyone to articulating the problem of form in relation to a disintegrating material and, in the process, to illuminating Adorno's concept of *une musique informelle*, the vanishing endpoint of his concept of the historical dialectic of musical material:

What I am saying does not mean that there will henceforth be no form in art. It only means that there will be new form, and that this form will be of such a type that it admits the chaos and does not try to say that the chaos is really something else. The form and the chaos remain separate. The latter is not reduced to the former. That is why the form itself becomes a preoccupation, because it exists as a problem separate from the material it accommodates. To find the form that accommodates the mess, that is the task of the artist now.[42]

3   Concluding remarks

It remains to draw this study to a close with some final comments on Adorno's interpretative method. In going 'against the grain' of his sociological aesthetics, separating out the different strands of his approach and identifying and contextualizing the conceptual 'constellations' with which he works, what emerges most strikingly is the extent of the interpenetration of different levels of analysis. It has to be admitted that this is a very real problem with Adorno's approach, because he often gives the impression that there is a smooth continuum between technical analysis, sociological critique and philosophical-historical interpretation,[43] in spite of the calculatedly fragmented form in which he presents his ideas. This is the ideological moment in Adorno's theory, the concealing of the fractures within his critical interpretations and an inability at times to resist the temptation to naturalize his interpretations by presenting them as the inevitable outcome of his technical analyses and sociological critique. However, while it is essential to recognize such discontinuities as the flaws and blind spots they are, they do not undermine the larger importance of his work – his key role in identifying and exploring areas which should be the concern of any critical musicology or analytical theory, but which have remained largely ignored in the academic study of music. Indeed, the identification of blind spots serves to emphasize that Adorno's critical aesthetics of music demands critique to reveal its lacunae. This is part of the necessary demystification of the terminology and approach which will enable this work to play a significant part in the gradual transformation of historical musicology, music analysis and music theory into less rigidly divided and more critical sub-disciplines. Furthermore, Adorno's project needs not only to be viewed as fragmentary, but also as necessarily *incomplete*. In *Einleitung in die Musiksoziologie* he hints at this himself, when criticizing the tendency of historical musicology and musical analysis to dismiss the idea of a specifically social content of music and to undervalue the importance of sociological perspectives:

If so many dismiss that specifically social element as a mere additive of sociological interpretation, if they see the thing itself in the actual notes alone, this is not due to the music but to a neutralized consciousness. The musical experience has been insulated from the experience of the reality in which it finds itself – however polemically – and to which it responds. While compositorial analysis was learning to trace the most delicate ramifications of the facture, and while musicology was accounting at length for the biographical circumstances of composer and work, the method of deciphering the specific social characteristics of music has lagged pitifully and must be largely content with improvisations. If we wished to catch up, to release the cognition of music from its inane isolation, it would be necessary to develop a physiognomics of the types of musical expression.[44]

That Adorno himself ultimately failed in this project should not blind us to the magnitude of his achievement. Almost single-handed within the discipline of music he has created the conditions for a debate on the social content of 'autonomous' music and its relation to its social context – a debate which he also developed towards a theory of the avant-garde appropriate to the complexities of late industrial society. Likewise, and in spite of his own clearly visible prejudices, he could also be said to have pioneered the debate on mass and popular culture through taking seriously areas of culture which had previously been regarded as of no significance. But most valuable of all is the dialectical 'method' itself. The web of concepts upon which he draws, and which allows the most subtle distinctions and connections to be made in the interpretation of musical phenomena, cannot be taken as a set of static givens. It is not a 'system' or a 'framework' which can be extracted as a separate thesis, but exists only as a dynamic field of debate. That his critical aesthetics of music cannot be understood, interpreted and reapplied to changing historical conditions without us actively entering that debate and, in the process, very likely changing its terms is a sign of its authenticity. As critical theory, it exists and develops only as a continuing reinterpretation and critique of existing systems of thought. It is in this spirit that Adorno's incomplete project itself demands continuing reinterpretation and critique: not in order to systematize and 'complete' it, but, through locating its terms and revealing its lacunae, to go beyond it.

Appendix

Berg's Sonata op. 1 and its relation to Wagner's Tristan

In his analysis of Berg's Piano Sonata op. 1 Adorno focuses on the work very much from the perspective of its extreme motivic economy, and consequently mainly in relation to Schoenberg's Chamber Symphony op. 9. He also, of course, discusses it in terms of 'continuous transition,' but certainly, and rather curiously, gives this aspect of the work less emphasis. The relation to Wagner is not really mentioned in the analysis of the Sonata in *Berg: Der Meister des kleinsten Übergangs*, although the Wagnerian influence is considered at some length in connection with Berg's music in general. But although Adorno, in emphasizing the importance of Wagner's influence on Berg, does not follow this through in his analysis, he does drop some hints in the article 'Berg and Webern – Schönberg's heirs' (1930) suggesting a link with *Tristan* which I would like to pursue in more detail here. In doing this I hope to show that, even where Adorno's own interpretations are fragmentary and lacking in careful and consistent analysis to back up his insights, they can, if regarded as *aperçus* needing critique and further development, lead to valuable new perceptions.

The suggestion that there is a strong link between Berg's music in general and Wagner's *Tristan* in particular warrants being followed up by means of immanent analysis – particularly in the case of the Sonata op. 1, given the special significance Adorno attaches to it within Berg's total compositional output. This may also serve to throw into greater relief the particular bias of Adorno's approach to analysis – what he assumes to be of most significance, and therefore gives most attention. His focus on the motivic–thematic dimension of the music at the expense of its harmonic directionality – so clearly also of great importance in Berg's music almost above all other composers of his period – has been commented upon in Chapter 4 and reasons for it suggested. I have argued that it is not that Adorno was unaware of the extraordinary importance of the harmonic dimension of Berg's music, but that his analytical 'method' was, by his own admission, of the reductive, formal and motivic variety, and thus, at the period of these analyses in particular, contained what would now be seen as serious blind spots. In focusing on the influence of Wagner on Berg in what follows, therefore, I am also focusing mainly on the harmonic dimension of the Sonata. In casting light on these blind spots the hiatuses in Adorno's approach can be seen both as a critique of that approach (as revealing the limitations of his 'immanent analysis') and, paradoxically, as a means of validating certain of his fragmentary and, at times, seemingly unfounded insights and assertions. The analytical points which follow make use of Adorno's analysis as outlined in Chapter 4, and make reference to his motivic examples from his Berg book. Adorno's numbering of bars in the Sonata is also retained for ease of reference, even though incorrect (Adorno counts the first incomplete bar as bar 1).

With the Wagner connection in mind (together with Adorno's emphasis on features like 'transition' (*Übergang*), 'dissolution' (*Auflösung*), and 'motivic remnants' (*motivische Reste*)), it is perhaps not so surprising that a cursory examination of the Sonata reveals a significant appearance of the '*Tristan* chord'. This appears at the end of the big climax at bar 95 in the 'development' (notated f–b–eb–ab). It emerges out of the 'tonal flux' and provides the most effortless transition to the passage in fourths which immediately follows it at bar 96. Adorno focuses on the way in which the climax is built up – indeed, it is a distinctly Wagnerian climax – and on the way it dissolves into the ensuing fourth-chord passage. Berg's tiny quotation – surely the most subtle of the many examples of *Tristan*-quoting among composers it inevitably calls to mind (including his own *Lyric Suite*) – passes unremarked by Adorno, doubtless because, although surely intended by the composer to serve as a hidden reference, it also performs its function as a transitional device so superbly, and thus seems to merge with its surroundings completely. But I would argue that the affinity with the harmonic and motivic world of *Tristan* goes beyond the straightforward, albeit subtle quotation of this one celebrated chord out of context. I will attempt to demonstrate briefly, through comparing the end of the big climax of the development in the Berg (especially bars 89–102) with three points in the *Tristan* Prelude (the opening, especially bars 10–17, the end of the big climax of the 'development', especially bars 77–85, and the ending, especially bars 106–10), how Berg takes substantial sections of the Wagner Prelude as his model for the Sonata.

I suggest that Berg's main model here was the particular appearance of the *Tristan* chord which occurs at the end of the big climax in the Prelude, bars 81–3, after which the music subsides and 'dissolves' into the return of the opening theme, over a pedal point, emphasizing the semitone motif in both its ascending and descending forms, as well as the interval of the descending (diminished) seventh (bars 83–5). When this passage is compared with Berg (bars 95–100) some interesting evidence of borrowing, adaptation and re-composition comes to light. As well as the citation of the

Tristan chord in the Berg, at the same pitch as the original (Berg spells the chord at this point with a b♮ rather than with Wagner's c♭), there are a number of other features worthy of note. For example, the significance of the interval of the tritone throughout the Berg is obvious enough; at this point, as the interval f–b, it features prominently both as a motif and as a significant component of the *Tristan* chord. In the Wagner it also features as a motif (in bars 81–2, upper woodwind), but as c♭–f. Seen in the context of these two passages, Berg would appear to have set up a correspondence with Wagner through inversion at this point (whatever the 'original' derivation of the motif within the context of the Sonata). Trivial as this observation may initially appear, it does nevertheless lead to a further interesting observation if the passage leading up to these climaxes in both works are then compared, keeping the idea of inversion in mind.

Not only can the Berg (bars 88–94) be read thematically (i.e. the piano r.h. octaves) as a free inversion of the Wagner (bars 77–82, vlns I and II), with the rhythmic pattern of the Wagner also taken over, but there is furthermore a common direction in the harmony, with distinct points of correspondence, marked particularly, as one would expect, through the progression of the bass line. This is striking from bar 89 onwards in the Berg, precisely because, as Adorno points out in his analysis (*Berg*, in *GS* 13, p. 381; trans., p. 45), the climax is achieved in the Development through a *simplification* of the texture, rather than, as in the Exposition and Recapitulation, through an increase of contrapuntal and harmonic complexity (which, as he had suggested in relation to early Schoenberg, tends to undermine the bass line as foundation for the harmony and to turn it into an independent part within the contrapuntal texture). The fact that the music becomes very homophonic at this stage therefore seems to emphasize its links with the Wagner (likewise homophonic here – indeed, Adorno argues that Wagner's counterpoint is always essentially homophonic in conception – see *Versuch über Wagner, GS* 13, pp. 53–4; trans., p. 56). Thus, comparing the harmonic direction of the Berg from bar 89 with that of the Wagner from bar 78, the bass line moves through c–g♭–f in both cases (in the Berg over two 3/4 bars, in the Wagner over one 6/8 bar), harmonically the progression being that from a half-diminished seventh on c (to which Berg adds an a♭ as an appoggiatura to g♭), via the neapolitan function of the g♭, to the half-diminished seventh on f. (The *Tristan* chord can itself also be understood as a half-diminished chord at this point, of course, and the half-diminished seventh on f gives the *Tristan* chord at its original pitch – to which Berg adds a b♭ as an appoggiatura to the a♭.) Various interpretations are possible of the correspondences between the two works in the next few bars leading up to the appearance of the *Tristan* chord at the peak of the climax in both. I would suggest that Berg's adaptation has to be seen as complex, involving both contraction and expansion of the original at certain points, and even possibly 'harmonic superimposition', where a harmony could be interpreted as the result of the superimposition of two harmonies from the original. This no doubt merits further examination of a kind for which there is no space here. I shall simply sketch and compare the general direction of the harmony as it continues in the two works: to e♭ minor (Wagner, bar 79; Berg, from bar 90 to the big climax at bar 92), then through b♭⁷ (Wagner, bar 79; Berg, not as such, but via sliding descending semitone-step movement which emphasizes the pitch b♭ in the bass line at bar 93, and then perhaps more significantly the whole-tone harmony built over the g♭ at the end of bar 94), to the important restatement of the *Tristan* chord as the f half-diminished seventh (Wagner, bar 80, Berg, bar 95).

The passage from bar 95 to bar 101 in the Berg acts, according to Adorno, as 'a caesura' in the piece along the lines of similar passages in the Schoenberg Chamber Symphony op. 9, in that it features perfect fourths used both harmonically and melodically. In stressing the perfect fourths and making the comparison with sections of the Chamber Symphony (presumably bars 368–77 of the Schoenberg are particularly what he has in mind here) he seems also to be emphasizing the essentially static character of chords built of perfect fourths, and therefore seems to be implying that this passage in the Berg also has a certain 'static' function within the Sonata. What Adorno does not really discuss, however, is the function of bars 95–100 in the Berg as a 'field of dissolution' (*Auflösungsfeld*), making use of motivic 'remnants' – particularly from bars 26–9 in the Exposition, leading into the second subject, as well as the semitone-step motif (c) (see Chapter 4, p. 164, Ex.2) from the opening – to dispel the tension of the *Tristan* chord and the climax which led up to it, and to dissolve the material into the varied statement of the second subject which follows at this point in the Development (at bar 101). The perfect fourths actually emerge out of the *Tristan* chord at bar 95, and continue to alternate with its reordered elements over the next two bars, together with the descending semitone-step motif commencing on b♭ (and when elements of the *Tristan* chord are superimposed above it, strongly implying an incomplete dominant eleventh chord in E♭). This passage could be felt as a kind of echo of bars 81–3 of the Wagner, where the corresponding bars lead to a varied reprise of the opening material of the Prelude. In the Wagner (bars 81–2) the harmony oscillates between the *Tristan* chord and a dominant seventh/ninth on b♭, again implying E♭. In both works, in fact, having implied E♭ by means of a version of II–V⁷–I, the music actually slips via the semitone step to E – or rather, to a V⁷/⁹ on E implying A (minor) (Berg, bar 101; Wagner, bar 84). What is particularly intriguing is how the Berg at this point blends in yet another element, again made up of what Adorno calls 'motivic remnants' (the rising semitone version of motif (c) plus the superimposed major thirds of motif (b) with their whole-tone associations, over a figure reminiscent of the triplet motif at bars 28–9, now characterized by a rising augmented fourth and a descending minor seventh, which could even be understood as a variant of motif (a) through interversion or 'axis rotation'). This passage at the same time models itself closely on a corresponding passage from the beginning of the *Tristan* Prelude, as well as alluding to fragments of its ending. Thus, if the semitone-step motif (c) e♯–f♯ and its underlying harmony in bars 98–100 of the Berg are compared with the prominent appearance of the e♯–f♯ motif in bars 11–16 of the Wagner (itself a 'motivic remnant' retained from the opening theme), again with the underlying harmony, the following connections can be observed. In both cases the motif and its harmonic function are the same – the e♯ as an appoggiatura to the f♯ in the context of $B^{7/9}$ (the identity of the chord to some extent concealed in the Berg by being spelled with an e♭ instead of d♯) leading, as $V^{7/9}$ in E, to a V^9 in A minor. This can also be seen as making reference to bars 93–4 towards the end of the Prelude, the Berg even suggesting the striking interrupted cadence of the Wagner which continues the progression (Berg, bar 102; Wagner, bars 17 and 94).

Once such correspondences have been noticed, one begins to see that there are numerous other features of the *Tristan* Prelude which find more than an echo in both the harmonic and the *motivic* make-up of the Berg Sonata, quite apart from the general influence of Wagner's harmonic language to which Adorno points. Thus the influence of Wagner on Berg is, as Adorno insists, something quite distinctive in its own right – even more so, perhaps, than Adorno suspected, if the correspondences uncovered above are regarded as convincing – and not simply filtered through Mahler and Schoenberg. The main point which emerges both from Adorno's own analysis of the Berg Sonata and from my 'supplementary' analysis above, however, is the sheer complexity of what is to be understood by the term 'musical material'. The Sonata op. 1 provides evidence of a relationship to the material which is at the same time both highly conscious (at times even self-conscious, in the sense of direct quotation or 'recomposition') and highly intuitive (in the sense of a remarkable assimilation and internalization of the musical–cultural value-system of the Austro-German tradition, as *Formgefühl*). The material is thoroughly 'mediated' in all its aspects – a striking example of intertextuality. (Other aspects, such as the question of 'stasis' in Berg's music, the influence of French music and of Debussy in particular, of German Expressionism, and of the Viennese Classical composers, are all mentioned by Adorno, but have not been pursued here for lack of space.) Adorno's assertion that Berg's 'style' is the result of a synthesis of Schoenberg's art of motivic economy and Wagner's art of transition, with its aim 'disintegration through integration', is validated, I would argue, through a critical extension of Adorno's immanent analysis in the light of the claims of his aesthetic theory.

Notes

INTRODUCTION

1 T. W. Adorno, 'The actuality of philosophy', translator unacknowledged, *Telos* 31 (1977), p. 126. Cf. original German, 'Die Aktualität der Philosophie' (1932), *GS* 1 (Frankfurt/Main: Suhrkamp Verlag, 1973), p. 334.

2 Thomas Mann, *Doctor Faustus* (1947), trans. H. T. Lowe-Porter (Harmondsworth: Penguin Books, 1968), p. 232.

3 For an account of the writing of the novel, see Thomas Mann, *The Story of a Novel: The Genesis of Doctor Faustus*, trans. Richard and Sarah Winston (New York, 1961).

4 See Adorno, *Philosophie der neuen Musik* (1949), *GS* 12 (1975), p. 126. Cf. *Philosophy of Modern Music*, trans. Anne G. Mitchell and Wesley V. Blomster (London: Sheed & Ward, 1973), p. 133.

5 '"Lonely discourse" reveals more about social tendencies than does communicative discourse. Schoenberg hit upon the social character of loneliness by developing this lonely discourse to its ultimate extreme.' Adorno, *Philosophy of Modern Music*, p. 43. Cf. original German, *GS* 12, p. 48.

6 See Martin Jay, *Adorno* (London: Fontana/Collins, 1984), pp. 11–14; also Gillian Rose, *The Melancholy Science: An Introduction to the Thought of Theodor W. Adorno* (London: Macmillan, 1978), p. x.

7 Adorno, 'Ohne Leitbild: Anstelle einer Vorrede', *Ohne Leitbild: Parva Aesthetica*, GS 10.1 (1977), p. 291.

8 For biographical details I have made particular reference to the following: *Theodor W. Adorno: Gesammelte Schriften Dossier* (Frankfurt/Main: Suhrkamp Verlag, 1978); Carlo Pettazzi, 'Studien zu Leben und Werk Adornos bis 1938', in *Theodor W. Adorno – Text + Kritik*, ed. Heinz Ludwig Arnold (Munich: Edition Text + Kritik, 1977); Martin Jay, *The Dialectical Imagination* (London: Heinemann, 1973); Susan Buck-Morss, *The Origin of Negative Dialectics: Theodor W. Adorno, Walter Benjamin, and the Frankfurt Institute* (Sussex: Harvester Press, 1977); Rose, *The Melancholy Science*; and Gerhard P. Knapp, *Theodor W. Adorno* (Berlin: Colloquium Verlag, 1980).

9 Adorno, 'Vierhändig, noch einmal', *Impromptus* (1968), *GS* 17 (1982), p. 303.

10 See Adorno, 'Der wunderliche Realist: über Siegfried Kracauer', *Noten zur Literatur III* (1965), *GS* 11 (1974).

11 Among his very earliest published essays is 'Expressionismus und künstlerische Wahrhaftigkeit: Zur Kritik neuer Dichtung', *Die Neue Schaubühne* 2/9 (1920), pp. 233–6. *GS* 11. During the 1920s and early 1930s Adorno also wrote

many concert and opera reviews, as well as reviews of new books and scores, particularly for the journal *Die Musik*. Only those which have been used in writing the present study are included in the Bibliography. For a full list of Adorno's opera, concert and book reviews, see Rolf Tiedemann, 'Editorisches Nachwort', in Adorno, *GS* 19 (1984), pp. 648–54.

12 Ernst Bloch (1885–1977). German neo-Marxist philosopher. Bloch's Marxism is strongly Hegelian in orientation, with elements of Jewish mysticism – a mixture which has much appeal to radical theologians. His most influential books are *Geist der Utopie* (Spirit of Utopia, 1918, rev. edn 1923) and *Das Prinzip Hoffnung* (The Principle of Hope, 1938).

13 Max Horkheimer (1895–1973). German social theorist and philosopher. Apart from Marx, the main influences on his work were the neo-Kantian philosophy of Hans Cornelius, the phenomenology of Husserl, and the *Existenzphilosophie* of Heidegger. One of the founders of Critical Theory, Horkheimer was director of the Frankfurt Institut für Sozialforschung from 1931 to 1959.

14 Walter Benjamin (1892–1940). German literary theorist and philosopher. A neo-Kantian by training, Benjamin's work is characterized by a unique and idiosyncratic fusion of Hegelian-Marxism and Kabbalistic metaphysics.

15 Edmund Husserl (1859–1938). German philosopher who developed the philosophy of consciousness known as phenomenology. In the Preface to his *Ideen zu einer reinen Phänomenologie und phänomenologischen Philosophie* (1913), Husserl writes: 'the work here presented seeks to found a new science ... covering a new field of experience ... that of "Transcendental Subjectivity" ... an absolutely independent realm of direct experience...'. Husserl, *Ideas: General Introduction to Pure Phenomenology*, trans. W. R. Boyce Gibson (New York/London: Collier/Macmillan, 1962), p. 5.

16 Adorno, 'Die Transzendenz des Dinglichen und Noematischen in Husserls Phänomenologie' [1924], *GS* 1.

17 Walter Benjamin, *Charles Baudelaire: Ein Lyriker im Zeitalter des Hochkapitalismus* [1935–9], Benjamin, *Gesammelte Schriften*, ed. Rolf Tiedemann and Hermann Schweppenhäuser, vol. 1 no. 2 (Frankfurt/Main: Suhrkamp Verlag, 1974). Translated as: *Charles Baudelaire: A Lyric Poet in the Era of High Capitalism*, trans. Harry Zohn (London: NLB, 1973).

18 Walter Benjamin, 'Das Kunstwerk im Zeitalter seiner technischen Reproduzierbarkeit', *GS* 1.2 (1974). Translated as: 'The work of art in the age of mechanical reproduction', in *Illuminations*, trans. Harry Zohn (London: Fontana/Collins, 1973).

19 Adorno, 'Über den Fetischcharakter in der Musik und die Regression des Hörens' (1938), *GS* 14 (1973, 1980). Translated as: 'On the fetish character in music and the regression of listening', trans. unacknowledged, in *The Essential Frankfurt School Reader*, ed. Andrew Arato and Eike Gebhard (Oxford: Basil Blackwell, 1978).

20 Adorno, 'Reminiscence', *Alban Berg*, trans. Juliane Brand and Christopher Hailey (Cambridge: Cambridge University Press, 1991), p. 13. Cf. original German, *GS* 13 (1971), p. 340.

21 Adorno, *Sechs Bagatellen*, for voice and piano, op. 6 (1923). Published in T. W. Adorno, *Kompositionen*, ed. Heinz-Klaus Metzger and Rainer Riehn, vol. 1: *Lieder für Singstimme und Klavier* (Munich: Edition Text + Kritik, 1980). The

list of Adorno's compositions includes Six Trakl Songs, Two George Songs, Two Pieces for String Quartet op. 2 (1925–6), Three Poems of Theodor Däubler for four-part unaccompanied women's chorus (1923–45), and arrangements for small orchestra of Schumann piano pieces: *Kinderjahr* (1941). Although seldom performed, a number of Adorno's works have been recorded (see *Theodor W. Adorno: Kompositionen*, on CD Wergo WER 6173–2).

22 Adorno, *Sechs kurze Orchesterstücke* op. 4 (1929). Published originally by Ricordi in 1968; also in Adorno, *Kompositionen*, vol. 2: *Kammermusik, Chöre, Orchestrales* (Munich: Edition Text + Kritik, 1980).

23 Adorno, *Der Schatz des Indianer-Joe* (1932–3) (facsimile of fragments), ed. Rolf Tiedemann (Frankfurt/Main: Suhrkamp Verlag, 1979).

24 Buck-Morss, *The Origin of Negative Dialectics*, p. 16.

25 René Leibowitz, 'Der Komponist Theodor W. Adorno', in *Zeugnisse: Theodor W. Adorno zum 60. Geburtstag*, ed. Max Horkheimer (Frankfurt/Main: Europäische Verlagsanstalt, 1963), p. 359.

26 Adorno, 'Der Begriff des Unbewußten in der transzendentalen Seelenlehre' (1927), *GS* 1.

27 Georg Lukács (1885–1971). German-Hungarian philosopher and literary theorist. Lukács's Marxism is strongly Hegelian in character, but influenced by both Georg Simmel and Max Weber. His *Geschichte und Klassenbewußtsein* (History and Class Consciousness, 1922) is probably the single most influential book in Western Marxism.

28 For an account of the dispute between Adorno and Lukács, see Rose, *The Melancholy Science*, pp. 114–30.

29 'Kierkegaard: Konstruktion des Ästhetischen' (*Habilitationsschrift*, Universität Frankfurt/Main, 1931; revised and first published 1933), *GS* 2 (1979).

30 See Jay, *The Dialectical Imagination*, for an account of the development of the Institut für Sozialforschung in the years 1923–50.

31 Herbert Marcuse (1898–1979). German neo-Marxist social philosopher. Marcuse's Marxism was heavily Hegelian in character. Of all the members of the Institut für Sozialforschung, Marcuse had the greatest popular influence on the student movement of the 1960s in the United States.

32 Erich Fromm (1900–80). German psychoanalyst and social psychologist. One of the early members of the Institut für Sozialforschung, Fromm subsequently severed connections with the Frankfurt School in the United States after fundamental differences of approach became increasingly apparent. His main contribution to Critical Theory was the integration of Freud and Marx.

33 Leo Löwenthal (*b.* 1900). German sociologist of literature. Member of the Institut für Sozialforschung between 1926 and 1949. Taught at Columbia University, and in 1956 became Professor of Sociology at Berkeley. His ideology-critique of the novels of Knut Hamsun was published in the *Zeitschrift für Sozialforschung* vol. VI in 1937, and provides interesting parallels with Adorno's critique of the music of Jean Sibelius. See Adorno, 'Fußnote zu Sibelius und Hamsun' (1937), in *GS* 20.2 (1986), p. 804.

34 Friedrich Pollock (1894–1970). German economist. One of the founding members of the Institut für Sozialforschung.

35 Paul Connerton, *Critical Sociology: Selected Readings* (Harmondsworth:

Penguin Books, 1976), pp. 11–12.

36 When Hitler came to power, Horkheimer was astute enough to move the Institut's assets out of Germany, and to set up branches in other European capitals. He unobtrusively established headquarters first in Paris and then in New York.

37 Paul Lazarsfeld, a German *émigré* sociologist, was a member of the Institut für Sozialforschung in the United States. He set up the Bureau of Applied Social Research which, as its name implies, made extensive use of empirical research methods.

38 The differences between Lazarsfeld and Adorno came to a head in late 1939, when Lazarsfeld wrote to Adorno complaining: 'Your disrespect for possibilities alternative to your own ideas becomes even more disquieting when your text leads to the suspicion that you don't even know how an empirical check upon a hypothetical assumption is to be made'. Letter from Lazarsfeld to Adorno, cited in Jay, *The Dialectical Imagination*, p. 223.

39 Adorno *et al.*, *The Authoritarian Personality* (New York: Harper and Brothers, 1950).

40 Paul Lazarsfeld writes: 'When, after the war, the majority of the Frankfurt group returned to Germany, they at first tried to convey to their German colleagues the merits of empirical social research which they had observed in the United States. In 1951 they convened a general meeting on the role of empirical social research ... Adorno presented the main report. [He] provided many concrete examples to demonstrate how all aspects of sociology can be enriched by empirical studies. ... Within a period of five years, however, the situation changed completely. Adorno embarked on an endless series of articles dealing with the theme of theory and empirical research. These became more and more strident, and the invectives multiplied.... According to Adorno the research worker was only interested in verbalized subjective opinions of individuals in whom he had naive confidence...'. Paul Lazarsfeld, *Main Trends in Sociology* (1970) (London: Allen & Unwin, 1973), pp. 60–61.

41 Schoenberg clearly found Adorno irritating. He wrote to Rufer in 1949, on reading *Philosophie der neuen Musik*: 'The book is very difficult to read, for it uses this quasi-philosophical jargon in which modern professors of philosophy hide the absence of an idea. They think it is profound when they produce lack of clarity by undefined new expressions ... naturally he knows all about twelve-tone music, but he has no idea of the creative process... He seems to believe that the twelve-note row, if it doesn't hinder thought, hinders invention – the poor fellow ... the book will give many of my enemies a handle, especially because it is so scientifically done.' Letter from Schoenberg to Rufer, cited in H. H. Stuckenschmidt, *Schoenberg: His Life, World and Work*, trans. Humphrey Searle (London: Calder, 1977), p. 508.

42 Thomas Mann weaves numerous references to Adorno into the text of *Doktor Faustus*. At one point, the musician Kretschmar, giving an illustrated talk on Beethoven's piano sonata op. 111, sings to the Arietta theme: 'Dim-da-da ... mea-dow-land'. In German Wiesengrund means 'meadowland' (see Thomas Mann, *Doctor Faustus*, trans. p. 56).

43 Hanns Eisler [with Adorno], *Composing for the Films* (New York: Oxford University Press, 1947).

44 Adorno, 'Wissenschaftliche Erfahrungen in Amerika' (1968), in *Stichworte: Kritische Modelle 2, GS* 10.2 (1977), p. 734.

45 Adorno, *Einleitung in die Musiksoziologie* (1962), *GS* 14. Translated as: *Introduction to the Sociology of Music*, trans. E. B. Ashton (New York: Seabury Press, 1976).

46 Adorno, *Vorlesungen zur Ästhetik 1967–68* (Zurich: H. Mayer Verlag, 1973). This is a pirated edition of Adorno's 1967–8 lecture series on aesthetics, published in typescript with many of the lectures incomplete. Dubious as its origins are, it is instructive to read the collection in conjunction with *Ästhetische Theorie*.

47 Adorno *et al., Der Positivismusstreit in der deutschen Soziologie* (Neuwied and Berlin: Hermann Luchterhand Verlag, 1969). Translated as: *The Positivist Dispute in German Sociology*, trans. Glyn Adey and David Frisby (London: Heinemann, 1976).

48 Jay, *Adorno*, p. 51.

49 Adorno, *Aesthetic Theory*, trans. Christian Lenhardt (London: Routledge and Kegan Paul, 1984), p. 465. Cf. original German, *GS* 7 (1970), p. 504.

50 See Georg Picht, 'Atonale Philosophie', *Merkur* 13 (October 1969), pp. 889–92.

51 Adorno, 'Of barricades and ivory towers – an interview with T. W. Adorno', *Encounter* 33 (September 1969), p. 63.

52 *Ibid.* A note from *Der Spiegel* quoted in this article describes the event as follows: 'After the distribution of a leaflet entitled "ADORNO ALS INSTITUTION IST TOT", three young revolutionary females from the 'Basisgruppe Soziologie' circled around Professor Adorno, at first waving their bouquets of flowers, then kissing him, exposing their breasts, and confronting him with erotic pantomime. Professor Adorno, who had called the police last semester when 76 student radicals occupied his Institute for Social Research, tried to protect himself with his briefcase, and then left the lecture hall. He has since announced that his lectures and seminar on "Dialectics" would be indefinitely postponed' (p. 65).

53 See Friedemann Grenz, *Adornos Philosophie in Grundbegriffen: Auflösung einiger Deutungsprobleme* (Frankfurt/Main: Suhrkamp Verlag, 1975); Lucia Sziborsky, *Adornos Musikphilosophie: Genese, Konstitution, Pädagogische Perspektiven* (Munich: Wilhelm Fink Verlag, 1979); Martin Zenck, *Kunst als begriffslose Erkenntnis: Zum Kunstbegriff des ästhetischen Theorie Theodor W. Adornos* (Munich: Wilhelm Fink Verlag, 1977).

54 Adorno, *Philosophy of Modern Music*, trans. Anne G. Mitchell and Wesley V. Blomster (New York: Seabury Press, 1973).

55 Martin Jay, *The Dialectical Imagination: A History of the Frankfurt School and the Institute of Social Research 1923–1950* (London: Heinemann, 1973).

56 Susan Buck-Morss, *The Origin of Negative Dialectics: Theodor W. Adorno, Walter Benjamin, and the Frankfurt Institute* (Sussex: Harvester Press, 1977).

57 Gillian Rose, *The Melancholy Science: An Introduction to the Thought of Theodor W. Adorno* (London: Macmillan, 1978).

58 These are now collected in Rose Rosengard Subotnik, *Developing Variations: Style and Ideology in Western Music* (Minneapolis: University of Minnesota Press, 1991).

59 See Jürgen Habermas, 'Modernity – an incomplete project', in *Postmodern Culture*, ed. Hal Foster (London: Pluto Press, 1985), pp. 10–15; and Jean-François Lyotard, *The Postmodern Condition: A Report on Knowledge*, trans. Geoff Bennington and Brian Massumi, with a Foreword by Frederic Jameson (Manchester: Manchester University Press, 1984; orig. French, Editions de Minuit, 1979), pp. 72–3.

60 See Fredric Jameson, 'Postmodernism and consumer society', in *Postmodernism and its Discontents*, ed. E. Anne Kaplan (London/New York: Verso, 1988), pp. 16–18.

61 See Shierry M. Weber, 'Aesthetic experience and self-reflection as emancipatory processes: two complementary aspects of critical theory', in *On Critical Theory*, ed. John O'Neill (London: Heinemann, 1976), p. 79.

62 Adorno, *Minima Moralia*, trans. E. F. N. Jephcott (London: NLB, 1974), p. 15. Cf. original German, *Minima Moralia. Reflexionen aus dem beschädigten Leben* (1951), *GS* 4 (1980), p. 13.

63 Raymond Geuss, *The Idea of a Critical Theory: Habermas and the Frankfurt School* (Cambridge: Cambridge University Press, 1981), p. 2.

64 Horkheimer had recourse to religion in his later years. See Max Horkheimer, *Die Sehnsucht nach dem ganz Anderen* (Hamburg: Furche-Verlag, 1970).

65 Adorno, *Minima Moralia*, trans., p. 25. Cf. original German, *GS* 4, p. 26.

66 See Juri Dawydow, *Die sich selbst negierende Dialektik: Kritik der Musiktheorie Theodor Adornos* (Berlin: Akademie-Verlag, 1971).

67 See Connerton, *Critical Sociology*, p. 15.

68 Adorno and Horkheimer, *Dialectic of Enlightenment* (1947), trans. John Cumming (New York: Herder & Herder, 1972), p. 4. Cf. original German, *Dialektik der Aufklärung*, *GS* 3 (1981), p. 20.

69 See Paddison, 'Adorno's *Aesthetic Theory*', *Music Analysis* 6/3 (October 1987), p. 356.

70 Samuel Beckett, 'Three dialogues with Georges Duthuit' (1949), in *Proust and Three Dialogues* (London: John Calder, 1965), p. 101.

71 In the Introduction to *Negative Dialektik* Adorno writes: 'The name of dialectics says no more, to begin with, than that objects do not go into their concepts without leaving a remainder, that they come to contradict the traditional norm of adequacy. ... Yet the appearance of identity is inherent in thought itself, in its pure form. To think is to identify. Conceptual order is content to screen what thinking seeks to comprehend. The semblance and the truth of thought entwine. Contradiction is nonidentity under the aspect of identity. ... Dialectics is the consistent sense of nonidentity. It does not begin by taking a standpoint. My thought is driven to it by its own inevitable insufficiency...'. *Negative Dialectics*, p. 5. Cf. original German, *GS* 6 (1973, 1977), pp. 16–18.

72 The 'bourgeois period', as Adorno understands it, is the historical period characterized by the rise to political power of the middle classes in Western Europe and the United States, from the eighteenth century to the present day.

73 Adorno, *Negative Dialektik*, *GS* 6, p. 25 (my translation). Cf. *Negative Dialectics*, trans. E. B. Ashton (London: Routledge & Kegan Paul, 1973), p. 14.

74 'To proceed dialectically means to think in contradictions, for the sake of the

contradiction once experienced in the thing, and against that contradiction. A contradiction in reality, it is a contradiction against reality. But such dialectics is no longer reconcilable with Hegel. Its motion does not tend to the identity of the difference between each object and its concept; instead, it is suspicious of all identity. Its logic is one of disintegration: of a disintegration of the prepared and objectified form of the concepts which the cognitive subject faces, primarily and directly. Their identity with the subject is untruth.' Adorno, *Negative Dialectics*, pp. 144–5. Cf. *GS* 6, p. 148.

75 See Georg Lukács, *Die Theorie des Romans* (Berlin: P. Cassirer, 1920). Lukács writes: 'But as the objective world breaks down, so the subject, too, becomes a fragment; only the 'I' continues to exist, but its existence is then lost in the insubstantiality of its self-created world of ruins. Such subjectivity wants to give form to everything, and precisely for this reason succeeds only in mirroring a segment of the world'. Lukács, *The Theory of the Novel*, trans. Anna Bostock (London: Merlin Press, 1971), p. 53.

76 Cf. Buck-Morss, *The Origin of Negative Dialectics*; Jürgen Ritsert, *Vermittlung der Gegensätze in sich: Dialektische Themen und Variationen in der Musiksoziologie Adornos* (Frankfurt/Main: Studientexte zur Sozialwissenschaft, Fachbereich Gesellschaftswissenschaften der J. W. Goethe-Universität, 1987); Thomas Müller, 'Die Musiksoziologie Theodor W. Adornos – ein Model ihrer Interpretation am Beispiel von Musikstücken Alban Bergs' (diss. J. W. Goethe-Universität, Frankfurt/Main, 1988).

77 In spite of discipline boundaries, musicologists like Rose Rosengard Subotnik and Susan McClary have made a significant contribution to the debate on the importance of Adorno's work for 'cultural musicology'.

78 See the introductory note to the Bibliography.

79 Samuel Weber, 'Translating the untranslatable', in Adorno, *Prisms*, trans. Samuel and Shierry Weber (London: Neville Spearman, 1967), pp. 9–15; see also Paddison, 'Adorno's *Aesthetic Theory*', pp. 360–61.

80 See Rose, *The Melancholy Science*, pp. 11–26.

81 Friedrich Nietzsche, *The Genealogy of Morals* (edition includes *The Birth of Tragedy*), trans. Francis Golffing (New York: Doubleday Anchor, 1956), p. 157. Cf. *Zur Genealogie der Moral* (1887) (Munich: Wilhelm Goldmann Verlag, undated), p. 14.

82 Adorno and Ernst Krenek, *Briefwechsel*, ed. Wolfgang Rogge (Frankfurt/Main: Suhrkamp Verlag, 1974).

83 Adorno, 'Letters to Walter Benjamin', in *Aesthetics and Politics*, ed. Ronald Taylor, with an Afterword by Frederic Jameson (London: NLB, 1977), pp. 110–33.

84 Cf. Adorno, *Vorlesungen zur Ästhetik (1967–68)*.

85 Adorno, 'Zum Probleme der musikalischen Analyse' [1969] (unpublished talk, Library of the Hochschule für Musik und Darstellende Kunst, Frankfurt/Main, Tape No. 102). Translated as : 'On the problem of musical analysis', trans. Max Paddison, *Music Analysis* 1/2 (July 1982), pp. 169–87.

86 Ernst Krenek, 'Vorwort' to Adorno–Krenek, *Briefwechsel*, p. 8.

87 Adorno, 'Der Essay als Form', *GS* 11, pp. 9ff. See also Rose, *The Melancholy Science*, pp. 11–26.

88 Adorno, 'The actuality of philosophy', p. 133. Cf. *GS* 1, p. 344.

89 See Rolf Tiedemann, 'Editorische Nachbemerkung', in Adorno, *GS* 13, p. 517.
90 'The whole is the false [*das Ganze ist das Unwahre*]'. Adorno, *Minima Moralia*, trans. Jephcott p. 50. Cf. *GS* 4, p. 55.
91 Fredric Jameson, 'T. W. Adorno; or, historical tropes', in *Marxism and Form: Twentieth-Century Dialectical Theories of Literature* (Princeton: Princeton University Press, 1971), p. 3.
92 'An historical materialist ... regards it as his task to brush history against the grain', Walter Benjamin, 'Theses on the philosophy of history', in *Illuminations*, ed. and introduced by Hannah Arendt, trans. Harry Zohn (London: Fontana/Collins, 1973), pp. 258–9. See also Andreas Huyssen, *After the Great Divide: Modernism, Mass Culture, Postmodernism* (Bloomington and Indianapolis: Indiana University Press, 1986), pp. 3–4.
93 Max Horkheimer, 'On the problem of truth', in *The Essential Frankfurt School Reader*, ed. Andrew Arato and Eike Gebhardt (Oxford: Basil Blackwell, 1978), pp. 426–7. Cf. original German in *Zeitschrift für Sozialforschung*, vol. 4 (1935).

1 CONSTELLATIONS: TOWARDS A CRITICAL METHOD
    1 Adorno, 'The idea of natural-history', trans. Bob Hullot-Kentor, in *Telos* 60 (Summer 1984), p. 124. Cf. original German: 'Die Idee der Naturgeschichte' [1932], in *GS* 1, p. 365.
    2 Friedemann Grenz, *Adornos Philosophie in Grundbegriffen*, p. 12.
    3 Rolf Tiedemann, 'Editorische Nachwort', in Adorno, *GS* 13 (1971), p. 517. Cf. Grenz, *Adornos Philosophie in Grundbegriffen*, p. 14.
    4 See Buck-Morss, *The Origin of Negative Dialectics*, p. 98.
    5 *Ibid.*, p. 98.
    6 Adorno, (a) '"Die Hochzeit des Faun". Grundsätzliche Bemerkungen zu Bernhard Sekles' neuer Oper', *Neue Blätter für Kunst und Literatur* 4 (Heft 3/4, 2 December 1921), republished in *GS* 18 (1984), pp. 263–8; (b) 'Bernhard Sekles', *Frankfurter Zeitung* (20 June 1922), republished in *GS* 18, pp. 269–70.
    7 Adorno, 'Béla Bartók', *Neue Blätter für Kunst und Literatur* 4 (Heft 8, 1 May 1922); republished in *GS* 18, pp. 275–8.
    8 Adorno, 'Paul Hindemith', *Neue Blätter für Kunst und Literature* 4 (Heft 7, 20 March 1922), incorporated into 'Ad vocem Hindemith: Eine Dokumentation', in *Impromptus* (1968), *GS* 17, pp. 212–17.
    9 Adorno, (a) 'Béla Bartóks Tanzsuite', *Pult und Taktstock* 2 (Heft 6, June 1925), republished in *GS* 18, pp. 279–81; (b) 'Über einige Werke von Béla Bartók', *Zeitschrift für Musik* 92 (Heft 7/8, July/August 1925), republished in *GS* 18, pp. 282–6; (c) 'Béla Bartóks Drittes Streichquartett', *Anbruch* 11 (Heft 9/10, November/December 1929), republished in *GS* 18, pp. 287–90.
    10 Adorno, (a) 'Kammermusik von Paul Hindemith', *Die Musik* 29 (Heft 1, October 1926); (b) 'Kritik des Musikanten', *Frankfurter Zeitung* (12 March 1932): both incorporated into 'Ad vocem Hindemith: Eine Dokumentation', *Impromptus* (1968), *GS* 17, pp. 217–22 and pp. 222–9.
    11 For a detailed list of Adorno's shorter concert, opera, score and book reviews from the period of the 1920s and early 1930s, see *GS* 19 (1984), pp. 648–51.
    12 See Adorno, 'Zuschrift über Bartók', *Lippisches Volksblatt* (21 October 1965), *GS* 18, p. 295.
    13 Adorno, 'Ad vocem Hindemith: Eine Dokumentation', in *Impromptus* (1968),

GS 17, pp. 210–46.

14 Adorno, 'Johann Sebastian Bach: Präludium und Fuge cis-moll aus dem ersten Teil des Wohltemperiertes Klaviers', *Vossische Zeitung* (3 March 1934), *GS* 18, pp. 179–82.

15 Adorno, 'Spätstil Beethovens', *Der Auftakt. Blätter für die tschechoslowakische Republik* 17 (Heft 5/6, 1937); republished in *Moments musicaux* (1964); *GS* 17, pp. 13–17.

16 Adorno, 'Schubert', *Die Musik* 21 (Heft 1, 1928); republished in *Moments musicaux* (1964); *GS* 17, pp. 18–33.

17 Adorno, (a) 'Notiz über Wagner', *Europäische Revue* 9 (Heft 7, 1933); republished in *GS* 18, pp. 204–9; (b) 'Fragmente über Wagner', *Zeitschrift für Sozialforschung* 8 (Heft 1/2, 1939/40), pp. 1–48 (Chapters I, VI, IX and X of what was later published as *Versuch über Wagner* (1952)).

18 Adorno, 'Hoffmanns Erzählungen in Offenbachs Motiven', *Programmschrift der Städtischen Bühnen Düsseldorf* 8 (1932); republished in *Moments musicaux* (1964); *GS* 17, pp. 42–6.

19 Adorno, 'Mascagnis Landschaft', *Vossische Zeitung* (7 December 1933); republished in *Impromptus* (1968); *GS* 18, pp. 271–2.

20 Adorno, 'Ravel', *Anbruch* 12 (Heft 4/5, 1930); republished in revised version in *Moments musicaux* (1964); *GS* 17, pp. 60–65.

21 Adorno, (a) 'Mahler heute', *Anbruch* 12 (Heft 3, March 1930); *GS* 18, pp. 226–34; (b) 'Marginalien zu Mahler', *"23". Eine Wiener Musikzeitschrift* (no. 26/7, 18 May 1936); republished in *GS* 18, pp. 235–40.

22 Adorno, 'Richard Strauss', *Zeitschrift für Musik* 91 (Heft 6, June 1924); republished in *GS* 18, pp. 254–62.

23 Adorno, (a) 'Fußnote zu Sibelius und Hamsun', *Zeitschrift für Sozialforschung* 6 (Heft 2, 1937); republished in *GS* 20.2, p. 804; (b) 'Glosse über Sibelius', *Zeitschrift für Sozialforschung* 6 (Heft 3, 1938); republished in *Impromptus* (1968); *GS* 17, pp. 247–52. See also the Introduction, note 33, concerning parallels with Leo Löwenthal's 1937 analysis of the nature symbolism of the novels of the Norwegian Nobel prize-winning writer Knut Hamsun, who in 1942 revealed himself to be a Nazi collaborator. As well as criticizing it for technical shortcomings, Adorno also suggests that, in its historical regressiveness and its nature symbolism, Sibelius's music shares certain features of Nazi nature mysticism: 'The Great God Pan, according to need also "Blood and Soil", promptly puts in an appearance. The trivial stands for the natural and fundamental, the inarticulate for the sound of unconscious creation.' Adorno, 'Glosse über Sibelius', *GS* 17, p. 249 (my translation).

24 Adorno, (a) 'Hanns Eisler: Duo für Violine und Violoncello, op. 7 Nr. 1', *Musikblätter des Anbruch* 7 (Heft 7, 1925); republished in *GS* 18, pp. 518–21; (b) 'Eisler: Klavierstücke, op. 3', *Die Musik* 19 (Heft 10, July 1927); republished in *GS* 18, pp. 522–3; (c) 'Eisler: Zeitungsausschnitte, op. 11', *Anbruch* 11 (Heft 5, May 1929), *GS* 18, pp. 524–7.

25 Adorno, (a) 'Zur Dreigroschenoper', *Die Musik* 21 (Heft 6, March 1929), republished in *GS* 18, pp. 535–40; (b) 'Kurt Weill: Kleine Dreigroschenmusik für Blasorchester', *Anbruch* 11 (Heft 7/8, September/October, 1929); republished in *GS* 18, pp. 541–3; (c) 'Mahagonny' [I], *Der Scheinwerfer* 3 (Heft 14, 1930); republished in *Moments musicaux* (1964); *GS* 17, pp. 114–22; (d)

'Mahagonny' [II], *Anbruch* 14 (Heft 2/3, February/March, 1932); republished in *GS* 19, pp. 276–7.

26 Adorno, (a) 'Kreneks Operneinakter in Wiesbaden', *Neue Musikzeitung* 49 (Heft 22, 1928); republished in *GS* 20.2, pp. 777–9; (b) 'Zur Deutung Kreneks', *Anbruch* 14 (Heft 2/3, February/March 1932); republished in Adorno–Krenek *Briefwechsel*, and in *GS* 18, pp. 571–6; (c) 'Ernst Krenek', appeared anonymously in an English translation in *The Listener* (London, 23 October 1935); republished in Adorno–Krenek *Briefwechsel*, and the original German in *GS* 18, pp. 531–4; (d) 'Ernst Krenek, Über neue Musik', *Zeitschrift für Sozialforschung* 7 (Heft 3, 1938); republished in Adorno–Krenek *Briefwechsel*, and in *GS* 19, pp. 366–8.

27 Adorno, 'Schönberg: Serenade, op. 24 (I)', *Pult und Taktstock* 2 (Heft 7, September 1925); republished in *GS* 18, pp. 324–30.

28 Adorno, 'Alban Berg: Zur Uraufführung des "Wozzeck"', *Musikblätter des Anbruch* 7 (Heft 10, December 1925), republished in *GS* 18, pp. 456–64.

29 Adorno, 'Anton Webern: Zur Aufführung der Fünf Orchesterstücke, op. 10, in Zürich', *Musikblätter des Anbruch* 8 (Heft 6, June/July 1926); republished in *GS* 18, pp. 513–16.

30 For a list of articles on the music of Schoenberg, Berg and Webern published by Adorno between the years 1927 and 1937, see the chronological list in the Bibliography, Section 1.2.

31 Adorno, 'Der dialektische Komponist', *Arnold Schönberg zum 60. Geburtstag* (Vienna, 13 September 1934); republished in *Impromptus* (1968), *GS* 17, pp. 198–203.

32 Adorno, 'Zur gesellschaftlichen Lage der Musik', *Zeitschrift für Sozialforschung* 1 (Heft 1/2, 1932), pp. 103–24, and (Heft 3, 1932), pp. 356–78; republished in *GS* 18, pp. 729–77. Translated as: 'On the social situation of music', trans. Wesley Blomster, *Telos* 35 (Spring 1978), pp. 128–64.

33 For reference to Debussy see, for example, Adorno, 'On the social situation of music', p. 157. Cf. original German, *GS* 18, pp. 767–8. Adorno's interpretation of Debussy is discussed briefly in Chapter 6 of this study.

34 Adorno, 'Zum Problem der Reproduktion', *Pult und Taktstock* 2 (Heft 4, April 1925); republished in *GS* 19, pp. 440–44.

35 See Joan Allen Smith, *Schoenberg and his Circle: A Viennese Portrait* (New York: Schirmer Books, 1986), pp. 107–8.

36 The fragments, as *Theorie der Reproduktion*, are to be published at an unspecified date by the Editionen des Theodor W. Adorno Archivs. See introductory comments to the Bibliography for further details.

37 Adorno, 'Nadelkurven', *Musikblätter des Anbruch* 10 (Heft 2, February 1928); republished in *GS* 19, pp. 525–9.

38 Adorno, 'Bewußtsein des Konzerthörers', *Anbruch* 12 (Heft 9/10, November/December 1930); republished in *GS* 18, pp. 815–18.

39 Adorno and Krenek, 'Arbeitsprobleme des Komponisten: Gespräch über Musik und soziale Situation', *Frankfurter Zeitung* (10 December 1930); republished in Adorno–Krenek *Briefwechsel* (1974), and in *GS* 19, pp. 433–9.

40 Adorno, 'Reaktion und Fortschritt', *Anbruch* 12 (Heft 6, June 1930); republished in revised version in *Moments musicaux* (1964), in *Briefwechsel*, and in *GS* 17, pp. 133–9.

41 Krenek, 'Fortschritt und Reaktion', *Anbruch* 12 (Heft 6, June 1930); republished in *Briefwechsel*, pp. 181–6.

42 Adorno, *Introduction to the Sociology of Music*, trans. E. B. Ashton (New York: Seabury Press, 1976), p. 233n. Cf. *Einleitung in die Musiksoziologie* (1962), *GS* 14, p. 425n.

43 Adorno, 'Ideen zur Musiksoziologie', *Schweizer Monatshefte* 38 (Heft 8, November 1958); republished in *Klangfiguren* (1959), and in *GS* 16 (1978), pp. 9–23.

44 Adorno, 'Thesen zur Kunstsoziologie', in *Ohne Leitbild: Parva Aesthetica* (1967, 1968); republished in *GS* 10.1, pp. 367–74. Translated as: 'Theses on the sociology of art', trans. Brian Trench, *Birmingham Working Papers in Cultural Studies* 2 (1972), pp. 121–8.

45 For a discussion of Adorno's use of Marxian and Freudian terminology, see Chapter 3; for a discussion of his sociology of music, see Chapter 5.

46 Adorno, 'Über den Fetischcharakter in der Musik und die Regression des Hörens', *Zeitschrift für Sozialforschung* 7 (1938); republished in *Dissonanzen* (1956), and in *GS* 14, pp. 14–50. Translated as: 'On the fetish character in music and the regression of listening', trans. unacknowledged, in *The Essential Frankfurt School Reader*, pp. 270–99.

47 Adorno, 'The Radio Symphony', *Radio Research 1941* (New York, 1941), pp. 110ff. Original in English. Omitted from *Gesammelte Schriften*.

48 Adorno, 'On popular music' (with the assistance of George Simpson), *Studies in Philosophy and Social Sciences* 9 (1941), pp. 17–48. Original in English. Omitted from *Gesammelte Schriften*.

49 Adorno, 'A social critique of radio music', *Kenyon Review* 7 (1945), pp. 208–17. Original in English. Omitted from *Gesammelte Schriften*.

50 Adorno and Hanns Eisler, *Komposition für den Film* (Munich: Rogner & Bernhard, 1969); *GS* 15 (1976), pp. 7–155. Originally published in English as: Hanns Eisler (Adorno's name omitted), *Composing for the Films* (New York: Oxford University Press, 1947). See Bibliography, Section 1.2 under 1947, for full publishing history.

51 Adorno, 'Volksliedersammlungen', *Die Musik* 17 (Heft 8, May 1925), pp. 583–5; republished in *GS* 19, pp. 287–90.

52 See Adorno, 'Zur gesellschaftlichen Lage der Musik', *GS* 18, p. 771; 'On the social situation of music', p. 160.

53 See Max Paddison, 'The critique criticised: Adorno and popular music', in *Popular Music 2: Theory and Method*, ed. Richard Middleton and David Horn (Cambridge: Cambridge University Press, 1982), pp. 201–18.

54 Adorno, 'Schlageranalysen', *Anbruch* 11 (Heft 3, March 1929); republished in *GS* 18, pp. 778–87.

55 *Ibid.*, pp. 780–81.

56 Adorno, 'Kitsch' [*c.* 1932?], in *GS* 18, p. 793.

57 Adorno, 'Abschied vom Jazz', *Europäische Revue* 9 (Heft 5, 1933); republished in *GS* 18, pp. 795–9.

58 Adorno, 'Über Jazz' [1936] (under the pseudonym 'Hektor Rottweiler'), *Zeitschrift für Sozialforschung* 5 (1937); republished in *Moments musicaux* (1964), and in *GS* 17, pp. 74–108.

59 Adorno, 'Zeitlose Mode: Zum Jazz', *Merkur* (June 1953); republished in

Prismen (1955), and in *GS* 10.1, pp. 123–37. Translated as: 'Perennial fashion – jazz', trans. Samuel and Shierry Weber, in *Prisms* (London: Neville Spearman, 1967), pp. 119–32.

60 See Adorno, 'Wissenschafliche Erfahrungen in Amerika', *GS* 10.2, p. 719.

61 *Ibid.*, pp. 702–38.

62 Adorno, 'Bach gegen seine Liebhaber verteidigt', *Merkur* (1951); republished in *Prismen* (1955), and in *GS* 10.1, pp. 138–51. Translated as: 'Bach defended against his devotees', in *Prisms*, pp. 133–46.

63 Adorno, *Versuch über Wagner* (1952), *GS* 13, pp. 7–148. See the Bibliography, Section 1.2 for a full publishing history.

64 Adorno, 'Arnold Schönberg (1874–1951)', *Die Neue Rundschau* (1953); republished in *Prismen* (1955), and in *GS* 10.1, pp. 152–80. Translated as: 'Arnold Schoenberg, 1874–1951', in *Prisms*, pp. 147–72.

65 Adorno, 'Das Altern der neuen Musik', *Der Monat* (May 1955); revised and republished in *Dissonanzen* (1956); *GS* 14, pp. 143–67. Translated as: 'Modern music is growing old', trans. Rollo Myers, *The Score* (December 1956), pp. 18–29.

66 Adorno, 'Musik und Technik', *Gravesaner Blätter* 4 (Heft 11/12, 1958); republished in *Klangfiguren* (1959); *GS* 16, pp. 229–48. Translated as: 'Music and technique', trans. Wesley Blomster, *Telos* 32 (Summer 1977), pp. 79–94.

67 Adorno, 'Verfremdetes Hauptwerk: Zur Missa Solemnis', *Neue Deutsche Hefte* (Heft 54, 1959); republished in *Moments musicaux* (1964), and in *GS* 17, pp. 145–61. Translated as: 'Alienated masterpiece: the Missa Solemnis', trans. Duncan Smith, *Telos* 28 (1976), pp. 113–24.

68 Adorno, *Mahler: Eine musikalische Physiognomik* (Frankfurt/Main: Suhrkamp Verlag, 1960); *GS* 13, pp. 149–319. See the Bibliography, Section 1.2 for a full publishing history.

69 Adorno, 'Musik und neue Musik', *Merkur* (May 1960); republished in *Quasi una Fantasia* (1963), and in *GS* 16, pp. 476–92. Translated as: 'Music and the new music: in memory of Peter Suhrkamp', trans. Wesley Blomster, *Telos*, 43 (Spring 1980), pp. 124–38.

70 Adorno, 'Vers une musique informelle', *Darmstädter Beiträge* (1961); republished in revised form in *Quasi una Fantasia* (1963); *GS* 16, pp. 493–540.

71 Adorno, 'Richard Strauss: Zum hundertsten Geburtstag: 11. Juni 1964', *Neue Rundschau* 75 (Heft 4, 1964); republished in *GS* 16, pp. 565–606. Translated as: 'Richard Strauss: born June 11, 1864', trans. Samuel and Shierry Weber in *Perspectives of New Music* (Fall–Winter, 1965), pp. 14–32 and 113–29.

72 Adorno and Max Horkheimer, *Dialektik der Aufklärung: Philosophische Fragmente* (Amsterdam: Querido, 1947); *GS* 7 (1981). Translated as: *Dialectic of Enlightenment*, trans. John Cumming (New York: Herder & Herder, 1972).

73 Adorno, *Philosophie der neuen Musik* (1949), *GS* 12, p. 11. Cf. *Philosophy of Modern Music*, pp. xvii–xviii.

74 Adorno, *Minima Moralia*, trans. Jephcott, p. 15. Cf. original German *GS* 4, p. 13.

75 Adorno, *Zur Metakritik der Erkenntnistheorie* (Stuttgart: W. Kohlhammer, 1956); *GS* 5 (1970). Translated as: *Against Epistemology: A Metacritique*, trans. Willis Domingo (Cambridge, Mass.: MIT Press, 1983).

76 Adorno, *Jargon der Eigentlichkeit: Zur deutschen Ideologie* (Frankfurt/Main:

Suhrkamp Verlag, 1964); *GS* 6, pp. 413–526. Translated as: *Jargon of Authenticity*, trans. Knut Tarnowski and Frederic Will, with a Foreword by Trent Schroyer (London: Routledge & Kegan Paul, 1973).

77 Adorno, 'Über das gegenwärtige Verhältnis von Philosophie und Musik', *Archivio di Filosophia* 1 (Rome, 1953); republished in *GS* 18, pp. 149–78.

78 Adorno, 'Fragment über Musik und Sprache', *Jahresring 1956/57* (Stuttgart, 1956); republished in *Quasi una Fantasia* (1963), and in *GS* 16, pp. 251–6.

79 Adorno, 'The idea of natural-history', trans. Hullot-Kentor, in *Telos* 60 (Summer 1984).

80 *Ibid.*, p. 111.

81 *Ibid.*

82 *Ibid.*

83 See Arnold Schoenberg, *Theory of Harmony*, trans. Roy E. Carter (London: Faber & Faber, 1978), p. 48. See also Chapter 2.

84 George Lukács, *History and Class Consciousness*, trans. Rodney Livingstone (London: Merlin Press, 1971).

85 *Ibid.*, p. 91.

86 *Ibid.*, p. 83.

87 See Buck-Morss, *The Origin of Negative Dialectics*, pp. 25–8.

88 Georg Lukács, *The Theory of the Novel*, trans. Anna Bostock (London: Merlin Press, 1971).

89 Cf. Martin Jay, 'The concept of totality in Lukács and Adorno', *Telos* 32 (Summer 1977), pp. 120–37.

90 Lukács, *The Theory of the Novel*, p. 37.

91 *Ibid.*, pp. 38–9.

92 *Ibid.*, p. 41.

93 *Ibid.*, p. 53.

94 Cf. *Ibid.*, p. 62.

95 *Ibid.*

96 *Ibid.*, p. 64.

97 *Ibid.*

98 Lukács, *History and Class Consciousness*, p. 234.

99 Lukács, *The Theory of the Novel*, p. 64. Cf. Adorno, 'The idea of natural-history', p. 118.

100 Adorno, 'The idea of natural-history', p. 118.

101 See Buck-Morss, *The Origin of Negative Dialectics* for an account of the friendship between Adorno and Benjamin.

102 Buck-Morss (*ibid.*) draws attention to the influence of Benjamin's terminology and use of language in Adorno's early essay 'Schubert' (1928), in *Moments musicaux* (1964); *GS* 17, pp. 140–44. See Buck-Morss, *ibid.*, p. 208; also p. 206n.

103 *Ibid.*, p. 22.

104 See Adorno, 'Letters to Walter Benjamin', in *Aesthetics and Politics*, ed. Ronald Taylor (London: NLB, 1977).

105 Walter Benjamin, *Ursprung des deutschen Trauerspiels* [1928], in Benjamin, *Gesammelte Schriften* 1.1 (Frankfurt/Main: Suhrkamp Verlag, 1974), pp. 203–430. Translated as: *The Origin of German Tragic Drama*, trans. John Osborne (London: NLB, 1977).

106 Rose, *The Melancholy Science*, pp. 37–8.
107 Adorno, 'The idea of natural-history', p. 119.
108 *Ibid.*, p. 119.
109 Rose, *The Melancholy Science*, p. 39.
110 Benjamin's concept of *Urgeschichte* as 'primeval history' refers to the idea of the 'return of the archaic' as myth. Adorno saw a danger of the concept assuming a new ontological status, and thus of losing the dialectical tension between 'history' and 'nature'.
111 Adorno, 'The idea of natural-history', p. 120.
112 Göran Therborn has argued that the social analysis and cultural critique put forward by the Frankfurt School was frozen by the 'Medusa's head' of fascism, by the rise of Nazism in Germany and the Hitler–Stalin pact of 1939. He suggests that the Critical Theorists were unable to go beyond their philosophical revulsion at the rise of authoritarian regimes during the inter-war period, even after the defeat of Nazism. See Göran Therborn, 'The Frankfurt School', in *Western Marxism – A Critical Reader*, ed. *New Left Review* (London: NLB, 1977), pp. 118–20. This kind of criticism of the Frankfurt School has noticeably subsided since the events of 1989, and the subsequent re-emergence of extreme right-wing nationalist movements in Germany and Eastern Europe.
113 Lukács, *The Theory of the Novel*, p. 22.
114 Adorno, *Philosophy of Modern Music*, p. 36. Cf. *GS* 12, pp. 41–2.
115 Adorno, 'Béla Bartók' (1921), *GS* 18, p. 278 (my translation).
116 *Ibid.*, p. 274.
117 Adorno, 'Béla Bartóks Tanzsuite' (1925), *GS* 18, p. 280 (my translation).
118 *Ibid.*, pp. 280–81.
119 *Ibid.*, p. 281.
120 *Ibid.*
121 Adorno, 'Über einige Werke von Béla Bartók' (1925), *GS* 18, p. 282 (my translation).
122 Cf. *ibid.*, p. 283.
123 *Ibid.*
124 Adorno, 'Béla Bartóks Drittes Streichquartett' (1929), *GS* 18, p. 289 (my translation).
125 Adorno, 'Paul Hindemith' (1922), in 'Ad vocem Hindemith: Eine Dokumentation', *GS* 17, pp. 212–17.
126 See Adorno, 'Ad vocem Hindemith', *GS* 17, p. 121.
127 See Adorno, 'Kammermusik von Paul Hindemith' (1926), in 'Ad vocem Hindemith: Eine Dokumentation', *GS* 17, pp. 217–22.
128 *Ibid.*, p. 221 (my translation).
129 See Geoffrey Skelton, *Paul Hindemith: The Man behind the Music* (London: Gollancz, 1975), p. 86.
130 Adorno, 'Kritik des Musikanten' (1932), in 'Ad vocem Hindemith: Eine Dokumentation', *GS* 17, pp. 222–9.
131 I am grateful to Raymond Geuss for drawing my attention to this point.
132 Wolfgang Sandner suggests that Paul Whiteman's enormously popular dance-band music was taken to be jazz by Adorno in the 1920s and 1930s, when, due to the effects of radio and gramophone records, the music became as well known in Europe as it was in the United States. Sandner argues that

Adorno never revised his opinion that jazz was simply part of the entertainment industry, in spite of Charlie Parker and the 'bebop' revolution which took place in the post-war years, because his views had been shaped by his experience of the 'mass music' of the inter-war period, and in particular by that of Whiteman. See Wolfgang Sandner, 'Popularmusik als somatisches Stimulans. Adornos Kritik der "leichten Musik"', in *Adorno und die Musik*, ed. Otto Kolleritsch (Graz: Universal Edition, 1979), pp. 125–32.

133 Adorno, 'Ad vocem Hindemith', *GS* 17, p. 228 (my translation).

134 *Ibid.*, p. 224.

135 *Ibid.*

136 *Ibid.*, p. 228.

137 *Ibid.*, p. 229.

138 Adorno, 'Hindemiths *Unterweisung im Tonsatz*' [1939], in 'Ad vocem Hindemith: Eine Dokumentation', *GS* 17, pp. 229–35.

139 *Ibid.*, p. 233 (my translation).

140 *Ibid.*

141 Adorno, 'Die stabilisierte Musik' [1928], *GS* 18, p. 725 (my translation).

142 *Ibid.*

143 See Adorno, *Philosophy of Modern Music*, pp. 35n–6n. Cf. *GS* 12, pp. 41n–2n.

144 Adorno, 'Die stabilisierte Musik', *GS* 18, pp. 725–6.

145 *Ibid.*, p. 726 (my translation).

146 *Ibid.*

147 *Ibid.*

148 Adorno, 'On the social situation of music', p. 133. Cf. original German, *GS* 18, p. 735.

149 *Ibid.*, pp. 154–5. Cf. original, *GS* 18, p. 764. See also note 178 below on 'ideology'.

150 Adorno, 'Schönberg: Serenade, op. 24' (1925), *GS* 18, pp. 326–7 (my translation).

151 *Ibid.*, p. 327.

152 Adorno, 'Der dialektische Komponist' (1934), *GS* 17, p. 200 (my translation).

153 Adorno, 'Schönberg: Fünf Orchesterstücke, op. 16', *Pult und Taktstock* 4 (Sonderheft: Arnold Schönberg und seine Orchesterwerke, 36–43; March/April 1927); republished in *GS* 18, p. 337.

154 *Ibid.*, p. 341.

155 Adorno, 'Berg and Webern – Schönberg's heirs' (1930), *GS* 18, p. 446.

156 Adorno, *Philosophie der neuen Musik*, *GS* 12, p. 56. Cf. *Philosophy of Modern Music*, p. 52 (translation modified).

157 Adorno, 'Berg and Webern – Schönberg's heirs', *GS* 18, p. 446.

158 *Ibid.*, pp. 446–7.

159 *Ibid.*, p. 447.

160 George Perle, *The Operas of Alban Berg* vol. 1, *Wozzeck* (Berkeley/Los Angeles/London: University of California Press, 1980), p. 4.

161 Hans Redlich, *Alban Berg: The Man and his Music* (London: Calder, 1957), p. 48.

162 René Leibowitz, *Schoenberg and his School: The Contemporary Stage of the Language of Music*, trans. Dika Newlin (New York: Da Capo Press, 1949, 1975), p. 141.

163 See Adorno, 'Letters to Walter Benjamin', in *Aesthetics and Politics* (1977), pp. 110ff.
164 Adorno, 'Berg and Webern – Schönberg's heirs', *GS* 18, p. 449.
165 *Ibid.*, p. 447.
166 *Ibid.*
167 *Ibid.*
168 *Ibid.*, p. 448.
169 *Ibid.*
170 *Ibid.*
171 *Ibid.*
172 Adorno, 'Anton Webern: Zur Aufführung der Fünf Orchesterstücke, op. 10, in Zürich' (1926), *GS* 18, p. 513 (my translation).
173 *Ibid.*
174 *Ibid.*
175 *Ibid.*
176 *Ibid.*, p. 514.
177 Göran Therborn, 'The Frankfurt School', p. 96.
178 '... the sociology of knowledge inherited from Marx not only the sharpest formulation of its central concepts, among which should be mentioned particularly the concepts of "ideology" (ideas serving as weapons for social interests) and "false consciousness' (thought that is alienated from the real social being of the thinker)'. Peter Berger and Thomas Luckmann, *The Social Construction of Reality* (Harmondsworth: Penguin, 1967), p. 18.
179 '... there is some practical convergence between (i) the anthropological and sociological senses of culture as a distinct "whole way of life", within which, now, a distinctive "signifying system" is seen not only as essential but as essentially involved in *all* forms of social activity, and (ii) the more specialized if also more common sense of culture as "artistic and intellectual activities", though these, because of the emphasis on a general signifying system, are now much more broadly defined, to include not only the traditional arts and forms of intellectual production but also all the "signifying practices" – from language through the arts and philosophy to journalism, fashion and advertising – which now constitute this complex and necessarily extended field'. Raymond Williams, *Culture* (London: Fontana/Collins, 1981), p. 13.
180 The term 'monad' (*Monade*) is taken originally from Leibniz's *Monadology* (1714). Adorno's use of the concept is distinctly filtered through Hegel, however. In his *Logic* (1817, 1827) Hegel writes: 'the definition, which states that the Absolute is the Object, is most definitely implied in the Leibnizian Monad. The Monads are each an object, but an object implicitly "representative", indeed the total representation of the world. In the simple unity of the Monad, all difference is merely ideal, not independent or real. Nothing from without comes into the Monad: it is the whole notion in itself, only distinguished by its own greater or less development. None the less, this simple totality parts into the absolute multeity of differences, each becoming an independent Monad. In the Monad of Monads, and the Pre-established Harmony of their inward developments, these substances are in like manner again reduced to "identity" and unsubstantiality. The philosophy of Leibniz, therefore, represents contradiction in its complete development.' (Hegel's

Logic, trans. W. Wallace (Oxford: Clarendon Press, 1975), p. 260.) In *Ästhetische Theorie* Adorno writes: 'In relation to one another, art works are hermetically closed off and blind, yet able in their isolation to represent the outside world. ... the interpretation of a work of art in terms of a crystallized, immanent process at rest approximates the idea of a monad'. (Adorno, *Aesthetic Theory*, pp. 257–8. Cf. *GS* 7, p. 268.)

181 Adorno, 'Jene zwanziger Jahre' (1962), *Eingriffe, GS* 10.2, p. 506 (my translation).

182 Adorno, in Lucien Goldmann, 'To describe, understand and explain', *Cultural Creation in Modern Society*, Appendix 3, trans. Bart Grahl (St Louis: Telos Press, 1976), p. 145.

183 Kant, *Kritik der Urteilskraft* (1790), Bd. I, §10. Cf. *The Critique of Judgement* (1928), trans. with analytical indexes, James Creed Meredith (Oxford: Clarendon Press, 1952, 1982), Bd. I, §10, pp. 61–2. The Meredith translation renders *Zweckmäßigkeit* as 'finality', and obscures the sense of 'purposefulness', or 'purposiveness'.

184 Adorno, *Aesthetic Theory*, p. 137. Cf. *GS* 7, p. 143.

185 For Adorno's concept of 'rationality' see Max Weber, *Wirtschaft und Gesellschaft* (1922), §2. Cf. Weber, *Selections in Translation*, ed. W. G. Runciman, trans. Eric Matthews (Cambridge: Cambridge University Press, 1978), pp. 28–30.

186 Adorno, *Aesthetic Theory*, p. 402. Cf. original German, *GS* 7, p. 428.

187 An earlier version of this model originally appeared in Paddison, 'Adorno's *Aesthetic Theory*', pp. 368–71.

188 'Moment' in this sense refers to the German *das Moment*, defined in Jay, *The Dialectical Imagination*, p. 54n, as 'a phase or aspect of a cumulative dialectical process. It should not be confused with *der Moment*, which means a moment in time in the English sense.'

189 Adorno, *Philosophy of Modern Music*, p. 26 (translation modified). Cf. *GS* 12, p. 33.

190 For a criticism of Adorno's musical analyses, see Diether de la Motte, 'Adornos musikalische Analysen', in *Adorno und die Musik*, ed. Otto Kolleritsch (Graz: Universal Edition, 1979), pp. 52–63.

191 Adorno, *Introduction to the Sociology of Music*, p. xi. Cf. *GS* 14, p. 175.

192 For a criticism of Adorno's sociology of music, see K. P. Etzkorn, 'Sociologists and music', in *Music and Society: The Later Writings of Paul Honigsheim*, ed. Etzkorn (New York: Wiley and Sons, 1973), p. 23. See also Wesley Blomster, 'Sociology of music: Adorno and beyond', *Telos* 28 (1976), pp. 81–112.

193 Adorno, *Aesthetic Theory*, p. 490. Cf. *GS* 7, p. 531.

194 In *Ursprung des deutschen Trauerspiels* Walter Benjamin writes: 'In the last analysis structure and detail are always historically charged. The object of philosophical criticism is to show that the function of artistic form is as follows: to make historical content, such as provides the basis of every important work of art, into a philosophical truth. This transformation of material content into truth content makes the decrease in effectiveness, whereby the attraction of earlier charms diminishes decade by decade, into the basis for a rebirth, in which all ephemeral beauty is completely stripped off, and the work stands as a ruin ...'. (Walter Benjamin, *The Origin of German Tragic Drama*, p. 182.)

195 Adorno, *Aesthetic Theory*, p. 480 (translation modified). Cf. original German, *GS* 7, p. 529.
196 For criticism of Adorno's philosophy of history, see Carl Dahlhaus, *Foundations of Music History*, pp. 29–32.
197 Adorno, *Vorlesungen zur Ästhetik (1967–68)*, p. 2 (my translation).

2 THE DEVELOPMENT OF A THEORY OF MUSICAL MATERIAL
1 Adorno, *Philosophy of Modern Music*, p. 32. Cf. *GS* 12, pp. 38–9.
2 Eduard Hanslick, *Vom Musikalisch-Schönen* (Leipzig, 1902, 10th edn), p. 81 (my translation). See also Wolfgang Burde, 'Versuch über einen Satz Theodor W. Adornos', *Neue Zeitschrift für Musik* 132 (1971), p. 583n.
3 In his essay 'The sculptor's aims' (1934), Henry Moore writes: 'Each sculptor through his past experience, through observation of natural laws, through criticism of his own work and other sculpture, through his character and psychological make-up, and according to his stage of development, finds that certain qualities in sculpture become of fundamental importance to him. For me these qualities are [and he then offers a list, within which is]: *Truth to material*. Every material has its own individual qualities. It is only when the sculptor works direct, when there is an active relationship with his material, that the material can take its part in the shaping of an idea. Stone, for example, is hard and concentrated and should not be falsified to look like soft flesh – it should not be forced beyond its constructive build to a point of weakness. It should keep its hard tense stoniness.' (Henry Moore, *Modern Artists on Art*, ed. Robert I. Herbert (New York: Prentice Hall Press, 1964), pp. 138–9 (italics in original).)
4 Paul Hindemith, *The Craft of Musical Composition*, p. 9. Cf. original German, p. 23.
5 *Ibid.*, p. 32. Cf. original, pp. 14–15.
6 *Ibid.*, p. 22. Cf. original, p. 39.
7 *Ibid.*, p. 108. Cf. original, p. 124.
8 *Ibid.*, p. 152. Cf. original, p. 172.
9 Adorno, 'Ad vocem Hindemith: Eine Dokumentation', *GS* 17, p. 230 (my translation).
10 Adorno, *Aesthetic Theory*, p. 312. Cf. *GS* 7, pp. 325–6.
11 *Ibid.*, p. 312. Cf. original, p. 326.
12 Cf. Brian Stimpson, *Paul Valéry and Music: A Study of the Techniques of Composition in Valéry's Poetry* (Cambridge: Cambridge University Press, 1984).
13 W. N. Ince, *The Poetic Theory of Paul Valéry: Inspiration and Technique* (Leicester: Leicester University Press, 1970), p. 71.
14 Paul Valéry, 'The idea of art' (1935), trans. R. Manheim, in *Aesthetics*, ed. Harold Osborne (Oxford: Oxford University Press, 1972), p. 30.
15 Friedemann Grenz, *Adornos Philosophie in Grundbegriffen*, p. 11.
16 Carl Dahlhaus, *Schoenberg and the New Music*, trans. Derrick Puffett and Alfred Clayton (Cambridge: Cambridge University Press, 1987), p. 27.
17 Juri Tynyanov, cited in Peter Bürger, 'Das Vermittlungsproblem in der Kunstsoziologie Adornos', in *Materialien zur ästhetischen Theorie Th. W. Adornos: Konstruktion der Moderne*, ed. Burkhardt Lindner and W. Martin

Lüdke (Frankfurt/Main: Suhrkamp Verlag, 1979), p. 175 (my translation).

18 *Ibid.*, p. 184 (my translation).

19 Arnold Schönberg, *Harmonielehre* (Vienna: Universal Edition, 1911; 3rd edn 1922). Translated as: *Theory of Harmony*, trans. Roy E. Carter (London: Faber & Faber, 1978).

20 Cf. Arnold Schoenberg, *Theory of Harmony*, pp. 314–15.

21 *Ibid.*, p. 21.

22 Arnold Schoenberg, *Style and Idea: Selected Writings*, ed. Leonard Stein, trans. Leo Black (London: Faber & Faber, 1975), p. 253.

23 Arnold Schoenberg, *Theory of Harmony*, p. 19.

24 *Ibid.*, p. 29.

25 *Ibid.*, p. 48.

26 August Halm, *Von zwei Kulturen der Musik* (Munich: Georg Müller, 1913).

27 Adorno, *Aesthetic Theory*, p. 288. Cf. original German, *GS* 7, p. 299.

28 *Ibid.*, p. 505n. Cf. original, p. 299.

29 Halm, *Von zwei Kulturen der Musik*, p. 252 (my translation).

30 *Ibid.*, pp. 252–3.

31 *Ibid.*, p. 253.

32 Ernst Bloch, *Geist der Utopie* (1918, rev. edn 1923; Frankfurt: Suhrkamp Verlag, 1964); *Gesamtausgabe* Bd. 3 (Frankfurt/Main: Suhrkamp Verlag, 1977).

33 Ernst Bloch, *Essays on the Philosophy of Music*, trans. Peter Palmer, with an Introduction by David Drew (Cambridge: Cambridge University Press, 1985), p. 94. This selection, a translated version of Bloch, *Zur Philosophie der Musik*, selected and ed. Karola Bloch (Frankfurt/Main: Suhrkamp Verlag, 1974), contains substantial sections from *Geist der Utopie* and *Das Prinzip Hoffnung*.

34 Schoenberg, *Theory of Harmony*, p. 238.

35 Bloch, *Essays on the Philosophy of Music*, p. 98.

36 Adorno, 'Reaktion und Fortschritt', in Adorno–Krenek, *Briefwechsel*, p. 175.

37 Adorno, *Philosophy of Modern Music*, pp. 34–6. Cf. original German, *GS* 12, pp. 40–42.

38 Bloch, *Essays on the Philosophy of Music*, p. 117.

39 *Ibid.*, p. 133.

40 Adorno, *Aesthetic Theory*, p. 332. Cf. original German, *GS* 7, p. 347.

41 David Drew, 'Introduction', Bloch, *Essays on the Philosophy of Music*, p. xxxv.

42 Ernst Bloch, *Das Prinzip Hoffnung* (1938), *Gesamtausgabe* Bd. 5 (Frankfurt/Main: Suhrkamp Verlag, 1977).

43 Bloch, *Essays on the Philosophy of Music*, p. 200.

44 *Ibid.*, pp. 200–201.

45 *Ibid.*, p. 201.

46 For a discussion of the relationship between Eisler and Adorno, see Günter Mayer, 'Adorno und Eisler', in *Adorno und die Musik*, ed. Otto Kolleritsch (Graz: Universal Edition, 1979), pp. 133–55.

47 Hanns Eisler, 'Die Erbauer einer neuen Musikkultur', in Eisler, *Reden und Aufsätze*, ed. Winfried Höntsch (Leipzig, 1961), pp. 25–52. Translated as: 'The builders of a new musical culture', in Eisler, *A Rebel in Music* (Berlin: Seven Seas Publishers, 1978), pp. 36–58.

48 Hanns Eisler, 'The builders of a new musical culture', p. 52.

49 *Ibid.*, p. 42.
50 *Ibid.*, p. 41.
51 *Ibid.*, p. 44.
52 *Ibid.*
53 *Ibid.*, p. 45.
54 *Ibid.*, p. 46.
55 *Ibid.*
56 See Adorno, 'Engagement' (1962), in *Noten zur Literatur III* (1965), *GS* 11, pp. 409–30. Translated as: 'Commitment', trans. Francis McDonagh, in *The Essential Frankfurt School Reader*, pp. 300–318; see p. 304.
57 Claudia Maurer-Zenck, 'Die Auseinandersetzung Adornos mit Krenek', in *Adorno und die Musik*, ed. Otto Kolleritsch (Graz: Universal Edition, 1979), p. 227.
58 Adorno, 'Atonales Intermezzo?', *Anbruch* 11 (Heft 5, May 1929); *GS* 18, pp. 88–97.
59 See Adorno, 'Kreneks Operneinakter in Wiesbaden' (1928), *GS* 20.2 (1986), pp. 777–9.
60 See Maurer-Zenck, 'Die Auseinandersetzung Adornos mit Krenek', p. 227.
61 Willi Reich, *Alban Berg: Mit Bergs eigenen Schriften und Beiträgen von Theodor Wiesengrund-Adorno und Ernst Krenek* (Vienna/Leipzig/Zürich: Herbert Reichner Verlag, 1937).
62 Adorno–Krenek, *Briefwechsel*, ed. Wolfgang Rogge (Frankfurt/Main: Suhrkamp Verlag, 1974).
63 Adorno–Krenek, 'Arbeitsprobleme des Komponisten: Gespräch über Musik und soziale Situation', *Frankfurter Zeitung* (10 December 1930): republished in Adorno–Krenek, *Briefwechsel* (1974), and *GS* 19, pp. 433–9.
64 The exception is 'Zur gesellschaftlichen Lage der Musik' (1932). This has been translated as: 'On the social situation of music', trans. Wesley Blomster, in *Telos* 35 (Spring 1978), pp. 128–64.
65 Adorno to Krenek, 9 April 29, *Briefwechsel*, p. 12.
66 *Ibid.*
67 *Ibid.*
68 *Ibid.*
69 *Ibid.*, p. 13.
70 *Ibid.*
71 Cf. Bloch, *Essays on the Philosophy of Music*, p. 7.
72 Adorno to Krenek, 9 April 29, *Briefwechsel*, pp. 13–14.
73 *Ibid.*, p. 14.
74 *Ibid.*
75 *Ibid.*
76 *Ibid.*, p. 15.
77 *Ibid.*
78 *Ibid.*, p. 16.
79 *Ibid.*, pp. 16–17.
80 *Ibid.*, p. 17.
81 Krenek, 'Vorwort', in Adorno–Krenek, *Briefwechsel*, p. 8.
82 Adorno, 'Zur Zwölftonmusik' (1929), *Briefwechsel* (Anhang), p. 168.
83 'The failure of the technical work of art is evident in all dimensions of

composition. Enchaining music by virtue of unchaining it – a liberation which grants it unlimited domination over natural material – is a universal process. The definition of the row in terms of the twelve tones of the chromatic scale is proof of this process.' (Adorno, *Philosophy of Modern Music*, p. 71. Cf. *GS* 12, pp. 71–2.)

84 Adorno, *Aesthetic Theory*, p. 1. Cf. original German, *GS* 7, p. 9.
85 Adorno, 'Reaktion und Fortschritt' (1930), *Briefwechsel* (Anhang), pp. 174–5.
86 *Ibid.*, p. 175.
87 *Ibid.*, p. 176.
88 *Ibid.*
89 *Ibid.*, p. 177.
90 *Ibid.*, p. 178.
91 *Ibid.*, pp. 178–9.
92 *Ibid.*, p. 179.
93 Georg Lukács, *History and Class Consciousness*, p. 234.
94 Rose, *The Melancholy Science*, p. 39.
95 Adorno, 'Reaktion und Fortschritt', *Briefwechsel* (Anhang), p. 179.
96 *Ibid.*, pp. 179–80.
97 *Ibid.*, p. 180.
98 Adorno and Krenek, 'Arbeitsprobleme des Komponisten: Gespräch über Musik und soziale Situation' (1930), *Briefwechsel* (Anhang), p. 187.
99 *Ibid.*
100 *Ibid.*, p. 188.
101 *Ibid.*
102 *Ibid.*
103 *Ibid.*, p. 189.
104 *Ibid.*, p. 190.
105 *Ibid.*, p. 191.
106 *Ibid.*, p. 192.
107 *Ibid.*
108 *Ibid.*, p. 193.
109 Rose, *The Melancholy Science*, p. 35.
110 Adorno to Krenek, 30 September 1932, *Briefwechsel*, p. 36.
111 *Ibid.*
112 Adorno, 'On the social situation of music', p. 128. Cf. *GS* 18, p. 729.
113 *Ibid.*
114 *Ibid.*, p. 129. Cf. original, p. 729.
115 The term *Mündigkeit* can be translated as 'coming of age', 'growing up', 'adulthood' or 'maturity'. In *Ästhetische Theorie* Adorno writes: 'The history of aesthetic modernism is art's straining towards maturity' (*Aesthetic Theory*, p. 64. Cf. original German, *GS* 7, pp. 70–71). In using the concept in relation to music, Adorno is referring once again to what he sees as the ever-increasing control of all aspects of musical material through technique. That is to say, increasing technical control means increasing *consciousness* of musical processes (which also constitutes their demythologization) – together with a tendency towards increasing integration of the elements of the work. Given that it is through technique and technology that the Subject is 'objectified' and becomes increasingly conscious of itself in musical terms, it is this process of

'Subject-objectification' which constitutes, for Adorno, music's 'straining towards maturity'.

116 Adorno, 'On the social situation of music', p. 129. Cf. original German, *GS* 18, p. 730.
117 *Ibid.*, p. 130. Cf. original, p. 731.
118 *Ibid.*
119 *Ibid.*
120 *Ibid.*
121 *Ibid.*
122 *Ibid.*, p. 130. Cf. original, p. 732.
123 *Ibid.*
124 *Ibid.*, p. 140. Cf. original, p. 744.
125 While Adorno, in *Philosophie der neuen Musik*, is not accusing Stravinsky personally of being a Fascist, focusing rather on what he sees as the 'authoritarian character' of his music, it nevertheless does need to be pointed out that Stravinsky had an admiration for Mussolini in the 1920s and 1930s which must also be seen as an indication of his own political sympathies at that time. In a letter to the Italian music critic Alberto Gasco, Stravinsky wrote: 'I don't believe that anyone venerates Mussolini more than I. To me, he is the *one man who counts* nowadays in the whole world. I have travelled a great deal: I know many exalted personages, and my artist's mind does not shrink from political and social issues. Well, after having seen so many events and so many more or less representative men, I have an overpowering urge to render homage to your Duce. He is the saviour of Italy and – let us hope – of Europe.' A. Gasco (1939), cited in Harvey Sachs, *Music in Fascist Italy* (New York and London: W. W. Norton, 1987), p. 168 (italics in original).
126 *Ibid.* (translation modified).
127 *Ibid.*
128 *Ibid.*, p. 131. Cf. original, p. 733.
129 *Ibid.*
130 *Ibid.*
131 *Ibid.*, p. 132. Cf. original, p. 733.
132 *Ibid.*, p. 132. Cf. original, p. 743.
133 Cf. Adorno, 'Letters to Walter Benjamin', *Aesthetics and Politics*, p. 123.
134 In *Einleitung in die Musiksoziologie* Adorno writes: 'The social function of jazz coincides with its history, the history of a heresy that has been received into the mass culture. Certainly, jazz has the potential of a mass breakout from this culture on the part of those who were either refused admittance to it or annoyed by its mendacity. Time and again, however, jazz became a captive of the culture industry and thus of musical and social conformism; famed devices of its phases, such as "swing", "bebop", "cool jazz", are both advertising slogans and marks of that process of absorption.' (Adorno, *Introduction to the Sociology of Music*, pp. 33–4. Cf. original German, *GS* 14, p. 213.)
135 Adorno, 'On the social situation of music', p. 132. Cf. original German, *GS* 18, p. 734.
136 *Ibid.*
137 *Ibid.*
138 *Ibid.*

139 *Ibid.*, pp. 132–3. Cf. original, p. 734.
140 *Ibid.*, p. 133. Cf. original, p. 734.
141 *Ibid.*, p. 133 (translation modified). Cf. original, pp. 734–5.
142 *Ibid.*, p. 133. Cf. original, p. 735.
143 *Ibid.*
144 *Ibid.*
145 *Ibid.*, p. 134. Cf. original, p. 736.
146 *Ibid.*
147 *Ibid.*, p. 135. Cf. original, p. 737.
148 *Ibid.*, p. 135 (translation modified). Cf. original, p. 738.
149 *Ibid.*, p. 136. Cf. original p. 739.
150 *Ibid.*
151 *Ibid.*

3 THE PROBLEM OF MEDIATION

1 Adorno, 'Der Essay als Form' [1954–8], in *Noten zur Literatur I* (1958), *GS* 11, p. 29 (my translation).
2 Adorno, 'On the social situation of music', p. 140. Cf. *GS* 18, p. 744.
3 Cf. Michael Rosen, *Hegel's Dialectic and its Criticism* (Cambridge: Cambridge University Press, 1982), p. 178.
4 *Ibid.*, p. 177.
5 See Paul Connerton, 'Introduction', *Critical Sociology* (Harmondsworth: Penguin, 1976), pp. 34–5. Connerton writes, discussing the different, and potentially confusing, uses of the term *critique* in Adorno's critical theory and in Popper's critical rationalism: 'for Adorno critique does not refer to the critical testing of hypotheses, but rather to the development of the contradictions in social reality through a knowledge of them'.
6 Adorno, 'Theses on the sociology of art' (1967), trans. Brian Trench, *Birmingham Working Papers in Cultural Studies* 2 (1972), p. 128 (translation modified). Cf. original German: 'Thesen zur Kunstsoziologie' (1967) in *Ohne Leitbild: Parva Aesthetica* (1967, 1968), *GS* 10.1, p. 374.
7 Adorno, *Negative Dialectics*, p. 186. Cf. *GS* 6, pp. 186–7.
8 Alfred Schmidt, 'Begriff des Materialismus bei Adorno', in *Adorno-Konferenz 1983*, ed. Ludwig von Friedburg and Jürgen Habermas (Frankfurt/Main: Suhrkamp Verlag, 1983), p. 26 (my translation).
9 Adorno, *Philosophy of Modern Music*, p. 15 (translation modified). Cf. *GS* 12, p. 21.
10 See Hans-Georg Gadamer, *Hegel's Dialectic: Five Hermeneutical Studies*, trans. with Introduction, P. Christopher Smith (New Haven and London: Yale University Press, 1976), p. 75. Gadamer argues that *Wissenschaft der Logik* is, in fact, Hegel's central systematic work – more so, even, than *Phänomenologie des Geistes*. *Wissenschaft der Logik* is certainly more central to Adorno's aesthetic theory than are Hegel's actual writings on aesthetics.
11 G. W. F. Hegel, *Logic (Encyclopaedia of the Philosophical Sciences, Part I (1830))*, trans. William Wallace, with a Foreword by J. N. Findlay (Oxford: Clarendon Press, 1975), p. 41.
12 G. W. F. Hegel, *Science of Logic* (1812), trans. A. V. Miller, with a Foreword by J. N. Findlay (London: George Allen & Unwin, 1969), p. 44.

13 Hegel, *Logic*, p. 42.
14 Adorno, 'Fortschritt' (1964), *Stichworte: Kritische Modelle 2* (1969), *GS* 10.2, p. 634 (my translation).
15 Adorno, *Aesthetic Theory*, p. 129. Cf. *GS* 7, p. 134.
16 *Ibid.*, p. 128. Cf. original p. 134.
17 It is interesting to compare Krenek's attempt to schematize the intersection of individual and collectivity diagrammatically in terms of a theory of musical material in the essay 'Basic principles of a new theory of musical aesthetics', which originally appeared in a German version in *Über neue Musik* (Vienna: Verlag der Ringbuch-handlung, 1937). See English version in Ernst Krenek, *Exploring Music: Essays*, trans. Margaret Shenfield and Geoffrey Skelton (London: Calder and Boyars, 1966), p. 149.
18 Hegel, *Phänomenologie des Geistes* (1807) (Frankfurt/Main: Suhrkamp Verlag, 1970), p. 145 (my translation).
19 Adorno, 'Ideen zur Musiksoziologie' (1958), *Klangfiguren* (1959), *GS* 16, p. 18 (my translation).
20 Adorno, *Aesthetic Theory*, p. 238. Cf. *GS* 7, p. 248.
21 Adorno, *Mahler: Eine musikalische Physiognomik* (1960), *GS* 13, p. 182 (my translation).
22 Wolfgang Gramer, *Musik und Verstehen: Eine Studie zur Musikästhetik Theodor W. Adornos* (Mainz: Matthias-Grünewald-Verlag, 1976).
23 Lambert Paul Zuidervaart, 'Refractions: truth in Adorno's *Aesthetic Theory*' (diss., Vrije Universiteit te Amsterdam, 1981).
24 Adorno, *Aesthetic Theory*, p. 137 (translation modified). Cf. *GS* 7, p. 144.
25 Adorno, 'Reaktion und Fortschritt', *Briefwechsel*, p. 175.
26 Adorno, *Aesthetic Theory*, p. 49. Cf. *GS* 7, p. 50.
27 Adorno, *Introduction to the Sociology of Music*, p. 216 (translation modified). Cf. *GS* 14, p. 418.
28 *Ibid.*, p. 216 (translation modified). Cf. original, p. 419.
29 Adorno, *Introduction to the Sociology of Music*, p. 57. Cf. *GS* 14, p. 239.
30 *Ibid.*, p. 57. Cf. original, p. 238.
31 Michael de la Fontaine, 'Der Begriff der künstlerischen Erfahrung bei Theodor W. Adorno' (diss., J. W. Goethe-Universität, Frankfurt/Main, 1977).
32 Adorno, 'On the social situation of music', p. 160. Cf. *GS* 18, p. 771.
33 *Ibid.*, p. 160 (translation modified). Cf. original p. 771.
34 Jürgen Ritsert, *Vermittlung der Gegensätze in sich: Dialektische Themen und Variationen in der Musiksoziologie Adornos* (Frankfurt/Main: Studientexte zur Sozialwissenschaft, Fachbereich Gesellschaftswissenschaften der J. W. Goethe-Universität, 1987).
35 Adorno, 'Letters to Walter Benjamin', in *Aesthetics and Politics*, p. 123.
36 Ritsert, *Vermittlung der Gegensätze in sich*, p. 4.
37 *Ibid.*
38 Adorno, 'On the fetish character in music and the regression of listening', trans. unacknowledged, in *The Essential Frankfurt School Reader*, p. 275. Cf. original German, *GS* 14, p. 20.
39 Karl Marx, *A Contribution to the Critique of Political Economy*, trans. S. W. Ryazanskaya, ed. Maurice Dobb (Moscow/London: Progress Publishers/Lawrence & Wishart, 1970), p. 194.

40 *Ibid.*
41 Karl Marx, *Capital* vol. I, trans. Ben Fowkes, introduced by Ernest Mandel (Harmondsworth: Penguin, 1976), p. 711.
42 Adorno, 'Ideen zur Musiksoziologie' (1958), *GS* 16, p. 9 (my translation).
43 Adorno, *Aesthetic Theory*, p. 324. Cf. original German *GS* 7, pp. 338–9.
44 Marx, *Capital* vol. I, p. 165.
45 Cf. I. Mészaros, *Marx's Theory of Alienation* (London: Merlin Press, 4th edn, 1975), p. 91.
46 Cf. Rose, *The Melancholy Science*, pp. 41–2.
47 Karl Marx, 'Preface' to *A Contribution to the Critique of Political Economy*, in Marx, *Early Writings*, trans. Rodney Livingstone and Gregor Benton (Harmondsworth: Penguin, 1976), p. 425.
48 *Ibid.*
49 Cf. G. A. Cohen, *Karl Marx's Theory of History: A Defence* (Oxford: Clarendon Pres, 1978), pp. 28ff.
50 *Ibid.*, p. 426.
51 Marx, *A Contribution to the Critique of Political Economy*, trans. Ryazanskaya, p. 215.
52 Connerton, *Critical Sociology*, pp. 26–7.
53 For a critique of Adorno's reception of Marx, see Russell Berman, 'Adorno, Marxism and art', *Telos* 34 (Winter 1977–8), pp. 157–66.
54 For a commentary on Adorno's application of Marxian categories like the 'forces and relations of production' to the case of art, see Rose, *The Melancholy Science*, pp. 118–21.
55 Adorno, *Introduction to the Sociology of Music*, p. 233 (translation modified). Cf. *GS* 14, p. 425.
56 *Ibid.*, p. 201 (translation modified). Cf. original p. 402.
57 Adorno, Max Horkheimer, Herbert Marcuse, Erich Fromm and Walter Benjamin all incorporated aspects of Freudian psychoanalytic theory into their own, highly idiosyncratic versions of Marxian theory.
58 See David Drew, 'Introduction' to Ernst Bloch, *Essays on the Philosophy of Music* (Cambridge: Cambridge University Press, 1985), p. xxxviii.
59 Adorno, *Aesthetic Theory*, p. 11. Cf. original German *GS* 7, p. 19.
60 *Ibid.*, p. 12. Cf. original, p. 20.
61 *Ibid.*
62 *Ibid.*, p. 13. Cf. original, p. 21.
63 *Ibid.*
64 *Ibid.*, p. 15. Cf. original p. 23.
65 Cf. Charles Rycroft, *A Critical Dictionary of Psychoanalysis* (Harmondsworth: Penguin, [1968], 1972), pp. 159–60.
66 Freud, *New Introductory Lectures on Psychoanalysis*, trans. and ed. James Strachey (Harmondsworth: Penguin, 1973), p. 129.
67 Sigmund Freud, *Art and Literature*, trans. and ed. James Strachey and Albert Dickson (Harmondsworth: Penguin, 1985), p. 229.
68 Adorno, 'On the fetish character in music and the regression of listening', p. 270. Cf. original German, *GS* 14, p. 14.
69 Adorno, 'Sociology and psychology' (1955), trans. Irving N. Wohlfahrt, *New Left Review* 47 (January/February 1968). pp. 86–7. Cf. original German: 'Zum

Verhältnis von Soziologie und Psychologie' (1955), *GS* 8, p. 70.

70 Jay, *The Dialectical Imagination*, pp. 86–112.

71 Cf. Rose, *The Melancholy Science*, pp. 91ff.

72 Erich Fromm, (a) 'Über Methode und Aufgabe einer analytischen Sozial-psychologie', in *Zeitschrift für Sozialforschung* I (Hefte 1/2, 1932); English version: 'The method and function of an analytic social psychology', in Fromm, *The Crisis of Psychoanalysis: Essays on Freud, Marx and Social Psychology* (London: Jonathan Cape, 1970, 1971), pp. 135–62. (b) 'Die psychoanalytische Charakterologie und ihre Bedeutung für die sozial-psychologie', in *Zeitschrift für Sozialforschung* I (Heft 3, 1932); English version: 'Psychoanalytic characterology and its relevance for social psychology', in Fromm, *The Crisis of Psychoanalysis*, pp. 163–89.

73 Cf. Jay, *The Dialectical Imagination*, pp. 103–6.

74 Erich Fromm, 'The method and function of an analytic social psychology', pp. 147–8.

75 *Ibid.*, p. 154.

76 *Ibid.*, p. 156.

77 *Ibid.*, p. 162.

78 *Ibid.*

79 Cf. Jay, *The Dialectical Imagination*, pp. 103–4.

80 Adorno, 'Social science and sociological tendencies in psychoanalysis' [unpublished, 1946, Löwenthal Collection]. Cited in Jay, *The Dialectical Imagination*, p. 104.

81 *Ibid.*

82 Adorno, *Introduction to the Sociology of Music*, p. 189. Cf. *GS* 14, p. 388.

83 Adorno, *Aesthetic Theory*, p. 189. Cf. *GS* 7, p. 196.

84 Adorno, *Minima Moralia*, p. 111. Cf. original German, *Minima Moralia* (1951), *GS* 4, p. 123.

85 *Ibid.*, p. 214. Cf. original, p. 242.

86 Adorno, *Introduction to the Sociology of Music*, p. 207 (translation modified.) Cf. *GS* 14, p. 409.

87 Don Martindale and Johannes Riedel, 'Max Weber's sociology of music', in Weber, *The Rational and Social Foundations of Music* (Carbondale: Southern Illinois University Press, 1958), p. xviii.

88 *Ibid.*, p. xix.

89 *Ibid.*, pp. xx–xxi.

90 See Adorno, *Dissonanzen: Musik in der verwalteten Welt* (1956), *GS* 14, pp. 7–167.

91 Max Weber, *Selections in Translation*, trans. Eric Matthews, ed. W. G. Runciman (Cambridge: Cambridge University Press, 1978), p. 28.

92 *Ibid.*

93 *Ibid.*

94 *Ibid.*

95 Weber, like Freud, uses the term 'sublimation' (*Sublimierung*). The difference between the two usages would seem to lie in the extent to which the process of 'sublimation' is considered to be *conscious*. Weber talks of the conscious control and discharge of emotion; with Freud the process does not appear to be conscious, and the distinction between sublimation and repression is not

always clear in psychoanalytic theory.

96 Weber, *Selections in Translation*, p. 28.
97 *Ibid.*, p. 29.
98 *Ibid.*
99 *Ibid.*
100 Max Weber, *Die rationalen und sozialen Grundlagen der Musik* [1911] (Tübingen: J. C. B. Mohr, 1921). Translated as: *The Rational and Social Foundations of Music*, trans. and ed. Don Martindale, Johannes Riedel and Gertrude Neuwirth (Carbondale: Southern Illinois University Press, 1958).
101 The Frankfurt Institute for Social Research, *Aspects of Sociology*, with a Preface by Max Horkheimer and Theodor Adorno, trans. John Viertel (London: Heinemann, 1973), p. 110.
102 Weber, *Selections in Translation*, p. 30.
103 The Frankfurt Institute, *Aspects of Sociology*, p. 110.
104 Cf. Ferenc Feher, 'Negative philosophy of music – positive results', *New German Critique* 4 (Winter 1975), p. 107.
105 Adorno, *Aesthetic Theory*, p. 81. Cf. original German, *GS* 7, p. 87.
106 *Ibid.*, p. 81. Cf. original p. 88.
107 Richard J. Bernstein argues that Adorno, Horkheimer and Lukács generalized Weber's concept of *Zweckrationalität* and came dangerously close to interpreting it as 'historical necessity'. See *Habermas and Modernity*, ed. Bernstein (Cambridge: Polity Press, 1985), pp. 6–7.
108 Adorno, cited in Michael Cahn, 'Subversive mimesis: T. W. Adorno and the modern impasse of critique', in *Mimesis in Contemporary Theory* vol. I, ed. Mihai Spariosu (Philadelphia/Amsterdam: John Benjamin's Publishing Company, 1984), p. 31.
109 *Ibid.*, p. 32.
110 *Ibid.*, p. 33.
111 Helga Gripp, *Theodor W. Adorno: Erkenntnisdimensionen negativer Dialektik* (Paderborn: Schöningh, 1986), pp. 124–7.
112 Adorno, *Against Epistemology; A Metacritique*, trans. Willis Domingo (Cambridge, Mass.: MIT Press, 1983), p. 143n. Cf. original German: *Zur Metakritik der Erkenntnistheorie* (1956), *GS* 5, p. 148.
113 Cahn, 'Subversive mimesis', p. 36.
114 Adorno, *Aesthetic Theory*, pp. 403–4. Cf. *GS* 7, p. 430.
115 Adorno, 'Funktionalismus heute' [1965], *Ohne Leitbild: Parva Aesthetica* (1967, 1968), *GS* 10.1, p. 378 (my translation).
116 Adorno, *In Search of Wagner*, pp. 34–5 (translation modified). Cf. *GS* 13, p. 32.
117 Adorno, *Aesthetic Theory*, p. 163. Cf. *GS* 7, p. 170.
118 *Ibid.*
119 *Ibid.*, p. 167. Cf. original p. 174.
120 *Ibid.*
121 *Ibid.*
122 *Ibid.*, p. 164. Cf. original p. 171.
123 Adorno and Horkheimer, *Dialectic of Enlightenment*, pp. 17–18. Cf. *GS* 3, p. 34
124 Adorno, *Aesthetic Theory*, p. 164. Cf. *GS* 7, p. 171.
125 *Ibid.*, p. 167. Cf. original p. 174.

126 Schoenberg, *Style and Idea*, pp. 254–5.
127 Schoenberg, *Theory of Harmony*, p. 127.
128 Cf. Jessica Benjamin, 'The end of internalization: Adorno's social psychology', *Telos* 32 (1977), p. 48.
129 Adorno, *Aesthetic Theory*, p. 238. Cf. *GS* 7, pp. 248–9.
130 Ritsert's original model is as follows:

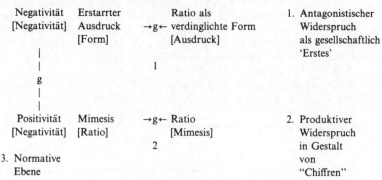

Negativität   Erstarrter   Ratio als   1. Antagonistischer
[Negativität]   Ausdruck   →g←   verdinglichte Form   Widerspruch
                [Form]   [Ausdruck]   als gesellschaftlich
  | 'Erstes'
  | 1
  g
  |
  |
Positivität   Mimesis   →g←   Ratio   2. Produktiver
[Negativität]   [Ratio]   [Mimesis]   Widerspruch
                                  2   in Gestalt
3. Normative   von
   Ebene   "Chiffren"
            g = Gegensatzbeziehung [oppositional relationship]
            See Jürgen Ritsert, *Vermittlung der Gegensätze in sich*, p. 11.

131 While the 'Vermittlung' chapter of *Einleitung in die Musiksoziologie* is devoted to the problem of mediation in music, it does not claim to put forward a 'theory of mediation' in any systematic sense.

4 A MATERIAL THEORY OF FORM

1 Adorno, *Aesthetic Theory*, pp. 9–10 (translation modified). Cf. *GS* 7, p. 18.
2 *Ibid.*, p. 213. Cf. *GS* 7, p. 222.
3 Cf. Carl Dahlhaus, 'Adornos Begriff des musikalischen Materials', in *Zur Terminologie der Musik des 20, Jahrhunderts: Bericht über das zweite Kolloquium, 9–10 März, 1972*, ed. H. H. Eggebrecht (Stuttgart, 1974), pp. 12–13.
4 Adorno, 'Form in der neuen Musik', *Darmstädter Beiträge zur Neuen Musik* vol. X (Mainz, 1966); republished in *Musikalische Schriften III* (1978), *GS* 16, p. 617.
5 Adorno, *Aesthetic Theory*, p. 203, Cf. *GS* 7, p. 211.
6 Cf. Adorno, 'Form in der neuen Musik', *GS* 16, p. 607.
7 Adorno, *Aesthetic Theory*, p. 207. Cf. *GS* 7, pp. 215–16.
8 G. W. F. Hegel, cited in Adorno, *Philosophy of Modern Music*, p. 3. Cf. *GS* 12, p. 13.
9 Cf. Adorno, *Aesthetic Theory*, p. 213, Cf. *GS* 7, p. 222. Also *Philosophy of Modern Music*, pp. 71–104. Cf. *GS* 12, pp. 38–42.
10 Adorno *Aesthetic Theory*, p. 213. Cf. *GS* 7, p. 222.
11 *Ibid.*, pp. 213–14. Cf. original, pp. 222–3.
12 *Ibid.*, p. 205. Cf. original, p. 213.
13 *Ibid.*
14 *Ibid.*, p. 208 (translation modified). Cf. original, p. 216.

15 Adorno, *Aesthetic Theory*, p. 212. Cf. *GS* 7, p. 221.
16 Carl Dahlhaus describes 'genre' as 'a congruence between a social function and a compositional norm ... [the] nexus of "external" social function and "internal" musical technique which tradition handed down to later composers ...'. Dahlhaus, *Foundations of Music History*, trans. J. B. Robinson (Cambridge: Cambridge University Press, 1983), p. 149. See also Jim Samson, who writes that 'a genre is dependent for its definition on context, function and community validation and not simply on formal and technical regulations. Thus a genre can change when the validating community changes, even where the notes remain the same.' Samson, 'Chopin and genre', *Music Analysis* 8/3 (October 1989), p. 213.
17 Adorno, *Aesthetic Theory*, p. 286. Cf. *GS* 7, p. 297.
18 *Ibid.*, p. 261. Cf. original, p. 471.
19 *Ibid.*, p. 288. Cf. original. p. 300.
20 Cf. Ferdinand de Saussure, *Course in General Linguistics*, introduced by Jonathan Culler, ed. Charles Ball and Albert Sechehaye, trans. Wade Baskin (London: Fontana/Collins, 1974), pp. 7–17.
21 Adorno, *Aesthetic Theory*, p. 293 (translation modified). Cf. *GS* 7, p. 305.
22 *Ibid.*, p. 292. Cf. *GS* 7, p. 304.
23 *Ibid.*
24 Adorno, 'On the problem of musical analysis', p. 173.
25 Cf. Carl Dahlhaus, 'Form', *Darmstädter Beiträge zur Neuen Musik*, vol. X (1966), pp. 72–3.
26 Adorno, 'On the problem of musical analysis', p. 173.
27 *Ibid.*
28 Adorno, 'Form in der neuen Musik', *GS* 16, pp. 607–8 (my translation).
29 Adorno, *Aesthetic Theory*, p. 4. Cf. *GS* 7, p. 12.
30 *Ibid.*, p. 7. Cf. original, p. 15.
31 Apart from the usual meanings associated with the term 'musicality' it seems possible that Adorno is using the concept *Musikalität* in a manner analogous to the Russian Formalists' use of the concept 'literariness' (*literaturnost*). That is to say, 'musicality' is that quality or attribute which separates and distinguishes an 'authentic' musical work in its use of musical material from the everyday, functional use of music as 'entertainment'. It is the way in which material is organized within the structure of the work, or the insight with which the work is performed, which renders the conventionalized or otherwise familiar musical gesture unfamiliar once more, and thus capable of conveying new meanings.
32 Adorno, 'Form in der neuen Musik', *GS* 16, p. 608 (my translation).
33 Adorno, *In Search of Wagner*, p. 48. Cf. *GS* 13, p. 46.
34 Cf. Adorno, *Aesthetic Theory*, p. 201. Cf. *GS* 7, p. 209.
35 Adorno, 'Form in der neuen Musik', *GS* 16, p. 617.
36 Willi Reich, *Alban Berg: Mit Bergs eigenen Schriften und Beiträgen von Theodor Wiesengrund-Adorno und Ernst Krenek* (Vienna/Leipzig/Zürich: Herbert Reichner Verlag, 1937). Contained the following analyses of Berg's works by Adorno: 'Klaviersonate op. 1' (pp. 21–6); 'Vier Lieder op. 2' (pp. 27–31); 'Sieben frühe Lieder' (pp. 31–3); 'Streichquartett op. 3' (pp. 35–42); 'Vier Stücke für Klarinette und Klavier op. 5' (pp. 47–51); 'Drei Orchester-

stücke op. 6' (pp. 52–61); 'Lyrische Suite fur Streichquartett' (pp. 91–101); 'Konzertarie "Der Wein"' (pp. 101–5).

37 Adorno, *Berg: Der Meister des kleinsten Übergangs* (1968), *GS* 13 (1971), pp. 321–494. Translated as: *Alban Berg: Master of the Smallest Link*, trans. Juliane Brand and Christopher Hailey (Cambridge: Cambridge University Press, 1991). See the Bibliography, Section 1.2, for full details of contents.

38 See, for example, 'Alban Berg: Violinkonzert', in *Der getreue Korrepetitor* (1963), *GS* 15, pp. 338–68.

39 Adorno, On the problem of musical analysis', p. 184.

40 *Ibid.*

41 Adorno, 'Klaviersonate', in *Berg: Der Meister des kleinsten Übergangs*, *GS* 13, pp. 374–82.

42 Adorno, 'Berg and Webern – Schönberg's heirs' (1930), *GS* 18, pp. 446–55.

43 Adorno, 'Klaviersonate', in *Berg: Der Meister des kleinsten Übergangs*, *GS* 13, p. 375 (my translation). Cf. English translation, p. 40.

44 *Ibid.*, p. 374 (my translation).

45 *Ibid.*

46 *Ibid.*, p. 377.

47 *Ibid.*, p. 375.

48 *Ibid.*

49 Cf. Hans Redlich, *Alban Berg: The Man and his Music* (London: Calder, 1957), p. 47.

50 Adorno, 'Klaviersonate', *GS* 13, p. 375. See also Adorno, 'Berg and Webern – Schönberg's heirs', *GS* 18, p. 448.

51 Cf. George Perle, *The Operas of Alban Berg*, vol. I, p. 4. Also Redlich, *Alban Berg*, p. 47.

52 Adorno, 'Klaviersonate', *GS* 13, p. 377. Cf. English translation, p. 42.

53 *Ibid.*, p. 377.

54 Adorno, 'Form in der neuen Musik', *GS* 16, p. 617.

55 Adorno, 'Klaviersonate', *GS* 13, p. 376.

56 *Ibid.*, p. 373.

57 *Ibid.*, p. 376.

58 Adorno, 'Berg and Webern – Schönberg's heirs', *GS* 18, p. 448.

59 Hans Redlich writes of the Berg Sonata op. 1: 'A family-likeness between theme-fragments in its first and thirty-first bars and motives in Schoenberg's Op. 9 has elicited frequent comment. The common thematic link is, of course, the interval of the fourth. However, while Schoenberg treats the fourth as thematic raw material [*Rohstoff*], Berg presents already in the very first bars a highly organized combination of motives, the thematic possibilities of which determine the plan of the whole sonata.' (Redlich, *Alban Berg*, p. 48.)

60 Adorno, 'Klaviersonate', *GS* 13, p. 376.

61 Adorno, 'Berg and Webern – Schönberg's heirs', *GS* 18, p. 449.

62 Adorno, 'Klaviersonate', *GS* 13, p. 377.

63 *Ibid.*, p. 378.

64 *Ibid.*

65 *Ibid.*

66 *Ibid.*

67 *Ibid.*, p. 379.

68 *Ibid.*
69 *Ibid.*
70 *Ibid.*
71 *Ibid.*, p. 380.
72 *Ibid.*
73 *Ibid.*
74 *Ibid.*
75 *Ibid.*, p. 381. Cf. English translation, p. 45.
76 *Ibid.*, p. 381.
77 *Ibid.*
78 *Ibid.*, p. 382.
79 *Ibid.*
80 *Ibid.*
81 *Ibid.*
82 Adorno, 'Berg and Webern – Schönberg's heirs', *GS* 18, p. 449.
83 *Ibid.*
84 *Ibid.*
85 Stefan Askenase, in an interview with Joan Allen Smith discussing Berg's interests, recalls that 'at the end, it was very narrowed to one chord and that was the first chord of *Tristan*. He was fascinated by it … when he saw a piano, he always played that.' (Joan Allen Smith, *Schoenberg and his Circle: A Viennese Portrait* (New York: Schirmer Books, 1986), p. 154.)
86 See Adorno, *Berg: Der Meister des kleinsten Übergangs, GS* 13, pp. 368–74.
87 See Adorno, 'On the problem of musical analysis', pp. 169–87.
88 See Paddison, 'Adorno's *Aesthetic Theory*', p. 372.
89 The German composer Hans Ulrich Engelmann, who had received composition lessons from Adorno in the early 1950s, told me that Adorno had struck him as rather conservative in his reception of the 'New Music' of that period in Darmstadt. In illustration of this he said that Adorno always insisted on evidence of traditional categories like exposition–development–recapitulation in his students' compositions. (Conversation with Hans Ulrich Engelmann, Darmstadt, 20 July, 1980.) This should, however, be seen in context. In his essay 'Vers une musique informelle', initially given as a talk at Darmstadt in 1961, Adorno writes: 'Contemporary music itself is not to be tied to what appear to be such general categories as first and second subject, as if they were irrevocable.... Nevertheless, for its articulation [*Artikulation*] it is certainly in need of musical–linguistic categories, however modified, if we are not to remain satisfied with [undifferentiated] accumulations of tones [*Tonhaufen*]. The old categories are not to be restored, but their equivalents [need to be] developed out of the mass of new materials, in order to achieve with transparency what those categories in the old materials achieved irrationally and therefore inadequately. The material theory of form that I have in mind would have this as its most worthy object.' Adorno, 'Vers une musique informelle', *GS* 16, p. 504 (my translation).
90 See Adorno, 'On the problem of musical analysis', pp. 174–5.
91 *Ibid.*, p. 184.
92 See Diether de la Motte, 'Adornos musikalische Analysen', in *Adorno und die Musik*, ed. Otto Kolleritsch (Graz: Universal Edition, 1979), pp. 52–63. Cf.

Juliane Brand and Christopher Hailey, 'Translators' introduction', in Adorno, *Alban Berg* (Cambridge: Cambridge University Press, 1991), p. xiv.
93 Adorno, 'On the problem of musical analysis', p. 184. Cf. 'Analyse und Berg' section of the Berg book, on which Adorno was working when he gave his talk 'On the problem of musical analysis'.
94 Adorno, *Berg, GS* 13, pp. 326–7 (my translation).
95 *Ibid.*, p. 326 (my translation).
96 Richard Wagner, Letter of 29 October 1859 to Mathilde Wesendonck; cited in Adorno, *In Search of Wagner*, p. 66. Cf. original, *GS* 13, p. 63, and p. 147n. (note 4 to Chapter IV).
97 Adorno, *Berg, GS* 13, p. 327 (my translation).
98 *Ibid.*, p. 328.
99 *Ibid.*
100 See Adorno, 'On the problem of musical analysis', p. 182.
101 Adorno, *Berg, GS* 13, p. 372 (my translation).
102 See Adorno, *Philosophy of Modern Music*, pp. 30–31. Cf. *GS* 12, pp. 37–8.
103 Adorno, *GS* 12, p. 37 (my translation). Cf. *Philosophy of Modern Music*, p. 30.
104 Adorno, *GS* 12, p. 38 (my translation). Cf. *Philosophy of Modern Music*, pp. 31–2.
105 Adorno, 'On the problem of musical analysis', p. 185.
106 Adorno, *Mahler: Eine musikalische Physiognomik, GS* 13, pp. 193–4 (my translation).
107 Adorno, 'On the problem of musical analysis', p. 185.
108 Adorno, *Aesthetic Theory*, pp. 227–8 (translation modified). Cf. *GS* 7, p. 238.
109 Adorno, *Aesthetic Theory* p. 150. Cf. *GS* 7, p. 156.
110 Adorno, 'Neunzehn Beiträge über neue Musik' [1942], *GS* 18, pp. 57–87.
111 *Ibid.*, pp. 68–9 (my translation).
112 Adorno, *Aesthetic Theory*, p. 204. Cf. *GS* 7, p. 212.
113 *Ibid.*, p. 204 (translation modified). Cf. original German, *GS* 7, p. 212.
114 Adorno, 'Form in der neuen Musik', *GS* 16, p. 612 (my translation).
115 *Ibid.*, p. 613.
116 Adorno, *Aesthetic Theory*, p. 228 (translation modified). Cf. *GS* 7, p. 238.
117 Adorno, 'Form in der neuen Musik', *GS* 16, p. 613 (my translation).
118 *Ibid.*, p. 616.
119 *Ibid.*, p. 624.
120 *Ibid.*, p. 622.
121 *Ibid.*, p. 624.
122 *Ibid.*, p. 617.
123 Adorno, *Aesthetic Theory*, p. 228. Cf. *GS* 7, p. 239.
124 *Ibid.*, p. 34. Cf. original p. 42.
125 *Ibid.*
126 *Ibid.*, p. 35. Cf. original, p. 42.
127 Adorno, *Aesthetic Theory*, p. 212 (translation modified). Cf. *GS* 7, p. 221.
128 *Ibid.*, p. 211. Cf. *GS* 7, p. 220.
129 *Ibid.*, p. 223. Cf. original, p. 233.
130 *Ibid.*, p. 314. Cf. original, p. 328.
131 *Ibid.*, p. 313. Cf. original, p. 327.
132 Adorno, 'On the problem of musical analysis', p. 184.

133 Adorno, *Aesthetic Theory*, p. 212. Cf. *GS* 7, p. 221.
134 *Ibid.*
135 Adorno, 'Vers une musique informelle', *Darmstädter Beiträge* (1961); republished in *Quasi una Fantasia* (1963). *GS* 16, pp. 493–540.
136 Martin Zenck, 'Auswirkungen einer "musique informelle" auf die Neue Musik. Zu Theodor W. Adornos Formvorstellung', *International Review of the Aesthetics and Sociology of Music* 10/2 (December 1979), p. 137.
137 Cf. Adorno, 'Vers une musique informelle', pp. 504–5. See also Chapter 4 note 89.
138 See Zenck, 'Auswirkungen einer "musique informelle" auf die Neue Musik'. It is useful to cite the Summary to this article here in full: 'The article proceeds from the demand made by Adorno upon any theory of aesthetics, that it be both on a par with contemporary aesthetic production and that it offers through its reflections a generative impulse to new musical composition. The intention is to verify the fulfillment of this postulation in the case of Adorno's idea of "musique informelle". The informal conception of form originated in the critique of ontological form, traditional closed form, the pre-formed form of serialism and the renunciation of all formal connexion in open and mobile form. It is to be found positively, even when only as an approximation, in the athematicism and free atonalism of the third piece of Arnold Schönberg's op. 11 and in *Erwartung*. These two instances represent Adorno's point of departure, from which he derives an idea of informal form to be applied to the compositional situation of 1960. Despite faults in the construction and transference of a nominalistic form from free atonality to post serialism, Adorno's idea of free form had nevertheless compositional consequences. This thesis is demonstrated in three steps: Firstly, in the theoretical appropriation of Adorno's idea of "musique informalle" in György Ligeti's musical thought; secondly, in an applied critique of compositional procedure in Stockhausen's *Klavierstück I*, evolved from Ligeti's general critique of serialism; and thirdly, in the compositional consequences which Ligeti derived from Adorno's ideal of informal form evident in *Aventures/Nouvelles Aventures*. The result is a form which is determined by its global character of movement but free in detail as far as succession and stratification are concerned: a form of indeterminate determination.' Zenck, 'Auswirkungen', p. 164.

5 SOCIAL CONTENT AND SOCIAL FUNCTION
1 Adorno, *Introduction to the Sociology of Music*, p. 63 (translation modified). Cf. *GS* 14, p. 245.
2 Adorno, 'Theses on the sociology of art', trans. Brian Trench, *Birmingham Working Papers in Cultural Studies* 2 (1972), p. 121. Cf. 'Thesen zur Kunstsoziologie' (1967), *GS* 10.1, p. 367.
3 The term 'theoretical model' is used here in the general sense of representing stages of an argument in such a way that it is possible to identify the terms and map the relations between them for the purposes of discussion. The aim is to identify assumptions and reveal patterns through limiting the scope of the discussion at any particular stage. This always involves the simplification of otherwise complex processes, in order to enable a model to fulfil its heuristic and explanatory function – i.e. to suggest schematically the relationship of

parts to whole. This process of simplification only has value, however, if the model, having served its limited purpose, is then seen in relation to the true complexity of the original – in this case, Adorno's 'antisystematic' theory. The reductive model may then be dispensed with. This use of the term 'model', derived from sociology, has some similarities with Max Weber's notion of the 'ideal type'. It is not to be understood in the sense of *Leitbild*, and is not prescriptive.

4 Adorno uses the term 'social fact' (*fait social*) in the sense given to it by Durkheim and other 'founding fathers' of sociology. John A. Rex writes: 'According to Durkheim, a fact is social only in so far as it exists externally to the individual and exercises constraint over him. . . . Unfortunately such facts are not directly observable. . . . The problem of theory and method in sociology . . . becomes one of showing how hypotheses about these external constraining forces can be treated. Such hypotheses will be sociological, i.e. about a social subject matter, provided that they make reference not simply to the biological and psychological constitution of an individual, but to the demands made upon that individual by social norms and other people.' (John A. Rex, entry: 'fact; social fact', in G. Duncan Mitchell (ed.), *A New Dictionary of Sociology* (London: Routledge & Kegan Paul, 1979), pp. 79–80.)

5 Adorno, *Aesthetic Theory*, p. 48. Cf. *GS* 7, p. 56.

6 Adorno, *Introduction to the Sociology of Music*, p. 213. Cf. *GS* 14, p. 416.

7 Adorno, *Philosophy of Modern Music*, p. 36. Cf. *GS* 12, p. 42.

8 *Ibid.*, pp. 36–7. Cf. original, p. 42.

9 Schoenberg, cited in Tibor Kneif, *Texte zur Musiksoziologie* (Cologne, 1975), p. 112. Translation in Wesley Blomster, 'Sociology of music: Adorno and beyond', *Telos* 28 (1976), p. 91.

10 Adorno, *Aesthetic Theory*, p. 255 (translation modified). Cf. *GS* 7, p. 266.

11 Adorno, 'On the problem of musical analysis', p. 181.

12 Adorno, *Aesthetic Theory*, p. 253. Cf. *GS* 7, p. 263.

13 *Ibid.*, p. 253. Cf. original, p. 264.

14 Adorno, 'On the problem of musical analysis', p. 178.

15 *Ibid.*, pp. 178–9.

16 Adorno, *Aesthetic Theory*, p. 253. Cf. *GS* 7, p. 264.

17 *Ibid.*

18 Adorno, 'On the social situation of music', p. 146. Cf. *GS* 18, pp. 752–3.

19 *Ibid.*, p. 146. Cf. original, p. 753.

20 Adorno, 'Zur gesellschaftlichen Lage der Musik', *GS* 18, p. 753 (my translation). Cf. 'On the social situation of music', p. 146.

21 Adorno, 'On the social situation of music', p. 146. Cf. *GS* 18, p. 753.

22 *Ibid.*

23 *Ibid.*

24 *Ibid.*, p. 147 (translation modified). Cf. original, p. 753.

25 *Ibid.*, pp. 147–8. Cf. *GS* 18, p. 753.

26 *Ibid.*, p. 147. Cf. original, pp. 753–4.

27 *Ibid.*, p. 147. Cf. original, p. 754.

28 *Ibid.*

29 *Ibid.*

30 *Ibid.*

31 *Ibid.*
32 *Ibid.*
33 *Ibid.*, p. 147. Cf. original, pp. 754–5.
34 *Ibid.*, p. 148. Cf. original, p. 756.
35 Adorno, 'Zur gesellschaftlichen Lage der Musik', *GS* 18, p. 756. Cf. 'On the social situation of music', pp. 148–9.
36 Adorno, 'On the social situation of music', p. 149 (translation modified). Cf. *GS* 18, p. 756.
37 *Ibid.*
38 Lucia Sziborsky, *Adornos Musikphilosophie: Genese, Konstitution, Pädagogische Perspektiven* (Munich: Wilhelm Fink Verlag, 1979), p. 132.
39 Adorno, 'Zum Problem der Reproduktion' (1925), *GS* 19, pp. 440–44.
40 Joan Allen Smith writes: 'Kolisch developed what he termed a methodology of performance involving extensive study of the score before realization could be attempted. He outlined this procedure as follows:

  1. *Study of the score*
    Macro-structure
    Retrace every thought process
    Motif vocabulary
  2. *Mental concept*
  3. *Instrumental preparation independently*
    Formation of 'raw material'
    Realization
  4. *Confrontation with concept*
  5. *Act of performance: Subconscious re-creation*
    Objective vs. Romantic

It must be stressed here that, although Kolisch's theories of performance arose from his association with Schoenberg and his concern for the performance of new music, he in no way envisaged his methodological contributions as being limited to music in that sphere.' (Smith, *Schoenberg and his Circle*, pp. 105–7.)

As Smith makes clear, Kolisch's approach, derived from his analysis and performance of Schoenberg's music and from his contact with Adorno, was applied retrospectively to all music of the Austro-German (and specifically the Viennese) tradition. This is very much in accord with Adorno's insistence that 'Bach can only be understood in the light of Schoenberg'.
41 Adorno, 'Zum Problem der Reproduktion', p. 140 (my translation).
42 *Ibid.*, p. 441.
43 *Ibid.*, pp. 441–2.
44 *Ibid.*, p. 442.
45 Adorno, *Aesthetic Theory*, p. 183. Cf. *GS* 7, p. 190.
46 *Ibid.*, p. 156. Cf. original, pp. 162–3.
47 *Ibid.*, p. 156. Cf. original, p. 163.
48 *Ibid.*
49 *Ibid.*, p. 146. Cf. original, p. 153.
50 *Ibid.*, pp. 146–7. Cf. original, pp. 153–4.
51 Adorno, *Introduction to the Sociology of Music*, p. 199. Cf. *GS* 14, p. 400.
52 *Ibid.*, p. 39. Cf. original, p. 219. See also Hans Heinrich Eggebrecht, 'Funktionale Musik', in *Musikalisches Denken* (Wilhelmshafen: Heinrichshofen's

Verlag, 1977), pp. 153–92.

53 Adorno, *Introduction to the Sociology of Music*, p. 41. Cf. *GS* 14, pp. 221–2.
54 *Ibid.*
55 Adorno, 'On the fetish character in music and the regression of listening', p. 284. Cf. *GS* 14, p. 31.
56 Adorno, *Introduction to the Sociology of Music*, p. 199. Cf. *GS* 14, p. 400.
57 *Ibid.*, p. 40. Cf. original, p. 220.
58 *Ibid.*
59 Adorno, *Dialectic of Enlightenment*, p. 120. Cf. *GS* 3, p. 141.
60 *Ibid.*, p. 121. Cf. original, p. 142.
61 *Ibid.*
62 *Ibid.*
63 Adorno, 'Culture industry reconsidered', trans. Anson G. Rabinbach, *New German Critique* 6 (1975), p. 12. Cf. 'Resumé über Kulturindustrie' (1963), in *Ohne Leitbild: Parva Aesthetica* (1967, 1968), *GS* 10.1, p. 337.
64 *Ibid.*
65 *Ibid.*, p. 14. Cf. original, p. 339.
66 *Ibid.*
67 *Ibid.*, p. 17. Cf. original, p. 343.
68 *Ibid.*, pp. 18–19. Cf. original, p. 345.
69 Adorno, 'On the social situation of music', p. 128. Cf. *GS* 18, p. 729.
70 Adorno, *Introduction to the Sociology of Music*, p. 23. Cf. *GS* 14, p. 201.
71 Adorno, 'On the social situation of music', p. 161. Cf. *GS* 18, p. 772.
72 See Adorno, *Introduction to the Sociology of Music*, p. 25. Cf. *GS* 14, pp. 203–4.
73 For criticisms of Adorno's critique of popular music see: Wesley Blomster, 'Sociology of music: Adorno and beyond', *Telos* 28 (1976), pp. 81–112, Wolfgang Sandner, 'Popularmusik als somatisches Stimulans. Adornos Kritik der "leichten Musik"', in *Adorno und die Musik*, ed. Otto Kolleritsch (Graz: Universal Edition, 1979), pp. 125–32. A particularly thorough critique is to be found in Richard Middleton, *Studying Popular Music* (Milton Keynes: Open University Press, 1990), especially pp. 34–63.
74 See Paddison, 'The critique criticised: Adorno and popular music'.
75 Adorno, *Introduction to the Sociology of Music*, pp. 33–4. Cf. original German, *GS* 14, p. 213.
76 *Ibid.*, p. 14. Cf. original, p. 192.
77 See Paddison, 'The critique criticised: Adorno and popular music', pp. 214–18. See also Special Section on Musicology: 'Popular music from Adorno ... to Zappa, in *Telos* 87 (1991), pp. 71–136.
78 Cf. Adorno, *Aesthetic Theory*, p. 24, where the translator has rendered *Entkunstung* as 'desubstantialization'. Cf. also Richard Wolin, 'The Deaestheticization of art: on Adorno's *Ästhetische Theorie*', *Telos* 41 (Fall 1979), pp. 105–27. 'De-aestheticization' would seem a more appropriate translation of *Entkunstung* than 'desubstantialization'. It remains problematic, however.
79 Adorno, *Aesthetic Theory*, p. 24. Cf. *GS* 7, p. 32.
80 Adorno, *Introduction to the Sociology of Music*, p. 197. Cf. *GS* 14, p. 398.
81 *Ibid.*, p. 1. Cf. original, p. 178.
82 *Ibid.*
83 *Ibid.*, p. 3. Cf. original, p. 180.

84 *Ibid.*
85 *Ibid.*
86 *Ibid.*
87 See Adorno, 'On the social situation of music', pp. 154–64. Cf. *GS* 18, pp. 763–77. This is not a 'typology' of listeners, but Adorno does prepare the ground in this essay for the versions of his typology which follow in later writings.
88 See Adorno, 'On the fetish character in music and the regression of listening', pp. 291ff. Cf. *GS* 14, pp. 41ff.
89 See Adorno, 'Anweisungen zum Hören neuer Musik' (1963), in *Der getreue Korrepetitor, GS* 15, pp. 188–248.
90 See Adorno, *Philosophy of Modern Music*, pp. 197ff. Cf. *GS* 12, pp. 179ff.
91 Adorno, *Introduction to the Sociology of Music*, p. 4. Cf. *GS* 14, p. 182.
92 See Adorno, 'Anweisungen zum Hören neuer Musik' (1963), *GS* 15, pp. 245–8.
93 *Ibid.*, p. 245 (my translation).
94 Adorno, *Introduction to the Sociology of Music*, p. 5. Cf. *GS* 14, p. 182.
95 *Ibid.*, p. 5 (translation modified). Cf. original, p. 182.
96 *Ibid.*, p. 5. Cf. original, p. 183.
97 *Ibid.*
98 *Ibid.*, p. 6. Cf. original, p. 183.
99 *Ibid.*, p. 6. Cf. original, p. 184.
100 Adorno, 'Vierhändig, noch einmal' (1933), *GS* 17, pp. 303–6.
101 See Adorno, *Introduction to the Sociology of Music*, pp. xi–xii. Cf. *GS* 14, pp. 175–7.
102 *Ibid.*, p. 15. Cf. *GS* 14, p. 193.
103 It is ironic that, while both Brecht and Eisler recognized, like Adorno, the narcotic and culinary function of music in capitalist society, they attributed this function to art music as a whole, preferring to use elements of popular music in their theatre works to achieve the *Verfremdungseffekt*. In an essay written in 1935 Brecht wrote: 'Most "advanced" music nowadays is still written for the concert hall. A single glance at the audiences who attend concerts is enough to show how impossible it is to make any political or philosophical use of music that produce such effects. We see entire rows of human beings transported into a peculiar doped state, wholly passive, sunk without trace, seemingly in the grip of a severe poisoning attack. Their tense, congealed gaze shows that these people are the helpless and involuntary victims of the unchecked lurchings of their emotions. Trickles of sweat prove how such excesses exhaust them. The worst gangster film treats its audience more like thinking beings. Music is cast in the role of Fate, as the exceedingly complex, wholly unanalysable fate of this period of the grisliest, most deliberate exploitation of man by man. Such music has nothing but purely culinary ambitions left. It seduces the listener into an enervating, because unproductive, act of enjoyment. No number of refinements can convince me that its social function is any different from that of the Broadway burlesques.' (Brecht, 'Über die Verwendung von Musik für ein episches Theater', in *Schriften zum Theater* (1957); translated as 'On the use of music in an epic theatre', in *Brecht on Theatre: The Development of an Aesthetic*, trans. John Willett (London: Eyre Methuen, 1964, 1973), p. 89.)

104 Adorno, *Introduction to the Sociology of Music*, p. 8. Cf. *GS* 14, p. 186.
105 *Ibid.*, p. 7. Cf. original, p. 185.
106 Adorno, 'Husserl and the problem of Idealism' (original in English), *The Journal of Philosophy* 37/1 (January 1940), *GS* 20.1, p. 129.
107 Adorno, *Ästhetische Theorie, GS* 7, p. 153 (my translation). Cf. *Aesthetic Theory*, p. 146.
108 Adorno, *Aesthetic Theory*, p. 177. Cf. *GS* 7, p. 184.
109 *Ibid.*
110 *Ibid.*, p. 178. Cf. original, p. 185.
111 *Ibid.*, p. 179. Cf. original, p. 185.
112 Georg Lukács, *History and Class Consciousness*, p. 163.

6 THE HISTORICAL DIALECTIC OF MUSICAL MATERIAL
  1 Adorno, *Ästhetische Theorie, GS* 7, p. 272 (my translation). Cf. *Aesthetic Theory*, p. 261.
  2 Adorno, *Philosophie der neuen Musik, GS* 12, p. 44 (my translation). Cf. *Philosophy of Modern Music*, p. 43.
  3 See Michael de la Fontaine, 'Der Begriff der künstlerischen Erfahrung bei Theodor W. Adorno' (diss., J. W. Goethe-Universität, Frankfurt/Main, 1977).
  4 See also Carl Dahlhaus, 'Progress and the avant garde', in *Schoenberg and the New Music*, trans. Derrick Puffett and Alfred Clayton (Cambridge: Cambridge University Press, 1987), p. 19.
  5 Friedrich Nietzsche, *The Genealogy of Morals*, p. 250. Cf. *Zur Genealogie der Moral*, p. 102.
  6 Adorno, *Dialectic of Enlightenment*, p. 93. Cf. *GS* 3, p. 112.
  7 *Ibid.*, p. 19. Cf. original, p. 35.
  8 E. J. Hobsbawm writes: 'Not until the 1848 revolutions destroyed the romantic hopes of the great rebirth of man, did self-contained aestheticism come into its own. The evolution of such 'forty-eighters' as Baudelaire and Flaubert illustrates this political as well as aesthetic change, and Flaubert's *Sentimental Education* remains its best literary record. Only in countries like Russia, in which the disillusion of 1848 had not occurred (if only because 1848 had not occurred), did the arts continue to remain socially committed or preoccupied as before.' (Hobsbawm, *The Age of Revolution 1789–1848* (London: Weidenfeld & Nicolson, 1962; Sphere/Cardinal, 1988, 1989), p. 325.)
  9 Adorno, like Walter Benjamin, dates the rise of modernism from Baudelaire in the 1840s. See Adorno, *Vorlesungen zur Ästhetik 1967–68* (Zürich: H. Mayer Verlag, 1973), pp. 60–61.
  10 de la Fontaine, 'Der Begriff der künstlerischen Erfahrung', p. 65 (my translation).
  11 Lambert Zuidervaart, 'Refractions: truth in Adorno's *Aesthetic Theory*', p. 33.
  12 Dahlhaus, *Foundations of Music History*, p. 31.
  13 Adorno, 'Tradition' (1960), in *Dissonanzen* (3rd edn, 1963), *GS* 14, p. 133 (my translation).
  14 Adorno, 'Ideen zur Musiksoziologie', *GS* 16, pp. 13–14.
  15 *Ibid.*, p. 14.
  16 Cf. Peter Bürger, *Theorie der Avantgarde* (Frankfurt/Main: Suhrkamp Verlag,

1974). Translated as: *Theory of the Avant-Garde*, trans. Michael Shaw, Foreword by Jochen Schulte-Gasse (Manchester: Manchester University Press, 1984).

17 See Adorno, 'Zur Vorgeschichte der Reihenkomposition' [1958], in *Klang-figuren* (1959), *GS* 16 (1978), pp. 68–84.

18 Adorno, 'Bach defended against his devotees', in *Prisms*, p. 135. Cf. 'Bach gegen seine Liebhaber verteidigt' (1951), *GS* 10.1, p. 138.

19 *Ibid.*

20 *Ibid.*, p. 141. Cf. original, p. 145.

21 *Ibid.*, p. 142. Cf. original, p. 146.

22 Adorno, 'Ideen zur Musiksoziologie', p. 20 (my translation).

23 *Ibid.*

24 de la Fontaine, 'Der Begriff der künstlerischen Erfahrung', p. 74.

25 *Ibid.*, p. 72.

26 Cf. *Ibid.*

27 Adorno, 'Bach defended against his devotees', p. 138. Cf. *GS* 10.1, p. 141.

28 *Ibid.*, p. 139. Cf. original, p. 142.

29 *Ibid.*, p. 139. Cf. original p. 143.

30 de la Fontaine, 'Der Begriff der künstlerischen Erfahrung', pp. 73–4.

31 Adorno, 'Bach defended against his devotees', p. 139. Cf. *GS* 10.1, p. 143.

32 *Ibid.*

33 *Ibid.*

34 Cf. Wolfgang Gramer, *Musik und Verstehen*, p. 74.

35 Adorno, 'Bach gegen seine Liebhaber verteidigt', *GS* 10.1, p. 147. Cf. 'Bach defended against his devotees', p. 142.

36 Adorno, 'Bach defended against his devotees', p. 142 (translation modified). Cf. *GS* 10.1, p. 147.

37 Adorno, 'Johann Sebastian Bach: Präludium und Fuge cis-moll aus dem ersten Teil des Wohltemperierten Klaviers', *Vossische Zeitung* (3 March 1934). *GS* 18, pp. 179–82.

38 Carl Dahlhaus writes: 'The relatively invariant facts that make up the framework of history are ... , to the historian who is more than a mere archivist, interesting less for their own sake than for the function they fulfil in vindicating or refuting competing interpretative systems. To put it bluntly, historical facts have no other reason for being than to substantiate historical narratives or descriptions of historical systems, unless it is to serve the negative purpose of revealing flaws in the opinions of earlier historians.' Dahlhaus, *Foundations of Music History*, p. 43.

39 Adorno, 'Ideen zur Musiksoziologie', p. 21 (my translation).

40 Cf. Adorno, *Aesthetic Theory*, p. 300. Cf. *GS* 7, p. 313.

41 Adorno, *Introduction to the Sociology of Music*, p. 208. Cf. *GS* 14, p. 410.

42 *Ibid.*

43 *Ibid.*

44 Adorno, *Aesthetic Theory*, p. 4. Cf. *GS* 7, p. 12.

45 Adorno, *Introduction to the Sociology of Music*, p. 208. Cf. *GS* 14, p. 410.

46 Cf. Adorno, *Dialectic of Enlightenment*, p. 124. Cf. *GS* 3, p. 145.

47 Adorno, *Introduction to the Sociology of Music*, p. 208. Cf. *GS* 14, p. 410.

48 *Ibid.*, p. 209. Cf. original, p. 411.

49 *Ibid.*
50 *Ibid.*
51 *Ibid.*
52 *Ibid.*, p. 214 (translation modified). Cf. original, p. 416.
53 Cf. de la Fontaine, 'Der Begriff der künstlerischen Erfahrung', p. 76.
54 Adorno, *Philosophy of Modern Music*, p. 55 (translation modified). Cf. *GS* 12, p. 54 (my translation).
55 Adorno, 'On the problem of musical analysis', p. 175.
56 Adorno, *Introduction to the Sociology of Music*, pp. 209–10 (translation modified). Cf. *GS* 14, pp. 411–12.
57 Cf. de la Fontaine, 'Der Begriff der künstlerischen Erfahrung', p. 76.
58 Adorno, *Philosophy of Modern Music*, pp. 73–4. Cf. *GS* 12, p. 69. See also de la Fontaine, 'Der Begriff der künstlerischen Erfahrung, p. 76.
59 Adorno, *Philosophy of Modern Music*, pp. 73–4. Cf. *GS* 12, p. 69.
60 de la Fontaine, 'Der Begriff der künstlerischen Erfahrung', p. 76 (my translation).
61 Adorno, *Introduction to the Sociology of Music*, p. 210 (translation modified). Cf. *GS* 14, p. 248.
62 *Ibid.*
63 Adorno, 'On the problem of musical analysis', p. 180.
64 *Ibid.*, p. 183.
65 de la Fontaine, 'Der Begriff der künstlerischen Erfahrung', p. 77.
66 Adorno, 'On the problem of musical analysis', p. 183.
67 Adorno, *Aesthetic Theory*, p. 303. Cf. original, *GS* 7, p. 316.
68 Adorno, 'Ludwig van Beethoven: Sechs Bagatellen für Klavier, op. 126' [1934], published posthumously in *GS* 18, pp. 185–8.
69 Adorno, 'Spätstil Beethovens', *Der Auftakt: Blätter für die tschecho-slowakische Republik* 17 (Heft 5/6, 1937); republished in *Moments musicaux* (1964). *GS* 17, pp. 13–17.
70 Adorno, 'Spätstil Beethovens', *GS* 17, pp. 16–17.
71 Adorno, 'Ludwig van Beethoven: Sechs Bagatellen für Klavier, op. 126', *GS* 18, pp. 185–6.
72 Adorno, 'Spätstil Beethovens', *GS* 17, p. 17 (my translation).
73 *Ibid.* (my translation).
74 Adorno, 'Verfremdetes Hauptwerk: Zur Missa Solemnis', *Neue Deutsche Hefte* (Heft 54, 1959); republished in *Moments musicaux* (1964). *GS* 17, pp. 145–61. Translated as: 'Alienated masterpiece: the Missa Solemnis', trans. Duncan Smith, *Telos* 28 (1976), pp. 113–24.
75 Adorno, 'Verfremdetes Hauptwerk: Zur Missa Solemnis', *GS* 17, p. 155 (my translation). Cf. 'Alienated masterpiece', p. 120.
76 *Ibid.*, p. 159 (my translation). Cf. 'Alienated masterpiece', p. 123.
77 Carl Dahlhaus, 'Zu Adornos Beethoven-Kritik', in *Adorno und die Musik*, ed. Otto Kolleritsch (Graz: Universal Edition, 1979), p. 171 (my translation).
78 *Ibid.*, p. 175.
79 Adorno, 'On the problem of musical analysis', p. 176.
80 Adorno, *Aesthetic Theory*, p. 279. Cf. *GS* 7, p. 291.
81 *Ibid.*
82 Adorno, 'Ideen zur Musiksoziologie', pp. 20–21 (my translation).

83 Adorno, *Introduction to the Sociology of Music*, p. 195. Cf. *GS* 14, p. 396.
84 *Ibid.*, p. 196. Cf. original, p. 396.
85 Adorno, 'Music and technique', trans. Wesley Blomster, *Telos* 32 (Summer 1977), p. 82. Cf. 'Musik und Technik', *GS* 16, p. 232.
86 'The leitmotiv has a history that goes back via Berlioz to the programme music of the seventeenth century, when a generally binding musical logic did not yet exist, and its origins here only begin to make sense in the context of allegory rather than the childish games with echo-effects and the like.' Adorno, *In Search of Wagner*, p. 45. Cf. *GS* 13, p. 43.
87 See Adorno, 'Music and technique'. Cf. 'Musik und Technik,' *GS* 16.
88 Adorno, 'Richard Strauss: born June 11, 1864', trans. Samuel and Shierry Weber, *Perspectives of New Music* (Fall–Winter 1965), pp. 20–21. Cf. 'Richard Strauss: Zum hundertsten Geburtstag: 11. Juni 1964', *GS* 16, p. 573.
89 Adorno, 'Music and technique', p. 82. Cf. *GS* 16, p. 232.
90 This discussion of Wagner draws mostly on Adorno's main work on the composer, *Versuch über Wagner* (Frankfurt/Main and Berlin: Suhrkamp Verlag, 1952). Also referred to are sections from *Philosophie der neuen Musik*, *Composing for the Films*, and the talk 'On the problem of musical analysis'. Other texts by Adorno on Wagner are: 'Notiz über Wagner' (1933), *GS* 18, pp. 204–9; 'Selbstanzeige des Essaybuches "Versuch über Wagner"' (1952), *GS* 13, pp. 504–8; 'Zur Partitur des "Parsifal"' (1956), *GS* 17, pp. 47–51; 'Wagners Aktualität' (1964), *GS* 16, pp. 543–64; 'Nachschrift zu einer Wagner-Diskussion' (1964), pp. 665–70; and 'Wagner und Bayreuth' (1966/7), *GS* 18, pp. 210–25.
91 Adorno, *In Search of Wagner* p. 66 (translation modified). Cf. *GS* 13, p. 63.
92 *Ibid.*, p. 137. Cf. *GS* 13, p. 128.
93 *Ibid.*, p. 54. Cf. original, p. 51.
94 *Ibid.*
95 *Ibid.*
96 In *Komposition für den Film* Adorno defends Wagner's use of the technique of leitmotif against its appropriation by film music (see Adorno and Hanns Eisler, *Komposition für den Film, GS* 15, pp. 15–16. Cf. *Composing for the Films*, pp. 4–6). In *Versuch über Wagner*, however, he suggests that the techniques of Hollywood film music are already implied in Wagner's *Gesamtkunstwerk* (see Adorno, *Versuch über Wagner*, pp. 102–3. Cf. *In Search of Wagner*, pp. 107–8).
97 Adorno, *Versuch über Wagner, GS* 13, p. 82 (my translation). Cf. *In Search of Wagner*, p. 85.
98 Adorno, *In Search of Wagner*, p. 97. Cf. *GS* 13, p. 92.
99 Cf. Walter Benjamin, *Reflections*, trans. Edmund Jephcott (New York: and London: Harcourt Brace Jovanovich, 1978), p. 152. Also Rose, *The Melancholy Science*, pp. 41–2.
100 Adorno, *In Search of Wagner*, p. 91. Cf. *GS* 13, p. 87.
101 *Ibid.*, p. 86.
102 Marx, *Capital*, vol. I (Harmondsworth: Penguin, 1976), p. 165. See also Adorno, *In Search of Wagner*, translator's note p. 85.
103 Adorno, *In Search of Wagner*, pp. 137–8. Cf. *GS* 13, p. 129.
104 Cf. Marc Jiminez, *Adorno: art, idéologie et théorie de l'art* (Paris: Union

Générale d'Editions, 1973), pp. 60–61.

105 Adorno, *In Search of Wagner*, p. 114. Cf. *GS* 13, p. 109.

106 *Ibid.*, p. 115. Cf. original, p. 110.

107 See Dahlhaus's criticism of Adorno's use of Lorenz in Carl Dahlhaus, 'Soziologische Dechiffrierung von Musik. Zu Theodor W. Adornos Wagnerkritik', in *International Review of Music, Aesthetics and Sociology*, 2 (1970), p. 141.

108 Adorno, *Versuch über Wagner, GS* 13, p. 46 (my translation). Cf. *In Search of Wagner*, p. 48.

109 Adorno, 'On the problem of musical analysis', p. 179.

110 *Ibid.*, pp. 179–80.

111 Adorno, *In Search of Wagner*, p. 33 (translation modified). Cf. *GS* 13, p. 31.

112 *Ibid.*

113 Cf. Dahlhaus, 'Soziologische Dechiffrierung von Musik', p. 140.

114 Adorno, *In Search of Wagner*, p. 33. Cf. *GS* 13, p. 31.

115 *Ibid.*, p. 34. Cf. original, p. 31.

116 Adorno, *Versuch über Wagner, GS* 13, p. 32 (my translation). Cf. *In Search of Wagner*, p. 34.

117 Adorno, *In Search of Wagner*, pp. 34–5 (translation modified). Cf. *GS* 13, p. 32.

118 Dahlhaus, 'Soziologische Dechiffrierung von Musik', p. 142 (my translation).

119 *Ibid.*, p. 144.

120 *Ibid.*, p. 146.

121 Adorno, *Philosophie der neuen Musik, GS* 12, p. 69. Cf. *Philosophy of Modern Music*, pp. 73–4.

122 Cf. Adorno, 'On the problem of musical analysis', pp. 183–4.

123 Benjamin, *Reflections*, p. 152.

124 Adorno, *Minima Moralia*, p. 214. Cf. *GS* 4, pp. 242–3.

125 *Ibid.*, pp. 214–15. Cf. original, p. 243.

126 Adorno, 'Eduard Steuermanns Brahms-Ausgabe', *Anbruch* 14 (Heft 1 January 1932), pp. 9–11. Republished in *GS* 18, pp. 195–9.

127 Adorno, 'Brahms aktuell' [1934], published posthumously in *Adorno-Noten*, ed. Rolf Tiedemann (Berlin, 1984), pp. 34–9. *GS* 18, pp. 200–203.

128 Schoenberg, 'Brahms the progressive' [1947], in *Style and Idea*, pp. 398–441.

129 Cf. Adorno, *Philosophy of Modern Music*, pp. 56–8. Cf. *GS* 12, pp. 59–61.

130 Cf. Adorno, *Introduction to the Sociology of Music*, pp. 63–5. Cf. *GS* 14, pp. 245–7.

131 Cf. Adorno, 'Brahms aktuell', *GS* 18, p. 201.

132 *Ibid.*, pp. 201–2 (my translation).

133 Adorno, *Philosophy of Modern Music*, p. 57 (translation modified). Cf. *GS* 12, p. 59.

134 *Ibid.*

135 Adorno, *Introduction to the Sociology of Music*, pp. 63–4. Cf. *GS* 14, pp. 245–6.

136 Cf. Adorno, 'Brahms aktuell', *GS* 18, p. 202.

137 *Ibid.*

138 Rose Rosengard Subotnik, 'The historical structure: Adorno's "French" model for the criticism of nineteenth-century music', *Nineteenth-Century Music* 2/1 (July 1978), p. 44.

139 Adorno, *Philosophy of Modern Music*, p. 149n. Cf. *GS* 12, p. 139n.

140 *Ibid.*

141 Cf. Adorno, *Aesthetic Theory*, p. 218. Cf. *GS* 7, p. 227.

142 Cf. Adorno, *Philosophy of Modern Music*, p. 189. Cf. *GS* 12, p. 172.

143 In *Philosophie der neuen Musik* Adorno writes: 'The undynamic nature of French music might well be traced back to its arch-enemy Wagner, who was accused of an insatiable appetite for dynamics. In Wagner's works progression is, in many places, actually mere displacement. Debussy's motivic technique is derived from this source; it consists of an undeveloped repetition of the simple tonal successions. Stravinsky's calculated and sterile melismata are the direct descendants of Debussy; they are almost physical. They allegedly signify "nature" – as do many of the Wagnerian melismata – and Stravinsky remained faithful to his belief in such primeval phenomena, even if he hoped to achieve this precisely by avoiding the expression of them.' (Adorno, *Philosophy of Modern Music*, p. 189. Cf. *GS* 12, p. 173.)

144 Adorno, *Philosophy of Modern Music*, p. 188. Cf. *GS* 12, p. 171.

145 Adorno, 'On the social situation of music', p. 157. Cf. *GS* 18, pp. 767–8.

146 This discussion of Mahler draws mainly on Adorno's main work on the composer. Other texts on Mahler by Adorno are: 'Mahler heute' (1930), *GS* 18, pp. 226–34; 'Marginalien zu Mahler' (1936), *GS* 18, pp. 235–40; 'Aus dem Ersten Mahler-Vortrag' [1960], *GS* 18, pp. 584–7; 'Zweiter Mahler-Vortrag' [1960], *GS* 18, pp. 588–603; 'Dritter Mahler-Vortrag' [1960], *GS* 18, pp. 604–22; 'Mahlers Aktualität' (1960), *GS* 18, pp. 241–3; 'Mahler: Wiener Gedenkrede' (1960), *GS*, 16, pp. 323–50; 'Zu einer imaginären Auswahl von Liedern Gustav Mahlers' [1964], *GS* 17, pp. 189–97; 'Zu einem Streitgespräch über Mahler' (1968), *GS* 18, pp. 244–50.

147 Adorno, *Mahler: Eine musikalische Physiognomik*, *GS* 13, p. 168 (my translation).

148 *Ibid.*, p. 164.

149 *Ibid.*, pp. 188–9.

150 Cf. Dahlhaus, 'Adornos Begriff des musikalischen Materials', *Zur Terminologie der Musik des 20. Jahrhunderts* (*Bericht über das zweite Kolloquium*, 9–10 März, 1972), ed. H. H. Eggebrecht (Stuttgart, 1974), p. 13.

151 Adorno, *Mahler: Eine musikalische Physiognomik*, *GS* 13, pp. 241–2 (my translation).

152 Adorno, *Philosophie der neuen Musik*, *GS* 12, p. 139n. (my translation). Cf. *Philosophy of Modern Music*, p. 150n.

153 Adorno, *Aesthetic Theory*, p. 21. Cf. *GS* 7, p. 29.

154 *Ibid.*, p. 39. Cf. original, p. 47.

155 Adorno, *Mahler: Eine musikalische Physiognomik*, *GS* 13, pp. 162–3 (my translation).

156 Adorno, *Aesthetic Theory*, p. 396. Cf. *GS* 7, p. 420.

157 Cf. J. Frow, 'Mediation and metaphor: Adorno and the sociology of art', *Clio* 12/1 (1982), pp. 37–66.

7 THE DISINTEGRATION OF MUSICAL MATERIAL

1 Adorno, *Aesthetic Theory*, p. 23 (translation modified). Cf. *GS* 7, p. 31.

2 Michael Rosen, 'Critical theory: between ideology and philosophy', in *The Need for Interpretation*, ed. Sollace Mitchell and Michael Rosen (London:

Athlone Press, 1983), p. 99.

3 Jay, *Adorno*, p. 162.

4 The most striking case of 'misunderstanding' Adorno's *Philosophie der neuen Musik* is Schoenberg's. In a letter to Stuckenschmidt on 5 December 1949 he wrote: 'So modern music has a philosophy – it would be enough if it had a philosopher. He attacks me quite vehemently in it. Another disloyal person . . . I have never been able to bear the fellow . . . now I know that he has clearly never liked my music . . . it is disgusting, by the way, how he treats Stravinsky. I am certainly no admirer of Stravinsky, although I like a piece of his here and there very much – but one should not write like that'. H. H. Stuckenschmidt, *Schoenberg: His Life, World and Work*, trans. Humphrey Searle (London: Calder, 1977), p. 508.

5 Cf. Giselher Schubert, 'Adornos Auseinandersetzung mit der Zwölftontechnik Schönbergs', *Archiv für Musikwissenschaft* 46/3 (1989), p. 254.

6 Cf. Jürgen Habermas, 'Dialectics of rationalization: an interview', *Telos* 49 (Fall 1981), pp. 5–31. See also James L. Marsh, 'Adorno's critique of Stravinsky', *New German Critique* 28 (Winter 1983), pp. 164–5.

7 Adorno, *Philosophie der neuen Musik, GS* 12, p. 13 (my translation). Cf. *Philosophy of Modern Music*, p. 3.

8 Adorno, *Philosophy of Modern Music*, p. 57 (translation modified). Cf. *GS* 12, p. 59.

9 *Ibid.*, pp. 67–8. Cf. original p. 68.

10 *Ibid.*, p. 68. Cf. original pp. 68–9.

11 Cf. Adorno, 'On the social situation of music', p. 141. Cf. *GS* 18, p. 746.

12 *Ibid.*, p. 141 (translation modified). Cf. original p. 746.

13 Adorno, *Philosophy of Modern Music*, p. 175. Cf. *GS* 12, pp. 160–61.

14 *Ibid.*, p. 136. Cf. original, p. 127.

15 Alfred Huber, 'Adornos Polemik gegen Strawinsky', *Melos* 38/9 (1971), p. 360 (my translation).

16 Adorno, 'Strawinsky: Ein dialektisches Bild', *Forum* (June/July/August 1962). Republished in revised version in *Quasi una Fantasia* (1963), *GS* 16, pp. 382–409.

17 Bürger, 'The decline of the modern age', *Telos* 62 (Winter 1984–5), p. 119. Cf. original German, 'Das Altern der Moderne', in *Adorno-Konferenz 1983*, pp. 179–80.

18 Adorno. *Philosophy of Modern Music*, pp. 4–5. Cf. *GS* 12, p. 14.

19 Adorno, 'Über das gegenwärtige Verhältnis von Philosophie und Musik', *GS* 18, p. 165 (my translation).

20 Adorno, 'Mißverständnisse', *Melos* 17/3 (1950), *GS* 12, pp. 203–6.

21 Walther Harth, 'Die Dialektik des musikalischen Fortschritts: Zu Theodor W. Adornos "Philosophie der neuen Musik"', *Melos* 16/12 (1949), pp. 333ff.

22 Adorno, 'Mißverständnisse', *GS* 12, p. 203 (my translation).

23 Dahlhaus, 'Adornos Begriff des musikalischen Materials', p. 13 (my translation).

24 Bürger, *Theory of the Avant-Garde*, trans. Michael Shaw (Manchester: Manchester University Press, 1984; original German 1974), p. iii.

25 Adorno, *Aesthetic Theory*, p. 5. Cf. *GS* 7, p. 13.

26 Adorno, 'Das Altern der neuen Musik', in *Dissonanzen: Musik in der*

verwalteten Welt (1956), *GS* 14, pp. 143–67. Translated as: 'Modern music is growing old', trans. (from a French version) Rollo Myers, *The Score* (December 1956), pp. 18–29.

27 Adorno, *Aesthetic Theory*, p. 359. Cf. original German, *GS* 7, p. 376.

28 Eisler [and Adorno], *Composing for the Films*, pp. 82–3.

29 Adorno, 'On the social situation of music', p. 128. Cf. *GS* 18.

30 Heinz-Klaus Metzger, 'Europe's opera: notes on John Cage's *Europeras 1 & 2*', trans. Jeremy Gaines and Doris Jones, in *John Cage: Europeras 1 & 2*', ed. Heinz-Klaus Metzger, Rainer Riehn and John Cage (Frankfurt/Main: Oper Frankfurt, 1987) (no page numbers).

31 Cf. Paddison, 'The critique criticised: Adorno and popular music', p. 215.

32 Adorno, 'On the fetish character in music and the regression of listening', p. 298. Cf. *GS* 14.

33 Heinz-Klaus Metzger, 'Just who is growing old?', *Die Reihe*, 4 (Pennsylvania: Theodor Presser, 1960), pp. 63–80

34 Metzger, 'Europe's opera: notes on John Cage's *Europeras 1 & 2*' (no page numbers).

35 In *Silence* Cage writes: 'Giving up control so that sounds can be sounds (they are not men: they are sounds)...', *Silence* (London: Marion Boyars, 1968), p. 72.

36 Dahlhaus, *Schoenberg and the New Music*, p. 277.

37 Metzger, 'Europe's opera: notes on John Cage's *Europeras 1 & 2*' (no page numbers).

38 Adorno, *Philosophy of Modern Music*, p. 159. Cf. *GS* 12, p. 147.

39 Adorno, 'Versuch, das Endspiel zu verstehen', in *Noten zur Literatur* II, *GS* 11, p. 313.

40 *Ibid.*, p. 283.

41 Adorno, *Aesthetic Theory*, p. 361 (translation modified). Cf. *GS* 7, p. 379.

42 Samuel Beckett, cited in Deirdre Bair, *Samuel Beckett: A Biography* (London: Jonathan Cape, 1978; Picador/Pan, 1980), pp. 441–2.

43 'The concept of musical material is a compositional/technical and simultaneously an aesthetic, historical/philosophical and sociological category... The different moments which are included within the concept of material flow into one another. In Adorno's aesthetic theory, which sets itself in opposition to the scientific division of disciplines, compositional/technical arguments are turned, without further ado, into historical/philosophical or sociological ones, without clear boundaries being drawn.' Dahlhaus, 'Adornos Begriff des musikalischen Materials', p. 13.

44 Adorno, *Introduction to the Sociology of Music*, p. 62. Cf. *GS* 14, p. 244.

Bibliography

At the time of his death in 1969 many of Adorno's published works were unavailable – either because the editions in which they had originally appeared or been collected were out of print, or because the large number of shorter texts, occasional articles, concert and book reviews, scripts of radio talks, magazine and newspaper interviews, record liner notes, etc., which he had produced every year between 1920 and 1969 had simply never been catalogued. There was, furthermore, a mass of important unpublished work, some of it (like the *Ästhetische Theorie*) unfinished.

Most of Adorno's writings have now appeared in the *Gesammelte Schriften*, edited by Rolf Tiedemann in collaboration with Gretel Adorno, Susan Buck-Morss and Klaus Schultz (Frankfurt/Main: Suhrkamp, 1970–86). This has been a massive project, and one carried out with impressive thoroughness. The edition has now reached Volume 20, which consists of miscellaneous shorter writings and which was published in two parts in 1986. Of these twenty volumes – a number of which are double volumes – nearly half are made up of texts on music. However, a number of previously unpublished (and incomplete) texts on music have yet to appear. These texts had originally been announced as forthcoming, but with no date of publication given (they were listed in the loose-leaf *Dossier* issued by the publishers in 1978 as 'Band 21 [= Fragmente 1]: Beethoven. Philosophie der Musik; Band 22 [= Fragmente 2]: Theorie der musikalischen Reproduktion; Band 23 [= Fragmente 3]: Current of Music. Elements of a Radio Theory', see *Theodor W. Adorno, Gesammelte Schriften, Dossier* (Frankfurt/Main: Suhrkamp Verlag, 1978, pages unnumbered)). As well as these there are many 'semi-improvised' talks which Adorno gave, particularly in the 1950s and 1960s, which have survived mainly as tape recordings, and typescripts and notes for his lecture series at Frankfurt University.

The situation regarding the remaining unpublished material in the Adorno-Nachlass (the Adorno Estate) has been clarified by Rolf Tiedemann in his 'Editorisches Nachwort' to *GS* 20.2. There Tiedemann explains that this, the final volume (1986) of the *Gesammelte Schriften*, also acts as the first publication of what has now becomed the *Theodor W. Adorno Archiv*, set up in 1985 by the Hamburger Stiftung zur Förderung von Wissenschaft und Kultur (now responsible for the Adorno Estate – see *GS* 20.2, p. 830). The plan for the 'Editionen des Theodor W. Adorno Archivs' includes the editing and publication of what is clearly still a very considerable amount of unpublished material in the Nachlass. This, we are told, has been identified as falling into seven main categories: (i) fragments of remaining books (3 vols: *Beethoven: Philosophie der Musik* (1993); *Theorie der musikalischen Reproduktion; Current of Music. Elements of a Radio Theory*); (ii) philosophical diaries (*c.* 5 vols.); (iii) poetical experiments (1 vol.); (iv) lectures (16 vols.); (v) improvised talks (*c.* 2 vols.); (vi) discussions and interviews (*c.* 3 vols.); and (vii) letters. When the Archiv has completed the task of editing and publishing this remaining material – and looking very much towards the future – work will then begin on a definitive *Gesamtausgabe* of Adorno's work (see *GS* 20.2, pp. 831–2).

There are a number of useful annotated bibliographies and bibliographical articles to which I am indebted in drawing up the present bibliography. The detailed bibliographical information contained in Rolf Tiedemann's editorial postscripts to the *Gesammelte Schriften* has been indispensable. With the completion of the *Gesammelte Schriften* this bibliographical information has come to supersede Klaus Schultz, 'Vorläufige Bibliographie der Schriften Theodor W. Adornos', in *Theodor W. Adorno zum Gedächtnis: eine Sammlung*, edited by Hermann Schweppenhäuser (Frankfurt/Main: Suhrkamp Verlag, 1971), pp. 178–239. A valuable selected bibliography, particularly focusing on selected published works written from 1920 to 1938 and providing a chronological listing, is to be found in Susan Buck-Morss, *The Origin of Negative Dialectics: Theodor W. Adorno, Walter Benjamin, and the Frankfurt Institute* (Sussex: Harvester Press, 1977), pp. 307–22. For an extensive bibliography of Adorno's works as published up to 1977, which also includes a selection of important secondary sources published in German and Italian, see Carlo Pettazzi, 'Kommentierte Bibliographie zu Th. W. Adorno', in *Theodor W. Adorno*, edited by Heinz Ludwig Arnold (Munich: Edition Text + Kritik, 1977), pp. 176–91. For a thorough survey of the reception of *Ästhetische Theorie* there is Peter Christian Lang, 'Kommentierte Auswahlbibliographie 1969–1979', in *Materialien zur ästhetischen Theorie Th. W. Adornos: Konstruktion der Moderne*, edited by Burkhardt Lindner and W. Martin Lüdke (Frankfurt/Main: Suhrkamp Verlag, 1979), pp. 509–56. And finally, for a comprehensive chronological list of Adorno's published books (including the collections of articles), together with an extensive list of writings on Adorno in German and English, there is René Görtzen, 'Theodor W. Adorno: Vorläufige Bibliographie seiner Schriften und der Sekundärliteratur', in *Adorno-Konferenz 1983*, edited by Ludwig von Friedeburg and Jürgen Habermas (Frankfurt/Main: Suhrkamp Verlag, 1983), pp. 402–71.

The present bibliography is divided into six sections. Under Section 1.1 Primary sources is provided a list of the volumes which make up the *Gesammelte Schriften*. This is followed, in Section 1.2, by a list of Adorno's main texts on music, giving their original date and place of publication as well as – where possible – references to their position in the *Gesammelte Schriften* (*GS*), together with details of available published translations into English. The purpose of this section, as well as being to acknowledge sources consulted in writing this study, is to provide a comprehensive and chronological reference list of Adorno's published texts on music. It includes a list of the posthumously published texts on music, most of which appeared for the first time in later volumes of the *Gesammelte Schriften*. It excludes, however, most of his numerous shorter concert, book and score reviews, as these have not been drawn on here to any great extent, and anyway are listed separately and chronologically (unlike the bulk of the musical texts) in Rolf Tiedemann's 'Editorisches Nachwort' to *GS* 19 (1984), pp. 648–52. In Section 1.3 a list of other

Adorno texts consulted is provided – writings in the areas of philosophy, sociology and social theory, psychology and psychoanalysis, literary and art criticism, together with available translations. And finally, in Section 1.4, is provided a list of other primary sources consulted. The secondary sources are divided into two parts: first, Section 2.1, specialist studies and articles on Adorno and the Frankfurt School; and secondly, Section 2.2, more general sources.

1 PRIMARY SOURCES

1.1 T. W. ADORNO: COLLECTED WRITINGS

Adorno, T. W., *Gesammelte Schriften*, 20 vols., ed. Rolf Tiedemann in collaboration with Gretel Adorno, Susan Buck-Morss and Klaus Schultz (Frankfurt/Main: Suhrkamp Verlag, 1970–86). The abbreviation *GS* is used below and in the Notes.

Vol. 1:	*Philosophische Frühschriften* (1973)
Vol. 2:	*Kierkegaard: Konstruktion des Ästhetischen* (1979)
Vol. 3:	*Dialektik der Aufklärung: Philosophische Fragmente* (with Max Horkheimer) (1981)
Vol. 4:	*Minima Moralia: Reflexionen aus dem beschädigten Leben* (1980)
Vol. 5:	*Zur Metakritik der Erkenntnistheorie. Drei Studien zu Hegel*, ed. Gretel Adorno and Rolf Tiedemann (1970; 2nd edn 1975)
Vol. 6:	*Negative Dialektik. Jargon der Eigentlichkeit: Zur deutschen Ideologie* (1973; 2nd edn 1977)
Vol. 7:	*Ästhetische Theorie*, ed. Gretel Adorno and Rolf Tiedemann (1970; 2nd edn 1972)
Vol. 8:	*Soziologische Schriften I* (1972)
Vol. 9.1:	*Soziologische Schriften II* (Part 1), ed. Susan Buck-Morss and Rolf Tiedemann (1975)
Vol. 9.2:	*Soziologische Schriften II* (Part 2), ed. Susan Buck-Morss and Rolf Tiedemann (1975)
Vol. 10.1:	*Kulturkritik und Gesellschaft I* (1977)
Vol. 10.2:	*Kulturkritik und Gesellschaft II* (1977)
Vol. 11:	*Noten zur Literatur* (1974)
Vol. 12:	*Philosophie der neuen Musik* (1975)
Vol. 13:	*Die musikalischen Mongraphien* (*Versuch über Wagner*; *Mahler: Eine musikalische Physiognomik*; *Berg: Der Meister des kleinsten Übergangs*) ed. Gretel Adorno and Rolf Tiedemann (1971; 2nd edn 1977)
Vol. 14:	*Dissonanzen. Einleitung in die Musiksoziologie* (1973; 2nd edn 1980)
Vol. 15:	*Komposition für den Film* (with Hanns Eisler). *Der getreue Korrepetitor* (1976)
Vol. 16:	*Musikalische Schriften I–III* (1978)
Vol. 17:	*Musikalische Schriften IV* (1982)
Vol. 18:	*Musikalische Schriften V*, ed. Rolf Tiedemann and Klaus Schultz (1984)
Vol. 19:	*Musikalische Schriften VI*, ed. Rolf Tiedemann and Klaus Schultz (1984)

Vol. 20.1:   *Vermischte Schriften I* (1986)
Vol. 20.2:   *Vermischte Schriften II* (1986)

1.2 T. W. ADORNO: A CHRONOLOGICAL LIST OF INDIVIDUAL TEXTS ON MUSIC

The following texts on music are listed chronologically, in order of year of original publication. Translations, where available, are listed together with the original text. Those texts on music which remained unpublished during Adorno's lifetime, but which were subsequently published, either in the *Gesammelte Schriften* (particularly in *GS* 18, 19 and 20) or elsewhere, are listed briefly (in alphabetical order) under 'Posthumous Publications'.

The list does not constitute a complete catalogue of Adorno's published writings on music. As already indicated, it omits the majority of reviews of books and scores (of which Adorno wrote a large number) as well as most of the concert reviews. A detailed and chronological list of Adorno's opera and concert reviews (for *Neue Blätter für Kunst und Literatur*, *Zeitschrift für Musik*, *Die Musik*, *Neue Musik-Zeitung* and *Anbruch*) is to be found in *GS* 19 (1984), pp. 648–50; of his reviews of scores (for *Zeitschrift für Musik* and *Die Musik*), in *GS* 19, pp. 650–51; and of his book reviews (for *Die Musik*, *Literaturblatt der Frankfurter Zeitung*, *Zeitschrift für Sozialforschung*, *Studies in Philosophy and Social Science*, *Kenyon Review*, *Frankfurter Allgemeine Zeitung*, *Neue Deutsche Hefte*, and *Der Spiegel*), in *GS* 19, pp. 651–2.

1921

'"Die Hochzeit des Faun": Grundsätzliche Bemerkungen zu Bernhard Sekles' neuer Oper', *Neue Blätter für Kunst und Literatur* 4 (Heft 3/4, 2 December 1921). *GS* 18 (1984), pp. 263–8

'Béla Bartók', *Neue Blätter für Kunst und Literatur* 4 (Heft 8, Frankfurt/Main, 1 May 1922); republished in *Béla Bartók: Musik-Konzepte* 22, ed. Heinz-Klaus Metzger and Rainer Riehn (Munich: Edition Text + Kritik, 1981). *GS* 18 (1984), pp. 275–8

1922

'Paul Hindemith', *Neue Blätter für Kunst und Literatur* 4 (Heft 7, 20 March 1922). *GS* 17 (1982), *Impromptus*, pp. 212–17

'Bernhard Sekles', *Frankfurter Zeitung* (20 June 1922). *GS* 18 (1984), pp. 269–70

1924

'Richard Strauss', *Zeitschrift für Musik* 91 (Heft 6, June 1924). *GS* 18 (1984), pp. 254–62

'Gebrauchsmusik', *Frankfurter Programmhefte* (1924). *GS* 19 (1984), pp. 445–7

1925

'Béla Bartóks Tanzsuite', *Pult und Taktstock* 2 (Heft 6, June 1925); republished in *Béla Bartók: Musik-Konzepte* 22, ed. Heinz-Klaus Metzger and Rainer Riehn (Munich: Edition Text + Kritik, 1981). *GS* 18 (1984), pp. 279–81

'Über einige Werke von Béla Bartók', *Zeitschrift für Musik* 92 (Heft 7/8, July/August 1925); republished in *Béla Bartók: Musik-Konzepte* 22 (1981). *GS* 18 (1984), pp. 282–6

'Volksliedersammlungen', *Die Musik* 17 (Heft 8, May 1925), *GS* 19 (1984), pp. 287–90

'Schönberg: Serenade, op. 24 (I)', *Pult und Taktstock* 2 (Heft 7, September 1925), *GS* 18 (1984), pp. 324–30

'Alban Berg: Zur Uraufführung des "Wozzeck"', *Musikblätter des Anbruch* 7 (Heft 10, December 1925). *GS* 18 (1984), pp. 456–64

'Hanns Eisler: Duo für Violine und Violoncello, op. 7 Nr.1', *Musikblätter des Anbruch* 7 (Heft 7, 1925). *GS* 18 (1984), pp. 518–21

'Zum Problem der Reproduktion', *Pult und Taktstock* 2 (Heft 4, April 1925). *GS* 19 (1984), pp. 440–44

1926

'Anton Webern: Zur Aufführung der Fünf Orchesterstücke, op. 10, in Zürich', *Musikblätter des Anbruch* 8 (Heft 6, June/July 1926). *GS* 18 (1984), pp. 513–16

'Drei Dirigenten', *Musikblätter des Anbruch* 8 (Heft 7, September 1926). *GS* 19 (1984), pp. 453–9

'Opernprobleme', *Musikblätter des Anbruch* 8 (Heft 5, May 1926). *GS* 10 (1984), pp. 470–75

'Kammermusik von Paul Hindemith', *Die Musik* 29 (Heft 1, October 1926): incorporated into 'Ad vocem Hindemith: Eine Dokumentation', in *Impromptus* (1969). *GS* 17 (1982), pp. 217–22

'Metronomisierung', *Pult und Taktstock* (Heft 7/8, September/October 1926); republished in *Impromptus* (1968). *GS* 17 (1982), pp. 307–10

1927

'Schönberg: Fünf Orchesterstücke, op. 16', *Pult und Taktstock* 4 (Sonderheft: Arnold Schönberg und seine Orchesterwerke, 36–43; March/April 1927). *GS* 18 (1984), pp. 335–44

'Eisler: Klavierstücke, op. 3', *Die Musik* 19 (Heft 10, July 1927). *GS* 18 (1984), pp. 522–3

1928

'Marginalien zur "Sonata" von Alexander Jemnitz', *Neue Musikzeitung* 49 (Heft 12, March 1928). *GS* 18 (1984), pp. 296–303

'Schönberg: Chöre, op. 27 und op. 28', *Musikblätter des Anbruch* 10 (Heft 9/10, November/December 1928). *GS* 18 (1984), pp. 354–7

'Schönberg: Suite für Klavier, drei Bläser und drei Streicher, op. 29, und Drittes Streichquartett, op. 30', *Die Musik* 20 (Heft 8, May 1928). *GS* 18 (1984), pp. 358–62

'Nadelkurven', *Musikblätter des Anbruch* 10 (Heft 2, February 1928). *GS* 19 (1984), pp. 525–9

'Schubert', *Die Musik* 21 (Heft 1, 1928)' republished in *Moments musicaux* (1964). *GS* 17 (1982), pp. 18–33

'Schönbergs Bläserquintett', *Pult und Taktstock* 5 (Heft 5/6, 1928); republished in *Moments musicaux* (1964). *GS* 17 (1982), pp. 140–44

'Kreneks Operneinakter in Wiesbaden', *Neue Musikzeitung* 49 (Heft 22, 1928). *GS* 20.2 (1986), pp. 777–9
'Situation des Liedes', *Musikblätter des Anbruch 10* (Heft 9/10, November/ December 1928), and elsewhere. *GS* 18 (1984), pp. 345–53

1929
'Béla Bartóks Drittes Streichquartett', *Anbruch* 11 (Heft 9/10, November/December 1929); republished in *Béla Bartók; Musik-Konzepte* 22, ed. Heinz-Klaus Metzger and Rainer Riehn (Munich: Edition Text + Kritik, 1981). *GS* 18 (1984), pp. 287–90
'Zur Zwölftontechnik', *Anbruch* 11 (Heft 7/8 September/October 1929); republished in Adorno–Krenek *Briefwechsel* (1974). *GS* 18 (1984), pp. 363–9
'Alban Bergs frühe Lieder', *Anbruch* 11 (Heft 2, February 1929). *GS* 18 (1984), pp. 465–8
'Berg: Sieben frühe Lieder', *Die Musik* 21 (Heft 10, July 1929). *GS* 8 (1984), pp. 469–71
'Die Oper Wozzeck', *Der Scheinwerfer, Blätter der Städtischen Bühnen Essen* 3 (Heft 4, November 1929). *GS* 18 (1984), pp. 472–9
'Eisler: Zeitungsausschnitte, op. 11', *Anbruch* 11 (Heft 5, May 1929). *GS* 18 (1984), pp. 524–7
'Zur Dreigroschenoper', *Die Musik* 21 (Heft 6, March 1929). *GS* 18 (1984), pp. 535–40
'Kurt Weill: Kleine Dreigroschenmusik für Blasorchester', *Anbruch* 11 (Heft 7/8, September/October 1929). *GS* 18 (1984), pp. 541–3
'Atonales Intermezzo?', *Anbruch* 11 (Heft 5, May 1929). *GS* 18 (1984), pp. 88–97
'Schlageranalysen', *Anbruch* 11 (Heft 3, March 1929). *GS* 18 (1984), pp. 778–87
'Nachtmusik', *Anbruch* 11 (Heft 1, 1929); republished in revised form in *Moments musicaux* (1964). *GS* 17 (1982), pp. 52–9
'Schönberg: Variationen für Orchester, op. 31', *Anbruch* 12 (Heft 1, January 1930). *GS* 18 (1984), pp. 370–75
'Zum Jahrgang 1929 des "Anbruch"', *Anbruch* 11 (Heft 1, January 1929). *GS* 19 (1984), pp. 605–8

1930
'Mahler heute', *Anbruch* 12 (Heft 3, March 1930). *GS* 18 (1984), pp. 226–34
'Schönberg: Variationen für Orchester, op. 31', *Anbruch* 12 (Heft 1, January 1930). *GS* 18 (1984), pp. 310–75
'Schönberg: Von heute auf morgen, op. 32 (I)', *Anbruch* 12 (Heft 2, February 1930). *GS* 18 (1984), pp. 376–80
'Schönberg: Von heute auf morgen, op. 32 (II)', *Die Musik* 22 (Heft 6, March 1930). *GS* 18 (1984), pp. 381–4
'Stilgeschichte in Schönbergs Werk', *Blätter der Staatsoper der städischen Oper Berlin* 10 (Heft 32, June 1930). *GS* 18 (1984), pp. 385–93
'Bewußtsein des Konzerthörers', *Anbruch* 12 (Heft 9/10, November/December 1930). *GS* 18 (1984), pp. 815–18
'Arbeitsprobleme des Komponisten: Gespräch über Musik und soziale Situation' [with Ernst Krenek], *Frankfurter Zeitung* (10 December 1930); republished in Adorno–Krenek *Briefwechsel* (1974). *GS* 19 (1984), pp. 433–9

'Kontroverse über die Heiterkeit' (with H. H. Stuckenschmidt), *Anbruch* 12 (Heft 1, January 1930). *GS* 19 (1984), pp. 448–52

'Neue Oper und Publikum', *50 Jahre Opernhaus* (Frankfurt/Main, 1930). *GS* 19 (1984), pp. 476–80

'Ravel', *Anbruch* 12 (Heft 4/5, 1930); republished in revised version in *Moments musicaux* (1964). *GS* 17 (1982), pp. 60–65

'Neue Tempi', *Pult und Taktstock* 7 (Heft 1, 1930); republished in *Moments musicaux* (1964). *GS* 17 (1982), pp. 66–73

'Mahagonny' [I] *Der Scheinwerfer* 3 (Heft 14, 1930); republished in *Moments musicaux* (1964). *GS* 17 (1982), pp. 114–22

'Reaktion und Fortschritt', *Anbruch* 12 (Heft 6, June 1930); republished in revised version in *Moments musicaux* (1964), and in Adorno–Krenek *Briefwechsel* (1974). *GS* 17 (1982), pp. 133–9

1931

'Gegen die neue Tonalität', *Der Scheinwerfer: Blätter der Städtischen Bühnen Essen* 4 (Heft 16, May 1931). *GS* 18 (1984), pp. 8–107

'Warum ist die neue Kunst so schwer verständlich?', *Der Scheinwerfer* 5 (Heft 2, October 1931). *GS* 18 (1984), pp. 824–31

'Musikstudio', *Anbruch* 13 (Heft 1, January 1931). *GS* 19 (1984), pp. 520–24

'Berg and Webern – Schönberg's heirs' [published in English – see original German version, 'Berg und Webern', below under Posthumous Publications], *Modern Music* no. 2 (New York, January/February 1931). *GS* 18 (1984), pp. 446–55

1932

'Zur gesellschaftlichen Lage der Musik', *Zeitschrift für Sozialforschung* 1 (Heft 1/2, 1932), pp. 103–24 and (Heft 3, 1932), pp. 356–78. *GS* 18 (1984), pp. 729–77. Translated as: 'On the social situation of music', trans. Wesley Blomster, *Telos* 35 (Spring 1978), pp. 128–64

'Zur Deutung Kreneks', *Anbruch* 14 (Heft 2/3, February/March 1932); republished in Adorno–Krenek *Briefwechsel* (1974). *GS* 18 (1984), pp. 571–6

'Exkurse zu einem Exkurs', *Der Scheinwerfer* 5 (Heft 9/10, January/February 1932). *GS* 18 (1984), pp. 108–13

'Parodie, je nachdem', *Frankfurter Zeitung* (14 July 1932). *GS* 18 (1984), pp. 788–9

'Arabesken zur Operette', *Die Rampe: Blätter des Deutschen Schauspielhauses Hamburg* (Heft 9, 1931/2). *GS* 19 (1984), pp. 516–19

'Mahagonny' [II], *Anbruch* 14 (Heft 2/3, February/March 1932). *GS* 19 (1984), pp. 276–7

'Kritik des Musikanten', *Frankfurter Zeitung* (12 March 1932); republished in *Impromptus* (1968) as part of the compilation 'Ad vocem Hindemith: Eine Dokumentation'. *GS* 17 (1982), pp. 222–9

'Hoffmanns Erzählungen in Offenbachs Motiven', *Programmschrift der Städtischen Bühnen Düsseldorf* 8 (1932); republished in *Moments musicaux* (1964), *GS* 17 (1982), pp. 42–6

'Die Instrumentation von Bergs Frühen Liedern', *Schweizerische Musikzeitschrift und Sängerblatt* (Heft 5/6, March 1932); republished in *Klangfiguren* (1959). *GS* 16 (1978), pp. 97–109

1933

'Notiz über Wagner', *Europäische Revue* 9 (Heft 7, 1933). *GS* 18 (1984), pp. 204–9

'Anton von Webern', *Vossische Zeitung* (3 December 1933). *GS* 18 (1984), pp. 517–18

'Abschied vom Jazz', *Europäische Revue* 9 (Heft 5, 1933). *GS* 18 (1984), pp. 795–9

'Vierhändig, noch einmal, *Vossische Zeitung* (19 December 1933); republished in *Impromptus* (1968). *GS* 17 (1982), pp. 303–6

'Mascagnis Landschaft', *Vossische Zeitung* (7 December 1933). *GS* 18 (1984), pp. 271–2

1934

'Johann Sebastian Bach: Präludium und Fuge cis-moll aus dem ersten Teil des Wohltemperierten Klaviers', *Vossische Zeitung* (3 March 1934). *GS* 18 (1984), pp. 179–82

'"Die Alte Orgel"', *Vossische Zeitung* (25 March 1934). *GS* 18 (1984), pp. 183–4

'Franz Schubert: Großes Rondo A-Dur, für Klavier zu vier Händen, op. 107', *Vossische Zeitung* (6 January 1934). *GS* 18 (1984), pp. 189–94

'Musik im Hintergrund', *Vossische Zeitung* (31 January 1934). *GS* 18 (1984), pp. 819–23

'Die Form der Schallplatte', *"23", Eine Wiener Musikzeitschrift* (no. 17–19, 15 December 1934). *GS* 19 (1984), pp. 530–34

'Der dialektische Komponist', *Arnold Schönberg zum 60. Geburtstag* (Vienna, 13 September 1934); republished in *Impromptus* (1968). *GS* 17 (1982), pp. 198–203

'Musikalische Diebe, unmusikalische Richter', *Stuttgarter Neues Tagblatt* (20 August 1934); republished in *Impromptus* (1968). *GS* 17 (1982), pp. 292–6

1935

'Ernst Krenek' [appeared anonymously in an English translation] in *The Listener* (London, 23 October 1935); republished in Adorno–Krenek *Briefwechsel* (1974). *GS* 18 (1984), pp. 531–4 (German original)

'Zur Krisis der Musikkritik', *"23". Eine Wiener Musikzeitschrift* (no. 20/21, 25 March 1935). *GS* 20.2 (1986), pp. 746–55

1936

'Marginalien zu Mahler', *"23". Eine Wiener Musikzeitschrift* (no. 26/7, 18 May 1936). *GS* 18 (1984), pp. 235–40

'Musikpädagogische Musik', *"23". Eine Wiener Musikzeitschrift* (no. 28/30, 10 November 1936); republished in Adorno–Krenek *Briefwechsel* (1974). *GS* 18 (1984), pp. 805–12

'Anton von Webern', *Auftakt* (1936), and elsewhere (originally given as a talk for Südwestfunk (Frankfurt) on 21 April 1932); republished in *Impromptus* (1968). *GS* 17 (1982), pp. 204–9

'Erinnerung an den Lebenden', *"23". Eine Wiener Musikzeitschrift* (no. 24/5, 1 February 1936). Adorno reworked material from this article in later reminiscences of Berg: 'Im Gedächtnis an Alban Berg' (1955) remained unpublished until *GS* 18 (1984), pp. 487–512; a version of it appeared as 'Erinnerung', in *Berg: Der Meister des kleinsten Übergangs* (1968), *GS* 13 (1971), pp. 335–67

1937

'Spätstil Beethovens', *Der Auftakt: Blätter für die tschechoslowakische Republik* 17 (Heft 5/6, 1937); republished in *Moments musicaux* (1964). *GS* 17 (1982), pp. 13–17

'Fußnote zu Sibelius und Hamsun', *Zeitschrift für Sozialforschung* 6 (Heft 2, 1937). *GS* 20.2 (1986), p. 804

'Über Jazz' [1936] [under the pseudonym 'Hektor Rottweiler'], *Zeitschrift für Sozialforschung* 5 (1937); republished in *Moments musicaux* (1964). *GS* 17 (1982), pp. 74–108

Eight analytical contributions to Willi Reich, *Alban Berg: Mit Bergs eigenen Schriften und Beiträgen von Theodor Wiesengrund-Adorno und Ernst Krenek* (Vienna/Leipzig/Zürich: Herbert Reichner Verlag, 1937): 'Klaviersonate, op. 1' (pp. 21–7); 'Vier Lieder, op. 2' (pp. 27–31); 'Sieben frühe Lieder' (pp. 31–5); 'Streichquartett, op. 3' (pp. 35–43); 'Vier Stücke für Klarinette und Klavier, op. 5' (pp. 47–52); 'Drei Orchesterstücke, op. 6' (pp. 52–64); 'Lyrische Suite für Streichquartett' (pp. 91–101); 'Konzertarie "Der Wein"' (pp. 101–6). With the exception of 'Konzertarie "Der Wein"', these analyses were republished, with slight revisions, in *Berg. Der Meister des kleinsten Übergangs* (1968). 'Konzertarie "Der Wein"' is included as an Appendix to *Berg* (1968) in *GS* 13 (1971)

1938

'Glosse über Sibelius', *Zeitschrift für Sozialforschung* 6 (Heft 3, 1938); republished in *Impromptus* (1968). *GS* 17 (1982), pp. 247–52

'Ernst Krenek, über neue Musik', *Zeitschrift für Sozialforschung* 7 (Heft 3, 1938): republished in *Adorno–Krenek Briefwechsel* (1974). *GS* 19 (1984), pp. 366–8

'Über den Fetischcharakter in der Musik und die Regression des Hörens', *Zeitschrift für Sozialforschung* 7 (1938); republished in *Dissonanzen* (1956). *GS* 14 (1973, 1980), pp. 14–50. Translated as: 'On the fetish character in music and the regression of listening', translator unacknowledged, in *The Essential Frankfurt School Reader*, ed. Andrew Arato and Eike Gebhard (Oxford: Basil Blackwell, 1978), pp. 270–99

1939

'Fragmente über Wagner', *Zeitschrift für Sozialforschung* 8 (Heft 1/2, 1939/40), pp. 1–48 [Chapters I, VI, IX and X of what was later published as *Versuch über Wagner* (1952)].

1941

'The Radio Symphony', *Radio Research 1941* (New York, 1941), pp. 110ff. (original in English). Omitted from *GS*.

'On popular music' (with the assistance of George Simpson), *Studies in Philosophy and Social Sciences* 9 (1941), pp. 17–48 (original in English). Omitted from *GS*. This, and the previous entry, are likely to be republished at some future date by the Theodor W. Adorno Archiv as part of the book planned by Adorno as *Current of Music: Elements of a Radio Theory* (cf. Rolf Tiedemann, 'Editorisches Nachwort', *GS* 20.2 (1986), pp. 830–32)

1945

'A social critique of radio music', *Kenyon Review* 7 (1945), pp. 208–17 (original in English). Omitted from *GS*. Likely to be republished at some future date by the Theodor W. Adorno Archiv as part of the book planned by Adorno as *Current of Music: Elements of a Radio Theory* (cf. Rolf Tiedemann, 'Editorisches Nachwort', *GS* 20.2 (1986), pp. 830–32)

1947

Composing for the Films [Hanns Eisler] (New York: Oxford University Press, 1947). Written as a collaboration between Adorno and Hanns Eisler in 1944 in the United States, but published (in English) in 1947 under Eisler's name alone. A British edition followed in 1951 (London: Dennis Dobson, 1951). Eisler published a German edition of the book in 1949, again under his name alone, as *Komposition für den Film* (Berlin: Verlag Bruno Henschel und Sohn, 1949). This varies in certain respects both from the content of the English editions and from that of the German edition published by Adorno in 1969, under both his and Eisler's names, as the first edition of the original version of 1944: Theodor W. Adorno and Hanns Eisler, *Komposition für den Film* (Munich: Verlag Rogner & Bernhard, 1969). It is this latter version which appears in *GS* 15 (1976), pp. 7–155, with some revisions, together with a postscript, 'Zum Erstdruck der Originalfassung'.

1949

Philosophie der neuen Musik (Tübingen: J. C. B. Mohr (Paul Siebeck), 1949); 2nd edn added a 'Notiz' (Frankfurt/Main: Europäischen Verlagsanstalt, 1958). Contents: 'Vorrede'; 'Einleitung'; 'Schönberg und der Fortschritt'; 'Strawinsky und die Reaktion'; 'Notiz' (1958, 1969). *GS* 12 (1975); this edition includes an Appendix: 'Mißverständnisse' (1950). Translated as: *Philosophy of Modern Music*, trans. Anne G. Mitchell and Wesley V. Blomster (London: Sheed & Ward, 1973)

1950

'Kurt Weill', *Frankfurter Rundschau* (15 April 1950). *GS* 18 (1984), pp. 544–7
'Mißverständnisse', *Melos* 17 (Heft 3, 1950). *GS* 12 (1975), pp. 203–6

1951

'Bach gegen seine Liebhaber verteidigt', *Merkur* (1951); republished in *Prismen* (Frankfurt/Main: Suhrkamp Verlag, 1955). *GS* 10.1 (1977), pp. 138–51. Translated as: 'Bach defended against his devotees', in *Prisms*, trans. Samuel and Shierry Weber (London: Neville Spearman, 1967), pp. 133–46
'Fur Alban Berg', *Die Neue Rundschau* 62 (Heft 1, 1951). *GS* 18 (1984), pp. 483–6

1952

Versuch über Wagner (Frankfurt/Main and Berlin: Suhrkamp Verlag, 1952); *GS* 13 based on 1964 edition (Munich/Zürich: Droemersche Verlagsanstalt Th. Knauer, 1964). Contents: I 'Sozialcharakter'; II 'Gestus'; III 'Motiv'; IV 'Klang'; V 'Farbe'; VI 'Phantasmagorie'; VII 'Musikdrama'; VIII 'Mythos'; IX 'Gott und Bettler'; X 'Chimäre'. *GS* 13 (1971), pp. 7–148. Translated as: *In*

Search of Wagner, trans. Rodney Livingstone (London: NLB, 1981) 'Huldigung an Zerlina', *Programmheft der Städtischen Bühnen Frankfurt* 4 (Heft 13, 1952/3); republished in *Moments musicaux* (1964). *GS* 17 (1982), pp. 34–5
'Selbstanzeige des Essaybuches "Versuch über Wagner"', *Morgenblatt für Freunde der Literatur* no. 3 (Frankfurt/Main and Berlin, 25 September 1952). *GS* (1971), pp. 504–9

1953

'Zeitlose Mode: Zum Jazz', *Merkur* (June 1953); republished in *Prismen* (1955). *GS* 10.1 (1977), pp. 123–37. Translated as: 'Perennial fashion – jazz', trans. Samuel and Shierry Weber, in *Prisms* (London: Neville Spearman, 1967), pp. 119–32
'Replik zu einer Kritik der "Zeitlosen Mode"' [reply to criticisms from Joachim Berendt], *Merkur* (September 1953); republished in *GS* 10.2 (1977), pp. 805–9
'Arnold Schönberg (1874–1951)', *Die Neue Rundschau* (1953); republished in *Prismen* (1955). *GS* 10.1 (1977), pp. 152–80. Translated as: 'Arnold Schoenberg, 1874–1951', trans. Samuel and Shierry Weber, in *Prisms* (London: Neville Spearman, 1967), pp. 147–72
'Die gegängelte Musik', *Monat* (May 1953); republished in *Dissonanzen* (1956). *GS* 14 (1973, 1980), pp. 51–66
'Über das gegenwärtige Verhältnis von Philosophie und Musik', *Archivio di Filosophia* 1 (Rome, 1953). *GS* 18 (1984), pp. 149–78

1954

'Kritik des Musikanten', *Junge Musik* (1954); republished in *Dissonanzen* (1956). *GS* 14 (1973, 1980), pp. 67–107
'Eduard Steuermann: Klaviertrio', *Die Neue Zeitung* (25 December 1954). *GS* 18 (1984), pp. 682–3

1955

'Das Altern der neuen Musik', *Der Monat* (May 1955); expanded version appeared in *Dissonanzen* (Göttingen: Vandenhoek & Ruprecht, 1956). *GS* 14 (1973, 1980), 143–67. Translated as: 'Modern music is growing old', trans. from the French by Rollo Myers, *The Score* (December 1956), pp. 18–29
'Bürgerliche Oper', *Theater*, ed. Egon Vietta (Darmstadt, 1955); republished in *Klangfiguren* (1959). *GS* 16 (1978), pp. 24–39
Prismen: Kulturkritik und Gesellschaft (Frankfurt/Main and Berlin: Suhrkamp Verlag, 1955); contains twelve essays, all previously published, of which three are on music (see above): 'Zeitlose Mode: Zum Jazz' (1953) (trans.); 'Bach gegen seine Liebhaber verteidigt' (1951) (trans.); and 'Arnold Schönberg (1874–1951)' (1953) (trans.). *GS* 10.1 (1977), pp. 9–287. Translated as: *Prisms*, trans. Samuel and Shierry Weber (London: Neville Spearman, 1967)
'Die Musik zur "Glücklichen Hand"', *Die Tribüne: Halbmonatsschrift der Bühnen der Stadt Köln* 24 (Heft 18, May 1955). *GS* 18 (1984), pp. 408–10
'Zum Verständnis Schönbergs', *Frankfurter Hefte* 10 (Heft 6, June 1955); later version published in *Programm Berliner Festwochen '67* (Berlin, September/ October 1967). *GS* 18 (1984), pp. 428–45
'Nach einem Vierteljahrhundert' (1955), *Programmheft der Städtischen Bühnen Düsseldorf* (Heft 6, 1955/6). *GS* 18 (1984), pp. 548–51

'Musikalische Warenanalysen' (written 1934–40), *Neue Rundschau* (Heft 1, 1955); republished in *Quasi una Fantasia* (1963). *GS* 16 (1978), pp. 284–97

'Fantasia sopra Carmen', *Neue Rundschau* (Heft 3, 1955); republished in *Quasi una Fantasia* (1963). *GS* 16 (1978), pp. 298–308

1956

Dissonanzen: Musik in der verwalteten Welt (Göttingen: Vandenhoek & Ruprecht, 1956; 2nd edn includes 'Zur Musikpädagogik'; 3rd edn 1963 includes 'Tradition'). Contains previously published essays (see above): 'Über den Fetischcharakter in der Musik und die Regression des Hörens' (1938) (trans.); 'Die gegängelte Musik' (1953); 'Kritik des Musikanten' (1954); 'zur Musikpädagogik' (1957); 'Tradition' (1960); 'Das Altern der Neuen Musik' (1955) (trans.). *GS* 14 (1973, 1980), pp. 7–167

'Alban Berg', *Merkur* 10 (Heft 7, July 1956); republished in *Klangfiguren* (1959). *GS* 16 (1978), pp. 85–96

'Zur Partitur des "Parsifal"', *Theaterzeitschrift der Deutschen Oper am Rhein* 1 (Heft 3, 1956/7); republished in *Moments musicaux* (1964). *GS* 17 (1982), pp. 47–51

'Neue Musik heute', under the title 'Zum Stand des Komponierens', in *Deutsche Zeitung und Wirtschaftszeitung* (21 January 1956), and elsewhere. *GS* 18 (1984), pp. 124–33

'Wozzeck in Partitur', *Frankfurter Allgemeine Zeitung* (18 April 1956). *GS* 18 (1984), pp. 480–82

'Vortrupp und Avantgarde', *Der Monat* 8 (Heft 90, March 1956). *GS* 18 (1984), pp. 800–804

'Widerspruch', *Ost-Probleme* 8 (no. 51/2, 21 December 1956). *GS* 18 (1984), pp. 834–5

'Kolisch und die neue Interpretation', *Frankfurter Allgemeine Zeitung* (20 July 1956); reprinted in *Melos* 23 (November 1956). *GS* 19 (1984), pp. 460–62

'Fragment über Musik und Sprache', *Jahresring 1956/57* (Stuttgart, 1956); republished in *Quasi una Fantasia* (1963). *GS* 16 (1978), pp. 251–6

'Musik, Sprache und ihr Verhältnis im gegenwärtigen Komponieren', *Jahresring 56/57* (Stuttgart, 1956). *GS* 16 (1978), pp. 649–64

1957

'Neue Musik, Interpretation, Publikum', *Neue Deutsche Hefte* (Heft 41, December 1957); republished in *Klangfiguren* (1959). *GS* 16 (1978), pp. 40–51. Translated as: 'New music and the public: some problems of interpretation', translator unacknowledged, in *Twentieth Century Music: A Symposium*, ed. Rollo Myers (London: Calder and Boyars, 1960; 2nd revised and enlarged edn 1968), pp. 63–74

'Die Funktion des Kontrapunkts in der neuen Musik', *Anmerkungen zur Zeit* (Akademie der Künste, Berlin, August 1957) and *Merkur* 12 (Heft 1, January 1958); republished in *Klangfiguren* (1959). *GS* 16 (1978), pp. 145–69

'Zur Musikpädagogik', *Junge Musik* (1957); republished in *Dissonanzen* (1956, 1963). *GS* 14 (1973, 1980), pp. 108–26

'Zur Physiognomik Kreneks', *Theaterzeitschrift der Deutschen Oper am Rhein* 2 (Heft 13, 1957/8); republished in *Moments musicaux* (1964), and in Adorno–

Krenek *Briefwechsel* (1974). *GS* 17 (1982), pp. 109–13
'Arnold Schoenberg' (I), *Die Großen Deutschen. Deutsche Biographie* vol. 4, ed. Hermann Heimpel, Theodor Heuss and Benno Reifenberg (Berlin, 1957). *GS* 18 (1984), pp. 304–23
'Fragen des gegenwärtigen Operntheaters', *Neue Deutsche Hefte* (Heft 31, January 1957); also in *Bayreuther Festspiele 1966. Programmheft zu "Tannhäuser"*. *GS* 19 (1984), pp. 481–93

1958
'Ideen zur Musiksoziologie', *Schweizer Monatshefte* 38 (Heft 8, November 1958); republished in *Klangfiguren* (1959). *GS* 16 (1978), pp. 9–23
'Die Meisterschaft des Maestro', *Merkur* 12 (Heft 10, October 1958); republished in *Klangfiguren* (1959). *GS* 16 (1978), pp. 52–67
'Musik und Technik', *Gravesaner Blätter* 4 (Heft 11/12, 1958); republished in *Klangfiguren* (1959), *GS* 16 (1978), pp. 229–48. Translated as: 'Music and technique', trans. Wesley Blomster, *Telos* 32 (Summer 1977), pp. 79–94
'Erwin Stein', *Frankfurter Allgemeine Zeitung* (20 September 1958). *GS* 19 (1984), pp. 463–4
'Naturgeschichte des Theaters', *Neue Deutsche Hefte* (Heft 50, 1958) [sections originally appeared in various journals between 1931 and 1933]. Republished in *Quasi una Fantasia* (1963). *GS* 16 (1978), pp. 309–20

1959
'Anton von Webern', *Merkur* 13 (Heft 3, March 1959); republished in *Klangfiguren* (1959, see below). *GS* 16 (1978), pp. 110–25
'Klassik, Romantik, Neue Musik', *Neue Deutsche Hefte* (Heft 56, March 1959); republished in *Klangfiguren* (1959, see below). *GS* 16 (1978), pp. 126–44
Klangfiguren: Musikalische Schriften I (Frankfurt/Main and Berlin: Suhrkamp Verlag, 1959). Contains twelve essays, ten of which had been previously published (see above): 'Ideen zur Musiksoziologie' (1958); 'Bürgerliche Oper' (1955); 'Neue Musik, Interpretation, Publikum' (1957) (trans.); 'Die Meisterschaft des Maestro' (1958); 'Zur Vorgeschichte der Reihenkomposition' (unpublished talk for Norddeutscher Rundfunk, 1958); 'Alban Berg' (1956); 'Die Instrumentation von Bergs Frühen Liedern' (1932, reworked); 'Anton von Webern' (1959); 'Klassik, Romantik, Neue Musik' (1959); 'Die Funktion des Kontrapunkts in der neuen Musik' (1957); 'Kriterien der neuen Musik' (based on unpublished lecture, Kranichstein 1957); 'Musik und Technik' (1958) (trans.). *GS* 16 (1978), pp. 7–248
'Verfremdetes Hauptwerk: Zur Missa Solemnis' (trans.), *Neue Deutsche Hefte* (Heft 54, 1959); republished in *Moments musicaux* (1964). *GS* 17 (1982), pp. 145–61. Translated as: 'Alienated masterpiece: the Missa Solemnis', trans. Duncan Smith, *Telos* 28 (1976), pp. 113–24
'Zu den Georgeliedern', in *Arnold Schönberg, Fünfzehn Gedichte aus 'Das Buch der Hängenden Gärten' von Stefan George. Für Gesang und Klavier* (Wiesbaden: Insel-Bücherei no. 683, 1959). *GS* 18 (1984), pp. 411–17

1960
Mahler: Eine musikalische Physiognomik (Frankfurt/Main: Suhrkamp Verlag, 1960); 2nd edn (1963) contains a 'Notiz'. Contents: I 'Vorhang und Fanfare'; II

'Ton'; III 'Charaktere'; IV 'Roman'; V 'Variante – Form'; VI 'Dimensionen der Technik'; VII 'Zerfall und Affirmation'; VIII 'Der lange Blick'; 'Notiz' (1963). *GS* 13 (1971), pp. 149–319

'Tradition', *Jahresring 1960/61* (Stuttgart, 1960), and *Musica* 15 (Heft 4, January 1961); republished in *Dissonanzen* (1956, 3rd edn 1963). *GS* 14 (1973, 1980), pp. 127–42

'Mahlers Aktualität', *Dichten und Trachten: Jahresschau des Suhrkamp Verlages* vol. 16 (Frankfurt/Main and Berlin: Suhrkamp Verlag, 1960). *GS* 18 (1984), pp. 241–3

'Verbindlichkeit des Neuen', *Melos* 27 (Heft 6, 1960). *GS* 18 (1984), pp. 832–3

'Rede über Bergs Lulu', *Frankfurter Allgemeine Zeitung* (19 January 1960); originally a talk given before the Frankfurt première of Lulu under George Solti. *GS* 18 (1984), pp. 645–9

'Mahler: Wiener Gedenkrede', *Neue Zürcher Zeitung* (July 1960); also *Neue Deutsche Hefte* (Heft 79, 1961). 'Epilegomena', *Forum* (September 1961), expanded. Republished in *Quasi una Fantasia* (1963). *GS* 16 (1978), pp. 323–50

'Wien', *Forum* (January/February 1960); republished in *Quasi una Fantasia* (1963). *GS* 16 (1978), pp. 433–53

'Musik und neue Musik', *Merkur* (May 1960); republished in *Quasi una Fantasia* (1963). *GS* 16 (1978), pp. 476–92. Translated as: 'Music and the new music: in memory of Peter Suhrkamp', trans. Wesley Blomster, *Telos* 43 (Spring 1980), pp. 124–38

1961

'Bilderwelt des Freischütz', *Programm der Hamburger Staatsoper* (Heft 5, 1961/2); republished in *Moments musicaux* (1964). *GS* 17 (1982), pp. 36–41

'Erwiderung', *Kölner Zeitschrift für Soziologie und Sozialpsychologie* 13 (Heft 4, 1961). *GS* 18 (1984), pp. 836–7

'Bergs Kompositionstechnische Funde', *Forum* (April/May 1961); republished in *Quasi una Fantasia* (1963). *GS* 16 (1978), pp. 413–32

'Vers une musique informelle', *Darmstädter Beiträge* (1961); republished in revised version in *Quasi una Fantasia* (1963). *GS* 16 (1978), pp. 493–540

1962

Einleitung in die Musiksoziologie: Zwölf theoretische Vorlesungen (Frankfurt/Main: Suhrkamp Verlag, 1962). A slightly revised edition appeared in 1968, which included a postscript, 'Musiksoziologie', in the series 'Rowohlts Deutsche enzyklopädie' (Hamburg: Rowohlt Verlag, 1968). Contents: 'Vorrede'; I 'Typen musikalischen Verhaltens'; II 'Leichte Musik'; III 'Funktion'; IV 'Klassen und Schichten'; V 'Oper'; VI 'Kammermusik'; VII 'Dirigent und Orchester'; VIII 'Musikleben'; IX 'Öffentliche Meinung, Kritik'; X 'Nation'; XI 'Moderne'; XII 'Vermittlung'; Nachwort: 'Musiksoziologie' (1968). *GS* 14 (1973), pp. 169–433, is based on the 1968 edition. Translated as: *Introduction to the Sociology of Music*, trans. E. B. Ashton (New York: Seabury Press, 1976)

'Strawinsky: Ein dialektisches Bild', *Forum* (June/July/August, 1962). Republished in revised version in *Quasi una Fantasia* (1963). *GS* 16 (1978), pp. 382–409

'Haringer und Schönberg', *Der Monat* 14 (Heft 163, April 1962). *GS* 18 (1984), p. 427

'Maria Proelss', *Frankfurter Allgemeine Zeitung* (18 September 1962). *GS* 19 (1984), pp. 465–7

1963

Der getreue Korrepetitor: Lehrschriften zur musikalischen Praxis (Frankfurt/Main: S. Fischer-Verlag, 1963). Contains eight essays: 'Die gewürdigte Musik'; 'Anweisungen zum Hören neuer Musik'; 'Anton Webern; Lieder op. 3 und op. 12'; 'Anton Webern: Sechs Bagatellen für Streichquartett op. 9'; 'Anton Webern: Vier Stücke für Geige und Klavier op. 7'; 'Arnold Schönberg: Phantasie für Geige mit Klavierbegleitung op. 47'; 'Alban Berg: Violinkonzert'; 'Über die musikalische Verwendung des Radios'. *GS* 15 (1976), pp. 188–248

Quasi una Fantasia: Musikalische Schriften II (Frankfurt/Main: Suhrkamp Verlag, 1963). Contains fourteen essays, of which eleven had been previously published (see above): 'Fragment über Musik und Sprache' (1956); 'Motive' [selected from the 'aphorisms' series:· 'Motive I' (*Anbruch*, Heft 4, 1927); 'Motive II' (*Anbruch*, Heft 6, 1928); 'Motive III' (*Anbruch*, Heft 7, 1928); 'Motive IV' (*Anbruch*, Heft 9/10, 1929); 'Motive V' (*Anbruch*, Heft 9/10, 1930); 'Kleiner Zitatenschatz' (*Die Musik, Heft* 10, 1932); 'Ensemble' ("23". Eine Wiener Musikzeitschrift, nos. 31/3, 1937, under the pseudonym 'Hektor Rottweiler'); 'Schlagzeug' (*Frankfurter Rundschau*, 1951); 'Glosse zu Richard Strauss' (*Anbruch*, Heft 6, 1929)]; 'Musikalische Warenanalysen' (written 1934–40, published 1955); 'Fantasia sopra Carmen' (1955); 'Naturgeschichte des Theaters' (1958); 'Mahler. Wiener Gedenkrede' (1960/61); 'Zemlinsky' (unpublished talk, NDR, 1959); 'Schreker' (unpublished talk, Hessische Rundfunk, 1959); 'Strawinsky' (1962, expanded); 'Bergs Kompositionstechnische Funde' (1961); 'Wien' (1960); 'Sakrales Fragment: über Schönbergs Moses und Aron' (unpublished talk, Berlin, 1963); 'Musik und neue Musik' (1960); 'Vers une musique informelle' (1960). *GS* 16 (1978), pp. 249–540

'Über einige Arbeiten Arnold Schoenbergs', *Forum* 10 (Vienna, Hefte 115/16 and 117, July/August and September 1963); republished in *Impromptus* (1968). *GS* 17 (1982), pp. 327–44

1964

Moments musicaux; Neu gedruckte Aufsätze 1928–1962 (Frankfurt/Main: Suhrkamp Verlag, 1964); contains sixteen essays, of which fifteen had been previously published (see above): 'Spätstil Beethovens' (1937); 'Schubert' (1928); 'Huldigung an Zerlina' (1952); 'Bilderwelt des Freischütz' (1961); 'Hoffmanns Erzählungen in Offenbachs Motiven' (1932); 'Zur Partitur des "Parsifal"' (1956); 'Nachtmusik' (1929, abridged version); 'Ravel' (1930, reworked version); 'Neue Tempi' (1930); 'Über Jazz' (1937); 'Zur Physiognomik Kreneks' (1957); 'Mahagonny' 1930); 'Zilligs Verlaine-Lieder' (unpublished radio talk, Bayerischer Rundfunk, July 1961); 'Reaktion und Fortschritt' (1930, abridged version); 'Schönbergs Bläserquintett' (1928); 'Verfremdetes Hauptwerk: Zur Missa Solemnis' (1959) (trans.). *GS* 17 (1982), pp. 7–161

'Früher Irrtum', *Schwietzer Monatshefte* 43 (Heft 10, January 1964); republished in *Impromptus* (1968) as part of the compilation 'Ad vocem Hindemith: Eine Dokumentation'. *GS* 17 (1982), pp. 235–9

'Nach Steuermanns Tod', originally under the title 'Nachruf auf einen Pianisten', *Süddeutsche Zeitung* (28/9 November 1964); republished in *Impromptus* (1968). *GS* 17 (1982), pp. 311–17

'Beethoven im Geist der Moderne', *Süddeutsche Zeitung* (22 December 1964). *GS* 19 (1984), pp. 535–8

'Wagners Aktualität', *Bayreuther Festspiele 1964: Programmheft 'Tristan und Isolde'*; also a later version in: *275 Jahre Theater in Braunschweig: Geschichte und Wirkung* (Braunschweig, 1965). 1965 version republished in *Musikalische Schriften III*; *GS* 16 (1978), pp. 543–64

'Nachschrift zu einer Wagner-Diskussion', *Die Zeit* (9 October 1964). *GS* 16 (1978), pp. 665–70

'Richard Strauss: Zum hundertsten Geburtstag: 11. Juni 1964', *Neue Rundschau* 75 (Heft 4, 1964). Republished in *Musikalische Schriften III*; *GS* 16 (1978), pp. 565–606. Translated as: 'Richard Strauss: born June 11, 1864', trans. Samuel and Shierry Weber, *Perspectives of New Music* (Fall–Winter 1965), pp. 14–32 and 113–29

1965

'Schwierigkeiten beim Komponieren', *Aspekte der Modernität* (Göttingen, 1965); republished in *Impromptus* (1968). *GS* 17 (1982), pp. 253–73

'Kleine Häresie', *Wege und Gestalten* (Biberach an der Riss, September 1965); republished in *Impromptus* (1968). *GS* 17 (1982), pp. 297–302

'Zuschrift über Bartók', *Lippisches Volksblatt* (21 October 1965). *GS* 18 (1984), p. 295

'Über einige Relationen zwischen Musik und Malerei', in *Pour Daniel-Henry Kahnweiler* (Stuttgart, 1965); also in *Theodor W. Adorno, über einige Relationen zwischen Musik und Malerei. Die Kunst und die Künste* (Berlin, Akademie der Künste, Anmerkungen zur Zeit 12, 1967); and *Protokolle 68. Wiener Jahresschrift für Literatur, bildende Kunst und Musik*, ed. Otto Breicha and Gerhard Fritsch (Vienna/Munich, 1968). Republished in *Musikalische Schriften III*; *GS* 16 (1978), pp. 628–42

1966

'Form in der neuen Musik', *Darmstädter Beiträge zur Neuen Musik* vol. X (Mainz, 1966); also in *Neue Rundschau* 77 (Heft 1, 1966). Republished in *Musikalische Schriften III*. *GS* 16 (1978), pp. 607–27

1967

'Anmerkungen zum deutschen Musikleben' (1966), *Deutscher Musikrat. Referate, Information* (5 February 1967); republished in *Impromptus* (Frankfurt/Main: Suhrkamp Verlag, 1968). *GS* 17 (1982), pp. 167–88

'Zu einer Umfrage: Neue Oper und Publikum', *Programmhefte der Städtischen Bühnen Frankfurt am Main*: supplement: *Neue Oper in Frankfurt* (1967/8). *GS* 19 (1984), pp. 494–5

'Klemperers "Don Giovanni"', *Süddeutsche Zeitung* (24 February 1967). *GS* 19 (1984), pp. 539–44

'Wagner und Bayreuth', *Bayreuther Festspiele 1967: Programmheft zu 'Das Rheingold'*. *GS* 18 (1984), pp. 210–25

1968

Berg: Der Meister des kleinsten Übergangs (Vienna: Verlag Elisabeth Lafite/ Österreichischer Bundesverlag, 1968). Contents: 'Ton'; 'Erinnerung'; 'Analyse und Berg'; 'Klaviersonate'; 'Lieder nach Hebbel und Mombert'; 'Sieben frühe Lieder'; 'Erstes Streichquartett'; 'Altenberglieder'; 'Klarinettenstücke'; 'Orchesterstücke'; 'Zur Charakteristik des Wozzeck'; 'Epilegomena zum Kammerkonzert'; 'Lyrische Suite'; 'Weinarie'; 'Erfahrungen an Lulu'. Parts of this book originally appeared as contributions to Willi Reich, *Alban Berg: Mit Bergs eigenen Schriften und Beiträgen von Theodor Wiesengrund-Adorno und Ernst Krenek* (Vienna: Herbert Reichner Verlag, 1937). *GS* 13 (1971), pp. 321–494. Translated as: *Alban Berg: Master of the Smallest Link*, trans. Juliane Brand and Christopher Hailey (Cambridge: Cambridge University Press, 1991)

'Schwierigkeiten in der Auffassung neuer Musik', *Neue Deutsche Hefte* 14 (Heft 5, 1968); republished in *Impromptus* (1968). *GS* 17 (1982), pp. 273–91

Impromptus: Zweite Folge neu gedruckter musikalischer Aufsätze (Frankfurt/Main: Suhrkamp, Verlag, 1968); contains fourteen essays, of which twelve had been previously published, although sometimes in different versions (see above): 'Anmerkungen zum deutschen Musikleben' (1967); 'Zu einer imaginären Auswahl von Liedern Gustav Mahlers' (previously unpublished); 'Der dialektische Komponist' (1934); 'Anton von Webern' (1932); 'Ad vocem Hindemith: Eine Dokumentation' (a compilation: 'Präludium' (previously unpublished), I 'Paul Hindemith' (1922), II 'Kammermusik von Paul Hindemith' (1926), III 'Kritik des Musikanten' (1932), 'Hindemith, Paul, *Unterweisung im Tonsatz, Theoretischer Teil*' (discussion intended for the *Zeitschrift für Sozialforschung*, V (1939), but which remained unpublished), 'Früher Irrtum' (1964), 'Postludium' (previously unpublished); 'Glosse über Sibelius' (1938); 'Schwierigkeiten' – I 'Beim Komponieren' (1965), II 'In der Auffassung neuer Musik' (1968); 'Musikalische Diebe, unmusikalische Richter' (1934); 'Kleine Häresie (1965); 'Vierhändig, noch einmal' (1933); 'Metronomisierung' (1926); 'Nach Steuermanns Tod' (under the title 'Nachruf auf einen Pianisten', 1964); 'Winfried Zillig. Möglichkeiten und Wirklichkeit' (talk for Bayerischer Rundfunk, 10 June 1964; previously unpublished); 'Über einige Arbeiten Arnold Schönbergs' (1963). *GS* 17 (1982), pp. 163–344

'Zu einem Streitgespräch über Mahler', in *Musik und Verlag: Karl Vötterle zum 65. Geburtstag*, ed. Richard Baum and Wolfgang Rehm (Kassel, 1968). *GS* 18 (1984), pp. 244–50

'Chormusik und falsches Bewußtsein', *Westfälische Rundschau* (Easter, 1968). *GS* 18 (1984), pp. 813–14

'Antwort des Fachidioten', *Der Spiegel* (22 April 1968). *GS* 19 (1984), pp. 570–72

'Reflexionen über Musikkritik', *Studien zur Wertungsforschung I: Symposium für Musikkritik* (Graz, 1968). *GS* 19 (1984), pp. 573–91

'Wilhelm Fürtwängler', in *Wilhelm Fürtwängler: Dokumente, Berichte und Bilder, Aufzeichnungen*, ed. Karla Höcker (1968). *GS* 19 (1984), pp. 468–9

'Orpheus in der Unterwelt', *Der Spiegel* (11 November 1968). *GS* 19 (1984), pp. 545–54

'Musik im Fernsehen ist Brimborium', *Der Spiegel* (26 February 1968). *GS* 19 (1984), pp. 559–69

1969

Komposition für den Film [with Hanns Eisler] (Munich: Rogner & Bernhard, 1969); the first publication of this book was in the English version of 1947, under Eisler's name only (see 1947 above for full history). *GS* 15 (1976), pp. 7–155

Nervenpunkte der Neuen Musik [selected essays from *Klangfiguren* (1959)], (Reinbeck bei Hamburg: Rowohlt Taschenbuch Verlag, 1969)

'Fragment als Graphik', *Süddeutsche Zeitung* (8/9 March 1969). *GS* 18 (1984), pp. 251–3

'Konzeption eines Wiener Operntheaters', *Studien zur Wertungsforschung* 2 (Graz, 1969). *GS* 19 (1984), pp. 496–515

'Oper und Langspielplatte', *Der Spiegel* (24 March 1969). *GS* 19 (1984), pp. 555–8

POSTHUMOUS PUBLICATIONS ON MUSIC

Briefwechsel [with Ernst Krenek], ed. Wolfgang Rogge (Frankfurt/Main: Suhrkamp Verlag, 1974). Contents: Krenek, 'Vortwort'; Adorno and Krenek, 'Briefe 1–64' [1929–64]; Appendix: Krenek, 'Freiheit und Technik. "Improvisatorischer" Stil' (1929); Adorno, 'Zur Zwölftontechnik' (1929); Adorno, 'Reaktion und Fortschritt' (1930); Krenek, 'Fortschritt und Reaktion' (1930); Adorno and Krenek, 'Arbeitsprobleme des Komponisten: Gespräch über Musik und soziale Situation' (1930); Adorno, 'Zur Deutung Kreneks' (1932); Krenek, 'Ansprache zum Abend zeitgenössischer Musik im österreichischen Studio' [1935, previously unpublished]; Adorno, 'Ernst Krenek' (1935, original in English); Krenek, 'Was erwartet der Komponist von der Musikerziehung' (1936); Adorno, 'Musikpädagogische Musik' (1936); Adorno, 'Besprechung zu: Krenek, Über neue Musik' (1938); Adorno, 'Zur Physiognomik Kreneks' (1957/8)

'Kammermusikwoche in Frankfurt am Main' [1923], *GS* 20.2 (1986), 771–6

'Ravel' [*c.* 1928], *GS* 18 (1984), pp. 273–4

'Die stabilisierte Musik' [1928], *GS* 18 (1984), pp. 721–8

'Berliner Memorial' [1928], (1984), pp. 259–66

'Berliner Opernmemorial' [1929], *GS* 19 (1984), 267–75

'Mahler heute' [1930], *GS* 18 (1984), pp. 226–34

'Berg und Webern' [1930], *GS* 20.2 (1986), pp. 782–92

'Bartók', [*c.* 1930], *GS* 18 (1984), pp. 291–4

'Eduard Steuermanns Brahms-Ausgabe' [1931], *GS* 18 (1984), pp. 195–9

'Der Wunderkantor' [*c.* 1932], *GS* 18 (1984), p. 790

'Anton von Webern' [1933], *GS* 18 (1984), pp. 517–18

'Arnold Schönberg (II)' [1934], *GS* 18 (1984), pp. 394–7

'Schönberg: Lieder und Klavierstücke' [1934], *GS* 18 (1984), pp. 398–400

'Brahms aktuell' [1934], *GS* 18 (1984), pp. 200–203

'Berg: Drei Stücke aus der Lyrischen Suite für Streichorchester' [1934], *GS* 20.2 (1986), pp. 797–801

'Ludwig van Beethoven: Sechs Bagatellen für Klavier, op. 126' [1934], *GS* 18 (1984), pp. 185–8

'Antwort eines Adepten' [1934]; corrected proof. Published posthumously in *"23".* *Eine Wiener Musikzeitschrift*, ed. Willi Reich (Vienna, 1971). *GS* 18 (1984), pp. 401–7

'Mozartfest in Glyndebourne' [1934]. *GS* 19 (1984), pp. 278–80

'Warum Zwölftonmusik?' [c. 1935], GS 18 (1984), pp. 114–17

'Marginalien zu Mahler' [1936?], GS 18 (1984), pp. 235–40

'Berg-Gedenkkonzert im Londoner Rundfunk' [1936], GS 20.2 (1986), pp. 802–3

'Drehorgel-Stücke' [1927–37], GS 18 (1984), pp. 37–44

'Zweite Nachtmusik' [1937], GS 18 (1984), pp. 45–53

'Exposé zu einer Monographie über Arnold Schoenberg' [1937], GS 19 (1984), pp. 609–13

'Was ist Musik?' [1939], GS 19 (1984), pp. 614–19

'Neunzehn Beiträge über neue Musik' [1942], GS 18 (1984), pp. 57–87

'The musical climate for fascism in Germany' [c. 1945], GS 20.2 (1986), pp. 430–40

'Die Geschichte der deutschen Musik von 1908 bis 1933' [c. 1949], GS 19 (1984), pp. 620–29

'Arnold Schönberg: Worte des Gedenkens zum 13. September 1951' [1951], GS 18 (1984), pp. 623–6

'Für Alban Berg' [1951], GS 18 (1984), pp. 483–6

'Entwicklung und Formen der neuen Musik' [1952], GS 18 (1984), pp. 188–223

'Alban Bergs Kammerkonzert' [1954], GS 18 (1984), pp. 630–40

'Einführung in die Zweite Kammersymphonie von Schönberg' [1954], GS 18 (1984), pp. 627–9

'Das Erbe und die neue Musik' [1954], GS 18 (1984), pp. 684–94

'Zur Uraufführung des Klaviertrios von Eduard Steuermann' [1954], GS 18 (1984), pp. 680–81

'Im Gedächtnis an Alban Berg' [1955], GS 18 (1984), pp. 487–512

'Kleiner Dank an Wien' [1955], GS 20.2 (1986), pp. 552–4

'Für die Kranichsteiner Idee' [1955], GS 19 (1984), pp. 630–32

'Musiksoziologie' [1955], GS 18 (1984), pp. 840–41

'Über einige Arbeiten von Anton von Webern' [1958], GS 18 (1984), pp. 573–9

'Zu den Georgeliedern' [1959], GS 18 (1984), pp. 411–17

'Mahlers aktualität' [1960], GS 18 (1984), pp. 241–3

'Aus dem Ersten Mahler-Vortrag' [1960], GS 18 (1984), pp. 584–7

'Zweiter Mahler-Vortrag' [1960], GS 18 (1984), pp. 588–603

'Dritter Mahler-Vortrag' [1960], GS 18 (1984), pp. 604–22

'Schönbergs Klavierwerk' [1961], GS 18 (1984), pp. 422–6

'Erwiderung' [auf Alphons Silbermann] [1961], GS 18 (1984), pp. 836–7

'Arnold Schönberg: Fünfzehn Gedichte aus "Das Buch der Hängenden Gärten" von Stefan George, op. 15. Anton Webern: Fünf Lieder nach Gedichten von Stefan George, op. 4' [1963], GS 18 (1984), pp. 418–21

'Schöne Stellen' [1965], GS 18 (1984), pp. 695–718

'Theodor W. Adorno; Vier Lieder nach Gedichten von Stefan George für Singstimme und Klavier, op. 7' [1967]; published posthumously in Adorno-Noten, ed. Rolf Tiedemann (Berlin, 1984), GS 18 (1984), pp. 552–6

'Von der Musik her' [1967], GS 20.2 (1986), pp. 527–9

'Wilhelm Furtwängler' [1968], GS 19 (1984), pp. 468–9

'Alban Berg: Oper und Moderne' [1969], GS 18 (1984), pp. 650–72

'Zu einer Auswahl aus den "Klangfiguren"' [1969], GS 16 (1978), pp. 645–8

'Zum Probleme der musikalischen Analyse' [1969]; improvised talk given at the Hochschule für Musik und Darstellende Kunst, Frankfurt am Main (24 February 1969; tape recording (Tonband no. 102) in the possession of the

Library of the Hochschule). As yet unpublished in German. Published in English as: 'On the problem of musical analysis', trans. with introduction and notes by Max Paddison, *Music Analysis* 1/2 (July 1982), pp. 169–87

1.3 OTHER WORKS BY ADORNO CONSULTED

Books

Dialektik der Aufklärung: Philosophische Fragmente [with Max Horkheimer] (Amsterdam: Querido, 1947). *GS* 3 (1981). Translated as: *Dialectic of Englightenment*, trans. John Cumming (New York: Herder & Herder, 1972)

The Authoritarian Personality, with contributions by Adorno, Else Frenkel-Brunswick, Daniel J. Levinson and R. Nevitt Sanford (New York: Harper and Brothers, 1950)

Minima Moralia: Reflexionen aus dem beschädigten Leben (Frankfurt/Main: Suhrkamp Verlag, 1951). *GS* 4 (1980). Translated as: *Minima Moralia: Reflections from Damaged Life*, trans. E. F. N. Jephcott (London: NLB, 1974)

Zur Metakritik der Erkenntnistheorie (Stuttgart: W. Kohlhammer, 1956). *GS* 5 (1970). Translated as: *Against Epistemology: A Metacritique*, trans. Willis Domingo (Cambridge, Mass.: MIT Press, 1983)

Soziologische Exkurse, by Institut für Sozialforschung, introduced by T. W. Adorno and Max Horkheimer (Frankfurt/Main: Europäische Verlagsanstalt, 1956). Translated as: *Aspects of Sociology*, by The Frankfurt Institute for Social Research, with a preface by Max Horkheimer and Theodor Adorno, trans. John Viertel (London: Heinemann, 1973)

Drei Studien zu Hegel (Frankfurt/Main: Suhrkamp Verlag, 1957, 1963). *GS* 5 (1970, 1975), pp. 247–381

Noten zur Literatur I (Frankfurt/Main and Berlin: Suhrkamp Verlag, 1958). *GS* 11 (1974), pp. 7–126

Noten zur Literatur II (Frankfurt/Main: Suhrkamp Verlag, 1961). *GS* 11 (1974), pp. 127–321

Eingriffe: Neun kritische Modelle (Frankfurt/Main: Suhrkamp Verlag, 1963). *GS* 10.2 (1977), pp. 455–594

Jargon der Eigentlichkeit: Zur deutschen Ideologie (Frankfurt/Main: Suhrkamp Verlag, 1964). *GS* 6 (1973, 1977), pp. 413–526. Translated as: *Jargon of Authenticity*, trans. Knut Tarnowski and Frederic Will, with a Foreword by Trent Schroyer (London: Routledge & Kegan Paul, 1973)

Noten zur Literatur III (Frankfurt/Main: Suhrkamp Verlag, 1965). *GS* 11 (1974), pp. 323–491

Negative Dialektik (Frankfurt/Main: Suhrkamp Verlag, 1966). *GS* 6 (1973, 1977) pp. 7–412. Translated as: *Negative Dialectics*, trans. E. B. Ashton (New York: Seabury Press, and London: Routledge & Kegan Paul, 1973)

Ohne Leitbild: Parva Aesthetica (Frankfurt/Main: Suhrkamp Verlag, 1967). *GS* 10.1 (1977), pp. 289–453

Der Positivismusstreit in der deutschen Soziologie with contributions from Adorno, Hans Albert, Ralf Dahrendorf, Jürgen Habermas, Harald Pilot and Karl Popper (Berlin: Hermann Luchterhand Verlag, 1969). Translated as: *The Positivist Dispute in German Sociology*, trans. Glyn Adey and David Frisby (London: Heinemann, 1976)

Stichworte: Kritische Modelle 2 (Frankfurt/Main: Suhrkamp Verlag, 1969). *GS* 10.2 (1977), pp. 595–738

Ästhetische Theorie (unfinished), ed. Rolf Tiedemann and Gretel Adorno (Frankfurt/Main: Suhrkamp Verlag, 1970; revised edition 1972). *GS* 7 (1970, 1972). Translated as: *Aesthetic Theory*, trans. Christian Lenhardt (London: Routledge and Kegan Paul, 1984)

Vorlesungen zur Ästhetik 1967–68 (Zürich: H. Mayer Verlag, 1973) ['Raubdruck', not included in *GS*]

Individual articles and essays

'Expressionismus und künstlerische Wahrhaftigkeit: Zur Kritik neuer Dichtung' (1920). *GS* 11 (1974), pp. 609–11

'*Die Aktualität der Philosophie*' [1931], *GS* 1 (1973), pp. 325–44. Translated as: 'The actuality of philosophy', translator unacknowledged, *Telos* 31 (1977), pp. 120–33

'Die Idee der Naturgeschichte' [1932]. *GS* 1 (1973), pp. 345–65. Translated as: 'The idea of natural-history', trans. Bob Hullot-Kentor, *Telos* 60 (Summer 1984), pp. 111–24

'Letters to Walter Benjamin' [1935–1938], trans. Harry Zohn, in Ernst Bloch *et al.*, *Aesthetics and Politics*, ed. Ronald Taylor (London: NLB, 1977), pp. 110–33

'Husserl and the problem of Idealism' (original in English), *The Journal of Philosophy* 37/1 (January 1940). *GS* 20.1 (1986), pp. 119–34

'Theses upon art and religion today' (original in English), *Kenyon Review* 7 (1945). *GS* 11 (1974), pp. 647–53

'Zum Verhältnis von Soziologie und Psychologie' (1955), in *Soziologische Schriften I, GS* 8 (1972), pp. 42–85. Translated as: 'Sociology and psychology', trans. Irving N. Wohlfahrt, *New Left Review* 46 (November/December 1967), pp. 67–80, and 47 (January/February 1968), pp. 79–97

'Der Essay als Form' (1958), in *Noten zur Literatur I* (1958). *GS* 11 (1974), pp. 9–33

'Kultur und Verwaltung' (1960), in *Soziologische Schriften I, GS* 8 (1972), pp. 122–46. Translated as: 'Culture and administration', trans. Wesley Blomster, *Telos* 37 (Fall 1978), pp. 93–111

'Engagement' (1962), in *Noten zur Literatur III* (1965). *GS* 11 (1974), pp. 409–30. Translated as: 'Commitment', trans. Francis McDonagh, in *The Essential Frankfurt School Reader*, ed. Andrew Arato and Eike Gebhardt (Oxford: Basil Blackwell, 1978), pp. 300–318

'Jene zwanziger Jahre', in *Eingriffe: Neun kritische Modelle* (1963). *GS* 10.2 (1977), pp. 499–506

'Resumé über Kulturindustrie' (1963), in *Ohne Leitbild: Parva Aesthetica* (1967, 1968). *GS* 10.1 (1977), pp. 337–45. Translated as: 'Culture industry reconsidered', trans. Anson G. Rabinbach, *New German Critique* 6 (1975), pp. 12–19

'Zweimal Chaplin' (1930/64), in *Ohne Leitbild: Parva Aesthetica* (1967, 1968). *GS* 10.1 (1977), pp. 362–6

'Fortschritt' (1964), in *Stichworte: Kritische Modelle 2* (1969). *GS* 10.2 (1977), pp. 617–38

'Funktionalismus heute' (1965/6), in *Ohne Leitbild: Parva Aesthetica* (1967). *GS* 10.1 (1977), pp. 375–95

'Gesellschaft' (1966). *GS* 8 (1972), pp. 9–19. Translated as: 'Society', trans. Fredric

Jameson, *Salmagundi* 10/11 (Fall 1969–Winter 1970), pp. 144–53
'Filmtransparente' (1966), in *Ohne Leitbild: Parva Aesthetica* (1967, 1968). *GS* 10.1 (1977), pp. 353–61. Translated as: 'Transparencies on film', trans. Thomas Y. Levin, *New German Critique* no. 24/5 (Fall/Winter 1981–2), pp. 199–205
'Über Tradition' (1966), in *Ohne Leitbild: Parva Aesthetica* (1967, 1968). *GS* 10.1 (1977), pp. 310–20
'Thesen zur Kunstsoziologie' (1967), in *Ohne Leitbild: Parva Aesthetica* (1967, 1968). *GS* 10.1 (1977), pp. 367–74. Translated as: 'Theses on the sociology of art', trans. Brian Trench, *Birmingham Working Papers in Cultural Studies* 2 (1972), pp. 121–8
'Erziehung nach Auschwitz' (1967), in *Stichworte: Kritische Modelle 2* (1969). *GS* 10.2 (1977), pp. 674–90
'Die Kunst und die Künste' (1967), in *Ohne Leitbild: Parva Aesthetica* (1967, 1968). *GS* 10.1 (1977), pp. 432–53
'Wissenschaftliche Erfahrungen in Amerika' (1968), in *Stichworte: Kritische Modelle 2* (1969). *GS* 10.2 (1977), pp. 702–40. Translated as: 'Scientific experiences of a European scholar in America', trans. Donald Fleming, in *The Intellectual Migration: Europe and America, 1930–1960*, ed. Donald Fleming and Bernard Bailyn (Cambridge, Mass.: Belknap-Harvard University Press, 1969)
'Zu Subjekt und Objekt' (1969), in *Stichworte: Kritische Modelle 2* (1969). *GS* 10.2 (1977), pp. 741–58. Translated as: 'Subject and Object', translator unacknowledged, in *The Essential Frankfurt School Reader*, ed. Andrew Arato and Eike Gebhardt (Oxford: Basil Blackwell, 1978), pp. 497–511
'Resignation' (1969), in *Kritische Modelle 3*, *GS* 10.2 (1977), pp. 794–9. Translated as: 'Resignation', trans. Wesley Blomster, *Telos* 35 (Spring 1978), pp. 165–8
'Kritik' (1969), in *Kritische Modelle 3*, *GS* 10.2 (1977), pp. 785–93
'Etwas fehlt . . . über die Widersprüche der utopischen Sehnsucht', in *Gespräche mit Ernst Bloch*, ed. Rainer Taub and Harald Wieser (Frankfurt/Main: Suhrkamp Verlag, 1975). Translated as: 'Something's missing: a discussion between Ernst Bloch and Theodor W. Adorno on the contradictions of utopian longing', in Ernst Bloch, *The Utopian Function of Art and Literature: Selected Essays*, trans. Jack Zipes and Frank Mecklenburg (Cambridge, Mass.: MIT Press, 1988), pp. 1–17
'To describe, understand and explain', a discussion between Adorno and Lucien Goldmann, Appendix 3 of Lucien Goldmann, *Cultural Creation in Modern Society*, trans. Bart Grahl (St Louis: Telos Press, 1976), pp. 131–47

1.4 OTHER PRIMARY SOURCES
Beckett, Samuel. *Proust and Three Dialogues with Georges Duthuit* (London: John Calder, 1965; original edns 1931 and 1949)
Benjamin, Walter. *Ursprung des deutschen Trauerspiels*, in Benjamin, *Gesammelte Schriften* 1.1, ed. Rolf Tiedemann (Frankfurt/Main: Suhrkamp Verlag, 1974), pp. 203–430. Translated as: *The Origin of German Tragic Drama*, trans. John Osborne and introduced by George Steiner (London: NLB, 1977)
'Das Kunstwerk im Zeitalter seiner technischen Reproduzierbarkeit', in Benjamin, *GS* 1.2 (Frankfurt/Main: Suhrkamp Verlag, 1974), pp. 431–508. Translated as: 'The work of art in the age of mechanical reproduction', in

Illuminations, ed. with introduction by Hannah Arendt, trans. Harry Zohn (London: Fontana/Collins, 1973), pp. 219–53

Reflections: Essays, Aphorisms, Autobiographical Writings, trans. Edmund Jephcott (New York/London: Harcourt Brace Jovanovich, 1978)

Bloch, Ernst; Lukács, Georg; Brecht, Bertolt; Benjamin, Walter; Adorno, Theodor. *Aesthetics and Politics*, ed. Ronald Taylor, Afterword by Fredric Jameson (London: NLB, 1977)

Bloch, Ernst. *Zur Philosophie der Musik*, selected and ed. Karola Bloch (Frankfurt/ Main: Suhrkamp Verlag, 1974). A version of this selection appeared in English as: *Essays on the Philosophy of Music*, trans. Peter Palmer with an introduction by David Drew (Cambridge: Cambridge University Press, 1985)

Geist der Utopie (1918, rev. edn 1923), *Gesamtausgabe* Bd. 3 (Frankfurt/Main: Suhrkamp Verlag, 1964)

Das Prinzip Hoffnung (1938), *Gesamtausgabe* Bd. 5 (Frankfurt/Main: Suhrkamp Verlag, 1977)

The Utopian Function of Art and Literature: Selected Essays, trans. Jack Zipes and Frank Mecklenburg (Cambridge, Mass.: MIT Press, 1988)

Brecht, Bertolt. 'Über die Verwendung von Musik für ein episches Theater' [1935], in *Schriften zum Theater* (1957). Translated as: 'On the use of music in an epic theatre', in *Brecht on Theatre: The Development of an Aesthetic*, ed. and trans. John Willett (London: Eyre Methuen, 1964, 2nd edn 1973), pp. 84–90

Bürger, Peter. *Theorie der Avantgarde* (Frankfurt/Main: Suhrkamp Verlag, 1974). Translated as: *Theory of the Avant-Garde*, trans. Michael Shaw, Foreword by Jochen Schulte-Sasse (Manchester: Manchester University Press, 1984)

The Decline of Modernism, trans. Nicholas Walker (Cambridge: Polity Press, 1992)

Cage, John. 'Storia dell'Opera', *Europeras 1 & 2. Programmheft* (Frankfurt/Main: Oper Frankfurt, 1987)

Silence: Lectures and Writings (London: Marion Boyars, 1968)

Dahlhaus, Carl. 'Form', *Darmstädter Beiträge zur Neuen Musik*, vol. X (1966), pp. 41–9

Musikästhetik (Cologne: Musikverlag Hans Gerig, 1967). Translated as: *Esthetics of Musics*, trans. William Austin (Cambridge: Cambridge University Press, 1982)

Grundlagen der Musikgeschichte (Cologne: Musikverlag Hans Gerig, 1967). Translated as: *Foundations of Music History*, trans. J. B. Robinson (Cambridge: Cambridge University Press, 1983)

Schoenberg and the New Music, trans. Derrick Puffett and Alfred Clayton (Cambridge: Cambridge University Press, 1987)

Eggebrecht, Hans Heinrich. 'Funktionale Musik', in *Musikalisches Denken* (Wilhelmshaven: Heinrichshofen's Verlag, 1977), pp. 153–92

Eisler, Hanns. 'Die Erbauer einer neuen Musikkultur' (1931), in *Reden und Aufsätze*, ed. Winfried Höntsch (Leipzig: Reclam, 1961), pp. 25–52. Translated as: 'The builders of a new musical culture', in Eisler, *A Rebel in Music: Selected Writings*, ed. with introduction by Manfred Grabs, trans. Marjorie Meyer (Berlin: Seven Seas Publishers, 1978)

Musik und Politik: Schriften 1924–1948 (Leipzig: VEB Deutscher Verlag für Music, 1973)

Musik und Politik: Schriften, Addenda (Leipzig: VEB Deutscher Verlag für Musik, 1983)

Materialien zu einer Dialektik der Musik (Leipzig: Reclam, 1973)

Komposition für den Film (with T. W. Adorno) (Munich: Rogner & Bernhard, 1969); first published in English as: *Composing for the Films* (Adorno's co-authorship not acknowledged) (New York: Oxford University Press, 1947)

Ejxenbaum [Eichenbaum], Boris M. 'The theory of the formal method', trans. L. R. Titunik, in *Readings in Russian Poetics: Formalist and Sructuralist Views*, ed. Ladislav Matejka and Krystyna Pomorska (Ann Arbor: MIT Press, 1978), pp. 3–37

Freud, Sigmund. *Neue Folge der Vorlesungen zur Einführung in die Psychoanalyse* (Vienna, 1933). Translated as: *New Introductory Lectures on Psychoanalysis*, trans. and ed. James Strachey (Harmondsworth: Penguin Books, 1973)

Eine Kindheitserinnerung des Leonardo da Vinci (Leipzig/Vienna, 1910). Translated as: 'Leonardo da Vinci and a memory of his childhood', in *Art and Literature*, trans. and ed. James Strachey and Albert Dickson (Harmondsworth: Penguin Books, 1985)

Fromm, Erich. 'Über Methode und Aufgabe einer analytischen Sozialpsychologie', *Zeitschrift für Sozialforschung* I, Hefte 1/2 (1932). English version: 'The method and function of an analytic social psychology', in *The Crisis of Psychoanalysis: Essays on Freud, Marx and Social Psychology* (London: Jonathan Cape, 1971), pp. 135–62

Gadamer, Hans-Georg. *Philosophical Hermeneutics*, trans. and ed. David E. Linge (Berkeley/Los Angeles: University of California Press, 1976)

Hegel's Dialectic: Five Hermeneutical Studies, trans. with an introduction by P. Christopher Smith (New Haven and London: Yale University Press, 1976)

Habermas, Jürgen. *Philosophical-Political Profiles*, trans. Frederick G. Lawrence (London: Heinemann, 1983)

'Modernity – an incomplete project', in *Postmodern Culture* [original title: *The Anti-Aesthetic* (Bay Press, 1983)], ed. Hal Foster (London: Pluto Press, 1985), pp. 3–15

Halm, August. *Von zwei Kulturen der Musik* (Munich: Georg Müller, 1913)

Hanslick, Eduard. *Vom Musikalisch-Schönen* (1854) (Leipzig, 1902; 10th edn)

Hegel, G. W. F. *Phänomenologie des Geistes* (1807) (Frankfurt/Main: Suhrkamp Verlag, 1980)

The Phenomenology of Mind, trans. with an introduction and notes by J. B. Baille, and with an introductory essay by George Lichtheim (New York and Evanston: Harper & Row, 1967)

Science of Logic (1812), trans. A. V. Miller, with a Foreword by J. N. Findlay (London: George Allen & Unwin, 1969)

Logic (Encyclopaedia of the Philosophical Sciences, Part I (1830)), trans. William Wallace, with a Foreword by J. N. Findlay (Oxford: Clarendon Press, 1975)

Introduction to Aesthetics (The Introduction to the Berlin Aesthetics Lectures of the 1820s), trans. T. M. Knox, with an interpretative essay by Charles Karelis (Oxford: Oxford University Press, 1979)

On Art, Religion, Philosophy: Introductory Lectures to the realm of Absolute Spirit, ed. with an introduction by J. Glenn Gray, trans. Bernard Bosanquet,

E. B. Speirs, J. Burdon Sanderson and E. S. Haldane (New York: Harper & Row, 1970)

Hindemith, Paul. *Unterweisung im Tonsatz* (Bd. I, Theoretischer Teil) (Mainz: B. Schott's Söhne, 1937). Translated as: *The Craft of Musical Composition* (Bk. I, Theoretical Part), trans. Arthur Mendel (London/Mainz/New York: Schott/ Associated Music Publishers, 1942)

Horkheimer, Max. *Traditionelle und kritische Theorie: Vier Aufsätze* (Frankfurt/ Main: Suhrkamp Verlag, 1970)
'Zum Problem der Wahrheit', *Zeitschrift für Sozialforschung* 4/3 (1935), pp. 321–64. Translated as: 'On the problem of truth', in *The Essential Frankfurt School Reader*, ed. Andrew Arato and Eike Gebhardt, translator unacknowledged (Oxford: Basil Blackwell, 1978), pp. 407–43

Husserl, Edmund. *Ideen zu einer reinen Phänomenologie und phänomenologischen Philosophie* (1913). Translated as: *Ideas: General Introduction to Pure Phenomenology*, trans. W. R. Boyce Gibson (New York/London: Collier/Macmillan, 1962)

Kant, Immanuel. *Kritik der Urteilskraft* (1790). Translated as: *The Critique of Judgement* (1928), trans. James Creed Meredith (Oxford: The Clarendon Press, 1952, 1982)

Kojève, Alexandre. *Introduction to the Reading of Hegel: Lectures on the Phenomenology of Spirit*, assembled by Raymond Queneau, ed. Allan Bloom, trans. James H. Nichols (Ithaca and London: Cornell University Press, 1969; original French edition, 1947)

Krenek, Ernst. *Exploring Music: Essays*, trans. Margaret Shenfield and Geoffrey Skelton (London: Calder and Boyars, 1966)
Horizons Circled: Reflections on my Music, with contributions by Will Ogden and John L. Stewart (Berkeley/Los Angeles: University of California Press, 1974)
'Freiheit und Technik: "Improvisatorischer" Stil', *Anbruch* 11 (Heft 7/8, September/October 1929). Republished in Adorno–Krenek, *Briefwechsel*, ed. Wolfgang Rogge (Frankfurt/Main: Suhrkamp Verlag, 1974), pp. 161–6
'Fortschritt und Reaktion', *Anbruch* 12 (Heft 6, June 1930). *Briefwechsel* (1974), pp. 181–6
'Arbeitsprobleme des Komponisten. Gespräch über Musik und soziale Situation' (with T. W. Adorno), *Frankfurter Zeitung* (10 December 1930). *Briefwechsel* (1974), pp. 187–93; Adorno, *GS* 19 (1984), pp. 433–9

Lazarsfeld, Paul. *Main Trends in Sociology* (1970) (London: Allen & Unwin, 1973)

Löwenthal, Leo. 'Knut Hamsun', *Zeitschrift für Sozialforschung* vol. 6 (1937). Translated as: 'Knut Hamsun', trans. anonymous, in *The Essential Frankfurt School Reader*, ed. Andrew Arato and Eike Gebhardt (Oxford: Basil Blackwell, 1978), pp. 319–45.

Lukács, Georg. *Die Theorie des Romans* (Berlin: P. Cassirer, 1920). Translated as: *The Theory of the Novel*, trans. Anna Bostock (London: Merlin Press, 1971)
Geschichte und Klassenbewußtsein (1922) (Berlin and Neuwied: Luchterhand Verlag, 1968). Translated as: *History and Class Consciousness*, trans. Rodney Livingstone (London: Merlin Press, 1971)

Lyotard, Jean-François. *La Condition postmoderne: rapport sur le savoir* (Paris: Editions de Minuit, 1979). Translated as: *The Postmodern Condition: A Report on Knowledge*, trans. Geoff Bennington and Brian Massumi (Manchester:

Manchester University Press, 1984)

Mann, Thomas. *Doktor Faustus* (Stockholm: Bermann-Fischer Verlag, 1947). Translated as: *Doctor Faustus*, trans. H. T. Lowe-Porter (Harmondsworth: Penguin Books, 1968)

The Story of a Novel: The Genesis of Doctor Faustus, trans. Richard and Sarah Winston (New York, 1961)

Marcuse, Herbert. *Die Permanenz der Kunst: Wider eine Bestimmte Marxistische Ästhetik* (Munich: Carl Hanser Verlag, 1977). Translated as: *The Aesthetic Dimension: Towards a Critique of Marxist Aesthetics*, trans. Herbert Marcuse and Erica Sherover (London: Macmillan, 1979)

Marx, Karl. *Ökonomische–Philosophische Manuskripte* (1984), *Marx–Engels Gesamtausgabe*, Bd. 1.3 (Moscow, 1932). Translated as: *Economic and Philosophic Manuscripts of 1844*, trans. Martin Milligan (Moscow/London: Progress Publishers/Lawrence & Wishart, 1977)

Zur Kritik der politischen Ökonomie (1859), *Marx–Engels Werke*, Bd. 13 (Berlin, 1975). Translated as: *A Contribution to the Critique of Political Economy* (1859), trans. S. W. Ryazanskaya, ed. Maurice Dobb (Moscow/London: Progress Publishers/Lawrence & Wishart, 1970). Also in: *Early Writings*, trans. Rodney Livingstone and Gregor Benton, introduced by Lucio Colletti (Harmondsworth: Penguin Books, 1975)

Das Kapital, Bd. 1 (1867), *Marx–Engels Werke*, Bd. 23 (Berlin, 1968). Translated as: *Capital*, vol. 1, trans. Ben Fowkes, introduced by Ernest Mandel (Harmondsworth: Penguin Books, 1976)

Marx, Karl, and Engels, Friedrich. *On Literature and Art* (Moscow: Progress Publishers, 1976)

Nietzsche, Friedrich. *Zur Genealogie der Moral* (1887) (Munich: Wilhelm Goldmann Verlag, undated). Translated as: *The Genealogy of Morals* [ed. also includes *The Birth of Tragedy*], trans. Francis Golffing (New York: Doubleday Anchor, 1956), pp. 147–299

Reich, Willi. *Alban Berg: Mit Bergs eigenen Schriften und Beiträgen von Theodor Wiesengrund–Adorno und Ernst Krenek* (Vienna/Leipzig/Zürich: Herbert Reichner Verlag, 1937)

de Saussure, Ferdinand. *Course in General Linguistics*, introduced by Jonathan Culler, ed. Charles Ball and Albert Sechehaye, trans. Wade Baskin (London: Fontana/Collins, 1974)

Schoenberg, Arnold. *Harmonielehre* (Vienna: Universal Edition, 1911; 3rd edn 1922). Translated as: *Theory of Harmony*, trans. Roy E. Carter (London: Faber & Faber, 1978)

Style and Idea: Selected Writings, trans. Leo Black, ed. Leonard Stein (London: Faber & Faber, 1975)

Letters, trans. Eithne Wilkins and Ernst Kaiser, selected and ed. Erwin Stein (London: Faber & Faber, 1964)

Tynjanov [Tynyanov], Jurij, and Jakobson, Roman. 'Problems in the study of literature and language', trans. Herbert Eagle, in *Readings in Russian Poetics: Formalist and Structualist Views*, ed. Ladislaw Matejka and Krystyna Pomorska (Ann Arbor: MIT Press, 1978), pp. 79–81

Valéry, Paul. *Pièces sur l'art* (Paris: Gallimard, 1934)

Selected Writings, trans. C. Day Lewis *et al.* (New York: New Directions Books,

1950)

'The idea of art', trans. R. Manheim, in *Aesthetics*, ed. Harold Osborne (Oxford: Oxford University Press, 1972), pp. 25–3

'Remarks on poetry', in *Symbolism: An Anthology*, ed. and trans. T. G. West (London and New York: Methuen, 1980), pp. 42–60

Wagner, Richard. *On Music and Drama*, trans. H. Ashton Ellis, selected and arranged, with an introduction, by Albert Goldman and Evert Sprinchorn (New York: Da Capo Press, 1964)

Weber, Max. *Die rationalen und sozialen Grundlagen der Musik* [1911] (Tübingen: J. C. B. Mohr, 1921). Translated as: *The Rational and Social Foundations of Music*, trans. and ed. Don Martindale, Johannes Riedel and Gertrude Neuwirth (Carbondale: Southern Illinois University Press, 1958)

Die protestantische Ethik und der Geist des Kapitalismus, Archiv für Sozialwissenschaft und Sozialpolitik, Hefte 20/21 (1904–5). Translated as: *The Protestant Ethic and the Spirit of Capitalism*, trans. Talcott Parsons with a Foreword by R. H. Tawney (London: George Allen & Unwin, 1930, 1971)

Selections in Translation, trans. E. Matthews, ed. W. G. Runciman (Cambridge: Cambridge University Press, 1978)

On Capitalism, Bureaucracy and Religion: A Selection of Texts, ed. and in part newly translated by Stanislav Andrewski (London: George Allen & Unwin, 1983)

Wind, H. E. *Die Endkrise in der bürgerlichen Musik und die Rolle Arnold Schoenbergs* (Vienna: Krystall-Verlag, 1935)

2 SECONDARY SOURCES

2.1 WORKS ON ADORNO, CRITICAL THEORY AND THE FRANKFURT SCHOOL

Arato, Andrew *et al.* (eds.). *The Essential Frankfurt School Reader* (Oxford: Basil Blackwell, 1978)

Arnold, Heinz Ludwig (ed.). *Theodor W. Adorno* (Munich: Edition Text + Kritik, 1977)

Benhabib, Seyla. *Critique, Norm and Utopia: A Study of the Foundations of Critical Theory* (New York: Columbia University Press, 1986)

Benjamin, Jessica. 'The end of internalization: Adorno's social psychology', *Telos* 32 (1977), pp. 42–64

Berman, Russell. 'Adorno, Marxism and art', *Telos* 34 (Winter 1977–8), pp. 157–66

Blomster, Wesley. 'Sociology of music: Adorno and beyond', *Telos* 28 (1976), pp. 81–112

'Electronic music', *Telos* 32 (Summer 1977), pp. 65–78

Boehmer, Konrad. 'Der Korrepetitor am Werk – Probleme des Materialbegriffs bei Adorno', *Zeitschrift für Musiktheorie* 4 (1973), pp. 28–33

Bottomore, Tom. *The Frankfurt School* (London: Tavistock Publications, 1984)

Breuer, Stefan. 'Adorno's anthropology', *Telos* 64 (Summer 1985), pp. 15–31

Buck-Morss, Susan. *The Origin of Negative Dialectics: Theodor W. Adorno, Walter Benjamin, and the Frankfurt Institute* (Sussex: Harvester Press, 1977)

'The dialectic of T. W. Adorno', *Telos* 14 (1973), pp. 137–44

Burde, Wolfgang. 'Versuch über einen Satz Theodor W. Adornos', *Neue Zeitschrift für Musik* 132 (1971), pp. 578–83

Bürger, Christa. 'Expression and construction: Adorno and Thomas Mann', in *Thinking Art: Beyond Traditional Aesthetics*, ed. Andrew Benjamin and Peter Osborne (London: ICA, 1991), pp. 131–430

Bürger, Peter. 'Das Vermittlungsproblem in der Kunstsoziologie Adornos', in *Materialien zur ästhetischen Theorie Th. W. Adornos: Konstruction der Moderne*, ed. Burkhardt Lindner and W. Martin Lüdke (Frankfurt/Main: Suhrkamp Verlag, 1979), pp. 169–86

'Das Altern der Moderne', in *Adorno-Konferenz 1983*, ed. Ludwig von Friedeburg and Jürgen Habermas (Frankfurt/Main: Suhrkamp Verlag, 1983), pp. 177–200. Translated as: 'The decline of the modern age', trans. David J. Parent, in *Telos* 62 (Winter 1984–5), pp. 117–30 [see also Primary Sources 1. 4]

Cahn, Michael. 'Subversive mimesis: T.W. Adorno and the modern impasse of critique', in *Mimesis in Contemporary Theory* vol. I, ed. Mihai Spariosu (Philadelphia/Amsterdam: John Benjamin's Publishing Company, 1984), pp. 27–64

Connerton, Paul. *The Tragedy of Enlightenment: An Essay on the Frankfurt School* (Cambridge: Cambridge University Press, 1980)

(ed.) *Critical Sociology: Selected Readings* (Harmondsworth: Penguin Books, 1976)

Dahlhaus, Carl. 'Soziologische Dechiffrierung von Musik: Zu Theodor W. Adorno Wagnerkritik', *International Review of Music, Aesthetics and Sociology*, 1/2 (1970), pp. 137–47

'Zu Adornos Beethoven-Kritik', in *Adorno und die Musik*, ed. Otto Kolleritsch (Graz: Universal Edition, 1979), pp. 170–79

'Adornos Begriff des musikalischen Materials', in *Zur Terminologie der Musik des 20. Jahrhunderts: Bericht über das zweite Kolloquium*, ed. H. H. Eggebrecht (Stuttgart, 1974), pp. 9–21

'Vom Altern einer Philosophie', in *Adorno-Konferenz 1983*, ed. Ludwig von Friedeburg and Jürgen Habermas (Frankfurt/Main: Suhrkamp Verlag, 1983), pp. 133–7

Dahmer, Helmut. 'Psychoanalysis as social theory', *Telos* 32 (Summer 1977), pp. 27–41

Dallmyr, Helmut. 'Phenomenology and critical theory: Adorno', *Cultural Hermeneutics* 3/4 (1976), pp. 367–405

Dawydow, Juri. *Die sich selbst negierende Dialektik: Kritik der Musiktheorie Theodor Adornos* (Berlin: Akademie-Verlag, 1971)

Deathridge, John. 'Theodor Adorno, *In Search of Wagner*' [review], *Nineteenth Century Music* 8/1 (Summer 1983), pp. 81–5

Dreyfus, Laurence. 'Early music defended against its devotees: a theory of historical performance in the twentieth century', *The Musical Quarterly* 69/3 (Summer 1983), pp. 297–322

Feher, Ferenc. 'Negative philosophy of music – positive results', *New German Critique* 4 (Winter 1975), pp. 99–111

358   Bibliography

Finscher, Ludwig. 'Über den Kunstwerkbegriff bei Adorno', in *Adorno und die Musik*, ed. Musik, ed. Otto Kolleritsch (Graz: Universal Edition, 1979), pp. 64–70
de la Fontaine, Michael. 'Der Begriff der künstlerischen Erfahrung bei Theodor W. Adorno' (diss., J. W. Goethe-Universität, Frankfurt/Main, 1977)
   'Künstlerische Erfahrung bei Arnold Schönberg. Zur Dialektik des musikalischen Materials', in *Materialien zur ästhetischen Theorie Th. W. Adornos Konstruktion der Moderne*, ed. Burkhardt Lindner and W. Martin Lüdke (Frankfurt/Main: Suhrkamp Verlag, 1979), pp. 467–93
von Friedeburg, Ludwig, and Habermas, Jürgen (eds.). *Adorno-Konferenz 1983* (Frankfurt/Main: Suhrkamp Verlag, 1983)
Frow, J. 'Mediation and metaphor: Adorno and the sociology of art', *Clio* 12/1 (1982), pp. 57–66
Geuss, Raymond. *The Idea of a Critical Theory: Habermas and the Frankfurt School* (Cambridge: Cambridge University Press, 1981)
Gramer, Wolfgang. *Musik und Verstehen: Eine Studie zur Musikästhetik Theodor W. Adornos* (Mainz: Matthias-Grünewald-Verlag, 1976)
Grenz, Friedemann. *Adornos Philosophie in Grundbegriffen: Auflösung einiger Deutungsprobleme* (Frankfurt/Main: Suhrkamp Verlag, 1975)
Gripp, Helga. *Theodor W. Adorno: Erkenntnisdimensionen negativer Dialektik* (Paderborn: Schöningh, 1986)
Hansen, Miriam. 'Introduction to Adorno: "Transparencies on film" (1966)', *New German Critique* 24/5 (Fall/Winter 1981–2), pp. 186–98
Held, David. *Introduction to Critical Theory: Horkheimer to Habermas* (London: Hutchinson, 1980)
Hohendahl, Peter Uwe. 'Autonomy of art: looking back at Adorno's "Aesthetic Theory"', *The German Quarterly* 54 (1981), pp. 133–48
Honneth, Axel. 'Communication and reconciliation: Habermas' critique of Adorno', trans. Vincent Thomas and David Parent, *Telos* 39 (Spring 1979), pp. 45–61
   'Foucault and Adorno: two forms of the critique of modernity', trans. David Roberts, *Thesis Eleven* 15 (1986), pp. 48–59
Huber, Alfred. 'Adornos Polemik gegen Strawinsky', *Melos* 38/9 (1971), pp. 356–60
Huhn, Thomas. 'Adorno's aesthetics of illusion', *The Journal of Aesthetics and Art Criticism* (1985), pp. 181–9
Hullot-Kentor, Bob. 'Adorno's *Aesthetic Theory: the translation*' [review], *Telos* 65 (Fall 1985), pp. 143–7
   'Introduction to Adorno's "Idea of natural history"', *Telos* 60 (Summer 1984), pp. 97–110
Huyssen, Andreas. 'Critical theory and modernity', *New German Critique* 26 (Spring/Summer 1982), pp. 3–11
   'Adorno in reverse: from Hollywood to Richard Wagner', *New German Critique* 29 (Spring//Summer 1983), pp. 8–38
   After the Great Divide: Modernism, Mass Culture, Postmodernism (Bloomington and Indianapolis: Indiana University Press, 1986)
Jameson, Fredric. 'T. W. Adorno; or, historical tropes', in *Marxism and Form: Twentieth-Century Dialectical Theories of Literature* (Princeton: Princeton

University Press, 1971), pp. 3–59

'Introduction to T. W. Adorno', *Salmagundi* 10/11 (Fall 1969–Winter 1970), pp. 140–43

Jay, Martin. *The Dialectical Imagination: A History of the Frankfurt School and the Institute of Social Research 1923–1950* (London: Heinemann, 1973)

'The concept of totality in Lukács and Adorno', *Telos* 32 (Summer 1977), pp. 117–37

Adorno (London: Fontana/Collins, 1984)

Marxism and Totality: The Adventures of a Concept from Lukács to Habermas (Berkeley/Los Angeles: University of California Press, 1984)

Jiminez, Marc. *Adorno: art, idéologie et théorie de l'art* (Paris: Union Générale d'Editions, 1973)

Johnson, Pauline. *Marxist Aesthetics: The Foundations within Everyday Life for an Enlightened Consciousness* (London: Routledge & Kegan Paul, 1984)

'An aesthetics of negativity/an aesthetics of reception: Jauss's dispute with Adorno', *New German Critique* 42 (Fall 1987), pp. 51–70

Kaiser, Gerhard. *Benjamin, Adorno: Zwei Studien* (Frankfurt/Main: Fischer Verlag, 1974)

Kappner, Hans-Hartmut. *Die Bildungstheorie Adornos als Theorie der Erfahrung von Kultur und Kunst* (Frankfurt/Main: Suhrkamp Verlag, 1984)

Knapp, Gerhard P. *Theodor W. Adorno* (Berlin: Colloquium Verlag, 1980)

Kolleritsch, Otto (ed.). *Adorno und die Musik* (Graz: Universal Edition, 1979)

Leibowitz, René. 'Der Komponist Theodor W. Adorno', in *Zeugnisse: Theodor W. Adorno zum 60. Geburtstag*, ed. Max Horkheimer (Frankfurt/Main, Europäische Verlagsanstalt, 1963), pp. 355–9

Lenhardt, Christian. 'Reply to Hullot-Kentor', *Telos* 65 (Fall 1985), pp. 147–52

Lindner, Burkhardt, and Lüdke, W. Martin (eds.). *Materialien zur ästhetischen Theorie Th. W. Adornos: Konstruktion der Moderne* (Frankfurt/Main: Suhrkamp Verlag, 1980)

Lunn, Eugene. *Marxism and Modernism: An Historical Study of Lukács, Brecht, Benjamin and Adorno* (London: Verso, 1982, 1985)

Maurer-Zenck, Claudia. 'Die Auseinandersetzung Adornos mit Krenek', in *Adorno und die Musik*, ed. Otto Kolleritsch (Graz: Universal Edition, 1979), pp. 227–39

Mayer, Gunter. *Weltbild – Notenbild: Zur Dialektik des musikalischen Materials* (Leipzig: Verlag Philipp Reclam, 1978)

'Adorno und Eisler', in *Adorno und die Musik*, ed. Otto Kolleritsch (Graz: Universal Edition, 1979), pp. 133–55

'Zur Dialektik des musikalischen Materials', *Alternative* 69 (December 1969), pp. 239–58

Metzger, Heinz-Klaus. 'Just who is growing old?', *Die Reihe* 4 (Pennsylvania: Theodor Presser and Co., 1960), pp. 63–80

'Adorno und die Geschichte der musikalischen Avantgarde', in *Adorno und die Musik*, ed. Otto Kolleritsch (Graz: Universal Edition, 1979), pp. 9–14

'Europas Oper: Notizen zu John Cages *Europeras 1 & 2*', in *Europeras 1 & 2. Programheft* (Frankfurt/Main: Oper Frankfurt, 1987) [no page numbers], with parallel English translation as: 'Europe's opera: notes on John Cage's *Europeras 1 & 2*', trans. Jeremy Gaines and Doris Jones

Mitchell Culver, Anne G. 'Theodor Adorno's Philosophy of Modern Music: evaluation and commentary' (diss., University of Colorado, 1973)

Mohanty, J. N. 'The concept of intuition in aesthetics: apropos a critique by Adorno', *The Journal of Aesthetics and Art Criticism* 39/1 (1980), pp. 39–45

de la Motte, Diether. 'Adornos musikalische Analysen', in *Adorno und die Musik*, ed. Otto Kolleritsch (Graz: Universal Edition, 1979), pp. 52–63

Müller, Thomas. 'Die Musiksoziologie Theodor W. Adornos – ein Model ihrer Interpretation am Beispiel von Musikstücken Alban Bergs' (diss. J. W. Goethe-Universität, Frankfurt/Main, 1988)

Paddison, Max. 'The critique criticised: Adorno and popular music', in *Popular Music 2: Theory and Method*, ed. Richard Middleton and David Horn (Cambridge: Cambridge University Press, 1982), pp. 201–18

'Adorno's *Aesthetic Theory*' [review article], *Music Analysis* 6/3 (October 1987), pp. 355–77

'The language-character of music: some motifs in Adorno', *Journal of the Royal Musical Association* 116/2 (1991), pp. 267–79

Pettazzi, Carlo. 'Studien zu Leben und Werk Adornos bis 1938', in *Theodor W. Adorno*, ed. Heinz Ludwig Arnold (Munich: Edition Text + Kritik, 1977), pp. 21–9

Rath, Norbert. *Adornos Kritische Theorie: Vermittlungen und Vermittlungsschwierigkeiten* (Paderborn: Schöningh, 1982)

Ritsert, Jürgen. *Vermittlung der Gegensätze in sich: Dialektische Themen und Variationen in der Musiksoziologie Adornos* (Frankfurt/Main: Studientexte zur Sozialwissenschaft, Fachbereich Gesellschaftswissenschaften der J. W. Goethe-Universität, 1987)

Rose, Gillian. *The Melancholy Science: An Introduction to the Thought of Theodor W. Adorno* (London: Macmillan, 1978)

Rosen, Michael. 'Critical theory: between ideology and philosophy', in *The Need for Interpretation: Contemporary Conceptions of the Philosopher's Task*, ed. Sollace Mitchell and Michael Rosen (London: Athlone Press, 1983)

Rosen, Philip. 'Adorno and film music: theoretical notes on *Composing for the Films*', in *Cinema/Sound: Yale French Studies* 60 (1980), pp. 157–82

Sandner, Wolfgang. 'Popularmusik als somatisches Stimulans. Adornos Kritik der "leichten Musik"', in *Adorno und die Musik*, ed. Otto Kolleritsch (Graz: Universal Edition, 1979), pp. 125–32

Sauerland, Karol. *Einführung in die Ästhetik Adornos* (Berlin/New York: Walter de Gruyter, 1979)

Schmidt, Alfred. 'Begriff des Materialismus bei Adorno', in *Adorno-Konferenz 1983*, ed. Ludwig von Friedeburg and Jürgen Habermas (Frankfurt/Main: Suhrkamp Verlag, 1983), pp. 14–34

Schnebel, Dieter. 'Einführung in Adornos Musik', in *Adorno und die Musik*, ed. Otto Kolleritsch (Graz: Universal Edition, 1979), pp. 15–19

Schubert, Giselher. 'Adornos Auseinandersetzung mit der Zwölftontechnik Schönbergs', *Archiv für Musikwissenschaft* 46 (Heft 3, 1989), pp. 235–54

Schweppenhäuser, Hermann (ed.). *Theodor W. Adorno zum Gedächtnis: eine Sammlung* (Frankfurt/Main: Suhrkamp Verlag, 1971)

Schweppenhäuser, Hermann et al. *Über Theodor W. Adorno* (Frankfurt/Main: Suhrkamp Verlag, 1968)

Slater, Phil. *Origin and Significance of the Frankfurt School: A Marxist Perspective*

(London: Routledge & Kegan Paul, 1977)

Stephan, Rudolf. 'Adorno und Hindemith: Zum Verständnis einer schwierigen Bezierhung', in *Adorno und die Musik*, ed. Otto Kolleritsch (Graz: Universal Edition, 1979), pp. 180–201

Subotnik, Rose Rosengard. 'The historical structure: Adorno's "French" model for the criticism of nineteenth-century music', *Nineteenth-Century Music* 2/1 (July 1978), pp. 36–60

Developing Variations: Style and Ideology in Western Music (Minneapolis: University of Minnesota Press, 1991)

Sziborsky, Lucia. *Adornos Musikphilosophie: Genese, Konstitution, Pädagogische Perspektiven* (Munich: Wilhelm Fink Verlag, 1979)

'Das Problem des Verstehens und der Begriff der "Adäquanz" bei Th. W. Adorno', in *Musik und Verstehen: Aufsätze zur semiotischen Theorie, Ästhetik und Soziologie der musikalischen Rezeption*, ed. Peter Faltin and Hans-Peter Reinecke (Cologne: Arno Volk Verlag/Hans Gerig KG, 1973), pp. 289–305

Tar, Zoltán. *The Frankfurt School: The Critical Theories of Max Horkheimer and Theodor W. Adorno* (New York: John Wiley and Sons, 1977)

Therborn, Göran. 'The Frankfurt School', in *Western Marxism – A Critical Reader*, ed. New Left Review (London: NLB, 1977), pp. 83–139

Weber, Samuel. 'Translating the untranslatable', in Adorno, *Prisms*, trans. Samuel and Shierry Weber (London: Neville Spearman, 1967), pp. 9–15

Weber, Shierry, M. 'Aesthetic experience and self-reflection as emancipatory processes: two complementary aspects of critical theory', in *On Critical Theory*, ed. John O'Neill (London: Heinemann, 1976), pp. 78–103

Weitzman, Ronald. 'An introduction to Adorno's music and social criticism', *Music & Letters* 52/3 (July 1971), pp. 287–98

Wellmer, Albrecht. 'Wahrheit, Schein, Versöhnung. Adornos ästhetische Rettung der Modernität', in *Adorno-Konferenz 1983*, ed. Ludwig von Friedeburg and Jürgen Habermas (Frankfurt/Main: Suhrkamp Verlag, 1983), pp. 138–76

Williams, Alastair. 'Mimesis and construction in the music of Boulez and Cage', in *Thinking Art: Beyond Traditional Aesthetics*, ed. Andrew Benjamin and Peter Osborne (London: ICA, 1991), pp. 145–55

Wolin, Richard. 'The De-aestheticization of art: on Adorno's *Ästhetische Theorie*', *Telos* 41 (Fall 1979), pp. 105–27

Zenck, Martin. *Kunst als begriffslose Erkenntnis: Zum Kunstbegriff des ästhetischen Theorie Theodor W. Adornos* (Munich: Wilhelm Fink Verlag, 1977)

'Phantasmagorie – Ausdruck – Extrem: Die Auseinandersetzung zwischen Adornos Musikdenken und Benjamins Kunsttheorie in den dreißiger Jahren', in *Adorno und die Musik*, ed. Otto Kolleritsch (Graz: Universal Edition, 1979), pp. 202–26

'Auswirkungen einer "musique informelle" auf die Neue Musik: Zu Theodor W. Adornos Formvorstellung', *International Review of the Aesthetics and Sociology of Music* 10/2 (December 1979), pp. 137–65

Zuidervaart, Lambert Paul. 'Refractions: truth in Adorno's *Aesthetic Theory*' (diss., Vrije Universiteit te Amsterdam, 1981)

2.2 OTHER SOURCES

Bair, Deirdre. *Samuel Beckett: A Biography* (London: Jonathan Cape/Picador, 1978, 1980)

Ballantine, Christopher. *Music and its Social Meanings* (New York: Gordon and Breach Science Publishers, 1984)

Benjamin, Andrew and Osborne, Peter (eds.). *Thinking Art: Beyond Traditional Aesthetics* (London: ICA, 1991)

Berger, Peter, and Luckmann, Thomas. *The Social Construction of Reality* (Harmondsworth: Penguin, 1967)

Betz, Albrecht. *Hanns Eisler Political Musician*, trans. Bill Hopkins (Cambridge: Cambridge University Press, 1982)

Bleicher, Josef. *Contemporary Hermeneutics: Hermeneutics as Method, Philosophy and Critique* (London: Routledge & Kegan Paul, 1980)

Brand, Juliane *et al.* (eds.). *The Berg-Schoenberg Correspondence: Selected Letters* (London: Macmillan Press, 1987)

Bubner, Rüdiger. *Modern German Philosophy*, trans. Eric Matthews (Cambridge: Cambridge University Press, 1981)

Bujic, Bojan (ed.). *Music in European Thought 1851–1912* (Cambridge: Cambridge University Press, 1988)

Bungay, Stephen. *Beauty and Truth: A Study of Hegel's Aesthetics* (Oxford: Oxford University Press, 1984)

Cahoone, Lawrence E. *The Dilemma of Modernity: Philosophy, Culture, and Anti-Culture* (Albany: State University of New York Press, 1988)

Carner, Mosco. *Alban Berg: The Man and the Work* (London: Duckworth, 1975, 1983)

Deliège, Célestin. 'Stravinsky: ideology & language', *Perspectives of New Music* 26/1 (Winter 1988), pp. 82–106

Erlich, Victor. *Russian Formalism: History – Doctrine* (New Haven and London: Yale University Press, 3rd edn 1981)

Etzkorn, K. P. 'Sociologists and music', in *Music and Society: The Later Writings of Paul Honigsheim*, ed. K. P. Etzkorn (New York: John Wiley and Sons, 1973), pp. 3–40

Gay, Peter. *Weimar Culture: The Outsider as Insider* (Harmondsworth: Penguin, 1974)

Goehr, Alexander. 'Schoenberg's *Gedanke Manuscript*', *Journal of the Arnold Schoenberg Institute* 2/1 (October 1977), pp. 4–25

Heller, Agnes (ed.). *Lukács Revalued* (Oxford: Basil Blackwell, 1983)

Herbert, Robert L. (ed.). *Modern Artists on Art: Ten Unabridged Essays* (New York: Prentice Hall, 1964)

Hobsbawm, E. J. *The Age of Revolution 1789–1848* (London: Weidenfeld & Nicolson/Sphere Books, 1962, 1989)
The Age of Capital 1848–1875 (London: Weidenfeld & Nicolson/Sphere Books, 1975, 1977)

Ince, W. N. *The Poetic Theory of Paul Valéry: Inspiration and Technique* (Leicester: Leicester University Press, 1970)

Jameson, Fredric. *The Prison House of Language: A Critical Account of Structuralism and Russian Formalism* (Princeton: Princeton University Press, 1972)
'Postmodernism and consumer society', in *Postmodernism and its Discontents*, ed. E. Anne Kaplan (London: Verso, 1988)

Kneif, Tibor. *Musiksoziologie* (Cologne: Musikverlag Hans Gerig, 1971; 2nd edn 1975) (ed.). *Texte zur Musiksoziologie* (Cologne, 1975)

Lacey, A. L. *A Dictionary of Philosophy* (London: Routledge & Kegan Paul, 1976)

Laing, Dave. *The Marxist Theory of Art: An Introductory Survey* (Sussex: Harvester Press, 1978)

Leibowitz, René. *Schoenberg and his School: The Contemporary Stage of the Language of Music*, trans. Dika Newlin (New York: Da Capo Press, 1949, 1975)

Martindale, Don, and Riedel, Johannes. 'Max Weber's sociology of music', in Weber, *The Rational and Social Foundations of Music*, trans. and ed. Don Martindale, Johannes Riedel and Gertrude Neuwirth (Carbondale: Southern Illinois University Press, 1958)

Mertens, Wim. *American Minimal Music*, trans. J. Hautekiet (London: Kahn & Averill, 1833)

Middleton, Richard. *Studying Popular Music* (Milton Keynes: Open University Press, 1990)

Mitchell, G. Duncan. *A New Dictionary of Sociology* (London: Routledge & Kegan Paul, 1968, 1979)

Newton, K. M. (ed.). *Twentieth-Century Literary Theory: A Reader* (London: Macmillan, 1988)

O'Toole, L. M., and Shukman, Ann (eds.). *Russian Poetics in Translation:* vol. 5, *Formalism: History, Comparison, Genre* (Oxford: Holdan Books, 1978)

Perle, George. *The Operas of Alban Berg*, vol. 1: *Wozzeck* (Berkeley/Los Angeles/London: University of California Press, 1980)

Redlich, H. E. *Alban Berg – Versuch einer Würdigung* (Vienna: Universal Edition, 1957). Translated as: *Alban Berg: The Man and his Music* (London: Calder, 1957)

Reich, Willi. (ed.). *Alban Berg: Mit Bergs eigenen Schriften und Beiträgen von Theodor Wiesengrund-Adorno und Ernst Krenek* (Vienna: Herbert Reichner Verlag, 1937)

Schoenberg: A Critical Biography, trans. Leo Black (London: Longman, 1971)

Rose, Margaret A. 'Theories of nature from Hegel to Marx', *The British Journal of Aesthetics* 26/2 (Spring 1986), pp. 150–60

Rosen, Michael. *Hegel's Dialectic and its Criticism* (Cambridge: Cambridge University Press, 1982)

Rycroft, Charles. *A Critical Dictionary of Psychoanalysis* (Harmondsworth: Penguin, 1972)

Sachs, Harvey. *Music in Fascist Italy* (New York/London: W. W. Norton, 1987)

Samson, Jim. 'Chopin and genre', *Music Analysis* 8/3 (October 1989), pp. 213–31

Silbermann, Alphons (ed.). *Klassiker der Kunstsoziologie* (Munich: Verlag C. H. Beck, 1979)

Skelton, Geoffrey. *Paul Hindemith: The Man behind the Music* (London: Gollancz, 1975)

Smith, Joan Allen. *Schoenberg and his Circle: A Viennese Portrait* (New York: Schirmer Books, 1986)

Solomon, Maynard (ed.). *Marxism and Art: Essays Classic and Contemporary* (Sussex: Harvester Press, 1979)

Stimpson, Brian. *Paul Valéry and Music: A Study of the Techniques of Composition in Valéry's Poetry* (Cambridge: Cambridge University Press, 1984)

Stuckenschmidt, H. H. *Schoenberg: His Life, World and Work*, trans. Humphrey Searle (London: Calder, 1977)

Tertulian, Nicolae. 'Lukács' aesthetics and its critics', *Telos* 52 (1982), pp. 159–67

Willett, John. *Brecht in Context: Comparative Approaches* (London: Methuen, 1984)

Williams, Raymond. *Keywords: A Vocabulary of Culture and Society* (London: Fontana/Collins, 1976; rev. edn 1983)

  Marxism and Literature (Oxford: Oxford University Press, 1977)

  Culture (London: Fontana/Collins, 1981)

Index of names

Adorno, T. W. early years 4–5; composition studies with Berg 5–7; Institute for Social Research 7–8; exile in America 8–9; positivist dispute 9–11; Adorno and the New Left students 11; Critical Theory: modernism and postmodernism 12–13; reading Adorno 13–16; interdisciplinary character 16–17; problem of translation 17–19; antisystematic character of the texts 19–20; Adorno and Benjamin 4–5, 6, 34–5, 36; and Berg 49–50, 158–74; and Bartók 38–41; and Bloch 74–8; and Eisler 6, 9, 78–81; and Heidegger 10–11; and Hindemith 41–4, 67–9; and Horkheimer 4–5, 7–8, 11, 28; and Krenek 6, 24–5, 81–97; and Lukács 31–4; and Schoenberg 47–9, 103–4, 266–7; and Stravinsky 44–7, 267–70; and Webern 49–51; and the avant-garde 272–6; see Subject Index for details of main concepts in Adorno's theoretical writings on music
Aristotle 51

Bach, J. S. 24, 27, 64, 73, 74, 75, 77, 173, 193, 196, 197–8, 218, 220, 224, 225–31, 234, 236, 241
Bacon, Francis 14
Bair, Deirdre 276
Bartók, Béla 21, 23, 26, 37, 38–41, 44, 46, 47, 104, 222, 223
Baudelaire, Charles 5, 69, 222, 257
Beckett, Samuel 14, 78, 181, 267, 270, 275–6
Beethoven, Ludwig van 24, 73, 74, 75, 76, 77, 80, 88, 155, 161, 179, 193, 195, 198, 219, 221, 232, 233–40, 243, 246, 247,

254, 255, 261, 271, 273
Benjamin, Walter 4, 6, 7, 19, 20, 21, 30, 34, 35, 36, 50, 52, 77, 96, 107, 120, 124, 148, 201, 213–14, 245, 252
Berg, Alban 5–6, 21, 23, 28, 44, 49–51, 82, 157, 158–74, 230, 260, 279–84
Berlioz, Hector 219, 221, 233, 238, 240–42, 261
Bloch, Ernst 4, 6, 74–8, 84, 88, 134
Boulez, Pierre 182, 265
Brahms, Johannes 77, 84, 105, 219, 222, 243, 253–6, 260, 271, 273
Brecht, Bertolt 6, 80, 104, 223
Bruckner, Anton 73, 74
Buck-Morss, Susan 6, 11, 23
Bürger, Peter 70, 269, 271–2

Cage, John 274–5
Cahn, Michael 140–41
Calvelli-Adorno, Maria 4
Casella, Alfredo 101
Coat, Tal 14
Connerton, Paul 7, 126
Cornelius, Hans 4

Dahlhaus, Carl 70, 156, 218, 224, 225, 239–40, 242, 249, 250–51, 271, 274
Darmstadt Summer School 9, 177, 223, 265, 272
Debussy, Claude 24, 162, 219, 222, 256–8, 260, 269, 283
Drew, David 77
Durkheim, Emile 259, 318n

Eichenbaum, Boris 70
Eisler, Hanns 6, 9, 23, 24, 66, 78–81, 102, 105, 201, 223, 273

365

Film Music Project 81
Fontaine, Michael de la 118–19, 218, 224,
    225, 227, 236, 237, 242
Frankfurt School 7, 9, 11, 12, 16, 18, 21,
    116, 118–19, 128
Freud, Sigmund 2, 6, 13, 21, 109, 128–35,
    145, 147, 219
Fromm, Erich 7, 12, 131–3

Geuss, Raymond 12
Gluck, Christoph Willibald von 242
Goldmann, Lucien 56
Gramer, Wolfgang 116
Grenz, Friedemann 21, 70
Grünberg, Carl 7

Habermas, Jürgen 10, 12, 266
Halm, August 73–4, 134
Handel, G. F. 77, 193, 220
Hanslick, Eduard 66, 73, 76
Harth, Walter 270
Hauer, Josef Matthias 84
Haydn, Joseph 75, 77, 155, 221, 232, 234
Hegel, G. W. F. 2, 12, 13, 21, 31, 36, 49,
    52, 53, 63, 73, 108, 109–21, 122, 124,
    125, 131, 135, 144, 147, 150, 151, 158,
    177, 183, 188, 190, 198, 219, 228, 231,
    236, 255, 260, 264, 265
Heidegger, Martin 10, 28, 30, 35, 46, 55
Hindemith, Paul 4, 21, 23, 30, 37, 41–4,
    46, 47, 66–9, 72, 102, 105, 222
Hitler, Adolf 8, 9
Horkheimer, Max 4, 7, 8, 9, 10, 11, 12, 20,
    28, 108, 114, 125, 141, 143, 201–2, 219
Horney, Karen 133
Husserl, Edmund 5, 29, 30, 213, 215
Huysmans, J. K. 69

Ince, W. N. 70
Institute for Social Research (Institut für
    Sozialforschung) 7–8, 9, 133, 138, 139
Ives, Charles 259

Jakobson, Roman 70
Jameson, Fredric 20
Janáček 38, 44, 45, 46, 223
Jay, Martin 10, 264
Jephcott, E. F. N. 18

Kandinsky, Wassily 114
Kant, Immanuel 6, 30, 57, 138, 140, 145,
    148, 234, 260
Karplus, Gretel 8
Kierkegaard, Søren 6, 10
Klemperer, Otto 6
Kolisch, Rudolf 24, 195–6

Kracauer, Siegfried 4, 6
Kraus, Karl 106
Krenek, Ernst 6, 17, 19, 23, 24, 25, 42, 65,
    69, 73, 75, 77, 81–97, 127, 151, 188
Kurth, Ernst 170

Lazarsfeld, Paul 8
Leibniz, Gottfried Wilhelm 140, 300n
Leibowitz, René 6, 50
Lenya, Lotte 6
Ligeti, György 182
Liszt, Franz 194, 241–2
Lorenz, Konrad 170
Löwenthal, Leo 7
Lukács, Georg 6, 7, 16, 21, 30, 31, 32, 34,
    35, 36, 37, 52, 53, 57, 72, 74, 77, 91,
    107, 121, 148, 196, 216
Lyotard, Jean-François 12

Maeterlinck, Maurice 69
Mahler, Gustav 5, 24, 28, 45, 47, 116, 157,
    172, 174–5, 201, 219, 222, 238, 256, 260,
    261, 263, 269–70, 274, 283
Mallarmé, Stéphane 69
Mann, Thomas 1, 9
Mannheim School 79
Marcuse, Herbert 7, 11, 12
Martindale, Don 135–6
Marx, Karl 2, 6, 7, 12, 13, 21, 31, 42, 54,
    57, 61, 78, 79, 96, 97, 101, 107, 109, 117,
    121–8, 131, 132, 135, 145, 147, 185, 208,
    219
Mascagni, Pietro 24
McCarthy, Joseph 81
Messiaen, Olivier 265
Metzger, Heinz-Klaus 274–5
Moholy-Nagy, László 6
Motte, Diether de la 170
Mozart, W. A. 75, 77, 155, 204, 221, 232,
    234, 255, 273

New Left 11
New School for Social Research 26, 81
Nietzsche, Friedrich 13, 18, 219, 253

Offenbach, Jacques 204

Palestrina, Giovanni Pierluigi da 228
Perle, George 50
Pfitzner, Hans 244
Picasso, Pablo 269
Picht, Georg 11
Plato 12, 51
Pollock, Friedrich 7
Popper, Karl 10
Princeton Radio Research Project 8, 26,
    212

Ratz, Erwin 170
Ravel, Maurice 24
Redlich, Hans 50
Reger, Max 162, 172, 244
Reich, Willi 50, 58, 82, 171
Riedel, Johannes 135–6
Riemann, Hugo 86
Rimbaud, Arthur 69, 117
Ritsert, Jürgen 120, 146
Rose, Gillian 11, 34, 35, 91, 96
Rosen, Michael 109, 263–4
Rossini, Giaccomo 233
Rottweiler, Hektor 8
Rousseau, Jean-Jacques 257
Rubinstein, Anton 194

Saussure, Ferdinand de 154
Schenker, Heinrich 73, 170
Schoenberg, Arnold 5, 7, 9, 21, 23, 24, 28,
   31, 40, 44, 47–52, 64, 71–3, 75, 83, 85,
   87, 88, 104, 105, 106, 128, 145, 151, 157,
   158, 159–60, 162, 167, 168, 170, 173,
   174, 177, 181, 182, 189, 218, 222, 223–4,
   225, 253, 254–5, 256, 259–60, 262, 263,
   264, 265, 266–7, 270, 275, 279, 283, 284
Schmidt, Alfred 12, 111
Schopenhauer, Arthur 73, 135
Schubert, Franz 24, 90, 243, 254, 255, 271
Schumann, Robert 243, 254, 255, 271
Second Viennese School 24, 37, 104, 158,
   177, 218, 222, 224, 242
Sekles, Bernhard 4, 23
Shklovsky, Viktor 70
Sibelius, Jan 24, 293
Skryabin, Alexander 162
Stalin, Joseph 7
Stephan, Rudolf 170

Steuermann, Eduard 6, 254
Stockhausen, Karlheinz 182, 265
Stravinsky, Igor 21, 24, 27, 28, 30, 37, 40,
   44–7, 90, 101, 104, 128, 177, 222, 224,
   256, 258, 262, 264, 265, 266–70, 275, 306
Strauss, Johann 204
Strauss, Richard 24, 28, 241–2, 244
Subotnik, Rose Rosengard 11, 256
Sziborsky, Lucia 195

Tiedemann, Rolf 17
Tomasjevsky, Boris 70
Twain, Mark 5
Tynyanov, Juri 70

Valéry, Paul 69–70, 72
Verlaine, Paul 69
Vinci, Leonardo da 128, 130

Wagner, Richard 24, 28, 64, 75, 105, 142,
   156, 157, 159, 162, 168, 172, 173, 219,
   222, 243–53, 255, 256, 257, 260, 261,
   269, 273, 279–84
Weber, Carl Maria von 75
Weber, Max 2, 13, 18, 70, 84, 109, 114,
   117, 121, 128, 135–47, 219, 226, 241, 271
Webern, Anton 21, 23, 24, 44, 49–52, 158,
   162, 180, 182, 279
Weil, Felix 7
Weill, Kurt 6, 23, 24, 46, 47, 90, 104, 201,
   206, 223, 260
Wellmer, Albrecht 12
Whiteman, Paul 42

Zenck, Martin 182, 317
Zuidervaart, Lambert 116, 224

Subject index

absolute 14, 37, 238, 250
Absolute Spirit 265
abstract, abstraction 15
abstract value 97
absurd, the 20
accessibility 95
acoustics 38
actuality 29, 83–4
adaption 130, 133–4
administration (*Verwaltung*) 136; the
    administered world 12, 136, 194; *see also*
    bureaucratization, rationalization
advertising 222, 272; *see also* culture
    industry
aesthetics, the aesthetic, aesthetic theory
    1–3; Adorno's dialectical aesthetics
    59–64; impossibility of a normative
    aesthetics 2; sociological aesthetics 14;
    task of aesthetics 1, 11; the problem of
    Adorno's aesthetics of music 116, 276–8;
    aestheticism 322 n8
affirmation, 'affirmative' music 14, 102–3
alienation 1, 98, 104, 193, 196, 206, 222; in
    Stravinsky 268; *Entfremdung* 192;
    Entäußerung in Hegel 113; *Verfremdung*
    in Brecht 223; Beethoven's *Missa
    Solemnis*, 'alienated masterpiece' 238–40;
    see also de-aestheticization,
    objectification
allegory 34–5; allegory and stasis in
    Wagner 244, 246
amateur 211
anachronism 229
analysis 155–6; formal analysis 279;
    immanent analysis 2, 22, 60, 158–68;
    micrological analysis 15, 23; reductive
    analysis 279; critique of Adorno's
    'immanent analysis' 168–74

anomie 222; *see also* alienation
antagonisms 56, 120–21, 126–7, 146–7
anthropomorphism in Adorno 133
anti-art – *see* art
antinomy 13, 96 *see also* contradiction, the
    dialectic, mediation
anti-system – *see* system
aphorism 14, 18, 19, 28
appearance (*Erscheinung*) 12, 197
archaism 30, 226, 228, 238, 239; in
    Debussy 257
aristocracy 211
art (*Kunst*) 1, 5, 10, 31–2; after Auschwitz
    56; art anti-art 11, 206; art and the
    redemption of nature 56–9; art as closed
    world (*un monde fermé*) 3, 69–70; as
    commodity 204–7; as day-dreaming,
    wish fulfilment, escape from the reality
    principle 128–9; art as mode of
    cognition 99; as 'purposiveness without
    a purpose' 142; as rationality criticizing
    itself 140; as 'uncommitted crime' 134;
    art for art's sake (*l'art pour l'art*) 69,
    222, 257; autonomous art – *see*
    autonomy; hermetic art 106; critical
    character of art 100; art criticism 16; *see
    also* aesthetics, commitment, content,
    form
artefact 22, 189
artifice 245
assimilation 220
atonality, free atonality 5, 37
Aufhebung – *see* dialectics, mediation,
    sublation
aura 206
authenticity (*Authentizität*) 22, 38, 47,
    55–6, 62, 64, 91, 216–18, 261, 263, 273,
    275, 278; in Beethoven 239; in Brahms

255; in Mahler 259, 260; in Schoenberg 267; in Stravinsky 268; *Echtheit* 91; *Eigentlichkeit* 29; historical authenticity in performance and reception 195, 212, 226–7; *see also* truth

authoritarianism, authoritarian personality 7, 222

autonomy 1, 3, 31, 32, 97, 106, 148, 233–4; autonomy character 98; autonomous music 1, 2, 14, 224; autonomous work 120; threat to autonomy 200–202; critique of Adorno's concept of autonomy 272; refusal of autonomy in Berlioz, Liszt and Strauss 242; *see also* heteronomy

avant-garde 27, 54–5, 116–17, 120; and the rise of the bourgeoisie 118; radical works as messages in bottles (*Flaschenpost*) 1; decline 223; historical character 272–3; theory of the avant-garde 225

axis rotation (*Achsendrehung*) 163, 283

bagatelles, Beethoven op. 126 in Adorno's analysis 237–8

Baroque 193, 221, 231

base-superstructure 54, 117, 126–8

beauty (*das Schöne*) 13; natural beauty (*das Naturschöne*) 57–9

Becoming (*Werden*) 113; Becoming as negation in Berg 171; *see also* Being

beginning (*Anfang*) and the problem of ending (*Schluß*) 176, 179–81; *see also* form

Being and Becoming (*Sein und Werden*) 30, 113, 246–7; pure Being 30, 37, 112

borrowing 280

bourgeoisie (*Bürgertum*), bourgeois 3, 221, 233; bourgeois Period 31, 118, 211, 224; bourgeois Subject 117–20, 223; high bourgeoisie 211; petty bourgeoisie 211; rise of the bourgeoisie 233–4; *embourgeoisement* 225, 231; *see also* class

bureaucracy, bureacratization 136

cabaret 45

canon 228

capitalism 54, 119–20, 136, 222; pre-capitalist period 193

catastrophe 238

catharsis 133; *see also* desublimation

chamber music 4, 211

chance operations in Cage 275

change 11; historical change 3, 93–4, 113

charnel house 33

chaos 158, 275–6; *see also* disintegration, fragmentation

cheerfulness (*Heiterkeit*) 45

chromaticism 162, 172

cipher 1, 19, 34, 147; Wagner's music as cipher for the 'age of industry' 243

circus act 197

class, class origins 118–19, 125, 221, 233; *see also* bourgeoisie, aristocracy, proletariat

classical, classicism 4, 106, 154–5, 221, 283; *see also* neoclassicism

closed forms – *see* form

closure, ending (*Schluß*) 175–6, 259; inability to close 181; *see also* form

cognition (*Erkenntnis*) 2, 12, 150; cognitive character (*Erkenntnischarakter*) 99; in Brahms 255; philosophical cognition 112, 235–7

collage 201; *see also* montage

collectivity 27, 115–16

coming of age (*Mündigkeit*) – *see* maturity

commercialization 232; *see also* commodity, culture industry

commitment (*Engagement*), politically committed art 80–81

commodity (*Ware*) 38, 54–5, 96–7, 120, 123–4; commodity-character (*Warencharakter*) 98; commodification 15, 26, 204, 222, 225; commodification of inwardness 252–3; *see also* fetishism

common sense 13

communication 134, 271; communicative language 143

communism 37

community (*Gemeinschaft*) 27, 30, 54, 95; community music (*Gemeinschaftsmusik*) 38, 104, 105; natural community (*Naturgemeinschaft*) 37; political community 38; *see also* society

complex of meaning (*Sinnzusammenhang*) – *see* context of meaning

complexity 16

composition 4, 9, 23, 25, 38; Adorno as composer 5–6; compositional problems 92–3; relation of composer to material 188–9

comprehensibility (*Verständlichkeit*) – *see* intelligibility

concept (*Begriff*) 2, 10, 14, 15–16, 21, 22, 23; conceptless cognition (*begriffslose Erkenntnis*) 15; conceptual context 52–6

concert 4; concert agents 186, 199

conditioning 3

conflict theory 121

conformism 200, 212

consciousness (*Bewußtsein*) 10, 11, 13,
    112–13; advanced consciousness 118;
    critical consciousness 125; empirical
    consciousness 101; false consciousness
    (*falsches Bewußtsein*) 12, 54, 184, 300
    n178; limitations of 'mass consciousness'
    101; self-consciousness
    (*Selbstbewußtsein*) 113
consistency (*Stimmigkeit*) 14, 60, 86, 89,
    94, 96, 150, 158, 181, 182, 183, 189; in
    Adorno 64, 110; in Beethoven 239; in
    Hegel 112; in Schoenberg 267; immanent
    consistency 55, 89; *see also* truth
consolation 13
constellation 14, 19, 21, 35–7, 64, 120
construction 13, 96, 144–5, 157; freedom
    and construction 106
consumption 25, 121–4, 207–16; sphere of
    consumption 25; consumerism 222; *see
    also* reception
content (*Inhalt, Gehalt*) 19; collective
    content 115–16; content as 'what is
    going on' (*das Geschehende*) 151;
    historical content 218; form and content
    (*Form und Inhalt*) 151–2; social content
    (*gesellschaftlicher Gehalt*) 97–8, 111, 156,
    184–217; truth content (*Wahrheitsgehalt*)
    – *see* truth; *see also* material
context (*Zusammenhang*) 21; context (or
    complex) of meaning
    (*Sinnzusammenhang*) 190; eschatological
    context 33; socio-political context 13,
    184; contextualization 2
continuation (*Fortsetzung*) 176; *see also*
    form
continuity 35, 113; historical continuity ↔
    discontinuity 35, 240, 261–2
contradiction (*Widerspruch*) 1, 2, 12, 14,
    15, 18, 36, 98, 290–91 n74; in Hegel's
    Logic 112, 120; *see also* antimony,
    dialectics, mediation, sublation
contrast (*Kontrast*) 80, 176–7; *see also*
    form
conventions 35, 36; in Beethoven 237
copy 32
correctness (*Stimmigkeit*) – *see* consistency
cosmos 229, 238
counterpoint 228
craft, craft ethic 38, 54, 187, 229
creation 36
crisis 240–41; in composition and analysis
    174
criteria 56, 149; criterion of truth content
    in Bach and Beethoven 236
critical character of music 100
critical method 52–64

Critical Theory 7, 9, 10, 11, 12–13, 17, 57;
    and psychoanalysis 131–3
critique 2, 10, 32; critique v. critical
    rationalism 307 n5; ideology critique 8;
    sociological critique 3, 22, 60–62
culture 9, 13, 30, 53, 54, 55, 96; culture
    consumer – *see* listening types; mass
    culture (*Massenkultur*) 8, 222; museum
    culture 222; popular culture 8, 27
culture industry (*Kulturindustrie*) 16, 26,
    28, 88, 126, 199–203, 225, 232

Dadaism 201, 206
dance 3
de-aestheticization (*Entkünstung*) 206–7
decline of the Modern 271–6
definition 3, 31
dehumanization 258
delayed gratification 133
demythologization 91–2, 114, 129
density (*Dichte*) 176–7; *see also* form
depersonalization 268
derivation 63
desublimation (*Entsublimierung*) 133–4; *see
    also* catharsis
determinism 125; socio-economic 128
devaluation (*Entwertung*) of musical
    material 75, 90–91, 118
development 130; motivic development as
    material self-reflection 234–5; developing
    variation – *see* variation; total
    development in Brahms 255
deviation (*Abweichung*); schema and
    deviation 155–6
dialectics, the dialectic (*Dialektik*) 2, 35,
    112–13; dialectical composer 47–9;
    dialectical method 13; dialectical model
    59–64; dialectic of musical material 119;
    dialectical tension 18; historical dialectic
    of musical material 218–62; immanent
    dialectic of musical material 149–58;
    negative dialectics (*negative Dialektik*)
    10–11, 15, 19, 29, 111; social dialectic of
    musical material 185
difference (*Ungleichheit*) 177–8; *see also*
    sameness, similarity
dinner music – *see* *Tafelmusik*
discontinuity 6, 261; historical 63, 231;
    social discontinuities as structural
    deficiencies in art works 261; in
    Beethoven 238; in Berlioz 242; *see also*
    continuity
disenchantment (*Entzauberung*) 135–6
disintegration (*Zerfall*) 120, 225;
    disintegration and integration as
    problems of form 158, 284;

disintegration of musical material
263–76; logic of disintegration (*Logik des Zerfalls*) 16, 88; *see also* form
displacement 130, 133–4
dissolution (*Auflösung*) 176; fields of dissolution (*Auflösungsfelder*) 282; *see also* form
distance from centre (*Mittelpunkt*) 19, 176–7, 185; *see also* form
distribution 25, 121–4, 198–207
divertissement 80, 231
division of labour – *see* labour
dodecaphony – *see* twelve-tone technique
domination (*Beherrschung*) 28; of material 113; of nature 28; of inner and outer nature 219
drama, tragic drama 34–5
drives (*Triebe*) 103, 128–35; death-drive (*Todestrieb*) 173; instinctual drives 129; sex drives 130; *see also* libido, psychoanalysis
duration (*Dauer*) 151
dynamic markings 193
dynamics (*Dynamik*) 151

ego-development 130, 133; *see also* psychoanalysis
élitism 271
ellipsis 13, 18, 169
emancipation 12, 57, 62, 91–2; emancipatory potential 62
empiricism 7, 8, 9, 10, 12, 13, 109
ending – *see* closure
enigma – *see* riddle-character
Enlightenment 12, 202, 203, 266; dialectic of Enlightenment 28, 219, 267; Bach and the Enlightenment 226–7; Enlightenment and myth 141
entertainment 75, 80, 273; entertainment listener 211–12; *see also* listening types
epic theatre 80
epistemology (*Erkenntnistheorie*) 2
escape mechanisms 129, 134
essence 246
eternity 34
ethics 2
exchange 121–4
exchange-value 26; as an abstract value 97
exile 21, 26, 28
existence (*Dasein*) 275
existentialism, existentialist 6, 10, 29, 56
experience (*Erfahrung, Erlebnis*) 2, 8, 29, 112, 213–16; aesthetic experience (*ästhetische Erfahrung*) 2; blind experience 214; experience of art as second reflection 63

expression 2, 34, 105, 142–3; change in function of expression 105–6; mimesis and expressivity 143; construction and expression 144–6; gesture and expression in Wagner 248–50
Expressionism 4, 105, 283
extremes 120–21

fact, historical fact 323 n38; social fact (*fait social*) 187, 318 n4
facticity, concrete historical facticity 37
failure 56; failure as criterion of truth in late Beethoven 239–40; Adorno's failure 277
false consciousness – *see* consciousness
fanfare 248
fascism 7, 37, 101; Stravinsky and fascism 306 n125
fashion 204
fate (*Schicksal*), nature as fate in Wagner 245; in Debussy 257; twelve-tone technique as the fate of music 267
fetish, fetishism 13; commodity fetishism 31, 124; fetish-character (*Fetischcharakter*) 99–100, 130; fetishization 5, 8, 26; fetishization of performance 200; *see also* commodity
feudalism 79, 80
figures, figurations (*Figuren*) 88; micrological figures (*mikrologische Figuren*) 63
figured bass 225
film 186, 203; film music 9, 26, 244, 273; film music project with Eisler 9, 81; Wagner and the Hollywood movie 253; *see also* industry
first causes 63
folk 22, 26, 118; folklorism 30, 38, 46, 104; folk music 26, 37, 38–41; pseudo-folksong 27
force-field (*Kraftfeld*) 14; social force-fields 227
forces and relations of production 54, 124–8; *see also* production
form (*Form*) 2, 30, 38, 81, 120, 149–83; changing concepts of form 274–6; closed forms 181–2; contradictory character of form 57–8; dual-level concept of form 149, 150, 154; episodic forms 181; formal consistency 58; Fomalism 20; formal types 16, 27, 157; form as unfolding of truth 150; law of form (*Formgesetz*) 247; material theory of form (*materiale Formenlehre*) 174–82; *musique informelle* 181–2, 317 n138; open forms 181–2; pre-given form 149;

form (*cont.*)
  sense of form (*Formgefühl*) 144–5, 164,
    166, 283; static form 177; theory of form
    (*Formenlehre*) 149, 155; traditional
    forms 5, 19, 23; *see also* fracture,
    fragment, genre, content
fracture, rupture (*Bruch*) 12; *see also* self,
    form
fragment 1, 3, 14, 25, 28–9; fragmentation
    14, 31, 32, 37, 38, 225; fragmentation
    and antisystematization 19–20;
    fragmentation and unity in Beethoven's
    late style 237–8
freedom 28, 57, 106, 112–18; artistic
    freedom 94; liberation of form 276
fugue 73, 153, 227–9
function 26; social function 38, 78–80, 98,
    184–217; change in social function
    230–32
functionality 57; Riemann's
    Funktionsbegriff 86
functionlessness 199–200; functionless
    harmony 86
fundemental principle (*Grundgestalt*) 60

galant style 218–19, 225–7, 229, 230–32,
    240
Gebrauchsmusik – *see* utility
Gemeinschaftsmusik – *see* community
genius 4
genre (*Gattung*) 5, 16, 23, 31, 32, 157; form
    and genre 152–4; genre, social function
    and community validation 312–13 n16;
    see also form
germinal cell (*Keimzelle*) 159
gesture (*Gestus, Geste*) 142, 240, 243;
    unsublimated gestures 247–8
givens 11
Grundgestalt 163
guilds 118

happiness, art's promise of happiness
    (*promesse de bonheur*) 1, 76
harmony 105, 151; *basso continuo* 227–9;
    complementary harmony 86; diminished
    seventh chord 75–6; harmonic series,
    overtone series 43, 263; Schoenberg's
    liberation of harmony 259
Hegelian-Marxism 4, 7
hermeneutics 18, 170; hermeneutic circle
    63
hermetic art – *see* art
heroic epic 32
heteronomy 32, 273; heteronomous gesture
    148; *see also* gesture
historical necessity – *see* necessity

history 3, 21, 24, 28; natural-history
    (*Naturgeschichte*) – *see* nature;
    Benjamin's 'original history'
    (*Urgeschichte*) 36; Adorno's philosophy
    of music history 219–25; Hegel's
    philosophy of history 112–14; rejection
    of history 244; *see also* philosophy
holism 274
homology 261
homophony 227
horror 13
humanism 2, 230
humour 45
hyperbole 13

idea 60, 89
idealism 6, 13; idealist philosophy 2, 16,
    120
ideal types 136, 139
idée fixe 241
identity ↔ non-identity (*Identitat ↔
    Nicht-Identität*) 10, 15, 31, 112, 290 n71;
    identity theory 60
ideology 3, 8, 10, 12, 19, 22, 37, 46, 53–4,
    60–61, 132, 216, 300 n178; ideology
    critique (*Ideologiekritik*) 8, 184; ideology
    of immediacy 250–51
idiom 154, 222
illusion, semblance, appearance (*Schein*)
    29, 30, 35, 54, 124; art as
    illusion/semblance of nature 56–9;
    perfection of illusion in Wagner 248; *see
    also* phantasmagoria
image (*Bild*) 143–4; historical images 23;
    see also gestrue, language, mimesis, sign
imagination 129
imitation – *see mimesis*
immanence 15; immanent analysis – *see*
    analysis
immediacy 28, 30, 250–51
Impressionism 257
improvisation 27, 193, 195, 196–7
impulse 130
incidental music 248
incomprehensibility (*Unverständlichkeit*) –
    see unintelligibility
inconsistency, technical inconsistency in
    Wagner 248–50
individual 37; bourgeois individual,
    proletarian individual 118–20
individualism 45, 51, 104, 254–5
industry and Berlioz 240; industrialization
    3; Wagner and industrialization 242–53,
    257; film industry 203; industrialization
    of operetta; *see also* culture industry,
    orchestra

inspiration (*Einfall*) 235, 249, 251;
inspiration and technique in Valéry
69–70
instinct 129; *see also* drives (*Triebe*)
institution of art 3, 272
instrumental music 221
integration 120
intelligibility, comprehensibility
(*Verständlichkeit*) 192, 214
intentionality 116
interiorization (*Verinnerlichung*) 249;
interiorities 33; *see also* expression
intermezzo 255
internalization 141, 224
interpretation 28, 213; interpretative
personality 194; interpretative
understanding (*Verstehen*) and second
reflection 214–15; levels of interpretation
59–63; philosophical interpretation 15,
22, 62–3; interpretation and the
hermeneutic circle 64
intertextuality 283
invariance 53; invariants, invariables 14,
37
inwardness (*Innerlichkeit*) 6, 139;
technification of inwardness 251–2;
retreat into inwardness 254–5
inversion 6, 18
irony 56; in Bartók 39–40; in Stravinsky
45; in Schoenberg 47–8; in Adorno 133
irrationality 130–31, 136, 225; *see also*
rationality

jargon 29
jazz 26, 46, 100, 205; jazz Subject 27; jazz
as heresy 306 n134
judgement 2; *see also* aesthetics

kitsch 27; in Mahler 258–9
knowledge (*Erkenntnis*) – *see* cognition

labour (*Arbeit*) 124; alienated labour 124;
concealment of labour 244–5; division of
labour (*Arbeitsteilung*) 233
Ländler 157
language (*Sprache*) 10, 13; German
language 18; language-character of
music (*Sprachcharakter*) 143–4; musical
mass language (*musikalische
Massensprache*) 200–201, 225, 272;
langue-parole 154; regression to the
pre-linguistic 144, 248
laws of nature 37 – *see also* nature
legitimation 126
leitmotif (*Leitmotiv*) – *see* motif

libido 129; libido strivings 132; *see also*
drives
Lied 247
life; the good life 12; ordinary life 70
light music (*leichte Musik*) 26
listening types (*Hörtypen*) 186, 208–13;
adequate listening 210; culture consumer
212; emotional listener 212;
entertainment listener 211; expert
listener 210; good listener 210;
indifferent listener 212; jazz fan 212;
regressive listening 211–12; resentment
listener 212; structural listening 210
literary criticism 16
lived experience (*Erlebnis*) – *see* experience
logic 3, 36; alternative logical structure,
the 'constellation' 14, 35–7; Hegel's
dialectical logic 112–13; logical
consistency 60; logic of disintegration
(*Logik des Zerfalls*) 16, 88; crisis in
musical logic 241–2; musical logic as
philosophical cognition 235–7
lyric 143; Schumann lyric song 254;
Brahms lyric intermezzo 255

magic 10, 136, 141; magic spell 215; *see
also* disenchantment
mannerism 19
march 5, 27, 157
marketing 186, 199, 200; law of the market
46
Marxian theory 121–8
mass (*Missa Solemnis*) 238–40
mass culture – *see* culture
material, concept of (*Materialbegriff*) 21,
149, 151–2; musical material 1, 3, 6, 14,
22, 24, 25, 38, 119; development of a
theory of musical material 65–107;
historical tendency of the material 85–6;
material theory of form – *see* form; raw
material (*Rohstoff*) 30, 66, 67; devalued
material 90–91; changing concepts of
material and form 223, 274–6;
Dahlhaus's critique of Adorno's concept
of material 329 n43; *see also* matter
(*Stoff*)
matter (*Stoff*) 66; raw material (*Rohstoff*)
and nature in Hindemith 67–9; *matière*
in Valéry 69; second order matter 152,
in Mahler 175, 259, in Beckett 276; the
twelve-tone technique 267; *see also*
material
maturity (*Mündigkeit*) 99, 230, 252–3,
305–6 n115
meaning (*Sinn*) 1, 14; in Wagner 250;
meaning and historical change 93–4;

meaning (*cont.*)
meaninglessness 56; original meaning
(*Ursinn*) 90
means-ends rationality – *see* rationality
mediation (*Vermittlung*) 8, 10, 22, 28–30,
31, 55, 100–101, 108–48, 216; mediation
of opposites through their extremes
145–7; schematic model 185–7; Hegel
and mediation 109–21; Marx and
mediation 121–8; mediated immediacy
112; mediating middle term (*vermittelnde
Mitte*) 120
melody (*Melos*) 93, 96, 138, 151; in
Mahler 259; emancipation of *melos* in
Schoenberg 105, 259–60; *see also*
individual, Subject
membra disiecta 134
metaphor 13, 261
metaphysics 32, 34, 116; metaphysical
awakening 33
method, methodology 3, 13, 16, 21;
methodological disputes 9
middle classes – *see* bourgeoisie
mimesis 13, 135, 140–41; mimetic art 2;
mimetic language 143; mimesis and *ratio*
140–43; mimetic regression 243–4;
mimetic taboo 141; mimetic
understanding 214; mimicry 140
mind (*Geist*) – *see* Spirit
miniature, in Webern 180
models 317 n3; *ohne Leitbild* 2;
interpretative models 59–64; schematic
model 22
modernism 3, 12; anti-modernist 6;
modernist period 31; moderate
modernism 44; classical modernism 12;
modernity 117
moment (*das Moment*) 301 n188
monad 55, 190, 300–301 n180
montage 90, 180–81, 201
mortality of music 99
motif (*Motiv*) 151; leitmotif (*Leitmotiv*)
246–7, 325 n86; motivic economy 279,
284; motivic-thematic development 228,
as self-reflection in Beethoven 234, as
coming of age in Brahms 255; *Urmotiv*
in Wagner 244
museum exhibits 103
musical, the 204
musicality (*Musikalität*) 157, 313 n31
musical logic – *see* logic
musical criticism 9
music drama 250–51
musicology 4, 17, 73, 277
musique informelle – *see* form
myth, mythology 27, 28, 30, 34, 37, 136, 244

naïvity, *naïveté* 63
narcotics, composers as dealers in
narcotics 212, 321 n103; Berlioz and
opium 241
nationalism 37
national socialism, Nazism 10, 223
nature (*Natur*) 2, 24, 57; first nature (*erste
Nature*) 21; nature as myth in Wagner
244; nature as ideology 37; folk music
and nature 27; history and nature 28,
29, 35, 36; natural-history
(*Naturgeschichte*) 30–31; Benjamin and
the 'history of nature' 34–5; Lukács and
second nature (*zweite Natur*) 31–4;
nature in Hegel's philosophy 112–14;
human nature 133; natural laws in
Hindemith's music 43; nature as fate in
Wagner 245–6; *see also* beauty
nearness 185
necessity 12; historical necessity in
Schoenberg 71; loss of necessity 255–6
needs, expressive needs 16, 23, 117
negation 11, 19, 103–5, 112
negativity 13, 14
neoclassicism 41, 44–6, 101, 104, 222
New Music, the 1, 22, 27, 29, 30, 31;
pre-history of the New Music 223–5;
problem of the New Music 260–61
New Objectivity – *see* objectivity
nihilism, in Berg 171
niveau 76
nominalism 181
non-identity – *see* identity
norms 2; aesthetic norms 11
notation 69, 138, 225

Object (*Objekt*) 2, 10, 12; *Objekt ↔ Subjekt*
2; Debussy's capitulation to the Object
256–8; objectification (*Objektivation,
Entäußerung*) 113, 116, 119; *see also*
Subject
objectivism 101, 104
objectivity 2, 16, 18, 143–4; mechanical
objectivity 41; New Objectivity (*neue
Sachlichkeit*) 101
ontology 2, 29, 30, 35; ontological
certainties 11, 37
open forms – *see* form
opera 4, 246, 250, 252; Cage's *Europeras 1
& 2* 274–5
operetta 204
opposition 133–4
orchestra, orchestration in Berlioz 241; in
Wagner 243, 245, 248; instrumental
colour in Debussy 257; 'nature sounds'
in Mahler's orchestration 258; *see also*

industry, phantasmagoria, rationalization
organicism 57; in Berg 168
origins 68
other (*das Andere*) 260
overture 80, 232

paradox 13
parataxis 18
part 8, 110–12; *see also* whole
particular, particularity 2, 15
pastiche (*Stilkopie*) 91; reminiscence technique 90
pedagogy 42
pedal point 280
periodization 220–23
performance 23, 24; relation between performer and score 192–7
pessimism 1, 133
phantasmagoria 124, 244–5
phenomenology 7, 10, 29, 215
philosophy 1; Adorno's philosophy of art 2–3; early philosophical influences 4–5 (Kant, Husserl, Bloch), 6–7 (Marx, Kierkegaard, Freud), philosophy and the social sciences 7, 184; methodological disputes (with Popper, Heidegger) 10; negative dialectics and aesthetics 10–11; Critical Theory 12–13; Classical Greek philosophy 13; gulf between British empiricist and German Idealist traditions 13; negative dialectics as atonal philosophy 11; philosophy of history 27, 218–25; debates with Lukács and Benjamin 29–37; Hegel 109–21; Marx 121–8; Nietzsche 18, 219; conceptual context for Adorno's philosophical aesthetics of music 52–64
physiognomics 35, 258, 277
piano duet 4, 211
pietism 225
pitch 149–50
play, game (*Spiel*) 39, 45; illusion and play (*Schein und Spiel*) 196, 266; empty game (*Spielerei*) 39–40
pluralism 223
poetry, the poetic 13, 14, 18
polarization, polarity 13; Schoenberg–Stravinsky polarization 266–70
polemics 10, 265
politics 3, 10, 13, 19, 37, 54, 246; political action 11; political engagement – *see also* commitment
polyphony 138
popular music 9, 26–7, 100, 119, 133,
204–6; as affirmation 103; popular culture 120; *see also* culture industry, folk music, jazz, rock music
positivism 8, 12; the Positivist Dispute (*Positivismusstreit*) 10
postmodernism 12, 191
pragmatism 7, 13
praxis 80, 101; dialectic of music and social praxis 101–2
primitive, the 268
problematics 2, 15
production 25, 121–4, 187–92; forces of production 2, 124–6; production, reproduction, distribution, consumption 187
profit 200
programme music 241
progress (*Fortschritt*) 28, 35, 113–14, 230; Brahms the progressive 253–4; progress of the avant-garde 87–9
prohibition of the naming of God (*Bilderverbot*) 78
proletariat, proletarian individual 118, 125
promise – *see* happiness
propaganda 7, 222
proportion 2
prose style 13; Adorno as literature and the problem of translation 17–20
protest 56
pseudo-individualization (*Pseudoindividualisierung*) 8
psychoanalysis 2, 128–35; psychoanalytical concepts 26, 27
psychology 3, 4, 16, 17, 19; empirical psychology 8, 21, 26; social psychology 131–3; psychology of perception 66
purposiveness (or purposefulness) without a purpose (*Zweckmäßigkeit ohne Zweck*) 57, 138–40
puzzle, jig-saw puzzle 191; *see also* riddle-character

quality 56, 62

radio 17, 26, 186
rank – *see* quality
rationalism 13
rationality, rationalization (*Rationalität, Rationalisierung*) 26, 28, 84–5, 106, 114, 116, 135–47, 224, 229–30; aesthetic rationality 138–40, 141; Adorno's generalization of Weber's concept of *Zweckrationalität* 311 n107; 'iron cage' of rationality 114; means-ends

rationality (*cont.*)
    rationality/rationalization 135, 136–8;
    value rationality (*Wertrationalität*)
    136–8; progressive rationalization in
    Bach 229–30, Wagner 243–4; traditional
    behaviour as rationality 136–8; *see also*
    bureaucratization, administration
reaction 89–90
reading Adorno 13–16; reading habits
    18
ready-mades 274
realism 245; socialist realism 201
reality 19, 113; reality principle 129; social
    reality and artistic freedom 94–5
reason – *see* rationality
reawakening 33
recapitulation 178
reception 13, 24; *see also* consumption
reconcilement, reconciliation 10, 35, 113,
    120; false reconciliation 37
recomposition 283
recording 186
recurrence (*Wiederkehr*) 176; *see also* form
redemption (*Rettung*) 1; redemption of
    nature 56–9
referential system, frame of reference
    (*Bezugssystem*) 31
reflection, reflexivity 3, 112; critical
    reflection 12; material self-reflection
    234–5; second reflection (*zweite
    Reflektion*) 63, 213; self-reflection 12, 18,
    28, 99, 112–13, 229–30
regression 28, 130; of listening 5, 26;
    mimetic regression in Wagner 243–4;
    regression to the pre-linguistic 247–8
reification (*Verdinglichung*) 23, 31, 225
relations of production – *see* production
relativism 12, 223
religion 3, 13, 136
remnant (*Rest*) 160; motivic remnants in
    Berg 165, 172, 280, 283
Renaissance 136
repetition 178–9; *see also* form
representation 3, 23; *see also* mimesis
repression 28, 57, 130
reproduction 25, 31, 122, 195;
    reproduction as
    performance/interpretation 192–8;
    reproduction as technical/mechanical
    reproducibility 25; as distribution 5, 8,
    222, 198–207; theory of reproduction 24,
    195–7
residue (*Rest*) – *see* remnant
resistance 102, 141
retrograde 6
revisionism 133

revolution 80, 125, 220, 221, 233
revue 204
rhapsody, declamatory rhapsody in Bartók
    40
rhythm 151
riddle-character (*Rätselcharakter*) 76, 197,
    215
ritual 3
rock music 206
Romanticism 4
rondo 152; rondo as open form 181; *see
    also* form
rupture (*Bruch*) 27; rupture between the
    self and forms 16, 21, 23, 24, 26, 30, 31,
    36, 37–8, 49; in the sphere of
    reproduction as performance 196–7; *see
    also* fracture

salon music 75, 257
sameness (*Gleichheit*) 177–8; *see also* form
scales 138
schema 155–6; *see also* deviation, form
schizophrenia 268
science 10, 12, 33; science and magic
    136
score 26, 188, 190, 192, 198
second hand 175, 274
second nature – *see* nature
sedimentation of history 93
self, the 'I' (*das Ich*) – *see* rupture between
    self and forms; *see also* Subject, Object
self-consciousnessness – *see* consciousness
self-determination 9
self-reflection – *see* reflection
semblance (*Schein*) – *see* illusion
sense of form – *see* form
sequence 250
serenade 80, 232; Schoenberg's op. 24
serialism 9, 224; multiple serialism 225
shock 18; aftershock 56
sign (*Zeichen*) 143–4; sign-system 193–4;
    see also image
signification 36
similarity (*Ähnlichkeit*) 177–8; *see also*
    form
socialist realism – *see* realism
social sciences 7
social situation 25, 97–8
society (*Gesellschaft*) 34, 54, 245; consumer
    society 27; open society 10; true society
    10
sociology 2, 3, 4, 9, 16, 17, 30; Adorno's
    sociology of music 10, 24, 25–6, 96–7,
    184–217; empirical sociology 8, 21, 26
sonata 73–4, 76, 80, 232, 234; Berg Piano
    Sonata op. 1 159–69, 279–84

spell – *see* magic
spirit (*Geist*) 9, 58, 113, 125; problematic concept 114; objective spirit (*objektiver Geist*) 115, 147, 263, 271; subjective spirit (*subjektiver Geist*) 271; spiritualization (*Vergeistigung*) 57–8, 115–6; as rationality and technical progress 117; as alienated labour 124; as historical progress of the bourgeois Subject 117–19
spleen et idéal 116, 222
spontaneity 58
stabilization (*Stabilisierung*) 44, 222; stabilized music (*stabilisierte Musik*) 44–7, 104
Stalinism 223
standardization 8, 203
stasis 30, 177, 178, 179, 225; static form 177; stasis in Wagner 246, 251, 257; *see also* form
statement (*Setzung*) 176; *see also* form
statics (*Statik*) 176, 177; *see also* dynamics, form
structure (*Struktur*) 19, 154, 155–6; *see also* form
stuff (*Stoff*) – *see* matter
style 12, 13, 151, 154, 231; style change 230–32; stylistic norms 150; *see also* prose style
Subject (*Subjekt*), Subject–Object 2, 10, 32; Subject-objectification 225, 227–9; historical Subject 117–20; disappearance of the Subject 12; expressive Subject 16; survival of the expressive Subject in Mahler 258–60; subjectivity 2, 38, 144–5; *see also* bourgeoisie, Object, spirit
sublation (*Aufhebung*) 112–13, 158, 231
sublimation (*Sublimierung*) 118, 129–35, 224; sublimation in Freud and Weber 310–11 n95; in Debussy 257; unsublimated gestures in Wagner 247–8; – *see also* psychoanalysis
substance (*Gehalt*) – *see* content
succession (*Reihung*) 176; *see also* form
suffering 56, 105
superstition 114
superstructure – *see* base-superstructure
surrealism, surrealist music 104
survival of art 56, 140, 222
symbol 34; in Wagner 244, 247, 257
symbolism 2, 69–70, 247
symmetry 177
symphony 80, 157, 232
synthesis 112
system 2, 14; anti-systematic 19, 25; systemization 6, 14, 37, 222

tabula rasa 188
Tafelmusik 156, 232
taste 258
technique 70, 116–17; Berlioz and technique 240–41; *priëm* 70; technical progress 113–14; technical skills 185; technification of inwardness in Wagner 251–2; technical consistency in Brahms 255; *see also* construction, rationality
technology 116–17, 127; musical instrument technology and Max Weber's concept of rationalization 138; technical means and expressive needs 151; inspiration and technique in Valéry 69–70; *see also* rationality
teleology 36
television 186, 273
tendency of the material – *see* material
tension (*Spannung*) 191; *see also* force-field
terror 56
text 192–3
texture 151
thematicism – *see* development, motif
theology 116
theory, theoretical speculation 7, 8, 12, 17, 20; social theory 99
timbre 151
time 179–80
titanism 195
tonality 234–5
tone (*Ton*) 171–2
tone-colour (*Klangfarbe*) 179
torn halves 120
totalitarian 37
totality (*Totalität*) 7, 12, 28, 29, 32, 34, 37; totalizing form 19; partial totalities 180
total work of art (*Gesamtkunstwerk*) 244
tour de force 15, 197
tradition 24, 31, 113; traditional behaviour 136
transcendence 109
transience 34, 35, 36, 53
transition (*Überleitung*) 175, 176; fields of transition (*Übergangsfeldern*) 176; Wagner's art of transition (*die Kunst des Übergangs*) 172, 284; smallest transition (*der kleinste Übergang*) in Berg 162, 172, 174, 280; *see also* remnant
translation, problems of 11, 16; *see also* prose style
trope 216
truth (*Wahrheit*) 1, 2, 19, 20, 29, 60–64, 112, 150; scientific truth 10; truth content (*Wahrheitsgehalt*) 15, 22, 29, 56–9, 111, 150, 225; truth outside history 91

tuning systems 138; tempered tuning 193
typology 102; typology of music 102–05
twelve-tone technique 81, 83, 84, 85, 86–7,
   224–5; as the fate of music 267

unconscious, the 6, 57, 129
understanding (*Verstehen*) 213–14,
   immanent understanding 215; mimetic
   understanding 214
unintelligibility (*Unverständlichkeit*) 101,
   120
unity (*Einheit*) 20, 21, 133; of Subject and
   Object 12
universal, unversality, the general 15, 153;
   universal and particular 154–5
Unterhaltungsmusik 231
use-value (*Gebrauchswert*) 26, 42
utility music (*Gebrauchsmusik*) 38, 105
utopia 12, 74–8, 187, 202, 229; utopian
   promise 76

value (*Wert*) 2; aesthetic value 2
variant (*Variant*) 274; *see also* second-hand
   (second-order) matter

variations 20, 152; developing variation
   232
violence 11
virtuosity 15, 197, 221
voice-leading 86

waltz 157
'We' (*das Wir*) 76, 115–16; in Bloch 76
Whole, the (*das Ganze*) 8, 110–12;
   wholeness 12; false whole 19;
   fractured/fragmented whole 14, 19,
   119–20
will (*Wille*) 135; will of form (*Formwille*)
   135
wish-fulfilment – *see* art
work, concept of the (*Werkbegriff*) 189–92;
   the musical work 26, 189–92; as
   autonomous object 189; as score 192–7;
   as performance 197–8; as commodity
   204–7; as dynamic complex of meaning
   190; as force-field 190; as jig-saw puzzle
   191; as museum exhibit 191; as process
   189; as windowless monad 190; the
   mediated work 208